2nd EDITION

Entrepreneur MAGAZINE'S

ULTIMATE

HOMEBASED BUSINESS HANDBOOK

How to Start, Run and Grow
Your Own Profitable Business

JAMES STEPHENSON *with* RICH MINTZER

EP
Entrepreneur.
Press

Publisher: Jere L. Calmes
Cover Design: Beth Hansen-Winter
Composition: CWL Publishing Enterprises, Inc., Madison, Wisconsin, www.cwlpub.com

© 2008 by Entrepreneur Media, Inc.

This publication is designed to provide accurate and authoritative information in regard to the subject matter covered. It is sold with the understanding that the publisher is not engaged in rendering legal, accounting or other professional services. If legal advice or other expert assistance is required, the services of a competent professional person should be sought.

—From a Declaration of Principles jointly adopted by a
Committee of the American Bar Association and
a Committee of Publishers and Associations

ISBN 978-1-59918-185-1

Library of Congress Cataloging-in-Publication Data

Stephenson, James, 1966-
  Ultimate homebased business handbook / by James Stephenson with Rich Mintzer. — 2nd ed.
      p. cm. — (Ultimate Series)
  Includes index.
  Rev. ed. of: Entrepreneur's ultimate homebased business handbook / James Stephenson. 2004.
  ISBN 978-1-59918-185-1 (alk. paper)
  1. Homebased businesses—Management—Handbooks, manuals, etc. 2. New business enterprises—
Management—Handbooks, manuals, etc. 3. Small business—Management—Handbooks, manuals, etc.
  4. Success in business—Handbooks, manuals, etc I. Mintzer, Richard. II. Stephenson, James, 1966-.
Entrepreneur's ultimate homebased business handbook. III. Title.
  HD62.38.S678 2008
  658'.0412—dc22

                                                                            2008004944

Printed in Canada.

12 11 10 09 08   10 9 8 7 6 5 4 3 2 1

Contents

Introduction

As the name suggests, a home business is a business venture that you operate from a homebased location. This certainly does not mean that you have to spend your time working exclusively in your home for your business to be classified as a home business. Any business that is operated or substantially managed from a residential location is classified as a home business, including:

- Professionals such as dentists who set up homebased practices
- Consultants who manage their businesses from home, but spend most of their working time at their clients' locations
- Service repair technicians who work from mobile vans and trucks, but store equipment and tools at home
- People manufacturing or assembling products in the garage or creating craft products in the basement at home
- Anyone running a website to sell products or services from the comfort of his or her own home

In a nutshell, if your home address is the same as the address your business uses, then you are operating a homebased business.

You are in good company. According to the SBA, more than 750,000 new business ventures are started each year, with the vast majority of homebased business enterprises started by first-time entrepreneurs. Wow, that adds up to a lot of people taking a gigantic leap of faith! But it does beg the questions: Where do you find all the need-to-know information? Like, how do you get started? Where do you find customers? How do you manage your new home business enterprise?

These questions and hundreds more are answered in great detail in this book. *The Ultimate Homebased Business Handbook* was specifically developed for the thousands of people who start a home business each week and for the thousands more who are considering starting a home business venture in the near future. *The Ultimate Homebased Business Handbook* provides first-time and even seasoned entrepreneurs with all the vital information that they need to start, run and grow their own profitable businesses from the comforts of home. The information is presented in an easy-to-use, understandable, step-by-step format that acts as a road map to guide readers effortlessly through the entire process of starting a homebased business.

GETTING STARTED

My objective in creating *The Ultimate Homebased Business Handbook* was to give people who want to start their own home business a time machine that would enable them to flash forward into the future to see how their dreams of home business ownership have become a successful and profitable reality. So you may be wondering where is this time machine? You are looking at it. That's right, this book.

I can call this book a time machine because over the years I have owned and operated some successful home business ventures and some not so successful home business ventures. And as the old saying goes, "If I knew then what I know now, I would have done things much differently." Obviously, it's too late for me to go back and do things differently, but I do know now what I wished I'd known then. That is why I refer to this book as a time machine. The information featured in this book covers the steps you need to take to succeed and the actions that you should avoid so that in ten years you will not be saying, "I wish I knew then what I know now."

HOW TO USE THIS BOOK

Along with being a guide to starting and running a

homebased business, this is also a workbook and should be used as such. It is not a book that should be taking a restful nap on a dusty shelf. Use it incrementally through all phases of getting your new home business rolling, including:

- Identifying your personal strengths and weaknesses
- Setting attainable and realistic goals
- Identifying the right new home business idea
- Choosing the right legal structure
- Developing a workable business plan
- Finding the money needed to start, operate and grow your business
- Designing and organizing a productive home workspace
- Creating a marketing plan that's guaranteed to find and keep customers for life
- Managing the day-to-day operations like a pro

WHAT YOU WILL DISCOVER INSIDE

I have attempted to maintain a sense of order in this book by putting specific information in what I feel is the logical chapter, though out of order in the true sense of an A to Z, step-by-step format. I chose this format because of the sheer amount of information contained in *The Ultimate Homebased Business Handbook*, the largest and most comprehensive book available on the subject of starting and operating a home business. For example, in Chapter 3, Financial Issues, you will find information dealing with the financial aspects of starting and operating a home business—securing startup funding, establishing business bank accounts, the various payment options available to your customers and small business tax information. I have also included relevant financial issues in other chapters to help explain the specific topic being discussed.

I strongly advise you to read each and every chapter in this book, even if you feel the information featured does not apply to your particular situation or the type of business you intend to start. As businesses change and grow, what may not be applicable right now may be applicable in the future. You'll also find numerous business ideas, valuable marketing tips and resources in each chapter. After completing this book, you will have acquired the following information:

- Help identifying the right home business venture for you. Information in the book has been specifically provided to guide you effortlessly through the process of knowing which business may be right for you. Also included in the last chapter are 125 great home business startup ideas, as well as information on 101 premiere home franchise opportunities, as compiled by the staff at *Entrepreneur Magazine.*

- Answers to all of those tough financial and legal questions. Far too many business books leave you with more questions than answers in terms of the financial and legal issues that you need to understand to start and run a home business. Here, you will find information on legal business structures, ways to finance your new business, the permits and licenses that you will need, and how to make sure that Uncle Sam gets his portion of the pie, but not before you have gotten yours.

- How to develop your own business and marketing plans step by step, from how to begin to how you can use your plans to secure business startup and growth capital. And, of course, plans will act as a road map leading you to home business success and profits.

- How to set up and organize your home workspace. Once occupying a portion of a den, the modern homebased office is a command center of sorts, with a host of high-tech possibilities, if you so desire. For others the homebased office is a quiet space in which to create, design and manufacture with the tools of their trade. If you have never designed, planned and equipped a home workspace before, don't worry. A variety of possibilities, the tips and ideas are included to help you put together a workspace (even on a tight budget) that will prove to be efficient and productive.

- Tips that will show you how to build a better business team. No one person can build a successful business alone; it requires a business team composed of people who understand your goals and who are dedicated to making sure that you reach these goals. Here you will discover who the key players should be, why you need them, and how to recruit them onto your business team.

- The quick and easy route for home business management. One of the most difficult aspects of operating a home business is the hands-on, day-to-day management that is required to keep the ship on its course.

- Surefire ways to find and keep customers. Without customers you have no business, so the importance of finding and keeping customers cannot be overstated. Included here are the tools that you need to conduct customer research and create a target customer profile, the strategies that will take you to your customers, the words and actions that will make them buy, and the incredible customer service tips that will keep them coming back for life.

- Selling secrets that the pros use. Deep in the core of the earth you will find a chamber. In that chamber you will find a chest. Locked away in that chest are the selling secrets that the pros have used for centuries to win big every time. Guess what? I found the key, unlocked the chest, and at great risk to my personal safety swiped these closely guarded selling secrets while no one was watching. Best of all, I have included these selling secrets in this book for you to use freely so that you too can win big every time.

- Advertising that gets the results that you want and need. One of the biggest marketing challenges that home business owners face is determining the type of advertising that will give them the biggest bang for their precious marketing buck. Inside, you will learn what type of advertising gets the results you need and want—without putting a second mortgage on your home to pay for it.

- The internet is the way of the world, and you'll learn throughout the chapters how you can best use your website to your advantage. Provided are the steps to building a website that can allow you to promote and sell on even footing with companies 100 times your size.

125 HOMEBASED BUSINESS IDEAS AND 101 HOMEBASED FRANCHISES

Yes, you'll be tempted to jump to the end (Chapter 18, to be exact) before you read through the book. If you do, you will find that the businesses and franchise possibilities listed are just some among so many possible ideas that you can pursue.

Of course, within the book, you will gather the information necessary to make these and other homebased business ideas work. Marketing, promotion, advertising and sales— whether a service or a product—are part of what will make the businesses listed in Chapter 18 successful. While you may gather some ideas by sneaking a peak, you will ultimately benefit from taking the time to under-

stand the entire world of the home business entrepreneur—deciding which type of home business is best for you, developing the business plan, naming the business, establishing a productive home office environment, marketing and promoting your business, selling your goods and/or services, and even closing up shop or selling your business. Yes, there is a life cycle to a homebased business and as you read the chapters, you will discover how a business grows and evolves.

CHECKLISTS AND WORKSHEETS

Throughout *The Ultimate Homebased Business Handbook*, you will find many helpful checklists, worksheets and forms that you can use as featured. Alternately, you can use these as templates. Using your computer, with a basic word processing program, you can customize each checklist, worksheet or form to create ones that are relevant to your home business, products, services or marketing objectives. You will also find many helpful examples, such as a sample press release, a target customer profile sheet, and a media questionnaire, just to mention a few. Their purpose is to help explain visually information that is being featured and to give you a useful tool for your business that will save time and money. Worksheets and checklists can prove invaluable when setting up a new business, especially if this is your first time. Therefore, I encourage you to take advantage of these useful tools.

HOME BUSINESS RESOURCES

As you read through each chapter, you will notice that hundreds of business-related resources have been included in the text and at the end. The resources featured throughout the book include both American and Canadian business associations, government agencies, private corporations, individuals, websites, books and other publications, products, services and lots more. The three primary categories you will find are associations, books and websites.

Association Resources

At the end of each chapter and the end of the book you will find association resources and listings. Listed are important nonprofit business and industry associations, as well as government agencies, to help guide you through important business and marketing activities. Organizations like the American Home Business Association and government agencies like the U.S. Patent and Trademark Office are included, with full contact information. There are hundreds of association and agencies listed throughout this book, many of which you will find extremely helpful when you are establishing your business, operating your business, and marketing your products or services. In many cases, especially with government agencies, there are free programs in place to help entrepreneurs from every walk of life succeed in starting their own businesses. I encourage you to use these valuable resources so that you can take advantage of these programs, thereby greatly increasing your odds of enjoying long-term, profitable business success.

Book Resources

You will also find a list of recommended books and other publications at the end of each chapter.

The purpose of this list is not to promote or endorse any one author, book, publisher or program. The book resources are there to give you a research tool for finding additional information and advice about the specific information that was featured in the chapter. Likewise, the suggested readings are not meant to inspire you to run out and spend hundreds of dollars on books and publications, though investments made to help you become a better business operator and marketer are without question wise business and personal investments.

Websites

At the end of each chapter and at the end of the book, you will find numerous useful websites. The purpose of including these resources is not to promote or endorse any particular company, product, service, individual, website, agency or organization. These sites provide additional information on the areas discussed in the chapters and, in many cases, provide additional links to help you develop an online source of references. Be sure to bookmark sites of interest as you find them.

Entrepreneur Magazine's *Ultimate Homebased Business Handbook* is the most authoritative and comprehensive home business startup book available today. It gives you the answers to all of the questions that you have about starting, operating and growing your own home business for long-term profitable success.

CHAPTER 1

Why Start a Home Business?

SHOULD YOU START A HOME BUSINESS? Maybe you should—or maybe you shouldn't. That's probably not what you were expecting to hear or what you wanted to hear. But the truth is that some people are destined to succeed at operating their own business and others are not and will fail in business.

Not every person is suited for starting and operating a business—not because they are afraid, not because they do not want to succeed, and certainly not because they are stupid—mainly because starting and operating a home business is hard work, much harder than the vast majority of new entrepreneurs realize. In fact, it is not uncommon for home business owners to work in excess of 50 hours per week, week in and week out, with little time off and for much less financial compensation than most are willing to admit. And other statistics suggest that four out of every five businesses will fail within the first five years of operation, making for a very bleak forecast.

Personally, I think that the numbers of business failures actually may be skewed to a degree. If a person starts a business and a year later decides to close the business because it turns out he or she does not enjoy being self-employed, would that be classified as a business failure? Statistically yes, but in reality I do not believe this example would constitute a business failure. These people may be guilty of not fully understanding what they were getting into or not taking enough time to rationalize their decision to start a business or possibly found another full-time opportunity that sounded better. This is definitely not failing. Besides, *success* and *failure* are relative terms. As explained above, a person who starts a business and decides to close the business after a year because he or she doesn't like being self-employed may very well consider the experience fulfilling and a success. He or she may have learned a lot from the experience. Another person in similar circumstances may consider the event to be one of the greatest failures of his or her life. It is relative to each person's individual situation, goals and way of thinking. In reality, failing in business is not about trying something new that doesn't work out. Failing is wanting to do something but never giving it a whirl. You cannot succeed if you do not try.

Still, why do so many new businesses fail? For many reasons. But most business failures can be traced to three main problems—lack of proper research, lack of proper planning and lack of money—with the last being the main problem. Additional reasons why businesses fail include:

- Lack of business skills
- Starting the business for the wrong reasons
- Having a bad business idea, product or service
- Lack of self-confidence
- Events beyond the control of the owner
- No support structure
- Underestimating the strength and resolve of competitors
- Entering an oversaturated market
- Failing to market, promote and/or advertise the business
- Following the advice of the wrong people or getting involved with the wrong people
- Not putting in the necessary time and effort required to launch the business
- Unrealistic expectations
- Health or other personal issues

If you decide to start a home business, there is no question that it will be successful and you will reach all of your personal and financial goals. I can say this unconditionally because you have two secret weapons on your side: your determination to make it happen and the information contained in this book. For me personally, the rewards of being self-employed far outweigh the risks, hard work and other potential disadvantages. I believe that this is a very fair and objective assessment because I have started businesses that have been successful and businesses that have not, as is true of most entrepreneurs who stick with it long enough. Of course, at the end of the day you want more checks on your scorecard in the win column than the loss column, especially from a financial perspective. So if you are the type of person who longs for independence, wants to control your future, and can stomach a certain degree of risk without pulling out your hair in the process, then there is a better-than-average chance that you have what it takes to start and operate your own home business.

However, before you hang out the "open for business sign," make sure that you want to start a business for the right reasons, not the wrong ones. Quitting your job and starting your own home business because you hate your boss is definitely a wrong reason. As soon as you cool down, you'll probably realize that, providing it's not too late. Starting your own home business because you want to buy a really neat $100,000 sports car is also a wrong reason. If you don't believe me, give it a try.

Starting your own home business because you have a good idea, want the potential to improve your lifestyle, and have the focus and determination to see it through to the end are very good reasons. It's true, especially if you have thought out the entire process, weighed advantages against disadvantages, and still feel the same a day, week, month or even years later.

THE ADVANTAGES OF STARTING A HOME BUSINESS

There are many advantages associated with starting your own home business.

You Are Your Own Boss

Without question the greatest lure for starting and running a business is the fact that you become your own boss. Of course, this is only partly true, for the simple reason that your customers will always be your bosses. I have been self-employed in various ventures for a number of years, with the majority being operated from my home. For me the lure of self-employment is the freedom, hands down. It's not so much the potential to generate a substantial income or the ability to grow equity, but simply the sense of freedom and independence that being the boss affords. This means setting your own schedule, working at your own pace and wearing what you wish. As long as you get the work done, satisfy your customers/clients and meet your deadlines, you can work in your bathrobe if you so choose, if no one is coming over for a meeting. More significantly, you will not have to play office politics.

You Have the Potential to Earn More Money

While it may not be a good reason to start a business solely on the prospect of making big bucks, it is true that the majority of people do have the potential to make more money by owning and operating a business than they do working for a paycheck. Why? When you work for someone else, there is only you and so many hours in the day to work for an hourly wage or a commission. However, when you operate a business, you can duplicate yourself by hiring employees and sales people to increase revenues, you can duplicate your customers and find more to purchase your goods or services, you can duplicate your business model and open in new geographical areas, and you can duplicate and expand the number of products that you sell. Once you have built a business that is generating revenues and profits, duplicating what works can greatly increase your personal income and equity. Even without duplicating, you can set your own wages, put in more hours to complete a job if necessary, and remain in control of that project. Too often in a business, you'll have to wait for nine other departments to get on board before you can finish a task. Working

on your own, however, you can determine how long each task will take, charge accordingly, and complete the job on your own—if it is feasible.

You Can Create Your Own Work Environment

Having the ability to create your own work environment and the ability to be flexible in how you operate the business are two more of the major advantages of starting and operating a business from home. If you so choose, you can spend some of these "commuting hours" getting work done or enjoy more time with friends. The average employee commutes at least one hour each day. That's five hours a week in which you have flexibility to do as you choose. It you like, you can walk the dog at noon, pick the kids up after school, be at home to let the TV repairperson in, and do a host of other personal activities on your schedule, without sacrificing any of your business responsibilities.

You also have the opportunity to work in an office setting of your choice, decorate as you like, and decide which high-tech and no-tech appliances are to your liking. For the millions of people who have moved from cubicles to home offices, these personal choices are a major factor. Additionally, if you are "green" conscious, you can regulate your own heat, shut off unused lights and even go solar-powered if you so choose. While many businesses today are getting in step with the green environmental movement, plenty are not. You, as your own boss, can do so and feel that sense of doing something good for Mother Earth in your own little piece of the world.

You Can Take Advantage of Tax Benefits

Operating a business from home also qualifies you for any number of the tax benefits associated with operating a business, even if you work a "regular job" and operate your business only part time. As soon as you open for business, a portion of your utility bills are tax-deductible against business revenues, a portion of your transportation costs (equal to the percentage of time and mileage your car is used for business) are tax-deductible, and even this book that you just purchased is an allowable deduction for educational purposes. While you will pay some self-employment taxes, you can typically benefit by more deductions with a home-based business.

DISADVANTAGES OF STARTING A HOME BUSINESS

This book should come with an audio soundtrack. At the precise moment you reach this point, the menacing music would start. In scary movie terms, it's just before the axe falls. In this case, the axe is where we begin listing the disadvantages associated with starting and operating your own home business. Like the advantages, there are several.

Financial Risks

Without question, the biggest disadvantage to starting any business is the potential that you will lose your financial investment and possibly damage your credit rating should the business fail. You can go into personal debt, have creditors waiting to get their owed money and face outstanding bank loans.

Pressure

When you own and operate a business, there is little, if any, support system in place to help share the workload, worry and daily strains of running a business. Plus small business owners wear many hats. One day you are an accounting expert, the next day a customer service expert, the following day an advertising expert and the list goes on and on. To make matters worse, there is no escape. If things get to a snapping point at work, you simply

call in sick and take a day off to recharge your batteries. But when you operate your own business, this option is not so easy. Who will answer the phones? Who will sell the products or services? Who will meet with clients who are not so happy? Once you have made the decision to jump into business with both feet, there is no going back. The pressure will be there day after day. It's important that you learn to cope with the pressure.

Hard Work

If you have any allergies whatsoever to hard work, you will definitely consider this a disadvantage to starting your own business. As previously mentioned, small business owners as a rule work incredibly hard and have super long hours. It is not uncommon to put in more than 50 or even 60 hours a week, day in and day out, year round, with little more than the occasional weekend off. Hard work is especially important for new startups with no track record of reliability and performance. However, number of hours logged can be misleading. It is all about achieving your goals. Some people log numerous hours scheduling and rescheduling, rewriting their to-do list a dozen times, planning and replanning, coming up with schemes and ideas that will not fly. Keep in mind that if you work 35 hours getting things done efficiently and charging a rate that can allow you to reach your goals, you need not put in 60 hours.

Most people who claim to be putting in more than 50 hours a week are including a lot of wasted time. It is therefore about the rate of production and not about simply logging hours.

Lack of Motivation

This can be a tough one. Without a boss or someone else telling you what to do and when and even how, you will need to be self-disciplined, self-motivated and able to keep yourself on track. Yes, you can make your own schedule. However, you need to follow it. Many people who are self-employed complain that this can be their biggest predicament, not being motivated to get their work done. Use personal rewards if necessary until you get into a habit of getting into the work mode and staying there until you accomplish what you need to each day.

WHAT DOES IT TAKE TO SUCCEED?

Success never happens by accident. Success is a combination of ambition, research, planning, goal setting, hard work, persistence and the support of others. It requires never losing sight of why you are doing something and what you want to achieve, which will eventually lead you to success. At this point, if you are like most successful people, you will start searching for your next big challenge with the enthusiasm and focus that have made you successful.

I stress again that success is a relative term. Your definition of business success may be to start and operate a business that generates an extra $1,000 per month to help offset the cost of putting the kids through college, while the next person's definition of success might be to expand his small home business into an international corporation.

The key to knowing what it takes to succeed is really knowing your own personal definition of success, what you want to achieve, and then putting a plan in place to make it happen. Never get caught up in someone else's definition of success. That is like keeping up with the proverbial Joneses.

There are, however, certain things that are required to succeed in businesses large or small. Without them you will never obtain success, no matter how you define it. You have to want to be in business. You have to enjoy what you are doing. You have to be persistent. You have to have clear goals. And you have to be prepared to work hard and to be smart in order to achieve your goals.

25 Common Characteristics Shared by Successful Entrepreneurs

Regardless of your definition of success, there are, oddly enough, a great number of common characteristics that are shared by successful businesspeople. See the Entrepreneur Characteristics Checklist (Figure 1.1). You can place a check beside each characteristic that you feel that you possess. This way, you can see how you stack up. Even if you do not have all of these characteristics, don't fret. Most can be learned with practice and by developing a winning attitude, especially if you set goals and apply yourself, through strategic planning, to reach those goals in incremental and measurable stages.

Here are some of the most common characteristics shared by successful entrepreneurs.

THE HOME BUSINESS MUSTS

As in any activity you pursue, certain things are required to be successful. To legally operate a vehicle on public roadways, one must have a driver's license; to excel in sports, one must train and practice; to retire comfortably, one must become an informed investor and actively invest for retirement. If your goal is success in business, then the formula is no different. There are certain requirements. There are many business musts, but featured in this chapter are what I believe to be some of the more important musts that are required to start, operate and grow a profitable home business. Many of the ideas and much of the information discussed here are also featured in other chapters, but that is only because of their importance and the positive effects that these ideas can have on your business.

Do What You Enjoy

What you get out of your business in the form of personal satisfaction, financial gain, stability and enjoy-

FIGURE 1.1	Entrepreneur Characteristics Checklist

- ❑ Successful entrepreneurs have a strong desire to take control and guide their futures.
- ❑ Successful entrepreneurs are not afraid to work hard and put in long hours, if necessary, to achieve their personal and business goals.
- ❑ Successful entrepreneurs are very optimistic about what the future holds for their businesses and for themselves personally.
- ❑ Successful entrepreneurs are very self-confident in their abilities.
- ❑ Successful entrepreneurs set goals and develop an action plan to reach their goals and then reward themselves when they have reached and exceeded those goals (big and small).
- ❑ Successful entrepreneurs are prepared to handle stress and welcome challenges.
- ❑ Successful entrepreneurs are ambitious.
- ❑ Successful entrepreneurs are not procrastinators, but proactive in their approach to completing jobs and tasks in full, correctly and on time.
- ❑ Successful entrepreneurs have a competitive spirit by nature.
- ❑ Successful entrepreneurs are accountable, accepting personal responsibility for their decisions and actions.
- ❑ Successful entrepreneurs like to take charge, lead others and delegate.
- ❑ Successful entrepreneurs are independent thinkers and workers.
- ❑ Successful entrepreneurs will take calculated risks and understand that in the absence of risk, success is seldom if ever achieved.
- ❑ Successful entrepreneurs communicate well with other people and respect everyone's right to an opinion even when they disagree.
- ❑ Successful entrepreneurs are proficient time managers and use time-saving systems to squeeze the most productivity out of each day.
- ❑ Successful entrepreneurs work at maintaining good mental and physical health.
- ❑ Successful entrepreneurs are persistent and not easily discouraged.
- ❑ Successful entrepreneurs are organized.
- ❑ Successful entrepreneurs think and react logically and not emotionally.
- ❑ Successful entrepreneurs are knowledge hungry and never stop looking for ways to become better in all areas of business.
- ❑ Successful entrepreneurs have realistic expectations.
- ❑ Successful entrepreneurs are great planners.
- ❑ Successful entrepreneurs are proficient problem solvers and decisive decision makers.
- ❑ Successful entrepreneurs keep an open mind, are flexible and are adaptable to change when change is beneficial.
- ❑ Successful entrepreneurs know how to listen.

ment will be the sum of what you put into your business. So if you do not enjoy what you are doing, in all likelihood it is safe to assume that will be reflected in the success of your business—or subsequent lack of

success. In fact, if you do not enjoy what you are doing, chances are you will not succeed.

Most people start a business because they want to do something they enjoy, have control over their future, have the ability to make decisions and build a stable financial foundation for themselves and their families. Basically, the business that you start or purchase should be your dream. This is not to say there will not be bad days when you dislike what you are doing, but by and large the good days should outnumber the bad. The best way to guarantee this is to start a business that involves something you really enjoy doing. If you enjoy sailing, find a niche in the sailing industry that is not being filled and start a business to service that niche. If you enjoy selling, make sure that your business is sales-oriented and revolves around personal interaction. If you enjoy working with your hands, consider a homebased manufacturing business or a business in which you provide services. The old adage, "Do what you love and the money will follow," is great advice, especially coupled with solid research and planning.

Take What You Do Seriously

You cannot expect to be effective and successful in business unless you truly believe in your business and in the goods and services that you sell. Far too many home business owners fail to take their own businesses seriously enough, getting easily sidetracked, and not staying motivated and keeping their noses to the grindstone. They also fall prey to naysayers who do not take them seriously because they do not work from an office building, office park, storefront or factory. These skeptics probably do not know that the number of people working from home and making very good annual incomes has grown by leaps and bounds in recent years.

According to the National Association of Home Based Businesses, more than 50 million people in the United States work from a home office or workspace in some capacity full time or part time. Not surprisingly, almost 30 million are self-employed, owning and operating a home business venture. In

fact, home business enterprises create more jobs and employ more people annually in the United States than any other business classification or industry sector.

Your home business is not merely a hobby and should not be treated as such, even if you operate the business part time or seasonally. Starting a home business requires the input of three very valuable assets—an investment of money to start and then to grow the business, a substantial investment of time, and a significant investment of personal energy and motivation. All three are extremely valuable commodities that should never be wasted or taken lightly.

Plan Everything

I won't say that failing to plan means that you're planning to fail, because few people consciously set out to fail in business. But I will say that many people do not properly plan, generally for two reasons. First, they're lazy and do not want to commit the time, money and energy that is required to properly develop business, marketing and financial plans. Second, many people are intimidated by the planning process because they do not understand what it takes to create and implement a working plan. Both hurdles are easily overcome. In the first case, there are no shortcuts in business. You will greatly increase your odds of succeeding if you plan for success. In the second case, read books about business planning or contact the SBA and inquire about business planning courses and programs offered in your local area or online. Likewise, contact home business associations and inquire about business planning courses and programs.

Planning every aspect of your home business is not only a must, but it also builds habits that every home business owner should develop and maintain. The act of business planning is so important because it requires you to analyze each business situation, research and compile data, and make conclusions based mainly on the facts as revealed through the research. Business planning also serves a second function, which is having your goals and how you will achieve them on paper. You can use the plan that you create both as map to take you from point A to point Z and as a yardstick to measure the success of each individual plan or segment within the plan. This is not to say that every plan you create for your small business must be a hefty tome chock full of statistics, but the basics must be covered. Enough information must be revealed so that you can develop business, marketing and growth strategies. Key plans include a business plan, marketing plan, advertising plan, sales plan and financial forecasts and plans.

Manage Money Wisely

The lifeblood of any business enterprise is cash flow. You need it to buy inventory, pay for services, promote and market your business, repair and replace tools and equipment, and pay yourself so that you can continue to work. Therefore, all home business owners must become wise money managers to ensure that the cash keeps flowing and the bills get paid. There are two aspects to wise money management.

1. The money you receive from clients in exchange for your goods and services (income)
2. The money you spend on inventory, supplies, wages and other items to operate your business (expenses)

A good money manager is on top of all invoices that have been sent out and all money owed from customers. A good money manager is also on top of what needs to be paid to vendors, the landlord, the phone company and so on. Balancing the books carefully means staying on top of your financial picture. It means spending and not spending according to a list of priorities and not wasting money. For most good business money managers, this will mean budgeting the startup costs and the ongoing expenses and then watching the income and expense log closely.

Ask for the Sale

A home business entrepreneur must always remember that marketing, advertising or promotional activities are completely worthless, regardless of how clever, expensive or perfectly targeted they are, unless one simple thing is accomplished—ask for the sale. This is not to say that being a great salesperson, an advertising copywriting whiz or a public relations specialist isn't a tremendous asset to your business. However, all of these skills will be for naught if you do not actively ask people to buy what you are selling.

Home business owners do not have to be sales and marketing geniuses to be successful. In fact, you will win more times than not by following one simple rule—always ask for the sale. In all your advertising, ask people to buy. In your booth at the trade show, ask people to buy. In all your signage, ask people to buy. In all your promotional materials, ask people to buy. During sales presentations, ask people to buy. On your website, ask people to buy. The last eight words that you say to a prospect or current customer should be, "How do you want to pay for that?" Few people will offer you their hard-earned money unless you ask. This simple, yet time-tested and proven business premise can easily mean the difference between success and failure. Therefore, every time you talk about your business, products or services to prospects or current customers, you must ask for the sale.

Remember That It's All About the Customer

Your home business is not about the products or services that you sell. Your home business is not about the prices that you charge for your goods and services. Your home business is not about your competitors and how to beat them. Your business is all about your customers or clients—period. After all, your customers are the people who will ultimately decide if your business goes boom or goes bust. Everything you do in business must be customer-focused, including your policies, warranties, payment options, operating hours, presentations, advertising and promotional campaigns and website. In addition, you must know who your customers are inside out and upside down. You have to know what they need, the problems they have that must be solved, where the majority of them are based, how much money they want to spend for what you sell and how often they want to buy what you have to offer. Everything you do in business must be for the benefit of your customers and potential customers and no one else. Too many people become self-indulgent and start touting what they want to sell, even if nobody wants to hear them. This is a ticket to failure. In business, it's not about *you*, it's about *them*.

Become a Shameless Self-Promoter (Without Becoming Obnoxious)

One of the greatest myths about personal or business success is that eventually your business, personal abilities, products or services will get discovered and be embraced by the masses, who will beat a path to your door to buy what you are selling. But how can this happen if no one knows who you are, what you sell and why they should be buying?

Self-promotion is one of the most beneficial yet most underused marketing tools that most home business owners have at their immediate disposal.

Become a shameless promoter of your business and your goods or services by creating unique promotions on a regular basis and constantly seeking publicity. Build a network of people who believe strongly enough in you and your business that they, too, will become supporters and shamelessly spread the word for you via word-of-mouth advertising and referrals. Never stop asking everyone you come into contact with for new business.

Success never happens by accident or by a lucky break; success is always the result of planning, smart and hard work and tireless promotion. You must become a portable advertisement for your business, a walking and talking example of what your business does and sells. So finely tuned and refined is your ability as a mobile advertisement that in less than 30 seconds you can explain what you do and how others benefit. And most important, the people to whom you speak understand instantly your advertisement and associate you with your business and your goods or services. In addition, as a mobile advertisement for your business, you are always armed with information, promotional items, business cards and samples.

Project a Positive Business Image

You have but a passing moment to make a positive and memorable impression on people with whom you intend to do business. Home business owners must go out of their way and make a conscious effort to always project the most professional business image possible. The majority of home business owners do not have the advantage of elaborate offices or elegant storefronts and showrooms to wow prospects and impress customers. Instead, they must rely on imagination, creativity and attention to the smallest detail when creating and maintaining a professional image for their home business.

It is wise to budget and spend extra to have business cards, stationery and sales materials, such as catalogs and brochures, printed on high-quality paper that is rich in texture and heavy to the touch. The more you strive to create a professional business image, the more likely your prospects will see your business as credible, overlooking the fact that it is small and operated from a home office location.

Keep in mind when developing your business image that consistency is the main objective. Once you have created the image you want to create and be remembered for, be sure to use it in all areas of your business. This includes being consistent in color scheme, logo, sales messages and promotional campaign. If you consistently use a unified message and theme, people will begin to associate these things with your business and with the products and services you sell. Consistency is the foundation of branding.

Get to Know Your Customers: Personalize Your Business

One of the biggest features and often the most significant competitive edge the homebased entrepreneur has over the larger competitors is being able to offer personalized attention. In an age when modern technology has e-shoppers buying from faceless websites or mega superstores, often with horror stories should they need customer service, you can offer that personal attention and excellent customer service that is very much in demand today. Call it high-tech backlash, if you will, but customers are sick and tired of hearing that their information is somewhere in the computer and must be retrieved or being told to push a dozen digits to finally get to the right department, only to end up with voice mail—from which they never receive a return phone call.

The home business owner can actually answer phone calls, get to know customers, provide per-sonal attention and win repeat business by doing so. It's a researched fact that most business (80 percent) will come from repeat customers rather than new customers. Therefore, along with trying to draw newcomers, the more you do to woo your regular customers, the better off you will be in the long run. Personalized attention is very much appreciated and remembered in our high-tech world.

Level the Playing Field with Technology

You should avoid getting overly caught up in technology, but you should also know how to take advantage of it. One of the most amazing aspects of the internet is that a one- or two-person business operating from a basement can have a better website than a $50-million company and nobody knows the difference. Make sure you are keeping up with the technology as it suits your needs. This means getting the computer and software you need to be efficient (a laptop if you'll be out on the road), having a separate business phone and a cell phone and all of technological tools that you really need. It also means bypassing the technology that doesn't make sense for your business needs. Think about technology for practical purposes and use it only to benefit your business. The best graphics software program in the world is meaningless to someone who needs no graphic design. Also, look to keep up-to-date rather than ahead of the curve. This means that if you, your clients and your vendors are all using the 2006 version of a program, don't run out and buy the 2008 model if it will cause interfacing difficulties. The best technology is what helps you, not what impresses your neighbors.

Build a Top-Notch Business Team

No one person can build a successful business alone. It requires a team of people who are as committed as you to the business and its success. Your business team may include family members, friends, suppliers, business alliances, employees, subcontractors, industry and business associations, local government and the community. Of course the most important team members will be your customers or clients. Any or all may have a say in how your business will function and a share in your business future.

With so much at stake, it stands to reason that you should go out of your way to build the strongest business team that you can possibly muster. Your team should be composed of people who share your vision of the future and believe in your ability to make it happen. A common challenge facing home businesses is the lack of a support system, people who can help grow the business and help out in its day-to-day operations. In most cases midsize or large corporations have the advantage of in-house or on-hand support staff that the majority of small business owners cannot afford, either in employee wages or in service retainers. These people can include in-house public relations staff, sales and marketing specialists, bookkeepers and accountants, lawyers and financial analysts. So it is important that you take the time now, while your business is small, to build a top-notch team of true believers to ensure that your business is here for today and in the future. Look for an accountant, an attorney, a bookkeeper and others who can be called on as necessary for their specialized expertise. Nobody is expected to know everything. Then look for support from friends and family.

Become Known as an Expert

When you have a problem, do you seek just anyone's advice or do you seek an expert in the field to help solve it? Obviously, you want the most accurate information and assistance that you can get. You naturally seek an expert to help solve your problem. You call a plumber when the water heater leaks, a real estate agent when it's time to sell your home or a dentist when you have a toothache. Therefore, it only stands to reason that the more you become known for your expertise in your business, the more people will seek you out for your expertise, creating more selling and referral opportunities. In effect, becoming known as an expert is another way to prospect for new business, just in reverse. You don't go out to find new and qualified prospect; these people seek you out for your expertise.

Becoming an expert is not as difficult as you might think. By virtue of starting a business, to a certain degree you are already an expert when you get a business license, put up a website and sell your first product or service. You can also position yourself as an expert in your particular field by speaking at public and business functions on your specialty and by writing articles for magazines, newsletters, newspapers and websites. You can send your name, business information and some background to the local media so reporters can call you when they need information in the area of your specialty. The more widely you become known as an expert in your particular field, the more people will seek you out for help.

Create a Competitive Advantage

A home business must have a clearly defined, unique selling proposition. This is nothing more than a fancy way of asking the vital question, "Why will people choose to do business with you instead of with a competitor?" In other words, what one aspect or combination of aspects is going to separate your business from your competitors? Will it be better service, a longer warranty, better selection, longer business hours, more flexible payment options, lowest price, personalized service, better customer service, better return and exchange policies or a combination of several of these? Your competitive advantage must be beneficial to consumers, exclusive to your business and simple to offer. You should be able to sum up your unique selling proposition in one clear sentence that makes customers say, "I understand why I should buy from you."

Every entrepreneur needs a competitive advantage to survive in a highly competitive, global business environment. Because of the importance of your competitive advantage in positioning your business and your products or services in the marketplace, you should use it to anchor all your promotional activities and you should think of it as your main marketing tool.

You will also need to develop a message to describe your competitive advantage. This message should be brief, to the point and easy to understand and, above all, it should clearly state why people should do business with you and not your competitors. For example, if you provide personalized service, your promotions and ads should feature that your business is run by caring people with whom customers can talk and not by a faceless corporation.

Invest in Yourself

Successful entrepreneurs share a common denominator across all types of business ventures and in every industry sector—they never stop investing in products, services, information and education that will make them better, smarter and more productive. They know and believe that every dollar they invest in educational activities and improvement will pay back tenfold or greater. These investments will also give them a much-needed advantage in an extremely competitive global business environment.

Top entrepreneurs read business and marketing books, magazines, reports, journals, newsletters, website content and industry publications, knowing that these resources will improve their understanding of business and marketing functions and skills. They join business associations and clubs and they network with successful businesspeople to learn their secrets of success and help define their own goals and objectives. Top entrepreneurs attend business and marketing seminars, workshops and training courses, even if they have already mastered the subject matter of the event. They do this because they know that education is an ongoing process that never ends. There are usually ways to do things better, in less time and with less effort. They invest in home office and business equipment and technology to improve their business and marketing efficiency. Equipment such as a comfortable office chair, a fast computer, professional software and multifunction telephone systems and printers helps increase productivity and profitability. In short, top entrepreneurs never stop investing in the most powerful, effective and best business and marketing tool at their immediate disposal—themselves.

Be Accessible

We are living in a time when we all expect our fast-food lunch at the drive-through window to be ready in mere minutes, our dry cleaning to be ready for pickup on the same day, our money to be available at the ATM, and our pizza delivered in 30 minutes or it's free. You see the pattern developing—you must make it as easy as you can for people to do business with you, regardless of the home business you operate.

You must remain cognizant of the fact that few people will work hard, go out of their way or be inconvenienced just for the privilege of giving you their hard-earned money. The shoe is always on the other foot. Making it easy for people to do business with you means that you must be accessible and knowledgeable about your products and services. You must be able to provide customers with what they want, when they want it. Accessibility means you never dodge telephone calls, you reply to e-mails quickly, you do not skip meetings or appointments, and you do not employ other procrastination techniques to make things convenient for yourself rather than for your customers and prospects. "Accessible" means telling your prospects and customers in advance the hours and days that you can be reached and how they can reach you. It means a website that is easy to navigate, with "contact us" always a single click away—without requiring visitors to provide a ton of information first. It means never letting your prospects and customers down. If you make it difficult for people to do business with you, then you will likely lose them as customers.

Build a Rock-Solid Reputation

A good reputation is unquestionably one of the home business owner's most tangible and marketable assets. You can't simply buy a good reputation; you must earn it by honoring your promises. If you promise to have the merchandise in the customer's hands by Wednesday, you have no excuse not to have it there. If you offer to repair something, you need to make good on your offer. You must honor whatever promises you make to gain a good reputation.

Consistency in what you offer is the other key factor. If you cannot regularly provide the same level of services and products for clients, why should they trust you? Without trust you won't have a good reputation.

Fast-food chain restaurants are perfect examples of why building a rock-solid reputation is essential for business success. Seldom is the food the best, but customers know exactly what they

will get in return for their money. This is because fast-food restaurant chains spend time, money and energy creating reputations for fast service, affordable prices and clean environments. They're not promoting the lowest prices, the fanciest interiors or exotic menus.

To build a solid reputation, you must provide great customer service, you must sell products and services that people need, you must provide value, you must stand behind your products or services, and, above all, you must keep your promises.

Few people refer friends to a business that sells inferior products at low prices. But many will refer friends to a business that has treated them fairly and met their expectations, even if it did not have the lowest price or is not the biggest player in the market.

Sell Benefits

Pushing product features is for inexperienced entrepreneurs. Selling the benefits associated with owning and using products and services is what sales professionals worldwide focus on to create buying excitement and to sell, sell more and sell more frequently to their customers. Your advertising, sales presentations, printed marketing materials, product packaging, website, newsletters, trade show exhibit and signage are vital. Every time you communicate with your target audience in every medium you use, you must always be selling the benefits associated with owning your product or using your service. A treadmill may have 30 features, but the true benefit to the user is the fact that if you buy and use the treadmill on a regular basis, you will be more physically fit. In this case, it is a proven fact that people who exercise are more physically fit than those people who do not. This information can then be translated into exciting selling terms, such as that the customer will lose weight, become healthier and enjoy increased self-confidence—all of which are the potential benefits of buying and using a treadmill. A built-in radio, a wider track surface and a larger color selection are features, but not necessarily benefits. You also need to drop any long-winded explanations about what your business does or sells and develop a high-impact mini sales pitch to replace it. Keep the pitch short, simple and directly to the point, which should be what you sell and the biggest benefit your customers receive. Clearly demonstrate to prospects how your product or service will benefit them and you will sell more.

Get Involved

Always go out of your way to get involved in the community that supports your business. You can do this in many ways, such as pitching in to help local charities or the food bank, helping organize community events, and participating in local politics. You can join associations and clubs that concentrate on programs and policies intended to improve the local community. It is a fact that people like to do business with people they know, like and respect, and with people who do things to help them as members of the community.

Therefore, get involved in your community and you will open many doors in terms of networking, prospecting, referrals and increased selling opportunities, which can have enormous long-term benefits for your business. You will also improve your reputation as someone who cares about more than just making money and today, with so many issues on the minds of your consumers, that can make a difference.

One of the primary building blocks for successful businesses is the investment of time, money and energy in the people and the community that support the business. It's being a good business citizen and it's a responsibility shared by all business owners. In terms of building a positive business image and loyal customer base, no marketing effort can match giving back to the community that supports your business and helps to build your success. It also helps you benefit as a human being.

Grab Attention

One way for small business owners to stand out in the increasingly competitive business world is to develop a strategy of always aiming to grab the attention of your target audience. In every business, the marketing, promotional and publicity activity you engage in must be designed and implemented in a way that grabs and holds the attention of the target prospects and customers long enough for them to form a positive image of your business. You have to create print advertisements that leap off the page screaming, "Look at me!" Your car, job site and trade show signage must turn heads so forcefully that people run the risk of getting whiplash. Your radio advertisements must make people crank up the volume at the mere mention of your business's name, products or services. Your networking style at meetings and events must have people mentioning your business name in a positive way to others, even days, weeks and months later.

In short, if you want to stand out in today's business environment, everything you do to market or promote your business must be aimed at grabbing the attention of your target audience. Small business owners cannot waste time, money and energy on promotional activities aimed at building awareness solely through long-term, repeated exposure. If you do, chances are you will go broke long before you achieve this goal. Instead, each of your promotional activities must put money back into your pocket so that you can continue to grab more attention and grow your business.

Master the Art of Negotiation

The ability to negotiate effectively is unquestionably a skill that every home business owner must make every effort to master. It is perhaps second in importance only to asking for the sale in terms of home business musts. In business, negotiation skills are used daily. You negotiate with prospects and clients to sell more goods and services and for a higher price. You negotiate with your suppliers to receive a lower cost per unit or better payment terms. You negotiate with your bank to secure lines of operating capital, lower credit card merchant rates and no-fee banking services. You may even find yourself negotiating with your family and friends about personal activities, such as missed vacations or late meals, because your business is swamped and time is at a premium.

Always remember that mastering the art of negotiation means that your skills are so finely tuned that you can always orchestrate a win-win situation. These win-win arrangements mean that every party involved feels like he or she has won, which is really the basis for building long-term and profitable business relationships. You cannot expect customers, employees, business alliance partners and suppliers to be loyal to your brand, treat you with respect, and believe in your business unless you strive to build situations and relationships in which they all stand to win. Everyone wants to know, "what's in it for me?", so being able to negotiate terms under which all sides benefit will put you in an excellent position for future negotiations.

Design Your Workspace for Success

Carefully plan and design your home office workspace to ensure maximum personal performance and productivity and, if necessary, to project professionalism for visiting clients. If at all possible, resist the temptation to turn a corner of the living room or your bedroom into your office. Ideally, you'll want a separate room with a door that closes to keep business activities in and family members out, at least during prime business and revenue-

generating hours of the day. A den, a spare bedroom, a basement and a converted garage are all ideal candidates for your new home office. If this is not possible, you'll have to find a means of converting a room with a partition or simply find hours to do the bulk of your work when nobody else is home.

Your workspace needs to include a dedicated phone line, your computer and printer and other technology that you need (e.g., photocopier, scanner and shredder), a comfortable and roomy work station, plus places to keep your files, other paperwork and any books and magazines.

You also want to feel good while you are working. Therefore, if you have some reminders of things you enjoy in life, such as a sports trophy or a photo of your family, put it up on one of the shelves. Remember: one of the best things about working at home is that you can keep the other areas of your life nearby so that you never lose focus on why you are doing all of this hard work ... for a better life for yourself and your family.

Some people will tell you to eliminate any clutter and have a clean desk. However, if you need to keep some papers out and around to be most efficient, then do so. There is no one-size-fits-all manner in which to work and the benefit of a homebased business is that as long as you are efficient, you can work any way you choose. The end result should be business success; if that means working in a rebuilt walk-in closet, so be it. Set up your workspace in a manner that allows *you* to be most efficient.

Ensure that your office and workspace are ergonomically designed for maximum productivity. Ergonomic and medical experts agree that a appropriate design can increase productivity and quality of work by as much as 20 percent. Invest in books that will explain the basics of ergonomics, such as chair size, style and adjustment, sitting position, lighting, upper body position and placement of monitor and keyboard. Proper ergonomic office design and layout will create a healthy and productive work environment.

Get and Stay Organized

The key to staying organized is not about which type of file you have or whether you keep a stack or two of papers on your desk, but about managing your business, about having systems in place to do things. Therefore, you want to establish a routine by which you can accomplish as much as possible in a given workday, whether that's three hours for a part-time business or seven, eight or nine hours as a full-timer.

In fact, you should develop systems and routines for just about every single business activity. Small things such as creating a to-do list at the end of each business day or for the week will help keep you on top of important tasks to tackle. Creating a single calendar to work from, not one for each activity or set of activities, will also ensure that you complete jobs on schedule and keep appointments. Incorporating family and personal activities into your work calendar is also critical, so that you work and plan from a single calendar.

Carefully planning out-of-office client meetings in blocks, such as an entire morning, afternoon or day, may reduce the travel time if the clients are in one area. However, taking a large block of time to drive all over the place may leave you unavailable to other customers for too long. Therefore, you might schedule two short trips out of the office to two specific areas in which to meet clients.

Include both high-priority and low-priority items on your to-do list. Don't forget to take time to answer e-mails and return phone calls—both very important. Also, get to know the schedules of vendors and other people with whom you will need to interact regularly. If a vendor is reachable only in the mornings, make a note of it. You will learn to integrate your schedule with others as necessary and allow for differences in time zone. For example, some business owners on the East Coast may have West Coast customers or vendors, so they schedule any phone calls with the time difference in mind.

Take Time Off

The temptation to work around the clock is very real for some home business owners. After all, you do not have a manager telling you it's time to go home because the company can't afford the overtime pay. If you work from home, you must take time to establish a regular work schedule that includes time to stretch your legs and take lunch breaks, plus some days off and scheduled vacations. Create the schedule as soon as you have made the commitment to start a home business. Of course, your schedule will have to be flexible, so you should not fill every possible hour in the day. Allow yourself a backup hour or two. For example, if you have seven hours scheduled on Tuesday but your son or daughter gets sick at school and you end up taking care of your child for part of the day, you can catch up for an hour on Saturday afternoon when you have nothing planned. No matter how dedicated you are, you must mix work time with the rest of your life. All work and no play makes you burn out very fast and become impatient or grumpy with customers and other people.

You must also learn to say no, regardless of how difficult it can be. Saying yes too often is one of the biggest temptations faced by home business owners, and one of the most difficult to overcome and correct. We all say yes because we want to please clients, business allies and family. But usually we spread ourselves too thin and fail to do the important moneymaking business tasks properly. Few people near the end of their life reflect fondly on the times they spent working around the clock and forgoing everything else that life has to offer. Wouldn't you prefer to reflect on the good times spent with family and friends and on life's adventures?

Make it a personal goal to stay fit and healthy. If you do not feel good physically or mentally, it is very difficult to be 100 percent effective and productive. Eat right, get enough sleep and maintain a regular physical exercise program.

Limit the Number of Hats You Wear

It is difficult for most business owners not to take a hands-on approach. They try to do as much as possible and tackle as many tasks as possible. The ability to multitask is a common trait shared by successful entrepreneurs. However, once in a while you have to stand back and look beyond today to determine what is in the best interests of your business and yourself over the long run. Often, by analyzing what is best for your business in the long term, you will discover that farming out some business and marketing tasks that would be better handled by an expert is a wise decision. Most highly successful entrepreneurs will tell you that from the time they started out they knew what they were good at and what tasks to delegate to others.

Without question there is a cost associated with paying others to do work that could be completed in-house. Outsourcing can be especially difficult for home business owners with limited capital. But the cost of trying to do something that you know little if anything about could be substantially higher. There is the potential for losing sales and customers or for not getting the desired results. For example, if prospecting or lead generation is not your forte, but you excel at presenting and closing the sale, then hire professional direct marketers to collect qualified leads for you. In almost all situations, you'll find that by doing what you do best you will generate far more revenue and profit than you will spend on farming out some of your more unproductive tasks.

Follow Up Constantly

Every home business owner, new or established, should constantly contact, follow up and follow through with customers, prospects and business allies. Constant and consistent follow-up enables you to turn prospects into customers, raise the value of each sale, increase the buying frequency of current customers and build stronger business relationships with suppliers and your core business team.

Follow-up is especially important with your current customers, as the real work begins after the sale. It is easy to sell products or services once, but it takes work to keep customers coming back. In fact, according to the SBA, more than of 60 percent of consumers stop doing business with a company because they feel they are being ignored and forgotten after the original sale. Couple that startling statistic with the fact that it costs 10 times as much to find and convert a prospect into a customer as it does to maintain a current customer. So you see why the real work begins after the sale—the work of building and maintaining a business relationship with your customers.

Develop a system that enables you to follow up with prospects and customers on a regular basis. Keep in touch with them by e-mail, phone and mail. Let them know that you are always thinking of them and encourage them to call you to ask for help, advice and suggestions—or just to say hello.

RESOURCES
Associations

National Association of Home Based Businesses
10451 Mill Run Circle, Suite 400
Owings Mills, MD 21117
(410) 581-1373, (410) 363-3698
usahomebusiness.com

National Association of Women Business Owners (NAWBO)
8405 Greensboro Drive, Suite 800
McLean, VA 22102
(800) 55-NAWBO (556-2926)
nawbo.org

Small Office Home Office Business Group (SOHO)
Suite 1, 1680 Lloyd Avenue
North Vancouver, BC V7P 2N6
(604) 929-8250, (800) 290-SOHO (7646)
soho.ca

SOHO America, Inc. (Small Office Home Office)
P.O. Box 941
Hurst, TX 76053-0941
soho.org

Suggested Reading

Barnett, Rebecca. *Winning Without Losing Your Way: Character-Centered Leadership*. Bowling Green, KY: Winning Your Way, Inc., 2003.

Barrett, Niall. *Building the Custom Home Office: Projects for the Complete Work Space*. Newtown, CT: Taunton Press, 2002.

Gleeson, Kerry. *The Personal Efficiency Program: How to Get Organized to Do More Work in Less Time*. 3rd edition. New York: John Wiley & Sons, 2004.

Silber, Lee T. *Self-Promotion for the Creative Person: Get the Word Out About Who You Are and What You Do*. New York: Three Rivers Press (Crown Publishing), 2001.

Stephenson, James, and Courtney Thurman. *The Ultimate Small Business Marketing Guide*: Irvine, CA: Entrepreneur Press, 2007.

Weltman, Barbara. *The Complete Idiot's Guide to Starting a Home-Based Business*. 3rd edition. New York: Alpha Books, 2007

Websites

Brian Tracy International: Sales and motivational expert. Provides coaching, information, products, programs and services. *briantracy.com*

Entrepreneur Online: Small business information, products and services portal. *entrepreneur.com*

Ergonomics Online: Ergonomics information, articles, industry links and resources. *ergonomics.org*

Guerrilla Marketing Online: Small business marketing tips, information, seminars, books and links. *gmarketing.com*

International Customer Service Association: The ICSA offers members information, products, services and education aimed at improving customer service skills and relationship building. *icsa.com*

Organized Times: Information, advice, tools and services aimed at getting the home office organized and productive. *organizedtimes.com*

WorkSpaces: Information, advice and links on setting up, organizing and furnishing a home office. *workspaces.com*

CHAPTER 2

What Type of Home Business Should You Start?

WHAT TYPE OF HOME BUSINESS should you start? Ultimately, there is only one person who knows that answer: you. Once you have decided that you want to start your own home business or are leaning in that general direction, the next step is to decide what type of business to start. There are many factors that will weigh on your decision, some much more than others, including:

- Your personal life situation
- The suitability of your home for running a business
- What you enjoy doing
- Your experiences and special skills
- Your personal and financial goals
- Available resources
- Sources of financing
- Finding a good match

Owning and operating a business is very much a balancing act—you often have to make personal compromises and almost always have to make financial compromises to get the business up and running successfully. As with anything in life that is worthwhile, you must make sacrifices along the way to build a successful business enterprise. However, if the sacrifices cause you to lose focus or hate the business that you started, chances are you will be miserable and ultimately the business will fail. Therefore, while weighing all factors might take a lot of time and effort, it is critical in the business planning process.

More detailed information about starting your business and related topics is to be found in later chapters. This section is specifically designed to help you decide on the right home business startup.

Your Personal Life Situation

One of the most important factors to consider prior to starting or purchasing a home business is to analyze carefully your reasons for starting a business. You need to make sure your reason is valid before embarking on such a quest. You also need to consider how such a transition to a homebased business will affect your family or the other significant people in your life.

There are no right or wrong answers here. This is meant to help you determine what new home business venture is right for you, if any. For question #1, does your answer reflect a desire to run a business on your own or perhaps to spend more time with your family? These are good answers. If you are tired of your commute, have friends who have home businesses or are doing this for a reason that doesn't suggest something positive in your future, you need to rethink the idea.

Likewise, question #2 is a bit tricky in that it asks you to consider whether your decision is based on being tired of your present job or boss (or both). Remember: Walking away from something is fine, but unless you have the attitude that one door closing means another one opening—and truly believe in a business idea—you'll be going into your own business for the wrong reason. Don't start a business simply as a way out of what you are doing now. Also, don't start a business to show up your boss or anyone else. Start a business because you believe it's time to do so. If you bought this book in haste, because you are

---

FIGURE 2.1   Taking Stock of Your Personal Life Situation Worksheet

1. Describe why you want to be self-employed and operate your own home business.

    _____

    _____

2. Are you dissatisfied with your current job or career? If so, why?

    _____

    _____

3. Do you want your family to be included in the decision-making process when selecting the right home business?

    _____

    _____

4. Will your family situation limit your ability to work at home?

    _____

    _____

5. If you are single, will you be able to work at home and still maintain a social life?

    _____

    _____

unhappy with your current job, put it down for a few days and wait before picking it up again.

Question #3 asks about your family's involvement in your business (if you have a family) and how that will affect your decision. This is simply a means of having you think about their role in your plan. It's OK to answer no and have your family simply be supportive while you make the decisions. Just make sure you have open communication with your family about your plan. Likewise, question #4 asks about family in a more practical manner. Some homes are just not ready to have a business going on in the midst of chaos. It may mean waiting a few years or working around homework time and various family activities. And finally, as noted in question #5, not everyone has a family. If you are single, can this type of arrangement work for you? It may mean less social interaction than you'll find in a busy office and it may mean you'll have a little less time available for dating. For many people, this is fine. Know what you need.

As for the type of business to choose, look at your priorities. If you rank wanting to spend more time with your family as very important to you, then a business that keeps you in the home office would be a better choice than one that requires visiting clients or working on job sites. If you have five young children at home, you'll probably want to choose a business that does not require you to have clients visit frequently. Also, keep in mind that when you start a business, you are making decisions for more than yourself, so it is vital to include your family members in the decision-making process.

Is Your Home Suitable for a Business?

Is your residence a good place to start and operate a home business? Lots of people decide to start a home business without giving this question much thought. Not every residence is a suitable location for a business. In fact, in some municipalities in the United States and Canada, local zoning laws prohibit home business ventures entirely. Therefore, long before you invest substantial amounts of cash to get your new home business venture rolling, you should determine if your residence is the right location for operating a business and if the venture will be legal. Considerations in terms of setting up a business in your home include:

- Zoning regulations
- Space requirements
- Access for clients and/or employees
- Neighbors and neighborhood issues
- Suitable and adequate parking
- Privacy for yourself and family
- Adequate storage space for business needs
- Security issues
- Laws involving employees working from your home
- Safety issues
- Special insurance needs
- Pollution concerns (noises, odors, wastes)
- Mechanical requirements, including electrical and phone lines

Additional information about setting up your home business workspace, legal issues and employees can be found in Chapters 4, 7 and 8, respectively. There is no side-stepping this issue. If your residence is not suitable for running a business, you will have to make whatever changes are necessary to make it right. This may mean getting a variance from the local zoning board or having a licensed electrician review and rewire your home to meet your increased electrical needs. One of the most important concerns that you will want to address is that you do not make your home unsafe with wiring, high-tech equipment or other changes to run your business.

Remember: You do not want to invest large amounts of time and money in starting or purchasing a business venture only to discover that you cannot run a business from your home.

What Do You Want to Do?

Another factor influencing your choice of home-based business is doing something that you really enjoy. Without question, potential profit should be a motivation for starting your own business. But enjoyment, pride and self-fulfillment must also factor into the business mix. If you do not enjoy what you are doing, money will be of little comfort. It is important to carefully consider what you enjoy doing. You may be investing substantial capital and operating your business for a long time.

You can be a little creative in terms of doing what you enjoy doing. For instance, if you enjoy carpentry, you can look at providing more than just carpentry services. You can also train others to become carpenters, write books or articles about carpentry or sell carpentry-related products and services to other carpentry fanatics. One way that you can focus on what you might enjoy is to create categories and match other criteria, such as income and capital available. The list below does not include every category, so you may want to expand it. Likewise, the businesses featured under each category are for example purposes only. Once again, you will want to expand them once you have created your own categories.

If you enjoy helping others, then consider:

- Nonmedical home care
- Wedding/event planning
- House inspection
- Catering

If you are creative, then consider:

- Interior decoration
- Photography
- Homebased crafts
- Desktop publishing

If you enjoy working with children, then consider:

- Homebased day care
- Birthday party planning
- Educational tutoring
- Running a nanny service

If you enjoy working with computers and other technology, then consider:

- Computer repair
- Website design and maintenance
- E-commerce
- Software development

If you enjoy providing information, then consider:

- Public relations
- Financial planning
- Advertising
- Consulting in your specialty

If you enjoy selling, then consider:

- Independent sales agent
- Business brokering
- Direct sales
- Running an import/export business

If you enjoy working with transportation, then consider:

- Being a driving instructor
- Automotive detailing
- Mobile auto inspections
- Running a delivery service

If you enjoy the outdoors and adventure, then consider:

- Adventure travel booking
- Teaching outdoor safety classes
- Creating adventure brochures
- Outdoor or sports instruction

If you enjoy working with your hands, then consider:

- Homebased manufacturing business

- Cabinetmaking
- Home improvement business
- Craft making

If you enjoy working with pets, then consider:

- A dog walking service
- Pet grooming
- Pet photography
- Pet training

If you enjoy writing, then consider:

- Writing books
- Writing web content and/or magazine articles
- Editing
- Writing resumes

If you enjoy health and fitness, then consider:

- Running yoga classes
- Being a fitness instructor
- Being a personal trainer
- Setting up training programs

The purpose of this exercise is to identify what it is you really enjoy doing in broad terms, so you can then consider home business ventures that fall into the appropriate categories and eliminate those that do not. For instance, if you enjoy working with your hands, skip home businesses that will keep you planted in a chair in front of a computer.

While most businesses, even in an area that you love, will include some tasks you do not enjoy, such as the outdoor enthusiast sitting behind the computer screen printing out invoices, you want to find a business opportunity with minimal discomfort. Think about all the tasks involved in your business idea and determine to what degree each is important. If, for example, you do not like working with numbers, you will have to suck it up, since all businesses in which money is involved will include some number crunching. However, some will focus more heavily on numbers or using high-tech equipment, while others will have you spending less time in such areas as craft making or having a career in the arts.

With that in mind, in order of priority, use the Things You Dislike Doing Worksheet (Figure 2.2) to list 10 things you dislike doing.

What Experience and Special Skills Do You Have?

While you certainly do not have to possess all the skills necessary for running a home business, identifying your personal strengths and weaknesses prior to starting a business is logical and enables you to

FIGURE 2.2 Things You Dislike Doing Worksheet

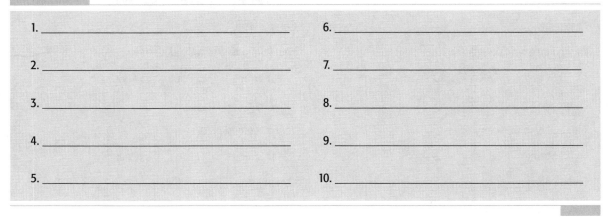

1. _____ 6. _____

2. _____ 7. _____

3. _____ 8. _____

4. _____ 9. _____

5. _____ 10. _____

correct weaknesses and build on your strengths. The Special Skills Checklist (Figure 2.3) is a good starting point for identifying your strengths and weaknesses as they relate to common business skills.

| FIGURE 2.3 | Special Skills Checklist |

Your ability to work independently is:

❑ Strong   ❑ Fair   ❑ Poor

Comments: _____

Your research skills are:

❑ Strong   ❑ Fair   ❑ Poor

Comments: _____

Your planning skills are:

❑ Strong   ❑ Fair   ❑ Poor

Comments: _____

Your sales and marketing skills are:

❑ Strong   ❑ Fair   ❑ Poor

Comments: _____

Your customer services skills are:

❑ Strong   ❑ Fair   ❑ Poor

Comments: _____

Your ability to lead/delegate is:

❑ Strong   ❑ Fair   ❑ Poor

Comments: _____

Your communication skills are:

❑ Strong   ❑ Fair   ❑ Poor

Comments: _____

Your ability to think logically is:

❑ Strong   ❑ Fair   ❑ Poor

Comments: _____

Your problem-solving skills are:

❑ Strong   ❑ Fair   ❑ Poor

Comments: _____

Your record-keeping/bookkeeping skills are:

❑ Strong   ❑ Fair   ❑ Poor

Comments: _____

Your competitive spirit is:

❑ Strong   ❑ Fair   ❑ Poor

Comments: _____

Your organizational skills are:

❑ Strong   ❑ Fair   ❑ Poor

Comments: _____

Your time management skills are:

❑ Strong   ❑ Fair   ❑ Poor

Comments: _____

Your risk assessment skills are:

❑ Strong   ❑ Fair   ❑ Poor

Comments: _____

Your computer/software skills are:

❑ Strong   ❑ Fair   ❑ Poor

Comments: _____

Your internet skills are:

❑ Strong   ❑ Fair   ❑ Poor

Comments: _____

FIGURE 2.3	Special Skills Checklist, continued

Your listening skills are:

❑ Strong ❑ Fair ❑ Poor

Comments: _____

Your ability to handle stress is:

❑ Strong ❑ Fair ❑ Poor

Comments: _____

Your ability to stay focused is:

❑ Strong ❑ Fair ❑ Poor

Comments: _____

Your networking skills are:

❑ Strong ❑ Fair ❑ Poor

Comments: _____

Your ability to set goals is:

❑ Strong ❑ Fair ❑ Poor

Comments: _____

Your money management skills are:

❑ Strong ❑ Fair ❑ Poor

Comments: _____

Your financial budgeting skills are:

❑ Strong ❑ Fair ❑ Poor

Comments: _____

Your public speaking skills are:

❑ Strong ❑ Fair ❑ Poor

Comments: _____

Your decision-making abilities are:

❑ Strong ❑ Fair ❑ Poor

Comments: _____

Your Personal Goals

Starting a business should involve knowing what you want to achieve in life. Whether your goals are grandiose or modest, they are important to you. Personal goals might include the desire to travel the world, be more physically fit, work less, attain more education, find a life partner or start a family. If a business does not help you reach your goals, it is not the right business for you. For instance, if one of your personal goals is to take time every year to travel extensively, a seasonal homebased business, such as a lawn maintenance service in a northern climate, would be a wise startup choice, while a home business that requires daily hands-on management, such as a commercial office cleaning service, would not fit well with your personal goal. Using the Defining Your Personal Goals Worksheet (Figure 2.4), list your short-term and long-term personal goals.

Family Goals

You may want to consider the goals of your entire family. These goals can influence your decision on the type of home business that you choose. Once again, you must prioritize all the goals in order of importance so that you can create an action plan for working toward each goal. Using the Defining Your Family Goals Worksheet (Figure 2.5), list your short-term and long-term family goals.

Financial Goals

You must also consider financial goals when choosing a business startup. These may include

FIGURE 2.4	Defining Your Personal Goals

In order of priority, list your personal goals for the short term (one to five years):

1. _____
2. _____
3. _____
4. _____
5. _____

In order of priority, list your personal goals for the long term (10 years and beyond):

1. _____
2. _____
3. _____
4. _____
5. _____

stashing away enough money to put the kids through college, paying off the mortgage, buying a vacation home or amassing enough wealth to retire comfortably by age 55. There are many reasons why people operate homebased businesses. For example:

- To enjoy some added cash flow for their family
- To continue working and earning after retiring from a full-time career
- To fulfill a dream to do something they love, regardless of whether they earn $20,000 or $200,000 doing it

Financial goals span a wide spectrum. The choice of a business is not necessarily all about making X amount of dollars. In fact, many homebased business owners are more than happy to earn $60,000, from the comfort of their own

FIGURE 2.5	Defining Your Family Goals Worksheet

In order of priority, list your family members' goals for the short term (one to five years):

1. _____
2. _____
3. _____
4. _____
5. _____

In order of priority, list your family members' goals for the long term (10 years and beyond):

1. _____
2. _____
3. _____
4. _____
5. _____

home, spending additional time with their children, instead of commuting for two or more hours per day and earning $75,000. There are advantages to working at home, including paying less in taxes and having far more flexibility. Therefore, your financial goals will tie in very closely to your personal goals, life situation, and various other factors. Of course, you will want to select a business that can meet your financial needs. However, you also need to remember that the more time, effort and marketing you put into a business, the more financial returns you will typically enjoy.

Using the Defining Your Financial Goals Worksheet (Figure 2.6), list your short-term and long-term financial goals.

with a spouse earning $35,000 and family expenses of $65,000 a year will need to make up the remaining $30,000 after taxes. However, two people who are retired, with grown children out on their own, may be looking for only an additional $20,000 on top of their pension income to use for traveling, playing golf, spoiling the grandchildren and saving for possible medical needs. (See Figure 2.7, Income Needs Worksheet.)

Income, to some degree, factors into the business startup equation for everyone. Even if you seek only a little money from a part-time or retirement business, you still want to make sure that the business you start will break even.

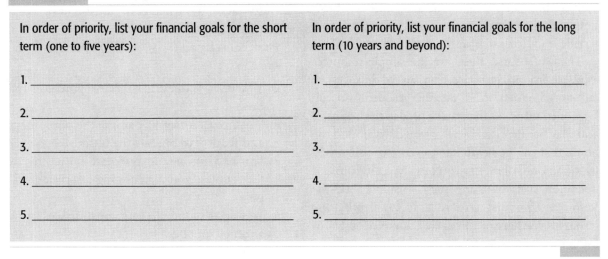

FIGURE 2.6   Defining Your Financial Goals Worksheet

In order of priority, list your financial goals for the short term (one to five years):	In order of priority, list your financial goals for the long term (10 years and beyond):
1. _____	1. _____
2. _____	2. _____
3. _____	3. _____
4. _____	4. _____
5. _____	5. _____

The amount of income you will need will depend on your life situation. Are you the sole supporter of a family? Do you have only yourself to support? Are you part of a two-income family (a very common situation)? Are you maintaining a "traditional" job and operating a homebased business for some extra income? Answers to these questions will determine the income you will need. For example, a full-timer in a two-income family

Additional Resources Available

Additional available resources can also greatly influence your choice of home business. Resources come in two forms: intangible (such as contacts, listings and connections) and tangible (such as money and property).

The less obvious resources, those that the astute entrepreneur will use, are means of gaining a competitive advantage. For example, do you know

FIGURE 2.7	Income Needs Worksheet

How much income do you feel you need to earn per year based on your life situation and personal and/or family needs?

❑ less than $15,000   ❑ $30,000–$45,000   ❑ $60,000–$75,000
❑ $15,000–$30,000   ❑ $45,000–$60,000   ❑ $75,000 or more

someone who has skills in your field of interest and might serve as a mentor? Perhaps you have a friend or a family member with some leads to advisors, consultants or even reputable vendors or suppliers. If you are starting up a business in a field in which you have worked or a related field, here is an opportunity to renew some old contacts and possibly even find a few part-time helpers. These are the most valuable types of resources. Such contacts and connections can get you launched into a new business with great enthusiasm, not to mention some terrific leads for gathering clients/customers.

Then, of course, there are the simple resources available around the house, from an old desk to your current computer. What tangible resources do you have or could access that can be used in the business? You may be surprised by what you have around the house that can be helpful and even more surprised by the amount of money you can save in startup and operation costs by using such resources. Use the Resource Checklist (Figure 2.8) to identify the resources you have or can easily acquire. Modify this list to meet your specific needs.

Sources of Financing

The first question is, Do you have the money to start a business?

One of the more important factors affecting your decision about which home business to start or purchase is the amount of money needed. Do you have the money in savings or have access to the money? Do you then have access to additional money for working capital to operate the business?

Unless you are purchasing an operating business, you're not likely to be generating a profit immediately. Every new business venture requires financing beyond the initial startup costs to achieve positive cash flow and, believe me, a lot of time can pass before a business shows a profit or even breaks even.

If you do not have the money readily available, the next question is whether or not you have access to the financing.

First, consider all the money you need and why it is needed:

- You need money to start or purchase the business.
- You need money to pay for the equipment and fixtures to operate the business.
- You need money to purchase initial inventory (unless you are running a service business).
- You need money to buy consumables, such as office supplies.
- You need money to pay yourself an income until the business generates enough to cover your income requirements.
- You need money to pay fixed operating costs, such as utilities, insurance, taxes, telephone and your website, until the business breaks even.
- You need money to pay employees and professionals providing services to your business.

FIGURE 2.8   Resource Checklist

Do you have good contacts within the local or business industry for networking and generating business?
    ❏ Yes   ❏ No

Comments: _____

Do your friends and/or family members have some good contacts to help you start your business?
    ❏ Yes   ❏ No

Comments: _____

Are there business clubs and associations in your local community that you can join to develop your networking opportunities?
    ❏ Yes   ❏ No

Comments: _____

Do you know any professionals or current business owners who can assist you with business decisions?
    ❏ Yes   ❏ No

Comments: _____

Do you know anyone who could serve as a mentor?
    ❏ Yes   ❏ No

Comments: _____

Do you have any former co-workers, employees or even employers who could benefit you with wisdom, leads or resources?
    ❏ Yes   ❏ No

Comments: _____

Do you have access to business listings or directories that could be beneficial?
    ❏ Yes   ❏ No

Comments: _____

Do you have computer equipment and software that could be used in the business?
    ❏ Yes   ❏ No

Comments: _____

Do you have general office equipment and fixtures that could be used in the business?
    ❏ Yes   ❏ No

Comments: _____

- You need money to pay for advertising and marketing materials.

Every business needs money not only to get rolling, but also to stay rolling. Cash flow is king. Unfortunately, one of the most common errors entrepreneurs make when starting a business is not calculating the true startup investment needed to reach positive cash flow. More information about raising capital and financing for your home business startup is in Chapter 3, "Financial Issues." At the end of this chapter you will find a Home Business Startup Costs Estimator (Figure 2.9) that you can use in calculating the amount of money needed to start your business. There is also a Fixed Monthly Overhead Calculator (Figure 2.10) to help you calculate the money needed to pay the monthly business bills.

The other questions to ask yourself are these:

- Do you have a good credit rating, so you can get a loan?
- Do you have any backers, supporters, family members or friends who could back your business financially?
- How would you feel about such support?

Finding a Good Match

Finally, the home business that you choose must

be a compatible match for you. Finding a good match is really the result of combining all the information previously discussed. Asking yourself the questions featured on the Finding a Good Match Worksheet (Figure 2.11) will help you to determine if the business you want to start suits you well.

You can copy this worksheet and complete information for each home business that you are considering.

FIGURE 2.11   Finding a Good Match Worksheet

Type of Business:

Is this a business I am really excited or passionate about?
❑ Yes ❑ No

Comments: _____

Is my home a suitable location for this business?
❑ Yes ❑ No

Comments: _____

Do I have the financial resources needed to start or purchase this business?   ❑ Yes ❑ No

Comments: _____

Do I have enough money to support this business and pay the bills until the business can generate an income and profit?   ❑ Yes ❑ No

Comments: _____

Can this business potentially generate the income I am seeking?   ❑ Yes ❑ No

Comments: _____

Am I physically healthy enough to handle the potential physical strains of starting and running this business?
❑ Yes ❑ No

Comments: _____

Am I mentally healthy enough to handle the potential mental stresses of starting and running this business?
❑ Yes ❑ No

Comments: _____

Will operating this business enable me to reach my personal goals?   ❑ Yes ❑ No

Comments: _____

Do I have experience in this type of business and industry in which the business operates?   ❑ Yes ❑ No

Comments: _____

Do I possess any special skills that can be used in this business?   ❑ Yes ❑ No

Comments: _____

Are there any special certificates or educational requirements to start and operate this business? If so, can I acquire the certification or education?
❑ Yes ❑ No

Comments: _____

Would I enjoy operating this business?   ❑ Yes ❑ No

Comments: _____

Does this business opportunity match my personality?
❑ Yes ❑ No

Comments: _____

Does this business match my level of maturity?
❑ Yes ❑ No

Comments: _____

Can I see myself still excited about this business 10 years from now?   ❑ Yes ❑ No

Comments: _____

FIGURE 2.11   Finding a Good Match Worksheet, continued

Can I commit to this business long term and am I prepared to work hard to succeed? ❑ Yes ❑ No Comments: _____	Is this the type of business I initially envisioned as a self-employment venture that would be suitable and a good match for me? ❑ Yes ❑ No Comments: _____

WHAT ARE YOUR HOME BUSINESS OPTIONS?

The businesses that can be started and operated from a homebased location are nearly limitless and expanding as new technologies and products are developed. However, before looking at specific home businesses, you first have to decide which of the following you wish to do:

- Start a new home business from scratch?
- Purchase and operate an existing business?
- Purchase and operate a home franchise business?
- Purchase and operate a business opportunity from home?

But, before you decide what type of home business to start or purchase, you should first decide how much time you are prepared to commit to your new business. Not everyone will be able to start a full-time home business and not everyone wants to make a full-time commitment to a home business. Therefore, you have to derive objectives from the goals and other issues that you identified earlier in this chapter, to decide whether you will operate a full-time, part-time, seasonal or post-retirement home business. Each option has its own unique set of advantages and disadvantages, depending on your objectives.

A Full-Time Home Business

The first option is to start a business that requires a 100-percent, full-time effort. As the commit-

ment would suggest, a full-time venture involves the most risk and offers the most rewards. Risks come in the form of your initial financial investment, suspension of current employee benefits if you are leaving a full-time job and no guarantee of a steady income. On the flip side of the coin, the rewards can include the potential to make more money than you could earn working full time for someone else or operating part time. Another reward is that you are pursuing your dream full time; you have assumed full control of your future and are prepared to work hard to realize your business dreams.

The majority of home business startups can be operated part time. Outside of a few seasonal businesses, almost all can be operated full time. However, some home business startups cannot be a part-time effort because of the nature of the business. A few of these would include:

- Property/house inspector
- Business broker
- Mobile on-call computer repair business
- Pest control

Again, your decision to operate your new business full time will largely be determined by your financial situation, the type of business and your own risk-reward assessment.

A Part-Time Home Business

Your second option is to start a part-time business. This will take a consistent time commitment, such as 10 or 20 hours every week, year-round. You might also decide to transition from your current job, decreasing the time you spend there each week and devoting more time to your new business. Of course, for this you need a good relationship with your current employer, who would have to approve of this working arrangement.

Unlike the leap of faith that a full-time effort requires, part-timers can enjoy the best of both worlds, while making the transition to a full-time business gradually. The advantages include keeping an income stream from your current job, taking advantage of current employee benefits (including health insurance) and building your business over a longer time, which should give it a more stable foundation. You can also spread out your initial investment in the business over a longer time, so you may not need to borrow money to finance needed equipment. Running a home business part-time allows you to test the waters without risking it all. By *all*, I mean money, your current job and self-confidence. If it turns out that you are not the type of person who is comfortable with owning and operating a business, you have risked little and still have the security of returning to your job full time. Once again, most home business ventures can be operated with a part-time effort. Examples include:

- Selling products via the web
- Website design and maintenance
- Wedding/event planner
- Commercial office cleaning

A Seasonal Home Business

The third option is to start a business that operates for only a few months a year. As the name suggests, seasonal businesses usually operate during one specific season or sometimes operate for two seasons. Even though a business is seasonal, it can still be operated full time or part time.

The potential to earn a very good living working only part of the year is real. I know entrepreneurs who are not only doing it, but also enjoying their time off to pursue other interests. Two very successful business people come to mind, both operating seasonal businesses from their homes. One with a wood lot spends the summer splitting logs into firewood and the fall delivering wood, and then takes the remainder of the year off to travel. The second operates a kayak tour business for only four months a year, but generates enough revenue to very comfortably enjoy other interests for the remaining eight months. When I say "successful" and "comfortable," I mean that both earn six-figure incomes from their seasonal businesses. Many "seasonal" businesses require work for at least 8 if not 10 months a year, since planning, bookkeeping, paperwork and ordering supplies and products must be done in the off seasons.

A seasonal home business is suited to people who want to follow other interests and are prepared to work very hard and smart to ensure that they can strike the balance required to do so. The balance is financial and time management, focus, planning and setting measurable targets to make sure they can stay on course. Home business ventures that could be operated on a seasonal basis include:

- Christmas tree sales/holiday decorating service
- Pool cleaning and maintenance in northern climates
- Preparing personal income tax returns
- A summer-only homebased day care

A Post-Retirement Home Business

The fourth option is to start a post-retirement business, working after you have retired from another business or career. This, too, can be operated full time, part time or even seasonally if it meets your personal, financial and business criteria.

Retirement businesses have become extremely popular in the past decade, for a number of reasons. First, the cost of living has dramatically increased, far outpacing wages in most cases. There have also been cuts in pension systems, many of which are underfunded and can no longer offer retirees the defined pension plans that recent generations of employees have received. The change in the stock market, from the 1990s bull markets, in which saving for retirement was much easier, to the downturn in the market since 2000 has been a major problem for baby boomer retirement plans, which generally are not growing quickly enough to cover the financial needs of those who will be receiving payments from them. Add to that the fact that life expectancy is longer and seniors are living more actively, so there is now a greater need for making money after retirement. Many retirees now want and need a steady income through their 60s, 70s and even 80s. The years of sitting on a porch in a rocking chair growing old are gone. People want to be vibrant and active. Operating a business is a way to stay active physically and mentally. Finally, many people have sacrificed their own personal dreams and goals for their children. Once their children have established themselves in careers and families, the parents want to take up the challenge and follow those dreams of business ownership that they have been putting off for years. If you choose to start a retirement business, you'll be in the company of many other eager entrepreneurs, with shifting demographics and the huge number of baby boomers set to retire over the next 20 years.

Keep in mind that in both the United States and Canada, people over age 65 who operate an income-producing business can face incremental decreases in benefits from Social Security in the U.S. and Canada Pension Plan (or Quebec Pension Plan) and Old Age Security, depending on the amount of income earned and their age. However, since the U.S. Social Security system benefits are only a drop in the financial bucket now and may be gone by the year 2012, the potential loss of some of these benefits may not be worth great concern.

Examples of post-retirement businesses include:

- Manufacturing woodcrafts
- Selling new and used goods on eBay or starting a web-based business
- Freelance photography or writing
- Consulting

STARTING A NEW HOME BUSINESS FROM SCRATCH

As mentioned previously, there are four basic options for getting into a home business. Your first option is to start from scratch—a business that is not a franchise, not a business opportunity and not an established business, but a totally new business from the idea on up.

The single most important advice about a new business startup is to not try to be too creative or innovative in terms of the idea. In other words, do not try to reinvent the wheel. Follow the KISS formula—"Keep It Simple, Stupid." I mention this because being the first to do anything burns money and plenty of it. Why? Because nobody will know what you have, how it works, what it will do for them, why they need it and, most important, why they should buy it from you. Therefore, to introduce your great new idea, get consumers to take notice and then convince them that they need it will be an uphill battle that takes time, energy and plenty of money. You also have nothing against which to compare yourself, no benchmark. Maybe in time you may want to branch out and sell some new and innovative products or services, but it is not the best way to start out.

If consumers already know, use, like, need and purchase from others what you intend to sell, most of your job is already done for you. You can then concentrate your marketing efforts on telling consumers why your business is the right one from which to purchase what they already know, use, like and need. You do this by adding value, making guarantees, providing incredible service and doing whatever else it takes to succeed.

Where Can You Find Home Business Startup Ideas?

Fortunately, home business ideas are easy to come by because they are everywhere—in your community, in books and magazines, on the internet and from friends. Chapter 18, "Home Business Startup Ideas and Home Franchise Opportunities," features 125 startup ideas plus the top 101 homebased franchises of the past year. Perhaps one of these ideas might even be right for you. But if not, don't fret. There are numerous sources you can tap to start identifying home businesses that you can start from scratch.

Books

There are many books that focus on home business startup ideas. Visit your local library or go to your local bookstore or the Amazon or Barnes & Noble websites to find a few. You'll also find several mentioned throughout this book. Of course, this is not to say that business startup books are the definitive word on the subject. They are a good point from which you can begin building a complete understanding of the startup possibilities and gathering details about businesses so that you can narrow the field. You might even want to pick up a copy of my first book, *Entrepreneur's Ultimate Start-Up Directory* (updated with Rich Mintzer). The updated edition features 1,500 great startup ideas, representing more than 30 industries, such as retail, manufacturing, advertising, sports, recreation, travel and transportation, and includes hundreds of home business oppor-

tunities, including eBay business possibilities. (The *Ultimate Start-Up Directory* is available online from Entrepreneur Press, *entrepreneurpress.com,* Amazon, *amazon.com,* and Barnes and Noble, *barnesandnoble.com* and at bookstores across the United States and Canada. The book is also found in most public libraries in the United States and Canada.)

The Internet

The internet is another great place to find home business startup ideas. There are tons of websites devoted to home businesses, business startups and business in general from which to draw ideas. Best of all, you can get much of this information for free. The Resources section at the end of this chapter features numerous home business and business opportunity websites where you can search for home business ideas.

Current Job

If you like what you are currently doing, perhaps you can consider turning your job into your new home business startup and maybe even land your current employer as your first client. The idea is not as crazy as it may seem at first.

Talk with your employer and find out about his or her plans for the future of the business. Maybe he or she wants to slow down, sell out or outsource some of the work. You never know unless you ask.

If turning to your current employer is not in the cards and you still want to pursue a business startup doing what you are currently doing, then go for it. Why not take advantage of the skills and knowledge you have acquired? However, do it ethically. Do not try to lure clients away from your employer while you're still employed and never compromise your current employer's intellectual or proprietary properties for your gain in your own business. These actions always catch up with the perpetrators, often in the form of unpleasant legal consequences.

Friends

You can ask friends and family members about what they think are good home business startup ideas. Of course, be cautious here. You do not want to pursue someone else's dreams; you just want a few suggestions to get the creative juices flowing. Open discussions with friends and family members on home business startup topics are a good idea. Usually, friends and family members will want to help and be very frank because they care about your future.

Community

Another option is to look around your community at businesses that are currently operating from a homebased location or could be operated that way. Are they successful? Do those types of businesses interest you? The advantage of this method is that you can see the business in operation, talk with its customers and check out its advertising, website and other marketing materials to get a good understanding of the business and the advantages and disadvantages associated with operating such a venture.

Hobbies and Interests

You can also start a business based on one of your hobbies or interests. You just need to make sure the business idea is sound and has the potential to flourish. The choice must be based on more than an emotional attachment. One benefit of starting a business from a hobby is that you know the subject well, expertise that could be an asset in marketing.

Market Research

There are numerous business publications and websites that can help you determine what is going on in the business world. Sites like *Entrepreneur.com* and *Allbusiness.com*, among many others, can help you get a feel for the hot up-and-coming businesses. Today, for example, businesses that are "green" or engaged in the environmental arena, such as green marketing or green career placement, are not only trendy but forging a new direction in response to the needs of our world.

Look at which businesses are popular, which products and services are in demand, and then determine whether or not you could make such a business work from your home. Personal life coaching and home organization are two of many growing fields. Also keep in mind that because of the internet, you are no longer limited to serving only your geographic region. Homebased businesses now can serve customers worldwide, so you need not think only in terms of the needs of your community.

The Advantages of Starting a Home Business from Scratch

Those who feel the need to blaze trails rather than walk familiar turf will be pleased to know that there are numerous advantages to starting your own home business from scratch as opposed to purchasing a business, a franchise or a business opportunity. Perhaps the biggest advantage, and one that is very attractive to many entrepreneurs who choose this route, is that it's possible to get started with little money, which can often be borrowed against credit cards, as a personal line of credit or from a family member with moderately deep pockets. Depending on the venture you start and the equipment and supply needs of the business, you can often get into business for less than $1,000. You can almost always start something with good potential for less than a $10,000 initial investment. Additional advantages of starting a home business from scratch would include:

- Most of your investment in the business is usually partially secured by inventory or equipment. Therefore, if things do not work out, these assets can be sold to recoup a portion of the money invested in the startup. Contrast this with a franchise, a situation in which you will be out the franchise fee and related intangible startup costs or an existing business, a situation in which some of the purchase price goes toward paying for goodwill, an investment that is lost if the business fails.

- When you start a home business from scratch, you are not buying into someone else's problems, which can be the case with buying an established business. The business may sound great, the equipment and inventory may be impressive, and the financials may appear to be in order, but until you are actually operating the business, you don't know what skeletons might be hiding in the closet.

- Starting a business from scratch allows you to have full control over the venture and enjoy independence from managing influences that are often found in franchise arrangements and some business opportunities. In addition, the growth and expansion potential in a startup is excellent and not limited geographically.

- You can set the wheels in motion however you wish. Being free without a lot of overhead is a marvelous way to start a business and the reason why most homebased businesses are started from scratch. You also have the advantage of scheduling your own hours.

The Disadvantages of Starting a Home Business from Scratch

In a perfect world, I would tell you that there are no disadvantages to starting a home business from scratch—but this is not a perfect world. In fact, according to the SBA, the highest percentage of business failures is in the new business startup category, businesses that have been started from scratch. This statistic can be attributed to many factors, but at the core are the usual three causes of business problems—lack of research, lack of planning and lack of financial resources. The major disadvantages with starting a home business from scratch are, unfortunately, the things that attract first-time entrepreneurs to start a business from scratch: low investment, little regulation and ease of starting. This combination can be a recipe for business disaster because you can get a business startup idea today and be open for business tomorrow, so there's little if any time for two of the three main essentials: research and planning. Additional disadvantages to starting a home business from scratch include:

- You are 100 percent responsible for everything in any business you start up. Being in your home means you must establish a system in which to begin running the business.

- Unlike buying an operating business, there are no revenues to help offset fixed operating costs. You have to build the business to the breakeven point and profitability from zero.

- It is hard to market and promote yourself to customers or clients in the traditional business world without an office address or storefront. However, with the emergence of homebased businesses and websites in particular, the stigma of working from home is quickly beginning to disappear.

- Self-motivation can be an issue. You have no boss to tell you to get to work and complete your tasks. Therefore, you need to be a good taskmaster—over yourself.

BUYING AN EXISTING HOME BUSINESS

A second option is to purchase a business that is currently operational and run the business from your home, whether the current owner is operating the business from a storefront, a commercial office or his or her home. You will still want to make sure the business you purchase is suited to be home based and, more important, suited to being run from your home.

For people who want quicker results and do not want to invest the time required to start a business and find customers from scratch, buying a business might be the best choice. If you choose this route, know that your approach to selecting the business, analyzing the potential and planning for the future is no less involved than when starting a business from scratch. In fact, it may be even more involved, because buying an operating business usually means investing a larger amount of money in the venture. It warrants extremely careful consideration, research and planning to limit or minimize the financial risk. You will still need to research the marketplace, create a target customer profile, identify competitors and develop business and marketing plans as you would for any business. In addition, you should get professional help for drafting and executing the purchase agreement. Enlist a lawyer and an accountant (and possibly a commercial real estate broker) with experience in business purchase agreements to advise you on all aspects of buying a business, especially if a considerable amount of money will be changing hands. The following are a few tips about buying an operating business:

- Ask the current owner for a customer list and talk with customers at random, asking if they are happy with the goods or services, the level of customer service provided and the price. Also ask them what they would like to see changed and why. Check with your local chapter of the Better Business Bureau to make sure that the business does not have any unresolved complaints.
- Ask the current owner for the audited financial statements for the business going back at least five years or, if the business has been operating less than five years, its entire history.
- Talk with current suppliers to find out about

payment history, amount of goods or services ordered, warranties and deliveries.

- If the purchase is for a substantial price, you may want to hire a business consultant to conduct a valuation of the business to make sure that you are paying a fair market value in relation to profit potential. You can conduct your own valuation of the business. Tips about how to value a business are included in Chapter 11, "Managing Your Home Business," in the Selling Your Business section.
- Make sure all agreements and contracts that the current owner has with clients, suppliers and manufacturers are transferable and will stay with the business upon transition to a new owner, without a fee.
- Make sure you have a non-competition clause built into the sale agreement. Non-competition clauses preclude the current owner, after the sale, from starting a similar type of business or selling similar goods and services within a set geographic area, for a fixed period of time.
- Make sure that the current owner of the business stays on with you after the sale for a reasonable amount of time to train and to help with the transition in other ways.

Where Can You Find a Business for Sale?

Once you have made the decision to purchase a business that is currently operating, you have many ways to begin looking for the business that meets all of your criteria. Business brokers, real estate agents, newspapers, the internet and specialty business publications are the best places to start searching, because these are a few of the main vehicles used to market and sell going business concerns.

Business Brokers
The first stop is to contact an independent business broker, because these are the people who spe-

cialize in the sale of operating businesses and the resale of franchises. Business brokers have access to thousands of businesses currently for sale and can perform detailed searches for you with the information you supply. Best of all, the business broker will do all of this legwork and more for free, because the owner who is selling pays the business broker a commission when the business is sold. The International Business Brokers Association, located online at *ibba.org*, contains links to more than 1,100 independent business brokers around the world.

Realtors

Many business owners sell their business using a local real estate broker to market their business. Therefore, contacting a local realtor is also a good way of finding out what businesses are currently for sale. Even if nothing is currently available that meets your criteria, your realtor will keep alert for the right opportunity. Consult your local telephone book to find real estate agents and brokers in your area that specialize in business and commercial property sales.

Newspapers

Another option is to check the classifieds section in your local newspapers under the heading Business for Sale or Business Opportunities. Some business owners opt to save business broker and real estate broker commission fees by marketing their business themselves. You may even want to run an advertisement describing the type of business you want to purchase and let business owners call you.

The Internet

The internet is full of business-for-sale portals and websites, which makes it a great place for gathering information about what types of businesses might be available for sale, where they are located and at what cost. The downside to shopping for a business, franchise or business opportunity on the internet is the fact that the web serves the world, so there is no guarantee that you will find the type of business you want for sale in your local area. Of course, if you are thinking about starting or purchasing a business that operates solely on the internet or even a mail order business, this is a great place to look, because such a business can be operated from any location. BizBuySell, located online at *bizbuysell.com*, is billed as the Internet's largest business-for-sale portal, with over 50,000 listings.

Specialty Publications

There are also specialty publications that cater solely to businesses-for-sale and commercial listings. Check your local newsstand for availability. You can also log onto *tradepub.com*, which lists hundreds of specialty publications indexed by subject.

The Advantages of Buying an Existing Home Business

For the vast majority of entrepreneurs who choose to purchase a business that is operational, the number-one advantage is that the business is generating revenue and has a customer base. The business may not be generating a profit and may not even be generating enough to pay you a wage, but revenue means cash flow. In business, cash flow is king! Cash flow enables you to keep the business running and to promote your goods and services so you can keep your current customers and attract new ones. Additional advantages for purchasing an operational business include:

- If the business has some level of name recognition, you are buying that, meaning you are not starting from scratch with a completely unknown brand.
- When you buy a business that is operating, you can make it part of the purchase agreement that the current owner stays on for a specified period of time to provide training

and transitional help. This is a built-in mentor of sorts.

- When you purchase an operating business, you can often negotiate terms, meaning you pay a portion of the purchase price upfront and the balance in installments or balloon payments. The advantage of buying on terms is that it gives you the ability to pay the installments out of business revenues, while maintaining more cash to use from day to day. In effect, you will actually be purchasing the business for no more than your down payment. Of course, you may be working for free for a while if the money that would normally be paying your wages goes to paying off the balance of the purchase.

The Disadvantages of Buying an Existing Home Business

Without question, the number-one disadvantage associated with buying an operating business is that you may be buying into the previous owner's problems, bad debts and outstanding invoices. You want to research the business as much as possible, but you cannot be sure exactly what you are getting until you are running the business. Do what you can to avoid inadvertently buying problems when you purchase what you think is your dream business. Additional disadvantages can include:

- You'll spend more money to get started. Nine times out of 10 it will cost more to purchase a business than it would to start the same business from scratch. This is usually because when you purchase a business, you pay a premium for the things that a new startup does not have, such as customers, goodwill, a proven management system and other valuable business assets, such as trade accounts, merchant payment systems, vendors, trained employees and more. Sometimes, all of this

can come at a high price.

- It's a slower process. When starting a business from scratch, you can get things running as quickly or as slowly as you choose. However, when buying a business, you will need to go at the pace of those around you. This means waiting until the valuation is complete, hammering out agreements and working through a variety of details, all of which can take time when you are eager to get started.

- You will not be able to do everything your way. It will be your business, of course, but it will have been established in such a way that has become familiar to the regular customers. Therefore, you will have to maintain some of what is already there and add your own personal touches more slowly as you go.

BUYING A HOME BUSINESS FRANCHISE

A third homebased business option is to purchase a franchise that can be operated/managed from a residential location. You could purchase either a new franchise, one that no other person has operated or a resale franchise, one that is currently operating.

Franchises can cost anywhere from a low of about $20,000, once you include franchise fees, startup costs, inventory and equipment, to well into seven figures for internationally known franchise operations. Purchasing and operating a franchise is a great option for someone who wants a proven management system, initial and ongoing training and support, and the benefits associated with branded names and products. However, if you choose to purchase a franchise, you still have to take the same precautions that you would when starting or purchasing any other type of business.

Do not assume that if you purchase a franchise you will be guaranteed success. Franchises, like any other type of businesses, fail; there is no franchisor

I am aware of that provides a 100 percent guarantee that any franchisee will stay in business and profit. It is, of course, in the franchisor's best interests to make sure that each franchise is successful and profitable so the franchisor can continue to expand the brand through franchising into new geographical areas. For that reason, most franchisors provide very good training and support services to all their franchisees. There are, however, franchise companies out there that are not entirely on the up and up. Therefore, you will need to do your research.

Before buying a homebased franchise you should:

- Make sure the type of franchise business is something you want to do and think you would enjoy. A good match is still a key requirement for success, whether the business is a franchise or not.
- Check out the franchisor and talk with current franchisees.
- Have your lawyer go over the franchisor's Uniform Franchise Offering Circular (UFOC), which is discussed later in this section.
- Conduct your own market research to make sure that the local market will support the franchise and that the franchisor's research, statements and forecasts are correct.
- Become a customer of the franchise to make sure that you like and believe in the products or services being sold.
- Make sure the franchise meets your needs. Below is a list of 10 criteria to use as a guide when determining which franchise is right for you.

Other issues to be concerned with are:

1. *Cost.* Stay within your comfort zone. This includes startup costs, franchising fees and available cash necessary to open the business.

Also, how much in commissions must you pay the franchisor? Eight to 15 percent is typical.

2. *Financing.* What does the franchise company provide and is third-party financing allowed?

3. *Marketing and promotion.* Does the company provide significant coverage in these important areas? This is typically the impetus for franchising, to have a business that people know about.

4. *Training and ongoing support.* You'll need to learn from other franchisees and from the company about these two *very* important areas.

5. *Saturation and competition.* Is this a business popping up on every street corner or does the franchisor limit the competition? Obviously, you want the latter, so you're not competing against people with the same franchise, the same brands and the same support.

6. *Franchisor relationships.* Again, learn from franchise owners. Do they have a good rapport with the franchise company? Do the company reps answer their questions quickly and solve their problems?

7. *Trends and popularity.* Health is "in." So are "green" businesses and quick-service-oriented companies. Look at what the public is buying and the services people want today.

8. *The bottom line.* Is the franchise company making money? Get sales figures. Is it making money from its franchisees or does it own some of its outlets? Look for companies that are close to 100 percent franchised. This indicates that they are product-driven and not selling franchises just to make money.

9. *Time and commitment.* You will put in long hours to build a business. However, businesses with inventories and lots of employees will mean a greater time commitment than a

service business you can run more easily from home. How much time are you willing to put in? A bigger business can have a greater pay-off. However, you may need to work that much harder.

10. *The fun factor.* Look for a business you will enjoy running. If you are not going to enjoy what you are doing, why not simply work for someone else? Can you find a franchise you feel good about?

Where Can You Find Home Business Franchises for Sale?

Much like finding business startup ideas and operating businesses for sale, franchise opportunities can be found everywhere and cover just about every type of business imaginable. Of course, your choices will be limited, as you cannot run a McDonald's from your living room. However, you can find many homebased possibilities. You should begin your search in the following places:

- Franchise magazines and books. *Entrepreneur* magazine publishes an annual issue featuring the best franchises indexed by industry. The magazine is available at newsstands nationwide or *Entrepreneur.com*.
- Franchise associations such as the American Franchisee Association, *franchisee.org*, International Franchise Association, *franchise.org* and the Canadian Franchise Association, *cfa.ca*.
- There are also numerous websites devoted to franchises, such as *Franchise Business Review, franchisebusinessreview.com*, which researches and reviews hundreds of franchises by getting reports and information from the actual franchisees.
- Local commercial real estate brokers and independent business brokers.
- Newspaper and magazine classified advertisements.
- Talking with current franchisees inside and outside of your local area.

Chapter 18, "Home Business Startup Ideas and Home Franchise Opportunities," features the top 101 homebased franchise opportunities from *Entrepreneur.com*. Many of the franchises featured in that chapter are nationally known chains with reputable management teams and multiple franchise units in operation. Each entry gives the name of the franchise as well as contact information and a brief description of the franchisor's business activities.

The Advantages of Buying a Home Business Franchise

There are a great number of advantages associated with purchasing a homebased franchise, especially for people who want the security of a supportive team, proven management systems and the benefits of branding on a large-scale basis. You have the combined strength of many franchises, as opposed to the possible weaknesses of one independent small business. The combined strength can lower costs through purchasing goods and services in bulk, reach a broader audience through collective advertising, and have an online presence managed through the head office, so an individual franchisee does not necessarily have to maintain and update a website for his or her franchise. A few additional advantages include:

- A franchise is often a good business startup choice for people who have never owned, operated or even managed a small business. A franchise comes with a complete operations manual and a proven management system. All you have to do is follow the steps as outlined, and there is a better-than-average chance your business will succeed.
- Franchises provide initial and ongoing training, support and education to maximize the

potential for success and profitability. Again, this is very beneficial for people with little or no business experience.

■ Almost all small homebased franchises can be started within a short time frame and generate cash flow in less than one month.

The Disadvantages of Buying a Home Business Franchise

Unfortunately, there are also disadvantages associated with purchasing a homebased franchise. You have to decide if the advantages outweigh the disadvantages. Refer to your earlier analysis of your personal situation, goals and possible good business matches prior to making the decision to purchase. A few disadvantages associated with purchasing and operating a home franchise include:

■ With a franchise, you have much less control and independence in all areas of your business than in a nonfranchise business. This is because one of the doctrines of the franchise model is conformity through consistent brand management. In fact, some of the more independent types reading this would find operating a franchise feels like managing someone else's business.

■ Franchisees pay monthly advertising and royalty fees, which can be a burden, especially if fees are fixed, rather than calculated on a percentage of total gross sales. Sales may be down for a few months in a row, but if your royalty and advertising fees are fixed, you are still required to pay them in full.

■ A potentially big disadvantage of a franchise, especially for entrepreneurs with ambitious growth plans, is it can be extremely limiting in terms of growth. Basically, if you want to expand geographically, your options are to purchase another franchise area if available,

buy out another franchisee or purchase a master or area franchise. All these options dramatically increase your overall investment.

■ There can be a large cost associated with buying a franchise.

GLOSSARY OF COMMON FRANCHISE AND FRANCHISE AGREEMENT TERMS

If you decide that a franchise is the right new business enterprise for you, then you will need to understand basic franchise terminology. Below is a Franchise-English glossary.

However, prior to signing on the dotted line to purchase a franchise, have a qualified lawyer experienced in franchise agreements go over the details section by section with you. Good legal advice does not come cheap; it could, however, save you the heartaches and financial hardship that could result if you find out later the franchise agreement is not what you expected.

Franchise. A business that offers to an individual, group of people or company a set range of products or services and specific and valuable intellectual properties, defined by geographic boundaries known as a *unit* or *area*. The franchise is governed by a franchise agreement, which spells out the details of the business activities, relationship, mutual expectations and financial obligations between the franchisee and franchisor.

Franchisor. The person, people or legal entity that owns the right to sell franchises for a specific business model, products and/or services. Often a successful business will choose to grow by selling opportunities to duplicate its business operations and model.

Franchisee. The franchisee is a person, group of people or company that owns one or more franchise units or franchised operating areas.

Generally, the franchisee also manages the day-to-day operations of the individual franchise or, if more than one is owned, hires managers or assistants to operate each franchise.

Uniform Franchise Offering Circular (UFOC). The Uniform Franchise Offering Circular is often referred to as a *disclosure document*. This mandatory document, created by the franchisor and presented to the potential franchisee, provides background information about the franchisor and a copy of the proposed agreement, listing all details and financial obligations between the franchisor and the franchisee. The franchise agreement will list and define the following:

- All the parties involved in the agreement
- All financial transactions between parties
- All terms of the franchise agreement, including franchisor's obligations, franchisee's obligations, date for opening the business, renewal of the agreement, assignment of the agreement and termination of the agreement
- All of the equipment, supplies and inventory that are included or needed and how these items will be procured and from whom
- The geographical territory covered by the franchise agreement
- All advertising and marketing plans and activities
- All aspects of initial and ongoing training and education
- All fees and royalties for which the franchisee is responsible.

Pro Forma. The *pro forma* details the franchisor's complete financial situation, including profit and loss statements, balance sheets and cash flow statements or projections, and asset and liability statements. Ideally, potential franchisees want financial information both on units owned and operated by individual franchisees and on units owned and operated by the company. Tangible financial information, if available, is always preferred over financial projections.

Minimum Capital Required. This is the amount of money required to purchase and operate the franchise. A franchisee is not always required to have the total investment amount upfront. Some of the amount may be financed or paid to the franchisor in installments. Many franchise agreements also contain a minimum net worth clause to qualify potential franchisees. This clause adds to the financial stability of the organization as a whole and protects the franchisor and current franchisees. To calculate net worth, the sum of all liabilities is subtracted from the sum of all assets.

Franchise Fee. This is the amount of money that a person must pay the franchisor to purchase a single franchise, multiple franchises or a master franchise area. The franchise fee almost always excludes the additional costs of inventory, equipment, operating capital, startup and initial marketing.

Total Investment. This figure generally includes the upfront franchise fee, startup fees and all inventory, marketing, supplies, and equipment required to purchase and start a franchise. The total investment amount will be segmented by category costs, as in the basic example below.

Franchise fee	$30,000
Startup fees and permits	$2,150
Initial inventory	$6,500
Equipment and supplies	$3,750
Initial marketing	$5,675
Total investment	$48,075

The total investment cost should include all fees and expenditures required to purchase and start the franchise. It does not include ongoing maintenance fees, marketing expenses, salaries, and product and services purchases once the franchise is operational.

Royalty Fees. The *royalty fee* is a monthly or sometimes quarterly amount that the franchisee pays to the franchisor for each franchise the franchisee owns and operates. A royalty fee can be a fixed amount (with a built-in cost-of-living or inflation index clause that automatically increases the fee annually on the anniversary of the franchise agreement by the amount stated in the clause) or based on a percentage of the franchisee's total gross or net revenues. (Net revenues are calculated as total sales minus the total costs of products sold.) Generally, royalty fees average between 5 and 10 percent of gross monthly revenues.

Advertising or Marketing Fees. This is the amount of money a franchisee pays to the franchisor each month in exchange for a communal-based (regional and/or national) advertising program for the benefit of all franchisees. The advertising fee can be a fixed amount or based on a percentage of the franchisee's total monthly revenues. Typically, the advertising or marketing fee is between 1.5 and 3 percent of the franchisee's gross monthly revenues, often with set minimum and maximum figures. Additional marketing materials and supplies generally fall under the "authorized supplier" section of the franchise agreement.

Company-Owned Units. These are franchises that are owned and operated by the franchise company. They are operated in the same manner as units owned by franchisees. Some companies own a significant number of their units; others sell almost 100 percent of their units to individual franchisees.

Exclusive and Protected Territory. This is the franchise area, which is almost always defined by geographic boundaries such as a subdivision, city, county, state or country. The franchisee retains the sole and exclusive right to operate the franchise in the specified territory under the terms and for the amount of time specified in the franchise agreement. The franchisor cannot sell any more franchises in the protected territory.

Master Franchise. This is an agreement that covers multiple franchise units or areas. The master franchise holder may sell individual franchise units to new franchisees under the direction of the franchisor or hold and develop each franchise unit within the master franchise area gradually over time. Owning a master franchise area or the right to develop a master franchise area is often a franchisee's best opportunity for long-term growth and increased revenues, whether through collecting franchise and maintenance fees or through operating multiple franchise units within the master franchise area.

Conversion Franchise. This is the result of a situation, not very common, in which an independent business joins a franchise program and becomes a franchise unit. Some franchisors have conversion programs to allow such a transformation. In most conversion situations, the new franchisee must pay franchise purchase fees and other expenses, even though he or she already owns and operates a business and owns the necessary equipment and supplies.

Operations Manual. In purchasing a franchise, the franchisee receives from the franchisor a manual that contains all the information on systems, training, products and procedures required to operate the franchise. The operations manual is the heart of the franchise system, as it contains specific intellectual materials, the combined experience of the franchisor and franchisees and marketing methods that provide competitive advantages. In most homebased franchise situations, the franchisee is purchasing access to a specific range of products for resale, plus training and knowledge about specialized services.

Franchisor Support. Support is in two main areas—between the franchisor and the franchisee and between the franchisor and each franchisee's customers. The degree of support from a franchisor varies greatly. For the franchisee, it will typically include marketing and advertising campaigns, website maintenance, centralized accounting and ongoing training. For the franchisee's customers, it will typically include a centralized customer service help desk, product or workmanship warranty underwriting, a company website, and research and development of new products and services or improvements of current products and services.

Authorized Suppliers. Most franchise agreements require that the franchisee purchase products and services for resale and/or consumption directly from the franchisor or through a supplier authorized by the franchisor. This is done for two reasons—to maintain consistency throughout the franchise organization and to create an additional revenue and control center for the franchisor. Generally, the use of authorized suppliers extends to all business activities and includes printed marketing materials, office or job equipment and uniforms.

BUYING A HOME BUSINESS OPPORTUNITY

The final home business option is to purchase a business opportunity that can be operated from a homebased location. *Business opportunity* is a broad term that covers many moneymaking opportunities, including sales agency, distribution, direct sales, multilevel marketing and vending.

Buying a business opportunity is not like starting a business from your own idea, because someone else has come up with the idea and generally has combined that idea into a package with the equipment, inventory and operations manual required for running the business. Buying a business opportunity is not like purchasing a franchise, because there are no royalty fees or franchise fees. You are on your own, although you may be

required to purchase inventory for resale from a distributor. Legally, you are not required to do so. Buying a business opportunity is not like purchasing an operationally independent business, because an opportunity does not come with customers and a cash flow.

Business opportunities can be many things, including the following:

- *Multilevel Marketing (MLM).* Most people are familiar with multilevel marketing, either because they have tried it or because friends or family members have tried to recruit them to do it. Multilevel marketing is selling goods or services directly to consumers, but the true focus is recruiting people into your *down line* (the salespeople whom you recruit or who are recruited by your recruits or by people recruited by your recruits and so on), because each recruit retains a percentage of the sales generated by his or her down line. This is how you expand your opportunity to make more money.
- *Direct Sales.* This could be selling cosmetics, health and fitness products, software, vitamins, cookware and fashion accessories directly to consumers via the internet, in-home parties, classified advertisements and out of your home or car.
- *Vending.* This is a business opportunity if you purchase a vending package, which generally includes vending machines, initial inventory for the machines, an operations manual, and guaranteed placement of the vending machines that you purchase. Guaranteed placement means that the machines will be installed in a retail, warehouse or factory environment, but with no guarantee that the location(s) will be good or profitable.

These examples are only three of the numerous business opportunities available. Homebased business opportunities can cost as little as a few hundred dollars or as much as $40,000. Most are around $5,000 or less, which includes the basic equipment, the operations manual and the inventory needed to start the business.

Where Do You Find Home Business Opportunities?

Like other types of home business operations discussed in this chapter, the ways to find home business opportunities are nearly unlimited. The first place to look is in the classifieds section of your local newspaper under "Business Opportunities." Generally you'll find numerous opportunities listed for sale, some legitimate and others suspect. You can also search the internet for "business opportunities" using Google, Yahoo! or any other search engine. You'll get thousands of hits. A third way to find a legitimate business opportunity, and perhaps the best, is to ask friends and family members if they or people they know are involved in a successful opportunity. The best aspect of using this method is that you can find out first-hand—without the hype of people who make money selling business opportunities—if an opportunity has merit and can be financially viable. Finally, look around your community for business opportunities in operation. Get out and talk with a few of the people who are running them. Ask if they are happy or if they are looking to sell.

The Advantages of Buying a Home Business Opportunity

The biggest advantage of buying a business opportunity is cost. Most are cheap to purchase and start. Some can be started for only a few hundred dollars, making them ideal for entrepreneurs with a determination to succeed but no money. Additional advantages of purchasing a homebased business opportunity include:

- Most business opportunities have been designed to be operated or managed from a

homebased location, which is great for people looking for a home business.
- Business opportunities are very quick to start and get rolling. In fact, you can purchase one today and be open for business tomorrow. Most can also be operated part time, nights, weekends or even seasonally, enabling you to keep your job until the business is self-supporting and can provide you with an income.
- Most business opportunities require no business experience to operate. If there's a learning curve, it takes hours or days, not weeks or months. This is perhaps the biggest lure of business opportunities for many people.

The Disadvantages of Buying a Home Business Opportunity

The number-one disadvantage of purchasing a business opportunity is that you have to be extremely cautious because there are many, many scams out there operated by slick con artists eager to get their hands on your money. There are additional disadvantages associated with purchasing and operating a business opportunity.

- Because business opportunities are not franchised or licensed, you do not receive a protected geographical territory, which means that you may very well be competing against other people operating exactly the same business opportunity as you, selling the exact same products or services as you, and within the same geographical territory as you, which could include your next-door neighbor.
- Business opportunities for the most part offer little or no real growth potential. There are exceptions, but business opportunities are usually very limited.
- Most business opportunities offer little or no initial training and almost none provide ongoing support. Once you have paid for the opportunity, you are essentially on your own.

■ Many business opportunities are not focused on selling products, but rather on adding more people to the flock. The more people you can recruit to buy the same business opportunity or at least to sell for you, the more money you can make. Unfortunately, there is typically no big payoff and, in many cases, like a pyramid scheme, it all comes crashing down, when the seller of these business opportunities disappears. Plus, you can alienate your friends, neighbors and family members by trying to recruit them as customers and salespeople. In short, buying one of these "incredible" business opportunities is often almost akin to joining a cult group.

HOME BUSINESS STARTUP COSTS ESTIMATOR

The Home Business Start-up Costs Estimator (Figure 2.9) is very comprehensive. Many items on the list will not be needed for every home business startup, especially part-time or basic ventures. Calculate only for the items that will be needed for the business you want to start and skip the other items. You may find it necessary to add items particular to your startup. You may also want to use this as an example for creating your own cost estimator on your computer, using any word processing or accounting program. Regardless of how you use the estimator, the value of knowing how much money you will need to start your business cannot be overestimated.

FIGURE 2.9	Home Business Startup Costs Estimator

Type of Business Startup: _____

Section 1. General Startup Costs	Quantity	$ Unit Cost	$ Total Cost
❑ Business/Name Registration	_____	$_____	$_____
❑ Business Incorporation	_____	$_____	$_____
❑ Legal Fees	_____	$_____	$_____
❑ Accounting Fees	_____	$_____	$_____
❑ Consultant Fees	_____	$_____	$_____
❑ Bank Account(s) Setup Charges	_____	$_____	$_____
❑ Merchant Account (Credit Card) Charges	_____	$_____	$_____
❑ Business Association Memberships	_____	$_____	$_____
❑ Industry Association Memberships	_____	$_____	$_____
❑ Professional Association Memberships	_____	$_____	$_____
❑ Distributor/Licensing Fees	_____	$_____	$_____
❑ Insurance Premiums			
1. _____	_____	$_____	$_____
2. _____	_____	$_____	$_____
3. _____	_____	$_____	$_____

FIGURE 2.9	Home Business Startup Costs Estimator, continued

4. _____	_____	$_____	$_____
❑ Special Training and Certificates	_____	$_____	$_____
❑ Other Permits	_____	$_____	$_____
❑ Trademarks, Copyrights, and Patents	_____	$_____	$_____
❑ Deposits	_____	$_____	$_____
❑ Other _____	_____	$_____	$_____
❑ Other _____	_____	$_____	$_____
		Section 1. Subtotal	$_____

Section 2. Office Furniture and Equipment Costs	Quantity	$ Unit Cost	$ Total Cost
❑ Desktop Computer (Including Monitor)	_____	$_____	$_____
❑ Notebook Computer or Laptop	_____	$_____	$_____
❑ Printer	_____	$_____	$_____
❑ Software Programs			
1. _____	_____	$_____	$_____
2. _____	_____	$_____	$_____
3. _____	_____	$_____	$_____
4. _____	_____	$_____	$_____
❑ Other Computer Peripherals	_____	$_____	$_____
❑ Photocopier	_____	$_____	$_____
❑ Digital Camera	_____	$_____	$_____
❑ Scanner	_____	$_____	$_____
❑ Telephone	_____	$_____	$_____
❑ Cell Telephone	_____	$_____	$_____
❑ Telephone Answering Machine	_____	$_____	$_____
❑ Telephone Answering Service	_____	$_____	$_____
❑ Pager	_____	$_____	$_____
❑ Fax Machine	_____	$_____	$_____
❑ Electronic Organizer	_____	$_____	$_____

FIGURE 2.9	Home Business Startup Costs Estimator, continued

	Quantity	$ Unit Cost	$ Total Cost
❑ Desk	_____	$_____	$_____
❑ Chair	_____	$_____	$_____
❑ File Cabinet(s)	_____	$_____	$_____
❑ Bookcase	_____	$_____	$_____
❑ Client Seating	_____	$_____	$_____
❑ Lighting	_____	$_____	$_____
❑ Shredder/Waste Receptacles	_____	$_____	$_____
❑ Small Office Equipment (Staplers, etc.)	_____	$_____	$_____
❑ General Office Supplies (Paper, etc.)	_____	$_____	$_____
❑ Reference Books/Directories	_____	$_____	$_____
❑ Other _____	_____	$_____	$_____
❑ Other _____	_____	$_____	$_____
		Section 2. Subtotal	$_____
Sections 3. Office Renovation Costs	**Quantity**	**$ Unit Cost**	**$ Total Cost**
❑ Building/Inspection Permits	_____	$_____	$_____
❑ New/Upgrades to Mechanicals	_____	$_____	$_____
❑ Fire/Security Alarms	_____	$_____	$_____
❑ Communications Upgrades	_____	$_____	$_____
❑ General Construction	_____	$_____	$_____
❑ Finish Carpentry	_____	$_____	$_____
❑ Windows/Doors	_____	$_____	$_____
❑ Paint/Wall Covering	_____	$_____	$_____
❑ Window Coverings	_____	$_____	$_____
❑ Flooring	_____	$_____	$_____
❑ Built-ins	_____	$_____	$_____
❑ Decorations	_____	$_____	$_____
❑ Other _____	_____	$_____	$_____
❑ Other _____	_____	$_____	$_____
		Section 3. Subtotal	$_____

FIGURE 2.9	Home Business Startup Costs Estimator, continued

Section 4. Inventory Costs	Quantity	$ Unit Cost	$ Total Cost
❑ Initial Product Orders			
1. _____	_____	$_____	$_____
2. _____	_____	$_____	$_____
3. _____	_____	$_____	$_____
4. _____	_____	$_____	$_____
5. _____	_____	$_____	$_____
6. _____	_____	$_____	$_____
7. _____	_____	$_____	$_____
8. _____	_____	$_____	$_____
9. _____	_____	$_____	$_____
10. _____	_____	$_____	$_____
❑ Product Packaging	_____	$_____	$_____
❑ Product Samples	_____	$_____	$_____
❑ Product Shipping Supplies	_____	$_____	$_____
❑ Point-of-Purchase Displays	_____	$_____	$_____
❑ Other _____	_____	$_____	$_____
❑ Other _____	_____	$_____	$_____
		Section 4. Subtotal	$_____

Section 5. Website and E-Commerce Costs	Quantity	$ Unit Cost	$ Total Cost
❑ Domain Registration	_____	$_____	$_____
❑ Website Design	_____	$_____	$_____
❑ Website Content	_____	$_____	$_____
❑ Web Optimization	_____	$_____	$_____
❑ Specialized Software			
1. _____	_____	$_____	$_____
2. _____	_____	$_____	$_____
3. _____	_____	$_____	$_____
4. _____	_____	$_____	$_____

FIGURE 2.9   Home Business Startup Costs Estimator, continued

❑ Special Equipment	____	$____	$____
❑ Search Engine Submission Fees			
1. ____	____	$____	$____
2. ____	____	$____	$____
3. ____	____	$____	$____
4. ____	____	$____	$____
❑ Online Payment Systems	____	$____	$____
❑ Online Shopping Cart	____	$____	$____
❑ Other ____	____	$____	$____
❑ Other ____	____	$____	$____
		Section 5. Subtotal	$____

Section 6. Marketing and Promotion Costs	Quantity	$ Unit Cost	$ Total Cost
❑ Initial Research/Planning Budget	____	$____	$____
❑ Initial Advertising Budget	____	$____	$____
❑ Advertising and Promotional Specialties	____	$____	$____
❑ Printed Promotional Literature			
1. ____	____	$____	$____
2. ____	____	$____	$____
3. ____	____	$____	$____
4. ____	____	$____	$____
❑ Signage			
1. ____	____	$____	$____
2. ____	____	$____	$____
3. ____	____	$____	$____
4. ____	____	$____	$____
❑ Trade Show/Event Marketing Booth	____	$____	$____
❑ Other ____	____	$____	$____
❑ Other ____	____	$____	$____

FIGURE 2.9	Home Business Startup Costs Estimator, continued

❏ Marketing and Promotional Items	_____	$_____	$_____
		Section 6. Subtotal	$_____

Section 7. Business Identity Costs	Quantity	$ Unit Cost	$ Total Cost
❏ Logo Design	_____	$_____	$_____
❏ Desktop Publishing/Design Fees	_____	$_____	$_____
❏ Business Cards	_____	$_____	$_____
❏ Stationery Package	_____	$_____	$_____
❏ Receipts/Invoices	_____	$_____	$_____
❏ Printed Specialties (Pens, etc.)	_____	$_____	$_____
❏ Uniforms	_____	$_____	$_____
❏ Other _____	_____	$_____	$_____
❏ Other _____	_____	$_____	$_____
		Section 7. Subtotal	$_____

Section 8. Transportation Costs	Quantity	$ Unit Cost	$ Total Cost
❏ Vehicle Purchase	_____	$_____	$_____
❏ Vehicle Lease/Loan Down Payment	_____	$_____	$_____
❏ Specialty Accessories (Toolbox, etc.)			
1. _____	_____	$_____	$_____
2. _____	_____	$_____	$_____
3. _____	_____	$_____	$_____
4. _____	_____	$_____	$_____
❏ Insurance	_____	$_____	$_____
❏ Registration	_____	$_____	$_____
❏ Signage	_____	$_____	$_____
❏ Other _____	_____	$_____	$_____
❏ Other _____	_____	$_____	$_____
		Section 8. Subtotal	$_____

FIGURE 2.9   Home Business Startup Costs Estimator, continued

Section 9. Specialized Equipment Costs	Quantity	$ Unit Cost	$ Total Cost
1. _____	_____	$_____	$_____
2. _____	_____	$_____	$_____
3. _____	_____	$_____	$_____
4. _____	_____	$_____	$_____
5. _____	_____	$_____	$_____
6. _____	_____	$_____	$_____
7. _____	_____	$_____	$_____
8. _____	_____	$_____	$_____
		Section 9. Subtotal	$_____

Calculating Total Startup Costs	
Section 1. General Startup Costs	$_____
Section 2. Office Furniture and Equipment Costs	$_____
Section 3. Office Renovation Costs	$_____
Section 4. Inventory Costs	$_____
Section 5. Website and E-Commerce Costs	$_____
Section 6. Marketing and Promotion Costs	$_____
Section 7. Business Identity Costs	$_____
Section 8. Transportation Costs	$_____
Section 9. Specialized Equipment Costs	$_____
Total Startup Costs	$_____
Reserve Fund (10%)	$_____
Estimated Number of Months Required to Reach Breakeven _____	
x Fixed Monthly Overhead Costs	$_____
Total Capital Needed to Start the Business	$_____

FIXED MONTHLY OVERHEAD CALCULATOR

Do you want to know how much money you will need every month to cover your fixed operating costs and wages? Of course! You can do so by using the Fixed Monthly Overhead Calculator (Figure 2.10) for any business you are considering starting, to get a good idea of the net sales that must be generated to cover wages and operating expenses. Then, once you have started a home business, you can use this form to keep track of your fixed operating costs every month. Much like the Home Business Startup Costs Estimator, the Fixed Monthly Overhead Calculator is very comprehensive. It does not list every expense for every home business. Complete only the items relevant to your particular business and skip the other items. The Fixed Monthly Overhead Estimator can be removed from the book and photocopied or you can use it as a model for creating your own on a computer using any word processing or accounting program.

FIGURE 2.10 Fixed Monthly Overhead Calculator

Type of Business Startup: _____

Section 1. General Office Expenditures	Quantity	$ Unit Cost	$ Total Cost
❑ Loan and Interest Repayments	_____	$_____	$_____
❑ Bank Charges	_____	$_____	$_____
❑ Credit Card Fees	_____	$_____	$_____
❑ Merchant Card Fees	_____	$_____	$_____
❑ Business Taxes	_____	$_____	$_____
❑ Business Permits and Registrations	_____	$_____	$_____
❑ Additional Utilities	_____	$_____	$_____
❑ Insurance Premiums			
1._____	_____	$_____	$_____
2._____	_____	$_____	$_____
3._____	_____	$_____	$_____
4._____	_____	$_____	$_____
❑ Workers' Compensation	_____	$_____	$_____
❑ Equipment Leases/Loans/Rentals			
1._____	_____	$_____	$_____
2._____	_____	$_____	$_____
3._____	_____	$_____	$_____
4._____	_____	$_____	$_____
❑ Equipment Repairs	_____	$_____	$_____
❑ Alarm Monitoring	_____	$_____	$_____
❑ Off-Site Storage Costs	_____	$_____	$_____

FIGURE 2.10   Fixed Monthly Overhead Calculator, continued

	Quantity	$ Unit Cost	$ Total Cost
❏ General Office Supplies	_____	$_____	$_____
❏ Postage	_____	$_____	$_____
❏ Courier/Delivery	_____	$_____	$_____
❏ Cleaning/Maintenance	_____	$_____	$_____
❏ Other _____	_____	$_____	$_____
❏ Other _____	_____	$_____	$_____
		Section 1. Subtotal	$_____

Section 2. Communications Expenditures	Quantity	$ Unit Cost	$ Total Cost
❏ Telephone	_____	$_____	$_____
❏ Toll-Free Line	_____	$_____	$_____
❏ Fax Line	_____	$_____	$_____
❏ Internet Connection	_____	$_____	$_____
❏ Cell Phone	_____	$_____	$_____
❏ Answering Service	_____	$_____	$_____
❏ Pager	_____	$_____	$_____
❏ Two-Way Radio	_____	$_____	$_____
❏ Communications Equipment Lease	_____	$_____	$_____
❏ Other _____	_____	$_____	$_____
❏ Other _____	_____	$_____	$_____
		Section 2. Subtotal	$_____

Section 3. Wages and Fees	Quantity	$ Unit Cost	$ Total Cost
❏ Personal Wages	_____	$_____	$_____
❏ Employees	_____	$_____	$_____
1. _____	_____	$_____	$_____
2. _____	_____	$_____	$_____
3. _____	_____	$_____	$_____
4. _____	_____	$_____	$_____

FIGURE 2.10   Fixed Monthly Overhead Calculator, continued

❑ **Employee Benefits**

1. _____   _____ $_____ $_____

2. _____   _____ $_____ $_____

3. _____   _____ $_____ $_____

4. _____   _____ $_____ $_____

❑ Accounting Fees   _____ $_____ $_____

❑ Legal Fees   _____ $_____ $_____

❑ Consultant Fees   _____ $_____ $_____

❑ Business Association Fees   _____ $_____ $_____

❑ Industry Association Fees   _____ $_____ $_____

❑ Professional Association Fees   _____ $_____ $_____

❑ Specialty Membership Fees   _____ $_____ $_____

❑ Other _____   _____ $_____ $_____

❑ Other _____ $_____ $_____

Section 3. Subtotal $_____

Section 4. Marketing Expenditures	Quantity	$ Unit Cost	$ Total Cost
❑ Yellow Pages	_____	$_____	$_____
❑ Newspaper Display Ads	_____	$_____	$_____
❑ Newspaper Classified Ads	_____	$_____	$_____
❑ Magazine	_____	$_____	$_____
❑ Radio	_____	$_____	$_____
❑ Television	_____	$_____	$_____
❑ Business Directories	_____	$_____	$_____
❑ Fliers	_____	$_____	$_____
❑ Direct Mail	_____	$_____	$_____
❑ Telemarketing	_____	$_____	$_____
❑ Trade Shows/Seminars	_____	$_____	$_____
❑ Public Relations	_____	$_____	$_____
❑ Outdoor Advertising	_____	$_____	$_____

FIGURE 2.10 Fixed Monthly Overhead Calculator, continued

	Quantity	$ Unit Cost	$ Total Cost
❑ Contests	_____	$_____	$_____
❑ Promotional Giveaways	_____	$_____	$_____
❑ Product Samples	_____	$_____	$_____
❑ Sponsorships	_____	$_____	$_____
❑ Surveys/Polls/Research	_____	$_____	$_____
❑ Customer Appreciation/Gifts	_____	$_____	$_____
❑ Graphic Design/Copy Fees	_____	$_____	$_____
❑ Other _____	_____	$_____	$_____
❑ Other _____	_____	$_____	$_____
Section 4. Subtotal			$_____

Section 5. Website and E-Commerce Expenditures	Quantity	$ Unit Cost	$ Total Cost
❑ Server/Host/Web Master	_____	$_____	$_____
❑ Maintenance	_____	$_____	$_____
❑ Content/Plug-In Fees			
1. _____	_____	$_____	$_____
2. _____	_____	$_____	$_____
3. _____	_____	$_____	$_____
4. _____	_____	$_____	$_____
❑ Internet Advertising			
1. _____	_____	$_____	$_____
2. _____	_____	$_____	$_____
3. _____	_____	$_____	$_____
4. _____	_____	$_____	$_____
❑ Search Engine	_____	$_____	$_____
❑ Paid Placements	_____	$_____	$_____
❑ Software/Web Tool Licenses			
1. _____	_____	$_____	$_____
2. _____	_____	$_____	$_____
3. _____	_____	$_____	$_____

FIGURE 2.10   Fixed Monthly Overhead Calculator, continued

4. _____	_____	$_____	$_____
❑ Online Payment System Fees	_____	$_____	$_____
❑ Order Fulfillment Fees	_____	$_____	$_____
❑ Equipment Leases/Loans	_____	$_____	$_____
❑ Equipment Maintenance	_____	$_____	$_____
❑ Other _____	_____	$_____	$_____
❑ Other _____	_____	$_____	$_____
		Section 5. Subtotal	$_____

Section 6. Transportation Expenditures	Quantity	$ Unit Cost	$ Total Cost
❑ Lease/Loan Payment	_____	$_____	$_____
❑ Fuel	_____	$_____	$_____
❑ Insurance	_____	$_____	$_____
❑ Repairs	_____	$_____	$_____
❑ Licensing/Registration	_____	$_____	$_____
❑ Parking	_____	$_____	$_____
❑ Cleaning	_____	$_____	$_____
❑ Other _____	_____	$_____	$_____
❑ Other _____	_____	$_____	$_____
		Section 6. Subtotal	$_____

Section 7. Miscellaneous Expenditures	Quantity	$ Unit Cost	$ Total Cost
❑ Travel	_____	$_____	$_____
❑ Entertainment	_____	$_____	$_____
❑ Uniforms/Dry Cleaning	_____	$_____	$_____
❑ Subscriptions			
1. _____	_____	$_____	$_____
2. _____	_____	$_____	$_____
3. _____	_____	$_____	$_____
4. _____	_____	$_____	$_____

FIGURE 2.10	Fixed Monthly Overhead Calculator, continued

❑ Charitable Donations   _____   \$_____   \$_____

❑ Other _____   _____   \$_____   \$_____

❑ Other _____   _____   \$_____   \$_____

                                Section 7. Subtotal   \$_____

Calculating Total Fixed Monthly Overhead

Section 1. General Office Expenditures   \$_____

Section 2. Communications Expenditures   \$_____

Section 3. Wages and Fees   \$_____

Section 4. Marketing Expenditures   \$_____

Section 5. Website and E-Commerce Expenditures   \$_____

Section 6. Transportation Expenditures   \$_____

Section 7. Miscellaneous Expenditures   \$_____

Fixed Monthly Overheads—Grand Total   \$_____

RESOURCES
Associations

American Franchisee Association
53 W. Jackson Boulevard, Suite 1157
Chicago, IL 60604
(312) 431-0545
franchisee.org

American Home Business Association
965 East 4800, Suite 3C
Salt Lake City, UT 84117
(866) 396-7773
homebusinessworks.com

Canadian Franchise Association (CFA)
5399 Eglinton Avenue West, Suite 116
Toronto, ON M9C 5K6
(416) 695-2896 or (800) 665-4232
cfa.ca

International Franchise Association (IFA)
1501 K Street NW, Suite 350
Washington, DC 20005
(202) 628-8000
franchise.org

U.S. Small Business Administration (SBA)
409 Third Street SW
Washington, DC 20416
(800) 827-5722
sba.gov

Suggested Reading

Caffey, Andrew A. *Franchises & Business Opportunities: How to Find, Buy, and Operate a Successful Business.* Irvine, CA: Entrepreneur Media Inc., 2002.

Edwards, Paul, and Sarah Edwards. *The Best Home Businesses for the 21st Century: The Inside Information You Need to Know to Select a Home-Based Business That's Right for You.* New York: J.P. Tarcher, 1999.

Hayes, Robert. *The Franchise Handbook: A Complete Guide to All Aspects of Buying, Selling or Investing in a Franchise.* Ocala, FL: Atlantic Publishing, 2006.

Huff, Priscilla Y. *The Self-Employed Woman's Guide to Launching a Home-Based Business: Everything You Need to Know About Getting Started on the Road to Success.* Roseville, CA: Prima Publishing, 2002.

Kowalski, Gary M. *The Franchise Ratings Guide: 3000 Franchisees Expose the Best & Worst Franchise Opportunities.* Lincoln, NE: iUniverse Inc., 2006.

Lesonsky, Rieva, and Maria Anton-Conley. *Ultimate Book of Franchises: From the Experts at Entrepreneur Magazine.* 2nd edition. Irvine, CA: Entrepreneur Press, 2007.

Pullen, Martha Campbell, and Lllly (Lillet) Walters. *You Can Make Money from Your Hobby: Building a Business Doing What You Love.* Nashville, TN: Broadman and Holman Publishing, 1999.

Sander, Jennifer Basye, and Peter Sander. *Niche and Grow Rich: Practical Ways of Turning Your Ideas into a Business.* Irvine, CA: Entrepreneur Press, 2003.

Stansell, Kimberly. *Bootstrapper's Success Secrets: 151 Tactics for Building Your Business on a Shoestring Budget.* Franklin Lakes, NJ: Career Press, 1997.

Stephenson, James, with Rich Mintzer. *Entrepreneur's Ultimate Start-Up Directory: 1500 Great Business Ideas!* 2nd edition. Irvine, CA: Entrepreneur Press, 2007.

Websites

Business Know-How: Small business information, advice, tools and services. ***businessknowhow.com***

Business Opportunities Classifieds Online: Online business opportunities portal listing hundreds of business opportunities indexed by category. ***boconline.com***

Canada Business/Entreprises Canada: A government information service for businesses and startup entrepreneurs in Canada, that serves as a single point of access for federal and provincial or territorial government services, programs and regulatory requirements for business (formerly *Canadian Business Service Center*). ***cbsc.org***

Entrepreneur Online: Online small business resource center providing entrepreneurs with information, advice, products, services and resources. ***entrepreneur.com***

Family Business Magazine Online: Information, tips, articles and advice about starting and operating a family business. ***familybusinessmagazine.com***

Franchise Direct: Comprehensive listings of franchise opportunities plus general information on franchising. ***franchisedirect.com***

Franchise Expo: Numerous franchise opportunities in the United States and worldwide. ***franchiseexpo.com***

Franchise Solutions: Information on the top franchise businesses for sale, including directories of opportunities. ***franchisesolutions.com***

Franchise Times Magazine Online: Electronic and print magazine providing the latest franchise news, information, products, services and industry resources. ***franchisetimes.com***

Franchising.org: Information on franchise opportunities, news, articles, books, a bulletin board and more. *franchising.org*

Home Based Business Opportunities: Online directory service featuring hundreds of homebased and small business opportunities listings. *home-based-business-opportunities.com*

Home-Based Working Moms: A professional association and online community for parents who work from home. *hbwm.com*

Home Business Magazine: Online magazine with information, advice, tools and links for home business owners. *homebusinessmag.com*

Home Working: A site based in the United Kingdom with information, advice, services and support by and for people working from home. *homebusinessmag.com*

PowerHomeBiz.com: Online information, advice and tools for home business owners. *powerhomebiz.com*

Small Business Now: Small business information, advice, tools, products, services and links of interest. *smallbusinessnow.com*

Small Business Opportunities Magazine Online: Electronic and print magazine providing readers with the latest small business opportunities news, information and industry resources. *sbomag.com*

CHAPTER 3

Financial Issues

FINANCIAL ISSUES FACING THE NEW HOME business owner are many and varied, but certainly manageable if you take the time to identify your personal financial requirements and those of your new venture. Home business owners must also educate themselves in such areas as banking, recordkeeping, payment processing, money management and small business taxation. Throughout this book, you will find additional information about financial issues facing the homebased business owner, especially in Chapter 11, "Managing Your Home Business."

The first step, prior to getting your business going, is to take stock of your personal financial situation to determine your net worth and the amount of income you need to generate each month to pay your bills. Knowing your personal financial situation is critical because it will enable you to determine how much money you can personally afford to invest in starting the business, how much you will have to borrow, and how much income you need to draw from your new business.

TAKING STOCK OF YOUR PERSONAL FINANCES

Complete the Personal Savings and Salable Assets Worksheet (Figure 3.1) and the Family Monthly Expenses Worksheet (Figure 3.2).

The Personal Savings and Salable Assets Worksheet will help you calculate how much money you have in savings or could have available and how much money you could raise by selling assets that are not essential. Some people consider taking their net worth into account when starting a business, but this is usually unnecessary, because you should not be planning to sell your home, getting rid of necessary insurance policies, or cashing out your retirement savings to open up a business. You should identify

FIGURE 3.1	Personal Savings and Salable Assets Worksheet

Include only assets that you could sell or use to raise capital.

	Asset Value	Liabilities Outstanding Balance
Real Estate (not including your primary residence)	$ _____	$ _____
Salable Personal Effects (furniture, electronics, etc.)	$ _____	$ _____
Cash in Bank Accounts	$ _____	$ _____
Stocks, Bonds and Other Money in Investments	$ _____	$ _____
Total Available Personal Savings and Salable Assets	$ _____	

sources of funding that are not necessary for your life and your living expenses.

The Family Monthly Expenses Worksheet is to help you calculate how much income you need to earn each month. You might want to complete both columns of the income worksheet. The first column calculates a subsistence income level, the minimum amount you need to pay your personal bills. The second column calculates a comfortable income level, the amount you need to maintain your current lifestyle. In these calculations it is presumed you are working full time at your home-based business and are a sole provider or responsible for a significant portion of the family income. If you are among the roughly half of the American households that are two-income families, you need to factor in your contribution to the family finances.

MAKING THE RIGHT FINANCIAL TRANSACTION INTO YOUR BUSINESS

Once you have determined your net worth and the income you need to pay your personal bills each month, you will be in a better position to identify the best financial transition into your new business. First, looking at your personal net worth, are you in a financial position to start the business you want to start? If so, are you prepared to risk a portion of your savings to start the business? Only you know the answer for sure, especially on the second question. If you are not in a position to start a new business, you must identify how to raise the money needed, which is discussed later in this chapter.

The second consideration in making the right financial transition into your new business is income. Does the business venture you intend to start have the potential to satisfy your income needs? If so, do you have enough money or access to enough money to manage comfortably until the business is providing an adequate income? Once again, only you know the answers.

As mentioned earlier, one option is to start your new business part time while working part time at your current job or another job until the business is able to provide enough income to meet your needs. Additional information about making a transition into a home business can be found in Chapter 2, "What Type of Home Business Should You Start?," under "What Are Your Home Business Options?," where you will find information about full-time, part-time, seasonal and retirement businesses.

FIGURE 3.2	Family Monthly Expenses Worksheet

Housing Expenses	Subsistence	Comfortable
Mortgage or Rent	$	$
Common Property Fees	$	$
Utilities	$	$
Telephone, Cable and Internet	$	$
Property Insurance	$	$
Property Taxes	$	$
Property Maintenance	$	$
Other	$	$

Transportation Expenses	Subsistence	Comfortable
Auto Loans or Leases	$	$
Fuel and Oil	$	$
Licensing	$	$
Maintenance	$	$
Insurance	$	$
Other	$	$

Personal Expenses	Subsistence	Comfortable
Food	$	$
Clothing	$	$
Pets	$	$
Health Care	$	$
Dental	$	$
Insurance	$	$
School	$	$
Retirement Plans	$	$
Entertainment	$	$
Recreation and Hobbies	$	$
Memberships and Subscriptions	$	$
Religious Contributions	$	$
Credit Card Payments	$	$

FIGURE 3.2	Family Monthly Expenses Worksheet, continued

Personal Expenses	Subsistence	Comfortable
Other	$ _____	$ _____
Total Expenses per Month	$ _____	$ _____
Less Other Income	$ _____	$ _____
(Spouse, Investment Income or Pensions)		
After-Tax Income Needed per Month	$ _____	$ _____
After-Tax Income Needed per Year (monthly figure x 12)	$ _____	$ _____

FINDING MONEY TO START YOUR HOME BUSINESS VENTURE

Once you have taken stock of your personal financial situation, the next step is to identify where the needed business funding will come from and what must be done to secure this funding.

Capital

Heads up! If this is your first foray into the world of business ownership, you should know there are generally three types of capital required to start or purchase a business—*startup* capital, *working* capital and *growth* capital. All three are important, but the first two are vital; if you do not have or cannot get the first two, you would be well-advised to keep saving until you can satisfy these financing requirements or to find a source willing to put up the capital needed with few demands in terms of when they want it back.

Startup Capital

This is the money you use to start a business or purchase a business or a franchise. Startup capital is needed to purchase equipment and/or office furniture, to meet legal requirements, to pay for any necessary training, to cover licensing, and to pur-

chase initial inventory if the business will be selling products rather than services. There are ways of reducing the startup capital needed to get the business rolling, as you will see later in this section, but you will need some money.

Working Capital

This is the money needed to pay all the bills and give you an income until the business reaches the breakeven point. I believe working capital is most important, especially in the absence of adequate cash flow, which is almost always the situation with startups. Entrepreneurs have lost their startup investments because their new business ventures had insufficient operating capital to achieve a positive cash flow. Beyond startup investment, working capital is needed to achieve positive cash flow. "Working capital" should be the mantra of every entrepreneur thinking about starting a business.

Growth Capital

This third type of capital is the money needed should you decide to expand your business. The reason growth capital is generally required to grow a business is that many entrepreneurs have tried unsuccessfully to expand from their current cash flow and their businesses have failed. Using cash flow places an enormous financial strain on the current business and the expansion, ultimately starving both of adequate funding to stay operational. As you start out, growth capital is the least important of the three, especially if you do not plan to grow your business.

Personal Savings

Perhaps the best way to finance your new home business venture is by using your personal cash savings and/or your personal investments, as listed in Figure 3.1. There are many reasons why I feel this is the best way to fund your business. You stay in control of how, when and why funds are distributed. You do not have to pay the interest rates on a loan or satisfy the requirements of investors. You will not feel anxious about whether or not you can get the proper funding. You do not have to worry about accumulating debt. There is no loan and interest repayment to make each month.

To personally fund your home business startup, you can use your savings account, investment certificates, mutual funds, bonds, stocks or other investments. You can also take out a mortgage on your home or pull from your retirement fund (typically incurring penalties), but this puts increased pressure on you, since you do not want to risk your home or your retirement security. For that reason, these are not good choices. It is also not smart to borrow against your credit cards, because of the high interest rates and fees.

It is always wise to consult with a certified financial planner prior to cashing, selling or redeeming any personal investment or certificates. Keep in mind that, depending on the investment you want to liquidate, you might actually be earning a higher rate of return than the interest rate you could secure for a startup loan. Again, check with your financial planner and investigate all financing

options and avenues available to you before cashing in investments to fund your startup.

You can also liquidate or borrow against other personal assets, such as a boat, a recreational vehicle, a cottage or antiques. It's up to you to decide to what lengths you are prepared to go to finance your business ambitions personally. Some people are comfortable using savings and other assets to fund a business dream; others are not. Only you can make that decision and commitment.

Government Business Loans

In the United States and Canada, there are government programs that can assist individuals who are starting a new business or provide growth funding for small businesses. In the United States these programs are administered through the SBA. In Canada, most small businesses can receive loans through incentive programs administered through the Business Development Bank of Canada.

There are three financial assistance programs offered by the SBA of particular interest to small business owners—Business Loans Program, Investment Program and Bonding Program.

SBA's Business Loans Program. These programs are available to new business enterprises with startup funding loaned from micro lending institutions (participating banks and credit unions) and guaranteed in full or in part by the government. There are various levels of qualification for the Business Loans Program, so check with your local SBA office for more details and to see if you qualify.

SBA's Investment Program. This program is aimed at supplying new business ventures with funding and small- to medium-size businesses with venture capital that can be used for growth and expansion.

SBA's Bonding Program. The Security Bond Guarantee (SBG) program gives small and minority contractors opportunities to bid on supply and service contracts.

It should be noted that the government programs in the United States and Canada to assist small business ventures do not in any way guarantee financial assistance. Each application is based on the potential of the venture and the background and experience of the people that will be managing the business. Therefore, to pursue assistance through these programs, all the usual steps are required, such as creating a complete business and marketing plan. These programs are, however, more "small business friendly" than many lending institutions.

For all of these programs, you can contact your local SBA office for details.

United States

U.S. Small Business Administration (SBA)
Financial Programs
409 Third Street SW
Washington, DC 20416
(800) 827-5722
sba.gov/financing

Canada

Business Development Bank of Canada
BDC Building
5 Place Ville Marie, Suite 400
Montréal, QC H3B 5E7
(877) BDC-BANX (232-2269)
bdc.ca

Private Investors

Startup funds can come from private investors. Depending on the investor, a loan may or may not have strings attached. If the private investor is providing loans to what traditional lending institutions (banks and credit unions) consider "high-risk" businesses, then he or she may ask for a high interest rate in return. In other situations, private lenders want to have a controlling interest

in the business or be involved with day-to-day activities. A private investor may want a combination of these conditions for funding.

However, you should not approach a private investor with a negative attitude, assuming you will need to make great sacrifices or share your business dreams. There are private investors who see promise and growth in your business and simply want to help you launch your business and, in exchange, make some money off your success.

Therefore, you need to evaluate what a private investor wants before getting into any agreement. A silent investor can be ideal; in many cases such an investor will lend his or her experience and background.

In any event, when dealing with a private investor, you want to have a lawyer write or review the investment agreement or, if you decide to go that route, the partnership agreement. You will also want an accountant to look over the financial aspects of the deal to ensure your best interests. Also keep in mind the following:

- All parties should share a similar excitement for the business and have similar goals and ambitions, both personally and for the business.
- It is advantageous (although not essential) to find a private investor with specific experiences and access to additional resources that can be used in the business.

You can now search for investors in geographic regions far and wide. One way to find investors to help finance a business startup, expansion or product invention is by placing a classified advertisement in local newspapers in their communities or an industry magazine. This is a good means of generating smaller levels of funding. However, the larger amounts will typically come through referrals by your accountant, attorney, business contacts and/or associations, and even through personal contacts. You can also visit venture capital websites that maintain listings of entrepreneurs or venture capitalists seeking to invest in new and existing businesses.

Many venture capitalists are known as *angels*. They are generally wealthy entrepreneurs with tons of business experience who provide capital in return for being part of a growing, successful business. These angels are somewhat different from average private investors. They prefer to invest in businesses that have a successful operating track record or that have a great potential for profit because of a unique product, protected intellectual property or verifiable market demand. The benefits of building investor relationships with such angels are numerous: Most are experienced and can be useful additions to your business team, and they can supply low-risk capital quickly, free of the usual need for immediate repayments of principal and interest.

Of course, as is the case with any partnership, there may be drawbacks, which can include a controlling interest in the business or large profit demands. Seeking out a private investor to fund your home business startup is a strategy that has worked very well for other entrepreneurs. Just make sure to be cautious and use sound judgment.

- VentureDirect Worldwide, *venturedirect.com*
- Finance, Inc., *vfinance.com*
- NVST, Inc., *nvst.com*
- National Venture Capital Association, *nvca.org*
- CVCA: Canada's Venture Capital and Private Equity Association, *cvca.ca*
- VentureDeal, *venturedeal.com*
- Venture Capital Access Online, *vcaonline.com*

Borrowing from Family and Friends

Another way to fund your startup is to ask family members or friends for a loan. The downside to borrowing money from a family member or a friend is that it can place a strain on the relationship. While your intent to repay the loan quickly may be honorable, it can be a difficult and stressful time until the business shows a profit. In many cases businesses fail, which can be very unsettling in terms of the relationship.

There are many extremely successful business ventures have been built on money loaned by friends and family members. One such success story is that of the three men who created the board game Trivial Pursuit. They hit up friends and family members to invest in their idea and issued what they called "Love Stock" in the company in exchange for development and startup money. The last time I heard, an initial $1,000 investment made by these "Love Stock" holders is now worth about $3 million and climbing.

You need to borrow only from people who you are convinced understand the situation you are facing in starting a business. These people must truly understand the risk and be OK with the fact that they may never see this money again.

Nonetheless, you should approach this deal in the same manner as if you were borrowing from a lending institution. Have a promissory note drawn up (Figure 3.3), noting all the details of the agreement and creating a repayment schedule. Sign it and have the lenders sign it. Stick to your repayment schedule and show you are trying your best to repay the loan, with interest or a dividend if possible.

Bank Loans

Entrepreneurs with a good credit rating also have the option of applying for a business startup loan through banks and credit unions. The business loan can be *secured*, meaning it is guaranteed with some other type of investment, such as a *guaranteed investment certificate*. Alternately, the loan can be *unsecured*, with the funds advanced

FIGURE 3.3   Sample Promissory Note

This loan agreement is by and between:

Borrower

Name _____   Address _____

City _____   State_____ ZIP _____ Tel _____

Borrower (if more than one)

Name _____   Address _____

City _____   State_____ ZIP _____ Tel _____

Lender

Name _____   Address _____

City _____   State_____ ZIP _____ Tel _____

Lender (if more than one)

Name _____   Address _____

City _____   State_____ ZIP _____ Tel _____

(Borrower's[s'] name[s] here) _____, jointly and severally, promise to pay

(lender's[s'] name[s] here) _____ the sum of $ _____, bearing interest at the

rate of _____% per annum, and payable in _____ equal and consecutive monthly installments, com-

mencing on the _____ day of _____ and each and every month thereafter until paid, with a final

installment of $ _____, on the _____ day of _____, 20___, upon which the loan shall be repaid in full

with no further principal or interest amounts owing.

_____	_____	_____	_____
Borrower's Signature	Date	Borrower's Signature	Date
_____	_____	_____	_____
Lender's Signature	Date	Lender's Signature	Date
_____	_____	_____	_____
Witnessed by	Date	Witnessed by	Date

because of your personal creditworthiness. The advantage of a secured loan is that the interest rate is generally lower. However, many first-time entrepreneurs do not have investments or other resources to secure the loan; otherwise, they would be able to finance the startup with those investments or other resources.

Another option is to talk to your bank or trust company about setting up a secured or unsecured *line of credit*. The interest rate for secured lines of credit is much lower than for unsecured credit lines. An advantage of a line of credit over a standard business loan is that you have to repay interest based only on the amount of money you use and not on the principal. For example, a $30,000 line of credit fully extended (that is, you borrow the full amount) with a per annum interest rate of 5 percent would require minimum monthly payments of $125 (5% × $30,000 ÷ 12 months = $125). Of course, you would not be paying down the principal of the line of credit. But this flexibility is exactly what new business startups need: breathing space in the early stages to get established and grow without the pressure of repaying on the loan, as well as paying interest every month. Of course, a line of credit typically won't provide enough money to start up a more expensive enterprise. Lines of credit are usually for ongoing business needs, such as inventory, remodeling and expansion.

If you decide to seek a business loan or a line of credit, go armed with a bulletproof business plan and a marketing plan. Bankers want to know they are investing in sound and well-researched ideas that have the potential to succeed. Listed below are a few financial institutions with small business loan programs. You'll find many others by searching the internet and by talking with other small business owners.

- Bank of America, *bankofamerica.com*
- Wells Fargo, *wellsfargo.com*
- RBC Royal Bank, *royalbank.com/sme*
- Key Bank, *key.com*
- Business Finance (a portal to small business loans), *businessfinance.com*

Credit Cards

Probably more home business ventures have been started with credit cards than with any other financing. The obvious drawback here is that many credit cards have very high annual interest rates, some as high as 20 percent. This makes them a less attractive option for financing your home

business option if you cannot pay off the balance for an extended period. Considering that millions of people are in credit card debt, this could be a rather dangerous way to start a business. In fact, credit card companies are essentially banking on your falling behind and paying high interest rates.

If you do elect to use credit card loans, use them for smaller needs, not to finance your entire business. You should always be sure you can pay off your balance in full each month.

You can certainly use your credit cards to do some small business shopping. Shop for credit cards with the lowest interest rates and no annual fees and for cards that reward purchases with air miles or redeemable shopping points. I would also suggest that you apply for credit cards specifically for small business use, such as the Visa Small Business Card. Business credit cards generally charge a lower annual interest rate and include such benefits as cards for employees, online bookkeeping and access, business travel perks, business insurance options and no extra charges for cash advances. The following are a few popular choices for small business credit cards.

- MasterCard Business, *mastercardbusiness.com*
- Visa Small Business, *usa.visa.com/business*
- American Express Small Business, *americanexpress.com*
- Advanta Business Credit Cards, *advanta.com*
- Citibank CitiBusiness®, *citibank.com*

Barter

Bartering your way into business is yet another option for the more creative entrepreneurial set. Barter clubs for small business owners have become extremely popular over the past decade, especially with the advent of the internet, which allows goods and services to easily be exchanged, without cash changing hands and all with the simple click of a mouse.

The premise behind barter is basic. You offer the goods or services you sell in exchange for goods and services you need to operate or promote your business. For instance, if you own a janitorial service and need printed fliers, you might offer your local printer office cleaning services in exchange for a few thousand promotional fliers.

The key element of bartering is very often time. If you are putting in your time, you need to be getting X dollars worth of value in return. Therefore, you do not want to tie yourself up for five hours in exchange for something that is worth $50.

Bartering will not produce the money you need to start and operate your homebased business, but it can greatly reduce the amount of hard cash you need. Listed below are online barter clubs for small business owners.

- National Trade Association, *ntatrade.com*
- VIP Barter, *vipbarter.com*
- ITEX: The Membership Trading Community, *itex.com*
- TradeAway, *tradeaway.com*
- The Barter Club, *thebarterclub.com*
- BarterNews (all about barter clubs), *barternews.com*

Leasing and Renting

Leasing or renting equipment is another financing strategy that can greatly reduce the amount of hard cash you need to get things rolling. First, you should understand the difference between leasing and renting. When you rent equipment or tools, you do not take ownership in any form; you simply pay for the amount of time you need the item and then return the item when you no longer need it. When you lease, you also do not own the equipment, but you are legally bound to pay for a portion of the entire value of the equipment plus interest through scheduled lease payments, which are generally monthly.

The benefit to new startups that rent or lease equipment, tools or fixtures is that you do not need to pay a lot of money upfront. An additional benefit of renting or leasing equipment is the fact that in most cases the total rental or lease payment is a 100-percent business expense, as opposed to a sliding scale of depreciation on owned equipment for tax purposes. When the lease or rental term is over, you can upgrade to a new model without having to worry about selling or trading in the old one or simply not replace the equipment if it is no longer required.

Of course the disadvantage of leasing or renting is that the items leased or rented are not assets, since you do not own them. You can also end up paying more than the value of the item if you lease it over a period of time. One New York–based PR company was leasing a coffee pot. In time, they realized that they had spent nearly $300 for a $30 coffee pot. They went out of business in the late 1990s. It wasn't a surprise to those who worked there.

With that story in mind, get into the habit of leasing only short-term items or large items such as a copier, which is one piece of office equipment that businesses frequently lease because they can upgrade more easily and (like leasing a car) have the best model around without spending several thousand dollars to own it. But, so you never get carried away with leasing, always remember the coffee pot story.

- LeaseSource, *leasesource.net*
- Tiger Leasing, *tigerleasing.com*

Credit Terms from Suppliers and Associates

Another way to finance your startup is to ask your new suppliers for a revolving credit account that gives you up to 90 days to pay for the goods and services you need to operate your business or to sell to customers. Keep in mind, though, just asking nicely may not work; you have to demonstrate to your suppliers you are a worthy credit risk. Usually the supplier will conduct a credit check on you or require you to provide some sort of security guarantee. If your credit history is good enough to establish revolving credit accounts that allow you up to 90 days to pay for goods, this is essentially a loan for three months with no interest charge. This is a favorite financing strategy for many home business owners simply because it works.

PROVIDING CUSTOMERS WITH PAYMENT OPTIONS

Consumers have come to expect payment options, so a steadfast cash-only payment policy is no longer acceptable. Instead, most business owners must now provide customers with numerous purchase payment options—cash, check, debit card, credit card and, for major purchases, financing options and leasing options. The downside to providing credit, debit, financing and leasing options are the fees charged back to the business—account fees, transaction fees, fixed monthly and annual equipment rental fees, and, for credit cards and debit cards, a merchant user fee based on a percentage of the total sales value.

Payment processing fees and commissions must be viewed as a cost of doing business now. Consumers expect or demand choices in paying for their purchases. If you elect not to provide payment options that meet their needs, in all likelihood they will go to your competitors. You can recoup fees and commissions by including them in product and service costs when calculating pricing formulas. In most cases, the higher volume of sales from offering more payment options will offset fees and commissions charged.

Cash

Cash is still the best way to get paid for your goods or services. Cash is instant. There is no processing time required. As fast as the cash comes in, you can use it to pay expenses and wages, buy more goods for resale or grow your business. There is a downside, however. Cash can be lost or stolen and there is no proof or paper trail. Collecting from your insurance company could prove difficult.

In all likelihood, you won't see very much cash unless you are selling small items or running a basic service, like dog walking, babysitting or window washing. For safekeeping, you can always buy a home safe. If you find yourself collecting too much cash, you can always make daytime deposits at the bank.

Credit Cards

Any business owner worth his or her salt is able to process credit cards, especially if doing business over the internet. In fact, the majority of consumers have replaced paper money altogether in favor of plastic.

There are two disadvantages from a business owner's perspective. First, there are fees that the credit card company charges merchants. The merchant fee ranges from 1 to 8 percent of the total sales value, based on your arrangement with the credit card service provider. One way to reduce the merchant rate for credit cards is through association membership. Often business associations like the Chamber of Commerce negotiate lower merchant rates with banks and credit card companies for their members, based on the number of members who use the service. Check whether your local Chamber of Commerce or other small business association in your area offers members reduced merchant rates. The second disadvantage is that it takes time to process the transaction. The cash is not available immediately, although modern technology makes it available quickly.

Despite these two relatively minor disadvantages, if you plan on selling goods and services to consumers, you will need to accept credit cards. If you choose not to, your sales and bottom-line profits will suffer because consumers will go elsewhere. Here are the major merchant accounts:

- Visa Financial Services, *visa.com*
- MasterCard, *mastercard.com*
- Discover Card, *discovercard.com*
- American Express, *americanexpress.com*
- Charge.com (service for Visa, MasterCard, American Express and Discover), *charge.com*
- USA Merchant Account, *usa-merchantaccount.com*
- Merchant Accounts Express, *merchantexpress.com*
- MerchantSeek, *merchantseek.com*
- Merchant Systems, *merchant-systems. com*
- Network Solutions Merchant Account, *merchantaccounts.networksolutions.com*

Debit Cards

Most home business owners probably will not need to offer customers a debit card payment option unless they retail goods or services at trade shows, seminars and other direct selling events. If you will be selling goods and services directly to consumers, it would be wise to set up a debit payment system with your bank so that you can offer consumers a debit card payment option.

Be aware that there is a cost associated with providing debit-card payment options. First, you will need to purchase or rent the debit card processing equipment, which will set you back about $40 per month. There is also a transaction fee charged by the bank that you pay every time you make a debit card transaction. Currently, this fee ranges from 10 cents to 50 cents per transaction, based on variables such as dollar value and frequency of use. Most banks and credit unions offer their business clients debit card equipment and services. Therefore, if you feel that offering debit card pay-

ment options will help to increase sales, contact your bank to arrange to get the process up and running.

Paper and Electronic Checks

Paper and electronic checks are two other purchase payment options you might want to consider offering your customers.

If you decide to accept paper checks for purchases, make sure you ask for picture identification and write the customer's driver's license number on the back of the check. Also let customers know that you do not send out merchandise until the check clears. Too many small business owners have been burned by operating on the basis of good faith with customers, even ones they thought they knew.

Electronic checks are especially helpful if you will be selling goods and services online. E-checks work much like cash because once the purchase and payment amounts have been verified, the funds are directly deposited into your bank account electronically. Here are a few e-check payment services; you can learn more about them by visiting their websites:

- PayByCheck, *paybycheck.com*
- E Check Processing (Zytransact), *e-checkprocessing.com*
- Official Payments, *officialpayments.com*

Financing and Leasing Plans

Other options that many consumers want are for financing and leasing, especially for expensive purchases or when buying specialized equipment. Fortunately, from a home business owner's perspective, offering customers financing and leasing options is very easy. All that is required is to establish an account with any of a number of retail financing or leasing services that provide consumer financing options for just about any purchase imaginable. Listed below are the websites for a few retail financing and leasing services.

- CitiFinancial Retail Services Program, *citifinancialretailservices.com*
- Chase, *chase.com*
- LeaseSource, *leasesource.net*

In-House Financing Options

In-house financing is yet another payment option that you may want to extend to your customers. At some point, if your customers operate their own businesses, it will be inevitable that they will want to establish a revolving trade account with your business, with purchases payable in 30, 60 or 90 days. In-house financing means you are, in effect, loaning the money to your customers to make purchases from your business. If they do not pay for the purchases, you have to try to get them to pay by making demands, hiring a collection agency or taking them to small claims court.

These are the steps in extending credit:

1. Create a standard credit policy that includes acceptance and denial guidelines.
2. Develop a standard business credit application and a consumer credit application, if you plan on extending credit to nonbusiness customers.
3. Conduct credit and reference checks from information supplied by customers on their credit applications.
4. Approve or reject applications based on credit and reference checks or any extenuating circumstances.
5. If an application is approved, establish an initial credit limit and a schedule for raising the limit if the customer's creditworthiness remains in good standing.
6. If an application is rejected, work with the customer to find ways to secure credit from a third party.

7. Bill customers on time, as scheduled, and watch for signs of trouble.
8. Reward customers who continue to pay on time and in full. This can be done with small gifts, special discounts or value-added rewards.
9. Develop a collection policy, schedule and action plan for delinquent and nonpayment accounts.

Additional information about extending credit, credit checks, credit applications, collection agencies and small claims courts can be found in Chapter 11, "Managing Your Home Business."

TAXATION AND THE HOME BUSINESS

Operating a business from home, even a small, part-time venture, has tax advantages, but with that comes the disadvantage—bookkeeping paperwork and complicated tax forms to complete, especially if you have employees, are incorporated or import and export goods. Like personal income, business earnings are taxed by multiple layers of government: federal, state or provincial and municipal.

The best information that you can obtain about small business and income taxation will come directly from the source. In the United States that's the Internal Revenue Service (*irs.gov*) and in Canada it's the Canada Revenue Agency (*cra-arc.gc.ca*).

A good accountant and a bookkeeper can help you navigate the taxation waters. In addition, there are books specifically written to help the small business owner understand and prepare tax forms. Among the best tax books for small businesses are those by Bernard B. Kamoroff, whose book *Small Time Operator* (2008 edition), is as up-to-date as you can find. It's available from *Amazon.com* and *Barnesandnoble.com*, as well as at book retailers. The investment in such books can prove invaluable and the cost will certainly be returned many times over through discovery of business deductions and tax-saving tips.

Home Business Taxation Basics

Small business taxation is complicated. You are always well-advised to seek professional help in terms of business, income and employee taxation issues.

Income/Business Earnings Tax

Paying taxes on personal income and business earnings can be tied together if you operate a sole proprietorship or a partnership that is not incorporated. If you are a sole proprietor, the income your business earns after expenses is your personal income and you are taxed accordingly. If your business is incorporated, you are personally taxed on the income you receive from the corporation, and the corporation is taxed as a separate entity on the profits it earns after expenses. Additionally, post-tax profits are taxed once again when distributed to corporation shareholders in the form of dividends. More information about the advantages and disadvantages associated with the various business legal structures can be found in Chapter 4, "Legal Issues."

Employees

If you hire employees, you will need to obtain an employee identification number (EIN) from the IRS, prepare and submit employee income tax reporting forms, and withhold and remit the employee's and employer's portions of Medicare, employment insurance and Social Security. Additional information about hiring employees and employee issues can be found in Chapter 8, "Building Your Business Team."

Sales Tax

Almost all states and provinces now have some sort of sales tax in place that businesses must charge on consumer purchases and then remit to the appropriate government agency. Therefore, you will need to check with either your state department of taxation or your provincial tax agency or with either the SBA (*sba.org*) or Canada Business/ Entreprises Canada (*canadabusiness.ca*) to inquire about obtaining a sales tax number for your business. In Canada all businesses that anticipate yearly sales to exceed $30,000 must obtain a federal Goods and Services Sales/ Harmonized Sales Tax (GST/HST) number. A GST of 6 percent is charged on the sales of most products and services, collected by the business and remitted to the federal government monthly, quarterly or annually, depending on your bookkeeping preference. GST numbers can be obtained by contacting the Canada Revenue Agency, *cra-arc.gc.ca*.

IRS Small Business Tax Forms and Publications

The IRS provides small business owners with free publications that explain small business taxation issues and that can be used as guides for completing small business and self-employment tax forms. You can order IRS small business information, tax forms and publications in four ways:

- In person at your local IRS office
- Online at *irs.gov/businesses/small*
- TaxFax service at (703) 368-9694
- Toll-free, call (800) 829-4933 for assistance

To download tax guides and forms online, you will need Adobe Acrobat Reader because the files are in PDF (Portable Document File) format. You can download and install this program free from *adobe.com*. The following are the most popular and important publication guides for small business owners.

Sole Proprietorship

- Publication 334: Tax Guide for Small Business
- Publication 505: Tax Withholding and Estimated Tax
- Publication 533: Self-Employment Tax Partnerships
- Publication 541: Partnerships
- Publication 505: Tax Withholding and Estimated Tax
- Publication 533: Self-Employment Tax

Corporations

- Publication 542: Corporations
- S-Corporation—Form 1120S: U.S. Income Tax Return for an S Corporation

Limited Liability Companies (LLCs)

LLCs are classified as partnerships if they have no more than two of the following corporate characteristics: centralization of management, continuity of life, free transferability of interests or limited liability.

- Partnership—Publication 541: Partnerships
- Corporation—Publication 542: Corporations

Additional IRS Small Business and Taxation Publications:

- Publication 583: Starting a Business and Keeping Records
- Publication 587: Business Use of Your Home
- Publication 538: Accounting Periods and Methods
- Publication 509: Tax Calendars
- Publication 1066C: A Virtual Small Business Tax Workshop DVD (replaces Publication 1066: Small Business Tax Workshops Workbook)
- Publication 1635: Understanding Your Employee Identification Number (EIN)
- Publication 15: Circular E, Employer's Tax Guide

- Publication 15-A: Employer's Supplemental Tax Guide
- Publication 15-B: Employer's Tax Guide to Fringe Benefits
- Publication 946: How to Depreciate Property
- Publication 463: Travel, Entertainment, Gift and Car Expenses
- Publication 560: Retirement Plans for Small Business (SEP, SIMPLE and Qualified Plans)

Canada Revenue Agency Small Business Tax Forms and Publications

The Canada Revenue Agency also provides small business owners with free publications that explain small business tax issues and can be used as guides for completing small business tax and self-employment tax forms. You can order Canada Revenue Agency small business information, tax forms and publications in three ways:

- In person at Canada Business/Entreprises Canada provincial centers (contact information for each business service center in the Home Business Resources section in the Appendix)
- Online at *cra-arc.gc.ca/formspubs/re-quest-e. html*, or
- Toll-free for mail delivery at (800) 959-2221

Additionally, all businesses in Canada that anticipate annual business revenues to exceed $30,000 are required to register for the Goods and Services Tax/Harmonized Sales Tax (GST/HST) and obtain a federal business number, available through the Canada Revenue Agency website or Canada Business/Entreprises Canada provincial centers. The following are the most popular and important publication guides for small business owners.

Major Guides

- Sole Proprietorship—Publication T4002: Business and Professional Income

- Partnership—Publication T4068: Guide for the T5013 Partnership Information Return
- Corporation—Publication T4012 T2 Corporation—Income Tax Guide
- Contractor—Publication RC4110: Employee or Self-Employed?

Additional Canada Revenue Agency Small Business and Taxation Publications:

- Publication RC4022: General Information for GST/HST Registrants
- Publication RC4027: Doing Business in Canada—GST/HST Information for Non-Residents
- Publication RC4070: Guide for Canadian Small Businesses
- Publication T4001: Employer's Guide—Payroll Deductions and Remittances
- Publication T4130: Employer's Guide—Taxable Benefits
- Publication 14-1: Direct Sellers
- Publication IT518R: Food, Beverages and Entertainment Expenses
- Publication IT521R: Motor Vehicle Expenses Claimed by Self-Employed Individuals

Common Allowable Business Expenses for Homebased Businesses

As previously mentioned, there are tax advantages to operating a business from your home. Deductions for business expenses can reduce your tax bill, especially for the sole proprietor. The basic premise for all deductible home business expenses is that you are using the item or service for business. Therefore, if you are using your phone, car or anything else for business as well as personal usage, you will need to keep track of the amount of time it is used for business purposes and deduct that portion of your overall bill or payments.

The following are some of the most common allowable business deductions.

Communications

The costs of communications used for business are allowable business expenses, including the cost of monthly telephone service, long-distance calls, toll-free telephone lines, cell phones, answering services, pagers and internet connections. However, if you do not have a dedicated business line, then only a portion of the phone bill is an allowable business expense. For ease of record-keeping, as well as professionalism, it is best to have a dedicated telephone line for your home business if you can afford one. Otherwise, keep a phone log (which can be kept in a notepad by the phone), so you can calculate the percentage of your calls for business purposes. Remember: you also pay for most incoming calls on your cell phone. Also, don't forget text messages that are above your monthly plan limit.

Rent or Mortgage

A portion of your rent or mortgage will also be an allowable business expense. Determine what percentage of the area of your home is used for your home office and storage, if you have inventory and you can deduct that percentage of your rent or mortgage payments for the year. For example, if you have a 2,500-square-foot home, operate a service-oriented business and use 250 square feet for your office (no storage), you would deduct 10 percent of your rent or mortgage payments as a business expense.

Utilities

You can also write off against business earnings a portion of your utility bills, including heat, electricity, gas, water and sewer. Use the percentage you are using for your rent or mortgage deduction.

Property Tax and Maintenance Costs

You may be able to claim a deduction for a portion of your property tax and maintenance costs, if applicable.

Technology

The costs of purchasing, renting or leasing computers, printers, personal organizers, cell phones and software and the costs associated with building and operating your business website can all be written off as business tax deductions. If you purchase this equipment, rather than renting or leasing, you depreciate its value against business earnings over time.

Transportation

The transportation costs directly related to operating your business are allowable business expenses, including fuel, mileage, maintenance and repairs, insurance and a portion of lease payments. If you use your vehicle for other purposes, keep records of the mileage used for business and use the allotted mileage amount as determined by the IRS or the Canada Revenue Agency.

Employee Wages and Benefits

All money paid to employees in the form of wages and benefits is an allowable business expense, regardless of whether they are employed full time, part time, temporarily or seasonally.

Professional Services

The fees you pay to lawyers, accountants, or consultants for professional advice and services relating to your business are allowable expenses and deducted from business earnings before calculating taxable income.

Marketing Costs

The money you spend on marketing and promoting your business is an allowable business expense, regardless of the type of marketing. This includes advertising, public relations, seminars, brochures, catalogs, fliers, trade shows, seminars and listings in Yellow Pages and other directories.

Insurance Premiums

Premiums you pay on business-related insurance coverage—property, liability, casualty, workers' compensation, business income and so on—are allowable business expenses. You can also factor in a portion of your homeowner's insurance premiums.

Office Supplies

The costs of supplies that your business consumes (e.g., paper, printer ink, pens, paper clips and garbage bags) are all allowable business expenses.

Interest on Loans

The interest you pay on business loans is an allowable business expense. Tally up the amounts you paid in interest charges on all business loans during the year; the total comes directly off the total business revenues before calculating income.

Training and Educational Tools

The costs of training classes, books, audiotapes, CDs and other educational materials used for business purposes are allowable business expenses.

Additional Allowable Expenses

The deductible business expenses mentioned above are not all. This is one reason why money spent for professional accounting and taxation advice is money wisely invested in your business success. Additional business expenses that can be used as deductions, entirely or partly, include:

- Postage and courier charges
- Business travel and entertainment
- Gifts, donations to charity and sponsorships
- Membership dues for business associations
- Costs of business licenses, permits and registrations
- Business cards, stationery and letterhead

RESOURCES
Associations

Business Development Bank of Canada
BDC Building
5 Place Ville Marie, Suite 400
Montréal, QC H3B 5E7
(877) BDC-BANX (232-2269)
bdc.ca

Canada Revenue Agency
333 Laurier Avenue West
Ottawa, ON K1A 0L9
(888) 576-4444, (800) 959-2221
cra-arc.gc.ca

*CVCA: Canada's Venture Capital and Private
    Equity Association*
MaRS Centre, Heritage Building
101 College Street, Suite 120 J
Toronto, ON M5G 1L7
(416) 487-0519
cvca.ca

Internal Revenue Service (IRS)
U.S. Department of the Treasury
1111 Constitution Avenue, NW
Washington, DC 20224
Business Assistance (800) 829-4933
(202) 622-5164
irs.gov

National Business Incubation Association
20 E. Circle Drive, #37198
Athens, OH 45701-3571
(740) 593-4331
nbia.org

National Venture Capital Association
1655 N. Fort Myer Drive, Suite 850
Arlington, VA 22209
(703) 524-2549
nvca.org

Suggested Reading

Alterowitz, Ralph, and Jon Zonderman. *Financing
    Your New or Growing Business: How to Find
    and Get Capital for Your Venture.* Irvine, CA:
    Entrepreneur Press, 2002.

Daily, Frederick W. *Tax Savvy for Small Business:
    Year-round Tax Strategies to Save You Money.*
    11th edition. Berkeley, CA: Nolo Press, 2007.

Fishman, Stephen. *Working for Yourself: Law and
    Taxes for Independent Contractors, Freelancers,
    and Consultants.* 7th edition. Berkeley, CA:
    Nolo Press, 2008.

Fishman, Stephen. *Home Business Tax Deductions:
    Keep What You Earn.* 4th edition. Berkeley, CA:
    Nolo Press, 2007.

Kamoroff, Bernard B. *Small Time Operator.* 10th
    edition. Willits, CA: Bell Springs Publishing,
    2008.

Pinson, Linda. *Keeping the Books: Basic Record
    Keeping and Accounting for the Successful Small
    Business.* 6th edition. Chicago, IL: Kaplan
    Publishing, 2004.

Stemmy, Thomas J. *Top Tax Savings Ideas: A Small
    Business Tax Survival Kit.* 2nd edition. Irvine,
    CA: Entrepreneur Press, 2004.

Weltman, Barbara. *J.K. Lasser's Small Business
    Taxes 2008: Your Complete Guide to a Better
    Bottom Line.* New York, NY: J. Wiley & Sons,
    2007.

Websites

International Business Brokers Association, Inc.:
    Links to more than 1,800 business brokers in
    North America, Asia and Europe. *ibba.org*

National Venture Capital Association: Association
    membership consists of venture capital firms
    and organizations that manage pools of risk

equity capital to be invested in young, emerging companies. *nvca.org*

Nolo: Online legal self-help information, products, services, resources and links for consumers and business owners. *nolo.com*

M.Y.O.B (Mind Your Own Business) Software: Small business bookkeeping and accounting software. *myob.com*

PayPal: Online payment processing options. *paypal.com*

QuickBooks Software: Small business bookkeeping and accounting software. *quickbooks.intuit.com*

Small Business Loans Online: Online loan applications for financing new business startups and established businesses that are growing. *smallbusinessloans.com*

vFinance Investments: Directory of venture capital firms and angel investors. *vfinance.com*

CHAPTER 4

Legal Issues

I F YOU DON'T LIKE GOVERNMENT RED TAPE (and who does?), you're going to run into some brick walls along the way to starting and operating your new home business. You will encounter red tape at every level of government—municipal, county, state or provincial and federal. You do not want to try to fight the system. It is much easier to conduct your research, find out what is required to start your business, and go out of your way to meet and exceed all the obligations. Go with the flow. Besides, the vast majority of laws and regulations governing businesses have been established to help business owners, not hinder them.

The following are a few of the legalities of starting and operating a home business.

- You will have to choose the legal structure that works best for your business and personal situation.
- You will have to comply with zoning laws, local ordinances and property use restrictions.

- You might have to get building and mechanical permits.
- You will have to select and register your business name.
- You will need to obtain business licenses, permits and certificates, depending on the type of business you operate.
- You will need to protect your intellectual property through the use of copyrights, trademarks and patents.

There are lots of legal issues involved in starting a home business and just as many laws and regulations to satisfy in operating it. If you want to be in business, you have to become resigned to the fact that there will always be forms to complete, licenses to secure and laws with which you must comply. You may as well educate yourself on legal issues pertaining to small business.

Information about selecting and working with experienced small business lawyers can be found in Chapter 8, Building Your

Business Team. You can also contact the American Bar Association through its website, *abanet.org*, or the Canadian Bar Association through its website, *cba.org*, for information on finding a qualified small business lawyer. You can also look in the Yellow Pages, talk with your local Chamber of Commerce or ask other business owners for recommendations. While your brother-in-law may be a great divorce attorney, you need to politely decline his advice and opt for someone with small business skills, particularly working with home-based business owners.

HOME BUSINESS ZONING REGULATIONS

Can you legally operate a business from your current residence? Probably, although probably with some restrictions. Unfortunately there are no standard, across-the-board rules or federal set of rules, on allowing businesses to operate from a residential location. Each and every community in the United States and Canada has its own home business zoning regulations and specific usage guidelines. Most municipalities allow small home businesses to operate from residences, providing the business activities do not negatively affect the neighbors or the residential aspect of the neighborhood. Such rules are generally in place for the purpose of differentiating between commercial and residential areas. They are intended to limit traffic in areas where there are homes, to control garbage collection and parking, and to generally maintain the sanctity of residential neighborhoods.

In terms of zoning, the potential issues for home businesses include:

- Exterior signage
- Parking
- Noise
- Pollution
- Fire and hazardous substances

- Employees working in the home
- Client visits
- Deliveries and shipping
- Water runoff and drainage

Before you decide to start a home business, and certainly before you spend any money on one, you need to check out your local zoning rules, regulations and restrictions. This is a very important first step. You may need to get a variance from the local government to run the business, prior to getting your business license.

With so much at stake, don't try to sidestep zoning requirements. There are ways local officials can find out. You could be caught and fined or even forced to close your business for noncompliance. All it takes is a few noise complaints from neighbors or a call to the zoning department from a business competitor and it won't be long until local government officials are knocking on your door.

In some areas in the United States and Canada, because of the proliferation of new home business startups where "traditional" businesses have a strong voice and influence on local policy making, setting up a home business can be much more difficult. This is mainly because owners of traditional businesses operating from rented or owned commercial locations believe that the laws are inequitable and favor home business owners. Their contention is that home business owners are not hindered by as much red tape in starting and operating their businesses. In these areas, some business groups have successfully lobbied to make it more difficult to operate a business in a residential neighborhood. While this is not common in most neighborhoods, it's possible, depending on the strength of the local business community and the type of business you are operating.

Single-Family Residences

If you own or rent a single-family residence, in all likelihood you will have a much easier time meeting zoning regulations for your home business than if you are living in a multifamily complex. But even some single-family residential neighborhoods, especially affluent ones, have covenants in place restricting home business operations. Most often the concerns have nothing to do with zoning, but are put in place by active homeowners' associations. The typical concerns of such associations are safety, traffic (especially commercial vehicles) and parking, which is at a premium in some neighborhoods.

The zoning laws that can affect your residence focus on:

- Limiting the amount of a home's square footage that can be used for business purposes. It is generally indicated in percentage terms.
- Limiting or prohibiting exterior signage. If permitted, signs are almost always restricted to a certain size, style and placement on the home or around the property.
- Limiting the number of employees or contractors who can be working from a home. In some areas, only the legal owners are allowed to work from their homes. Other areas do not even mention employee restrictions in the zoning ordinances.

In addition to home business zoning regulations, you will also be forced to comply with building regulations and permits if you plan to alter your home. You will need to get permits to expand your home or build a secondary structure on your property. Your plans may or may not be acceptable, depending on your local building and zoning regulations.

In an increasingly green-oriented world, environmental laws may also come into play, depending on the type of business you plan to run. Laws may regulate the materials that can be used, sold or stored, any emissions that may emanate from the property, waste disposal, water runoff and impact on land use.

Vehicles used in the business are almost always restricted, by size, type and number parked on the property or on the street. Restrictions may also extend to deliveries and traffic caused by clients coming to your home. Again, some of these concerns may not come from zoning regulations, but from the local homeowners. Therefore, gauge what the feeling of the neighborhood will be if you plan to start a homebased business.

Multi-family Residences

Multifamily residential developments—such as condominiums, duplexes, town homes, mobile home parks, single-family strata communities and cooperative buildings—are much different from single-family residence properties in terms of a home business. The difference mainly lies in the fact that residents of multifamily properties have to contend not only with local zoning ordinances, but also with common property regulations (legally known as *covenants, conditions and restrictions*, CC&Rs) that govern all aspects of individual unit use within the common development. Restrictive covenants are put into place to protect the interests of the majority of residents, rather than the interests of the individual.

In almost all situations, rules pertaining to establishing and operating a home business are considerably stricter than those found in local zoning ordinances. There are also more safety and security concerns with operating a business within a multifamily residential development. Fire, crime, pollution and noise are all valid concerns for residents of the development. If your development allows home businesses, chances are it greatly restricts the types of businesses permitted and will almost certainly exclude any type of manufacturing or retail sales or any business that would bring clients to your home.

However, there are many business ventures that are perfectly suited to a multifamily residential unit or apartment, including internet ventures, consulting, freelance writing and/or editing, bookkeeping, photography and travel agencies.

Where Do You Find Out About Local Zoning Regulations?

There are two primary questions about zoning if you want to start a business in your home. Are home businesses allowed? If so, what are the restrictions?

The only way to find out for sure is to get a copy of your local zoning rules from city hall, the local public library or your lawyer and start investigating. Even if you discover that home businesses are permitted, you may find that some of the descriptions are vague and require further explanation. The zoning department staff or your lawyer should be able to clarify.

If you discover that you are not allowed to operate a business from your home, you can make a formal request to alter the zoning bylaws or get a variance so that you can proceed. Since many zoning laws were written prior to the advancements in technology, some laws that simply do not allow businesses might be easily waived for a homebased internet business that does not raise any of the zoning concerns about pollution, signage, traffic, etc.

This approach is generally successful, providing you can get the support of your immediate neighbors and are patient. It can take several months or, in some cases, even a year or more to work through all the proper channels and meetings. Do your homework in advance of any public meetings on your request and make sure to cover the important concerns, such as parking, noise and pollution, so that you can assure city councilors and neighbors that your business will be a benefit and not a deterrent.

Additional information about establishing a business at home and setting up your workspace can be found in Chapter 7, Establishing Your Home Workspace.

CHOOSING THE RIGHT BUSINESS NAME

When it comes time to choose and register a name for your business, you have to be forward thinking, consider potential domain name matches, think about the image you want to project, and decide how you will legally protect your business name. You definitely want a name that will describe exactly what your business does or sells. In short, the business name game is an involved process that requires some research and planning.

There are two basic options in terms of naming your new business. First, you can choose to name the business after your legal name, as in Joe Smith Marketing and Consulting. Second, you can choose to register and operate under a fictitious business name, such as Pacific Winds Marketing and Consulting. Even if you choose to incorporate your business as a numbered company (that is, using the corporation number assigned to it under the Canada Business Corporations Act), you will still need a proper or fictitious name in conjunction with the numbered company.

Most home business owners opt to create a fictitious name. Once you have selected your business name, the next step is to register it to make sure that you can legally use the name and that no other business is operating under that name in the jurisdiction in which you register. Business name registration in the United States and Canada is covered later in this section.

Important Tips for Choosing a Good Business Name

More than anything else, your business name will promote your business. So the importance of having the right business name cannot be overstated.

You will definitely want to test-drive a few name variations by creating a short list of possible business names and then running them by family, friends and other businesspeople to see which one they think works best for your business, image, products or services and target customers.

Above all, don't rush the process. Whatever name you choose, you will have to work with it for a long time. The following are some helpful tips.

- Your business name should be descriptive, so that it becomes an effective marketing tool. For instance, for your mobile computer repair business, On Call Mobile Computer Repair is far more descriptive than Zytech Computers, which says nothing about your selling point, mobility.
- Your business name should be short, easy to spell, easy to pronounce and very memorable. ABC Automotive Detailing may not be a very original business name, but it is easy to spell, pronounce and remember, and it instantly tells people what your business does—automotive detailing. When naming your business, think about visual impact and word-of-mouth referral; for both, names that are short, easy to spell and to remember and descriptive are better.
- Your business name should also project the image you want to project. For instance, Budget House Painting projects a low-cost image, while Opulence House Painting projects a more upscale image.
- Be forward thinking and do not limit growth opportunities because of your business name. For instance, choosing the name North Chicago Web Designs could greatly limit the number of customers you attract in other areas of Chicagoland, Illinois, the United States or beyond. Keep your options open with a name that is geographically universal, unless you can benefit more from

identifying your business with a specific geographic region. For example, the name North Chicago On Call Mobile Computer Repair suggests a limited geographic focus that would allow you to get to problem computers more quickly.
- Don't order business cards, signs and stationery until you have registered your business name. You do not want to risk spending money on materials that will be useless if you cannot get the business name you want.
- It's a good idea to prepare a list of three or four alternate names, so when you go to file you're prepared in case your first choice is taken.
- Think in terms of the internet, since you will want a domain name that is as close as possible to your business name. Is it easy to spell? People need to type out your business name accurately and quickly. (More on domain name searches later.)
- Is your business name easy to pronounce? Think of yourself answering the phone. Can you say it clearly? How do you feel about saying that name every time you receive or make a call?

Just as you want to find a name that is not being used in your geographic region, you want to register your name to protect it from being used by another business. Another reason for registering your business name is that, in some situations, you have to show proof of business name registration in order to establish bank accounts and credit card merchant accounts.

It is important to remember that you may be prohibited from using a specific business name because someone else is already using the name. Therefore, it is a good idea to select at least three names, so you have backup choices in case your first choice is already registered. You don't want to spend a small fortune on marketing the business and producing signs and stationery, only to discover later that another business has the legal right to the name and you must stop using it or face legal action.

Registering a Business Name in the United States

Where do you go to register your business name? It differs from state to state, so check with your local SBA office, Chamber of Commerce or the county clerk's office. Generally, business name registrations are handled by the county clerk's office, but not always. Be sure to ask about the procedure for registering a business name, as this varies.

To register a name at the state level, you first conduct a business name search to make sure that no other business is using the name. A name search is usually included in the cost of the name registration. Many states also require that the business name registration be published in the local newspaper to inform consumers and other business owners of the intent to do business. This cost may or may not be included in the registration fee, so be sure to ask.

The final issue to consider when registering your business name, to protect it locally, is whether your business name should also be trademarked, to protect it throughout the United States. If you plan on expanding your business beyond your local area into other states and countries, then it is a good idea to trademark your business name. By protecting your business name with a federal trademark, you are preventing any other business in the nation from using your exact business name. However, you should know that getting a federal trademark is a very costly process and best handled by an experienced trademark lawyer.

Registering a Business Name in Canada

Registering a business name in Canada is a very straightforward process; it can be done online, by mail or in person at any Canada Business/

Entreprises Canada provincial service center. The telephone number and website address for each province are shown below. Alternately, you can also register your business and business name through your local Chamber of Commerce. Consult your telephone book or go to the Canadian Chamber of Commerce website, *chamber.ca,* to find the office closest to you.

There is no fee for a preliminary search. For a comprehensive search, the fee is $100. Then there is a $350 fee for preparing and filing an application for registration of your trademark. You pay a final fee, $150, upon registration of your trademark, approximately eight months after you file your application. Trademarks are registered for 15 years, after which they can be renewed.

Canada Business/Entreprises Canada Provincial Service Centers

Alberta
(800) 272-9675
canadabusiness.ca/alberta

British Columbia
(604) 775-5525
canadabusiness.ca/bc

Manitoba
(800) 665-2019, (204) 984-2272
canadabusiness.ca/manitoba

New Brunswick
(506) 444-6140, (800) 668-1010
cbsc.org/nb

Newfoundland and Labrador
(709) 772-6022
cbsc.org/nf

Northwest Territories
(867) 873-7958
cbsc.org/nwt

Nova Scotia
(902) 426-8604, (800) 668-1010
cbsc.org/ns

Nunavut
(877) 499-5199
canadabusiness.ca/nunavut

Ontario
(800) 567-2345
canadabusiness.ca/ontario

Prince Edward Island
(902) 368-0771
canadabusiness.ca/pe

Quebec
(514) 496-4636, (800) 322-4636
infoentrepreneurs.org

Saskatchewan
(306) 956-2323, (800) 667-4374
canadabusiness.ca/sask

Yukon
(800) 661-0543, (867) 633-6257
canadabusiness.ca/yukon

LEGAL STRUCTURE OPTIONS FOR THE HOME BUSINESS OWNER

After you have decided to start a home business, you have to choose the type of legal structure within which the business will operate. The four most popular forms of legal structure are sole proprietorship, partnership, corporation and limited liability company. You will choose the legal structure based on one or more of the following factors:

- Your budget and financing requirements
- The type of business
- Personal liability concerns
- The number of owners
- Your goals and objectives for your business
- Tax concerns, as mentioned (in part) earlier

The Sole Proprietorship

The sole proprietorship is by far the most common type of home business legal structure for many reasons, but mainly because it is the simplest and least expensive to get started and maintain. In a nutshell, in a sole proprietorship your business is an extension of your personal life. You include income from your business on your personal income tax return, which makes tax payments simple. However, you are personally liable for all accrued business debts and actions, as well as control of all revenues and profits.

It is easy and straightforward to start a sole proprietorship, but it is still important to keep your business finances separate from your personal household and family finances as much as possible, mainly for record keeping and income tax reasons. For instance, interest payments on business loans and credit cards used for business purchases are 100-percent tax deductible, while interest payments on personal loans and credit cards used for personal purchases are not tax deductible. Therefore, it is advised for the sole proprietor to establish separate bank accounts, one for the business and one for personal use, and to separate other financial matters as much as possible.

Sole Proprietorship Advantages

- The process of establishing a sole proprietorship is simple, inexpensive and quick. You can decide to start a business today and be open for business tomorrow. A sole proprietorship can be started, altered, bought, sold or closed at any time very quickly and very inexpensively.
- You have complete control over your business and any revenues and profits that the business generates.
- Outside of routine business registrations, permits and licenses, there are few legal forms required, limited paperwork and not many government regulations to worry about.

Sole Proprietorship Disadvantages

- The biggest disadvantage of a sole proprietorship is unquestionably the issue of personal liability. You are 100-percent liable for any business activities, including debts incurred and any legal actions taken against the business. This includes lawsuits resulting from equipment or vehicles used for business purposes. In an age of litigation mania, your personal assets are at risk if anything goes wrong and you are sued.

- It can be more difficult to secure business startup and growth funds from banks, government sources and private investors because there is no formal organization: the legal entity is a person.
- Often businesses that are not incorporated or limited liability companies are not viewed as serious business contenders, a perception that can play against you when you are bidding for work against businesses that are incorporated.

Sole proprietorships work best for businesses where there is limited potential for lawsuits and where being an independent does not pit you against major companies. Freelance writing and editing businesses, photography, consulting, crafts, tutoring services and similar businesses can operate in this manner successfully. As a means of limiting liability concerns, when establishing relationships with clients, you can always have contracts drawn up (with a legal advisor) and lay out what you are and are not responsible for.

The Partnership

A partnership is another popular type of low-cost legal business structure. It allows two or more people to start and own a business. Each partner can specialize in her area of expertise within the business. There is no need for any documentation; intent and action are enough to form a partnership. However, all—and I repeat *all*—partnerships should be based on a written partnership agreement, not simply a verbal agreement, even if your partner is a close friend or family member, including your spouse. The partnership agreement should address all of the usual hot buttons, such as:

- The amount of money each partner is to invest initially, as well as ongoing capital infusions as needed
- Clearly defined responsibilities and duties for each partner
- An exit strategy for each partner, should the need arise

Many partnership agreements are informal, but the lack of a formal agreement can spell big trouble should disagreements arise or should one of the partners die or want out of the business.

As in a sole proprietorship, business profits, which are split between or among partners proportionate to their partnership agreement, are treated as taxable personal income.

Partnership Advantages

- Two heads are better than one. Two people with one goal can combine their skills, abilities, strengths and strategies and create a more successful business than either one could alone.
- The borrowing capacity of two or more people is generally greater than that of each individual separately.
- The cost of establishing a partnership is minimal, financial risks are shared equally, and there are very few regulations governing who or how many people can legally form a partnership. Also, bookkeeping and record keeping requirements are basic, as with a sole proprietorship.
- The partnership legal structure affords great opportunities for family members to work together building a business, with each

equally responsible for the success or failure of the business.

- With two or more people investing in the business, it's easier to finance it.
- A partnership may be equal or not. For example, you may have a 75-percent stake in the partnership and your partner may contribute 25 percent. Your partner may be a silent partner, meaning that he or she puts up money, but you handle the day-to-day operations.

Partnership Disadvantages

- Each partner is legally responsible, i.e., personally liable, for the other partner's or partners' actions in the business, and even outside of the business in terms of some financial issues. Why? Because a partnership provides no liability protection for the owners of the business, regardless of the percentage of ownership. Each partner is equally responsible personally for the business's debts, liabilities and actions. What this means is that if you are in a business partnership and the business fails, even if entirely because of your partner or partners, creditors can take legal action to seize assets, such as your home, to recoup their loans or debts, even if your home is co-owned by your spouse.
- Partners do not always agree on everything, and disagreements can cripple the decision-making process, resulting in lower productivity, less profitability and even closure of the business. Partnerships can lead to tension and great friction unless the obligations and responsibilities of the parties are spelled out clearly in writing in advance. This does not mean that partnerships are equal.
- A general partnership ends on the death or withdrawal of one of the partners. Unless the partners have planned for succession and continuity and included those arrangements in the written partnership agreement, the partnership and business are legally dissolved.

Partnerships can work for almost any type of business, but you must be careful with the potential for liability. It is also important that you and your partner or partners maintain excellent communication, so that neither or none of you is suddenly surprised by the consequences of the actions of the other or another.

The Corporation

The third type of business structure, and the most complicated for the home business owner, is the corporation. In forming a corporation, the owners of a business create a separate and distinct legal entity. The shareholders of the corporation can include the owners, family members, business partners and private investors. Because the company becomes a separate legal entity, it can assume debt, it can sue, it can be sued, and it must pay taxes on its profits. Also, because the corporation is a legal entity, unlike a general partnership or a sole proprietorship, the company's finances and financial records are completely separate from the finances of the owners (shareholders). Because the corporation is a legal entity, the owners (shareholders) must elect and authorize officers to conduct business and make all decisions for the company—day-to-day operations, borrowing money, making purchases and so forth.

Corporation Advantages

- Without question, the biggest advantage of incorporating your home business is that you can greatly reduce your own personal liability. Because the corporation is a separate legal entity, your personal assets are protected. Therefore, if you are sued, the lawsuit will most likely name the corporation and not you personally. Likewise, if the corporation borrows a substantial amount of money and cannot repay the debt, the corporation will be responsible for the debt and not you personally, unless you have personally guaranteed the loan.

It is worth noting, however, that this legal protection from personal liability for corporate debts and legal actions can be breached in a number of ways. First, lenders generally require home business owners, especially of businesses that are new and lack a track record of profitability, to personally guarantee to repay loans granted to the corporation. Second, if all corporate formalities and record keeping responsibilities are not followed carefully, the directors of the corporation can be held legally, financially and personally responsible for the actions of the corporation.

- It is generally much easier to arrange financing, procure loans and raise money in general for business expansion.
- Because a corporation is a separate legal entity, it is very easy to sell the business or a portion of it, to gift shares, and to continue business even if one or more shareholders die.
- Customers, business partners and bankers generally see a corporation as a more stable entity than a sole proprietorship.
- The company can sell ownership (shares) as a means of raising funds.

Corporation Disadvantages

- The major disadvantage associated with a corporation is double taxation. The corporation must pay taxes on its profits and then the shareholders must pay taxes on those profits as personal income when distributed as dividends. Still, double taxation can be significantly reduced if the shareholders are also employees in the corporation, drawing salaries. These wages provide the shareholder employees with personal income and decrease the corporation's taxable profits.

Unfortunately, it does not work the same way if the corporation loses money. If the corporation suffers a loss, the shareholders cannot each take his or her share of that loss as a personal income tax deduction.

- Of the business structures discussed in this chapter, corporations are the most expensive to form and maintain. Starting and running a corporation requires filing a lot of paperwork, taking minutes of meetings, and following government rules and regulations, at both the state and federal levels.
- As with any group, conflicts or disagreements among the stockholders in a small corporation, such as a home business, can disrupt the decision-making process and result in lower productivity, decreased profitability and even the demise of the business.
- The processes for making decisions and acting on new ideas is slower with more people involved.

Online Corporation Filing Services in the United States

- CorpAmerica, *corpamerica.com*
- CorpoMax, *corpomax.com*
- BizFilings, *bizfilings.com*
- The Company Corporation, *corporate.com*
- Active Filings, *activefilings.com*
- MyCorporation, *mycorporation.com*

Online Corporation Filing Services in Canada

- Ontario Business Central, *ontariobusinesscentral.ca*
- CanadianCorp.com, *canadiancorp.com*
- CorporationCentre.ca, *corporationcen-tre.ca*
- New Business Now.com, *newbusinessnow.com*

Corporations are best advised for companies where significant growth is anticipated and where potential for liability is greater. If you are manufacturing, you will certainly want to be protected, since numerous lawsuits result from products claimed to be defective. Typically larger businesses, with more complexities and greater sums of money involved ("deep pockets"), incorporate.

The Limited Liability Company

A limited liability company, a relatively new legal business structure, combines many of the characteristics of a corporation with those of a partnership. It is a legal entity that is separate and distinct from the owners who form it. It provides protection from personal liability like a corporation, but the tax advantages of a partnership. Limited liability companies can be formed by one or more people, called LLC *members.*

The advantages of a limited liability company over a corporation or partnership include:

■ Protection from personal liability that partnerships do not provide

■ Less expensive to form and maintain than a corporation

■ Fewer rules and regulations and less paperwork than a corporation

■ Simpler taxation rules than a corporation

An LLC allows for pass-through taxation, as the income is not taxed at the entity level, although a tax return must be filed for the LLC. Any income or loss is passed through to the members, who are each responsible for reporting their share of the income or loss on their personal tax returns and paying any necessary tax.

Because of the advantages that limited liability companies offer over partnerships and corporations, the limited liability company has become the fastest-growing business structure in the United States and one that is embraced by home business owners who are seeking an affordable way to limit their personal liability and protect their assets, while not obligating the company to follow the rules that a corporation must follow.

Disadvantages of Limited Liability Company

■ Unlike a corporation, a limited liability company is dissolved when a member dies or files for bankruptcy.

■ Business owners with plans to take their company public or issue employee shares cannot do so through an LLC.

Online Limited Liability Company Filing Services

■ MyCorporation, *mycorporation.com*

■ LLC.com, *llc.com*

■ USA Corporate Services, *usa-corporate.com*

■ legal-forms-kit.com, *legal-forms-kit.com/forming-LLC.html*

BUSINESS LICENSES, PERMITS AND PROFESSIONAL CERTIFICATIONS

Even though you will be operating from your home, there are certain business licenses, permits and certificates that you will need to operate your business legally. The types of licenses, permits and certificates required will vary depending on the kind of business and the area where you establish the business. The best way to find out what is needed is to contact your local chapter of the Chamber of Commerce or city hall. You can visit the United States Chamber of Commerce website, *chamber.com,* or the Canadian Chamber of Commerce website, *chamber.ca,* to find the nearest chapter. Most local Chambers of Commerce have their own websites, which you can find by searching under the name of your city or town.

If you are thinking about skipping the required licenses, permits and certificates, you should reconsider. In some cases, you will be required to show these documents to open a bank account, apply for loans and purchase goods for resale. Also, businesses operating without licenses can be subject to fines and, in extreme cases, to closure.

Business License

Almost all municipalities in the United States and Canada require home business owners to obtain a business license. The cost of your business license can vary depending on three factors—your geographic location, your expected sales and the type of business. Once again, city hall or your local Chamber of Commerce will be able to help you obtain a business license. Typically, such a license is not very costly.

Building Permits

If you plan on substantially renovating or altering your home to accommodate your new business or altering your home's mechanical system, plumbing or wiring, you will probably need to obtain a building permit and possibly electrical and plumbing permits prior to carrying out the work.

Vendor Permits

Most states and provinces also require home business owners to obtain vendor permits if they are reselling goods and, on occasion, if they are providing services, although that is not as common. Again, find out what you will need from your local SBA office or Canada Business/Entreprises Canada provincial service center or from your Chamber of Commerce.

Professional Certification

In addition to business licenses and permits, professionals such as dentists, veterinarians, electricians and plumbers will also be required to obtain relevant certification in order to provide professional services. Information on professional and trade certificates is available through the associations that represent those professions and trades and are generally issued at the state or provincial level.

Home Occupation Permit

In addition to a business license, some municipalities also now require home business operators to obtain a home occupation permit, which legally enables a business to be run from the residence specified in the permit. Your local zoning bylaws will indicate if you will require a home occupation permit and the requirements that must be satisfied to obtain one. Contact city hall, the county clerk's office or the city planning department to obtain a copy of your current zoning and land use bylaws.

Sales Tax Permits

Depending on the type of business you operate and the location of your business, you might also need to obtain a sales tax permit. In Canada, you will be required to obtain a goods and services tax/harmonized sales tax (GST/HST) number if your expected sales will exceed $30,000 per annum. Business taxation information is available in the United States through the Internal Revenue Service, *irs.gov*, and in Canada through the Canada Revenue Agency, *cra-arc.gc.ca*.

Additional Permits and Licenses

By now you're probably thinking the world has gone permit-and-regulation crazy—and you'd be right on the money. There may be other licenses, permits and certificates you must obtain and other laws and regulations with which you must comply prior to starting and operating your home business. The documents might include fire safety inspection permits, hazardous materials handling permits, import/export certificates and police clearance certificates. The rules might include environmental laws and laws pertaining to food and drug safety (U.S. Food and Drug Administration or Health Canada). Keep in mind that the obligation is on the home business owner to find out the laws and regulations that must be followed and the relevant permits and registrations that will be required.

PROTECTING YOUR INTELLECTUAL PROPERTY

Intellectual properties can consist of a training

manual that you have developed for your sales staff, a slogan that you use to help brand your business or a product or process that you have invented. An intellectual property is unique to your business and a very valuable asset that is well worth legally protecting.

Depending on the type of intellectual property you want to protect, you can use legally registered and documented copyrights, trademarks or patents. A copyright, automatic each time a new piece of work is created, protects your written words, photographs, songs and other original works. A trademark is used to protect your brand and distinguish your products or services from competitors' products or services. A patent is used by inventors to protect their inventions and prevent others from copying or benefiting from those inventions without permission.

Copyright Protection

The first, least expensive and simplest form of intellectual property protection is the copyright. A copyright is a legal right given to creators of original works such as books, poems, lyrics, photographs and paintings. The creators have exclusive right to publish, sell or reproduce their works or to determine through agreement who gets the right to publish, sell or reproduce their works. In the United States and Canada, when you create an original work, it is automatically protected by copyright, unless the work was created as an employee or as a work for hire, in which case the employer owns the copyright. Copyrights can be used to protect the following types of original works:

- Books, journals and maps
- Song lyrics and musical scores
- Sculptures, paintings and photographs
- Visual films and audio recordings
- Computer programs, databases and software code

As a home business owner, copyrights will protect you when you create a brochure or advertising copy, when you write a jingle to promote your business or a book to sell. Also, if you have business, marketing or promotional materials created for your business by others, you will want to make sure that it is clearly spelled out in your agreement to commission such work that you own the copyright to the work. If you want to use work created by others, you need to make sure you have the right to do so. For example, if you see a photograph that would look wonderful on your travel brochure, you need to get permission from the photographer to use it. It is a misconception that anything on the internet is fair game; this is not true. Seek out permissions to use any and all works copyrighted by others and make sure to let anyone using your material without your permission know that he or she is infringing on copyrighted work.

Copyrights protect only works that can be presented in a fixed format, not ideas you may have or facts that you have researched and recorded for your business. In the United States, the copyright for works created after 1977 lasts for the life of the author plus 70 years; in Canada the copyright lasts for the life of the author plus 50 years. Copyrighted materials are generally accompanied by the symbol ©.

Use the following contact information to register a formal copyright.

United States

U.S. Copyright Office
Library of Congress
101 Independence Avenue SE
Washington, DC 20559-6000
(202) 707-3000
copyright.gov

Canada

Canadian Intellectual Property Office
Place du Portage 1
50 Victoria Street, Room C-114

Gatineau, QC K1A 0C9
(866) 997-1936, (819) 997-1936
cipo.gc.ca

Trademark Protection

A trademark can be used to protect a word, name, symbol, sound or any combination of these that identifies your product or service and distinguishes it from your competitors' products or services. For instance, McDonald's trademarked golden arches are very distinguishable from Burger King's trademarked burger with a crown. Trademarked materials are generally accompanied by a "TM" or "®" symbol.

Trademarks can be registered with either the state or the federal government. A federal trademark is more expensive, but it provides protection in all states and U.S. territories. A state trademark provides protection only within the state in which the trademark was registered and granted. If you plan to do business outside your state or at some time to expand your business beyond your state, the extra cost to register a federal trademark is definitely worth it.

You have two options for searching and registering a trademark. The first option is to do the job yourself; be aware that this is a time-consuming process that involves lots of paperwork and forms. The second option is to hire a trademark agent or lawyer to conduct the trademark search and complete the registration process. This process is very expensive, costing possibly more than $5,000 for a federal trademark.

Use the following contact information to start the trademark search and registration process.

United States
U.S. Patent and Trademark Office
Trademark Assistance Center
James Madison Building, East Wing
600 Dulany Street

Alexandria, VA 22314
Commissioner for Trademarks
P.O. Box 1451
Alexandria, VA 22313-1451
(800) 786-9199, (571) 272-9250
uspto.gov

Canada
Canadian Intellectual Property Office
Place du Portage 1
50 Victoria Street, Room C-114
Gatineau, QC K1A 0C9
(819) 997-1936, (866) 997-1936
cipo.gc.ca

Patent Protection

A patent is a document protecting the rights of the inventor and offers the inventor exclusive rights to his or her creations. In the United States, patents are granted and issued by the U.S. Patent and Trademark Office; in Canada patents are granted and issued by the Canadian Intellectual Property Office. In both the United States and Canada, the life of the patent is 20 years from the filing date. That gives the inventor the right to prevent others from making, using, selling, offering for sale or importing the invention into the country that has issued the patent. Patents are effective only within the country that has issued the patent and in its territories. Patents can be filed individually in most countries, regardless of citizenship. The term "Patent Pending" indicates that the inventor has applied for a patent and it has not yet been granted.

Applying for a patent is both time-consuming and costly and best left to a patent agent or lawyer. Long before you decide to patent your product invention or process, you should conduct a market feasibility study to ensure not only that there will be a demand for your invention, but also that it will be worth the extremely high costs associated with obtaining a patent. The U.S. and Canadian patent offices provide lists of registered patent agents. If you're very brave, you can choose to do it yourself.

United States

U.S. Patent and Trademark Office
Inventors Assistance Center
James Madison Building, East Wing
600 Dulany Street
Alexandria, VA 22314
Commissioner for Patents
P.O. Box 1450
Alexandria, VA 22313-1450
(800) 786-9199, (571) 272-1000
uspto.gov

Canada

Canadian Intellectual Property Office
Place du Portage 1
50 Victoria Street, Room C-229
Gatineau, QC K1A 0C9
(819) 997-1936
cipo.gc.ca

RESOURCES

Associations

American Bar Association
321 N. Clark Street
Chicago, IL 60610
(800) 285-2221, (312) 988-5000
740 15th Street NW
Washington, DC 20005-1019
(202) 662-1000
abanet.org

American Intellectual Property Law Association
241 18th Street South, Suite 700
Arlington, VA 22202
(703) 415-0780
aipla.org

Canadian Bar Association
500-865 Carling Avenue
Ottawa, ON K1S 5S8
(800) 267-8860, (613) 237-2925, (613) 237-1988
cba.org

International Bar Association
1 Stephen Street, 10th Fl.
London, UK W1T 1AT
+44 (0)20-7691 6868
ibanet.org

U.S. Small Business Administration
409 Third Street SW
Washington, DC 20416
(800) 827-5722
sba.gov/indexbusplans.html

Suggested Reading

Fishman, Stephen. *Working for Yourself: Law and Taxes for Independent Contractors, Freelancers and Consultants.* 5th edition. Berkeley, CA: Nolo Press, 2004.

Hupalo, Peter I. *How to Start and Run Your Own Corporation: S-Corporations for Small Business Owners.* West Saint Paul, MN: HCM Publishing, 2003.

Mancuso, Anthony. *Form Your Own Limited Liability Company.* 5th edition. Berkeley, CA: Nolo Press, 2007.

Norman, Jan. *What No One Ever Tells You About Starting Your Own Business: Real-Life Start-Up Advice from 101 Successful Entrepreneurs.* 2nd edition. New York: Kaplan Business/Dearborn Trade Publishing, 2004.

Piper, Mike. *Surprisingly Simple: Independent Contractor, Sole Proprietor and LLC Taxes Explained in 100 Pages or Less.* Chicago: Piper Tax Group, 2007.

Spadaccini, Michael. *Entrepreneur Magazine's Ultimate Book on Forming Corporations, LLCs, Sole Proprietorships and Partnerships.* Irvine, CA: Entrepreneur Press, 2004.

Steingold, Fred S. *Legal Guide for Starting and Running a Small Business.* 9th edition. Berkeley, CA: Nolo Press, 2006.

Websites

All Business.com: Articles and advice on all areas of forming and running a small business. **allbusiness.com**

Canada Legal: Thousands of Canadian laws organized by categories, including small business. **canadalegal.com**

Entrepreneur Online: Resource center for small businesses, providing information, advice, products and services. **entrepreneur.com**

International Licensing Industry Merchandisers' Association: Representing 1,000 member companies and individuals engaged in the market-ing of licensed properties, both as agents and as property owners: manufacturers, consultants, publications, lawyers, accountants and retailers in the licensing business. **licensing.org**

Nolo: Online legal self-help information, products, services, resources and links for consumers and business owners. **nolo.com**

Ontario Business Central: Canadian business registration and incorporation services. **ontariobusinesscentral.ca**

Training Registry: National online directory listing professional business, management and employee training consultants. **trainingregistry.com**

USA Corporation Services: Online incorporation products and services. **usa-corporate.com**

National Business Institute: Customized legal and business seminars offered for all types of businesses. **nbi-sems.com**

CHAPTER 5

Home Business Insurance

WHAT TYPE OF INSURANCE DO YOU need to protect your home, assets, business, family and clients? The answer will depend greatly on the type of business you operate, the products you sell and the services you provide. But regardless of what you do and sell, one thing is for sure—if you operate a business from your home, you need the protection and peace of mind that home business insurance provides.

Many home business owners wrongly assume the insurance they already have in place to protect their home and its contents will also cover their business activities. This could not be further from the truth. In fact, insurance companies can reject property damage or liability claims if a business is operating from the home, but not included or fully disclosed in the insurance policy. The reasoning is that the insurance company and its agents cannot assume the risk of insuring what they do not know about

nor should they be required to cover claims arising from that business. For instance, your current homeowner's insurance policy probably provides coverage that protects you in the event a relative takes a nasty tumble on your icy driveway. But don't expect the same insurance coverage will be extended to someone who slips while visiting your home on business. What if your home burns to the ground because of faulty equipment used in your business? Once again, do not expect your insurance policy to cover the damage unless you have specifically informed the insurance company you are operating a business from home and this business use is reflected in your policy, coverage and premiums.

The vast majority of home businesses are registered as sole proprietorships. If there is a claim made against your business that is successfully litigated by the plaintiff, you could be held personally liable. In all likelihood, the plaintiff would attempt to go after your assets or possibly those of your immediate family. So you can see the importance of being fully insured when operating a business from home. If you rent the home or apartment from which your business operates, you should not only obtain separate home business insurance, but also disclose fully any and all business activities to your landlord's insurance company, to ensure your business interests are protected.

Don't worry if you feel frustrated by a lack of knowledge about home business insurance and insurance in general and don't be intimidated by the thought of having to figure out the ins and outs of insurance. This chapter will demystify home business and other insurance coverage by discussing the most common types of business insurance and the reasons for obtaining coverage, and citing resources to help you find additional information or suitable coverage for your specific needs.

WORKING WITH INSURANCE AGENTS AND BROKERS

Tracking down the right insurance can be time-intensive and frustrating because of the number of insurance companies, coverage types and programs available to home business owners, both in the United States and in Canada. For that reason, don't chance going it alone and getting the wrong insurance, paying too much or spending too much time on it. Instead, enlist the services of a qualified and licensed insurance agent or broker to do the research and legwork for you. The agent will be able not only to find the best coverage for you and at the lowest cost, but also to translate insurance jargon into plain English for you. Keep in mind, though, that you should select an agent knowledgeable about insurance needs specific to the home business owner, because they differ substantially from the needs of storefront retailers, manufacturers, distributors, franchisees, general

contractors and other businesses.

To find a suitable insurance agent, you can check with business associations such as your local Chamber of Commerce or call other home business owners in your area to inquire about the type of insurance coverage they carry and their insurance agent. You might also want to check with specific industry associations; they often offer members insurance programs and packages at lower costs due to volume. You can also go online to find a qualified insurance agent or broker. In the United States, you can contact the Independent Insurance Agents and Brokers of America at *iiaba.net*. This nonprofit association offers a free online agent search service on its website. In Canada, you can contact the Insurance Brokers Association of Canada at *ibac.ca*. This nonprofit association offers visitors access to a free online directory that geographically lists more than 30,000 licensed and certified insurance agents and brokers across all of Canada.

HEALTH INSURANCE

Home business owners have lots to do. The last thing you want to think about is your health. Unfortunately, it must be one of the first things you consider when starting a home business. As health care costs keep rising, if you have no health insurance, paying for an unplanned trip to the hospital can easily put your business future in jeopardy. There are substantial differences in health care services and insurance for home business owners between the United States and Canada. The insurance concerns for each is highlighted below.

Health Insurance in the United States

Home business owners have access to two types of health insurance—fee-based health services plans or managed health care plans. With a fee-based plan, you choose the medical professional and he or she submits the bill directly to the health insurer for payment or you pay for the services and file a claim with the health insurer for reimbursement. With a managed care plan, you are treated by a medical practitioner who belongs to the health maintenance organization (HMO) that underwrites the health insurance plan.

Regardless of the health insurance plan you choose, the premiums can be staggering. What can you do?

If you are currently employed or have been recently employed and covered by a health insurance plan provided by your employer, you should know about COBRA (Consolidated Omnibus Budget Reconciliation Act). Under COBRA, employers with 20 or more employees must let their employees and their dependents keep their group health coverage for a minimum of 18 months, and in some situations up to 36 months, after they leave their employment. Sometimes employees who worked for employers with less than 20 employees also qualify. The act states that you have the right to pay the current cost of coverage, which is usually much lower than it would be for individual health insurance.

If you are married and your spouse is covered at work, you could join your spouse's health insurance plan. This, too, can save you significant costs.

If your health is considered very good, you might consider obtaining catastrophic health insurance coverage. Under this type of plan, you pay for all visits to your doctor for minor treatments, but if something happens to you that requires medical treatment with major expenses, your health insurance would kick in and cover those expenses.

You can dramatically reduce your health insurance premiums by increasing your deductible. The higher your deductible, the lower your premiums. Of course, the risk with a higher deductible is if you make unanticipated multiple visits to medical practitioners over a short period of time.

Whatever health insurance coverage you select, the fact remains that your good health is your single largest asset and you must protect it. Georgetown University Health Policy Institute publishes electronic and print consumer guides for getting and keeping health insurance for all 50 states and the District of Columbia. The guides are available free online at *healthinsuranceinfo.net*. There are commonsense measures for protecting your health, such as eating right, getting periodic medical checkups, exercising and keeping informed on health concerns. You can also set up your home office in a manner that is beneficial to your health and safety, starting with an ergonomically designed computer chair and proper lighting. If you are manufacturing, use appropriate safety equipment.

Health Insurance in Canada

The cornerstone of the health care system in Canada is a legislated health act guaranteeing universal access, something the United States badly needs. In Canada, all citizens have equal access to necessary medical services. The health care system is publicly funded through federal and provincial taxes and provincial medical services premiums and is administered both federally and by provincial government agencies.

If you travel outside of your home province within Canada, there are limits on the medical services and benefits you can receive. If you travel to the United States or other countries, you will need to obtain third-party health insurance to provide medical coverage in the event of accident, disease or illness. Blue Cross and certain groups, such as the Canadian Automobile Association, provide third-party health insurance for Canadians who travel outside Canada. More information about Canadian health care can be found on the website operated by Health Canada, *hc-sc.gc.ca*, which provides health care information, resources and links of interest.

WORKERS' COMPENSATION INSURANCE

Workers' compensation insurance serves two primary functions. First, it protects employees injured on the job by providing short-term and, in some cases, long-term financial benefits, as well as by covering medical and rehabilitation costs directly resulting from an on-the-job injury. Second, it protects employers from claims by employees who are injured while on the job.

In the United States and Canada, workers' compensation insurance is mandatory for all employees, whether they are full time, part time or seasonal. If you have no employees and operate your business as a sole proprietorship or a partnership with one or more owners, workers' compensation insurance is not mandatory. If your business is incorporated, officers and employees must be covered by workers' compensation insurance.

Workers' compensation rates are based on industry classification; generally, the more dangerous the work, the higher the workers' compensation premiums you pay on each employee's taxable earnings. In addition, the more claims for workers' compensation your business files, the higher your rates will go. Workers' compensation classifications, forms, and guidelines can be especially confusing for first-time entrepreneurs to figure out.

Fortunately, information about workers' compensation coverage for businesses in the United States can be found on the U.S. Department of Labor's Office of Workers' Compensation Programs website, *dol.gov/dol/topic/workcomp*. In Canada, the Association of Workers' Compensation Boards of Canada, *awcbc.org*, provides links to all provincial and territorial workers' compensation boards or commissions.

DISABILITY INSURANCE

If you were sick or hurt and could not work, would you be able to pay your business expenses, pay someone else to keep the business going, and pay yourself an income? Given that most home business owners are sole operators of their businesses, chances are you would not. Disability insurance makes payments to you if a physical illness, mental illness or bodily injury prevents you from working.

More people working are at an age when they are more likely to become disabled than to die. Therefore, like life insurance, disability insurance is certainly something every home business owner should consider carrying. Disability insurance will provide an income for you in the event you are unable to work or conduct business because of an injury. There are basically two types of disability policies—short-term and long-term.

With a *short-term* disability policy, there's generally a waiting period of 30 days after the person insured becomes disabled before he or she can collect benefits, and a maximum benefits period of 24 months, after which full or partial benefits expire.

With a *long-term* disability policy, the waiting period ranges from 30 to 180 days after the person insured becomes disabled before he or she can collect benefits, and a maximum benefits period that can range from 24 months to life. Of course, the longer the potential to collect benefits in the event of a disability, the higher the premiums.

In addition to deciding on the waiting period and benefits period that best suit your anticipated needs, you should consider the following important points when purchasing disability insurance.

- Be sure to have a cost-of-living clause built into your disability policy, so your disability benefits increase proportionally with the consumer price index. You will pay a higher premium for this clause, but you'll be protecting any benefits against inflation.

- Consider getting professional overhead expenses coverage added to your disability policy. This coverage would reimburse you for employee salaries, property tax, equipment and tool depreciation and other overhead expenses.
- Tell your insurance agent you want your disability coverage to include partial disabilities, so you can collect partial benefits while working part time in your business if you cannot return to full time activity.
- Build in a clause that gives you the right to increase your disability insurance benefits as your business and income grow. This is known as an *additional purchase option* and can be extended to include key employee disability insurance, as well.

Additional information regarding disability insurance can be found on the About Disability Insurance website, *about-disability-insurance.com*. Free online quotes for disability insurance for the United States can be found at *disability-insurance-quotes-online.com*.

LIFE INSURANCE

Life insurance pays out a benefit claim if the insured policyholder dies. Whether you are self-employed or work for someone else, the basic function of life insurance remains the same: provide financial protection and stability to the beneficiaries named in the life insurance policy in the event that you die.

As with most other forms of insurance, you have options. With life insurance, these options come in two basic packages: term and whole (aka permanent). A term life insurance policy pays a fixed death benefit amount; a whole life insurance policy pays a death benefit amount and often has a savings element or cash value. Of course, there are

further choices for both basic types—the amount of the death benefit, the length of the policy, and the policy or savings benefit feature.

So what type of life insurance is best for you? You have probably received advice about each type of life insurance and why one is better than the other. The bottom line is that the best life insurance is the one that best suits your needs, your family needs, your business needs and your financial situation.

Term Life Insurance

Term insurance is the most basic form of life insurance. It provides financial protection for a specified time, such as 10 or 15 years. Term life insurance is relatively inexpensive and readily available, providing your current health is good. On the downside, when the term life policy expires, there is no cash or savings value built up in the account. The premiums you paid over the term of the policy were used to cover the costs of insuring the death benefit amount of the policy and nothing else. If your financial resources are limited at present, you should purchase term life insurance to protect your family—it's much better than no insurance at all. Additional benefits associated with term life insurance include:

- Simplicity—if the insured person dies, the policy pays out the stated death benefit to the beneficiary or beneficiaries.
- Term life insurance is widely available and straightforward, so it's easy to get comparative quotes, especially if you shop for insurance online.
- Term life insurance is inexpensive. You can carry it for the times in your life when you need it most, such as while you have children living at home and while you have a mortgage on your home.

Whole Life Insurance

Whole life insurance, or permanent life insurance, provides long-term financial protection for policyholders in two ways: it provides a minimum guaranteed death benefit at a premium that never changes and it provides dividends and a cash benefit that accumulate tax-deferred. The monthly premiums tend to be much higher than for term life insurance, so you should go this route only if you can afford it. The benefits of purchasing whole life insurance include:

- Coverage is guaranteed for your entire life, with fixed premiums that cannot increase if you pay the amount outlined in the plan.
- Depending on the plan, you can withdraw some or all of the value you have built in the policy or use the dividends to pay part of your premiums.
- Whole life insurance programs can be "forced savings," protecting your family's financial future.
- The total amount of the policy can go up significantly, because the insurance company is investing a portion of the money, yet you are guaranteed not to lose your original amount of coverage.
- The benefit can be taken as monthly payments instead of as a lump sum.

Call your local life insurance agent to find out more about whole life insurance options and rates. Free quotes for whole life insurance policies can be found online at Insure.com, *insure.com*, IntelliQuote, *intelliquote.com* or any other insurance websites.

KEY PERSON INSURANCE

Key person insurance is a catchall phrase for any type of insurance policy, such as life or disability, that can be taken out on anyone who is of critical importance to a business. These key people can include the business owners or employees.

Think of it this way. If a person important to the operations, success and profitability of your business were to become disabled or to die, would your business continue to operate, grow and be profitable without that person? If the answer is no, there is a good chance you need to take out life insurance or disability insurance on that person.

Most home business owners do not need to worry about insuring key people in their business other than themselves. In fact, if you are the sole owner of the business with few or no employees, your insurance situation is straightforward. Insure yourself to protect your family financially and your business in case of liability or disaster potential (which includes workers' comp) and that's about it.

However, if you own a business with one or more partners, you should consider insuring each of the owners individually. The reason is that if one of the owners dies or becomes disabled, the death or disability benefits can be used to purchase that person's share of the business from his or her beneficiaries. In the case of a key employee or spouse partnership, the money can be used to stabilize the business until other key people can be hired to help the business operate smoothly and profitably again.

PROPERTY INSURANCE

Property insurance is the most common type of home insurance. It generally covers structures on the property and the contents of those structures. Depending on how extensive your property insurance is, it could provide protection in the form of a cash settlement or paid repairs in the event of fire, theft, vandalism, flood, earthquake, wind damage, and other acts of nature or damages from malicious intent. Floods and earthquakes generally require separate insurance riders, extensions of the standard policy that provide coverage for a specific item or activity.

Property insurance is the starting point from which home business owners should build, branching out to include specialized tools and equipment, home office improvements, inventory and liability riders, depending on the type of business.

Contact your insurance agent and ask questions specific to your business and equipment. You should quickly discover what is or is not covered by your current policy. You likely will want to increase the value of the contents portion of the policy if you use expensive computer and office equipment in your business. Below is a list of some items you will want to be insured specifically:

- Your house, apartment, condo or townhouse, whether you own it or rent;
- Other structures on the property you own or in which you keep any possessions, including your garage, sheds, greenhouses, fences and decks;
- Improvements made to your home as a result of your home business;
- Office equipment, furniture and supplies, owned and leased;
- Cash on hand and account receivable records;
- Business-specific items, such as tools and specialized equipment;
- Intellectual and intangible property, such as customer lists and data.

BUSINESS INTERRUPTION INSURANCE

Business interruption insurance is another coverage that home business owners should carefully consider, especially once your business is generating profits and if it is your sole source of income. Business interruption insurance protects the business owner against losses resulting from significant interruptions to the normal course of business. Owners can claim loss of business income, business profits, and coverage of fixed operating overhead items such as licenses, in-place advertising, and utilities for the period of time the business is shut down due to any reason stated in the policy.

You must make sure the policy limits are sufficient to cover your expenses and loss of income for more than a few days. The price of the policy is directly related to the risk of a fire or other disaster damaging your premises. For example, all other things being equal, the price of interruption coverage would probably be higher for a home manufacturing business than a home consulting service, because of the greater risk of fire due to the business activity. Business interruption insurance is available in many levels of coverage. Ask your insurance agent to conduct a business interruption analysis to determine the level of protection necessary to adequately cover your financial situation. The higher the level of coverage, the higher the premiums.

As is the case with various types of insurance, the location in which you do business will also factor into your premiums. For example, you will pay more for property or business interruption insurance in areas where there is a higher potential of a hurricane or other type of natural disaster.

You will want to make sure your policy will cover the amount of time it should realistically take to get your business started up again and operating. There is also usually a 48-hour waiting period before the coverage kicks in. One way to limit your premiums and further protect your business is to determine ways you might be able to operate out of another location. For some businesses, obviously, this is more feasible than for others.

Keep in mind all business interruption insurance policies are extensions of other insured perils, such as fire, flood and theft. Business interruption insurance is not sold separately. It is typically added to a property insurance policy for home business owners or included in a business insurance package policy if the business operates from another location. For example, if your business were shut down for two weeks because of flooding, you would have to be covered for floods in your property insurance to claim loss of business profits and income because of the flood.

Multiple layers of insurance can become confusing when trying to figure out what will be best for your situation, which again makes the case for getting an insurance professional to guide you through the maze.

LIABILITY INSURANCE

Most homeowners have some sort of liability protection built into their home and property insurance policy. This is also true for people who rent their homes or apartments, as landlords are obligated by law in most places to carry property and liability insurance on buildings and lands they rent. But no matter how diligently you are in taking all necessary precautions to protect your customers and yourself by removing potential perils from your business and the products and services you sell, you could still be held legally responsible for events beyond your control. Product misuse, third-party damages and service misunderstandings have all been grounds for successful litigation in the United States and Canada.

Therefore, as the old adage goes, it's better to be safe than sorry. The best way to be safe is to get liability insurance that specifically provides protection for the type of activities in which your business is engaged and for the types of products and services you sell. Often this type of extended liability insurance is called *general business liability* or *umbrella business liability*.

General business liability coverage insures against accidents and injuries that might occur at the home business location or at clients' locations and against perils related to the products and services sold. General liability insurance provides protection for the costs associated with successful litigation or claims against your business or against you, depending on the legal entity of your business, and covers such things as medical expenses, recovery expenses, property damage and other costs typically associated with liability situations.

There are also more specific types of liability insurance some home business owners will need to protect their businesses and clients. The three most common are *professional liability insurance, completed operations liability insurance* and *product liability insurance*.

Professional Liability Insurance

Professional liability insurance, commonly known as *errors and omissions insurance*, is designed to protect you or your company from the financial losses that might arise if you are sued by a client for alleged negligence in rendering professional services or advice. Professional liability insurance is one of the most common types of specialized liability insurance. This type of insurance is never included in a homeowner's insurance policy or a basic home business insurance policy. It is always sold separately as a specialized insurance specific to the nature of the profession or business. In fact, in many states and provinces (e.g., Ontario), practicing professionals will find professional liability insurance, or errors and omissions insurance, is mandatory: without it they cannot practice legally.

What type of home businesses and business-people need professional liability insurance? Until recently, professional liability insurance was generally carried only by practicing professionals such as lawyers, notary publics, certified accountants and engineers. But it is now common for almost every type of business professional and consultant to carry such insurance. This would include public relations specialists, advertising and marketing consultants, stockbrokers, home and building inspectors, software developers, webmasters, financial and estate planners, insurance agents and real estate agents, just to mention a few. Anyone who charges a fee for advice or professional services should carefully consider carrying professional liability insurance to protect his or her business, personal finances and clients' interests.

Obtaining professional liability insurance is a relatively straightforward process. Begin by checking with your specific professional associations, because many offer insurance programs to their members. You can also ask your current insurance agent to recommend an agent who specializes in liability insurance coverage. American Professional Agency provides free professional liability quotes on its website, *americanprofessional.com*. The site is indexed by type of profession and then indexed geographically by state.

Completed Operations Liability Insurance

Completed operations liability insurance is less common than professional liability. This liability insurance is for home business owners who provide services to clients or customers on location. Its basic function is similar to that of professional liability insurance. It would protect you from a liability if a service you provided to a client or a customer caused harm to the property or the individual's body after you had completed the service and left the premises. For example, a plumber with completed operations liability insurance is protected if she or he fixes a pipe in a customer's home and the pipe then bursts and causes bodily harm or damage to the home.

Obtaining completed operations insurance ⅄ easy. You can contact your current insurance provider and ask for a quote or a referral to an agent who handles this specialized insurance. You can contact professional associations or unions to which you might belong and inquire about members' insurance options. You can always go online to find information and quotes by doing a simple search for "completed operations liability insurance." Also, you can talk with other business owners in your area who work at clients' locations.

Product Liability Insurance

Many home businesses are involved in manufacturing a product, entirely or through a value-added process, and therefore should obtain product liability coverage to protect their businesses and clients in the event one of their products malfunctions and causes property or bodily damage. Even if your business is not directly involved in manufacturing the products you sell, you still must be proactive in terms of product liability insurance concerns.

You can first protect yourself by making sure the manufacturers of the products you sell are reputable and fully insured. You can also talk with your current insurance agent about the need for extended product liability insurance coverage even if you do not manufacture the product. It is not uncommon in litigation situations for plaintiffs who have suffered as a result of product malfunctions to name numerous defendants in their claim, including the seller of the product. Because of this possibility, it's smart for home business owners to protect themselves. This includes providing warning labels, even if the dangers seem to you to be painfully obvious.

AUTOMOTIVE INSURANCE

There are so many automobile insurance policies available to home business owners—commercial policies for people who use their vehicles exclusively for business, policies for occasional business use or special-usage and driver-restricted policies. The type of automobile insurance you select will be directly related to your business needs and situation.

Many states and provinces have auto accident compensation laws permitting auto accident victims to collect directly from their own insurance companies for medical, hospital, recovery and related expenses, regardless of who was at fault in the accident. This is commonly called *no-fault insurance*. The name of this insurance is misleading, as most states and provinces still allow victims who were not at fault to sue the party who caused the accident. Many states and provinces also impose requirements for commercial use vehicles in terms of mandatory insurance coverage, specific maintenance schedules and driver certifications, all of which you must research for your area prior to using your vehicle for business purposes.

Basic Types of Automotive Insurance Coverage

Liability Insurance

The basic type of insurance for automobiles is liability insurance. Most states and provinces require that every vehicle licensed for the road be covered by basic liability insurance. Liability insurance protects you should you cause an accident and injure people or damage property. There is no set amount of liability insurance that must be carried, but because of our litigation-crazed society, most insurance agents recommend a minimum of $1 million in liability insurance. Of course, premiums increase as the amount of liability insurance protection increases.

Collision Insurance

In the event your car is damaged in an accident and you are responsible for the damages, collision insurance will cover the costs associated with repairing or, in the event it is beyond repair, replacing the vehicle (market value). Generally, the rule of thumb is to carry collision insurance on vehicles that have a value of $5,000 or more. Collision insurance is a must if your vehicle is leased or financed.

Comprehensive Insurance

Comprehensive is another optional insurance. It covers damage to your vehicle caused by an event other than a collision with another vehicle or object. Comprehensive insurance covers fire, vandalism, theft, collisions with animals and acts of nature such as hailstorms and falling tree branches. Once again, depending on the value of your vehicle and your dependency on it for business use, you should carefully consider comprehensive insurance.

Riders for Tools and Equipment

Do you transport tools, a laptop computer, inventory, expensive product samples or other business-related property in your vehicle? If so, I strongly recommend you get a rider on your automobile insurance to protect you should these items be stolen from your vehicle or damaged in a collision or by an act of nature. Tools and equipment insurance can also be extended to cover aftermarket items you install in or on your vehicle and use for business purposes, such as signage, generators, ladder racks and tool storage boxes.

Rental Insurance

Rental insurance or rental reimbursement insurance should be considered, especially for home business owners who rely on their vehicle daily for business use. In the event that your car is damaged or stolen and you must rent a car to conduct business, this insurance will cover the costs associated with the rental vehicle. But be aware that most policies have a set maximum reimbursement for car rentals. If you need a truck for business, then make sure your policy states you can rent a truck as a replacement.

Leasing and Loans

If you lease your transportation for business use or if you have financed the purchase of a vehicle, in all likelihood you will be required to name as an additional insured entity the leasing company or the company that holds the financing note, to protect its financial investment in the event that the vehicle gets damaged and is declared a total loss. This insurance also protects the leasing company if it's named in a lawsuit as a result of an accident.

If you are making lease or loan payments, you may want to consider getting *gap coverage*. This coverage ensures that you receive the total amount of the loan or lease in the event the vehicle is a total loss. Gap coverage is especially important for new expensive vehicles, because vehicles depreciate by 25 percent or more as soon as they are driven off the lot. Without gap insurance, if the vehicle is totaled you will receive only market value, not the loan or lease value.

Automotive Insurance Discounts

The following are a few ways to reduce the amount you pay for automobile insurance.

Safe Driving Habits

Just about every insurance company rewards good drivers with lower insurance premiums. So the easiest way to reduce your automobile insurance premiums is to drive safely, don't speed, and keep your vehicle well maintained to reduce the chances for an accident resulting from mechanical failures. In many states and provinces, demerit points on your driver's license from traffic violations will raise your insurance rates. Therefore, wear seatbelts (it's the law in most states and provinces) and adhere to traffic rules and regulations.

Anti-Theft Devices

Most insurance companies give discounts ranging from 5 to 10 percent to customers who install and use anti-theft devices such as alarms, ignition immobilizers and onboard GPS recovery devices. All are designed to eliminate or reduce the possibility of your vehicle being stolen or to expedite recovery, thus reducing financial risk to the insurer.

Defensive Driver Courses

In some states, defensive driver courses are offered through or sponsored by the department of motor vehicles to improve driving skills. Insurance companies generally reward graduates of defensive driver courses in the form of lower automobile insurance premiums. Check with your local department of motor vehicles to inquire about defensive driver courses. Ask your insurance agent if completion of these courses will lower your premiums.

Limit the Number of Drivers

Another way to reduce auto insurance premiums is to limit the number of people who can drive the vehicle. This works especially well in situations where one driver has a poor driving record, which dramatically increases the overall cost to insure the vehicle, even if all the other drivers have clean driving records.

Compare Prices

The final way to reduce your automobile insurance premiums is to compare prices to ensure you are receiving the best value for the coverage you need. The simplest way to do this is to go online and get free automobile insurance quotes. Check GEICO Direct at *geico.com*, Insure.com at *insure.com,* the Auto Insurance Section of Insurance.com at *Insurance.com/quotes/auto.aspx,* or, for Canada, Kanetix at *kanetix.ca.*

BUSINESS TRAVELERS' INSURANCE

Home business owners who frequently travel within and beyond their home state, province or country should carry short-term business travelers' insurance as needed or permanent coverage if frequent travel warrants. Business travelers' insurance can cover common problems, such as trip cancellation and lost luggage, and more extreme problems, such as political abductions, extended hostage situations, false imprisonments, kidnapping negotiations and related costs, and political evacuation and repatriation expenses. A few of these are extreme situations, but in the wake of 9/11, and the rise in global unrest, these extremes are becoming real threats for many travelers.

The Association of Business Travellers offers its members unique insurance options, including trip cancellation, political evacuation, repatriation and medical evacuation. The association's website, *abt-travel.com*, includes information about member benefits as well as general information about business travel. Many credit card companies and other business and industry associations also offer members and customers travel insurance options at lower costs than can generally be obtained by individuals.

PROTECTING OFF-SITE ASSETS AND SUBCONTRACTORS

Never assume that people who tell you they are fully insured actually are. You might have all the necessary insurance in place to protect your business, customers and family in the event of misadventure, disaster or accident. But are your business alliances and subcontractors also fully insured? Before you hire subcontractors to carry out any work for your clients or in your home business environment, make sure they can provide you with proof of relevant insurance coverage, including

workers' compensation and liability insurance. Without it, if there is a problem on the job, you can be held liable as the contractor or the entity hired for the project, even if another business or person conducts the work for you under a subcontract agreement.

Also make sure the people with whom you do business are adequately insured. This ranges from your accountant or bookkeeper to the self-storage facility where you keep inventory or equipment and the warehouse that fulfills your customer orders. If any of these people are not fully insured and a catastrophic event occurs, you can be left holding a bag full of financial losses that cannot be recouped. To protect yourself, your family and your clients, the only sure way to know that people with whom you do business are insured is to ask for and receive proof of insurance. If they cannot provide proof of adequate insurance coverage, start shopping around for people with insurance.

TIPS FOR SAVING MONEY ON BUSINESS INSURANCE

Insurance companies base insurance premiums on statistical and specific evaluated risks. As the risks (financial exposure) associated with insuring a particular activity, item or individual increase, so do the premiums charged. Of course, there are steps you can take to minimize your insurance costs.

- Obtain at least three quotes for each type of insurance you need and analyze each for the range of coverage, cost/protection value and reputation of the agent, broker and insurance underwriter. But remember: the lowest cost certainly does not necessarily mean the best coverage. However much you might save, if a policy does not properly meet your specific needs, it is not worth the savings.

- Contact local business associations such as the Small Office Home Office (SOHO), *soho.org*, the Small Office Home Office Business Group (SOHO), *soho.ca*, the U.S. Chamber of Commerce, *uschamber.com*, or the Canadian Chamber of Commerce, *chamber.ca*, or your local Chamber of Commerce to find out if they offer members group business and health insurance options. Most home business associations have business insurance programs in place for members at a much lower cost because of volume purchasing. Often the savings will pay for the price of membership. Specific industry associations generally offer members these same packages and services.

- Contact your current insurance broker and inquire about special home business riders. The popularity of home businesses has increased so much in the past decade that many insurance companies now offer their policy holders home business rider options, which can be tagged onto their homeowners policies for less than the cost of separate home business policies.

- Consider raising your claims deductible, the portion of any insurance claim you pay before the insurance coverage pays the balance. As a rule of thumb, the higher your deductible, the lower your premiums. But do not make your deductible so high you would not be able to pay it in the event of a misadventure. Weigh the odds and do the math carefully before raising your deductible or you could be risking more than you could afford to lose.

- Get creative and find out if there is an insurance agent or broker in one of the local business or barter clubs who would be willing to accept your products or services in exchange for decreasing or eliminating the cost of insuring your home business. Shoestring tactics such as these have contributed to building thousands of successful businesses.

- Take the logical approach to home business insurance and prioritize your true insurance needs. You can add or increase insurance coverage as your business grows and you become able to pay higher premiums. Start with the basic plans that will deliver the best protection for your family and clients now and then increase your insurance coverage as your means allow.

HOME BUSINESS INSURANCE COVERAGE WORKSHEET

You can use the Insurance Coverage Worksheet (Figure 5.1) to determine if you need specific insurance coverage for your home business and the costs associated with each type. In some cases, more than one insurance policy will be required to protect employees, partners or family members. In other cases, insurance policies may overlap in their coverage and you won't need quite as many as you think. By using riders and buying various umbrella policies, you may be able to save money. Check with your insurance agent before filling in the amounts in pen.

For now, you can search the web for quotes or call insurance companies and get rough estimates. Then, after you fill in the number of policies you need and the unit cost per month of each, you can calculate the cost per month for each specific type of insurance. Then add the coverage costs to calculate the total insurance cost per month.

BEING PREPARED FOR PROBLEMS AND READY FOR RECOVERY

Yes, writing a check every month for intangibles like insurance can be painful, especially for a busi-

FIGURE 5.1 Insurance Coverage Worksheet

Type of Insurance Coverage	Insurance Required		Number of Policies Needed	Unit Cost Per Month	Total Cost Per Month
Health	❑ Yes	❑ No	_____	$_____	$_____
Workers' Compensation	❑ Yes	❑ No	_____	$_____	$_____
Life	❑ Yes	❑ No	_____	$_____	$_____
Disability	❑ Yes	❑ No	_____	$_____	$_____
Property	❑ Yes	❑ No	_____	$_____	$_____
General Liability	❑ Yes	❑ No	_____	$_____	$_____
Business Interruption	❑ Yes	❑ No	_____	$_____	$_____
Errors and Omissions	❑ Yes	❑ No	_____	$_____	$_____
Professional Liability	❑ Yes	❑ No	_____	$_____	$_____
Product Liability	❑ Yes	❑ No	_____	$_____	$_____
Completed Operations	❑ Yes	❑ No	_____	$_____	$_____
Liability	❑ Yes	❑ No	_____	$_____	$_____
Auto	❑ Yes	❑ No	_____	$_____	$_____
Travel	❑ Yes	❑ No	_____	$_____	$_____
Additional	❑ Yes	❑ No	_____	$_____	$_____
Additional	❑ Yes	❑ No	_____	$_____	$_____
Additional	❑ Yes	❑ No	_____	$_____	$_____
			Total insurance cost per month		$_____
			Total insurance cost per annum		$_____

Notes:

_____

_____

_____

_____

_____

ness startup with limited working capital and cash flow. Yet, you need to consider this expense as an absolute must. Purchasing business, life, disability and liability insurance is the only way you can be 100-percent sure that in the event of a catastrophic event, a lawsuit or an injury, your family, your business and you are protected against a massive financial loss.

You want to be proactive and keep your business and personal records organized so you're ready to make an insurance claim if necessary. You want to be able to make the insurance claims process as easy as possible so you are reimbursed quickly. Therefore, keep your accounts receivable and payable records up-to-date, keep inventory and equipment lists current, make duplicates of all records (including—and especially—computer data), and store them off-site in a safety deposit box or with your accountant, your attorney or even with a friend or family member.

For extra peace of mind, you might want to take photos or a videotape of your home office, the improvements made and your inventory, supplies, and special tools and equipment you use in your business. You should store this visual record off-site, with copies of your business documents and data. The loss of business records as the result of a disaster is one of the main obstacles to quick and accurate insurance claims settlements.

THE COMMON SENSE APPROACH

As mentioned earlier, you can do a lot to minimize your insurance premiums by using good common sense. Here are seven tips.

1. Provide warnings on packaging and/or products or sell only products that have sufficient warning labels. While many safety and warning labels may seem obvious, they are a smart way of minimizing the possibility of problems, bad publicity and litigation.
2. Stay current with all applicable business codes, zoning ordinances and local and state regulations. This means ensuring that everything from following guidelines with your smoke alarms to complying with regulations in your manner of disposing of trash. Be careful about where and how you store your inventory. For example, if your basement has a history of flooding, it may be unwise to store your valuable merchandise there.
3. Avoid exposing clients or visitors to unsafe conditions. For example, if you are having your home office painted, keep people from walking under the scaffolding. Minimize risks; meet clients in a neutral location, like a coffee shop.
4. Maintain good relations with customers, vendors and employees. People who feel good about you are less likely to sue than people who are disgruntled.
5. Don't tempt fate. Displaying your wealth of high-end home technology for every vendor, client and passerby who can see through your window can encourage theft. Therefore, don't be ostentatious with your possessions, lock up expensive equipment and buy a home security alarm to guard your things when you are away.
6. Hire professionals for all home improvements, especially wiring and plumbing. Numerous fires are the result of people tampering with the wiring because they think they know enough about electricity. Also, make sure wiring is inside the walls or otherwise protected and that wires are properly insulated.
7. Test all products you make before selling them. Document your testing.

The bottom line is simple. Do what you can to protect your clients from harm, protect yourself from being held responsible and protect your business equipment, inventory and other property from being destroyed or stolen. No, you cannot protect against everything—hence the need for insurance—but you can significantly lessen the potential for disaster.

RESOURCES
Associations

America's Health Insurance Plans (formerly Health
   Insurance Association of America)
601 Pennsylvania Avenue, NW
South Building, Suite 500
Washington, DC 20004
(202) 778-3200
ahip.org

Canadian Chamber of Commerce
360 Albert Street, Suite 420
Ottawa, K1R 7X7
(613) 238-4000
chamber.ca

*Independent Insurance Agents and Brokers
   of America*
127 S. Peyton Street
Alexandria, VA 22314
(800) 221-7917
iiaba.net

Insurance Brokers Association of Canada
1230-155 University Avenue
Toronto, M5H 3B7
(416) 367-1831
ibac.ca

Insurance Information Institute
110 William Street, 24th Floor
New York, NY 10038
(212) 346-5500
iii.org

Property Casualty Insurers Association of America
   (formerly National Association of Independent
   Insurers and Alliance of American Insurers)
2600 S. River Road
Des Plaines, IL 60018 -3286
(847) 297-7800
pciaa.net

Small Office Home Office Business Group (SOHO)
Suite 1, 1680 Lloyd Avenue

North Vancouver, BC V7P 2N6
(604) 929-8250, (800) 290-SOHO (7646)
soho.ca

SOHO America, Inc. (Small Office Home Office)
P.O. Box 941
Hurst, TX 76053-0941
soho.org

Small Office Home Office Business Group (SOHO)
U.S. Chamber of Commerce
1615 H Street NW
Washington, DC 20062-2000
(202) 659-6000
uschamber.com

Workers' Compensation Research Institute
955 Massachusetts Avenue
Cambridge, MA 02139
(617) 661-WCRI (9274)
wcrinet.org

Suggested Reading

Baldwin, Ben G. *The New Life Insurance
   Investment Advisor: Achieving Financial
   Security for You and Your Family Through
   Today's Insurance Products.* 2nd edition. New
   York: McGraw-Hill, 2001.

Hungelmann, Jack. *Insurance for Dummies.* New
   York: Hungry Minds, 2001.

Rubin, Harvey W. *Dictionary of Insurance Terms.*
   4th edition. New York: Barrons, 2000.

The Insurance Information Institute offers two
brochures of interest to home business owners:

Insuring Your Business Against a Catastrophe

Insuring Your Home Business

These brochures are available free of charge: send
a self-addressed stamped envelope to Insurance
Information Institute, Publications Department,
110 William Street, 24th Floor, New York, NY
10038. These brochures may also be downloaded

from the Institute's website at *iii.org/individuals/ brochures.*

Websites

2Insure4Less.com: Free quotes for all types of insurance. *2insure4less.com*

The Association of Business Travellers (North Sydney, Australia): Insurance information and services for frequent business travelers. *abt-travel.com*

Chubb Group of Insurance Companies: Free quotes on all types of business and personal insurance; directory of Chubb agents and brokers. *chubb.com*

Digital Insurance: Employee health and benefits insurance programs and packages. *digitalinsurance.com*

GEICO Direct: Online automotive insurance quotes for personal and commercial applications. *geico.com*

Insurancevalues.com: Free quotes on all types of business, personal, health and life insurance as well as general insurance information and useful links. *insurancevalues.com*

Insure.com: Free online home business insurance quotes, representing more than 200 companies. *insure.com*

InsWeb: Free quotes on all types of business, personal, health and life insurance programs and packages. *insweb.com*

State Farm Insurance: Business in the Home Program. *statefarm.com*
Quick quote service and directory of agents: *statefarm.com/insurance/business/homebus.asp*

CHAPTER 6

Preparing a Business Plan

FIRST AND FOREMOST, THE IMPORTANCE OF a business plan is not the document itself, but the process that goes into creating the document. Anyone can write a business plan. There are hundreds, if not thousands, of sample business plans available on the internet and in books, and most are free to use as models in creating your plan. All you have to do is use one as a template and fill in your own information.

I cannot emphasize enough that business planning has little to do with the actual business plan document and everything to do with the process of creating it. Far too many entrepreneurs get caught up in creating a great document—unfortunately at the expense creating a great business plan.

GETTING STARTED

The first step in building a business plan is to consider who will be reading the finished product. Business plans are typically written for several types of people. There are poten-

tial investors, venture capitalists, lenders and others from whom you are seeking financial backing. There are potential partners and others whom you may want to become part of your business, now or down the road. Finally, you also write your business plan for yourself, to guide you through the process of planning, establishing and running the business.

In many cases, your plan will be written with all of these possible readers in mind. However, in the case of a small business, which you can financially support on your own, the plan may be for your eyes only.

In this case, your goal is to create more of an operations manual than a document to market your business idea. You want it to be a guide for managing and then making a profit. You need only to include the information that will enable you to identify each stage of business startup and growth, how you will raise money and use it in the business, what you need to operate the business, who your customers are and where they are, your business and marketing objectives, and how you will reach these objectives.

If you are going to be using your business plan to secure startup or growth capital, you will need to cover all the bases in creating the business plan and produce a polished, professional document.

You want to keep your business plan from falling into the hands of your competitors. Therefore, be careful to whom you show your plan and to whom others show your plan. You may even want to consider having a lawyer draft a confidential disclosure agreement, which basically states you own the information contained in your business plan and the recipients of the document cannot discuss the details of your business plan with others or use ideas and concepts from your plan for their own personal benefit. Most of the people to whom you will be handing your business plan will be familiar with confidential disclosure agreements and will not have any issues signing one.

Do It Yourself or Hire a Pro?

The second decision to make about your business plan is whether you will prepare it yourself or hire a business consultant or freelance writer to do it. If the purpose of your business plan is to be a road map detailing your objectives and the actions required to reach each objective, chances are you will want to save the money and do it yourself. Even if you do not have experience in business planning, fear not. As mentioned above, there are plenty of books and websites to assist you. A few of the more popular ones can be found at the end of this chapter in the "Resources" section.

There is also a plethora of business plan software and templates on the market that can help you with the contents and format, such as:

- Fundable Plans, *fundableplans.com*
- PlanMagic, *planmagic.com*

- Palo Alto Software, *paloalto.com*
- Planium Software, *planium.com*
- MyBusinessKit.com, *mybusinesskit.com*
- Business Resource Software, *brs-inc.com*

Some office and word processing programs, such as MS Office, also include basic business plan templates and tutorials that can help lead novice entrepreneurs through the business planning process step by step.

If you do not feel comfortable preparing your business plan because you want to use it to secure funding, you may want to hire someone.

If you want to use a freelance writer, you need to find someone with business plan writing experience, someone who can show you references of people for whom he or she has written business plans. You will also want to see a copy of one of those plans (with names and numbers removed).

If you want to work with a business consultant, make sure he or she understands you are starting a homebased business and is familiar with the needs of such startups. He or she will also need to have experience preparing such materials for investors and show you references. A good business consultant can conduct research, collect data from secondary sources, create target customer profiles, conduct SWOT (strengths, weaknesses, opportunities and threats) and PEST (political, economic, social and technological) analyses, and do whatever else is necessary to prepare your business plan.

The additional benefit of hiring a business consultant rather than a freelance writer is that the consultant will have the experience needed to critique your business concept and objectives, keeping you in touch with realities, and to assess your chances of success from the facts revealed in the process of planning. Before hiring a business consultant, interview a few and see who is most comfortable with your plans and ideas. After all, you need someone who understands your business and your vision, someone who is not simply selling you a standard business plan. Accountants, lawyers and bankers often have access to business consultants and should be able to offer recommendations. Expect to pay between $2,000 and $10,000, depending on the amount of research needed to compile, analyze and catalog data on competitors, to prepare financial budgets and forecasts, to create draft plans for review and to write the final plan.

I must stress that the majority of people who start small businesses can easily prepare proper business plans themselves that will meet their specific needs and more. Do not feel intimidated by the business planning process. It is nothing more than collecting, analyzing and recording the information you need to be successful in business. Think of the business planning process as planning for a family vacation: You need to know where you are going, what you need to take along and how you will reach your destination. The same principles can be applied to business planning.

Many new business owners, if writing a business plan to obtain financing, write a draft of the entire plan themselves and then hire a business consultant to review it or a freelance business plan writer to revise it. This will cost less and can be advantageous. Remember: The business plan must put all your plans, ideas and goals onto paper. Who is better qualified to do that than you? There are numerous stories of business owners hiring others to write business plans from scratch, only to receive a document that does not represent what they envisioned. This is your business, your baby, so don't expect someone else to see it as clearly as you do. After all, you wouldn't hire someone to write your autobiography. Here are reasons for bringing in someone after you have completed the plan:

- To notice flaws in the logic or planning;
- To find any problem in the writing style and phrasing and any errors in grammar and spelling;

- To give you an overall perspective on how it reads. Is it clear? To the point? Perhaps there is a better way to express something.

Business Plan Outline

For the structure, there are no standard rules, mainly because business plans vary by industry, type of business, location of the company, size of the company, stage of growth and target readers. If you cover the basics—that is, you answer the questions of who, what, why, when, where and how—the result will be a business plan that works for your particular business situation and meets your specific needs.

The basic business plan is broken into 10 sections:

1. Introduction
2. Executive summary
3. Industry analysis
4. Business overview
5. Products and/or services
6. Competitive analysis
7. Marketing plan
8. Management
9. Financials
10. Appendices or supporting documents

Some of these sections are broken down into subsections.

Business plans are generally printed on 8.5-by-11-inch standard white office paper, single-spaced, 12-point Times Roman or similar font, and spiral bound or placed in a soft-cover binder. If you really want to make a positive impression, you can use a heavy-stock paper, include color photographs of products, and use an upscale cover and binding. Basically you should match the look of your business plan to its purpose.

The following is a basic business plan outline for a small homebased business.

INTRODUCTION

The first section of the business plan is the Introduction, which consists of a cover, a title page with full contact information and a table of contents that lists the main sections and subsections.

Cover

The cover is the first page. If you choose to use a soft binder, get one with a business card pocket or a window so your business name is displayed. If you choose to go with a spiral binding, use a heavier stock of paper for the cover, perhaps even a dark color with your business name printed on the outside in silver or gold for visual impact. Personally, I like to keep the cover of the business plan simple, with only the name of the business printed on the front cover and nothing else. Others prefer to include a contact person and address on the cover. It is really up to you to decide how you want the cover to look and what information you want to include.

If you will be sending your business plan to a number of people, use a cover letter on your company letterhead and attach it to the front cover with a paper clip. The cover letter should include the name of the person to whom you are sending the business plan, along with the business name, title and contact information. The opening paragraph should state why this person is receiving the business plan—he or she requested it, a third party referred this person to you or whatever. The second paragraph should briefly describe your business venture and your product(s) or service(s). The last paragraph should ask the recipient to call you so you can discuss the details of your exciting business and opportunity. Depending on the nature of your business, the purpose of your plan and the person who will be reviewing the plan, you might want to have the person sign a confidential disclosure agreement before you send the business plan.

Title Page

The second page is the title page. This is where you will print your business name, contact person and full mailing address, along with contact telephone numbers, fax numbers, e-mail addresses and your website URL.

You may want to control the number of business plans in circulation to help ensure it does not fall into the wrong hands. One easy tracking system is to put an identifying number on the title page, handwritten and very small, starting at "1." Keep a log in which you record each number and the name of the person who receives the business plan with that number. For an extra measure of protection, you can also include a copyright mark at the bottom of the title page. You can apply for a formal copyright with the U.S. Copyright Office or the Copyright Office of the Canadian Intellectual Property Office if you like, although it certainly is not required, as any original work is automatically copyrighted by the author in the United States and Canada. (Additional information about copyrights can be found in Chapter 4, "Legal Issues.")

Sample Title Page

Business Plan
ABC Consulting Ltd.

Joe Smith, President
555 Main Street
Any Town, CA 90210
Tel: (555) 555-5555
Fax: (555) 555-5555
E-mail: youremail@yoururl.com
Website: yoururl.com

Business Plan Copy # _____
©2008 by ABC Consulting Ltd. All rights reserved.

Table of Contents

The table of contents is a single page that lists the major sections and subsections of the business plan in order, with the corresponding page numbers. If your business plan consists of only a few pages, a table of contents will not be necessary. But if your business plan is broken into sections with numerous supporting documents, a table of contents is required, especially if the purpose of the business plan is to secure funding.

EXECUTIVE SUMMARY

The Executive Summary describes key points from every section of the plan, but in a concise manner so it fits on a single page. Even though the Executive Summary comes at the beginning of the business plan, it is usually the last section of the plan you write. You create the Executive Summary last because it is composed of key points from each section of the plan and you do not know what these key points will be until each section is substantially completed.

The main purpose of the Executive Summary is to provide readers with a brief overview of the plan. Some will read it and move on, while others will continue into the plan.

You want to make the Executive Summary sound intriguing, although without using hype. In brief, you want to spell out the who, what, when, where, why and how of your business.

Begin with your goals and/or philosophies for starting the business. Most important, begin by stating a problem you want to address. For example, there is no one-stop educational tutoring service in your area that hires current and retired teachers and schedules them to come to students' homes. Or perhaps nobody sells do-it-yourself ecofriendly auto detailing kits, so people could learn the detailing process and save money, while avoiding environmentally unsafe chemicals. You

can solve that problem by … Then you explain in a sentence or two how your business will address this problem, highlighting your business idea, the market, your products or services, the pricing and the demographic groups you intend to serve.

Next, you pull a couple of sentences from your marketing section, so the reader knows you have a plan. Finally, you tell who you are and why you are the best person to run this business. Include how you plan to get it off the ground or your means of financing it. Anyone reading a business plan with the intent of lending money is happy to hear that he or she would not be the only investor. At least you should be investing in your business, even if no one else does.

There are differing schools of thought as to whether you mention at this point how much money you are seeking. Some people believe you should put the money upfront so that readers know exactly what you are seeking. Others believe this can seem pushy and you risk being rejected on the basis of this figure, not on the merits of the case you have worked hard to present in your plan. Your decision will depend largely on the amount of money you need, the type of business you're starting and the lenders who will be reading you plan.

The Executive Summary should also include some basic facts, such as where you will be based, when you plan to open for business, what type of business structure you will have, and if you plan to have employees, consultants and/or freelancers or you plan to be a one-person operation.

All of this—on only one page!

INDUSTRY ANALYSIS

Before anything else, familiarize your readers with the industry in which you are launching your business. Do your research and find out how the industry is faring at present. Are companies doing well? Is there growth in the industry? Are there new products, inventions, discoveries or innovative technology moving this industry forward?

Using primary and secondary research, try to get a grasp of the present and the future of the industry and provide a short description of the industry. Look for accurate and up-to-date statistics to include in support of your analysis.

Finally, end by explaining how your business will fit into this picture. Why are you venturing into this industry? The idea of the Industry Analysis is to set the stage for the reader, to provide a backdrop against which you will enter the field. Don't be flowery; just create the scene concisely.

BUSINESS OVERVIEW

This is where you will provide a comprehensive overview of your plans for the business. How will your business operate? What will it accomplish? What kind of business structure will you have? What resources will you need? Describe your business. You can explain the equipment that will be necessary and how it will be used and how you will store inventory, ship packages (from your home or a drop shipper?) and so on.

Operations

Some business plans take a separate section to include operations. However, since you are working from home, you can probably work it into this section. After all, it will not be as elaborate as explaining what nine departments do to manufacture, market, distribute and sell widgets. Instead, you should address the issue of working from a home base, since location is typically part of the operations section. Simply explain how you will run the business from your home, deal with distractions and maintain a professional atmosphere in which to make the business successful. What portion of the home will be used for business? What renovations are needed to make the space

suitable for your business needs? How will you address issues of clients visiting your location, parking, storage, communication requirements and shipping and receiving? You will also want to describe how the business will be managed on a day-to-day basis and detail key policies for customer service and human resources. If your business will involve manufacturing or assembling products at home or if you will be providing professional services such as dentistry, your operations descriptions will obviously be much more detailed than if you were operating a freelance writing business from home.

Whatever you plan to use to make the business work, include it here. Essentially, you want to give the details and highlight the selling points of what your business will offer and how it will benefit customers or clients. Again, do not use hype: present the facts to tell your story.

Security

In the Business Overview section you will include how you intend to protect your business. From insurance to home security systems to risk management plans and contingency plans, you should relate what you are doing to take care of your business, to avoid problems and to minimize the impact of problems.

Keep this subsection brief, but include the important details, such as how much of each type of insurance coverage you will buy.

Legal Issues, Zoning and Permits

Describe all business licenses, registrations and permits needed to start and operate your business. Which of these have you obtained so far? Which are yet to be obtained? Depending on the type of business, these licenses, registrations and permits could include:

- Business license

- Employer Identification Number
- Vendor's permit
- Sales tax permits
- Import/export certificates
- Professional certificates
- Police clearance
- Internet domain name registrations

Since you are starting a homebased business, you should also mention zoning laws for which you need a variance or other laws or local ordinances that could get in your way and how you plan to circumvent (legally) any problems.

Mission Statement

Finally, in the Business Overview, perhaps at the beginning, perhaps at the end, you may want to include your mission statement.

A mission statement is your declaration that clearly states, in 50 words or less, who you are as a business, what you do, what you stand for and why you do it. Think seriously about the words you choose to create your mission statement. It should express your core values and what you hold to be important or your purpose.

So who needs a mission statement? Basically any business—sole proprietorship, partnership, LLC or corporation—or other organization whose owners or managers want to publicly or privately state their purpose and what they stand for. Businesses both large and small should take the time to create a mission statement. For example: "The purpose of ABC Technical Consulting is to provide up-to-date, targeted, professional strategies, ideas and on-site solutions to meet the current and future needs of each individual client."

There are no hard-and-fast rules for creating a mission statement. Ask 100 experts how to write one and you will probably get 100 different answers. Most, however, agree that the following are key points to consider when developing a mission statement.

- Keep your mission statements brief: two or three sentences.
- A mission statement is not an advertisement, a business plan or a promotional message. However, you should be able to use it as a component of these and other marketing activities.
- Take enough time to create your mission statement and make it right. Draft it, revise it as necessary and edit it carefully.
- Look at other mission statements to get ideas about how they were crafted. You'll find plenty of examples online. But never copy a mission statement.
- Skip puffery (hype) about how great you are and what a great job you do. Stick with what your target customers or clients will receive, the benefits to them through quality, value and service.
- Most important, make sure your mission plan actually says something. Some mission statements are bunches of buzz words strung together that sound good but don't really have any meaning. This is not the place for rhetoric, even though you will find that in some mission statements. Be honest. Be straightforward. Be concise.

Business History

This part is necessary to include in your Business Overview only if you are purchasing a business or if you are already in business and are writing a business plan to finance growth. Here you explain how the business started, discuss the previous owners, list the challenges facing the business, and include the current customers, suppliers and vendors. If you are buying a business, give the reasons why the owners are selling it, explain how it will be transferred successfully to your home office and so on. Take the readers through a brief journey into the past and bring them up to date with all the significant details about the history of the business.

PRODUCTS AND/OR SERVICES

So, what are you selling? Tell the reader about your Products and/or Services.

Start off with a brief description of your products and/or services. Begin with what the products or services do. Then provide some details. How long do the products last? How long they take to install? What they are made of? Include information you feel is relevant to provide an overview of what you will be selling to customers. Don't get technical; focus on the main attributes, benefits and value of the products and services. Why do people buy them? What is important about these products or services? Again, give the reader a good sense of why you are enthusiastic about the products or services you will be offering.

While writing this section, describe the benefits customers will receive from your products and/or services. Do they save money, make money, get physically fit, become healthier, save time? Remember: You have stated there is a problem and your products and/or services provide the solution to that problem; they meet some need. So, how do they do that and what are the effects?

Again, when explaining the selling points of your products and/or services, don't use hype. People want facts, not claims and opinions.

COMPETITIVE ANALYSIS

This section requires solid research. Don't take shortcuts, because this can be one of the most important sections of your business plan.

As much as you might be tempted to "trash" your competitors, you need to take the high road, the professional approach. Discuss all your direct and indirect competitors. *Direct* competitors are similar businesses that offer exactly what you offer in your same geographic region or also via the web. *Indirect* competitors might be businesses such as a department store that also includes some of the same type of products as you sell or a carwash that details some cars on the side, vying for the same customers as your detailing business.

Provide information on your competitors, including their prices. Discuss their strengths, providing a fair assessment. After all, if they have been successful and you present only negatives, the reader will wonder, "Then, why are they still in business?" and "Do you really believe it will be so easy to succeed against these competitors?"

In the next part of this section, you show the weaknesses of your competitors. To make this section particularly strong, you need to provide a realistic picture of your competitors. Then mention the areas in which they do not excel, according to your research. Are there specific products or services they do not offer? Are they larger businesses that do not provide personalized attention? You want to use the information you have gathered on your competitors to show where you can do better and what will bring customers to your business. This is your competitive edge—what separates the successful entrepreneurs from the others.

Having already explained the industry, this is where you can put the pieces together, showing how you can carve a niche in the marketplace with what you are offering. Are your products or services unique? If so, how? Are you able to charge less? Can you complete the job faster? Can you special-order parts or supplies? Do you provide free installation? All of this is part of the Competitive Analysis—all-important because in it you justify the existence of your company and give reasons why you will succeed.

In the end, this analysis should help you to identify your position within the marketplace, explaining how consumers view your business, products or services in direct relationship to your competitors and their products or services.

MARKETING

The Marketing section is a key component of your business plan. (It is so important, in fact, that Chapter 12 is entirely devoted to creating a marketing plan. Included in that chapter are worksheets you can complete as the basis for creating a marketing plan. There are also numerous tips, ideas and resources throughout that chapter.) The purpose of the Marketing section in your business plan is to explain how you will identify your target prospects and reach them through advertising, promotional and marketing strategies.

Below is the marketing plan outline used in Chapter 12, along with a brief introduction to each section. My advice would be to complete the business plan and marketing plan as two separate documents. Then use in the Marketing section of your business plan portions of the marketing plan that do not overlap with the other sections of the business plan.

The main sections of the marketing plan are:

- Executive overview
- Company analysis (you may exclude this, since it is already in the business plan)
- Market analysis
- Customer analysis
- Competitor analysis (you may exclude this, since it is already in the business plan)
- Marketing objectives
- Marketing strategy
- Marketing budget
- Action plan
- Support documents

Executive Overview

Like the business plan, the Marketing section begins with an executive overview or introduction, in which you summarize in one page the key points from every section of your marketing plan. Although you put the executive overview at the beginning of your Marketing section, it is logically the last piece of the section that you write. The main purpose of the executive overview is to provide readers with the who, what, where, when, why and how of your marketing plan.

Market Analysis

Unlike the Industry Analysis, the market analysis provides information about the specific market in which your business will operate. This subsection is divided into three main areas—market size, market segmentation, and marketing environment, including a PEST analysis detailing current and emerging political, economic, social and technological trends and issues that can have a potential effect (positive or negative) on your business and marketing efforts.

Customer Analysis

The customer and prospect analysis subsection of the Marketing section is where you will answer the same important questions about the people you're targeting as customers. What decision-making process do they use when buying? What benefits do they consider critical when deciding which product or service to purchase? How do your target customers make choices between or among competitors? How sensitive are your potential customers to price, quality, service and value issues? What promotional or marketing activities are they most likely to notice?

Marketing Objectives

Every business needs to set concrete objectives so it will have a yardstick to measure progress. In the marketing objectives subsection, you outline objectives for your marketing efforts, objectives that are realistic and attainable. Marketing objectives should include many individual goals, such as increasing sales, increasing market share, decreasing customer complaints and improving products, combined into a cohesive statement.

Marketing Strategy

The marketing strategy subsection describes how you believe you can best reach your target customers, such as emphasizing quality over price or filling a well-defined niche in the marketplace. It should also indicate how your marketing strategy relates to the four marketing Ps—product, price, place (distribution) and promotion.

Marketing Budget

Your marketing budget subsection answers the obvious question: How much will each marketing strategy and activity cost to implement, manage and maintain? You have to know how much it will cost to implement marketing strategies to reach your marketing objectives, where the money will come from and how much money you believe will be generated as a result of each marketing activity.

Action Plan

The action plan subsection is really nothing more than a big to-do list broken into marketing categories with timetables outlining when each promotional activity described in your marketing strategy subsection will be implemented in the calendar year. Also included in the action plan subsection are the systems you will put in place to measure the results of your promotional and marketing activities and when these measurements will be taken and the results compared against the expectations in the marketing plan.

Support Documents

The final subsection of your Marketing section consists of such documents as summaries of the principles, research surveys, market studies, spreadsheets, supplier and vendor agreements, client testimonials and press clippings. Basically, include any document that can support the statements, forecasts, decisions, strategies and opinions in your Marketing section. Support documents are especially helpful if your business plan will be used as an instrument to help secure funding.

MANAGEMENT

The vast majority of homebased businesses are owned and run by one person. If that's your situation, it is most important that you provide a brief autobiography highlighting the information that is appropriate to your business endeavor. Think about what lenders and investors might want to know about you. No, they do not really care about the car wash you ran in your driveway when you were 12 years old. They are interested in seeing a pattern of responsible business successes if they are going to back you in this venture. The same holds true for potential business partners and for attracting top employees. Obviously, if you're creating this business plan only for yourself, you can simply attach your resume, for the time being, to remind yourself of what you have done to date. But if you need to show potential lenders or partners what you have to offer to this business, you will want to mention your applicable skills and explain how you have used them to reach goals and succeed. Your goal here is to show how well you will be able to run this business and why lenders and investors should consider you a good risk.

Next, you will want to include other people on your management team. This will include a brief description (a paragraph at the most) on your attorney, your accountant and any business consultants or others involved in the business. You can use their resumes, but often there is a lot to sift through to find the relative experience. For that reason, it's worthwhile for you to take the time to extract the key information. You can always include the resumes in the Supporting Documents section at the end of the plan. If you are seeking funding and have not yet hired employees, contractors or freelancers, you will list the skills and experience you are seeking in those areas or describe the types of people you anticipate finding to fill those jobs. When describing the management team, keep in mind that you want to specify the people your business needs to hire or align with to operate the business and meet your key objectives.

FINANCIALS

A word of advice when you tackle the Financials section of your business plan: do not be intimidated by having to create financial statements and projections and do not let this challenge prevent you from preparing a business plan. Many new entrepreneurs feel intimidated by financial planning because of a lack of experience. But remember: any section of your business plan can be as simple or as complex as you want to make it.

For a small home business venture, you have to cover the basics in financial planning and forecasting—funding requirements, sources of funding, a balance sheet, a breakeven analysis, a cash flow projection, an income projection and lists of equipment and inventory—all of which are discussed in detail below.

If you decide to purchase a business or a franchise, the Financials section of your business plan will be more involved; it will include current and past information, including profit and loss statements, cash flow statements and depreciation

schedules. This will require more research and less number crunching, since these already exist for the previous years of a business or for the franchising company.

The discussion here focuses more on the home business startup than the purchase of a business or a franchise. My intention is to explain, in a simple and straightforward manner, what you need to include in the Financials section of your business plan and why. You will notice the absence of financial statement templates and charts. Almost all business plan software and most accounting software, such as the programs listed below, include customizable templates for financial forecasting such as breakeven analysis, profit and loss statements and cash flow projections.

- Fundable Plans, *fundableplans.com*
- PlanMagic, *planmagic.com*
- Palo Alto Software, *paloalto.com*
- Intuit QuickBooks, *quickbooks.intuit.com*
- Peachtree (Sage Software), *peachtree. com*

Funding Requirements

The first financial information that you want to include are the funding requirements for your new business. How much money is needed to start the business and how will the money be used? Funding requirements should be broken into three subcategories—current funding requirements, use of the funds and future funding requirements.

Current Funding Requirements

What are your current funding requirements? In Chapter 2, "What Type of Home Business Should You Start?" there is a handy business startup costs estimator that will help you pinpoint the amount of money needed to start your business.

Use of Funds

In the second section, you explain how the money will be used, such as to purchase equipment, to market, to buy inventory for resale, to obtain business permits or to renovate your home workspace. Be specific, since lenders or investors of any type want to know what you intend to do with their money.

Future Funding Requirements

Describe future funding needs, including why and when you anticipate needing the money. Future funding requirements can include, for example, new equipment purchases, business expansion plans or hiring employees.

Funding Sources

Now that you have identified your funding requirements, the next step is to identify and describe the sources of those funds. If the purpose of your business plan is to obtain funding, this is where you describe the sources of the money you are seeking (bank loan, private investments or partnerships), how the money will be repaid (cash or equity), and where the money will come from to meet a repayment schedule (generally through the business revenues). If you will be seeking private investor funding, you must make the potential return on investment very attractive. However, you need to be realistic. Unrealistic funding or repayment plans can throw a monkey wrench into your business plan.

It is almost always easier to get money from lenders or investors when you show that you are putting money into the business yourself. They want the reassurance that you are taking some part of the financial risk. This shows you're dedicated to making the business a success.

If you are providing funding yourself, explain the source of the money, such as savings, borrowing against home equity or sale of an asset, as well as when the funds will be available. Chapter 3, "Financial Issues," provides information about funding your home business startup.

Balance Sheet

The balance sheet lists your assets and liabilities, allowing you to determine your net equity position. Assets are what your business owns of value, liabilities are what your business owes, and equity is the difference between the two. Balance sheets generally record in one column short-term (current) assets (such as accounts receivable) and fixed assets (such as land and building owned by the business) and in a second column short-term (current) liabilities (such as accounts payable) and long-term liabilities (such as business startup loans with amortizations greater than 12 months or debts payable beyond the current fiscal year). Not included on the balance sheet are intangible assets (such as goodwill) and contingent liabilities (such as future warranty claims). The purpose of the balance sheet is to show what your business is worth.

Current and Fixed Assets

- *Cash:* the sum of all cash, including cash on hand and cash in business bank accounts.
- *Inventory:* the total value of in-stock inventory.
- *Accounts Receivable:* completed and invoiced product/service sales owed to the business by customers.
- *Loans Receivable:* the total outstanding value of loans from the business made to employees, managers, owners, shareholders, officers, suppliers, vendors and other third parties.
- *Investments:* the sum of all investments, such as a guaranteed investment certificate owned by the business.
- *Fixed Assets:* the total value of physical assets owned by the business, including land, buildings, leasehold improvements, equipment, tools, transportation, furniture and fixtures, less depreciation.
- *Miscellaneous Assets:* miscellaneous assets include deposits prepaid and prepaid expenses.

FIGURE 6.1 Balance Sheet

Current Assets	$ _____	Current Liabilities	$ _____
Fixed Assets	$ _____	Long-Term Liabilities	$ _____
Total Assets	$ _____	Total Liabilities	$ _____
		Total Assets – Total Liabilities = Net Equity	$ _____

Current and Long-Term Liabilities

- *Accounts Payable:* the total sum of money owed to your product/service suppliers for outstanding invoices, including items such as inventory and telephone bills.
- *Accrued Expenses:* the total sum of monies owed but not yet due, such as wages, taxes, benefits and interest on loans.
- *Current/Short-Term Loans:* the total principal sum of short-term loans or notes to 360 days, less interest (accrued liabilities).
- *Long-Term Loans:* the total principal sum of long-term loans owed by the business to banks, investors and shareholders.

Breakeven Analysis

The breakeven analysis is used to determine how much product or service must be sold for the business to break even or the total amount of incoming revenues to match the total amount of outgoing expenses. To calculate your breakeven point, you will need to estimate your fixed expenses (overhead). (In Chapter 2, "What Type of Business Should Your Start?" you will find an overhead estimator worksheet.) You will need to know the variable costs for purchasing products, shipping products and providing services, as well as the gross margin for each sale, which can be found in Chapter 9, "What Price Will You Charge?" For example, if you sold bicycles from home and you sold each bicycle for $1,000, which included vari-

able costs and a gross margin of 25 percent, you would have $250 gross profit per sale. If your fixed costs are $50,000 per annum, you would need to sell 200 bicycles per year to break even. $50,000 in fixed costs divided by $250 gross profit margin equals 200 sales per year or roughly 17 sales per month.

Cash Flow Projection

The cash flow projection shows how money will flow into the business in the form of revenues and flow out of the business in the form of expenses (disbursements). For startups, the cash flow projection is important because it can tell you the times in the year when you can expect a cash surplus and the times in the year when you can expect a cash shortage. It also shows would-be investors and lenders that you have considered ongoing cash flow concerns in advance, since this is often an area in which businesses struggle.

If you know this information, you can manage your money more carefully, even before the money begins to come into the business, and you can secure working capital funding for the times when you anticipate a cash flow shortage.

It should be noted that a cash flow *projection* is not a cash flow *statement*. A cash flow projection is the anticipated revenues and disbursements over the next 12 months. A cash flow statement shows how cash has flowed in and out of a business over a specific past period, usually 12 months. If you are purchasing a business or an existing franchise, you should obtain cash flow statements from the owner; if you are purchasing a new franchise, you should obtain cash flow statements from similar franchises in your geographic region (if possible).

The cash flow projection consists of three parts—estimated monthly cash sales (products and services), estimated monthly cash disbursements (fixed and variable costs) and closing cash balance, which is the monthly cash sales less the monthly cash disbursements. The cash balance anticipated for each month, either plus or minus, is then carried forward to the next month, until you have projected your cash flow on a month-by-month basis for the entire year.

Income Projections

Income projections are the anticipated sales and expenses on a year-by-year basis moving forward. They should not be confused with income statements, also known as profit and loss statements, which are based on actual operating history, and again included when buying an existing business.

Income projections are prepared using your marketing objectives (sales target), cost of goods sold, estimated fixed overhead, estimated variable costs and gross margins or markups. Ideally, if you are starting a business, you will want to prepare income projections for at least three years and then measure performance by comparing the income statement for each year with your income projection for that year. Doing so enables you to tweak your marketing strategies if actual revenues and expenses do not meet your projections for revenues and expenses.

Obviously, lenders and investors will take a close look at your income projections, since they are looking to recoup their money and, in the case of investors, see a profit. Be forewarned that it is easier to procure funding by taking a more conservative stance in your income projections. Do your research and gather data on the profitability of similar businesses, homebased or not. Always take a more cautious approach. If you calculate your sales at 500 widgets a year, bring it down 20 percent to 400. Since many businesses do not make money in the first year, let it be known how many years you anticipate it will take for your business to get into the black. Most lending institutions, knowledgeable investors and venture capital firms understand it takes time for a business to grow. In fact, even if you are sure you can make money the first year (which is uncommon), do not show profits for that first year.

Equipment and Inventory Lists

Finally, the financial data section of your business plan includes equipment and inventory lists. You can separate the two lists or combine them into one (Figure 6.1).

Regardless of the form, equipment and inventory lists should include what you currently have, what is needed in the short term (less than 12 months) and what is needed in the long term (more than 12 months). You should also include the number of units that are required, the cost of the items and the date when the required items will be purchased. Equipment and inventory lists can be included in the financial data section of your business plan or in the financial support documents in the appendices of your business plan.

APPENDICES OR SUPPORTING DOCUMENTS

The appendices of your business plan are reserved for supporting documentation, such as resumes for the principals, research surveys, market studies, financial forecasts, supplier and vendor agreements, client testimonials and appropriate press clippings or newsworthy articles on you, businesses you have owned or the growth of the indus-

FIGURE 6.2	Capital Equipment and Inventory List

Current Equipment

Equipment Description	# of Units	$ Unit Cost	Total Cost	
_____	_____	$ _____	$ _____	
_____	_____	$ _____	$ _____	
_____	_____	$ _____	$ _____	
		$ _____	$ _____	

Needed Equipment

Equipment Description	# of Units	$ Unit Cost	Total Cost	Date Required
_____	_____	$ _____	$ _____	_____
_____	_____	$ _____	$ _____	_____
_____	_____	$ _____	$ _____	_____
_____	_____	$ _____	$ _____	_____

Current Inventory

Inventory Description	# of Units	$ Unit Cost	Total Cost	
_____	_____	$ _____	$ _____	
_____	_____	$ _____	$ _____	
_____	_____	$ _____	$ _____	
_____	_____	$ _____	$ _____	

Needed Inventory

Inventory Description	# of Units	$ Unit Cost	Total Cost	Date Required
_____	_____	$ _____	$ _____	_____
_____	_____	$ _____	$ _____	_____
_____	_____	$ _____	$ _____	_____
_____	_____	$ _____	$ _____	_____

try. Basically, include documents that can help support your research, your forecasts, your statements and the information contained in your business plan, as well as any plans in your business plan, such as a marketing plan, a sales plan, an advertising plan and an internet plan.

Supporting documents can be especially valuable if you are going to use your business plan to secure investment capital to start or grow your business. After reading the Executive Summary, bankers, accountants and venture capitalists often go straight to the supporting documents section to make sure that you have done your homework, that you are committed to the project, and that there is verifiable documentation indicating a great potential to succeed. In short, they want to know their money is going into the right venture and will be managed by capable individuals. Depending on the purpose of your business plan, you may or may not need to include copies of all or any of the supporting documents mentioned below.

Personal Documents

Personal support documents are generally focused on three areas—resumes, training and financial statements. The documents should include resumes for all the key players in the business, including owner(s), managers, key employees, sales agents and subcontractors, even if they are only simple one-page resumes highlighting experiences in bullet-list format. The documents should include copies of training certificates or specialized licenses held by the owner(s), managers or key employees relative to the business, the products sold or the services supplied. Finally, if the purpose of the business plan is to secure funding, you will need to include a personal assets statement for each of the people applying for the loan. The statement should list all personal assets (such as real estate, automobiles, equities and savings plans) and all personal liabilities (including property mortgages, personal loans and credit cards). For each statement, subtract the total liabilities or debts from the total assets to show the net worth.

Legal Documents

Copies of legal documents that should be included in the business plan are:

- Business and domain name registrations
- Business and home occupation licenses
- Business insurance coverage documents
- Patents, trademarks and copyright documents (if any)
- Product, workmanship and third-party warranties

- Vendor and supplier agreements already negotiated and in force

Financial Documents

Copies of financial documents that should be included in the business plan are:

- Short-term and long-term sales projections
- Breakeven analysis
- Audited financial statement (if a business is being purchased or if an operating business is applying for funds)
- Marketing budgets and projections
- Start-up costs estimates
- Equipment and supplies projections, estimates and lists
- Projections for fixed operating costs

Marketing Documents

You should include here documents supporting your marketing research, secondary data sources, and other marketing-related documents that support or prove marketing statements made in your business plan. It is through the process of researching the market, demand for the product, target customers and competitors that the true potential viability of the business is proven. Any or all of the following would qualify as marketing support documents:

- Primary research documents, including surveys, questionnaires and focus group results
- Secondary data documents
- Target customer profile
- PEST and SWOT analyses
- Any marketing materials (even mockups), including brochures, product photographs, catalogs, price lists and print advertisements
- Press clippings
- Client testimonials and company, individual or organizational endorsements

- Competitors' brochures, price lists, warranties and print advertisements

Other Documents

If you are using a drop shipper, provide a sheet on the pricing and the company. If you plan on building an office onto your home, show an architectural rendering. If you have won awards in the field in which you are starting your business, include the certificates or press clippings as evidence of winning these awards. If you have product photos or illustrations, you can include a few. If your business will be web-based, include a screen shot of the home page or a couple of pages from the site.

In short, you can include whatever can make your business shine for whoever will be reading your business plan. Of course, you don't want to overdo it. People will look at 10, even 20 supporting documents. However, if your appendices are rivaling the Yellow Pages in size and weight, you may need to select the key pages to include and leave out the others.

FINISHING TOUCHES

While it may sound obvious, you *must* edit and proofread your business plan. No first draft of anything this important is good enough. Read it and revise it. Then make sure to correct typos, rework awkward or faulty wording and eliminate anything that makes the plan look less impressive. Have someone you know and trust read the document carefully and slowly proofread it for the sole purpose of finding errors. Remember: If you want people to give you money, you need to make the best impression.

Finally, when you have the finished version, save a copy on a CD and print several hard copies, beyond those you will send out. You always want to

have one around for reference and several backup copies in case you spill coffee on it or you can't find it.

SUPPORTING YOUR PLAN

As mentioned at the start of the chapter, the actual business plan on paper, although it should be as professional as possible, is not the most important factor in developing a business plan. The facts, thoughts and feelings behind the plan are the key elements. Why do you believe in this business? What makes you think you can make it work? How will it succeed and show a profit? Are you prepared to oversee the many areas that make up a business? Why are you the best person to make this business a success? These are the questions you will want to answer as you prepare your business plan.

When bankers, venture capitalists, independent investors, business angels or anyone else reads your plan, you must be ready to answer questions and support your statements. To be ready to do so, you must review your plan to make sure there are no holes in your logic or gaps in your information. If a potential investor asks you a question to which you have no answer, your chances of obtaining funding from that source disappear. Therefore, everything you write needs to have validity.

For example, if you are asked how your previous business experience at XYZ Incorporated will help you in this endeavor, you will need to provide a succinct answer that supports and elaborates on whatever you wrote in the business plan. If you are asked about handling your home business during "family hours," you need to support whatever you wrote in the plan and provide a detailed answer.

In short, you must think through and work out

everything in your business plan. Prior to meeting with potential investors or lenders, ask someone you know and trust who has some understanding of your business concept to read through your plan and play devil's advocate. This way, you can prepare to answer any and all questions from anyone who reads your business plan.

RESOURCES
Associations

Business Development Bank of Canada
BDC Building
5 Place Ville Marie, Suite 400
Montréal, QC H3B 5E7
(877) BDC-BANX (232-2269)
bdc.ca

Canadian Chamber of Commerce
360 Albert Street, Suite 420
Ottawa, ON K1R 7X7
(613) 238-4000
chamber.ca

SCORE Association
409 3rd Street, SW, 6th Floor
Washington, DC 20024
1175 Herndon Parkway, Suite 900
Herndon, VA 20170
(800) 634-0245, (703) 487-3612
score.org

U.S. Chamber of Commerce
1615 H Street NW
Washington, DC 20062-2000
(202) 659-6000
uschamber.com

U.S. Small Business Administration (SBA)
409 Third Street SW
Washington, DC 20416
(800) 827-5722
sba.gov/indexbusplans.html

Suggested Reading

Bangs, David H., Jr. *The Business Planning Guide: Creating a Winning Plan for Success.* 9th edition. Chicago: Dearborn Trade Publishing, 2002.

Covello, Joseph, and Brian Hazelgren. *Your First Business Plan.* 5th edition. Naperville, IL: Sourcebooks, 2005.

Debelak, Don. *Successful Business Models: Surefire Ways to Build a Profitable Business.* Irvine, CA: Entrepreneur Media, Inc., 2003.

Hargrave, Lee E., Jr. *Plans for Profitability! How to Write a Strategic Business Plan.* Titusville, FL: Four Seasons Publishers, 1999.

Henricks, Mark. *Business Plans Made Easy: It's Not as Hard as You Think!* 2nd edition. Irvine, CA: Entrepreneur Media, Inc., 2002.

O'Donnell, Michael. *Writing Business Plans That Get Results: A Step-by-Step Guide.* New York: McGraw-Hill, 1991.

Sutton, Garrett. *The ABC's of Writing Winning Business Plans: How to Prepare a Business Plan That Others Will Want to Read — and Invest In.* New York, NY: Business Plus (Warner Business Books), 2005.

Websites

All Business.com: Articles and expert advice on all areas of business, including business plans. ***allbusiness.com***

Bplans: Sample business plans and plenty of advice on creating them. ***bplans.com***

Business Town: Section on structuring and writing a business plan. ***businesstown.com***

Center for Business Planning: Information about creating business plans, including free templates and samples, as well as business planning products and services. ***businessplans.org***

MarketResearch.com: Billed as the most comprehensive collection of published market research available on demand. **marketresearch.com**

National Venture Capital Association: Association of venture capital firms and organizations that manage pools of risk equity capital designated to be invested in young, emerging companies. **nvca.org**

Nolo: Online legal self-help information, products, services, resources and links for consumers and business owners. **nolo.com**

Palo Alto Software: Business Plan Pro, software for creating business plans. **paloalto.com**

Small Business Loans: Online loan applications for financing startups and established businesses. **smallbusinessloans.com**

Small Business Now: Small business information, advice, tools, products, services and links of interest. **smallbusinessnow.com**

U.S. Census Bureau: Market demographics, information and statistics. **census.gov**

vFinance: Directory of venture capital firms and angel investors. **vfinance.com**

CHAPTER 7

Establishing Your Home Workspace

THIS CHAPTER IS CALLED "ESTABLISHING Your Home *Workspace*," not home *office*, because every business that is operated or managed from home will require some sort of workspace, but not all will require an office in the traditional sense. If you operate a freelance photography business, for example, your main workspace in the home may be your darkroom. If you operate an automotive paint shop, then chances are your workspace will be the garage or a freestanding shop out back. If you operate a dental practice from home, then your workspace will probably be a portion of your home used for a waiting room, a treatment room and an office. In other words, workspace requirements will vary depending on the business you choose to operate.

While helping you determine your needs so you can create the right home workspace for your business, this chapter is broken into sections to help you establish your home workspace step by step:

1. Selecting your workspace based on your needs
2. Planning your workspace
3. Renovating your workspace
4. Equipping your workspace
5. Making your workspace secure and safe
6. Providing your workspace with furniture, equipment and supplies
7. Building a positive image for your new business

Working full or part time in the home requires much thought and planning to create a working environment suitable for your business and in balance with the needs of your family.

SELECTING YOUR WORKSPACE

The type of business you will be operating from home is key to determining the type, size and location of the workspace you need. You must also carefully consider day-to-day living as well as special occasions, seasonal activities and guests.

If you have a family and will be operating a business primarily from within your home, you will want to incorporate as many of the following ideas as possible to help achieve the best business–family balance:

- If available, choose a separate room as dedicated workspace. Then you can close the door to keep business in and family, friends and pets out.
- Pick a room or other space where you can minimize distractions, far away from kitchen, laundry room and PlayStation noises.
- Select a workspace that is large enough to operate your business. Working out of two or three separate areas of the home is far less productive than working from one area, although you can certainly use another part of the house, such as your basement or garage, for storage, if necessary.
- If clients will be coming to your home, the ideal is a workspace with a separate outside door or very close to an outside door.
- If you will be operating a business that creates noise or generates byproducts (dust, mess, fumes), consider the garage or an outside structure for your workspace.

Your Workspace Options

Your workspace options range from a corner of the home to a separate outside structure. This will depend on the size of your home and available rooms, the type of business you are running and other residents. Obviously, someone who is living alone has different options than someone whose home reminds visitors of the movie *Cheaper by the Dozen*.

Spare Corner

Though by far the least expensive way to set up a home workspace, using a spare corner of the house can have some disadvantages. If you are not alone, you will have to deal with a lack of privacy and noise. However, if all your budget allows is a secondhand desk in the corner of your living room to serve as the head office location for your new business, then go for it! Many successful business people have started with far less. Lillian Vernon started her massive catalog empire from her kitchen table.

Dining Room

Believe it or not, the dining room is the most popular room of the house to convert into a home business workspace, mainly because it is cheap and quick to do and because the dining room is an area often used only on occasion. Unfortunately, most dining rooms do not have doors that close, so that room may not be appropriate for client visits. Again, this will depend on other residents and the type of home business you are running. For example, a part-time seasonal homebased business doing income tax returns can work well from the dining room table, where all paperwork can be spread out after dinner while the kids are doing homework.

Kitchen

Desks in kitchens are not that uncommon now. If you need a place to pay the bills, make phone calls, handle paperwork and run a part-time business, this scenario can work out fine. You can use a fold-out desk, with a filing cabinet below and a hutch above. The lighting is probably appropriate and the atmosphere is usually cheery, so if you live alone or other residents are away at work or in school, doing business from your kitchen can be fine.

In one loft apartment, the homeowner simply extended the kitchen counter several feet and added onto the cabinets with shelving made of the same wood. Sliding wooden doors were installed on the counter top to hide the computer; in fact, a visitor would not know if behind the closed doors was a computer station or a breadbox. In fact, the only hint of an office in the kitchen was the computer chair, which could easily be wheeled out of sight.

However, if you require full-time office space, any portion of the kitchen will likely afford too many distractions. In most households, the kitchen is a busy room. In addition, the ever-present temptation to snack may make the kitchen a bad choice.

Extra Bedroom

A spare bedroom is the second-most popular choice for almost any type of homebased business that has no or few client visitors. Here, you can create the full office experience or use as much or as little space as you need. In addition, since this is a dedicated workspace, you can decorate as you choose and take care of all functional needs, such as installing an extra phone jack, stronger, insulated windows to keep out the cold of winter and so forth.

Converted Garage

The garage can be a great place for a business, especially if it is attached to the home, has a separate entrance, requires few alterations and is large enough to meet your needs. The downside is the large amount of money required to make the transformation from a typical garage to a fully functioning home workspace complete with electricity, heat, water, sewer and communications. Recently, an associate converted his double attached garage to home business use, leaving one side for storage, shipping and receiving, basically unchanged, while renovating the other into a very elaborate office that would rival any in a high-rise, high-rent downtown office district. The other downside to using your garage is that you may need to park your car outside, which may be inconvenient if you are living where it snows a lot.

Basement

Basements provide yet another good, and increasingly popular, option for home business space, if they have been altered for your climate and have good access, improved lighting and adequate headroom. Many people have built offices into finished basements, often taking up only a portion of the area, leaving other sections for storage or family use. One concern with basement workspaces is moisture, especially at certain times of the year. So, if you are considering this option, think carefully about the conditions, especially if you plan to store inventory, paper or documents that can be easily ruined or computer equipment that can be affected by heat, cold or dampness.

Attic Space

Attics can work, providing they have been altered to suit the climate and have good access. The downside is that there is almost no chance of having a separate outside entrance for client visits. Also, if the attic space is the third floor, walking up and down two flights of steps with documents, mail, products and job files can be tiring. In addition, most attics are shaped oddly, with low or slanted roofs that can reduce use of much of the space. Attics are usually subject to great changes in temperature, as well as unwanted visitors (bats, squirrels, mice, bugs, etc.) and many are not equipped with electrical outlets and phone jacks or even solid flooring to support your technical equipment.

New Addition

The much more costly option for workspace is to build an addition onto your home. On average, you can count on spending $30,000 to $50,000 on the addition, before you spend one dime on business equipment, inventory, marketing or other aspect of setting up and getting your business rolling. You will also have to comply with building codes, zoning regulations and other rules associated with adding square footage to your home.

The positive aspect is that you can design this addition exactly as you wish. Also, if you decide to sell your house, the extra space can be used as a family room or for some other reason, making your home that much more valuable when you put it on the market. Typically, such additions are more common for high-income professionals who need a large and well-designed separate area, such as doctors, dentists or physical therapists.

Outside Structures

Outbuildings on your property, such as tool sheds, enclosed cabanas and freestanding workshops, are another option, if the structure is suitable and large enough to meet your needs. The downside to outbuildings is that most do not have water or sewer connections and only basic electrical services, lacking proper heat and light. By the time you renovate and upgrade the mechanicals, you will be talking about a substantial amount of money that might be better spent renovating another space that does not require as many alterations, such as the attic or basement. Outbuildings are generally in the backyard, so you would have to address issues of client parking and access as well as access for deliveries and pickups. However, if you plan on operating a manufacturing or repair business, a renovated or new outbuilding on your property may be your only logical or legal option.

Other Workspace Issues

The type of home business you will be starting greatly influences your needs in terms of where in the house the workspace is established and, in many cases, even if you can operate your business legally from home. Here are a few additional workspace issues to consider prior to starting up.

1. Will you have clients visiting your home office? If so:
   - Do you have the space to accommodate visits?
   - Do you have suitable parking for clients and good access?

- Will you be able to separate your workspace from your living space to provide visiting clients with privacy?
- Is the appearance of your home suitable for client visits? Broken porch boards, peeling paint and worn carpets can send potential clients the wrong signals about your business.
- Can you provide clients easy and private access to washroom facilities in your home?

2. Will you have employees working from your home? If so:
   - Can employees or outside contractors legally work from your home?
   - Do you have the space required for employees to work?
   - Can you provide employees working from your home with enough privacy to do their work and offer your family enough privacy from your employees?
   - Can you provide employees separate and easy access to your home workspace and can you provide them with suitable parking?
   - Can you provide employees with the basic necessities, such as washroom facilities, space for breaks and lunch and closet space for coats?

3. Will you be manufacturing or assembling products at home? If so:
   - Do local zoning regulations allow home-based manufacturing businesses?
   - Will you have to upgrade or install new mechanical services, such as heating, cooling, electrical and plumbing to accommodate your business?
   - Will you need to install ventilation systems? If so, will the exhaust pollute? Will the noise bother your neighbors?
   - Do you have adequate access for parking, shipping, receiving and storage?

- Will you have to upgrade your home to meet fire safety standards because of your business or the product you manufacture?

4. Do you need storage space? If so:
   - Do you have enough room in your home to store inventory, equipment, business records and client files?
   - Is your storage space accessed easily and safely?
   - Is your storage space suitable for the things you need to store? Consider dampness, heat, critters and cold.
   - Is your storage space secure so that valuable business equipment, inventory and records are not at risk of being stolen?
   - If you do not have suitable storage space, is there a suitable self-storage facility close by with easy access? If so, how much does it cost?

5. Do you have the communications connectivity you require?
   - Are there phone jacks for landlines? Does your cell phone work clearly from your chosen location?
   - Can you connect your wireless routers from your workspace? There's nothing worse than realizing your wireless router, wireless phone and wireless computer do not work reliably.

PLANNING YOUR WORKSPACE

You will greatly maximize your chances of putting together the most productive, functional and visually appealing workspace at the lowest possible cost if you take the time necessary to plan your workspace well in advance of actually setting it up. Planning your workspace enables you to take into account all your needs and avoiding costly mistakes.

First, determine if there are renovations that must be done. It's always easier to get these completed in advance of setting up shop. After renovations or if no renovations are needed, completely clean the space and all surfaces—walls, ceiling and floor—and do any painting.

The next step is to take measurements of the room and make a scale drawing on a large piece of paper, noting on your floor plan windows, doors, electrical outlets, telephone jacks, cable outlets and lights. Once you have an accurate, scaled floor plan, you can move on to purchasing equipment and furniture that fit your space and suit your needs. After you have purchased all or most of what you need, install the furniture and equipment according to your plan.

This may seem like a time-consuming way of setting up your workspace, but you want to do the job only once, do it within your budget, and get exactly what you need to start your business right. The extra time spent planning your workspace now will ultimately save you time and money down the road, as it won't be necessary to interrupt business to redo your workspace or lose productivity because the space does not suit your business needs.

Hiring a Designer

Most home workspaces are basic enough so they can be planned without hiring a professional. However, if you intend to spend a substantial amount of money to create a workspace in your home or you have hired an architect to build an extension to your home, you might want to consider hiring an interior designer with home office experience. A key point to remember is that the ultimate goal of the designer is to create the perfect workspace to suit your specific business needs while saving you at least enough to pay his or her fee. That's right: in the end you will most likely find that a professional designer can save you enough money through his or her experience, contacts and trade discounts to cover the fee, especially on contracts in excess of $25,000. Additionally, the finished product will probably be far superior to what you can plan and design yourself—unless, of course, you're a contractor or a designer.

To find an interior designer with experience in home workspace design and planning, consult your local Yellow Pages directory, ask friends and associates if they know one, or visit the website of the International Interior Design Association at *iida.org*. Typically, a designer might be helpful for businesses that will be receiving visits from clients, businesses that will be employing several workers or businesses that require specialized professional facilities, such as a dentist's office with a waiting room, an X-ray room, etc. Otherwise, you can likely design your workspace yourself.

Creating an Environment-Friendly Workspace

You will want to be sensitive to the environment. Integrate your home business recycling with your household recycling for convenience. Find out how you can use recycled products in your business. Also, let your customers know that you support recycling and environmentally conscious business practices. In fact, include this information in all your advertising and business communications, because you will certainly not alienate customers in an increasingly environmentally conscious society. In fact, you will likely attract a few new customers because we all know that taking care of our planet is not only right, but necessary for this and future generations. Heidi Schimpl, Community Programs Coordinator at the North Shore Recycling Program in North Vancouver, British Columbia, advises these simple and inexpensive practices in your home office to save money and contribute to a healthier environment:

- Place paper recycling bins in convenient locations such as beside your desk, areas

where you pack and unpack shipments and near file cabinets. The more convenient you make recycling, the more you will recycle.
- Hang on to paper that has been printed only on one side and use the other side for printing draft documents and other materials that are for your eyes only, as well as for use in your fax machine. You can also cut paper that has only been printed on one side and staple the pieces together for use as note and memo pads.
- Purchase and use unbleached office paper with a high-recycled content; if available, 100-percent post-consumer waste is the best.
- Purchase and use ink and toner cartridge refill kits to cut down on waste and save money on cartridge costs. If your printer and toner cartridges are non-refillable, contact the manufacturer about recycling them; most cartridge manufacturers have programs for recycling.
- Edit documents on screen rather than printing draft copies.
- Reduce fax-related paper waste by using a computer fax-modem or scanning and e-mailing documents.
- Turn off lights when not in use and purchase energy-efficient office equipment with power-saving sleep options rather than power-wasting screensavers. Look for Energy Star office equipment.
- Use energy-efficient light bulbs and reusable items, such as rechargeable batteries and mechanical pencils and pens.
- Purchase office supplies in bulk to cut down on packaging waste. Purchase only what you need, regardless of what's on sale.
- Use environmentally friendly packaging materials rather than polystyrene foam peanuts and minimize your use of packing materials.

- Use large windows and skylights to provide light and heating, rather than lights and heating, whenever possible.
- Install insulated windows to keep heat in and cold out, to reduce energy consumption.
- Use workstations and office furnishing built from sustainable, earth-friendly materials.

Additional helpful information and tips about recycling practices and your home business, as well as environmental information, can be found on the North Shore Recycling Program's website at *nsrp.bc.ca*. Green Sites Online, at *greensites.com*, also offers recycling information, resources and links.

RENOVATING YOUR WORKSPACE

If you can use the space that you have selected with only minimal renovations, you are wise to do so. Sometimes, however, you will have to renovate your workspace or other areas of your home to accommodate your new business. This is especially true for professionals setting up practices at home and for people engaged in manufacturing or assembling products at home.

Renovating your workspace can be challenging for a number of reasons. There is the noise and disruption that result. Also, if the renovations are extensive, you'll have to deal with the mess. In addition, there's the time factor. Once you have decided to start a home business, you want to get moving as quickly as possible so you can begin to recoup some of the money you'll be spending. Finally, there's the cost. Renovating is not cheap, especially when you consider that skilled tradespeople charge upward of $50 per hour plus the cost of materials. If you can get by with the workspace you have without renovations, you should do so. However, if you must renovate your home to accommodate your new business, the information in this section should help.

Do It Yourself or Hire a Contractor?

Once you have action and design plans and know exactly what you need, the next step is to decide if you can do the work or if an experienced contractor is necessary. Certainly, if the job is uncomplicated and if you have the time, tools and talents necessary to do the work, by all means do it. It can save you a substantial amount of money on labor costs. If the job is small, but outside your comfort zone, you may be able to hire a local handyperson. If you do so, expect to pay about $40+ per hour plus the cost of materials. If however, your new workspace is a major renovation that includes upgraded mechanicals, removing walls, installing new doors and so forth, you will be well advised to hire a professional contractor.

If you decide to hire a contractor, the following are a few tips:

- Explain the type of business you will be starting and show the contractor your plans, equipment lists and other information relevant to the renovation. Doing so will help the contractor understand what you want and he or she may offer some cost-saving suggestions.
- Obtain three quotes, basing your decision not only on price, but also on value, quality and reputation.
- Call each contractor's references to make sure past clients were satisfied with the jobs. If possible, get a look at a home office the contractor has built or substantially renovated.
- Before selecting a contractor check with your local chapter of the Better Business Bureau to make sure the contractor has no unresolved complaints outstanding. I say "unresolved" because complaints that have been resolved are generally not a sign of trouble, but unresolved complaints usually are.

- Get a contract in writing, signed by both parties. Make sure it specifies the scope of work and all details.

- Obtain proof of liability insurance and workers' compensation insurance from the contractor before the job begins.

- Arrange for favorable payment terms in four installments: 25 percent deposit, 25 percent progress installment, 25 percent on substantial completion and the balance 30 days after full completion of the renovation.

- Inspect materials delivered to the job site before they are used to make sure they are what is specified in the scope of work and contract.

- Know which party is responsible for securing building permits and if the costs of these permits are included in the estimate. This is important. If you renovate without a permit and the required inspections from your local municipality, if any structural, electrical or other mechanical problems arise with the work that has been done, your insurance company may not compensate you if the work was completed illegally.

- Make sure all warranty information is included in the written agreement. The workmanship portion of the warranty should be a minimum of five years from the date of completion.

- Don't be totally focused on cost. Remember: This is a job you want to tackle only once. You may save $500 now by not installing an outside door into your workspace, but if you decide to install one later, the cost can easily be as much as five times what it would have cost when the crew and tools were there for the renovation.

- Make sure your contract specifies a completion date. Some renovation projects have taken far longer than expected. A "finish" date for the job is essential.

Renovation Costs

Whether you plan on doing the required renovations yourself or hiring a contractor, it is wise to have a general idea of the costs associated with the renovation before getting started or asking for quotes and bids on the job. Following is a basic Renovation Costs Worksheet (Figure 7.1) that you can use to estimate the costs of renovating your workspace. Add or delete items according to your specific needs. To arrive at the cost per unit or total cost of some items or services, you will need to make a few calls and visit your local home improvement store to check product prices.

EQUIPPING YOUR WORKSPACE

Equipping your home workspace with the furniture, equipment, technology, communications and supplies you will need to operate your business requires considering three main factors—business needs, personal comfort and budget.

The need for office equipment, furniture, technology and communications varies with the type of business planned. But every business will need at least a few items from each of the five main home workspace categories: furniture, equipment, technology, communications and supplies. Each of these categories is discussed in detail later in the chapter.

The second issue will be comfort, which is of particular concern for home business operators who will be putting in long hours at their desks in front of a computer or on the telephone. You cannot cut corners on comfort. In order to be productive over the long term, you have to be comfortable. In recent years, many new physical ailments, such as carpal tunnel syndrome, have been linked to long hours spent doing repetitive tasks, such as typing at a key-

FIGURE 7.1	Renovation Costs Worksheet

	Quantity	$ Unit Cost	$ Total Cost
❑ Building and inspection permits	_____	$_____	$_____
❑ General construction	_____	$_____	$_____
❑ Finish carpentry	_____	$_____	$_____
❑ Plumbing and heating	_____	$_____	$_____
❑ New or upgraded electrical	_____	$_____	$_____
❑ Security alarms	_____	$_____	$_____
❑ Fire alarms and extinguishers	_____	$_____	$_____
❑ New or upgraded communications capabilities	_____	$_____	$_____
❑ Windows	_____	$_____	$_____
❑ Window coverings	_____	$_____	$_____
❑ Doors and locksets	_____	$_____	$_____
❑ Paint	_____	$_____	$_____
❑ Wall covering	_____	$_____	$_____
❑ Flooring	_____	$_____	$_____
❑ Build-ins	_____	$_____	$_____
❑ Decorations	_____	$_____	$_____
❑ Other _____	_____	$_____	$_____
❑ Other _____	_____	$_____	$_____
	Total		$_____

board. Therefore, you need to focus on the long-term physical effects of improper furniture and lighting. Ergonomics, the study of the correct positioning of your body while at rest or work, can play a major role in ensuring comfort and maintaining good physical health over the long term. When setting up and equipping your home workspace, you will want to ensure it is ergonomically correct. To help you plan, you can purchase a book on ergonomics or visit Ergonomics Online, *ergonomics.org*, which provides in-depth information, links and resources related to ergonomics.

The third main factor when equipping your home workspace is your budget. Here are five ways a financially challenged entrepreneur can substantially reduce the cost of home office furniture, equipment, computers and communication products or minimize the amount of money needed upfront:

1. *Barter.* You can barter and trade for office furniture and equipment. For instance, if you operate a painting service, ask local office suppliers if they would be interested in trading office furniture for a paint job. You can also join a local

barter club and trade whatever products or services you sell with members who sell office furniture and equipment. BarterNews, *barternews. com*, is an online magazine dedicated to the world of business barter clubs, organizations and industry information. There are many barter clubs on the web. To locate a bartering exchange group, check out Bartermax, *bartermax.com* or the International Reciprocal Trade Association, *irta.com*. Or network with other local business owners and see what you can do for each other.

2. *Borrow.* Create a list of all needed office furniture, equipment and supplies you need and distribute copies to friends and family members. You will be amazed at how many of the things that you need to start and run your business are stored away in basements, garages and attics, just waiting to be borrowed. Most of your friends and family members won't mind if you borrow these items. In fact, many will probably be happy to get rid of them and free up some space for more clutter.

3. *Buy seconds or floor models.* Call around to your local office outfitters and inquire about factory seconds and the floor models they have available. Often you can save as much as 25 percent of the retail price by purchasing seconds with slight blemishes or floor models with nothing wrong other than a few fingerprints and smudges.

4. *Purchase secondhand.* Buy used office equipment and furniture and save as much as 75 percent or more off the retail price. Good places to begin your search for used office equipment include auctions, business closeouts, newspaper classifieds, garage sales and retailers that sell secondhand office furniture, equipment and computers. Also look for businesses that are moving or closing; if you find what you want, you can get great discounts.

5. *Lease.* Take the no-money-down route and lease new office furniture, equipment and computers. You will have to pay for these items monthly, but you will not be spending capital to buy them, capital that can be used for marketing. Lease payments can be written off taxes and you will have the use of new equipment with full warranties. The downside of leasing is that you cannot count things you lease as assets. You can also rent furniture and equipment. Definitely rent specialized equipment for select jobs as you need it, so you do not have to spend as much as to purchase it. Be careful when leasing and renting that you do not end up paying more for an item than if you bought it and financed it.

Getting the Office Furniture and Equipment You Need

Every business has different needs for office furniture and equipment. If clients will be visiting your home office, your furniture and equipment will need to reflect this use, both in appearance and function. If you do not have clients visiting your home office, you will have a little more leeway in your equipment and furniture choices. It won't really matter if the colors are mismatched, if you purchased your desk secondhand at your neighbor's garage sale or even if you choose to build a few of the items yourself. All that really matters is that your furniture and equipment do what you need them to do and are reliable and comfortable. So what are the basics that every home workspace needs, regardless of business type?

Desk or Workstation

Depending on the percentage of time you will spend at a desk not working with a computer, you will decide whether you want a traditional desk with a computer on it or a computer table with some desk space. Often, a used desk can serve the purpose. The same holds true with secondhand computer tables, which are often good, low-cost alternatives to new. Either way, the reason you should look for specific computer furniture is because it is designed to be at the right height for computer chairs plus strong and roomy enough to hold computer equipment. Computers have gotten lighter and most chairs are adjustable, making alternatives to computer furniture more feasible than in previous years.

If you need drawers to hold plenty of things at your disposal, but out of site, then by all means find a desk with drawers. If you are comfortable with rolling a couple of filing cabinets under your computer table, than perhaps drawers are unnecessary. Consider that rearranging your workspace is more difficult with older, heavier traditional desks, especially with large drawers that tend to accumulate plenty of junk. Yet some people just don't feel like they are working if they aren't sitting at a big desk. Wooden desks often appear more impressive to clients, which may score points for your business.

When buying a desk, check that the drawers have adequate space for your needs and open and close smoothly. Metal suspension rollers last longer than plastic or other alternatives. The wood and the construction will indicate the quality of the desk. Look underneath and see if the quality of the materials is consistent throughout and not just on the surface. For example, if staples underneath are holding drawers together, it is not a sign of quality. Heavier woods are used in the better desks and the construction is more solid. Also, if a wooden desk has rounded corners, it's more likely a higher-end model. Most office furniture suppliers today sell wooden desks with a laminate finish, which can help the wood resist scratches and dents.

Measure your office space before shopping for furniture, so you will know exactly what will fit. Then, when shopping, measure the height of desks, tables and standing furniture so you know how much room they allow underneath for filing cabinets or other type of storage.

Computer desks are created to position the computer at a comfortable height, assuming the monitor is on a stand. For this reason, desktop computers are preferred for computer desks, since laptops or notebooks can cause back pain if the user is constantly leaning toward the screen. Some people like movable keyboard trays; others don't care. Again, your preference is what matters. Also, keep in mind that unless you are doing computer programming or similar work exclusively, there will be a need for space to do tasks away from the computer. Many people focus all their attention on the position of the computer and tend to forget there will be a need for reference books, papers and a desk lamp. Make sure you leave adequate room for whatever you anticipate needing on the desk—including some open space.

Lastly, take computer wiring into consideration before you make your purchase. Modern desks and computer tables are typically designed for computer wiring. Older desks, however, are not. You will want to position the desk in such a way as to minimize the length of the wires between the desk and the wall. Don't cut into any older desk that has potential value. It's easier to hide wiring in some manner, such as taping it to the bottom of the desk.

Desk Alternatives

If your home office is part of another room, you might opt for creating desk space out of an armoire, a piece of furniture with doors that hide drawers or other storage space. Created specifically for home office use, many armoires allow you to have a workspace with shelves, storage and even a sliding computer keyboard tray in one unit with doors that can be closed when company comes over. Built as work centers, armoires are often equipped with file drawers, adjustable shelves and nooks and crannies for storing supplies. You also want to look for accommodations for computer wiring, which are included in the newest models.

Countertops or other such flat areas are not usually roomy or sturdy enough to be considered as workstations. Some home offices have counters built around part or all of the perimeter, extending far enough to hold a computer and/or a printer, but needing extra reinforcement to support technological equipment. Cutouts in the back can accommodate wiring and drawers can be built. If you have such counters or workstations extending from a wall, measure carefully for both depth and height from the floor. Sit comfortably and see at what height you would like to be working with your feet on the floor.

Comfortable Chair

If you can splurge on only one piece of office furniture, a comfortable and ergonomically correct chair should be that luxury item, especially if your business keeps you in front of the computer or on the telephone for long periods. I endured many uncomfortable chairs until I decided a few years ago to splurge on a comfortable and high-quality chair for my office. All I can say is that I should have done it 10 years earlier. Sitting in an uncomfortable chair all day is like running a marathon in sneakers that are two sizes too small; both will leave you in physical agony.

Key things to check are distance from the seat to floor (or adjustable heights), adjustable armrests and adjustable seating positions. Try chairs out to find one that feels comfortable. You will likely buy a computer chair on wheels, so you can roll it over to a filing cabinet if necessary.

Filing Cabinets

There are plenty of choices when buying filing cabinets, most of which are inexpensive, particularly secondhand. The portable two-drawer cabinets for hanging files are popular, since you can slide one under a computer table or tuck one in a corner and move it when necessary. In fact, some people roll them into their closets when not using them, as they also fit under hanging clothes.

Three- and four-drawer tower files can obviously accommodate more and usually come with options, such as drawers designed to accommodate CD/DVDs. Lateral filing cabinets will work only if you have enough wall space. The disadvantage is that they are heavier to move and require bending to access the files. An advantage is that if they are a good height you can set fax machine and/or printer on top.

If money is tight, you do not have to invest in a file cabinet for client files immediately. Instead, for about $5 you can purchase an accordion-style file storage box that can hold up to about 100 documents. That is enough file storage space to get you going, especially if you purchase one for business records and a second for client files. Obviously, as your business grows, you will want to invest in quality cabinets with locking mechanisms.

Bookshelves

Bookshelves are indispensable for the home workspace. In addition to the obvious use of holding books, they can be used for office supplies, in and out boxes, mail, a radio or CD player, CDs, DVDs and just about anything else you need to be easily accessible. There are numerous office supply websites as well as office supply stores in any major shopping area. Ikea is one place to check for shelving (*ikea.com*) if you don't mind assembling the shelves yourself.

Lighting

As the years roll on, things may get a little more out of focus. Natural lighting from windows and skylights is terrific, but you will also need quality electrical lighting, which can make a huge difference in reducing eyestrain and increasing productivity. In addition to bright overhead lighting, invest a few dollars in a good desk or a clamp-on work lamp that can be positioned to illuminate specific tasks.

Office Furniture and Equipment Costs

Figure 7.2, Office Furniture and Equipment Costs Worksheet, will help you calculate the costs of obtaining furniture and equipment for your workspace. Once again, ignore items that are not relevant to your business and add items that are specific to it.

Getting the Technology You Need

There is basic technology every business needs: a computer, a monitor, an operating system, software, a modem, a printer and a digital camera.

Computer

Assuming you know how to use a computer (if not, sign up for computer training at your local community college), the main considerations will be processing speed and data storage capabilities.

Whether you are planning to buy a desktop computer or intend to use one you already have, you should look for the following:

FIGURE 7.2   Office Furniture and Equipment Costs Worksheet

	Quantity	$ Unit Cost	$ Total Cost
❑ Desk	_____	$_____	$_____
❑ Office chair	_____	$_____	$_____
❑ Client seating	_____	$_____	$_____
❑ File cabinets	_____	$_____	$_____
❑ Bookcases	_____	$_____	$_____
❑ Worktable(s)	_____	$_____	$_____
❑ Work lighting	_____	$_____	$_____
❑ Fireproof safe	_____	$_____	$_____
❑ Storage boxes	_____	$_____	$_____
❑ Photocopier	_____	$_____	$_____
❑ Postage meter	_____	$_____	$_____
❑ Radio or CD player	_____	$_____	$_____
❑ Paper shredder	_____	$_____	$_____
❑ Recycling bin	_____	$_____	$_____
❑ Labeling machine	_____	$_____	$_____
❑ Wastebasket	_____	$_____	$_____
❑ Other _____	_____	$_____	$_____
❑ Other _____	_____	$_____	$_____
		Total	$_____

- At least 1 gigabyte (GB) of RAM
- At least 200, if not 250 or more, gigabytes (GB) of hard drive (the more the better)
- At least 2.3 or 2.8 gigahertz (GHz) processing speed
- At least four USB (universal serial bus) connections for peripherals, typically including a printer and perhaps a scanner
- A DVD drive/burner
- A CD burner
- Windows XP operating system (Vista has thus far not been as "amazing" as billed, which means you can get XP for less money and interface with the many other people who are also not yet taking a chance with Vista)
- An internal modem
- A 3D graphics card, which will allow you to use the latest software programs
- 5.1 Surround Sound (not essential for your purposes, but always a plus for quality sound, such as background music while you're working)
- A firewall and antivirus software (The firewall should be part of your purchasing deal; for antivirus programs, consider PC-cillin, Norton 2008 or another leading anti-virus program.)

The main part of your computer, the processor (aka central processing unit, CPU), is the component that runs the programs. A CPU typically costs between $400 and $1,000 and is usually packaged (or bundled) with a keyboard, a monitor, speakers and a mouse, providing a discount against buying them all separately.

Monitors

For years the typical home computer monitor has been the familiar bulky kind with the big back, resembling a TV. It has that look because it uses a cathode-ray tube (CRT) like the televisions we've

watched for years, with numerous tiny phosphor dots inside the glass tube, each forming a line, with all the lines together creating an image.

The latest trend in monitors is the flat-panel LCD (liquid crystal display) monitor, which uses plasma and light-emitting diodes. While LCD monitors are more technical to explain, they offer a sleeker look than their CRT counterparts. The flat-panel monitors take up less room and are lighter, often weighing less than 20 pounds, far less than CRT monitors, generally weighing 35 to 45 pounds. Here are some basic differences to make shopping for a monitor less confusing:

- LCD monitors cost a little more than CRTs.
- LCD monitors typically have sharper pictures than CRTs, although not sharper colors.
- LCD monitors don't have that occasional flicker that you may sometimes experience on a CRT monitor.
- To see an LCD monitor clearly, you need to be in front of it; otherwise, the image on screen can look distorted. A CRT monitor, however, can be seen clearly from various angles.
- LCD monitors are more energy-efficient than CRT monitors.

Monitors range anywhere from $170 to $2,000, depending primarily on size and clarity. Most people purchase good-quality monitors in the $300 to $700 range. Again, look for a deal or work a deal with the CPU.

Keyboard and Mouse

Studies have shown that ergonomics should play a major role in your decision about what keyboard and mouse to purchase for your computer. The reason is that hand, wrist, arm and shoulder positions are affected by your mouse and keyboard. Each has to be in balance to reduce the potential for injury. You may also want to consider purchasing a wireless keyboard-and-mouse set because it frees space on your desk and eliminates those pesky wires that seem to get wrapped around everything. Plan to spend about $50 to $70 on a keyboard, $20 to $60 on a mouse or $70 to $130 on both. These are very often worked into the cost of the package—CPU, monitor, keyboard and mouse—since it is worthwhile to the seller to get you to buy a slightly better monitor by practically throwing in the keyboard and mouse. Look at package deals, but don't be afraid to ask that one item be changed if you prefer another.

Modem

Most computers now come with a standard 56K modem, which is needed to connect to the internet. You can also opt for a more expensive modem, giving you the ability to connect to high-speed cable internet. This allows you to download files up to 20 times faster than with a dial-up internet connection, which is now becoming a thing of the past.

Wireless Modems

You can opt to go the wireless route with a wireless router. These routers are small and include an antenna. They can be set up in any location in the house, so you can use your computer in any room. It's almost like having your own personal radio station signal tower, only much smaller. From this "hot spot," the wireless connections will go in all directions. Therefore, you may want to select a location that is not only central for your current computer, but also good for a laptop, should you decide to work in other parts of the home. You can also use the router for the computers of family members, although beyond that, I would not opt for networking between a business computer and one being used for computer games. Depending on the speed and distance you need, you can buy a wireless router for anywhere from $25 to $250.

Laptops and Notebooks

If you like working in different places around your office ... or around the house ... or in the backyard, there are many laptop and notebook computers available. Many weigh less than four pounds and are powerful enough to handle the same functions as a desktop, if not more.

The biggest disadvantages of laptop and notebook computers are the smaller screen and keyboard. While this may take getting used to while on the road, in your home office you can use a docking station, which magically turns your laptop into a desktop. No, this has nothing to do with the Starship Enterprise. A docking station is actually a platform into which you can install your portable computer so you can use a full-size monitor, a full-size keyboard, your printer and other peripheral devices.

When you are shopping for a laptop, the same rules apply as for a desktop. The feel of the keys, the size of the screen and the feel of the trackball, TrackPoint™ or touchpad will all be a matter of comfort. How does it look or feel to you? Last, remember: The smaller the components, the higher the prices, so you can expect to pay a little more for a notebook. Popular laptops and notebooks are available from Dell, Hewlett-Packard, Compaq, Toshiba, IBM, Sony, Gateway, Fujitsu, Acer, eMachines and, of course, Apple. You can walk away with a good quality model for around $800.

Printers

There are two types of printers, laser and inkjet. Which one you need will depend on the type of business you are running and your primary need for a printer.

Laser printers are fast, some printing as much as 30 pages per minute. These are strong workhorse printers for someone who has a higher volume of material and needs printed words more than high-quality graphics and photos. Laser printers typically cost between $200 and $700, but cartridges, although not inexpensive, cost less than those for inkjet printers.

Inkjet printers are slower than their laser counterparts, but they can produce a higher level of color than color laser models and are priced lower. The cost of ink, however, will make them higher in the long run. These are printers for businesses that need a higher level of graphic and photographic materials and do not have as high a volume of printed matter. You'll find inkjets for $300 to $500.

Yes, some business owners have both to meet their various needs.

Once you have zeroed in on your printer needs, try a few models in stores and ask friends and neighbors which printers they have bought. It's easy to compare prices online and salespeople will tell you all the positives. However, since printers can be frustrating when they stop working properly, you'll want to get some good reviews and recommendations from people you know and trust.

Popular printer models manufacturers are Canon, Epson, Oki Data, Brother, Lexmark and Hewlett-Packard.

Computer Data Storage

You'll want to stock up on CDs for your computer to store your data and back up all important material. It can't be stressed often enough that you need to back up your files frequently so you do not suddenly lose valuable customer, vendor and personal data if your computer crashes or you have a power outage. You can also use a USB flash drive, which is a small, lightweight, removable and rewritable device used to save computer data, much like disks were used in the past, only sturdier, since disks could get bent or accidentally erased more easily.

Digital Camera

Digital cameras are indispensable to home business owners. You can take pictures of products, clients, completed jobs or your trip to Florida, and then transfer them easily to your website, e-mails or desktop publishing programs. You can easily create brochures, presentations, catalogs and fliers using your own photographs. Good-quality digital cameras cost in the range of $200 to $500. Nikon, Canon, Sony, Panasonic and Olympus USA are among the leading companies making digital cameras.

High-Tech Shopping Tips

When shopping for your high-tech business equipment, it's advantageous to buy from well-known reputable companies that have been in business for some time and will likely still be there should you need them if you have problems with your business equipment. Here are some other general high-tech shopping tips:

- Look for good deals. Don't be afraid to walk away if you are not getting what you need.
- Don't buy into the wealth of features offered on top models, whether it's computers or digital cameras. Look for the functions you need.
- Don't jump at the latest innovations. You can often buy the previously "hottest" items for a better price when the latest models come out. Unless the newest model has a feature you absolutely need, go with last year's model.
- Shop for a good warranty.
- Make sure you get all paperwork that comes with technical equipment and keep it in a safe place.
- Buy from companies and businesses that provide excellent tech support.

Computer Hardware, Accessories and Software Costs

The following Computer Hardware, Accessories and Software Costs Worksheet (Figure 7.3) can help you calculate the costs of equipping your new home workspace with common technology. Ignore items that are not relevant to your business and add items that are specific to your business, as required.

FIGURE 7.3	Computer Hardware, Accessories and Software Costs Worksheet

	Quantity	$ Unit Cost	$ Total Cost
❏ Desk	_____	$_____	$_____
❏ Desktop computer	_____	$_____	$_____
❏ Desktop monitor	_____	$_____	$_____
❏ Keyboard and mouse	_____	$_____	$_____
❏ Modem	_____	$_____	$_____
❏ Notebook or laptop computer	_____	$_____	$_____
❏ Printer	_____	$_____	$_____
❏ PowerPoint projector	_____	$_____	$_____
❏ Palm organizer	_____	$_____	$_____
❏ Scanner	_____	$_____	$_____
❏ Digital camera	_____	$_____	$_____
❏ Surge protector	_____	$_____	$_____
❏ UPS (uninterruptible/universal power supply)	_____	$_____	$_____
❏ Word processing program	_____	$_____	$_____
❏ Accounting software	_____	$_____	$_____
❏ Contact management software	_____	$_____	$_____
❏ Database management software	_____	$_____	$_____
❏ Website building software	_____	$_____	$_____
❏ Website maintenance software	_____	$_____	$_____
❏ E-commerce software	_____	$_____	$_____
❏ Payment processing software	_____	$_____	$_____
❏ Inventory management software	_____	$_____	$_____
❏ Desktop publishing software	_____	$_____	$_____
❏ Multimedia software	_____	$_____	$_____
❏ Antivirus software	_____	$_____	$_____
❏ Other _____	_____	$_____	$_____
❏ Other _____	_____	$_____	$_____
		Total	$_____

Getting the Communication Devices You Need

The proliferation of high-tech communication devices in recent years makes it easy to spend a whole lot of money in a short time. But, once again, if you can get by with just the basic communication devices at first, you can always upgrade to new and better communication devices when your business is generating profits. For basic communication, you will need all or some of the following.

Telephone

If you are going to have a workspace, you'll want to install a separate telephone line or multiline system, depending on the volume of calls you anticipate. Ideally this phone will have business features and functions such as conferencing, redial, speakerphone, call waiting, caller ID and so on. Get what you need if it's not included. The payments can be added to your telephone bill.

Fax Machine

Although fax transmissions have greatly declined in popularity in the last few years as e-mail use has increased, many businesses will still need a fax machine. Most contracts and agreements that must be signed are legal when faxed if both parties agree and it is so stipulated in the contract. If you do not want to purchase a separate fax machine, you can get fax software for your computer.

Cell Phone

It seems that everyone has a cell phone now. They're convenient for anyone who wants to stay in touch and necessary for anyone who needs to do business while away from home.

Shop around for a good rate. Although the newer models have more features, you will primarily need only the basics for communication purposes. You may, however, consider purchasing a cell phone with internet features, as it is conven-ient to be able to check e-mail when you are away from your computer. In fact, cell phones have become so popular and the services and features so varied that many home business owners are also using simple and inexpensive cell phones as their main phone. It's always advisable to have a landline, however, since cell phones drop calls and cell phone batteries tend to need recharging when you need your phone the most. Therefore, have both.

Telephone Headset

A telephone headset will be a definite need if your business keeps you working at a computer all day or if you use a phone in your car. It enables you to use your phone and leaves your hands free to work on the computer or, when you are out of the office and on your cell phone, to drive your car, walk down the street or work in your garden. Headsets, both wired and wireless, are available for both desktop phones and cellular phones. Count on spending $30 to $90 for either type.

Internet Connection

You will need an internet connection. A good internet service provider is a must for anyone in business today. Most internet service providers (ISPs) charge about $20 to $30 per month for broadband, meaning cable or DSL hookup, and give you unlimited web and e-mail access. Dial-up access will cost less, but tie up a phone line, so it can end up costing you more—as well as being too slow for business purposes. Therefore, you need to sign up for cable or DSL.

Communications Costs

The Communications Costs Worksheet (Figure 7.4) will help you calculate the costs of equipping your home workspace with common communication devices. Ignore items that are not relevant to your business and add items that are specific to your business.

FIGURE 7.4 Communications Costs Worksheet

	Quantity	$ Unit Cost	$ Total Cost
❑ Specialty wiring and networking	_____	$_____	$_____
❑ Telephone with business functions	_____	$_____	$_____
❑ Install dedicated telephone line	_____	$_____	$_____
❑ Install dedicated fax line	_____	$_____	$_____
❑ Toll-free line/number	_____	$_____	$_____
❑ Internet connection	_____	$_____	$_____
❑ Cordless telephone	_____	$_____	$_____
❑ Cell phone (perhaps with internet features)	_____	$_____	$_____
❑ Headset	_____	$_____	$_____
❑ Answering machine or service	_____	$_____	$_____
❑ Fax machine (or fax software)	_____	$_____	$_____
❑ Pager	_____	$_____	$_____
❑ Other _____	_____	$_____	$_____
❑ Other _____	_____	$_____	$_____
		Total	$_____

Home Office Library

All successful entrepreneurs share a common trait—they never stop searching for ways to become better businesspeople through education. And because time is always in high demand but short supply, the best way to educate themselves and find information that will make them better businesspeople is by purchasing and reading books, reports, magazines, directories and journals. In fact, most successful businesspeople take pride in their business libraries.

For these reasons, you should start purchasing business-related publications so you can build your own valuable business library. Even with the internet as a powerful research and educational tool, books are handy: you can take them on the plane or read them in bed. They help you check facts quickly, without having to log onto the Net and conduct searches for the information. The internet is an invaluable business tool, but the combination of a well-stocked and varied business library and key websites gives businesspeople access to all the information they need.

You will want to subscribe to journals aimed at your specific business or industry. When you come across ideas in print or on the internet that will work for your business, cut out the article or print the page and place it in an idea folder for later use. Prime topics you should include in your business library include:

- Small business accounting, bookkeeping and taxation
- Sales and marketing
- Business and marketing planning

- Administration and management
- Internet, website building and e-commerce
- Advertising and public relations
- Personal and business goal setting
- Customer service
- Industry, product, service and manufacturers' directories and source books
- Time management and organization

A good source for used books is AbeBooks, *abebooks.com*, which boasts in excess of 45 million used books for sale in every imaginable category. Amazon, *amazon.com*, is a good source for new and used books. PubList.com, *publist.com*, is an online directory listing in excess of 150,000 domestic and international print and electronic publications, including magazines, journals, e-journals and newsletters. Also check with your local library about book sales; most sell titles for a fraction of what they cost new.

HOME BUSINESS SECURITY AND SAFETY

Protecting your family from criminal intrusion and creating a safe working environment should be high on your list of priorities. Unfortunately for home business owners, the most common crime in the United States and Canada is home burglary. The potential loss is even greater for business owners with expensive computer equipment, cash and specialized tools commonly on-site, making residences a tempting target, because experienced burglars know which homes contain businesses.

As a rule of thumb, criminals look for items that are small, valuable and easy to sell, such as notebook computers and digital cameras. Even worse, with the increase in identity theft and e-fraud, your clients could also become crime victims if their financial and confidential information is stolen from your business. For these reasons, all home business owners have to go out of their way to secure their homes and businesses for the pro-

tection of their families, businesses, clients and neighbors.

Building Alliances with Neighbors

One of the simplest and least expensive ways to begin securing your home, family and business is to forge close relationships with your neighbors, so you all can help each other by watching out for suspicious activities. Knock on a few doors and introduce yourself to your neighbors and suggest setting up a simple neighborhood watch, if there is none already in place. Establish a system so that when residents are away their neighbors will pick up their mail and park in their vacant driveways so the home seems occupied. Property crimes can be greatly reduced when neighbors report suspicious activities to the local police. And most police departments have information available about how to set up neighborhood watch programs; some even have neighborhood watch programs in place already.

It helps to keep shrubs and trees trimmed back from your exterior entrances and window areas, to make your home more visible from the street and from your neighbors' homes so they can keep an eye on your property and you can watch their properties.

Home Security Alarms

The next logical step in protecting your family and business is to purchase and install a good quality, monitored home alarm system complete with glass-break detectors, interior motion detectors and window and door contact point detectors. Home security alarms provide three major deterrents to theft. The small alarm company sign that can be displayed around the outside of the home informs thieves the home is protected. There are also window and door stickers to reinforce this message, which is another deterrent. Last, the alarm that blasts an ear-piercing screech after a contact point has been disrupted or a motion detector triggered is definitely a deterrent.

You can buy home surveillance systems that are hooked up to a digital video recorder and installed for less than $500.

Most home alarm companies offer free, comprehensive written quotations. Be sure to get three, so you can compare features, benefits, and costs of having the alarm system installed and the monthly monitoring fee. There are also monitored alarm systems available that detect smoke and carbon monoxide, as well as break-ins. Two major players in the home security industry are ADT Security Services, *adt.com*, and Brinks Home Security, *brinkshomesecurity.com*. Both companies offer numerous home alarm systems and monitoring options that can be tailored to individual needs and financial budgets.

Securing Doors and Windows

In over 70 percent of home thefts, entrance was gained through a door or window using no more than a simple screwdriver or pry bar. Consequently, you want to beef up locks, consider installing heavy-duty entrance doors, and take a few other simple measures that will make your home less of a target for theft and more secure for your family and business.

Entrance Doors

If your home or apartment does not currently have steel or solid wood entrance doors, you should consider upgrading to heavy-duty steel doors. It is a wise investment that not only can help keep your home secure, but also can be a business tax deduction if the improvements are made in conjunction with starting your home business. Deadbolts can be installed to prevent entrance by means of twisting or prying on locks and jambs. These heavy-duty locks are not expensive, easy to install and are available at your local hardware store.

Patio Doors

Sliding glass doors, commonly known as patio doors, are another easy entrance point for thieves, mainly because of inferior and defective locks. The doors are also easily lifted from their tracks. However, if you spend just a few dollars on an anti-lift device, such as a pin that extends through both the sliding and fixed portion of the door track at the bottom, you can make it impossible for an outsider to slide the door open or lift it from the track. Locking pins are cheap, quick to install with basic hand tools and available at any hardware store.

Windows

Windows make easy entrance points for brazen thieves; windows are often left open for ventilation in warmer weather, making a thief's job that much easier. Ground-floor windows, of course, are more susceptible to break-ins; upper-floor windows become attractive targets if they can be accessed from stairs, a tree, a fence or an extension ladder left lying beside the house. Most windows have basic latches instead of keyed locks, but the addition of simple blocks and pin locks can prevent an outsider from prying windows up, out or over. They are easy to install, cheap and available at your local hardware store. You can also install security bars on the windows. But be cautious here: the design of some window bars can prevent people inside the home from escaping through the window in case of emergency.

Security Lighting

Indoor and outdoor lighting plays a major role in home security, especially when darkness makes your home more vulnerable to burglars. You should purchase and install good-quality exterior lighting with motion detectors to keep the outside of your home illuminated at night as needed. Motion-sensitive lights will serve a dual purpose. First, when thieves approach your home, a sudden light may surprise them into fleeing. Second, a motion-sensitive light makes it safer for you to enter your home. Exterior motion-detector lights are inexpensive, approximately $50 each, and can be installed in a few minutes by novices with nothing more than basic hand tools.

Interior lighting is important, as it indicates activity inside your home. If it's dark, especially for extended periods of time, burglars are likely to assume nobody is home. To confuse burglars, you can purchase inexpensive light timers and connect them to key interior lighting visible through front and back windows. When interior lights come on and turn off at various times, it appears that someone is home, which is the number-one deterrent to thieves.

Going High Tech

The latest in high-tech home integration packages, with HD CCTV (high-definition closed-circuit TV), can provide clear photos of who is outside your front door or on your property—and even send you photographs via e-mail. If you prefer to watch your home over your cell phone, the Motorola Q Phone is one cell phone that gives you that possibility. Full-integration technology can now allow you to see visitors at your front door either on your computer or even, if you are away from your desk, on your laptop or notebook. The latest devices also allow you to regulate lighting from afar via your computer, so if you are away for a few days, you can still turn the lights on from time to time and get alerts if anyone is on your property, so you can call the local police if necessary. Ask security companies in your area about home integration technology.

Home Office Safes

Purchasing and installing a safe is another way a home business owner can protect his or her valuables and important personal and business documents. There are various styles of home office safes available at many price points: flush wall-mounted safes, portable lockbox safes, floor-mounted safes and safes that are disguised as pieces of office furniture and equipment. Ideally, you want a safe with a long burn rating and one that can be securely anchored to the floor or in a wall to prevent thieves from stealing the safe to get its contents. In addition to cash, safes can be used to store key client files on disk, business documents such as incorporation papers, backup CDs of customer data, insurance policies, personal and family documents and copies of important documents, such as your will or your drivers' license.

You should do a little research to determine which safe will best meet your specific needs. You can learn more about home business safes, features and costs by visiting these websites:

- Liberty Safe & Security Products, *libertysafe.com*
- Sentry Group, *sentrysafe.com*
- Gardall Safe Corporation, *gardall.com*
- Hidden Safes, *hiddensafes.com*
- American Security Products, *amsecusa.com*

Fire Safety

Like property and personal security, fire safety is another high-priority issue for home business owners. While having sufficient fire insurance is certainly a must, it is not the sole answer to all fire safety concerns. The following are a few tips to help protect your family and your business:

- Carry sufficient fire insurance.
- Install hardwired smoke detectors with a battery backup system on each floor and in the home office.
- Install emergency battery-powered lighting in hallways and stair corridors.

- Purchase fire extinguishers and keep them in key areas of the home, such as the kitchen, your home office and the upstairs hall closet.
- Install carbon monoxide detectors.
- Install second-story fire safety ladders or ropes.
- Purchase fireproof lock boxes for important business and personal documents.
- Develop an emergency fire plan and make sure all family members know it well. It should include an exit strategy for each room of the house, contingency exit points in case of fire blocks, and a central meeting place outside, at a safe distance.

To find out more about fire safety, visit the U.S. Fire Administration website at *usfa.fema.gov*. On the site you will find fire safety tips for your home and business.

Home Office Safety

In addition to security and fire concerns, you want to ensure that your home office is a safe working environment for you, your family and visitors. Believe it or not, the vast majority of preventable accidents and injuries happen at home, not on the highways, so take extra precautions to make sure that you develop and maintain a safe working environment. Here are a few great tips to help you:

- Keep emergency numbers for the police, ambulance and fire department in a visible place by the telephone.
- All electrical outlets should be the grounded, three-pronged type. It's easy and inexpensive to switch from ungrounded outlets to grounded outlets, which are readily available at hardware stores everywhere.
- Use surge protectors to protect expensive computer equipment against voltage spikes in your electricity service. You can also get an

uninterruptible/universal power supply (UPS), so you're prepared in the event of a power outage. This will keep your computer running so you can close down all important files rather than losing them.

- Do not store toxic materials, such as paints and cleaners, in your home office.
- Secure top-heavy or unstable furniture and equipment such as file cabinets firmly to the floor or walls.
- Avoid loose wiring. Make sure all wiring, cables and extension cords are secured to the walls or floor.
- Keep a flashlight in an easily accessible location in case of power outages.

HOME OFFICE FURNITURE, EQUIPMENT AND SUPPLIES

Here is a handy checklist to help you determine the furniture, equipment and supplies you will need (Figure 7.5). This checklist is comprehensive; chances are you will not need everything featured on it. If your budget is a concern, you can prioritize the items and purchase what you need most to get the business generating revenues and profits right away and then purchase the other items as you earn.

BUILDING A POSITIVE BUSINESS IMAGE

The majority of home business owners do not have the advantage of elaborate offices or elegant storefronts to wow prospects and impress customers. Instead, they must rely on imagination, creativity, and attention to the smallest detail when creating and maintaining a professional business image.

Yes, there are disadvantages in operating a business from home in terms of projecting a positive and professional business image, but these disad-

FIGURE 7.5   Home Office Furniture, Equipment and Supplies Checklist

Office Furniture and Equipment

❑ Desk	❑ Comfortable chair	❑ Filing cabinets
❑ Work/computer table(s)	❑ Overhead and work lighting	❑ Client seating
❑ Fireproof safe	❑ Desktop and pocket calculators	❑ Bookcases
❑ Postage meter	❑ Wall whiteboard and markers	❑ Storage boxes
❑ Label maker	❑ Photocopier	❑ Radio
❑ Paper shredder	❑ Air conditioner	❑ Wastebasket
❑ Insulated windows	❑ Recycling bin	❑ Desktop fan
❑ Space heater	❑ Outside courier delivery box	❑ Home alarm system
❑ Fire extinguisher	❑ Telephone Yellow Pages	❑ Smoke director
❑ Telephone White Pages	❑ Rechargeable flashlight	❑ Office decorations
❑ Business and industry directory	❑ Reference books and product catalogs	

Computer Hardware and Accessories

❑ Desktop computer, keyboard, mouse and monitor	❑ Surge protector	❑ UPS
	❑ Printer	❑ Scanner
❑ Notebook or laptop computer	❑ Modem	
❑ Wireless router	❑ PowerPoint projector	
❑ Palm organizer	❑ Digital camera	
❑ USB flash drive	❑ Computer and equipment manuals	

Computer Software   Specific Program or Brand

❑ Word processing program   _____

❑ Accounting software   _____

❑ Contact management software   _____

❑ Database management software   _____

❑ Website building software   _____

❑ Website maintenance software   _____

❑ E-commerce software   _____

❑ Payment processing software   _____

❑ Inventory management software   _____

❑ Delivery tracking software   _____

FIGURE 7.5   Home Office Furniture, Equipment and Supplies Checklist, continued

❑ Desktop publishing software   _____
❑ Multimedia software   _____
❑ Antivirus software   _____
❑ CD storage case   _____
❑ Fireproof lock box (disks)   _____
❑ Industry-specific software programs _____

Home Office Communications

❑ Dedicated telephone line	❑ Internet connection	❑ Dedicated fax line
❑ Toll-free line/number	❑ Cordless telephone	❑ Fax machine
❑ Answering machine/service	❑ Cordless headset	❑ Speakerphone
❑ Cell phone (possibly with internet features)		❑ Pager
❑ Tape recorder	❑ Telephone (possibly multiline) with business features and functions	

Home Office General Supplies

❑ Business cards (paper)	❑ Business cards (CDs)	❑ Envelopes
❑ Promotional items (e.g., pens)	❑ Mailing labels	❑ Letterhead
❑ Postage stamps	❑ CD	❑ DVD
❑ Index cards	❑ Printer cartridges	❑ In box
❑ Out box	❑ Pens	❑ Pencils/erasers
❑ Accordion files	❑ File folders	❑ File labels and tabs
❑ Markers	❑ Hanging files	❑ Pencil holder
❑ Pencil sharpener	❑ Printer paper	❑ Note pads
❑ Fax paper	❑ Paper clips	❑ Hole puncher
❑ Stapler/staples/staple remover	❑ Paper cutter	❑ Packing tape
❑ Tape	❑ Rubber bands	❑ Glue
❑ Ring binders	❑ Scissors	❑ Cleaning supplies

vantages can be easily overcome and often turned into competitive advantages. In most instances, your startup costs will be lower than those of a similar business that operates from a commercial office or storefront. Therefore, you can spend more to project your image. This means putting more money into brochures, promotional materials, public relations, customer service and descriptive advertising campaigns. Since you do not commute, you have extra time and money to prospect, build strong relationships with customers and develop business and marketing plans. Your overhead will most likely be a fraction of what competitors are paying to maintain commercial office space or storefronts, so you can devote some of the money you save into more productive activities to attract new clients—advertising, product demonstrations and trade show marketing. You may also want to set aside some of the money you saved to incorporate or form a limited liability company right from the start.

Logos and Slogans

Logos and slogans can brand your business and build consumer awareness of your business, products or services in a simple and easy-to-remember manner. Good slogans have been used effectively to communicate a message as attention spans are getting shorter. Logos provide visual images that can serve as imprints for businesses. Visual images are powerful tools that people remember. They can also transcend language barriers.

Of course, the key here is consistency. Once you have decided on a logo design and a promotional or descriptive slogan, you must consistently incorporate these into every aspect of your business. Branding requires time. The more often consumers are exposed to your brand, the more they will remember it, giving you brand recognition.

Business logos and promotional slogans play a major role in branding, especially logos because we recognize them as soon as we see them. You see the "swoosh" and you instantly think Nike. You see the golden arches and McDonald's instantly comes to mind. You hear or read "like a good neighbor" and think State Farm Insurance. This is what logos and slogans do: They act as beacons in the swirling fog of competition to attract consumers instantly to brands they know, like and trust.

Slogans are straightforward to develop. Simply think about the biggest benefit that people receive

from doing business with you. Build a slogan around that benefit. Then, keep editing until you have a few powerful words that perfectly sum up your big benefit and are easy to remember. No, it's not necessarily easy. If it were, advertising agencies wouldn't make millions of dollars coming up with slogans. You also need a slogan that is not being used by another company.

Logos can be tricky to create unless you have design experience. Fortunately, there are many logo and business image design services that will be more than happy to help you create a professional logo for your business—a logo that makes sense and builds brand awareness. Logo design starts at about $50 and can go as high as a few hundred dollars, depending on your needs. Make sure your logo is not being used by another business. You can copyright your slogan and trademark your logo once you are happy with what you have created.

Listed below are a few online logo design services to get you on your way to creating a powerful business image through instant brand identification:

- Logo Design, *logodesign.com*
- LogoBee, *logobee.com*
- The Logo Company, *thelogocompany.net*
- OnlineLogo.com, *onlinelogo.com*
- E-Logo Design, *e-logodesign.com*

Print Identity Package

Your print identity package is composed of the print elements that you use daily in your business—business cards, letter stationery, receipts, envelopes, estimate forms, presentation folders, marketing brochures, catalogs, simple fliers and account statements. High-quality printing is well worth the extra expense, especially for home business owners. Even though high-quality printing on heavy stock paper may be more expensive than a standard print job, it is still relatively cheap when compared with other overhead expenses, such as office rent, that home business owners do not have to pay. Therefore, you can spend a little extra on items that will project a positive business image.

The key to a great print identity package is consistency throughout the entire package, just as in your entire marketing program. You want to develop a standard color scheme, logo, slogan and type of font, and use these consistently so customers and prospects visually link your business with your identity program. Use colors and a design appropriate for your business and your clients. For example, you might use brighter colors and a more youthful design if you are selling children's toys than you would as a legal consultant.

Consult your local telephone directory for printers near you or ask other business owners for recommendations. Remember to obtain three quotes for all your printing needs. Do not decide on price alone. Instead, base your purchasing decision on quality, value, reputation and turnaround time. You can also visit the PrintUSA website at *printusa.com* to get free online printing quotes for hundreds of business products, from mouse pads to business cards and everything in between.

Website

Whether you are handling e-commerce or not, your business needs a web presence. In simple terms, you need a website.

The type and complexity of the site will depend on the type of business you are running and your budget. If, for example, you are running a local tutoring service, you may need only a simple web page that provides your basic information. In this case, you can probably design a workable site yourself with a web design program or through Yahoo!

or another search engine. However, if you intend to engage in business through your website, the design should be professional. You want it to sell merchandise, present content that interests and/or informs visitors and promote your business and whatever you're selling.

Your online presence is a very important aspect of your overall business and marketing strategy and you should treat it as such. Again, consistency is one of the keys to success. You want your offline business and your online business image to be uniform and appropriate. This is not to say that you or someone you know cannot design and build your website. However, for a more complex site, with a shopping cart or other such functions, you should bring in a professional web designer.

Whatever you decide, take the time to plan carefully how you want the site to look, how you want it to work and how you expect it to achieve your business and marketing objectives. In Chapter 17, "Internet and E-Commerce," you will find additional information, resources and tips about building, hosting and maintaining a website and using it to market your business and its products and/or services.

Communications

Communications systems and devices play a major role in projecting a positive and professional business image. You can use communications to project your business as much larger and to reach more prospects, especially when you consider the following simple communications tips that every home entrepreneur can use:

- Install a dedicated business telephone line and promote the number in all marketing activities and business correspondence.
- Purchase and carry a cell phone so important clients can keep in constant communication with you and vice versa. Poor access is always

one of the biggest complaints in any customer service survey.

- Provide customers with a toll-free calling option for inquiries and product orders. This option makes your business appear larger, especially when the toll-free number is featured in all your advertising.
- Always return telephone messages and e-mails the same day when possible, especially to your best customers and your hottest prospects. Never wait longer than 48 hours.
- If you operate a service business, use an answering service to take after-hours calls. You can also use a voice-mail system, since people are now more comfortable leaving messages. Answering machines, while they serve the purpose, do not project the same business image. However, for a part-time business or a business run primarily via e-mails, an answering machine with a business message (not recorded by your kids) will usually be sufficient.
- Record promotional on-hold messages featuring special offers or information on new products or services so you can take advantage of the time prospects or customers are placed on hold. Be careful not to overdo it or you will turn customers off.

Powerful Image-Building Business Letters

People receive lots of letters, especially business-people and professionals. If you want your business letters to attract attention and achieve your objectives, you must get to the point quickly and have a clear and concise message.

Start by letting your reader know right away what's in it for him or her. What will he or she get by continuing to read your letter? Write in short paragraphs, using subheadings for each new section to ensure that skimmers get the message and stay engaged and interested. Perhaps most impor-

tant, write from the reader's viewpoint. Anticipate questions, concerns and objections the reader might have and try to answer them. Here are a few more tips for writing powerful business letters:

- Write a first draft, wait a day, and then review it. Often you will notice points that you want to expand—or delete.
- Include a call to action: e.g., "Give me a call" or "Visit my website" or "Stop by our trade show booth."
- Avoid technical words or explanations. Use basic, easy-to-understand language. Never make your reader work or think too hard to understand your points.
- Edit and proofread for errors at least twice before sending.
- At the bottom of all written communications, include a postscript (P.S.) that restates the main theme of your message and the big benefit for the reader if he or she takes action and responds to your communication.

E-Mails

The world is e-mail crazy, with employees sending e-mails to co-workers 50 feet away and family members sending e-mails from room to room in the same house. While it is not always the best means of communication, since they consist of words alone without intonation or expressions and gestures, e-mail is a strong means of communicating business messages quickly and inexpensively.

Word all e-mails to clients and customers carefully, as if they were business letters, and take the time to proofread for errors and typos. Here are a few other tips for business e-mails:

- Do not send unsolicited e-mails to prospective customers. Make sure you have permission to use their e-mail addresses before sending.
- Use your business name in the From line so

that people become familiar with your company and don't see just your name.

- Don't use acronyms, such as LOL (laughing out loud) and other lingo.
- Don't use all caps. It's considered the same as shouting.
- Keep your messages brief, professional and to the point. Don't ramble.
- If replying to an e-mail question, inquiry or complaint, address the sender's situation first and respond appropriately. Resist the urge to sell until after you've addressed the issue.
- Don't continue endless threads. Start a new e-mail or, if you are returning an e-mail, delete the older text that is no longer necessary. Change the Subject line to make it appropriate to the current communication.
- If you have a spam filter on, check your spam inbox briefly on occasion to make sure nothing you need got routed there. Then delete all of the unwanted spam you received.

E-mails are a very common means of communication now. However, there are some matters that merit picking up the phone or meeting in person. Try to judge accordingly, based on the nature and significance of the message to be communicated.

Dress for Success and Uniforms

You may hate them, but stereotypes sell. Resist the urge to stand out or make a statement in terms of how you dress for work. Leave fashion trends to the Hollywood types. Society in general has expectations about the way businesspeople and professionals should dress. We expect doctors to be in white lab coats, mechanics in coveralls and bankers in business wear. It stands to reason that if you want to make the sale, don't let your choice of business fashion be an obstacle. Dress for success

by wearing what the majority of your customers expect you to be wearing. If their expectation is a suit, wear a suit. If it is smart casual, wear smart casual. If it is a uniform, wear a uniform.

Enter Business Competitions

Winning business, product and customer service awards is a fantastic way to earn credibility, attract new business and build a great business image and reputation. This is especially important for service providers, who often build their entire sales and marketing campaign around trust, reliability, credibility and a good reputation. Just about every community, city and state has some sort of annual business competition classified by type, sector or industry. Often these business excellence awards and competitions are sponsored and administered by local business groups such as the Chamber of Commerce, the economic committee of local government or even local newspapers, radio and TV stations. Many industry associations hold annual best-of-business award ceremonies. It is more than worthwhile to take the time to enter your business.

Check with community business groups, your local newspaper and industry associations for competitions and awards appropriate for your business. Study the details of each and then apply or get nominated for the ones that interest you and that offer the best opportunities to benefit your business. The publicity and free advertising that winning can generate are priceless and the marketing opportunities associated with being the best are limitless.

Custom Postcards

Another great way to project a positive business image is with custom-designed postcards emblazoned with your company name, logo and promotional message. Not only do they scream professionalism, but also they are a terrific way to keep in touch with current customers and new prospects. In bulk, custom-printed postcards can be designed and printed for less than 10 cents each, making them less expensive than sending an ordinary run-of-the-mill sales letter. Use the postcards to promote a new product or service or just to let customers know that you are thinking of them.

RESOURCES
Associations

American Home Business Association
965 East 4800, Suite 3C
Salt Lake City, UT 84117
(866) 396-7773
homebusinessworks.com

National Association of Professional Organizers
15000 Commerce Parkway, Suite C
Mount Laurel, NJ 08054
(856) 380-6828
napo.net

National Association of Women Business Owners (NAWBO)
8405 Greensboro Drive, Suite 800
McLean, VA 22102
(800) 55-NAWBO (556-2926)
nawbo.org

Small Office Home Office Business Group (SOHO)
1680 Lloyd Avenue, Suite 1
North Vancouver, BC V7P 2N6
(604) 929-8250 or (800) 290-SOHO (7646)
soho.ca

Suggested Reading

Allen, David. *Ready for Anything: 52 Productivity Principles for Work and Life.* New York: Viking Press, 2003.

Carter, David E., and Suzanna MW Stephens. *American Corporate Identity 2008.* New York: Collins Design (HarperCollins Publishers), 2007.

Kanarek, Lisa. *Home Office Life: Marking a Space to Work at Home.* Gloucester, MA: Rockport Publishers, 2001.

Allen, David. *Getting Things Done: The Art of Stress-Free Productivity.* New York: Viking (Penguin Putnam), 2001.

Websites

Apple Computers: Wide range of computers and peripherals. *apple.com*

Best Buy: Wide range of computers, printers, digital cameras, etc. *bestbuy.com*

CNet: Comprehensive website for reviews and vendors of every type of technology. **cnet.com**

Dell Computers: Wide range of computers and peripherals. **dell.com**

DigitalCameraInfo.com: Comparisons, reviews and data. **digitalcamerainfo.com**

Download Superstore: Business software with shareware downloads. **downloadsuperstore.com**

Ergonomics Online: Ergonomics information, articles, industry links and resources. **ergonomics.org**

Gateway Computers: Wide range of computers and peripherals. **gateway.com**

Hewlett-Packard: Printers, computers, etc. **hp.com**

Ikea: Retailer of home office furniture. **ikea.com**

Office by Design: Retailer of home office furniture and design services. **officebydesign.com**

Office Depot: Office supplies, furniture and equipment. **officedepot.com**

OfficeFurniture.com: Retailer of home office furniture. ***officefurniture.com***

Office Max: Office supplies, furniture and equipment. ***officemax.com***

PC Magazine: Leading authority on all technical equipment. ***pcmag.com***

PopPhoto.com: Buying guide for digital and all other cameras. ***popphoto.com***

PowerHomeBiz.com: Home business information portal. ***powerhomebiz.com***

Staples: Office supplies, furniture and equipment. ***staples.com***

Steve's Digicams: Detailed revews and comparisons of digital cameras and related devices. ***stevesdigicams.com***

WorkSpaces: Information, advice and links on setting up, organizing and furnishing a home office. ***workspaces.com***

CHAPTER 8

Building Your Business Team

BUILDING YOUR BUSINESS TEAM IS JUST AS important as any other step in starting a home business and generally much more involved than new entrepreneurs even realize. Your business team has five divisions: the front-line business team, employees and agents, trade accounts, professional services and alliances.

I have purposely left out the most important member of your business team—your customers. I have chosen to place customer issues in Chapter 10, "Finding and Keeping Customers," and Chapter 12, "Creating a Marketing Plan." That approach keeps the information together. Customer information can then be directly linked to research, customer service issues and your marketing plan, rather than spread throughout the book.

Homebased Business Team: Outline

Group 1. Front-Line Business Team
- Your family
- Your friends
- Your neighbors
- Your pets

Group 2. Employees and Agents
- Hired full-time and part-time employees, including contractors and freelancers
- Sales agents

Group 3. Trade Accounts
- Product and service suppliers
- Vendors

Group 4. Professional Services
- Lawyers
- Accountants
- Bankers
- Insurance agents/brokers
- Consultants

Group 5. Alliances
- Business and industry associations
- Community businesspeople
- Government agencies
- Media personnel
- Business and competitor partnerships

As you can see from the outline, your business team is very comprehensive and broad. Consequently, you have to develop a plan that addresses how you will build your business team, the players to be involved, and how you will maintain and grow it for your benefit, the benefit of your business and the benefit of your business team members. In fact, all successful businesses share a common denominator—every person involved with the business benefits in his or her own way from that involvement.

BUILDING YOUR FRONT-LINE BUSINESS TEAM

I like to refer to your front-line business team as the people (and pets) affected most immediately by your decision to start and operate a homebased business—your family members, your pets, your friends and your neighbors.

Working with Your Family at Home

Your front-line business team consists of your family members, especially the ones sharing your home with your business. Of course, you may not have a family, in which case your team may consist of others living in your home, such as a significant other or a roommate, so some of the following will be applicable. If you are living alone, we'll address your needs later in this chapter.

If you have a family, your business will affect everyone in the household and everyone in the household will affect your business. This is inevitable. Consequently, the goal of the business owner is twofold.

First, you must have the support of the family for the venture. Not necessarily 100-percent support, but enough that they understand the reason why you want to start such a business and are supportive.

Second, you have to develop ground rules for the benefit of both your family and your business.

For example, the home workspace is off limits for anything but work; no bending or breaking this rule. If possible, set regular work hours so your business does not also become your entire life. If you have young children and they are home during busy or important business days, you'll need to hire a babysitter or nanny to take care of them. If you have older children, set rules about not interrupting your business unless there is something urgent—and review what "urgent" means. Of course, working from home allows you to take an hour off in the afternoon to spend with your kids after school, if you so choose. All in the family will have to adjust to the new living/work situation and make compromises, and perhaps even a few sacrifices, such as lost living space, no loud music and no gang of friends over after school. But as long as there is an open discussion before starting the business, so all family members can voice concerns and make suggestions, none of these small challenges will be insurmountable.

I offer two final pieces of advice in terms of your home business and your family. Don't be upset if your family members do not share your level of enthusiasm for your new business. Remember that in most cases the new business will be your dream, not theirs. As in any new business venture, there are inherent financial risks, which may make some of your family members very nervous. Perhaps more important, do not view your family members, especially the ones living at home, as a pool of temporary help or assume that they will want to work in the business now or in the future. The decision whether or not to work in the family business must be left up to each member to decide, free of pressure from you.

The Single Homebased Business Owner

Being on your own clearly allows you the freedom to set up and run the business any way you choose, since you are not interfering with anyone else's lifestyle. However, your living situation may change as a significant other spends more time at your home or you get married and/or have or adopt children.

So you will want to structure your business in such a way that it does not take over your home and "become your home." There are examples of people living in homes that have become one massive office space or even a warehouse. One woman ran a lampshade business in New York City from a one-bedroom apartment and soon she could barely be seen in the warehouse of lampshades that was once a apartment. Without others around to say, "Leave me some space," she lost sight of having a living area.

It is very important if you're single, divorced or widowed to leave yourself some place to walk away from your business, take breaks and enjoy other aspects of your life. Often, someone who is very enthusiastic and living alone will soon be working round the clock. Do not let this happen to you.

Friends and the Home Business

People who do not work from home, like many of your friends, tend to believe that if you are home during the day, you are not really working. You are definitely available for whatever reason: a quick chat, a game of golf or a movie. While this perception is slowly changing as telecommuting and home businesses grow rapidly, some of those who are not also running businesses from their homes may not get it completely. Therefore, you will have to clearly spell out to your friends in no uncertain terms that you will be operating a business and that you are not simply hanging around in your pajamas all day watching soaps, snacking and taking naps. You do not have to be mean-spirited when you explain, just firm and directly to the point.

Even after more than a decade of working from home, on occasion friends still call or stop by during working hours to ask if I want to join them in whatever activity they are doing that day. When I am swamped, it can be very frustrating to take the time out and once again explain that I am working. I tell you this because once you start working from home, you will experience similar interruptions and you will need to learn to be firm and say no. Do not yield to the temptation to play hooky occasionally. It can easily become habitual, especially when you are the boss and you do not have anyone to keep your nose pressed to the grindstone but yourself.

Of course, one of the reasons for working from home is to set up your own schedule. Many home-based business owners take a specific hour daily to go to the gym, meet friends for lunch or do something that they enjoy. You can do that; after all, you are in control. You may put in the same number of hours as your friends in their jobs—even more, since you are working while they are commuting, *but* you can make your own hours. Therefore, you can leave work between noon and 1:30 every day to for a visit to the gym and a quick lunch or for a yoga class or whatever you choose. Then you can work from 5:30 to 7 p.m. if you like, while office workers are on the train or the bus or in their cars on the commute home. Remember: be strict with your personal schedule, but build it to suit your needs.

Working with Pets at Home

Don't consider your pet a potential disadvantage to working from home. In fact, if you do not currently have a pet, consider this the opportune time to get one. Sure, working from home with a pet under foot or always under the desk occasionally creates a challenge, as does the odd awkward moment when clients visit and are greeted by a barking dog or a cat that likes to rub up against legs. But there are many advantages to having a pet at home while you work, including these:

- If you have a dog, you have a reason not to become a workaholic. Schedule two or three walk times per day. This allows you to get out and get some exercise and a much-needed break from work.
- Pets can be great companions, especially for home business owners who are accustomed to working in a busy office atmosphere. Don't feel silly if you catch yourself talking to Fido or Mimi about business-related issues. If they answer you, however, you know it's probably time for human contact again.
- As mentioned in Chapter 7, "Establishing Your Home Workspace," dogs also provide for a great sense of security. Home business owners have real concerns about security because the expensive equipment and cash around the home provides a great temptation for thieves. However, a barking dog will scare off even the most brazen burglar.

As you can probably tell, I am a big fan of dogs. My 100-pound Rottie, Dana, spends most of her time under the desk in my home office and I often take her with me when I go to see clients. In fact, many clients call and request that I bring her along so they can visit.

There are some legitimate concerns in terms of working from home with pets, but all are manageable:

- Keep your pet out of your office and the door closed when you're on the telephone.
- Keep your pet in the yard or in another area of your home when clients come to visit. Not everyone will share your enthusiasm for your pet and lots of people have allergies to pet dander.
- Don't leave anything lying around in your workspace that your pet could take and/or destroy or that could potentially harm it.
- Pets like to be on a schedule. Try to feed your pet at the same time of the day, walk it at the

same time and set aside a little play time so that it does not get bored and terrorize you while you work.

If you have a cat, it can fit comfortably on your lap or sit next to you on the windowsill while you work. However, cats can sometimes take a stroll across your keyboard, which can result in poorly planned sentences or internet searches to places you don't want to go. Don't fear: the software program called PawSense can cat-proof your keyboard. For more information go to *pawsense.com*.

Keeping the Neighbors Happy

The neighbors living beside you, behind you, above you, below you, across the street, down the road and even a few blocks away also have to be considered as part of your business team because your homebased business could have an impact on their lives. As soon as you tell neighbors you are starting a business that will be operating from home, many or most will immediately think of negatives. If neighbors decide they want to make it tough on you because you are operating a home business, they can. And some will if you do not go out of your way from the start to appease all parties. To keep the peace with your neighbors, you must address certain issues, even if your property is zoned for a homebased business.

Exterior Signage

If you are going to install exterior signage, choose wisely and carefully consider how your signage impacts your neighbors. Will they be able to see it from their windows? If it is a lit sign, will it shine in their windows? Is the type of sign appropriate for the neighborhood? Regarding signage, you should meet with your neighborhood association (or co-op or condo board) to review its guidelines. Many neighborhoods will prohibit any type of signage, other than the signs for a professional, such as a doctor, dentist or therapist.

You will have to respect such rules and regulations if your neighborhood association has explained them and is not open to a compromise solution.

Parking

Another issue that you will have to address with your neighbors is parking, especially if you expect lots of deliveries and client visits. Ideally, you want to contain parking for your business within your own property and keep it off the road. You will also not want delivery vans or larger trucks with noisy diesel motors idling for long periods of time while they drop off or pick up materials. If you anticipate the need for many delivery services coming and going, you may need to set up a postal box or have another location to handle shipping.

Visiting Clients

You will also need to set some "open hours" for visiting clients so your neighbors are not disturbed late into the evening or on Sundays. Try to schedule client visits during the hours that most of your neighbors will be at work. If necessary, create a waiting area in your hallway or foyer where they can sit and wait their turn. Better yet, space visits out so you minimize inconveniences. You will also have to clearly identify your business and the access to your workspace so clients and other visitors to your business do not wander around your neighborhood trying to find you, disturbing your neighbors.

Pollution

Without question, noise and airborne pollution will be two of the biggest concerns your neighbors are likely to have about your business. Therefore, you have to make sure that you eliminate the potential for any type of pollutant. Install extra insulation to reduce noise transfer or build fences and install hedges. If airborne pollutants will be a problem because of a manufacturing or assembly process, install high-quality ventilation and air-purification systems to eliminate that potential. If you are operating a business with water runoff, make sure to have a water reclamation system.

Safety Issues

You also want to assure your neighbors that there are no potential safety or environmental issues because of your home business. Comply with local safety and fire regulations for storing and handling toxic materials and install high-quality smoke detectors and extinguishing systems.

On the upside, working from home enables you to keep an eye on your neighbors' homes and the neighborhood in general for suspicious activity. Use this as a selling point when it comes time to talk with your neighbors about your new home business and safety-related issues. In fact, you can join the neighborhood watch or become involved in the neighborhood association, since you are in and around the neighborhood during hours when many of your neighbors are not.

Be respectful of your neighbors and be the kind of neighbor that you would want living around you. Understand that, as with you, their homes are probably their largest or only major assets. Should you receive complaints, address them politely, listening to your neighbors and letting them know that you will work on a solution—and then do it. Show your neighbors that you are working with them to solve a problem, rather than encouraging a potential conflict.

GETTING STARTED WITH EMPLOYEES

Most homebased businesses start without any employees. The vast majority are one-person operations, sometimes with contractors and/or free-lancers.

In time, as your business grows, you may reach a point when you will be thinking about hiring employees. You have to weigh your options carefully. Employing adds lots of administrative work to what most homebased business owners already consider excessive. When you have employees, your business opens up to labor laws, minimum wages, health and safety workplace issues, work hours and workers' compensation insurance coverage. You are also required to withhold and remit income taxes and Social Security insurance contributions for your employees. Moreover, home business owners have additional concerns that employers in conventional environments do not face:

- Can employees or outside contractors legally work from your home?
- Do you have the space required for one or more employees to work from your home?
- Can you provide employees working from your home with enough privacy to do their work?
- Will employees have separate and easy access to your home workspace? Can you provide them with suitable parking?
- Can you provide employees with the basic necessities, such as washroom facilities, space for breaks and lunch and closet space for coats?
- Can you trust them? More than 50 percent of business theft today happens from within.

You have alternatives to hiring to fill needed roles within your business. For example, you can hire temporary workers as needed, engage agents or contractors or build alliances with other home business owners and farm out overflow work to them. Telecommunications supports another option: you do not need to worry about where to put these people in your home, as they can work

from their own homes, provided you are able to e-mail, overnight or snail-mail them their work assignments or necessary materials.

Ultimately, if you decide that hiring is the best available option, you will need to familiarize yourself with labor laws and obtain an Employer Identification Number (EIN). Labor laws can be researched in the United States by contacting the Department of Labor or visiting the DOL website and in Canada by contacting Human Resources and Social Development Canada or visiting the HRSDC website:

U.S. Department of Labor
Frances Perkins Building
200 Constitution Avenue, NW
Washington, DC 20210
(866) 4-USA-DOL (487-2365)
dol.gov

Human Resources and Social Development Canada
140 Promenade du Portage
Gatineau, QC K1A 0J9
(800) 567-6866
hrsdc.gc.ca

To obtain an Employer Identification Number in the United States, visit your local Internal Revenue Service office or the IRS website. In Canada, visit your local Canada Revenue Agency office or the CRA website and download the EIN form.

Internal Revenue Service
500 N. Capitol Street, NW
Washington, DC 20221
(202) 874-6748
irs.gov

Canada Revenue Agency
333 Laurier Avenue West
Ottawa K1A 0J9
(800) 959-5525
cra-arc.gc.ca

Hiring and Keeping Good Employees

If you need to hire employees, you will soon learn there is a great deal of truth to the old adage that a business is only as good as its employees. Poor customer service will alienate customers and salespeople who prefer to talk when they should be listening can drive business away to competitors. Unfortunately, discovering that you have hired the wrong person for the job generally comes too late, after the damage has occurred.

One way to make sure you hire the right person is to insist that the candidate supply you with customer references. Don't rely solely on a resume and character references supplied by the candidate; go directly to the source by asking the candidate to furnish customer references—people to whom they have sold or whose accounts they have serviced. No one is better qualified to give you the honest lowdown on a candidate's work ethic and people skills than the customers with whom the candidate has worked.

If you are new to the process of interviewing and hiring, you also need to know what characteristics make a good employee, what employees need and what job benefits they prize most.

- What are the characteristics of a good employee?

Productive	Professional
Honest	Loyal
Pleasant	Respectful
Punctual	Confident

- What do employees need?
  - A fair salary so they can pay their bills and maintain a lifestyle
  - Job security and an opportunity to advance
  - Challenges, so they do not get bored and become less productive
  - The ability to make some independent decisions
  - Recognition for a job well done, because we all need to feel as though we are positively contributing to a larger cause

- What are the benefits that employees rate as the most important?
  - Health care, insurance and dental plans
  - Employer contributions to a retirement saving plan
  - A good work atmosphere in which they feel comfortable
  - Rewards based on productivity
  - Flexible work schedules

How to Increase Employee Productivity

Here are a few sure ways to motivate your employees to be more productive:

- Give your valued employees the opportunity to earn more money through a pay structure of salary plus performance-based commission. Once they discover how much more money they might earn, productivity should improve.
- Give employees job titles befitting their loyalty and the respect they have earned. When people feel needed and respected, they work harder to fulfill their responsibilities.
- Implement a profit-sharing program. The program can be based on all profits or, perhaps preferably, on profit increases based on productivity on a year-over-year basis. Since new businesses take time to make profits, profit sharing typically will come later. Also, as we learned from the dotcoms, don't make promises you cannot keep.
- Recognize your employees. Recognition is a very powerful motivator. Set targets and reward achievement with perks, dollars or time off. Recognize employees for a job well done by putting their names on a plaque, throwing a party in their honor and/or publishing a news item in the local paper

about their achievement and how they were honored.

- Add to their responsibilities. Believe it or not, this is also a very powerful way to motivate employees to increase productivity. If you delegate a job or task that you would normally do, the employee will feel that he or she has earned your trust and will work harder to keep that trust.

- Seek out feedback from employees and listen to their ideas. Employees who feel that they are part of the business, rather than just doing tasks, will be more productive. You don't have to use all their ideas, but if you use one or two, they will feel a sense of belonging to the business and take greater pride in their work.

These are only a few ideas for increasing employee productivity. Regardless of the method you choose, increasing productivity is one of the fastest and least expensive ways to increase business revenues and profits. Therefore, the goal of the home business should include developing programs that will increase productivity without increasing overhead. Ideally, keeping productivity high will result in higher profits. While awards and statues are only a gesture, they make employees feel good and appreciated. Motivation USA (Successories), *motivationusa.com*, offers employee motivation products, services and programs.

Hire Temporary Help as Needed

Instead of hiring full-time or part-time employees, you might want to consider enlisting the services of a temporary help agency to supply experienced workers to meet your short-term labor requirements. There are both advantages and disadvantages to working with a temp agency.

The advantages include:

- The agency screens all workers, so the work-

ers should be competent.

- The agency does all bookkeeping and arranges to pay all payroll deductions, so all you have to do is write one check to cover it all.

- The agency in some cases arranges for workers' compensation and other specialized insurance coverage as needed. (Check with the agency first.)

- The service is fast and convenient. Most temporary help positions can be filled within 24 hours and often within hours of the call.

Perhaps the biggest advantage of using temporary help as opposed to hiring employees is the fact that once you no longer require their services, you are under no obligation to the workers and need pay no severance outside of that which is required under labor laws.

The disadvantages include:

- Many temp agencies try to fit round pegs into square holes, bending the truth to place people in jobs even if they are not qualified.

- Temp employees are often not very enthusiastic, doing the job only until something better comes along, so their level of productivity may not be very high.

- The cost of hiring workers through a temp agency is generally 25 percent higher per hour on average than you would be paying an employee.

Consult your Yellow Pages telephone directory or local online directory to find a temp agency in your area or do a search on the web for local temp agencies.

Choosing Gray Power

The average age of North Americans is rising. As a business owner, you have to carefully consider hiring older workers. In some cases, you might have no choice as the competition heats up for the limited supply of younger workers entering the workforce. Don't despair. With age often come wisdom and experience. Tapping into gray power can benefit a business immensely because the business and sales know-how of retirees can be especially beneficial to small and new businesses. Never underestimate an older person's value to your organization when hiring employees or searching for contractors or consultants. Older people are generally more loyal, have a better work ethic and are more reliable, but you can also tap into their business and marketing experience for ideas to help your business grow. Not to mention the fact that people who have 30, 40 and even 50 years of business, marketing or sales experience also have extensive customer and business contact lists that may be of value to you.

Working with Sales Agents

To expand revenues and market share, home business owners often hire seasoned sales professionals to prospect for new business and sell their goods or services. That can be a very wise and profitable decision. Not only can you tap into their sales and marketing knowledge, but many also have a large base of contacts to whom they can market, generating quick sales.

Most sales agents (also known as sales consultants or freelance sales representatives) prefer to work on contracts for tax purposes and to remain able to represent more than one business client at a time. This kind of arrangement is good for the home business owner. You do not need to worry about extra paperwork, labor laws and employee benefits and the agents come with the tools that they need to sell, including transportation, portable computers and cell phones.

One of the best aspects about hiring or contracting with independent sales agents is that they bring one skill to the table that the majority of home business owners lack—the ability to

prospect effectively for new business. Prospecting is without question one of the most difficult sales disciplines to master. The ability to read people and markets is what sales agents do best; they find people who need and are willing to purchase your goods and services.

Of course, these skills and experiences come at a cost, but don't worry. Outside of the cost of business cards, promotional literature and products samples, many independent sales agents work on a performance-based fee system, retaining a portion of their total sales as a fee. The fee is typically between 5 and 30 percent, depending on the products being sold, sales, value and the costs associated with selling the products.

You do have to take some precautions when hiring sales agents or other subcontractors for your business. The agents or contractors represent your business, so their performance is viewed as a reflection of your performance and your business in the eyes of your customers. Therefore, the agents or contractors you choose will definitely have to be reading from the same page as you. You will also want to ensure the following:

- Make sure the agents or contractors are fully insured, if appropriate.
- Find out what types of warranties or guarantees they offer on their work.
- Ask for references. Make sure that their reputations are spotless. Once again, their reputations will become your reputation.
- Be sure they are reliable to a fault.
- Make sure they work only for you and not direct or indirect competitors in your same marketplace. It is also wise to insist that agents and contractors sign a confidentiality and noncompete agreement, which can be drawn up by your lawyer.
- Always work from a written and binding contract that spells out all the details, including payment, performance and liability

issues and sets beginning and ending dates. You can always extend the time frame of the contract, but don't leave it open-ended.

To find independent sales agents, you can run classified ads under the Help Wanted section of your local newspaper or in newspapers that serve areas into which you want to expand your business. You can also place ads on websites that find employment. The Manufacturers' Agents National Association is a good source, at *manaonline. org*, where you can view listings of sales consultants.

BUILDING TRADE ACCOUNTS

The third group of people on your business team are your product and service suppliers and your vendors. (We will use "suppliers" for the businesses from which you purchase goods and services, such as products for resale or the courier service that delivers your packages, and "vendors" for the businesses that sell your products or services to their customers, such as distributors or retailers.) Just like other member of your business team, suppliers and vendors can play a major role in your ultimate success or failure. Therefore, these relationships need to be carefully developed and managed.

Building Strong Relationships with Your Suppliers

In order to sustain long-term stability, your working relationships with your product and service providers must be mutually beneficial and equitable. Decisions to select one supplier over another cannot be based solely on price; you also have to consider other factors.

- *A good match.* The first rule of working with suppliers is that you are selecting people as much as you are a business, product or service. If you do not like, trust or respect the people who operate the business, there is no hope

for establishing a long-term, stable, equitable business relationship. Distrust and personality clashes only get worse over time and always undermine the relationship. Do business with people you like, trust and respect.

- *Reliability and performance.* If your suppliers cannot deliver what you need, when you need it, it will have a very negative effect on your business. Supplier reliability and performance are perhaps the two most important criteria that you should consider when establishing trade accounts. The promises that your suppliers make to you become the promises that you make to your customers. Therefore, if your suppliers let you down, you in turn let your customers down. Everybody loses when this happens.

- *Warranty programs.* You also have to consider in your decision the suppliers' warranty programs. What kind of product warranties do they offer? What is their workmanship warranty? How do they handle warranty and claim issues? And how will their warranty programs affect your business and customers?

- *Payment terms.* Often more important than a lower cost are the payment terms you can negotiate with your suppliers. With the right terms, you can often sell what you have purchased before paying your supplier. That keeps your capital free and cash flow moving. Ideally, you want to secure 90-day payment terms on a revolving account. You will generally find most suppliers prefer 30 days and offer discounts for cash orders. A word of advice: treat all supplier accounts with respect and pay on time and in full when required to do so. Credit is a privilege for those who deserve it, not a right.

In written agreements with suppliers, try to build in as many of the following features as possible, because all will protect your position and benefit your business.

- If you will be handling a product line, you want an agreement in writing that gives you the exclusive right to sell the products in question and any new or expanded models based on that product line, within a specific geographical area.
- You want the ability to transfer the agreement should you decide to sell your business. These types of exclusive product line agreements can dramatically increase the value of your business.
- You want the right to cancel the agreement on short notice, without having to give a reason and with no financial penalty.
- You do not want to be obligated to purchase a certain amount of the product or meet sales quotas, although most suppliers will

push hard for this. If you find that you must yield on this point, make sure the agreement stipulates that the more of the product you sell, the lower the unit cost will go.

- You do not want to have to commit to spending a certain amount of money each month, quarter or year to promote and market the product line. Many suppliers or manufacturers will want this in the agreement, but avoid this one if possible. Try to turn it around so they have to spend a certain amount promoting the product in your exclusive sales area. At the very least, they should match your promotional expenditures dollar for dollar.
- You do not want to pay a premium for an exclusive product line. You want the product at the same unit cost or less. You should also never pay an upfront fee for the right to sell the product on an exclusive basis.

FIGURE 8.1	Trade Account Support Checklist

Cooperative Advertising

❑ Newspaper and magazine display advertisements

❑ Newspaper and magazine classified advertisements

❑ Radio ads and program sponsorships

❑ Television ads and program sponsorships

❑ Internet and electronic publications advertising

❑ Print newsletters and specialty publication advertising

❑ Yellow Pages ads and business directory listings

❑ Direct mail, flier drops, telemarketing and coupons

❑ Outdoor advertising, including billboards and transit ads

❑ Advertising specialties such as pens, notepads and hats

Product

❑ Product samples   ❑ Product displays

FIGURE 8.1	Trade Account Support Checklist, continued

Product (continued)

❏ Product deliveries	❏ Product installations
❏ Product packaging	❏ Product labels
❏ Product brochures and catalogs	❏ Extended product warranties
❏ Exclusive product lines	❏ Product training and upgrading

Promotional and Printed Materials

❏ Business cards	❏ Customer management software
❏ Contest support and prize	❏ Gift certificates
❏ Stationery package	❏ Estimate and presentation forms and folders
❏ E-mail and fax blasting	❏ Event posters, banners and table tents

Signage

❏ Special event signs for trade shows and seminars

❏ Vehicle signs, fixed and magnetic

❏ Product display signs for point-of-purchase and countertop displays

❏ Exterior and site signs

❏ Window and bumper stickers

Additional Assistance and Items

❏ Education and training	❏ Office furniture and fixtures, new and used
❏ Technical assistance	❏ Website design and maintenance assistance
❏ Customer service support	❏ Staff for special events and demonstrations
❏ Specialized equipment as required	❏ Storage, meeting and boardroom space
❏ Public relations support	❏ Bookkeeping and general office support

Tap Your Trade Accounts for the Works

What tools, equipment or marketing materials that can be used in your business do your suppliers offer for free or at greatly reduced costs? Chances are, there will be more than a few useful items. Home business owners must learn to tap their suppliers' generosity. By this I mean that many of your suppliers will have programs for offering their trade accounts (like you) valuable equipment, marketing materials and cooperative advertising opportunities that will enable those accounts to be more efficient, productive and profitable. The benefit to your suppliers is, of course, that as your business grows you will need to purchase more goods or services from them, increasing their revenues and profits. So it's a win-win situation. Use the Trade Account Support Checklist (Figure 8.1) to identify items that you need in your business and that your trade accounts can potentially supply to you for free or at reduced costs.

Building Strong Relationships with Your Vendors

If you sell products or services through vendors such as retailers, wholesalers, distributors and resellers, vendors are a very important part of your business team. After all, they are your customers. An often-overlooked aspect of working with vendors is that no one knows the benefits of your products or services better than you. That is why it is of vital importance for you to take a hands-on approach to training each and every person who will be selling your product or service, even if it means training the staff members of retailers, manufacturers and distributors or managers. You have to educate them about your goods or services and the reasons why they should be pushing your products or services to their customers instead of your competitors' goods or services. You may even want to develop a few creative incentives for people selling your products or services so they will be inclined to sell more and more often. Remember that your vendors' strengths and weaknesses are your strengths and weaknesses.

Here are a few training ideas for your vendors:

- Provide your vendors with comprehensive product knowledge through initial and ongoing training and through support materials such as manuals, videos and toll-free help lines.
- Ensure that all vendors thoroughly understand your warranty program and your repair, return and refund policies.
- Clearly explain and demonstrate the competitive advantages of your products—durability, price, user-friendliness, reputation and exclusivity—so that vendors can tell their customers about these advantages with confidence and excitement.

- Make sure that your vendors know what the most common objections to the sale will be and, more important, give them the tools and knowledge to overcome these objections and close the sale.

GETTING STARTED WITH PROFESSIONAL SERVICES

The fourth group that defines your business team is high-priority professional service providers such as bankers, lawyers, accountants and consultants. When selecting professional service providers, it is important to keep the following criteria in mind:

- *Experience.* You want to work with professionals who are highly experienced in their fields. You're relying on their experience, knowledge and advice to keep you in business, grow your business, keep you out of trouble and help you with many issues in setting up and managing your business.
- *Accessibility.* You want to be able to contact your team professionals and have their undivided attention (within reason) when you need their advice and guidance. Waiting a few days to get an appointment is acceptable, but not a week, two weeks or even longer. That's out of the question. Business decisions must often be made quickly, so your professional service providers need to be accessible.
- *Affordability.* Good business advice can come at a cost. However, you must select professional services that you can afford.

Working with a Lawyer

Anyone who has ever been in business knows that operating a business and having access to good legal advice go hand in hand. I can't imagine trying to take a business from start-up to operations and on to eventual sale without legal advice during each step and many times in between. Competent lawyers with experience working with small businesses will be able to advise you on which legal business structure best meets your needs, insurance and liability issues, drafting legal documents, money collection and small claims courts matters, estate planning and continuation of your business, supplier and vendor agreements and many other legal issues. In short, lawyers will decipher the legalese for you and help make sense of complicated matters pertaining to business. Sound professional advice comes at a cost and a lawyer's time is his or her product. Therefore, to minimize legal costs, follow these timesaving tips:

- Always be fully prepared when meeting with your lawyer. Know what you want to talk about, explain the situation briefly and prepare questions in advance of the meeting.
- Stay focused on the task at hand. Don't engage in social chitchat. Remember: lawyers sell their time and you are on the clock the minute you walk through their door or pick up the telephone to talk to them.
- Copy your documents yourself prior to meeting with your lawyer because all lawyers charge for copying and the time spent copying documents.

Additional information on the legal aspects of setting up and operating a homebased business can be found in Chapter 4, "Legal Issues." To find a lawyer, you can contact the American Bar Association or Canadian Bar Association at the addresses below. They will help you locate a lawyer in your area who specializes in small businesses. You can also ask other businesspeople in your area, those who also belong to associations and/or friends and family members for recommendations. Make sure the attorneys with whom you meet understand your specific business needs.

American Bar Association
321 North Clark Street
Chicago, IL 60610
(312) 988-5000
740 15th Street, NW
Washington, DC 20005-1019
(202) 662-1000
abanet.org

Canadian Bar Association
500–865 Carling Avenue
Ottawa K1S 5S8
(800) 267-8860, (613) 237-2925, (613) 237-1988
cba.org

Working with a Banker

Establishing a relationship and working with a banker means working with all employees at the bank where you establish your business accounts, from the manager to the loan officers to the tellers to the guards who make sure no one takes off with your loot. Having a good working relationship with a bank or other financial institution, such as a credit union, is a critical factor in small business success—you never know when you will need to borrow working capital, growth capital or just a quick loan to get you through the next 60 days until a client contract is completed, billed and collected. Not only do you need a good working relationship with your bank people so they will meet your special needs and requests, but you also must go out of your way not to blemish that relationship. Make all loan payments on time and in full to keep in good standing.

Working with an Accountant

Even with the proliferation of accounting and bookkeeping software, hiring an accountant to take care of more complicated money matters is a wise decision. Like many professionals, the vast majority of accountants pride themselves on the fact that they do not cost you money, but rather save you money by discovering items overlooked on tax returns, by identifying business deductions you never knew existed, by creating financial plans that will enable you to enjoy the fruits of your labor later in life and by answering your financial questions and preparing in advance for any potential dilemmas, such as changes in tax laws or—the ultimate fear—a tax audit.

Even if you decide to keep your books yourself, you will still want to make contact with an accountant familiar with small business money and tax issues. If you decide to sell your business, expand your business or merge with another business, you will want to have a competent accounting professional on your team to make sure that your financial best interests are being served. If you are unsure about your bookkeeping abilities, even with accounting software, you may want to hire a bookkeeper to do your books monthly and a CPA accountant to audit your books quarterly and prepare year-end business statements and tax returns. Additional information about homebased business financing, money management and bookkeeping can be found in Chapter 3, "Financial Issues."

Keep in mind that a bookkeeper is different than an accountant. You can hire someone to come in and handle your books for much less than it would cost you to have a CPA do the job. The accountant should oversee the bookkeeping and be involved in the decision-making process.

Important reminder: never let your money matters get too far away from you. Regularly review your financial situation with your bookkeeper and your accountant. Review all your account statements and stay on top of all money matters. Too many business owners have entrusted too much financial responsibility to others and regretted it afterward.

To locate a qualified accountant or bookkeeper for your business, you can contact the following

U.S. and Canadian associations. You can find a good accountant by asking other small business owners whom they would recommend or talking to people in local associations and/or organizations.

United States

Association of Chartered Accountants in the
   United States
341 Lafayette Street, Suite 4246
New York, NY 10012-2417
(212) 334-2078
acaus.org

American Institute of Professional Bookkeepers
6001 Montrose Road, Suite 500
Rockville, MD 20852
(800) 622-0121
aipb.com

Canada

Chartered Accountants of Canada (Canadian
   Institute of Chartered Accountants)
277 Wellington Street West
Toronto, ON M5V 3H2
(416) 977-3222
cica.ca

Working with an Insurance Agent

Having the right insurance to protect you, your family, your business and your customers is imperative. But there are so many types of small business insurance programs out there that trying to find the right one could be time-consuming and frustrating. Don't chance going it alone and ending up with the wrong insurance. Instead, enlist the services of a qualified and licensed insurance agent or broker to advise you on small business insurance matters. The agent will be able not only to decipher insurance legalese into easily understandable English for you, but also to find the best coverage for your specific needs and at the lowest cost.

In the United States you can contact the

Independent Insurance Agents and Brokers of America, at *iiaa.org*. This nonprofit association offers a free "Find an Agent" search on its website, indexed geographically. In Canada you can contact the Insurance Brokers Association of Canada, at *ibac.ca*. This nonprofit association also offers visitors access to a free online directory that geographically lists in excess of 25,000 licensed and certified insurance agents and brokers across Canada. You will find more information and resources for finding and working with insurance agents and brokers in Chapter 5, Home Business Insurance.

Working with Business Consultants and Trainers

Professional consultants have long played a role in helping small business owners meet and exceed their business and marketing objectives through coaching, planning, new business development and training strategies. There are consulting experts in almost every business discipline, including:

- Small business consultants
- Logistic consultants
- Marketing consultants
- Sales and sales training consultants
- Financial planning consultants
- Computer, internet and website consultants
- Advertising and public relations consultants
- Direct marketing consultants
- Franchise and licensing consultants

Quite literally the list goes on and on.

The first step in hiring a business consultant is to define your objectives. What do you want to fix, improve or venture into? Once you know your objectives, then you can select and interview a few potential candidates. The key to selecting the right consultant is to make sure that he or she has experience in the specific area. Ask for references—and check them. Ask each consultant to provide a brief written proposal outlining how he or she would be able to help you achieve your objectives.

As always, don't base your final decision on costs. Make sure the fit feels right and that the consultant has a firm grasp on your specific situation and your objectives. Once you select the consultant, ask for a detailed proposal that includes payment terms, a scope of work and applicable guarantees.

The Training Registry at *trainingregistry.com* is a directory service listing thousands of experienced, professional consultants. The site is indexed both by topic and geography.

A word of caution. Many people have jumped onto the consulting bandwagon. They may have good intentions and a background in a specific field, but that doesn't necessarily mean they are able to help you. A consultant must be an excellent listener and current on the latest trends, technologies and economic news. A consultant should be at least one step ahead of you on the learning curve. Find someone with training, experience and excellent communications skills.

COMPLETING YOUR TEAM WITH ALLIANCES

The final component of your business team are the alliances you establish within your industry and the community in which your business operates. These alliances include business and industry associations, other community business owners, competitors, government agencies, schools and the media. Business alliances can play a major role in helping you achieve your business and marketing objectives, success and profitability.

Business and Industry Associations

You first want to align your home business with business and industry associations, such as your local Chamber of Commerce and industry associations relevant to your business or profession. Many home business owners neglect to join business and industry associations because of the cost and the time. Membership dues can cost between a few hundred and a few thousand dollars per year, depending on the association. Once you join there are various functions and events that will require a time commitment. However, it is important not to view membership in business or industry associations just in terms of cost and time. Instead, you should base your decision on whether joining will help you reach your goals and objectives through the events and the opportunities for education, advocacy and networking.

It is important to remember that business and industry associations must provide value and benefits to their members in order to secure new members and retain current ones. Most associations provide great opportunities, but the rest is up to you. Profiting through membership requires a plan and participation to realize the value and benefits to the fullest extent.

Member Services

The services that associations often provide can be very beneficial to home business owners. Start by asking if this association has the resources and specialized services that would help your business and if you can easily take advantage of these resources and services. Resources and services could include a print and electronic library of industry-related information, meeting space and boardroom rentals and equipment you could borrow, such as trade show displays and PowerPoint projection systems. Are there experts on staff to answer questions and provide assistance when needed? Many small business and industry associations have economists, business planners and marketing specialists to assist members with their specific business challenges.

Member Discounts

Discounts on products and services that small

business owners routinely need are another potential benefit of joining small business or industry associations. The second question to ask before joining is whether this association offers member discounts on products and services that you need in your business. Common member discounts include reduced merchant rates with major credit card providers, lower courier fees, savings on office products and supplies and fleet rate fuel cards through major gas companies. There may also be weekly and monthly specials on business travel and small business insurance and reduced fees for seminars, trade shows and other marketing events.

Business-Building Opportunities

Depending on your marketing objectives, business-building opportunities may be more important than member services or discounts. Consequently, you will want to find out if the members of the association match your target audience. If so, are there opportunities to market your products or services directly to association members? Business-building opportunities include trade shows, networking meetings, advertising opportunities in the association's publication and on its website and direct promotional mailings to members.

Educational Opportunities

The potential to learn can also be an important reason for joining a business association. Prior to signing up, you will want to know if the association provides educational opportunities. These opportunities could include workshops, training classes and seminars featuring keynote speakers. Also, does the association provide members with valuable and up-to-date industry research, news and information on emerging trends? Generally you will find that most business associations host educational events monthly on a wide variety of topics, including sales, advertising, public relations, logistics, management, bookkeeping, and networking.

Advocacy

For many home business owners, having a voice in the business community is important, but nearly impossible for a small business. Therefore, if advocacy is important to you, it is important to know if the association has a strong voice within the industry and is respected enough that it can influence the decision-making process at the regional and federal levels of government. Business associations take a strength-in-numbers approach to making their voices heard on issues important to members and the business community.

To locate business and industry associations specific to your needs, contact Marketing Source at *marketingsource.com/associations*. Marketing Source publishes a print and electronic business association directory containing information on more than 35,000 associations. Additionally, the Chamber of Commerce offers home business owners good value for specific products and services, and useful business information and networking opportunities. There are Chamber of Commerce chapters throughout the United States and Canada. To find one close to you, do a web search for "Chamber of Commerce" and the name of your town or city or visit *uschamber.com* or *chamber.ca*. More information about creating new business and selling opportunities through business and industry associations can be found in Chapter 14, Public Relations and Networking.

Cross-Promotional Partners

You also want to establish relationships with other businesses in your community so you can create and benefit from cross-promotional opportunities and referrals. The business world is abuzz with terminology such as "strategic alliances," "relationship marketing," and "joint ventures" as the global

marketplace becomes more competitive. One of the best ways to grow your home business is by joining forces with other small business owners to create cross-promotional activities. You should develop these activities so they increase awareness of your brand, enable you to reach a broader audience and attract new business to you while driving down the cost for each partner to market and promote his or her business. In a nutshell, cross-promotional activities enable entrepreneurs who share similar goals and objectives to band together and reduce financial risk and share financial rewards.

Lifestyle Packages

Creating lifestyle packages is one of the best ways to build your business through cross-promotional opportunities because packages allow you to be extremely creative and clearly separate your business from your competitors. For instance, if you design and install custom sundecks, logical matches to create a lifestyle package are with a retailer of custom patio furniture and accessories and a retailer of hot tub spas. Together you could create a Family Outdoor Living Package that includes a custom sundeck, matching custom patio furniture and a hot tub, at a lower price than if each were purchased separately.

Sponsorships

Form a team of businesses to share the expense of community sponsorships, but still receive the full impact of beneficial exposure. The sponsorships could be in the form of a youth baseball team, a Clean-Up-the-Park Day or a local charitable cause.

Advertising

An obvious but effective cross-promotional activity is to form an advertising club with other small businesses that are not in competition with you. In doing so, you will generally find that you can negotiate lower costs for print and broadcast media and for printed promotional literature such as brochures, coupons and product catalogs because of your greater buying power based on volume.

Government Officials

Building your business team also means opening lines of communications with elected or appointed public officials at all levels of government, especially local. By including local officials such as politicians, planners and members of police and fire services in your business team and keeping lines of communication open, you can help local government understand how its decisions affect your business by expressing your perspectives. You will also better understand the issues and challenges facing the community and how they relate to policy making. When you take an active role in your community, you help to shape the kind of community in which you want to live and conduct business.

The Media

The media can also be important members of your business team if you take the time and steps necessary to include them. Of course, the benefits of doing so can include very valuable media exposure for your business, products or services. Through continued media exposure, you can also position yourself as an expert in your field, which can have a very positive impact on your business.

Get to know the local media by sending out a letter introducing your business and the products or services that you sell and let it be known that you welcome any questions they have about your business, industry, products or services. Also get into the habit of regularly sending out press releases to announce company news and writing letters to the editor of newspapers to voice your

opinions. Additional ideas about how to target and work with the media can be found in Chapter 14, "Public Relations and Networking."

Schools

Home business owners are wise to establish working relationships with local schools and educational institutions because many have co-op work programs that are designed to bring community businesses and young people together so that students can receive much needed, hands-on work experience and business can benefit from the students' ideas and creativity. Students can also be great teachers, helping home business owners with computer hardware and software training, marketing research and planning and access to a pool of eager part-time, seasonal or temporary help as needed. And many of these students may very well be your customers in the not-too-distant future.

Competitors

Yes, even your competitors can be on your business team, especially if you join those competitors who operate outside of your geographical trading area to build strong business coalitions. Companies that share similar goals and objectives can band together to share risks and rewards. In doing so, you may find that as a group you are able to negotiate lower supply costs through increased purchasing power. By building and collaborating in a coalition, you will be able to identify and overcome marketing and business challenges facing the industry through collective brainstorming and the planning process. You can also build working relationships with local competitors, offering to assist each other with overflow work during busy times.

RESOURCES
Associations

American Home Business Association
965 East 4800, Suite 3C
Salt Lake City, UT 84117
(866) 396-7773
homebusinessworks.com

Human Resources and Social Development Canada
140 Promenade du Portage
Gatineau, QC K1A 0J9
(800) 567-6866
hrsdc.gc.ca

SCORE Association
409 Third Street, SW, 6th Floor
Washington, DC 20024
1175 Herndon Parkway, Suite 900
Herndon, VA 20170
(800) 634-0245, (703) 487-3612
score.org

Small Office Home Office Business Group (SOHO)
Suite 1, 1680 Lloyd Avenue
North Vancouver, BC V7P 2N6
(604) 929-8250, (800) 290-SOHO (7646)
soho.ca

U.S. Department of Labor
Frances Perkins Building
200 Constitution Avenue NW
Washington, DC 20210
(866) 4-USA-DOL (487-2365)
dol.gov

Suggested Reading

Blanchard, Kenneth H., and Spencer Johnson. *The One Minute Manager*. New York: Berkley Publishing Group, 1983.

Carnegie, Dale. *How to Win Friends and Influence People*. Reissue. New York: Pocket Books (Simon & Schuster), 1994.

Cobe, Patricia, and Ellen H. Parlapiano. *Mompreneurs: A Mother's Practical Step-by-Step Guide to Work-at-Home Success*. New York: Perigee/Berkley Publishing Group (Penguin Putnam), 2002.

Collins, Jim. *Good to Great: Why Some Companies Make the Leap … And Others Don't*. New York: HarperCollins, 2001.

Hiam, Alex. *Making Horses Drink: How to Lead and Succeed in Business*. Irvine, CA: Entrepreneur Press, 2002.

Nelson, Bob. *1001 Ways to Energize Employees*. New York: Workman Publishing Company, 1997.

Websites

Advanced Research: Background checks on job applicants. *arsbackgrounds.com*

All Business: Articles and expert advice on growing a business. *allbusiness.com*

Better Business Bureau: Consumer and business protection group. *bbb.org*

BusinessTown.com: Small business online directory. *businesstown.com*

Employment Screening Services, Inc.: Screening service for job applicants. *employscreen.com*

Entrepreneur: Online small business resource center. *entrepreneur.com*

ExpertClick.com: Online directory listing expert services for media members and contacts. *expertclick.com*

Family Business Magazine Online: Information, tips, articles and advice about starting and operating a family business. *familybusinessmagazine.com*

Free Management Library: Extensive online business directory. *managementhelp.org*

Marketing Resource Center: Online directory listing more than 37,000 business associations indexed by industry. *marketingsource.com/associations*

Teambuilding Adventures: Team-building adventure programs. *teambuilding.com*

Training Registry: National online directory listing professional business, management and employee training consultants. *trainingregistry.com*

CHAPTER 9

What Price Will You Charge?

PRICING IS A VERY IMPORTANT ELEMENT of the marketing mix and your marketing strategy. If your prices are too high, you will meet with great resistance trying to sell your goods or services. If your prices are too low, you may meet with great resistance selling your goods or services because of perceptions of quality. ("You get what you pay for.") Clearly, you must take a balanced approach when setting your prices and developing your pricing polices and strategies. Factors influencing pricing formulas and strategies include:

- Product costs
- Costs of delivering services
- Fixed operating overheads
- Market supply and demand
- Economic conditions
- Competition for market share
- Desired return on investment
- Method of distribution
- Seasonal pressures
- Political pressures

- Psychological factors (consumer perceptions)
- How you want to position your business, products or services within the marketplace and in comparison to competitors

As you can see, there are a great many factors influencing the formula used to set your prices initially and how you deal with changes in the marketplace and product life-cycles (growth, decline, static) moving forward. A key concept to keep in mind when devising pricing strategies is that consumers see prices in simple terms—the price you charge for your product or service relative to how that product or service will fill their needs and provide value.

When was the last time you purchased a loaf of bread and thought about all the costs associated with it—the costs of growing the wheat, seeds, fertilizers, equipment, fuel and labor; the costs of milling the flour; the costs of baking the bread and wrapping the loaf;

the costs of transporting the wheat to the mill, the flour to the bakery and the loaf of bread to the supermarket; the costs of advertising; and the costs of stocking the shelves and selling the loaf to you? If you are like most consumers, you don't give it a second thought. All you see are loaves of bread on the shelf. One is 10 cents cheaper than the next; the one next to that is 50 cents more, but claims to be better for you. Once again, you have to evaluate the price in terms of your needs and the value.

When your pricing is correct for what you sell, consumers don't think twice because they feel the price is fair for what the product or service will do for them. However, as soon as your price goes below or above the threshold of what consumers feel is the fair range for your goods or services, you will meet resistance. At this point, consumers must begin to justify buying from you—and you never want your target consumers to have to convince themselves to buy your products or services. That is always your job and you do it through proper pricing, promotion and positioning strategies.

THE BASICS

You first have to determine the costs associated with selling and delivering your goods and services from an internal perspective, excluding outside influences such as competition or economic conditions. The internal factors include fixed costs, direct costs, incomes and wages and profit. These costs will help you determine what prices you have to charge for your goods and services to pay your expenses. This can be seen as your base price—the bottom line of what you need to break even.

Covering Direct Costs and Consumables

Direct costs and *consumables* are the costs specifically associated with selling and delivering your products or services. Examples of direct costs include the wholesale cost of a product (inventory) that you resell to a customer or equipment or tools you have purchased or rented and used on a specific job for a client.

Start with the basics of what you are selling. For example, you're in the business of selling tennis rackets. Each racket costs you $40; that is the first direct cost. Next, you need to consider how much you are spending to sell that tennis racket. This includes all of your other costs—advertising, marketing, web expenses and so on. You must break down these expenses to determine how much you need to show a profit. You could simply decide on a 20-percent markup and sell the tennis racket for $50, but would that cover the costs you incur to buy it and sell it and leave you with a profit?

Covering Fixed Costs

Your *fixed costs* are also known as your *overhead*. This is the cost of doing business. Even though these fixed costs cannot directly generate a profit, you must pay them to operate the business.

Use the worksheet Monthly Overhead Estimator (Figure 9.1) to determine your fixed monthly expenses for each month and for the year. Complete only the sections relevant to your business. Remember to separate out expenses specific to your business from your personal expenses.

Determining Profit and Pricing

This is where you start to put together the various components. If your overhead comes to $3,000 per month or $36,000 per year including a part-time employee, you would now figure that amount into the cost of selling your product.

Now, you need to first determine the price for the item you're selling. Our example is tennis rack-

FIGURE 9.1	Monthly Overhead Estimator (Home Business Portion Only)		
Rent or mortgage	$_____	Transportation parking	$_____
Utilities	$_____	Advertising	$_____
Property taxes	$_____	Public relations	$_____
Business taxes	$_____	Direct marketing	$_____
Alarm monitoring	$_____	Event marketing	$_____
Workspace cleaning and maintenance	$_____	Website hosting	$_____
Business loan and interest repayments	$_____	Website content and software	$_____
Bank charges	$_____	Website maintenance	$_____
Accounting or bookkeeping fees	$_____	Equipment loans and leases	$_____
Business licenses and permits	$_____	Equipment repairs and maintenance	$_____
Business insurance	$_____	Off-site storage	$_____
Workers' compensation	$_____	General office supplies	$_____
Dedicated telephone line	$_____	Business or industry association dues	$_____
Toll-free telephone line	$_____	Uniforms and dry cleaning	$_____
Cellular telephone	$_____	Subscriptions	$_____
Answering service	$_____	Other _____	$_____
Pager	$_____	Other _____	$_____
Two-way radio	$_____	Other _____	$_____
Transportation lease or loan payment	$_____	Other _____	$_____
Transportation fuel and oil	$_____	Other _____	$_____
Transportation insurance and license	$_____	Total overhead per month	$_____
Transportation repairs and maintenance	$_____	Total overhead per year	$_____

ets. If this particular tennis racket that costs you $40 sells in the stores for $70 and higher, you will make $30 over your product cost. You would need to sell 100 per month to cover your overhead of $3,000 per month and break even, about 25 each week.

But your goal is not just to break even, of course, but to make money. How much are you trying to make? That will depend on your income needs, discussed earlier in the book. (Do you have a spouse or significant other who is also bringing in income? Are you supporting a family or only yourself? Do you have other sources of income?) You need to look at your expenses and determine how much of them this business can cover. If, for example, you want to bring in an annual income of $40,000, then you need to add that into your equation. Now you need to cover $36,000 in business expenses plus $40,000 in income, or $76,000. At a margin of $30 per racket, you need to sell 2,533 rackets a year or

211 a month or about 53 a week or nearly 9 a day if you are selling six days per week.

Do you have enough potential contacts to reach such totals? Do you have access to advertise at tennis camps, local courts and tennis clubs? Is there some accessory you can offer? Can you work stringing the rackets for free into the equation? Clearly, you need to punch these kinds of numbers early on when deciding what business to start so you do not end up with a product you cannot sell in sufficient quantity to cover your costs. If this racket is selling in stores for $80 and you can sell it for $70, you can use this price difference as your competitive edge and perhaps sell 3,000 per year, exceeding your initial goal.

Clearly, the best opportunities for homebased businesses are those with the lowest overhead costs, the most demand, the biggest markups and the opportunity for repeat business. The head of one of the leading mail order associations suggested wine (via mail order) as a viable business option. There is a growing interest in wine and a great markup, so if you used the internet to promote your business, you could have a lucrative possibility. Plus, wine enthusiasts keep coming back for more. Tennis players typically don't need a new racket very often.

This is the numbers game you need to play to determine whether or not you can price a product or a service to make it work for your business. The plus is that you can often keep the overhead low, since you are not paying rent. The negative is that if you are not a good salesperson with plenty of leads, you will have a hard time selling your product or services.

It's critical to include a profit when setting your prices; it's not enough to just cover your expenses and break even. There is no standard formula. Most business owners use a cost-plus formula when setting prices, with the "plus" in the equation being profit. There are, however, factors that may not allow you to use this approach, such as the prices of your competitors, supply, demand and market conditions—all covered in detail later in this chapter.

Tying It All Together

Finally, you have to be able to tie together all the internal factors to create a pricing formula for your goods or services. New entrepreneurs often use a cost-plus formula to establish prices for their products or services. For example, I sell gizmos, my costs are $10, and so I will mark up my costs by 30 percent and sell my gizmos for $13 each. The danger in a cost-plus approach is that it does not take into consideration how many products you must sell to break even or make a profit or how many hours you have to work to break even or make a profit.

Therefore, a more logical approach is to use a cost-plus pricing formula but also create a breakeven analysis, which will tell you how many products you must sell at your cost-plus pricing to break even or how many hours you must work to break even. The breakeven analysis enables you to know your pricing is reasonable in terms of expected sales volume, as the following example indicates:

Unit cost price	$10
50% markup	$5
Retail selling price	$15
	(33.333% gross margin)
Estimated business expenses per year	$15,000
Number of units to sell per year to break even	3,000
	250 per month
Breakeven revenues	$45,000 per year
	$3,750 per month

Once you have determined how many units of a product or service you need to sell to break even, it can help you to establish your pricing formula based on your projected sales. Of course, at this point, external factors can also influence your pricing formulas. Economic conditions or competitor pricing may affect your ability to charge what you need to charge. Additional information about breakeven analysis and sales projections can be found in Chapter 6, "Preparing a Business Plan," and in Chapter 12, "Creating a Marketing Plan."

Pricing a Service

The difference between a product and a service is that you are not paying for a tangible item when you sell a service, which is why there are so many homebased service businesses. Psychologists are not selling anything beyond their own knowledge and abilities to help the client. Therefore, if your cost of running a service business is $36,000 a year, plus $5,000 to repay the loans for attending schools or getting certification, that is all you need in revenues to cover your expenses and start making a profit.

If, for example, it costs a consultant $40,000 to run the business, including advertising and promotion and all other expenses, he or she then needs to determine an hourly rate. Service providers use an hourly rate. If this consultant chooses to work 1,000 hours a year (only about 20 hours a week), he or she needs to charge only $40 an hour to break even. If the going rate for consultants in the region is $60 an hour and so that's what the consultant charges, this brings in $60,000 (1,000 × $60)—a profit of $20,000. If billable hours increase to 30 hours weekly (1,500 hours), the consultant brings in $90,000 (1,500 × $60), for a $50,000 profit.

Again, this is determined by a variety of factors, including how many hours the consultant can book in a year. Ten clients at just 150 hours a year would be enough. This isn't to say that the consultant does not need another 5 to 10 hours weekly to handle paperwork. However, while the hourly rate will

drop, the income will not, since there are minimal extra expenditures to doing paperwork.

DETERMINING YOUR PRICING STRATEGY

Setting your prices and determining your pricing strategy have much to do with positioning your business and your goods or services in the marketplace and with external factors that can potentially influence your prices. You can position yourself to become known for low prices, moderate prices or prestige prices. However, once you have determined your pricing strategy, you should stick with it. Do not change back and forth, because doing so will confuse customers, as they won't know what to expect. The only exception to this would be circumstances that require you to be flexible or promotional pricing in connection with a special event. Your pricing positioning strategy must also match your marketing positioning strategy and the rest of your business strategy.

Your positioning strategy answers two vital questions:

1. Where do your business and products or services fit into the market?
2. How do your target customers and prospects view your products or services in relation to those offered by your competitors?

Obviously price makes up a large part of the answers. You might position your business as the low-price leader in the marketplace (if you can sell enough units to make a profit) or perhaps you will choose a quality-first philosophy and opt to charge a premium for your goods or services by providing personalized attention or something else to justify the higher prices. Much of your positioning is affected by your competitors and where they are positioned in the market, by perceptions and expectations of consumers for the type of products or services you sell, and by the benefits you can create for consumers purchasing from your business.

You can try to alter consumer perceptions and buying habits, but this is a costly and long-term process that most home business owners with limited capital cannot attempt. A more logical approach to defining your pricing strategy is to analyze the current marketplace, identifying what competitors are charging and how consumers respond to those prices.

Factors Influencing Pricing

External factors will sometimes influence your pricing strategy. Sometimes external factors will be positive for your business; other times these factors will be negative and have a detrimental effect on your business. Here are a few of the more common external influences on pricing:

- *Demand factor.* If what you sell is in high demand, you can charge a premium or at least not have to discount. Alternately, if supply is high and demand is low, you might have to lower your prices to increase sales and capture market share. However, there's a bottom-line price below which you cannot make a profit, so know that price before you start selling and determine whether what you will be selling will be in demand.
- *Economic factors.* The state of the local economy will also play a role in your pricing strategies. If the economy is robust, then consumers have more discretionary income to spend, which generally keeps prices stable to high. If the economy stumbles, usually this results in lower prices. You can protect against problems in the economy by having a "staple" product or service that people need in good or bad times, such as diapers for their babies, as opposed to leisure items, such as shower massagers. If the economy is projected to take

a downturn, don't start a business that sells high-end luxury products or services unless you know you have a solid market.
- *Competitive factors.* You also have no control over what your competitors charge for the same goods and services, unless you operate in a regulated industry for which a commission or agency sets all market pricing. Your competitors can choose to sell for less than you, more than you or the same price. Of course, their pricing affects what you will charge. In most industries, prices are in a general range in a given region and it's hard for companies to undercut each other significantly. It's easy to find manufacturers' retail prices, especially on the internet, so consumers today are price-savvy. You will probably set your prices generally in line with what your competitors are charging, perhaps charge a little less because of lower overhead.
- *Phantom factors.* Political unrest in the Middle East drives up the price of crude oil, affecting what we pay for gas at the pumps. Pine beetles devour thousands of trees in the Pacific Northwest of the United States and Canada, driving up the price of softwood lumber and affecting what we pay for lumber to build a deck. Early frost wipes out half of the Florida citrus crops, affecting what we pay for oranges at the market. All of these are examples of phantom factors that are difficult if not impossible to predict, but can dramatically affect the prices you charge. If you have some diversity in your line of products or services, you may be able to offset some of these factors.

Four Basic Pricing Strategies

There are a great number of pricing strategies, some which are aimed at market entry, others at specific promotional activities and still others at competitors. Four pricing strategies are worth looking at in detail—low pricing, moderate pricing, prestige pricing and discount pricing.

Low Pricing

Selecting a low-price strategy means that you will strive to sell your goods or services at the lowest or near lowest price in the marketplace, a bargain-basement approach to pricing, if you will. A low-pricing strategy means you will have to sell a greater volume of goods or to produce an equivalent profit margin.

Most home business owners wisely choose not to compete in the marketplace based on low prices. Many chain retailers and national franchise services providers have already adopted a low-price strategy, making it difficult for the small independent business to compete on this level. Also, since you are not as well known as a chain store, consumers may consider low prices from you as an indicator of poor quality or shoddy service.

Moderate Pricing

"A good-quality product or service delivered to consumers at a fair price" best sums up moderate pricing. This is the pricing strategy the majority of home business owners choose. It leaves enough financial leeway to develop and introduce competitive advantages to separate their offerings from what their competitors offer. The moderate pricing strategy gives home business owners the most flexibility in terms of combining value and good service at a fair price, which is difficult to achieve if you adopt a low-price strategy.

Prestige Pricing

Generally, a high-quality product or service is delivered in an upscale or exclusive environment. Personalized service, attention to detail, extras (such as engraving), and other features can be the selling points behind prestige prices, along with selling top designer products and projecting an image of quality and exclusivity. Consumers pay a substantial premium for the quality and the prestige generally associated with purchasing the product or service.

Discount Pricing

Discounting is a pricing strategy that can be used to achieve business and marketing objectives such as entering a new market, celebrating a company milestone or rewarding the most loyal customers. The downside of discounting is that you are selling your products or services for less than the full price you had established. There are a number of discounting methods you can use.

- You can offer a *straight cash* discount, represented in monetary terms, such as $25 off or as a percentage, such as 25 percent off the retail price.
- You can offer a *quantity* discount: the more a customer buys, the lower the unit price.
- You can offer a *rebate* discount: the consumer must first pay full price and apply for the specified rebate or the rebate can be given instantly at the point of purchase.
- You can offer a *trade* discount to commercial clients, which is standard practice.
- You can offer a *seasonal* discount to liquidate off-season inventory, such as selling swimwear in the winter or boosting off-season service sales, such as a discount if you replace your roof in the winter months when few people think of roofing.
- You can offer *promotional* discounts, such as "save the sales tax." Most promotional discounts are tied to specific events or holidays, such as your company's anniversary or Christmas. One of the best strategies is to get customers to buy more because they are spending less. Of course you don't promote it as such, but the idea is to sell the customers one $90 item for $75 and then sell

them at usual price a $19 accessory that they might not have purchased otherwise. Hey, you're $4 ahead!

Why You May Have to Change Your Prices

Home business owners must plan for price changes, generally annually, to keep up with inflation or other issues affecting pricing. Depending on the situation, your prices may have to move upward or downward. In either case you will need to determine the best way to control fluctuating prices while retaining customers.

Why Prices Increase and What You Can Do About It

You may have to raise your prices for reasons including the following:

- Increased costs of products, supplies and/or labor
- A shortage of supply and heavy consumer demand
- Need for a higher gross profit margin

You should act with sensitivity when raising your prices. You do not want to lose a loyal customer because you have to charge more; at the same time you do not want to eat higher costs and earn less per sale. Ultimately, you have two options. You can explain to your customers why prices have increased or you can work with your customers to find ways to hold the line on prices, which generally means reducing service or lowering the quality or quantity of product.

Why Prices Decrease and What You Can Do About It

You may also lower your prices. Reasons for price decreases include:

- Your supplier lowers prices or you find a less

expensive supplier and pass the savings on to your customers.
- Supply is abundant in the marketplace and demand is low, forcing lower pricing.
- You want to increase sales volume and attract new business with lower prices.

Obviously, it's easier to deal with lowering your prices than with raising them. Don't expect your customers to complain or go elsewhere.

ADDITIONAL PRICING INFORMATION FOR SERVICE PROVIDERS

Although the fundamentals of price setting are similar for product sellers and service providers, there are other issues that service providers should consider when setting their prices, especially if they provide a specialty or niche service. One commonality among service providers that more often than not the service they provide is worth more than the price they charge. This is generally due to a "trading skills for an hourly rate" mind-set or because the service is not a necessity to the consumer.

In setting their prices, all service providers should first clearly identify and list what their service does for their customers. For instance, do customers save money as a direct result of using your service? If so, how much, and can you clearly demonstrate that savings to prospects and customers? If you can, should you set your price for your service as a percentage of the savings? Saving a client $10,000 and asking for only 50 percent of the savings as a fee is realistic and fair, especially if you can prove it with client testimonials and tangible documentation or guarantee it in writing. But in that case you would probably have to promise to refund some or all of the payment if your clients do not save money as you have assured them or guaranteed.

You have to be able to justify the price you charge for the value you provide. When developing service pricing, you must not think of the value of your service in terms of an hourly or daily fee. Value your service based on what it will do for your customers. There are limits, of course, especially in very competitive service industries, such as cleaning and home services. If the average going rate for carpet cleaning is $40 per hour, you might have a difficult time convincing customers that they should pay $80.

Working with Budgets

Another factor that should be considered is your client's budget for the service or services. This is an area in which service providers should remain flexible to the possibilities. "Flexible to the possibilities" means that if your client's budget is $1,000 for a project and you have quoted $2,000, don't view this situation as a lost cause. Instead, determine what services you can provide to meet your client's budget by prioritizing them for the job and eliminating those with the lowest priority. You will be amazed at how many more jobs you can close by remaining flexible. Also, once your foot is in the door, budgets have a way of increasing as the benefits of the service become apparent to the client.

Index Your Contracts

Before you sign any long-term contracts to provide services, make sure you have included a provision for indexing the contract. Inflationary and deflationary pressures on the economy can affect the costs of labor, materials and transportation, and all other direct costs associated with providing a service. These costs can rise dramatically or drop dramatically, affecting your business and your ability to generate a profit. To protect yourself, you should consider having an indexing clause written into all your service supply contracts.

For instance, you could tie the indexing clause

to a specific indicator, such as the cost of living inflation index. The contract would then be automatically adjusted annually to match this selected indicator. For example, if the rate of inflation the previous year was 3 percent, then the pricing in your service contract for the following year would rise by 3 percent to keep pace with inflation. You and your client could create your own indexing system, basing the index on key components of the contract, such as labor, materials and transportation. Select a median number, such as 100, based on today's prices. Then, if the index goes up or down beyond a certain point, perhaps 10 points in either direction, the indexing clause would automatically change the contract pricing to reflect economic conditions.

You want to minimize the potential effects of external factors on your ability to generate a profit, especially the external factors you cannot control. Consequently, it is wise to develop an indexing formula that can be used to automatically adjust long-term service contracts, keeping in mind the major external influences that can have the biggest impact on your profit:

- Inflation
- Currency fluctuation
- Interest rates
- Supply and demand
- Political influences

Choosing Your Contracts Carefully

Choosing your contracts carefully is not a pricing strategy, but it is nonetheless important. More than any other industry, service providers have long been plagued by not being paid on time (if at all) for work completed. This is especially prevalent for service providers that subcontract in the construction and home improvement industry.

Before signing a contract to provide services, you must stand back, study the situation and ask yourself if the contract is work that you really want. Before agreeing to a job, always question your customer's motives for wanting to contract with your service.

For instance, if you run a house painting service and a general contractor or home builder asks you to paint five houses, a red flag should go up. Assuming the contractor is established, why is his or her usual house painter not painting these houses? Is the contractor slow to pay or is the contractor simply seeking new subcontractors?

Secondary service providers are often the last in line to get paid and the first to lose out when money runs short for whatever reason. Before jumping at that great opportunity to expand your business, make sure you protect yourself, and know the client and the situation, and how and when you will be paid. Make sure to do some due diligence on potential clients. In Chapter 11, "Managing Your Home Business," you will find additional information about extending credit,

establishing payment terms and collecting on completed contracts.

Be Detail Oriented

It is in the service provider's best interest to keep a detailed log of each client's job, noting the exact amount of time spent on the job and the time related to the job, such as estimating, picking up supplies and administrative work. If your client challenges the invoice, you will have documentation to support your billing. And, by keeping an accurate log of each contract, you will not overlook small items and time spent on the job, which can cost you money if you neglect to include them in your invoice. A basic Client Job Log for Time template is presented here (Figure 9.2) that you can create on your computer and customize to meet your specific needs. Also, presented here is a basic Client Job Log for Direct Costs (Figure 9.3) that you can also create on your computer and customize to meet your specific needs.

FIGURE 9.2   Client Job Log for Time

Client Name: _____

Client Address: _____

Telephone Number: _____

Job Number: _____

Start Date: _____ Completion Date: _____

Time Log

Date	Time Started	Time Finished	Hours/Minutes	Total Time to Date
_____	_____	_____	___/___	_____
_____	_____	_____	___/___	_____
_____	_____	_____	___/___	_____
_____	_____	_____	___/___	_____
_____	_____	_____	___/___	_____
_____	_____	_____	___/___	_____

FIGURE 9.2	Client Job Log for Time, continued

Date	Time Started	Time Finished	Hours/Minutes	Total Time to Date
_____	_____	_____	____ / ____	_____
_____	_____	_____	____ / ____	_____
_____	_____	_____	____ / ____	_____
_____	_____	_____	____ / ____	_____
_____	_____	_____	____ / ____	_____
_____	_____	_____	____ / ____	_____
_____	_____	_____	____ / ____	_____
_____	_____	_____	____ / ____	_____
_____	_____	_____	____ / ____	_____
_____	_____	_____	____ / ____	_____
_____	_____	_____	____ / ____	_____
_____	_____	_____	____ / ____	_____
_____	_____	_____	____ / ____	_____
_____	_____	_____	____ / ____	_____

Total billing hours _____

Rate per hour $ _____

Total labor costs $ _____ (A)

FIGURE 9.3	Client Job Log for Direct Costs

Client Name: _____

Client Address: _____

Telephone Number: _____

Job Number: _____

Start Date: _____ Completion Date: _____

Direct Cost Log

Date	Description	# of Units	$ Cost per Unit	$ Total Cost
_____	_____	_____	_____	_____
_____	_____	_____	_____	_____

FIGURE 9.3	Client Job Log for Direct Costs, continued

Date	Description	# of Units	$ Cost per Unit	$ Total Cost

Total direct costs $ _____ (B)

Invoicing

Total labor costs (A) $ _____

Total direct costs (B) $ _____

Markup $ _____

Total invoice $ _____

(Plus applicable taxes)

RESOURCES

Associations

American Marketing Association
311 S. Wacker Drive, Suite 5800
Chicago, IL 60606
(800) AMA-1150 (262-1150), (312) 542-9000

webmarketingpower.com

Business Marketing Association
1601 N. Bond Street, Suite 101
Naperville, IL 60563
(800) 664-4BMA (4262), (630) 544-5054
webmarketing.org

Canadian Marketing Association
1 Concorde Gate, Suite 607
Don Mills, ON M3C 3N6
(416) 391-2362
webthe-cma.org

Marketing Education Association
P.O. Box 27473
Tempe, AZ 85285-7473
(602) 750-6735
webnationalmea.org

Suggested Reading

Daly, John L. *Pricing for Profitability: Activity-Based Pricing for Competitive Advantage.* New York: John Wiley & Sons, 2002.

Dolan, Robert J., and Hermann Simon. *Power Pricing: How Managing Price Transforms the Bottom Line.* New York: Free Press (Simon & Schuster), 1997.

Nagle, Thomas T., and John E. Hogan. *The Strategy and Tactics of Pricing: A Guide to Growing More Profitably.* 4th edition. New York: Pearson Prentice Hall, 2002.

Reilly, Tom. *Value-Added Selling: How to Sell More Profitably, Confidently, and Professionally by Competing on Value, Not Price.* New York: McGraw-Hill, 2002.

Weiss, Alan. *Value-Based Fees: How to Charge—and Get—What You're Worth.* New York: Jossey-Bass/Pfeiffer, 2002.

Websites

Entrepreneur Online: Small business information products and services portal featuring marketing planning advice and custom Marketing Calculator software. ***entrepreneur.com***

More Business: Marketing and business information, advice and free templates. ***morebusiness.com***

SBA: U.S. Small Business Administration. ***sba.gov***

Society for Marketing Professional Services: Nonprofit association representing professional marketing organizations and consultants in architectural, engineering, planning, interior design, construction and specialty consulting firms located throughout the United States and Canada. Website offers information about the services provided by marketing professionals. ***smps.org***

CHAPTER 10

Finding and Keeping Customers

THIS CHAPTER COVERS THREE MAIN TOPics—conducting research and collecting data to identify your target customers, understanding your competitors and building competitive advantages, and learning how to provide incredible customer service to make sure you keep the customers coming back. These important topics are grouped because:

1. You need to identify the target customers for your business, so you will know to whom you will be selling your products or services.
2. You need to know who your competitors are and how you can gain an edge on them.
3. You need to know how to provide customer service that keeps your customers coming back to your business.

In short, every business needs customers and cannot survive without them. As you continue reading, you will notice that this chapter is closely tied to Chapter 12, "Creating a Marketing Plan," which details the steps needed to identify markets and their potential and to develop marketing strategies. There is also information about the research and data-collection methods necessary to create sections of your marketing plan. I have identified and noted the crossover areas in both chapters for your convenience.

STARTING YOUR RESEARCH

Through research you gain insights into your business, industry, competition, customers, products or services and the marketplace, enabling you to make fact-based forecasts and decisions, which are vital when planning your business activities. Without research to back up your statements and forecasts, your plans are nothing more than fiction, based not on what you know but on what you hope will happen.

Research will reveal:

- If there is a market for your invention before you spend $150,000 to have prototypes designed and apply for a patent.
- If the marketplace can support another office cleaning company.
- Which consumers you should target.
- Where you should position your business and products in the market.
- What types of user benefits consumers need and want.
- What motivates people to buy and whether or not they are likely to buy your products or services.

In short, research will reveal if there is the potential for your business or product and what marketing strategies you need to use to succeed.

Types of Data

Before you begin your research, you first have to identify the types of data needed to completely research and analyze specific business and marketing activities—primary data, secondary data, quantitative data, qualitative data, geographic data, demographic data and psychographic data.

Primary Data

Primary data is the information and facts that you get by conducting your own research. If you are already in business, you can collect primary data for free by talking with your customers, suppliers, competitors, other businesspeople and business alliances about your products, services and marketplace. If you are not currently in business, another method of collecting free primary data is making general observations about your target customers, about the goods or services you will be selling, about your competitors and about the marketplace and the industry you are about to enter. There are additional key methods of collecting primary data, such as conducting formal surveys, hosting focus groups, giving product or service demonstrations and doing mystery or comparison shopping. Some are discussed later in this chapter.

Secondary Data

Secondary data is information and facts that you did not generate personally, but instead obtain from outside sources. Most secondary data can be acquired for free from books, journals, websites, newspapers, studies and material found on audio or videotapes, CDs or DVDs. You can obtain secondary data at schools, through business and industry associations, in your local library, in bookstores, on the internet, through private and publicly held corporations, and from government agencies and other places that collect such materials.

You must, however, be careful and not get too far ahead of yourself. You must first identify your research objectives, that is, what you are seeking and what you can do with the data you collect. Data, information and statistics are available on just about every person or every product or every place that you can think of.

Some of the statistical information that may be of use will include:

- Patent, copyright and trademark data from the copyright office and trademark and patent offices both in the United States and Canada;
- Manufactured product specifications, available through manufacturers' associations and manufacturers' product directories (print and electronic);
- Demographic statistics and psychographic data reports, available through government agencies, the media, almanacs, the internet and research organizations;
- Public opinion polls and media surveys, available through research organizations, government agencies, schools and private companies;

- Transportation data, available through transportation-related associations, almanacs and government agencies;
- Legal and crime data, available at the federal level and local levels though court, police and media services;
- Business statistics, available through business and industry associations, as well as government agencies and business websites;
- International statistics, available through business and industry associations and government agencies;
- Political statistics and data, available through political groups and government agencies;
- Weather statistics, available through government agencies, the media and almanacs;
- Personal finance and monetary markets data, available from banks, government agencies, business and industry associations, consumer groups, the internet and the media.

Endless volumes could easily be filled about the types of data, statistics and information available from secondary sources. So identify what you want to learn and then contact the sources that have compiled the type of data you are seeking. Keep in mind that you are (usually) looking for current data, so check the dates before you proceed through documents or web pages.

Quantitative Data

Quantitative data is always expressed in numbers and percentages. Most data analyzed and used by small business owners to create business and marketing plans is quantitative. Because quantitative data is expressed numerically, they are objective, easily measured and therefore easy to understand and transfer into charts, lists and graphs for planning purposes.

Quantitative data is valuable to small business owners because the data enables them to under-

stand the marketplace in broad terms at a glance. For instance, if you circulate a questionnaire that asks yes-or-no questions, the resulting answers can be easily tabulated, either as numbers, such as 106 yes and 94 no, or as percentages, such as 53 percent yes and 47 percent no. Another example is comment cards that ask customers to rank your service on a scale of 1 to 5. Once again, the results are expressed in numbers, such as "15 people of the 30 who ranked our service gave us 5 out of 5" or "our average ranking was 4.3," or in percentages, such as "50 percent of our customers are 100 percent satisfied with the level of service we provide."

You can gather quantitative data (primary) or seek it out in research (secondary). The positive of quantitative data is that the data is easy to use and can be easily used for comparative purposes. The downside is that numbers provide only part of an answer. They do not explain *why* the results came out as they did.

Qualitative Data

Qualitative data is not expressed in numbers, but rather in specific answers and statements. It is what people say about your business, products, services, prices, quality or anything else they reveal in responses that cannot be presented numerically. Examples of qualitative data include information gained in the following ways:

- From open-ended questions designed to encourage people to answer freely;
- From discussion groups composed of members of your target group(s), who are encouraged to talk about how they feel or what they think about a certain topic, such as a product, service, price, value or quality;
- From informal discussions with customers, suppliers, vendors, employees or other people.

Qualitative data is valuable to small business owners because the data can reveal more precise details and information about what your customers or target consumers think and feel about specific issues relevant to your business or the products or services you sell. The downsides are that the data can be biased, the person using it may interpret it in a manner in which it was not intended, and it is difficult or impossible to aggregate and represent simply, either in numbers or in graphics.

Geographic Data

Geographic data is information segmenting your target groups by country, region, state, county, city, neighborhood and even street. There are five basic questions in terms of collecting geographic data about your target groups:

1. Where are your target customers located?
2. Is the target group in the geographic area large enough to be profitable?
3. What is required to access the geographic area where your target group resides?
4. What means of promotion will enable you to tap the target market in that specific geographic area?
5. Will the target group respond to your promotional activities?

Even on a basic level, geographically segmented information about your target audience, whether obtained through primary or secondary research, is extremely valuable. For example, if you operate a pool cleaning service, you would want to know where in the town or city you'll find the most people who have swimming pools. Having this basic information enables you to target your advertising and promotion activities to that area.

Demographic Data

Demographic data is statistical information about the population. It can be used for segmenting a target group by gender, age, race, religion, education, income, marital status and profession. Demographic data can be further expanded to include information such as the type of car your typical target consumer drives or the average number of people in his or her household.

If you are already in business, you can collect demographic information from your current customers to create a demographic profile of your target groups. If you are in the research or start-up phases, you can contact local government agencies, libraries and business associations, and visit local websites, as well as those of federal agencies. For the United States, a good place to start is FedStats, *fedstats.gov*, "making statistics from more than 100 agencies available to citizens everywhere." For Canada, Statistics Canada, *statcan.ca*, the national statistics agency, "produces statistics that help Canadians better understand their country—its population, resources, economy, society and culture."

Whether obtained through primary or secondary research, demographic data plays a significant role in creating the profile of your target customers. From this information you can determine how to plan your marketing strategy to best connect with groups of potential customers. The downside is that demographic data can be misinterpreted based on stereotypes, generalizations and broad assumptions.

Psychographic Data

Psychographics is segmenting your customers by their common characteristics, such as lifestyle, values, behavior and opinions. Psychographics is used as a continuation of geographic and demographic data. Once you know where your target group is located (geographic) and who your target group is (demographic), you can begin to find out what the members of the group think and care about (psychographics) in terms of your business, industry, competitors, pricing issues and goods and services. Psychographic data can answer a variety of questions.

- What do most members of my target group

have in common? Do they go to church or belong to a certain social club?

- What do most members of my target group care about most—price, quality, fast service, value or a wide selection of goods and services?
- What publications do most members of my target group read, what television shows do they watch, what radio stations do they listen to and what recreational activities do they pursue?

Basic assumptions can be made in terms of psychographic profiling of your target market, providing they are logical assumptions. For instance, it is a safe assumption that most members of the target market for custom-designed and -manufactured golf clubs are not university students. As noted above, be careful when you make assumptions.

Research Methods

Next, you need to consider the research methods. But before you do, you will have to decide if you will conduct your own research, hire a research firm or consultant or perhaps combine the two options. (If you decide to conduct your own research, start by not overlooking one of the easiest and least expensive ways of conducting research—looking out your window to see what is going on in your own community.)

Research can answer your questions about the area in which you plan to start conducting business, such as the following.

- Is the economy hot?
- In what lifecycle stage are the product and the market—growth, decline or static?
- How many other businesses are selling the same products and services?
- Is unemployment high, low or static?
- Are there any current issues or emerging trends that will affect the market?

This type of research is more than looking out your window in the literal sense. It is done by keeping your finger on the pulse of the community at all times to stay current on local trends. Then, you will have the knowledge and information needed to make business and planning decisions for the future.

One way to keep in touch with what is going on in your own community is to conduct informal research. You have to make an effort to get out and talk with people, such as your potential suppliers, target customers, community leaders, business associations and other small and homebased business owners. Informal research can happen over a cup of coffee, at the point of purchase, during a business or social function or just about any other place or time. There are also many other ways of collecting primary data, including hosting formal focus groups, looking through your local Yellow Pages business directory and going online.

Focus Groups

One of the best ways to research the viability of a new product or service is to conduct a focus group to see what a sampling of people think of your products or services and the features, benefits, competitive advantages, durability, reliability, performance and price points. Unfortunately, a professionally run focus group can be very costly for budding entrepreneurs with little money for research.

To save some money, consider creating your own homemade focus group. Choose people who are from your intended primary target group and who are OK with you either videotaping or audiotaping the discussion to ensure you do not overlook any information when analyzing it. Ideally, a focus group should have 6 to 12 participants, which will allow everyone to contribute to the discussion and give you enough varying responses.

Prior to conducting a focus group, you need to

prepare. First, you want to create an outline of the topics, points and ideas you would like the focus group to consider. Decide how you want to conduct the discussion. Ask questions? Present a slide show? Throw out points for discussion? You need a way to start the focus group off and keep it running. The session should last no more than 90 minutes or perhaps two hours—longer than that and you tend to lose people. You should provide some food and perhaps an incentive, which could be anything from cash to free samples of your product(s).

Every participant in the group should be made aware of the fact that his or her input, ideas, suggestions and complaints are important and you are interested in any contributions. After all, that is the whole idea behind the process. Each person in the group should have the opportunity to voice his or her opinions.

You need to be able to keep the discussion going and cover the topics without swaying the contributions. The participants should always feel free to express their thoughts, feelings and opinions. Some businesses will hire someone with an outgoing personality and some experience to lead a focus group.

No matter how you arrange and run the focus group, the purpose is to gather the data and analyze it afterward. Compile and review the results to determine what these people thought and felt about your products, services, advertisements and so on.

Research Online

Just over a decade ago, finding a foreign distribution source for your widget or even learning about out-of-state laws and regulations pertaining to business expansion was time-consuming and often frustrating. Countless hours could be spent on the telephone, writing letters or purchasing expensive books and directories just to get the information needed to start a business, find products and services and learn more about potential customers.

Fortunately, all of that has changed thanks to the internet. Facts, information, leads and just about anything you could want to know or need to know about a business, an industry or a market, domestically or internationally, are now just a mouse click away.

To use the web effectively, try a variety of searches, including using different keywords and even different search engines. When checking the web pages resulting from a search, look for a date on the page to make sure the material is recent. Be sure to discern fact-based sites from blogs (personal journals) and other sites that are based on someone's opinions—although sometimes those can be beneficial, as well. Once you find helpful websites, look for links to other sites that may prove worthwhile.

You can find out a lot about your competitors by perusing their websites. In addition, you can compare suppliers and vendors; look for demographic data for your town, city, state or region; and seek out articles on trends, news and changes in the industry. For future reference, bookmark the best research websites you find so you can access them again. Also, print out statistics or other documents you want to keep at your fingertips.

Using Surveys for Research Purposes

Surveys have long been used by small business owners and marketers as a highly effective business and marketing research tool. Like most research activities, there are numerous options for conducting consumer surveys for business research and planning purposes, including by mail, by telephone, in person or online. Of course a survey is viable only if you ask the right questions and use the answers to provide data you need.

Mail Surveys

Mail surveys are a popular way to find out what

consumers think, but they can also be costly when you factor in time, postage, advertising and renting mailing lists. The first mail survey option is to rent consumer mailing lists of people who match your primary target consumers and mail a survey to them with a postage-paid return envelope. The second method is to create your survey in a tear-away response card format and have it inserted in a newspaper, magazine, newsletter or trade journal read by your primary target consumers and ask readers to complete the survey and mail it back. In both cases you will likely have to provide some sort of incentive to motivate people to take the time to complete and mail in the survey. The incentive could be automatic entry into a contest, a discount coupon, a gift certificate or any number of rewards that would entice people to complete and send in the survey. While you can get some good results, often mailed-in surveys contain a higher degree of junk data or useless information because people don't always take them seriously or because the respondents are not totally representative of your target consumers. (Some people like to participate in surveys and some people always avoid them.)

Telephone Surveys

Calling members of your target group at their home or office is another method of conducting surveys, but one that requires skill, time and patience. In fact, you might even want to leave this method to the professional telemarketers and phone survey folks who have the communications skills, equipment and ability to tolerate the 90 percent of people who will say, "No thanks!" or just hang up.

However, if you decide to try telephone surveying yourself, make sure you call consumers in the early evenings (best between 6:00 and 7:00 p.m.) and business consumers during the day (best between 10:00 a.m. 4:00 p.m.). Try to get a listing of targeted customers, since calling at random would be a colossal waste of time, as most people hate phone solicitors. In fact, you might want to make sure that random telephone surveys are not prohibited by the Do Not Call listings. For the United States, visit the National Do-Not-Call Registry website at *fcc.gov/cgb/donotcall* for additional information. For Canada, the Canadian Radio-television and Telecommunications Commission, *crtc.gc.ca*, has contracted to have the National Do Not Call List operational by September 30, 2008.

In-Person Surveys

In-person surveys are another way of finding out what your customers and target consumers think about your proposed or current products and services. In-person surveys can be conducted at malls on weekends with permission, at trade shows and seminars or out on the street. The benefits of surveying consumers personally is that it enables you to ask questions that are more qualitative, as respondents will often answer these kinds of questions face to face, but not take the time if they have to write their answers down. You can get a better quality of answers from people in a one-to-one situation, especially if there is some incentive for answering the questions, such as a discount coupon or a free gift.

Online Surveys

A quick and cheap way to survey your target group is to use your website. An online survey is a great option for small business owners who are on tight budgets and need results quickly.

General Guidelines. Regardless of the survey method you choose, there are some general guidelines for creating a survey that is unbiased and will get the results you need for your business.

- The first rule to creating an effective survey is to ask questions that will elicit quality answers to help you make decisions about your products, services, advertising and/or your business in general.

- If you want *quantitative* results, ask closed-ended questions that require a yes or no response or that require only one response from multiple choices. (For example, a carpet cleaning service might ask, "How many times a year do you have your carpets cleaned? ❏ 1 ❏ 2 ❏ 3"

- If you want *qualitative* results, ask open-ended questions that require people to reveal what they think or how they feel. (For example, a carpet cleaning service might ask, "What is the biggest benefit you receive from having your carpets cleaned?")

- Try to word your questions in such a way as to not influence how people respond. The key is objectivity. Therefore, the surveying exercise must be focused on finding out how people think and feel and believe, without bias from the questioning techniques.

- Word and phrase your questions to make them easy to understand, free of technical expertise, ambiguity, jargon and abbreviations. Questions should also be easy to answer. The harder you make it for people to answer your questions, the less likely they are to complete the survey accurately and truthfully, if at all.

- Don't ask personally identifying information. You do not need any Social Security numbers or other information that could be deemed too personal. Instead of asking for specific numbers, use ranges. For example, "Is your income between $20,000 and $30,000, between $30,000 and $50,000, . . . ?"

- Keep your surveys short. People get tired of taking a survey after about 10 questions, especially if you are surveying by phone.

- Before conducting a survey, test it on a small segment of your intended target group to make sure your questions follow a logical sequence, are free of errors in grammar and spelling, can be answered in a reasonable amount of time and will elicit answers that will help you achieve your survey objectives.

Creating a Target Customer Profile

Once you have compiled and analyzed your research data, you should have a good idea of who your target customers are and their special characteristics. At this point, you should create a simple profile of your target customer to use as a handy reference when planning advertising, marketing and promotional activities. You will know where to allocate your marketing budget so you will have the best chance of reaching your target consumers and get the most bang from your promotional bucks.

Below, you'll find a Primary Target Customer Profile Worksheet (Figure 10.1). You may want to delete some of the items to suit your specific needs and/or to add items, such as the types of TV programs your target consumers watch, the types of sports they participate in or the types of music they listen to. Of course, while you want to zero in on a target group, you do not want to make the profile so narrow that the group of people who fit the criteria is very small. This won't give you a large enough market to succeed unless you are selling high-end products or services. You want to narrow the field enough to market most effectively and yet include in your profile enough potential customers to generate the profits you expect.

GETTING STARTED WITH IDENTIFYING YOUR COMPETITORS

Evaluating your competitors is tricky, to say the least. You do not want to overestimate or, of course, underestimate your competitors' ability to effectively compete in the marketplace and their resolve not to lose

FIGURE 10.1	Primary Target Customer Profile Worksheet

Where do my target customers live?

Country: _____ State: _____

County: _____ City: _____

Neighborhood: _____

How many people match my target customer profile in the geographical area in which I will be doing business? _____
_____

What is most important to my target customers when making purchasing decisions?

❑ Price _____% ❑ Value_____% ❑ Quality_____% ❑ Service _____%

What percentage of my target customers is male? _____% How old are they?

❑ 0–17 _____% ❑ 18–29 _____% ❑ 30–39 _____% ❑ 40–49 _____% ❑ 50–64 _____%

❑ 65 + _____%

What percentage of my target customers is female? _____% How old are they?

❑ 0–17 _____% ❑ 18–29 _____% ❑ 30–39 _____% ❑ 40–49 _____% ❑ 50–64 _____%

❑ 65+ _____%

What is the marital status of my target customers?

❑ Single _____% ❑ Married _____% ❑ Divorced _____% ❑ Widowed _____%

What level of education do my target customers have?

❑ Grade School _____% ❑ High School _____% ❑ Post-Secondary _____%

What do my target customers do to earn a living?

❑ Labor _____% ❑ Office Work _____% ❑ Retail _____% ❑ Management _____%

❑ Sales _____% ❑ Professionals _____% ❑ Executives _____% ❑ Self-Employed _____%

❑ Retired _____% ❑ Other _____%

How much do my target customers earn per year?

❑ $0–$15,000_____% ❑ $15,000–$25,000 _____% ❑ $25,000–$40,000 _____%

❑ $40,000–$55,000 _____% ❑ $55,000–$70,000 _____% ❑ $70,000+ _____%

What is my target customers' household income per year?

❑ $0–$20,000 _____% ❑ $20,000–$35,000 _____% ❑ $35,000–$50,000 _____%

❑ $50,000–$75,000 _____% ❑ $75,000–$100,000 _____% ❑ $100,000+ _____%

Do my target customers own or rent their homes?

❑ Own _____% ❑ Rent_____%

FIGURE 10.1	Primary Target Customer Profile Worksheet, continued

In what types of homes do my target consumers live?

❑ Apartment _____% ❑ Condo _____% ❑ Single Family _____% ❑ Town House _____%

❑ Duplex _____% ❑ Cooperative _____%

How many people are currently living in the home?

❑ 1 _____% ❑ 2 _____% ❑ 3 _____% ❑ 4 _____% ❑ 5 _____% ❑ 6+ _____%

Which types of pets do my target customers have?

❑ Dog _____% ❑ Cat _____% ❑ Fish _____% ❑ Bird _____% ❑ Other _____%

What type of automobiles do my target customers drive?

❑ Sports Car _____% ❑ Family Car _____% ❑ Truck _____% ❑ Van_____% ❑ SUV _____%

How many vacations do my target customers take each year?

❑ 1 _____% ❑ 2 _____% ❑ 3 _____% ❑ 4+ _____%

market share to new competitors. Competing businesses have to realize they are engaged in war with each other and that to the victors will go the spoils of war, which in business means customers. Regardless of the type of business you operate or the kinds of products or services you sell, you will always be competing for customers and their money.

You have two options, which you can combine if you like. The first is to go toe-to-toe with your competitors and beat them by developing competitive advantages and by providing more benefits to the consumer. The second option is to carefully research and analyze all areas of your industry, marketplace, business and competing businesses to identify niche markets presently being ignored or underserviced and "specialize" your business so you can succeed in that niche market.

The latter is probably the easier path for home business owners, because their competitors are almost always better financed, longer established and more resources. But before you decide whether to specialize within the industry or market, you should be able to identify the various types of competition and learn how to develop a competitive advantage. Both topics are covered later. A comprehensive Competition Comparison Worksheet (Figure 10.2) is provided to enable you to better understand your competitors, their products, and services in comparison with your products and services and their position in the marketplace relative to your position.

The Four Kinds of Competition

Like all businesses, homebased businesses face four types of competition—direct, indirect, phantom and future.

Direct Competition

Direct competition is by far the easiest to identify because it is the most obvious. These are the competitors operating in the same geographic area as you, selling a similar product or service, and targeting the same primary consumers. An example of direct competitors would be two lawn care services that offer clients similar services in the same geographical area.

Indirect Competition

The second type of competition your home business will face is indirect—businesses that sell numerous products or services, some of which are the same or similar to your core product or service line. For instance, if you exclusively sell and install rain gutters, indirect competitors would include home improvement centers that sell rain gutter products and contractors who occasionally install gutters in the course of a larger project.

Phantom Competition

As the name suggests, phantom competition is tough to nail down with any great accuracy because it can be in many forms—self-help books, do-it-yourself kits, unusual weather patterns, media influences that sway or change consumer opinion, factors that cause consumers to choose not to buy for whatever reason, other things that compete for their money and/or time and so forth. For instance, the individual who washes his or her car at home is competing with the local car wash, but not directly since he or she is not in business.

Future Competition

The final type of competition business owners face is competitors who have not yet opened for business. Future competitors come in two forms: businesses yet to open and businesses that will expand their offerings to include the products or services you sell. For instance, if you operate the only pet taxi in town and are swamped with business, expect that in the near future someone will open a pet taxi service to cash in on the obvious demand for the service. Alternately, a people taxi service might decide, because your pet taxi service is so successful, to expand the services they offer to include transporting pets, as well as people. When there is demand, supply will always follow.

Building a Competitive Advantage

As discussed earlier, every business, product and service needs a competitive advantage. In fact, in an extremely competitive business environment, a competitive advantage is crucial if you hope to compete, survive and grow your business. Think of your competitive advantage as the main reason why someone will choose your business over your competitors!

For that reason, the competitive advantage you create should be used in all business and marketing activities to describe how your business excels and what special advantage people can expect when they do business with you. Thus, you will need to develop a central message to describe your competitive advantage. It should be brief, to the point, and easy to understand and, above all, clearly state why people should do business with you, not the competition.

But what is your competitive advantage and how do you discover it? First, your competitive advantage must be beneficial to your customers. People want to know upfront what they will get out of doing business with you. Simply put, if there is no benefit to doing business with you, then why do it? Do you offer the lowest price? Can people make money by purchasing your products or services? Do the products or services that you sell help people solve a problem, make people feel better, or enable people fill a special need that isn't being filled by your competitors? If you want to beat the competition, you must have or create an advantage that your competitors do not have and that advantage must benefit your target consumers enough to attract them to your business.

Competitive Possibilities

There are numerous possibilities for creating and maintaining a competitive advantage. Here are a few areas to consider.

Personalized Attention. As mentioned earlier, in an age of impersonal communications, you might offer personalized attention. The bigger your competitors, the less likely they can offer to take the time with each customer that you can provide.

New and/or Specialized Technology. For example, Detail Plus Appearance Systems offers unique, top-of-the-line technology to auto detailers, most of whom are still buying and using the same, basic equipment that was being used in the industry nearly 20 years ago. Owner Bud Abraham says he found a new way to run detailing businesses by using new, specialized technology designed for the industry.

A Special Skill. If your competitors are all in the party-performance business, doing clowning and magic, and you are the lone fire eater, you've got an edge. Likewise, if all the local gardening businesses are cutting grass and planting, but you can do lawn sculptures, you've got an edge. Look at your skills and determine which ones you can work into your business that your competition cannot.

A Special Look. It doesn't matter what business you are in, appearances count. The children's dentist with the coolest waiting room (the one with kid-friendly designs, videos and the latest games) will have more patients than the dentists with the standard fish tank and magazines. Packaging can also dress up ordinary products, so if you can package your products in a more exciting manner, that can gain you an advantage over your competitors.

Value. Value doesn't always mean lowest price. It may mean more for your money—and that appeals to customers. For example, if you are running a housecleaning service and charging $80 an hour while your competitors are charging $70 an hour, but your cleaners do laundry and exterior windows but your competitors do not, then which is the better deal? Determine what your competitors include in their prices and see what you can include in your price. Even with products, you can add in a low-cost accessory and provide the better value.

In addition to beneficial, your competitive advantage must be exclusive to your business. This does not necessarily mean that no other business sells the same products or services, but "exclusive" more in the way that you sell your products or provide your services. Creating a beneficial competitive advantage that is exclusive to your business does not have to be difficult or costly. In fact, it can be something as simple as a plumber offering a 10-year warranty for workmanship instead of a 5-year warranty, which is the typical industry standard. This is an exclusive competitive advantage that will definitely appeal to many people needing plumbing services. An exclusive competitive advantage does not have to reinvent your business or the industry; it just has to be something you do or sell that is different and not available from competitors in your area.

Your competitive advantage must also be easy to remember, simplistic in nature, and easily identified and linked to your business. However, it is best if it is something people can evaluate. The advantage of the pizzeria promises to get your pizza to you in less than 30 minutes or it's free is easy to evaluate—just look at the clock.

This is also a challenge of sorts and people like that. But what could be a competitive advantage could also be a problem. For example, a wedding planner boasts, "We guarantee a stress-free wedding day or we'll pay for the cake." That guarantee is easy to remember, beneficial to the customer and exclusive to the business, but it is hard to prove. How can the wedding planner or a customer prove the big day was or was not "stress-free"? Therefore, the wedding planner should be planning to pay for a lot of wedding cakes—or arguing with customers about whether an event was stress-free. If such a guarantee brings the business enough customers to keep it in the black, even though it pays for a cake on occasion, then it can use this approach. The point is that any claim that cannot be evaluated objectively or at least quantifiably can be tricky, so a business making a subjective claim should prepare for the added expense.

Competition Comparison

Even with a SWOT (Strengths, Weaknesses, Opportunities and Threats) analysis, featured in Chapter 12, "Creating a Marketing Plan," it can prove difficult to get a firm grasp on the competitors and how your business, products and services compare with theirs. Below is a Competition Comparison Worksheet (Figure 10.2) that I created for *Entrepreneur Magazine's Ultimate Small Business Marketing Guide* and have revised for this book. You can copy it and use it to rate each of your competitors. Once you've completed this worksheet, use this information to identify and build on your strengths and opportunities in the marketplace, while correcting internal weaknesses and eliminating external threats. Complete only the items relevant to your specific business or industry. You may also discover a few items you want to add that are specific to your business, industry, market or target groups.

FIGURE 10.2	Competition Comparison Worksheet

Competitor Information

Competitor Company Name: _____

Years in Business: _____ Estimated Annual Sales: $_____

Number of Employees: _____ Estimated Market Share: _____%

How is their market share? ❏ Increasing   ❏ Decreasing

What is this competitor's number-one specialty? _____

Business location   ❏ Homebased   ❏ Storefront   ❏ Office   ❏ Other _____

How would you rate this competitor's reputation impartially?	Poor	Fair	Good	Great
Company reputation	❏	❏	❏	❏
Product(s) reputation	❏	❏	❏	❏
Service(s) reputation	❏	❏	❏	❏
Customer service reputation	❏	❏	❏	❏
Pricing reputation	❏	❏	❏	❏

How would you rate this competitor's product(s) impartially?	Poor	Fair	Good	Great
Benefits	❏	❏	❏	❏
Positioning	❏	❏	❏	❏
Quality	❏	❏	❏	❏
Value	❏	❏	❏	❏

FIGURE 10.2   Competition Comparison Worksheet, continued

How would you rate this competitor's product(s) impartially?	Poor	Fair	Good	Great
Reliability	❏	❏	❏	❏
Performance	❏	❏	❏	❏
Ability to meet market trends	❏	❏	❏	❏
Ability to meet market needs	❏	❏	❏	❏
Availability	❏	❏	❏	❏
Packaging	❏	❏	❏	❏
Labeling	❏	❏	❏	❏
Private label/exclusive product(s)	❏	❏	❏	❏
Product(s) warranties	❏	❏	❏	❏
How would you rate this competitor's service(s) impartially?	Poor	Fair	Good	Great
Benefits	❏	❏	❏	❏
Positioning	❏	❏	❏	❏
Quality	❏	❏	❏	❏
Value	❏	❏	❏	❏
Reliability	❏	❏	❏	❏
Performance	❏	❏	❏	❏
Ability to meet market trends	❏	❏	❏	❏
Ability to meet market needs	❏	❏	❏	❏
Availability	❏	❏	❏	❏
Exclusive/proprietary service(s)	❏	❏	❏	❏
Service(s) warranties	❏	❏	❏	❏
Workmanship warranties	❏	❏	❏	❏
How would you rate this competitor's marketing impartially?	Poor	Fair	Good	Great
Advertising	❏	❏	❏	❏
Yellow Pages	❏	❏	❏	❏
Radio	❏	❏	❏	❏
TV	❏	❏	❏	❏

FIGURE 10.2	Competition Comparison Worksheet, continued

How would you rate this competitor's marketing impartially?	Poor	Fair	Good	Great
Direct mail	❑	❑	❑	❑
Magazines	❑	❑	❑	❑
Trade Shows	❑	❑	❑	❑
Seminars	❑	❑	❑	❑
Publicity	❑	❑	❑	❑
Contests	❑	❑	❑	❑
Coupons	❑	❑	❑	❑
Catalogs	❑	❑	❑	❑
Signage	❑	❑	❑	❑
Newsletters	❑	❑	❑	❑
Networking	❑	❑	❑	❑
Seasonal promotional events	❑	❑	❑	❑
Telemarketing	❑	❑	❑	❑
Event sponsorships	❑	❑	❑	❑
Cross marketing/promotional activity	❑	❑	❑	❑
Customer clubs/loyalty programs	❑	❑	❑	❑

How would you rate this competitor's operations?	Poor	Fair	Good	Great
Customer policies	❑	❑	❑	❑
Reliability	❑	❑	❑	❑
Consistency of message	❑	❑	❑	❑
Leadership	❑	❑	❑	❑
Proactive thinking/planning	❑	❑	❑	❑
Customer service	❑	❑	❑	❑
Communications	❑	❑	❑	❑
Technological state	❑	❑	❑	❑
Community involvement	❑	❑	❑	❑
Charity involvement	❑	❑	❑	❑
Corporate citizenship	❑	❑	❑	❑

FIGURE 10.2 Competition Comparison Worksheet, continued

How would you rate this competitor's operations?	Poor	Fair	Good	Great
Business associations	❏	❏	❏	❏
Better Business Bureau report	❏	❏	❏	❏
Vendor(s) support	❏	❏	❏	❏
Manufacturing capabilities	❏	❏	❏	❏
Research/development	❏	❏	❏	❏
Distribution channels	❏	❏	❏	❏
Equipment	❏	❏	❏	❏
Transportation	❏	❏	❏	❏
Overall financial stability	❏	❏	❏	❏
Accept credit cards	❏	❏	❏	❏
Accept paper/e-checks	❏	❏	❏	❏
Offer financing options	❏	❏	❏	❏
Pay suppliers on time	❏	❏	❏	❏
Pay employees on time	❏	❏	❏	❏
Business hours	❏	❏	❏	❏
Computerized	❏	❏	❏	❏

How would you rate this competitor's employees?	Poor	Fair	Good	Great
Loyalty	❏	❏	❏	❏
Training	❏	❏	❏	❏
Remuneration	❏	❏	❏	❏
Benefits	❏	❏	❏	❏
Work conditions	❏	❏	❏	❏
Education	❏	❏	❏	❏
Specialized	❏	❏	❏	❏
Subcontractors	❏	❏	❏	❏
Professional appearance	❏	❏	❏	❏
Energized/motivated	❏	❏	❏	❏

FIGURE 10.2   Competition Comparison Worksheet, continued

How would you rate this competitor's website?	Poor	Fair	Good	Great
Regularly updated	❑	❑	❑	❑
Relevant content	❑	❑	❑	❑
Efficient shopping model	❑	❑	❑	❑
Customer service support	❑	❑	❑	❑
Visitor-interactive (community)	❑	❑	❑	❑
Fast/efficient	❑	❑	❑	❑
Relevant to audience	❑	❑	❑	❑
Links	❑	❑	❑	❑
Navigation	❑	❑	❑	❑
Helpful user tools	❑	❑	❑	❑
Keyword search	❑	❑	❑	❑
Opt-In/e-zine/e-newsletter	❑	❑	❑	❑
Online advertising	❑	❑	❑	❑

Result Analysis

Based on how you have rated this competitor, answer the following questions.

What do you think is this company's biggest competitive advantage within the marketplace? Why?

_____

_____

What do you think is this company's greatest strength? _____

_____

_____

What do you think is this company's greatest weakness? _____

_____

_____

What opportunities do you see in terms of competing against this company or filling a niche within the market that it does not?

_____

_____

_____

FIGURE 10.2   Competition Comparison Worksheet, continued

What is the greatest threat that this company poses to your business?

_____

_____

What is the greatest threat that your business poses to this company?

_____

_____

What is your greatest advantage in terms of competing against this company?

_____

_____

What does this company do well enough that you should also be doing?

_____

_____

Now that you know this company better, what products or services can you provide to lure its customers away to your business?

_____

_____

What marketing activities can you implement to reach this company's core target audience?

_____

_____

GETTING STARTED WITH CUSTOMER SERVICE

Your ability to survive in business will be based on many factors, but perhaps the biggest contributing factor will be your ability to retain customers and foster long-term and profitable selling relationships with them. Just how important is customer service in terms of the survival of your home business? Well, a recent survey conducted by the SBA revealed that the number-one reason customers stop doing business with a particular business and choose to start doing business with a competitor was poor customer service. In fact, in excess of 60 percent of respondents to the survey cited poor customer service as the number-one reason why they no longer did business with certain companies. It was more important than all other reasons—moving away, death or changing priorities—combined. Specifically, the SBA survey found:

- 1 percent of customers died or become physically immobile and unable to continue shopping at a particular business.
- 4 percent of customers move out of the geographic trading area.
- 15 percent of customers go to competitors because of lower prices.

- 15 percent of customers stop shopping because they are dissatisfied with what they buy.
- 65 percent of customers stop shopping because of poor service they receive.

The results of the SBA survey provide business owners a picture of what will eventually happen to their customer base if providing great customer service is not one of their highest priorities. Providing great customer service is easier and cheaper than trying to find and satisfy new customers constantly. According to the maxim, "It is 10 times easier and less expensive to keep the customers you have than it is to find new ones."

But you don't need surveys to show the negative effects of poor customer service. You've likely experienced it personally or heard numerous stories from friends, neighbors and relatives.

For example, one couple had purchased $2,500 in hardwood floors for their home from a major chain store. When the installers were installing the floor, they blew out the electricity. When the couple complained, they got the response, "Not our fault." After writing letters to the VP of the chain, they were finally reimbursed for the $600 in damages to their electrical system. Another example comes from the service industry. The owners of a therapy center in Bedford, New York, berated and essentially kicked out a long-time client who they thought owed them a mere $30.

The point of these stories, among thousands and thousands of such stories, is that if you own a business, you must assess how to handle customer relations so you do not lose customers. You need to acknowledge when something is or could be your fault. You also need to choose your battles wisely, rather than losing a long-time client for a few dollars or some other insignificant matter. You can learn from these examples of terrible customer service.

The best way to provide great customer service is to treat your customers the way you like to be treated when you trade your hard-earned money for products and services with other businesses. In fact, using the How I Like to Be Treated as a Customer Worksheet (Figure 10.3) to list both how you like to be treated as a customer and how you dislike being treated is one of the best ways of developing customer service policies for your business.

FIGURE 10.3 How I Like to Be Treated as a Customer Worksheet

As a customer I like:

1. _____

2. _____

3. _____

4. _____

5. _____

As a customer I dislike:

1. _____

2. _____

3. _____

4. _____

5. _____

Key Customer Service Components

One of the easiest customer service concepts to grasp is the fact that people like to do business with people whom they like. When was the last time you returned to a business run by someone you disliked, just for the privilege of giving them your hard-earned money? I hope never. Therefore, it stands to reason that you should go out of your way to be likable. It is not tough to do. Smile, be presentable, take an interest in your customers, treat them fairly, do not be condescending and thank them for their continued support of your business. That's about all it takes to make your customers like you. In addition to being someone who people like to do business with, there are three other important components to providing great customer service—reliability, flexibility and contact.

Reliability

All home business owners, especially service providers, should be reliable. If you say you'll be there at 10:00, arrive five minutes early. If you guarantee your work and then something goes wrong, fix it, no questions asked. And if you promise to give a customer or prospect more information about a specific topic, make it a priority and get it done. Reliability is a characteristic of all successful businesses, especially those that provide services, because their track record of happy clients is often their main marketing tool. Make a pledge to all customers that they can trust you to do what you say you will do when you say you will do it. We all want to know that when we purchase a product or a service the company that sells it to us is reliable and will be there for us in the future should there be problems.

Flexibility

A huge advantage that home business owners have over large competitors with highly developed chains of command and customer service policies set in stone is the ability to be flexible with customers. Recognize that customers are not all the same; they want and need different things. You must view each person as an individual, not merely as part of a group. Be willing to bend the rules once in a while when your customers need you to, even if it is an inconvenience to you and your business. Ask customers what they truly want and develop solutions to meet each individual's needs. Let them know that customer satisfaction really is your primary concern and you will go that extra mile when called on to do so.

If you find yourself using the phrase, "If I do it for you, then I'll have to do it for everyone," rethink your customer service policy. Likewise, never allow the computer to be your boss: "The computer says we need to do such and such." Computers are programmed and maintained by humans. Remember that and always be flexible.

If you provide good customer service, price will be less of a factor in the buying decisions of your customers. It is also the way to build a positive reputation with each customer. Remember: Customers know other customers and potential customers and they can spread the word quickly, especially about poor customer service. Considering that it costs more to find a new customer than maintain a current one, you are smarter to keep your customers satisfied.

Customer Contact

The third important component to great customer service is contact. In business, it is easy to become complacent when it comes to "regular" customers. There are two reasons for this complacency. First, these are good customers, so you just expect that they will always be there. We also tend to become engrossed in looking for new customers and, as a result, we forget about our current customers.

Unfortunately, if over time customers do not feel you appreciate them or you value their business, they will go elsewhere. Don't let this happen to you.

Stay in constant contact with all your customers, big and small. Do this by sending them e-mails, offering special perks for frequent customers (like a special sale by invitation only, as Bloomingdale's and other major stores have done for years), or making occasional telephone calls and letting them know you appreciate their business. Ask if they have special requests, such as new products or services. Send out greetings to your clients on their birthdays and anniversaries, during the holidays and for other special occasions. The more you stay in contact with your customers, the better you will be able to serve them, which makes them less likely to take their business elsewhere.

Customer Service Surveys

Customer surveys have long been one of the best methods for finding out what consumers think about the level of customer service. You can conduct customer service surveys just as you would conduct any surveys: by mail, in person, by telephone and through your website. Your budget will probably determine which method is the best for your business. Regardless of the method you use,

once you have identified a surveying method that gets the results you want, continue to use this method quarterly to ensure that your business keeps up with ever-changing customer needs and wants. Even a basic please-rate-our-service comment card that customers complete can provide you with valuable information about the level of service you provide and overall customer satisfaction.

Developing a customer service survey is straightforward. Simply ask specific questions about each area of your business, from initial contact right through to completion of the sale or job and about overall satisfaction of doing business with you. If you mail your customer service survey, include a self-addressed stamped envelope, which makes it easy for people to respond, ensuring a higher response rate.

Use the results of your ongoing customer surveys to identify problems or weaknesses in your business so you can correct them and to identify strengths in your business so you can build on them and expand them into other areas of your business. Here is a basic Sample Customer Service Survey Form (Figure 10.4) you can use as an outline to create one suitable for your business and needs.

FIGURE 10.4 Sample Customer Service Survey Form

[Put your business name and contact information here.]

We greatly value our customers! Please help us serve you better by rating our service.

Your personal information and responses will not be shared with anyone outside of our business. Ignore personal information spaces if you do not want to identify yourself. Thank you for your help.

❑ Mr. ❑ Mrs. ❑ Ms. Name _____

Address _____ Apartment _____

City _____ State/Province _____ ZIP/Postal Code _____

Home Telephone _____ Work _____ Fax _____ E-Mail _____

FIGURE 10.4	Sample Customer Service Survey Form, continued

	Great	Good	Poor
How was your initial inquiry to our business handled?	❑	❑	❑
How knowledgeable are we about our products and services?	❑	❑	❑
How would you rate the value of our service?	❑	❑	❑
How would you rate the price of our products and services?	❑	❑	❑
How would you rate your overall experience with our service?	❑	❑	❑
How would you rate the quality of our service?	❑	❑	❑
How would you rate the performance and reliability of our service?	❑	❑	❑
Would you like to receive free and valuable information occasionally?	❑ Yes	❑ No	
Would you refer other people to our business?	❑ Yes	❑ No	
Would you be prepared to provide a written testimonial?	❑ Yes	❑ No	

We welcome additional comments, questions or concerns you may have.

_____

_____

_____

_____

Thank you! We appreciate your comments and your business.

Cultivating Customers

No businesses, regardless of size, are actually in the business of selling products or services. They are, in fact, in the business of finding and keeping customers who want to trade their cash for products and services.

If you have customers who are loyal to you, believe in you and want to give you their money, you have won their respect and their trust. That is what business is all about—winning people over by catering to their wants and needs. So it makes sense that to truly understand your customers, you have to identify them, know what they buy, know how often they buy and figure out ways to sell them more of what they want and need.

There are some steps you can take to identify and track your most profitable customers and build lifetime selling relationships with them. It is a five-step process to set up, manage and maintain on a regular basis.

Step 1. Develop a Customer Management Database

The first step is to set up a customer database so you can gather and store information about your customers. You want to define them and know more about all of their buying habits. Along with this, you will need contact information and data such as birthdays. Every business owner should take the time and invest the money required to build a customer database. It is an essential business and marketing tool that is necessary to survive in a hyper-competitive business environment. You can then use this information to make special offers based on each client's needs or wants.

Get started by asking every new customer to take a few minutes to complete a new customer form. Ask questions that can be used to determine what your customers really want or problems they need addressed, along with getting their contact information, especially an e-mail address. Your database should be built using sales or customer management software, such as Maximizer, *maximizer.com*.

Step 2. Rank Your Customers

Next, based on the information you capture in your customer management database, develop a simple customer ranking system so you can identify your best customers and similarities they might share. Assign each customer an alphabetical or numerical ranking, from weakest to strongest, based on factors such as buying frequency, types of products or services bought, profitability associated with these purchases, special requests or complaints, and payment behavior (i.e., if they pay on time or are slow to pay).

Step 3. Concentrate on Your Most Profitable Customers

Ranking your customers will enable you to pinpoint your best and most profitable customers. Then you will be able to direct more of your marketing efforts at your core target group to increase sales, introduce new products and ask for referrals. Additionally, through customer ranking and analysis, you will generally discover that 80 percent of sales and profits come from 20 percent of your customers. This is commonly referred to as the *80/20 Rule*, a widely accepted rule of thumb. It is the top 20 percent of your best and most profitable customers on whom you should focus most of your marketing efforts and activities. Once again, it is 10 times easier and less expensive to sell more and more frequently to current customers than to find new customers. Ultimately, the goal is to turn every current customer and every new customer into a lifetime customer. But start with your core group of best customers who give you the largest profits with the least amount of trouble.

Step 4. Look for Ways to Increase Buying Frequency

Now that you know who your best customers are, look for ways to sell them more products or services more frequently. You can do this in many ways. For example, you might introduce a product- or service-of-the-month club, a gift registry service, an automatic replenishment service, a reminder or alert service, or whatever you feel is relevant to your business, your customers and your products and services. The point here is to know who your best customers are and then use promotions specifically to entice them to buy more and more often.

Step 5. Build Relationships with Customers for Life

The final step in cultivating great customers is to go out of your way to secure every customer for life. Do this by catering to each customer's individual needs and by paying close attention to the small details of each of your best customer accounts. People love attention—and when you pay a little attention to your customers it goes a long way. Institute customer loyalty programs, rewards and appreciation gifts. Work with customers to keep prices low, value high and service a top priority. Doing so will go a long way to cement lifelong business relationships with your best customers and ensure that your business remains strong and profitable.

Overcoming Customer Complaints and Challenges

The first rule of overcoming customer complaints and challenges is to make it a policy to deal with each one in a reasonable time. In many cases, you can rectify a problem by the end of the working day. In cases in which you need to contact a supplier or do repairs, you may need a couple of days to solve a problem. The point is to take action as soon as possible, to not delay and to never try to brush a complaint under the rug.

The vast majority of customer complaints are nothing more than the result of a simple miscommunication between buyer and seller. However, even the smallest of complaints can quickly turn into a full-blown problem unless it is dealt with in a timely and decisive fashion. Never let yourself procrastinate: "I'll look after it tomorrow." Instead, make a conscious effort to clear all customer challenges by the end of each business day and to carry over only those that require input from a source that is temporarily unavailable, such as a sales rep, manufacturer or distributor. If you are unable to fix the problem, let your customer know why and when the problem will be corrected. Give your customer a firm call-back time and tell him or her that you are making his or her concern priority number-one. People want to know that their problem is now your problem, too. As part of the business–customer relationship, you need to acknowledge and accept your role in this relationship, whether or not you believe you are at fault. Ignoring a complaint at the risk of losing a customer is a terrible business practice that too many business owners allow to occur.

Log Complaints

Develop your customer service savvy by recording all customer complaints, questions and concerns you receive. Then use the information you collect to find weak areas in your business, products, services, staff or customer service policies.

Basically, look for recurring problems that need to be corrected. Also look for customers who are always complaining so you can determine whether you are doing something wrong or you simply have customers who like to complain. Once you have identified your weaknesses, you will be able to look for solutions and ways to fix the problems.

Even homebased businesses can benefit by recording all customer complaints. Simply write them in a daily journal notepad or enter a few notes on your computer. By recording complaints, you will have the information needed to measure the performance of your suppliers' products and services, as well. If you find that patterns start to develop with a particular supplier, you'll have the information you need to confront the supplier and look for a mutually beneficial way to fix the deficiencies or find a better supplier source.

Appease the Customer First

Regardless of the source of the customer service complaint or problem, always look for ways to appease the customer first, quickly and without hesitation. Once you have done this, turn your attention to the source of the problem or complaint. "I'll get back to you" or "That is a manufacture's problem" is not good enough in a highly competitive business environment.

If you have an angry customer on the telephone or standing in front of you, you can do something to help resolve the customer's problem. In all likelihood, you cannot do anything about the problem itself at that moment; what caused the problem is probably out of your immediate control. But it is in your immediate control to assure the customer, who deserves your immediate and undivided attention, that you can do something and will take on the problem—you are not ignoring it or passing the buck. Too many people look to find another source for the blame rather than taking the responsibility. It's your business, so whether you believe the customer's complaint is valid or not, you should take the responsibility.

Maintain a Complaint File

It's to your advantage to maintain a file of complaints, for two reasons. First, you can determine any patterns emerging. If you are getting several complaints about your pricing or your return policy, you may want to look into it and determine if you can make a change. The other reason for holding onto complaints, as well as problems that occur with customers, is to also hold on to your solutions. By recording how you solved each dilemma and saving that information, you can refer to it if you encounter a similar problem or complaint in the future.

Make Friends

Remember the old adage that an unhappy customer will tell 10 times as many people about an experience with your business than a happy customer. It is still true now—and even more so as customers are going public with their dissatisfaction on the web. You need to make unhappy customers happy. You can make friends and allies from even your angriest customers by trying a few of the following actions when you receive complaints.

- Don't interrupt. Let the customer express what is on his or her mind. Interruptions only further infuriate a customer who is already angry, frustrated and upset. By interrupting, you are telling customers that you do not care about them or their problem.
- Once the customer has finished venting, empathize with him or her and show that you understand the situation and how he or she feels about it. Use the customer's name so he or she feels valued and important.
- Ask the customer to restate the chain of events that led to the complaint. Ask for details such as other people in the company with whom they might have spoken or who were involved, specifics about product or service problems and problems resulting from those problems.

- Don't start pointing fingers. First make sure there have been no miscommunications on either side. Then start seeking solutions by asking the customer how he or she would like the problem resolved.
- Fix what you can immediately. If the problem cannot be fixed during the first contact, promise to call the customer by a specific time and restate the solution that both the customer and you feel will be appropriate to correct the situation.

Post-Resolution Follow-Up

Sometimes problems that appear to have been resolved are not. It is wise to implement a post-customer complaint-and-resolution follow-up program. Wait a few days or perhaps a week after the complaint should be resolved and then call your customer to find out if he or she is truly satisfied with the way the problem was handled. Develop a checklist of questions that you ask:

- "Are you satisfied with the way we responded to your complaint?"
- "Are you happy with the way the problem was resolved?"
- "Would you purchase from our business in the future?"
- "Would you refer our business to other people?"

You can also develop more specific questions that are suited to your business and the problem. But keep in mind that what's most important is to find out if the customer is truly satisfied with the solution.

Show Your Customers You Appreciate Them

Business is going well. Now you want to thank the people who made it happen—your customers. But how will you go about showing your customers that you appreciate their continued support? Here are a few ideas.

Customer Appreciation Events

Host a customer appreciation party and invite your best customers and hottest prospects. The party can be held at local restaurant or, if your budget is tight, you can host the party at your home, perhaps a backyard barbecue if weather permits. Customer appreciation parties are a way to say, "Thank you for your business," and reinforce your business relationships. Make it an annual event and you'll soon discover that customers start looking forward to it.

Subscriptions

Find out what newspapers or magazines your customers like to read and give them a monthly subscription. Every time they receive and read the magazine or newspaper, they will automatically think of you and your business.

Hobby Gifts

Get to know your clients by asking them questions about their hobbies and the activities they enjoy when they are not working. Armed with this information, you can purchase gifts for them that are relevant to their hobbies and interests, anything and everything from concert tickets to continuing education classes or a custom kite.

Referrals

Make an effort to send quality and qualified referrals to customers who own small businesses or professional practices. After all, what better gift is there than helping someone build a business, a practice or a career?

Imprinted Items

Have your business name, logo and marketing message emblazoned on items such as key chains, pens, notepads, calendars, coffee mugs, travel mugs, clocks or mouse pads. Give these to prospects and customers as gifts. These items make good customer appreciation gifts because they are things that most people use daily, so your name is constantly in front of them and fresh in their memory. PromoMart, at *promomart.com,* offers a huge selection of imprinted promotional and advertising specialties.

RESOURCES

Associations

American Marketing Association
311 S. Wacker Drive, Suite 5800
Chicago, IL 60606
(800) AMA-1150 (262-1150), (312) 542-9000
marketingpower.com

Business Marketing Association
1601 N. Bond Street, Suite 101
Naperville, IL 60563
(800) 664-4BMA (4262), (630) 544-5054
marketing.org

Canadian Marketing Association
1 Concorde Gate, Suite 607
Don Mills, ON M3C 3N6
(416) 391-2362
the-cma.org

International Customer Service Association
401 N. Michigan Avenue
Chicago, IL 60611
(800) 360-4272, (312) 321-6800
icsa.com

Marketing Research Association
110 National Drive, 2nd Fl.
Glastonbury, CT 06033-1212
(860) 682-1000
mra-net.org

Suggested Reading

Abraham, Jay. *Getting Everything You Can out of All You've Got: 21 Ways You Can Out-Think, Out-Perform, and Out-Earn the Competition.* New York: St. Martin's Press, 2000.

Bacal, Robert. *Perfect Phrases for Customer Service: Hundreds of Tools, Techniques, and Scripts for Handling Any Situation.* New York: McGraw-Hill, 2005.

Colombo, George W. *Killer Customer Care: Five Star Service That Will Double and Triple Profits.* Irvine, CA: Entrepreneur Press, 2003.

Evenson, Renee. *Customer Service Training 101: Quick and Easy Techniques That Get Great Results.* New York: AMACOM, 2005.

Grossnickle, Joshua, and Oliver Raskin. *Handbook of Online Marketing Research: Knowing Your Customers, Using the Net.* New York: McGraw-Hill, 2001.

Porter, Michael E. *Competitive Strategy: Techniques for Analyzing Industries and Competitors.* New York: Free Press (Simon & Schuster), 2004.

Smith, Jaynie L., and William G. Flanagan. *Creating Competitive Advantage: Give Customers a Reason to Choose You over Your Competitors.* New York: Currency/Doubleday, 2006.

Stephenson, James with Courtney Thurman. *Entrepreneur Magazine's Ultimate Small Business Marketing Guide: 1500 Great Marketing Tricks That Will Drive Your Business Through the Roof! 2nd Edition.* Irvine, CA: Entrepreneur Press Inc., 2007.

Websites

Better Business Bureau: Nonprofit consumer protection organization that encourages reputable business practices. To register your business with the BBB, visit its website to find a chapter near you (United States and Canada). ***bbb.org***

Canadian Chamber of Commerce: Business association offering members information, advice and business building opportunities. Visit the website to find a chapter near you. ***chamber.ca***

Customer Service.com: Large portal to customer service sites and directories. ***customerservice.com***

Marketing Masters: Survey Said™ Survey Software, including custom applications for phone, internet, paper, laptop and kiosk surveys. ***surveysaid.com***

Maximizer Software: Contact and customer relationship management software. ***maximizer.com***

Salesforce.com: Contact and customer relationship management software. ***salesforce.com***

SRDS Media Solutions, Inc.: Publishers of print and online lifestyle and demographics sourcebooks. ***srds.com***

U.S. Census Bureau: Market demographics information and statistics. ***census.gov***

U.S. Chamber of Commerce: Business association offering members information, advice and business-building opportunities. Visit the website to find a chapter near you. ***uschamber.com***

CHAPTER 11

Managing Your Home Business

YOU HAVE RESEARCHED, PLANNED, financed, set up your home workspace, opened your business and have a few customers. Now it is time to manage your business on a day-to-day basis for success and long-term growth. This is exactly the point where lots of new entrepreneurs become unglued, because every aspect of the home business must be managed and maintained—not one single element can be ignored. This can be overwhelming day in and day out. Just think: on any one day, you might have to manage any or all of the following:

- Your time
- Customer complaints
- Banking and record keeping
- Employees, sales agents and contractors
- Supplier and vendor accounts
- Shipping and receiving
- Account receivables and payables
- Sending invoices

- Client jobs and contracts
- Website maintenance
- Communications, including phone, e-mail and snail mail
- Sales and networking
- Advertising and public relations
- Distractions
- Equipment malfunctions
- Warranty questions, problems and claims
- Permit and insurance renewals
- Tax payments
- And on and on and on and …

There is a lot to manage when you own a business, regardless of the size or type of business. It is a never-ending task. Of course, the savvy business operator develops systems and schedules for every activity imaginable so that he or she can stay on top of management tasks, maximize his or her time and become more productive.

Much of this chapter revolves around time management because of the importance it plays in business, especially homebased businesses, which are often run by one person, with little if any support structure. This chapter also covers handling the pressure of operating your own business, making wise decisions, managing money and debt, growing your business, and—when the time is right—closing or selling your home business.

HANDLING THE PRESSURES OF OPERATING A HOME BUSINESS

Business owners face all kinds of pressures each day, ranging from finding good suppliers to dealing with irate clients to collecting payment and everything in between. Being under continual pressure to deliver, correct and explain can take a toll on home business owners, because they rarely have any support staff or resources available to help them deal with these pressures. Therefore, entrepreneurs must master ways to face pressure and deal with it to be effective in business and avoid stress-related illnesses.

Below is a five-step process that will help you handle the pressures associated with operating your home business:

1. *Identify each source of pressure.* Customer complaints, supplier problems, tight deadlines and financial troubles are among the leading sources of pressure, although there are many other culprits. Knowing you are under pressure gets you no closer to fixing the problem; you must identify the source of the pressure so you can develop a plan to overcome or eliminate it.

2. *Remain flexible.* Keep your mind open so you can seek compromise solutions. If a problem involves other people, work with them and be flexible to their needs to create mutually beneficial solutions. This can only happen through remaining flexible and keeping the lines of communication open.

3. *Seek advice.* Talk with people around you whom you trust and respect. Almost all the most successful people in business know their limitations and turn to professionals and experts for advice and assistance. Don't try to go it alone, even if you are working alone.

4. *Use separation techniques.* Sometimes the problem is a combination of unavoidable business pressures. At this point you have to be able to separate your business life from your personal life and take a break, even if it is just a day or two. Getting away from pressure for a short time can often help us gain a new perspective.

5. *Take corrective action.* Finally, once you have identified the source of the pressure, you must take action to reduce or eliminate it entirely. Otherwise, pressure could grow and lead to health problems. Assess the possible solutions and choose the one that seems best for you.

Making Wise Decisions

Many new homebased entrepreneurs also struggle with decisions. This is mainly because a bad decision usually causes more negative results when you're the owner and the boss than when you're an employee. Also, your decisions affect you personally—and perhaps your family. This puts further pressure on you to make the right decisions.

Operating a business requires the ability to make fast, concise and wise decisions. Learning how to make wise decisions takes practice. Certainly not all the decisions you make will be the right ones. Some will probably have a negative impact on your business. However, what separates the winners from the losers is that winners learn from their mistakes and become better at making decisions. Here are a few tips that can help you make wise decisions.

- Carefully consider all the consequences or repercussions that may arise from a single decision. You have to weigh each, while keeping in mind your objectives. Remember: this is not only from a money perspective; you must consider other factors, such as your time and how decisions may affect other people in your life. Determine whether the advantages outweigh the disadvantages. The more decisions you make, the more easily and quickly you will be able to weigh the alternatives and the consequences.

- Never make snap decisions about spending money. Instead, set a monetary limit on business purchases. For instance, any purchasing decision that involves more than $1,000 must wait for at least 24 hours. This time allows you to think about purchasing decisions more carefully and not act impulsively or emotionally.

- Once you have decided to take action, do it immediately. Don't procrastinate. If not, as time passes, you will begin to second-guess yourself and this can quickly become habitual. Entrepreneurs who continually procrastinate or cannot be decisive generally find themselves out of business soon.

- All successful entrepreneurs are able to take risks when necessary. By nature, entrepreneurs are calculated risk takers; this is a key trait that separates them from the working masses. Taking risks means different things to different people. As you start out, you must determine what your level of risk tolerance will be. How much can you spend before you make money? How long can you go without a profit? How much can you bid on projects? How many hours can you afford to seek out new clients? These are all a matter of taking risks. To be successful, you must take some risks. The trick is to know your limits and make calculated risks.

- When in serious doubt, seek second opinions from trusted sources. Never let your pride get in the way of asking for help. Just make sure that the person dispensing the advice is an expert on the topic.

- Keep learning. The more you know about the products and services you are offering, the easier it will be to make good decisions. Know your field and know your industry. After a while, you will be able to make many key decisions instinctively because you will know more about your situation and the larger context.

TIME MANAGEMENT

Managing your time is just about as important as any business discipline. At the top of the list of most common complaints of business owners is that they never have enough time. Managing your time will enable you to be more productive and get more done in less time. Good time management allows you to spend your time where it can make the greatest difference. It also allows you time off to recharge your batteries.

Most time management gurus agree that the first rule of productivity is having the right tools on hand to do the job properly. This means that to squeeze the most productivity from the time you have available, you must invest in business tools that enable you to be 100-percent efficient—training, education, equipment, technology, supplies and so on. Having to dart out to purchase a new ink cartridge in the middle of preparing an important and time-sensitive presentation is not an efficient use of your time. Having to tear down your home office and set it up again day after day because you use the kitchen table as your workspace is not an efficient use of your time.

Heather Cartwright, noted integrated logistics and supply chain management systems expert and owner of Logixsource Consulting Ltd., *logix-source.com*, offers entrepreneurs the following valuable advice. To be successful as an entrepreneur in a small, homebased business, it is critical to manage the business effectively and efficiently and yet be flexible enough to change when market conditions or key customers require you to do so.

There is a plethora of information available about business planning and financing. However, this information is focused on critical success factors from the perspective of business management. For entrepreneurs, time is a critical success factor. Entrepreneurs face an overwhelming number of decisions to make because typically there are a limited number of people responsible for making business decisions. You can use the well-known Time Management Decision Matrix in Figure 11.1 as a guide.

In making decisions, you can be guided by these three important questions:

1. Is what I am doing now leading me closer to my short-term and long-term goals? If not, what should I be doing to get back on track, focused on my goals and objectives?
2. What would happen if I didn't do this task? Can I learn to say no to some requests? Learning to say no is one of the biggest challenges for small business owners. We all feel the need to accommodate every client request, but sometimes saying no is smart for our business and for good time management.
3. By working on this task, am I putting my time to the best possible use? If not, what could I be doing that would be the best, most productive and potentially most profitable use of my time?

At an operational level, major business, management and marketing decisions can be categorized in four key areas—skills and experience, business processes, technology infrastructure and business organization.

FIGURE 11.1   Time Management Decision Matrix

Urgent and Important Activities	Not Urgent but Important Activities
❏ Crises	❏ Prevention
❏ Pressing problems	❏ Learning
•	❏ Recreation outside the business
•	❏ Client and alliance relationship building
•	❏ Business and marketing planning
•	❏ Business-building opportunities
Urgent but Not Important Activities	**Not Urgent, Not Important Activities**
❏ Interruptions	❏ Trivia
❏ Some telephone calls	❏ Procrastination
❏ Mail	❏ Junk mail
❏ Reports	❏ Personal calls during business hours
❏ Some meetings	❏ "Escape," such as reading and TV

1. Skills and experience
   - Experience or access to knowledge and best practices
   - Support networks, including accountant, lawyer, banker and business advisor
   - Core and other suppliers of products and services
   - Tools and techniques to design, develop and deliver products and services
2. Business processes
   - Marketing and sales management
   - Quality and risk management processes
   - Financial analysis and management
   - Continuous improvement procedures
3. Technology infrastructure
   - Facilities and equipment
   - Computer hardware and software
   - Telecommunications
   - Managing historical records
4. Business organization
   - The organization of the business, including how work gets performed and how decisions are made
   - The business governance structure and how decisions will be made
   - The key business processes performed internally and outsourced to suppliers
   - Who is responsible for what decisions and how they will be implemented
   - Communications process to employees, customers, alliances and suppliers—and, for home business owners, also family members

Daily To-Do List

Before ending your workday, try to get into the habit of making a to-do list of important activities for the following day. If you prefer, on Friday afternoon, Sunday night or first thing Monday morning, make a to-do list for the upcoming week. List each task or project and how many hours you anticipate needing. During the week, you can pull from the larger list and fill in each day's to-do list on your daily schedule.

In making your list, you can combine business and personal tasks, so you do not inadvertently overlap tasks and times. I would also suggest that you include important telephone calls to make or return and e-mails to send. You can create your to-do list in print or electronically, such as with time management software, on a handheld organizer or with a word processing program, since it's basically just a list. You can even write it out by hand and tape it to your computer or workstation. You can purchase time planner books and calendars at your local office supplier.

Below is a Sample Weekly and Daily To-Do List Worksheet (Figure 11.2) you can use as guidelines to create your own, using any word processing program. Photocopy or print it for each day. Regardless of how you make a daily to-do list, this simple management tool is important. It is guaranteed to save you time and frustration over missing tasks and overlapping activities.

Daily and Weekly Planners

For some people, a better means of time management is making out a more detailed list for the week, specifying what needs to be done and when. For many specific appointments, with clients, prospective clients, vendors and/or affiliates, you may want to fill in the daily details prior to the week. Certainly doctors, dentists, contractors, therapists (physical or psychological) and anyone with an appointment schedule will use such a weekly planner.

Below is a Sample Daily and Weekly Planner Worksheet (Figure 11.3). Simply circle the appropriate day and fill in your appointments and projects as needed. You can use this form as is or create a customized one on your computer. Keep in mind

| FIGURE 11.2 | Sample Weekly To-Do List Worksheet |

Project or task   # of hours for the week   Comments

Date: _____ Day: _____

Specific Tasks and Projects

Task	Comments	Completed
		❑
		❑
		❑
		❑
		❑
		❑
		❑
		❑

Telephone Calls to Make

Time	Person	Comments	Completed
			❑
			❑
			❑
			❑
			❑
			❑
			❑
			❑
			❑

FIGURE 11.2   Sample Weekly To-Do List Worksheet, continued

E-Mails to Send

Person	Purpose	Completed
_____	_____	❑
_____	_____	❑
_____	_____	❑
_____	_____	❑
_____	_____	❑
_____	_____	❑
_____	_____	❑
_____	_____	❑

that the key to success in using planners is to use them conscientiously to save time and be more productive.

But remember: Do not spend (waste) an inordinate amount of time moving appointments around and around, as this or that little thing comes up, as many people do. Try to set a schedule and make only necessary changes.

Monthly and Yearly Planners

In addition to daily and weekly planners, monthly and yearly planners are great for keeping track of long-term appointments and projects. However, you have to get into the habit of using these regularly so you remember to transfer important meetings and activities into your daily and weekly

FIGURE 11.3   Sample Daily and Weekly Planner Worksheet

Date _____   Day • S • M • T • W • T • F • S • *(circle)*

Time	Activity	Comments	Completed
7:00	_____	_____	❑
7:30	_____	_____	❑
8:00	_____	_____	❑
8:30	_____	_____	❑
9:00	_____	_____	❑
9:30	_____	_____	❑
10:00	_____	_____	❑
10:30	_____	_____	❑
11:00	_____	_____	❑

FIGURE 11.3	Sample Daily and Weekly Planner Worksheet, continued

Time	Activity	Comments	Completed
11:30			❑
12:00			❑
12:30			❑
1:00			❑
1:30			❑
2:00			❑
2:30			❑
3:00			❑
3:30			❑
4:00			❑
4:30			❑
5:00			❑
5:30			❑
6:00			❑
6:30			❑
7:00			❑
7:30			❑
8:00			❑
8:30			❑
9:00			❑
9:30			❑

planners. Erasable yearly planners and markers can be purchased for less than $25 from most office supply stores that generally include a monthly and yearly calendar space for recording important information. Following is a Sample Monthly Planner Worksheet (Figure 11.4) you can use as is or as a template to create your own using word processing program.

Time Management Tips

The greatest time management tip is that you must be healthy. If you are not feeling physically or emotionally well because of burnout, it will always be difficult to be productive and manage your business and time efficiently. Small business burnout is the result of a combination of factors—trying to do too much, lack of a support structure, long

FIGURE 11.4	Sample Monthly Planner Worksheet

Month • J • F • M • A • M • J • J • A • S • O • N • D • *(circle)*

Date	Key Appointments and Projects	Comments	Logged
1			❏
2			❏
3			❏
4			❏
5			❏
6			❏
7			❏
8			❏
9			❏
10			❏
11			❏
12			❏
13			❏
14			❏
15			❏
16			❏
17			❏
18			❏
19			❏
20			❏
21			❏
22			❏
23			❏
24			❏
25			❏
26			❏
27			❏
28			❏
29			❏
30			❏
31			❏

working hours, and often the inability to say no to excessive work or work outside your field. You must get into the habit of scheduling time off and time away from your business on a regular basis. Make it a personal goal to stay fit and healthy by taking time off, maintaining a balanced diet, staying physically active and getting lots of rest. As familiar as this advice may be, it is still smart.

Here are more time management tips and ideas to help you do more in less time:

- Establish a primary workstation in your home office for working on client projects and other key moneymaking projects, and a secondary workstation for lower-priority tasks, such as sorting mail, filing and general administrative recording. Doing so will help you stay organized and focused on the areas of your business that make money while keeping other required business activities organized but clearly secondary.

- Try to set aside specific times when you open mail, pay bills and do administrative paperwork. This simple trick will save you an incredible amount of time over the year. Best of all, the time saved can be invested in more productive and money-making activities such as prospecting, closing sales and staying in contact with key clients.

- Plan out-of-the-office appointments and errands in blocks of time, such as an entire morning or day, so you can minimize time spent getting from place to place. Confirm all appointments twice, first a few days prior to the meeting and again before you leave the office for the appointment. A telephone call takes only a moment, but hours can be wasted if the person you are to meet is not available.

- Purchase and use color-coded file folders to indicate high-priority projects, perhaps red for the most important, green for medium

priority and blue for low priority. Invest in a good filing system so you can spend more time working on files and less time looking for them. Be sure to purge your paper files and electronic files of outdated or irrelevant information monthly, to keep your money-making files lean. Move the purged files to an archive system so you can occasionally revisit them. Remember: Back up all computer files often!

- Install an erasable board on the office wall or a SMART board™ (*smarttech.com*) to keep an ongoing list of office supplies that are running low, so you can replenish once a month instead of weekly or even daily.

- Most home business operators find it difficult to stay focused on work and not be distracted by their working environment. Temptations such as TV will sink productivity. Remember that you have to be the hard-nosed manager who keeps squawking to get back to work. So increase productivity by getting rid of temptations. Set rules for yourself, and write them down if necessary, such as "No TV before 7 p.m." or "Only one hour per day for personal phone calls (unless it's an emergency)."

- Plan telephone calls prior to dialing: Know to whom you want to talk, know what you want to say and know what you want to accomplish as a result of the call. If you need to refer to files, a website or e-mail, have it ready and in front of you when you dial. Such planning will greatly reduce the time you spend on the phone and the number of calls you make back to the party to get information you missed. Also, when leaving a voice message, include a specific day and time range when you can be reached, such as "I'll be in the office Tuesday morning between 9 and 11 a.m. Can you please call me then?" You can reduce time-wasting telephone tag this way.

- Keep all relevant e-mails in your inbox until you can read, respond or delete. Try to set aside a block of time each day for e-mails. If you receive hundreds of e-mails each day, use e-mail auto responders as a way to reduce the time you spend answering low-priority emails. Also, use a filter to reduce the junk.

- Learn to motivate yourself. Think of the little things you enjoy doing and set them up for after you accomplish X amount of work. Is there a TV show you enjoy? Do you want to go exercise? Do you have a favorite hobby? Use these things as motivational rewards. Sometimes being accountable to someone else can provide great motivation. For example, tell a friend what is on your agenda and that you will meet him or her for dinner—if you complete your work. There is something in being accountable to others that motivates people.

- Set up systems. No matter what business you are in, you can set up systems for getting things done in ways that are time- and money-efficient.

MONEY MANAGEMENT

Money comes in and money goes out. Managing your small business cash flow is tricky because cash keeps the business machine operating. Cash flow is what will keep you in business. Consequently, understanding money management must be a priority for all home business owners. Even if you hire an accountant or bookkeeper to manage your money, you will still need to familiarize yourself with basic bookkeeping and money management, understand credit, read bank statements and tax forms and make sense of accounts receivable and payable. All successful business owners are aware of their financial situation and never leave it solely in the hands of someone else.

The key aspects of money management are:

- Establishing a business bank account
- Developing a bookkeeping system
- Establishing payment terms
- Extending credit
- Getting paid on time in full
- Debt collection when necessary

Information about small business taxation, establishing merchant accounts and accepting credit cards, e-checks and debit cards are featured in Chapter 3, "Financial Issues."

Establishing a Bank Account

Once your business is registered and ready to roll, you will need to establish one or more business bank accounts. It's important to have a bank account separate from your personal savings or checking accounts, for at least two reasons. First, you will be able to separate your business finances from your personal finances, which will make it much easier to complete business sales-and-expense reports and tax forms. Second, you will be able to have checks printed with your business name and to establish a credit card merchant account. Banks and payment processing companies will not directly deposit into personal bank accounts, only into business bank accounts.

Setting up a business bank account is straightforward. Select the bank you want to work with (think "small-business-friendly") and set up an appointment to open an account. When you go, make sure you take personal identification, as well as your business name registration papers and business license, because these are usually required to open a business bank account. Deposit funds into your new account. (An opening deposit of only $100 is usually sufficient.) Then you are ready to go.

Keeping the Books

The next aspect of money management is keeping the books. You have two options—keep the books yourself or hire either an accountant or a professional bookkeeper. Some business owners choose to keep their books themselves but hire an accountant to prepare year-end financial statements and tax forms. You can also hire a bookkeeper to keep the books and then an accountant to do the taxes. (Personally, I prefer combining do-it-yourself for bookkeeping and an accountant for taxes.)

If you opt to do the bookkeeping yourself, you have lots of help available with accounting software such as QuickBooks. Accounting software enables you to create client accounts, invoices and mail merge options, as well as track bank account balances, merchant account information and accounts payable. Most of the accounting software available is very easy to use; the learning curve for even the more complex functions is only a few weeks of trial and error.

- QuickBooks, *quickbooks.intuit.com*
- Peachtree (Sage Software), *peachtree.com*
- Quicken, *quicken.intuit.com*

Accounting and Bookkeeping Resources

United States
American Institute of Certified Public Accountants
1211 Avenue of the Americas
New York, NY 10036
(212) 596-6200
aicpa.org

American Institute of Professional Bookkeepers
6001 Montrose Road, Suite 500
Rockville, MD 20852
(800) 622-0121
aipb.com

Association of Chartered Accountants in the United States
341 Lafayette Street, Suite 4246
New York, NY 10012-2417
(212) 334-2078
acaus.org

Canada
Canadian Institute of Chartered Accountants
277 Wellington Street West
Toronto, M5V 2H2
(416) 977-3222
cica.ca

Canadian Bookkeepers Association
283 Danforth Avenue, Suite 482
Toronto, M4K 1N2
c-b-a.ca

Establishing Payment Terms

Once you have established a bookkeeping and invoicing system, the next step is to establish your payment terms policy. Setting payment terms covers deposits, progress payments and extending credit. While you certainly want to standardize the way you will receive payment for products or services, you also have to be flexible enough to meet an individual client's needs. Providing customers with institutional or retail financing and leasing payment options are covered in Chapter 3, "Financial Issues."

It is important to establish clear, written payment terms and to have them printed on your estimate forms and included in formal contracts and work orders. Of course, they should also be on your final invoices. It is best if you provide signature space so clients can sign off on the agreed payment terms in writing. Should you need to go to court to collect payment, you will be glad you have taken the time to establish your payment terms in advance, in writing, with the client's signature.

Securing Deposits

All home business owners should get into the habit of asking clients for a deposit prior to ordering materials. The deposit should be for at least the value of the materials plus delivery costs. Any job or product orders over a certain dollar value also should require a deposit, usually based on a percentage of the total value, such as 25 percent. Most consumers expect to pay a deposit when ordering products, especially from a small business owner. If you are supplying labor only, try to secure a deposit of at least one-third to one-half the total value of the contract. Your order form or contract should state the deposit information clearly. It should also include information on canceled orders or contracts and the amount of the deposit that will be refunded. Securing a deposit is your best way of ensuring that at least basic out-of-pocket costs are covered if the customer cancels the job or contract.

Progress Payments

Progress payments are a way to ensure you do not expose yourself to great financial risk when working on larger jobs. In the home renovation industry, it is standard practice to invoice clients at various stages of completion. This practice could easily carry over into many industries and businesses, such as consulting, software programming and website design.

Establish your contract and payment terms to include progress payments. Agree on the amount that will be due at various stages of the project. You can use percentages to calculate the progress payments (such as 25 percent deposit, 25 percent on delivery of the product, 25 percent on substantial completion and the balance at completion or within 30 days of substantial completion) or you can base progress payments on indicators that are relevant to the scope of work, the job, the products

being sold or the services provided. Regardless of the system you use, progress payments on larger jobs can dramatically lessen your exposure to financial risk.

Extending Credit

Should you extend credit? In most cases, home business owners do not extend credit to consumers unless they provide a service that is billed on a monthly schedule or a major renovation. However, commercial clients (business to business) will generally require home business owners to extend some type of revolving credit account, 30, 60, 90 or sometimes 120 days after receiving the product or service. Ideally, you want to collect payment as quickly as possible, in full or in part, so you might want to offer clients a 2 percent discount for payment within one week.

The steps involved in extending credit should cover the following:

1. Create a standard credit policy that includes acceptance and denial guidelines.
2. Develop a standard business credit application and a consumer credit application if you plan on extending credit to nonbusiness customers.
3. Conduct credit and reference checks from information supplied by customers on their credit applications.
4. Approve or reject applications based on credit and reference checks or any extenuating circumstances.
5. If an application is approved, establish an initial credit limit and a schedule for raising the limit if the customer's creditworthiness remains in good standing.
6. If an application is rejected, work with the customer to find ways to secure credit from a third party.
7. Bill customers on time, as scheduled and watch for signs of trouble.

8. Reward customers who continue to pay on time and in full. This can be done with small gifts, special discounts or value-added rewards.

9. Develop a collection policy, schedule, and action plan for delinquent and nonpayment accounts.

Business Credit Application

The following is a basic Business Credit Application (Figure 11.5) that you can copy and use in your business as is or modify to suit your particular needs.

Credit Checks

Conduct a credit check when a new client asks you to establish a revolving credit account for his or her business. Checking credit is a straightforward process.

There are three major credit reporting agencies serving the United States and Canada—TransUnion,

FIGURE 11.5   Business Credit Application

Date: _____

Legal Business Name: _____

Doing Business As: _____

❑ Sole Proprietorship   ❑ Partnership   ❑ Limited Liability Company   ❑ Corporation

Address: _____ Apartment: _____

City: _____ State/Province: _____ ZIP/Postal Code: _____

Telephone: _____ Fax: _____ E-Mail: _____

Owner Name 1: _____

Owner Name 2: _____

Manager Name: _____

How long in business? _____ Credit line requested $_____

Bank Reference _____

Name: _____

Address: _____

Telephone: _____ Fax: _____ E-Mail: _____

Contact Person: _____ Title: _____

Account Number: _____

Trade Reference _____

Name: _____

Address: _____

Telephone: _____ Fax: _____ E-Mail: _____

FIGURE 11.5   Business Credit Application, continued

Contact Person: _____ Title: _____

How long have you had an account with this business? _____

How much is your credit line with this business? $ _____

Trade Reference _____

Name: _____

Address: _____

Telephone: _____ Fax: _____ E-Mail: _____

Contact Person: _____ Title: _____

How long have you had an account with this business? _____

How much is your credit line with this business? $ _____

Trade Reference _____

Name: _____

Address: _____

Telephone: _____ Fax: _____ E-Mail: _____

Contact Person: _____ Title: _____

How long have you had an account with this business? _____

How much is your credit line with this business? $ _____

The undersigned authorizes _____ (your business name) to conduct credit inquiries and checks as required and further acknowledges that credit may or may not be granted, and if credit privileges are granted, they may be withdrawn at any time.

_____   _____   _____
Applicant's Signature   Business Name   Date

_____   _____   _____
Co-Applicant's Signature   Business Name   Date

Office Use

❑ Bank Reference Checked/Date _____   ❑ Trade Reference #1 Checked/Date _____

Comments _____   Comments _____

❑ Trade Reference #2 Checked/Date _____   ❑ Trade Reference #3 Checked/Date _____

Comments _____   Comments _____

❑ Credit Rating Checked/Date _____   ❑ Credit Approved/Date _____ Credit Limit $ _____

Comments _____   ❑ Credit Declined/Date _____

Comments _____   Comments _____

transunion.com, Equifax, *equifax.com* and Experian, *experian.com*. All three agencies compile and maintain credit files on just about every person, business and organization that has ever applied for credit. Credit card companies, banks, and trust companies supply information to these credit-reporting agencies, as do other businesses that lend money or extend credit to people and businesses. From this information the credit bureaus assign a credit rating to each individual or business. Nonpayment of loans, bankruptcies, slow repayment of loans and litigation to collect funds can all affect a credit rating negatively.

Financial institutions, credit card companies, mortgage brokers, retail stores, leasing companies, and other businesses conduct credit checks to determine if the person or business applying for credit is a good credit risk; that is, if the person or business is likely to repay the debt and interest on time and in full as set forth in the agreement. Home business owners can subscribe to these credit reporting agencies and then for a fee they can have a credit report compiled on a person or business applying for a credit account. To conduct the credit check, you must first have the applicant's permission and a signed credit check and application form.

Returns, Refunds and Contract Cancellations

Inevitably, all home business owners will be faced with a customer who wants to return a product, requests a refund or wants out of a contract. Consequently, it is best to establish your return, refund and contract cancellation policies before that happens. In formulating your return/refund policies, consider:

- Will you allow customers to return products?
- What condition will be acceptable for a return?

- What time frame will be acceptable for a return?
- What will be the return options? A new product of equal value, an amount credited for a future purchase, a cash refund or something else?
- Will customers be allowed to return products purchased at less than your normal retail prices?
- Will all sales be final?

Put your return/refund policy clearly in writing and provide it to each customer prior to making a purchase, whether on your website (if you are selling via the internet) or on your printed material, such as brochures or catalogs.

Most states and provinces have consumer protection mechanisms in place that enable consumers to cancel contracts within a prescribed time, generally called "a cooling-off period." However, these laws do not set a standard time limit. You will need to contact the SBA, *sba.gov*, or your lawyer to inquire about your specific area and how the law is applied. You can find the FTC rule explained on the agency website, *ftc.gov/bcp/edu/pubs/consumer/products/pro03. shtm*. Contact in-formation for state consumer protection offices can be found here: *consumeraction.gov/state. shtml*. In Canada, check with the Office of Consumer Affairs, *ic.gc.ca,* the provincial agencies listed here: *ic.gc.ca/epic/site/oca-bc.nsf/ en/ca01506e.html*.

DEBT COLLECTION

No matter how careful you are in terms of extending credit privileges to customers, once in a while you will receive partial payment or no payment at all. What can you do to collect? You have a number of options.

First, you can keep the lines of communication

open with your delinquent customer and maintain pressure to get your money. In most cases, letters, telephone calls, and personal visits will generally lead to payment, at least in part. Keep in mind, however, that you cannot legally intimidate someone into paying you. All you can do is to stay on top of the situation and, if you are not receiving any indication of payment forthcoming, let the customer know that nonpayment will hurt his or her credit rating or that you will take the matter to court. It may be that the customer has not paid because of a financial problem; if it's short term, you can decide to carry the debt until the customer is able to pay up. If this is possible, it may well be worth the effort so that you can keep an otherwise good customer.

Your second option is to hire a collection agency. Under an assignment agreement, for a fixed fee or a portion (usually 50 percent) of the outstanding debt, the agency will attempt to collect the balance for you. The Association of Credit and Collection Professionals, *acainternational.org*, is a good starting point for finding a collection agency.

Your third option is to take the delinquent account to small claims court. This option is discussed in detail later in this section.

Your fourth and final option is to not collect the debt at all. Depending on the amount owed, the time involved in trying to collect the debt and other factors, you may decide to write off the account as a "bad debt." Before you choose this route, however, make sure you talk with your bookkeeper or accountant, because you may not be allowed to deduct the total amount of the debt.

Small Claims Court

If you choose not to enlist the services of a collection agency and you have exhausted all means of trying to collect the debt, without success, you may want to consider taking the debtor to small claims court. Just remember that small claims courts have limits on the amount for which a plaintiff can sue in that state or province. The following table (Figure 11.6) lists the maximum for each state and province at the time of writing. In some cases the maximum varies because of special circumstances. Filing fees vary by state and province. You must pay these fees upfront, but if you win, the fees can be added to your award amount.

Small business owners who take people to court for nonpayment of accounts or nonperformance of services and contracts generally represent themselves, as the amount of the potential award is usually small and does not justify the fees of an attorney. Even if you win, you do not necessarily receive the amount that you are awarded. You may win a judgment, but still have to chase the defendant through garnishment of income or seizure of assets to collect. You may need to work through the sheriff's office or another government body; sometimes this too can be more trouble than it is worth. If you schedule with the small claims court and you have the paperwork to make your case, the customer may opt to settle out of court. After all, losing a small claims court case does not look good on his or her credit report.

You can learn more about the small claims court process and filing fees by contacting your local courthouse.

OPTIONS FOR GROWING YOUR HOME BUSINESS

At some point, most home business owners must decide whether to grow their business. Of course, as with any business decision, you have to weigh the advantages and disadvantages of the decision for your business, you personally and your family. There are obvious benefits to business growth:

- The potential for increased revenues and profits

FIGURE 11.6   Small Claims Court Limits

United States

Alabama	$3,000	North Carolina	$5,000
Alaska	$10,000	North Dakota	$5,000
Arizona	$2,500	Ohio	$3,000
Arkansas	$5,000	Oklahoma	$6,000
California	$7,500	Oregon	$5,000
Colorado	$7,500	Pennsylvania	$8,000
Connecticut	$5,000		($10,000 in Philadelphia)
Delaware	$15,000	Rhode Island	$2,500
District of Columbia	$5,000	South Carolina	$7,500
Florida	$5,000	South Dakota	$8,000
Georgia	$15,000	Tennessee	$25,000
Hawaii	$3,500	Texas	$10,000
Idaho	$5,000	Utah	$7,500
Illinois	$10,000	Vermont	$5,000
Indiana	$6,000	Virginia	$5,000
Iowa	$5,000	Washington	$4,000
Kansas	$4,000	West Virginia	$5,000
Kentucky	$1,500	Wisconsin	$5,000
Louisiana	$3,000	Wyoming	$7,000
Maine	$4,500		
Maryland	$5,000	**Canada**	
Massachusetts	$2,000	Alberta	$25,000
Michigan	$3,000	British Columbia	$25,000
Minnesota	$7,500	Manitoba	$10,000
Mississippi	$2,500	New Brunswick	$6,000
Missouri	$3,000	Newfoundland	$5,000
Montana	$3,000	Northwest Territories	$5,000
Nebraska	$2,700	Nova Scotia	$15,000
Nevada	$5,000	Nunavut	No limit set yet
New Hampshire	$5,000	Ontario	$10,000
New Jersey	$3,000	Prince Edward Island	$8,000
New Mexico	$10,000	Quebec	$7,000
New York	$5,000	Saskatchewan	$10,000
	($3,000 in town and village courts)	Yukon Territories	$5,000

- Accelerating equity accumulation
- Greater visibility in the marketplace
- Increase in value

On the other hand, there are disadvantages in growing a home business. Many entrepreneurs who have decided to grow their business have not succeeded because the business model that generated success initially did not work on a larger scale.

Other potential disadvantages include not having enough technical equipment and needing to hire outside help, both of which bring additional problems. Sometimes, growing a home business means larger headaches, including problems resulting from making the business more visible in the neighborhood.

Additional disadvantages of growing a home business include:

- Increased overhead and greater financial risk
- A loss of some control if additional people are brought into the business to assume responsibilities
- Increased management responsibilities that can leave you less time to do what made the business successful

If you decide that growing your home business is the best option for you, your business and/or your family and that it will help you achieve your personal and business goals, you have numerous ways in which to grow—geographic growth, growth by people, growth in product or service lines, franchising and mergers and acquisitions.

Grow Geographically

There are basically two ways to grow geographically: physically and/or electronically. The first is through building satellite locations in the same city, county, state or country or in other countries. The second way is by using the internet to sell products and possibly services to a global audience.

To grow your home business geographically in the real world, there are many choices, including agents, a mobile sales staff, licensees, new offices with managers, new business partners, franchising or mergers and acquisitions. All are discussed in detail in this chapter.

Growing your business via the internet is more common today because it is much easier and definitely less expensive than growing your business

physically. There is no need to rent office space and pay employees and managers, which is the reason why many people choose the comfort of a home-based business. If you decide to expand via the internet, you can move into foreign markets relatively quickly, efficiently and with virtually no red tape. More information about growing your business electronically can be found in Chapter 17, "Internet and E-Commerce."

Grow by People

You can substantially grow your home business by involving more people in the business. You can hire employees so that you can increase productivity and afford to take on new clients. Many home salespeople expand by hiring employees, usually part-time, as sales agents or to help with marketing and promotion. If you choose to grow your home business by bringing in people, you must be prepared to invest the time necessary to find people who share your enthusiasm for the business or are at least dedicated and reliable. You must also be prepared to invest the money required to train, equip, and support employees until they can contribute to the bottom line.

Before growing your business by adding people, consider the following questions:

- What type of training is required to bring new people up to speed on your business operations, your products or services and your customers?
- Who will perform the training? Will you do it yourself? Will you bring in outside trainers? If the latter, what is the cost and where will the training take place?
- Will your new employees, agents, or subcontractors work from their own homes or offices or will they be working from your home? If they will be working from your home, do you have the space to accommo-

date additional people and does zoning allow outside employees to work from your home?

- What type of new equipment must you acquire for your expanded work force, where will the equipment come from and how will you pay for it?

- How much will you be paying your workers and how will they be compensated? Will they receive a base salary, commissions or both? Do you have to supply employee insurance and benefits? If so, how much will this cost and where will you get the money?

These questions can help you prepare for adding people to your business. You must also consider labor laws, health and safety regulations, management issues and most definitely financial issues. If growing your business means adding people, you need to develop a strategy for doing so. Additional information about employee and contractor issues can be found in Chapter 8, "Building Your Business Team."

Grow by Expanding Product or Service Lines

Another way to grow your home business is to offer more products or services. This strategy for growing is highly advisable. You have valuable customer relationships in place. You do not immediately have to go searching for new customers for your new products or services; you can sell to your current customers.

However, your current customers must want and need your new products or services. Before expanding your line, you might want to talk with your customers and/or conduct a survey. Find out what additional products or services they might like and what they would be willing to spend. Check with your suppliers or find other suppliers and make a list of possible new products and services. Have your customers choose from this list the products or services that would interest them. If

you simply ask for suggestions, without structuring your request, they might ask for products or services you cannot provide and they would thus be disappointed.

As a word of caution, if you decide to expand your products or services, make sure any additions complement your current offerings and that the expansion is logical. For instance, if you operate an office cleaning service, then you might offer mobile dry cleaning pickup and drop-off services as a logical add-on service. That would be easy to manage, cheap to incorporate and likely to earn additional profits. One of the best parts of expanding products and services is that you do not necessarily need to add people. Many homebased business entrepreneurs build their online businesses by adding pages to their websites and expanding their online catalogs.

Grow by Franchising and Licensing

Many home businesses have expanded to become national and international corporations by franchising their business model or by licensing their products or intellectual and proprietary properties. The potential for growth through franchising and licensing is nearly limitless, but these are very tricky waters to navigate.

Home business owners who choose this route for growth are well advised to seek the services of a lawyer and an accountant well-versed in franchising laws and financial issues. You will also want to talk with a franchise consultant who can analyze your business, products and services and advise you on the viability of franchising your business.

The most successful franchises are ones that follow the KISS formula—"Keep It Simple, Stupid." The franchise must be easy to operate, sell something consumers want and have the potential to cover expenses and the operator's income. The best franchises do not try to reinvent the wheel, but rather improve on a current product or service and its distribution through a unique selling proposition. If your home business meets these criteria, it may very well be ideal for expanding into new geographic areas through a franchise agreement.

It is best to start a business and run it successfully for several years before venturing into franchising it. You will need to ensure that your business can run efficiently and profitably before people will be interested in operating franchises.

Additional information about franchising can be found in Chapter 2, "What Type of Business Should You Start?" or you can contact or visit the website of the International Franchise Association (*franchise.org*) for more information about franchising and licensing opportunities. IFA members include franchisors, franchisees and product and service providers to the franchise industry.

Grow by Mergers or Acquisitions

Mergers and acquisitions are a growth option for home business owners, although certainly not as popular as the growth options already discussed. It is, however, possible to merge your business with another business, whether competing or not. If you do, your options would include retaining a portion of ownership of the new operation or selling out completely and not retaining any ownership, but perhaps remaining involved as an employee or a consultant.

Growing a business by merging it with another business can be a wise growth strategy. When the two businesses become one, they benefit by being able to take advantage of their combined resources and strengths while offsetting weaknesses through specialization. It may also afford you the opportunity to own a piece of a larger pie with further growth potential, instead of a larger piece of a small pie with little or no opportunity for growth.

Business growth through acquisition can also prove a wise move. Purchasing direct or indirect competitors or businesses that sell complementary goods and service enables you to expand your current line.

There are advantages and disadvantages associated with growing your business through mergers or acquisitions. But provided that you do enough research and the new organization appears viable, you might want to merge with or acquire another business to move toward your business goals.

GETTING OUT OF YOUR HOME BUSINESS

Eventually, you will also face a decision about selling your business, passing it to a family member or closing out. At some point, this decision will be inevitable. Nothing lasts forever—or at least not we humans. There are many valid reasons for selling or closing a home business:

- The time is right to retire.
- You want to slow down to a part-time or seasonal home business operation.
- You want to move on to new business challenges and opportunities.
- You want to cash out your equity and enjoy the fruits of your labor.
- You want to return to the corporate world as an employee or a manager.
- Health-related issues make operating a business no longer possible.
- There are family-related issues, such as marriage, divorce or starting a family.
- You want to move to another city, state or country.

Whatever your reason(s) for selling or closing your home business, consult with your accountant before you take any action. There will probably be tax implications to consider, whether you sell your business, close it down, pass it on to a family member or employee or reduce the business to a seasonal or part-time effort.

Selling Your Business

Home business operations can be sold, provided you have something of value to attract new owners—inventory, a good customer base, protected intellectual properties, an exclusive line of products or services or a list of steady clients or customers. Of course, home businesses are not always easy to sell, since your strength may be in your own skills, contacts and/or personality, rather than in the business as an entity. This is not to say that you cannot sell your business. It just takes time to find the right buyer.

The next logical question is, How much is your home business worth? There are various approaches you can use to place a value on your business. If you feel you can sell your business for a substantial amount of money, it may be wise to hire a business broker or consultant to use standard valuation techniques to establish a value for your business. You may, however, choose one of the following easy and less costly routes:

- *Asset value.* The most basic way to value your business is to calculate the value of your physical assets (e.g., inventory, equipment and transportation) and sell the business for the total value of these physical assets. Selling your business based on a valuation of physical assets makes it very easy to find buyers, but harder to make much profit. You can sell the assets individually to many people or all to a single buyer. Competitors may be interested in some or all your business assets, including inventory, equipment, customer lists, telephone number and office fixtures. You can also run classified advertisements or hold an auction to liquidate your business assets.

- *Comparative value.* What have similar home business operations sold for in your area? What is the going rate for a similar homebased franchise? Comparative value is an easy way to place a basic value on your business. For instance, if you operate a lawn mowing service and if lawn mowing distributorships or franchises are selling for $25,000 in your area, then chances are you can place a value on your business close to $25,000, if not slightly more, depending on your equipment, customer base and net profits. You need some due diligence to find out the selling prices of other businesses. You can get an idea by looking for prices in newspapers or on the internet. Remember to look only for similar businesses in your geographic region. Find as many recent sales as possible. You may find asking prices for $45,000, but maybe the last similar business to sell in your area went for $25,000. Remember: Asking prices are not the same as sales prices, since an owner can ask for any amount. It is often very difficult to find similar homebased businesses that are selling in the same area. If you do use a comparative (market-based) valuation, add or subtract for differences between your business and the comparisons you find. If, for example, you are selling the lawn mowing business mentioned above for $25,000, the same as the sale price of a similar business, but you have three new state-of-the-art mowers, you can up your price by the asset values of those mowers.

- *Income value.* You can base the value of your business on the income that it is generating. If your business has few or no physical assets, but it generates a pretax income of $35,000 annually, you could use a factor such as two times the earnings to place a value on your business for sale purposes. In this example you would value your business at $70,000. After all, to most people the enticement to buy an independent, operating business is that the business is generating an income and the new owner can immediately draw a wage.

To calculate an income (earnings-based) valuation, you take into account historical financial figures, including debt payments, cash flow (past, present and projected) and revenues. Using the pro forma method, you can use the income statements of last five years to project out for the next five years, adding in some items and an end payment. Of course, all future projections are open to some debate. However, if you can show steady growth based on the numbers from recent years, you can present a strong argument for your valuation.

It's worth pointing out that before you multiply your income number by two or three or four, you need to also determine the market and the economic climate. In an oversaturated market, you may be fortunate to get the $70,000. If, however, you have a hot new business in a very trendy industry, you might ask for four or even five times the $35,000 income figure, for $140,000 or $175,000. You can always lower an asking price, but you can rarely ever raise it.

Here's the bottom line: if your business is generating an income, regardless of the amount, it has value and is a salable asset.

Of course, you can also use a combination of all three valuation techniques to arrive at a selling price. Regardless of the way you arrive at the selling price, you do not want to underprice your business and sell it for less than you could get or to overvalue your business and generate no interest.

Your reason for getting out of the business may factor into your decision. The seller does not need to know why you are selling, but you can determine your initial asking price based on your own personal needs. For example, if you or someone in your family is ill and you need the money now, you will likely lower the price to get cash more quickly. If, however, you'd like to sell, but are not in any hurry, you can start higher and then, if you don't attract interest, start lowering the price slowly. Obviously, there are many factors that will influence how much you ask for your business.

Also, remember that there are intangibles, such as the reputation you have built up in your area or even on the internet. Someone buying a business with an established name should be ready to pay more, since the buyer will be profiting from that reputation and saving money on advertising and marketing. That should be part of your sales pitch. This is why the more successful franchises sell more quickly than most other businesses—the name value.

Hiring Professional Help

If you decide to hire a professional to sell your business, you have some options. You can list your business for sale with a real estate firm in your area. If you choose this route, you will want to list with an agent who specializes in selling businesses and commercial properties. You can also enlist the services of a certified business broker who specializes solely in marketing businesses and franchises. The International Business Brokers Association, located online at *ibba.org*, has listings of more than 1,000 independent business brokers in North America, Asia and Europe. Whether you work with a real estate agent or a business broker, you will be required to pay a commission based on the total sale price of your business, generally between 5 and 10 percent. You can also work with a business valuation consultant to help you value your business and then go on your own to sell it. In that case, you might pay a flat fee for the valuation.

If you decide that you are best qualified to sell your business, you can advertise your business for sale locally, but be discreet. Do not include your business name in the advertisements; you do not want your current customers to find out that your business is for sale, because it might make them nervous and cause them to take their business elsewhere. There are also many business-for-sale print and electronic publications and websites that will list your business in exchange for a fee. Generally, these publications and online services are divided into business sections or industries such as home businesses, distributorships, retail, services and manufacturing. BizBuySell, at *bizbuysell.com*, is one of the largest business-for-sale websites.

Giving Your Business Away

Another option is to give away your home business, although not necessarily for free. You could give your business to one of your kids, an employee, a relative or friend with an interest in operating the business. Even though you may be giving the business to someone, you could still receive payments over a set period in exchange for fully training the new operator and providing occasional consulting services as needed. You could agree to a percentage of the sales for a specific time. In some cases, giving your business away, rather than selling it, makes a lot of sense, especially if the recipient is a family member. There are tax benefits that may be derived from this kind of arrangement. Of course, if you can give the business away and still generate income through consulting fees, royalty payments or part-time employment, as needed, then there is also a benefit in terms of financial security.

Taking Your Business to Part-Time

You can always decide not to sell, close down or give your business away. Instead you may choose to scale back your business to part-time or seasonal. If you decide on this route, keep your best and most profitable clients and hang onto a minimum amount of equipment, only what is needed to operate part time or seasonally. The rest of your business assets—such as excess inventory, equipment, fixtures and customer lists that you will no longer need—can be sold to competitors or other entrepreneurs seeking a fast start-up. Determine what you will need to continue and scale back accordingly. Professionals, such as accountants who work on their own, often turn some of their major clients over to family members starting out in the field, retaining only a few major clients.

There are two main benefits to taking your business part time instead of selling or closing it. First, you can continue to generate a part-time or seasonal income that is derived from your best customers, who should also be your most profitable. If 80 percent of your business comes from 20 percent of your customers, why not keep the most profitable 20 percent and do without the other 80 percent? Second, there are great tax benefits associated with keeping your business operating part time or seasonally, even if you decide to take an outside job. Deductible expenses from a part-time business are little different from those of a full-time business and can include a portion of your household expenses, transportation costs, insurance premiums, health care premiums and travel expenses. Of course, not all expenses will be 100-percent tax deductible. But any time you can reduce your taxable earnings through allowable business expenses, it is certainly wise to take advantage of the opportunity.

Closing Your Business

Many home business operations are unique in the sense that the value of the business really lies in the experience and special skills of the operator and not so much in the rest of the business. For that reason, it is not uncommon for home businesses to close instead of being sold or passed on to family members or others. This is especially true of professional practices and businesses that provide highly specialized services. If you choose to close your home business, know that you are in good company; many home business owners simply close their businesses when they decide to retire or move on to new adventures and challenges.

There are still issues that you must deal with before you can unplug the phone and call it quits, primarily your customers. You do not want to leave your loyal clients in the lurch, forced to find new product or service providers without notice or assistance. Plan your exit strategy carefully and give clients as much notice as possible. Offer to help them find new providers to fill their needs. Ideally, if you decide to shut your business, you want to go out on very good terms with all of your customers, suppliers and business associates. That's not just the right way to leave; it's also smart. If you decide to reopen the business or another business or to serve as a consultant to other entrepreneurs, these are valuable business relationships that can be reignited for your benefit if the need arises.

RESOURCES
Associations

American Home Business Association
965 East 4800, Suite 3C
Salt Lake City, UT 84117
(866) 396-7773
homebusinessworks.com

American Management Association
1601 Broadway
New York, NY 10019
(212) 586-8100
amanet.org

Association of Credit and Collection Professionals
P.O. Box 390106
Minneapolis, MN 55439
(952) 926-6547
acainternational.org

U.S. Small Business Administration
409 3rd Street SW
Washington, DC 20416
(800) 827-5722
sba.org

Suggested Reading

Allen, David. *Getting Things Done: The Art of Stress Free Productivity*. New York: Penguin Books, 2003.

Forsyth, Patrick. *Successful Time Management*. 2nd edition. London: Kogan Page, 2007.

Harvard Business Essentials. *Time Management: Increase Your Personal Productivity and Effectiveness*. Boston: Harvard Business School Press, 2005.

Hugos, Michael H. *Essentials of Supply Chain Management*. 2nd edition. New York: John Wiley & Sons, 2002.

McCormick, Blaine. *Ben Franklin's 12 Rules of Management*. Irvine, CA: Entrepreneur Press, 2000.

Pinson, Linda. *Keeping the Books: Basic Recordkeeping and Accounting for the Successful Small Business*. 7th edition. Chicago: Dearborn Trade Publishing (Kaplan Publishing), 2007.

Rickertsen, Rick, and Robert E. Gunther. *Sell Your Business Your Way: Getting Out, Getting Rich, and Getting on with Your Life*. Boston: AMACOM (American Management Association), 2006.

Stemmy, Thomas J. *Top Tax Savings Ideas: A Small Business Tax Survival Kit.* Irvine, CA: Entrepreneur Press Inc., 2004.

Websites

Canada Business/Entreprises Canada: A government information service for businesses and start-up entrepreneurs in Canada that serves as a single point of access for federal and provincial or territorial government services, programs and regulatory requirements for business (formerly *Canadian Business Service Center*). *canadabusiness.ca*

Home Business Magazine Online: Information, advice, tools and links for home business owners. *homebusinessmag.com*

Organize Your World: Home business organization tips, products and resources. *organizeyourworld.com*

PowerHomeBiz.com: Online information, advice and tools for home business owners. *powerhomebiz.com*

QuickBooks Software: Small business bookkeeping and accounting software. *quickbooks.intuit.com*

Quicken Software: Business and financial software. *quicken.intuit.com*

Time-Management-Guide.com: Tips and information on time management topics. *time-management-guide.com*

CHAPTER 12

Creating a Marketing Plan

WHAT WILL A MARKETING PLAN DO for your business? The answer is simple: You will be able to prove, based on your research and data, that there is sufficient consumer demand for your products or services. You will also be able to support your belief that you can compete in the marketplace based on benefits for consumers and competitive advantages and that the market is large enough to support your business.

Many small business owners "fly by the seat of their pants" in market planning, choosing to forgo any type of formal or even informal plans. They opt to make important marketing decisions day by day. Some are very successful; others struggle and eventually go out of business because of their lack of planning. Like most entrepreneurs, I can chalk up more than one bad marketing experience to a lack of planning. When I say "bad marketing experience," what I am really saying is "Ouch, that dumb idea just cost me a bundle! What was I thinking?"

This may be why I highly advise new entrepreneurs to create a marketing plan. By doing so, you can maximize your positive marketing experiences, minimize your bad marketing experiences, and reach your marketing goals in a clearly defined and measurable way, step by step.

Keep in mind, of course, that the small business marketing plan does not have to be sophisticated or highly detailed like those marketing plans that multinational corporations need to satisfy nervous bankers and investors. In fact, even just a few detailed and well-documented pages covering the basics are often sufficient to present the information you need to identify your customers, your product's beneficial advantages, your marketing goals, your marketing strategies and your action plan. The extent of your marketing plan is a function of its purpose. If you are going to use it to secure startup or growth financing, it will need to be comprehensive and satisfy the needs of those from whom you are seeking funding. If the purpose is to merely act as a road map that eventually helps you reach your marketing goals, the fit and finish only must satisfy your personal objectives and needs.

A final word of advice before you start your marketing plan or, for that matter, any business-related plan: Don't be intimidated by the planning process and do not let business gurus or academic terminology prevent you from developing your plans. They need not be business school models, as long as they are able to serve your purposes. Just make sure that the information you research, record, analyze, and document is valuable and specific to your business situation.

In Chapter 10, "Finding and Keeping Customers," we provided information about conducting market research, collecting secondary data and creating a target customer profile. All will be required to fully develop your marketing plan. Like a business plan, a marketing plan is grounded in as much fact as is possible, with perhaps a few safe assumptions. Simply stating in your marketing plan what you hope will happen or what you believe will happen is utterly useless. Therefore, take the time necessary to fully research, record, and analyze each section of your marketing plan before you put all your findings into a formal document. The result should be a step-by-step guide that acts as a road map to transport your business from where you are currently to where you want to be.

MARKETING PLAN OUTLINE

The format of a marketing plan has no rules set in stone because plans vary by industry, type of business, location, size of the company, stage of growth, intended target market and plan function (financing vs. management). The marketing plan you need to help guide your homebased lawn care service to success is much different than the marketing plan that The Coca-Cola Company needs to guide its multi-billion-dollar international business though the competitive waters of the soft drink industry. Remember: For the small business operator, the format is really not an issue. Format your marketing plan in such a way that it makes sense to you in terms of how the information is recorded and how the information can be applied to your particular business situation. The true value of the plan is the information about your business, products or services, customers, market, competitors, and the strategies you used in creating it. Provided that you cover the basics, the result will be a marketing plan that works for your particular situation. The following is a basic marketing plan outline for a small business:

- Executive Overview
- Company Analysis
- Market Analysis
- Customer Analysis
- Competitor Analysis
- Marketing Objectives
- Marketing Strategy
- Marketing Budget
- Action Plan
- Support Documents

Worksheets are included in this chapter for most sections of marketing planning so that you can begin the process of creating a marketing plan as you read, gather and record the basic information.

EXECUTIVE OVERVIEW

Just like a business plan, a marketing plan begins with an Executive Overview or Introduction. This section is a brief summary of key points from every section of your marketing plan, short enough to fit onto one page. Even though the Executive Overview is at the beginning, it is usually the last section you create. The Executive Overview comprises the key points extracted from each section of your plan, points that you do not know until you have substantially completed each section. The main purpose of this overview is to provide readers with the who, what, where, when, why and how of the marketing plan.

Depending on your business, industry, stage of growth and purpose, the Executive Overview could include any or all of the following information:

- Your business name and legal structure
- Mission statement or philosophy
- A brief mention of the owner, management team and relevant experience and training
- When your business will start
- The geographic area you will serve
- The type of product or service you will offer
- The unique benefits of your products or services

- Your target customers
- Market size and potential
- Position in the marketplace
- Company objectives
- How you will achieve your objectives
- Projected revenues
- Short-term and long-terms goals

Once you have substantially completed your marketing plan, you will be ready to create your Executive Overview. Answering the questions on the following Executive Overview Worksheet (Figure 12.1) with information extracted from the appropriate section of your marketing plan will enable you to create an Executive Overview. Of course not all the questions are relevant to your business. Answer those that are relevant and ignore the rest. Also, keep in mind that the Executive Overview is brief, so limit your answers to a few sentences.

FIGURE 12.1   Executive Overview Worksheet

What are your business name and legal structure? _____

What is your mission statement or purpose for being in business? _____

Who will manage the business? What special skills, experience or training do they have? _____

When did the business start? _____

Where is the business located? (city) _____

What geographic area does your business service? (city, county, state, country, world) _____

What type of products or services do you sell? _____

What are the unique user benefits of your products or services? _____

FIGURE 12.1	Executive Overview Worksheet, continued

What is your main competitive advantage? _____
_____

Who are your target customers? _____
_____

How big is your current market? _____
_____

How big is the potential market? _____
_____

What is your position in the marketplace or what is your positioning strategy? _____
_____

What are your company's key marketing objectives? _____
_____

How will you achieve your objectives? _____
_____

What is your first year's revenue projection? $ _____

What is your long-term revenue projection? (five years) $ _____

What are your short-term goals? _____
_____

What are your long-term goals? _____
_____

COMPANY ANALYSIS

The Company Analysis is a full description of your company, including in-depth information on the owner(s), key partnerships the business has entered into or will enter into, and the company's strengths and weaknesses. Of course, if you are doing a business plan, you need not overlap with the same information, since the idea of a marketing plan is to describe your market, your target audience and how you will market your business.

The Company Analysis will include as much of the following information as possible or as applicable to your type of business and situation.

- Business name and legal structure
- Business location (city) and the area that the business serves (city, county, state, country or world)
- If the company is established, its history: when it was formed and growth or decline in recent years
- If the business is new, a starting date and full description of why the business will succeed
- Your business goals and objectives
- Your business culture

- Relationships with key suppliers, vendors and other important players
- Company strengths
- Company weaknesses
- Any significant obstacles or challenges that stand in the way of reaching key marketing goals and objectives
- Special licenses and intellectual property ownerships, such as exclusive sales agreements, product representations, product or service licenses, patents, trademarks and copyrights
- Associations to which the business belongs—professional, industry or business
- Any accreditations or endorsements that the business has received from schools, private

industry, government agencies or nonprofit agencies

Answering the following questions on the Company Analysis Worksheet (Figure 12.2) and completing any descriptions or lists required will help you create a company analysis. Ignore questions that are not relevant and add any that you believe will paint a more accurate picture of your company. Now you want to go into great detail in terms of information, statistics, and facts when developing these other sections of your marketing plan. The goal of the marketing plan is to leave no unanswered questions in terms of the company and its marketing intentions, especially if the marketing plan will be used as a tool to secure funding.

FIGURE 12.2 Company Analysis Worksheet

What are your business name and legal structure? _____

What are the goals of your business? _____

Where is your business located? (city) _____

What is your business culture? _____

In detail, describe the trading area that your business serves. (city, county, state, country, world) _____

If your business is currently operating, give a brief history of the company, including when it was formed, successes to date, failures to date, current market share and growth or decline to date. Include yearly sales figures. _____

If your business is new, describe why you think it will be successful in terms of marketing. _____

List any joint venture or cross-promotional partners and the nature of the partnerships. _____

FIGURE 12.2   Company Analysis Worksheet, continued

List key suppliers or key vendors. _____

_____

Describe what you believe are your company's strengths. _____

_____

Describe what you believe are your company's weaknesses. _____

_____

Describe the obstacles that stand in the way of your company reaching its marketing goals and objectives. _____

_____

List any product or service licenses or exclusive sales/supply agreements your company has. _____

_____

List any intellectual property your company owns and describe the property protected. _____

_____

List any professional, industry or business associations to which your company belongs. _____

_____

List any accreditations or endorsements that your business has from schools, private industry, government agencies or nonprofit agencies.

_____

_____

MARKET ANALYSIS

A Market Analysis is information about the marketplace in which your business currently operates or will operate. The biggest benefit of conducting and recording a Market Analysis is that the information you discover enables you to greatly reduce your exposure to financial risk, while at the same time increasing your chances of capitalizing on marketplace opportunities. It also proves that there is a big enough marketplace to support your business. Use Figure 12.3 to help you.

Information included in your marketing plan will be based on your primary research, as well as data from secondary sources, such as schools, government agencies, private companies and the internet. Chapter 10, "Finding and Keeping Customers," describes the methods you can use to conduct primary research, such as focus groups and surveys. It also tells where you can find secondary sources of data and statistics so you can compile the information you will eventually use to support your statements, forecasts and objectives. The Market Analysis section of your marketing plan should include research based on in-depth information in three main areas: market size, market segmentation and marketing environment.

Market Size

The starting point is to define your market. Most home business owners will elect to use geographical boundaries, because most home businesses serve a specific market. So what is the current size of the market?

A pool-cleaning service might describe the current size of the market as 1,000 single-family homes of which 200, or 20 percent, currently have a swimming pool. Therefore, the current market is the 200 homeowners who have swimming pools. How big is the potential market? The city planning department estimates that 5,000 new single-family homes will be built over the next 10 years. If 20 percent of the new homes have pools, this would provide a potential market of 1,200 single-family homes with swimming pools.

Additionally, you would go on to describe the current stage of the market lifecycle—growing, declining or static (no growth or no decline). As you can see, the market size needs only to be detailed in broad, statistical terms. You will supply this information by your own primary research, as well as from secondary sources.

Market Segmentation

Market segmentation is breaking your target audience down into groups for easy identification and targeting. The three market segments researched, analyzed, and recorded are geographics, demographics and psychographics. Market segmenting is highly significant, because it allows you to get a much clearer picture of your customers. Such detailed information about the lifestyles, interests, spending habits, age, and so on of your customers will provide you with a means of gearing your promotional, marketing and advertising materials to your target customers.

In Chapter 10, "Finding and Keeping Customers," you will find geographic, demographic, and psychographic information, how each can be researched and how this information can be applied to your business and marketing planning activities.

Geographics

By determining where your target market is living, you can better determine where to direct your marketing efforts. Specify the country, state, county, city and even neighborhood. If you intend on servicing more than one geographic market, you will have to create a geographic profile for each. Of course, for a web-based business, your audience is global, so you won't be able to specify a single area. However, you will soon see which areas provide the most hits.

Demographics

The second step is to segment your target audience demographically by gender, age, race, religion, education, income and profession. Demographic data can be further expanded to include information such as number of people in the household and marital status. In Chapter 10, "Finding and Keeping Customers," you will find a customer profiling worksheet, which can help you segment your target audience demographically.

Psychographics

Psychographics is segmenting your customers by their common characteristics, such as lifestyle, values, behavior and opinions. This data is used as a continuation of geographic and demographic profiling. Once you know where your target audience is located (geographic) and who your target audience is (demographic), then you can begin to find out what your target customers have in common—the type of music they like, the type of social clubs they belong to, the type of cars they drive or whatever.

Marketing Environment

Marketing environment is the third area in the Market Analysis section. In it you answer the question, "What are the current issues or emerging trends that can positively or negatively affect my business and the marketing of my products or services?" The best way to research the marketing environment is to conduct a PEST (political, economic, social and technological) analysis, which divides the marketing environment into four key areas that can potentially affect your business and marketing efforts: political and legal issues, economic issues, social and cultural issues and technological issues. You should complete a PEST analysis for all of the geographic regions in which you intend to conduct business, because the economy in one area may be different than in another.

Political/Legal

When you research and analyze political and legal issues, you are looking for current issues or emerging trends that can influence the way you do business, either positively or negatively. Is the political situation stable in the area where you want to conduct business? Are there impending tax regulations that will affect your business? Are the zoning laws regulating home businesses in your area about to change? Are there any current or emerging environmental issues or laws that will affect your business? Basically, you want to take an in-depth look at the political and legal environment to determine if there are current issues or emerging trends that you should know about.

Economic

Researching and analyzing economic issues and trends is straightforward. You can start by conducting good old look-out-your-window research. Take a walk around your community to see what's going on. Is the economy hot, flat or declining? Is unemployment high, low or static? Are there many stores and businesses for rent or is it hard to find office or retail space? Current and emerging economic factors can also include issues such as fluctuations in interest rates or currency values or forthcoming mass layoffs or hiring campaigns by major employers. Consider economic factors that can affect the purchasing power of

your target customers.

Social/Cultural

Social and cultural factors revolve around demographics, social activities and cultural attitudes. For example, if you operate a fitness consulting business and the shift is toward health consciousness, this could have a positive impact on your business. It would certainly affect how you promote your fitness service. Research and analyze the changes taking place or trends emerging in demographics and social attitudes and activities. Look at population growth, age distribution, views on environmental issues, sports and recreational activities, personal safety and the actions people take as a result. These are all examples of social or cultural changes that can influence your business.

Technological

You do not have to look hard or far to see how much technology affects business and the way business is conducted, especially over the last few decades with the proliferation of internet users and with the introduction and wide consumer acceptance of digital technologies. When researching technology in relationship to your business, market and marketing plan, you want to look at current and emerging technologies and determine how they may impact your business and customers. Technology may influence how your target customers get their information, how they communicate with one another, what they purchase and how you can reach them most effectively.

CUSTOMER ANALYSIS

The Customer Analysis section of your marketing plan is really a fine-tuning of your target customer profile. You dig deeper to better understand what is important to your target customers.

I believe that the only way to accurately collect this information is through conducting your own

FIGURE 12.3   Market Analysis Worksheet

Summarize the research methods and the sources of data used in creating the market analysis, noting specific market size, market segmentation and marketing environment. _____

_____

_____

Market Size

Define your market. _____

_____

How big is the current market? _____

_____

How big is the potential market? _____

_____

Is the market large enough to be profitable? _____

_____

How many competitors are operating in the market? _____

_____

In what lifecycle stage is the market—growth, decline or static? _____

_____

Market Segmentation

Where are your target customers located geographically? (Be specific.) _____

_____

What means of promotion will enable you to reach your target audience within the specific geographical market(s)?

_____

_____

Demographically speaking, define your target audience by gender, age, race, religion, income, education, number of dependents and marital status (target customer profile). _____

_____

What are the common characteristics that members of your primary target audience share? _____

_____

What publications do members of your target audience like to read, what television shows do they watch, what radio stations do they listen to, and what recreational activities do they pursue in their free time? _____

_____

FIGURE 12.3   Market Analysis Worksheet, continued

Marketing Environment

Is the geographical area in which you will be conducting business politically stable? _____
_____

Are there new or forthcoming changes in any laws or regulations that will affect your business, products or services? If so, what will these effects be? _____
_____

Are there any current or emerging social or cultural issues that will affect your business? If so, why? _____
_____

What is your biggest concern in terms of the economy? How may this affect your business? _____
_____

Will an increase or decrease in interest rates affect your business? If so, why? _____
_____

Will an increase or decrease in employment rates affect your business? If so, why? _____
_____

Are there any current or emerging technologies that will affect your business? If so, what is the technology and how will it affect your business? _____
_____

Will the rate of technological change affect your business? If so, how? _____
_____

primary research, using methods such as surveys, focus groups and personal interviews. You have to get out, talk with your potential customers, and ask specific questions that will reveal how they choose between or among competitors. How sensitive are they to price, quality, service and value issues? What type of promotional or marketing activities do they typically respond to? These are commonly called *consumer drivers*. What drives your target customers to make their purchasing decisions? In terms of marketing, you have two choices. You can try to change consumer perceptions and buying habits so that they will buy what you are selling or you can follow the path of least resistance. You can attempt the first, but you better have really deep pockets, because altering consumer buying habits is a long and very costly process.

COMPETITOR ANALYSIS

The Competitor Analysis section is an important part of your marketing plan because it tells you about your direct competitors, the other businesses that sell the same or similar goods or services to the same target customers within the same geographical area. It sheds light on indirect competitors, such as the supermarket that rents carpet cleaning machines and competes with a carpet cleaning service. It also uncovers the phantom and future competitors discussed in Chapter 10, "Finding and Keeping Customers."

Not unlike the business plan, the purpose of conducting and recording a competitor analysis in the marketing plan is to take an objective and realistic look at the business practices, products, and services of your competitors in comparison with your own, so that you can identify internal strengths, correct internal weaknesses, capitalize on external opportunities and reduce or eliminate external threats. This method of competitor analysis, commonly called SWOT (strengths, weaknesses, opportunities and threats) analysis, is featured further along in this section. An additional benefit of completing a competitor analysis is that you'll be able to pinpoint why customers will choose to do business with you instead of a competitor. Or, if you discover that certain markets for specific products and services have reached saturation, you will be able to avoid those markets and concentrate on growth markets. Objectively analyzing the competition will enable you to:

- Identify direct competitors
- Identify indirect competitors
- Identify competitors' strengths and weaknesses
- Identify niche markets for products or services that are not being serviced by competitors
- Identify the advantages and benefits of a competitor's products and services, as well as the benefits and advantages of your own products and services
- See how each competitor is positioned in the marketplace compared with you or where you need to be positioned in the marketplace to take advantage of opportunities
- Identify your competitors' target customers and what promotional methods your competitors use to reach them
- Determine what share of the market they control and their estimated sales
- Understand how competitors change depending on the influences affecting the marketplace

In the Competition section in Chapter 10, "Finding and Keeping Customers," is all the vital need-to-know information for identifying competitors and for competing against other businesses in the markets your business serves.

SWOT Analysis

Business owners and managers will often conduct a SWOT analysis to determine their ability to compete against other businesses that sell similar products or services in the same marketplace and to the same target customers. A SWOT analysis will also help you identify your position within the marketplace, that is, how consumers view your business, products, or services in direct relationship to your competitors and their products or services.

When developing your marketing strategies, try to think about how your competitors will react to these marketing strategies. Remember Newton's third law: For every action there is an equal and opposite reaction. You have to remain aware that your competitors will react to your marketing efforts. The trick is to know beforehand what action they will take, so that you can stay two steps ahead, even when they think you are one step behind.

One positive about a homebased business is that it often takes a little longer for your competitors to find out what you are doing, as opposed to a storefront with a big sign in the window or a large company with a regular stream of media coverage. Smaller businesses operating from a homebase can fly under the radar while instituting changes and launching new products or services until their marketing and promotion hit the streets.

FIGURE 12.4	Customer Analysis Worksheet

Summarize the research methods and the data sources used in creating your customer analysis. _____
_____

What are the critical benefits that your target customers look for in your product or service? _____
_____

How and on what criteria are choices made between or among competitors? _____
_____

What do most of your target customers care about most—price, quality, fast service, value or a wide selection of
goods and services? _____
_____
_____

Strengths

Get started by identifying your internal strengths—those skills and resources you have currently that you can capitalize on and use to your advantage in reaching business and marketing objectives. For instance, your strength might be that you have 25 years' experience in your particular field. Answering questions, such as "What are your current competitive advantages in the marketplace?" and "What is the biggest benefit that people receive from your products or services?" will help you identify your internal strengths. List at least five points that you consider to be your greatest internal strengths. Once you have identified your greatest internal strengths, you can leverage them into other areas of your business.

What are your business's internal strengths?

_____
_____
_____
_____
_____

Weaknesses

Weaknesses are critical factors that can make you less competitive or obstruct your ability to reach specific business and marketing objectives. For example, if you lack specialized equipment that you need to bid on certain jobs, this would be considered an internal weakness. Cash flow problems, lack of credibility, and limited product selection are all examples of internal weaknesses. Make a list of such weaknesses, any factors that you believe diminish your ability to effectively compete within the marketplace, answering basic questions, like "What could we be doing better?"

What are your business's internal weaknesses?

_____
_____
_____
_____
_____

Opportunities

An opportunity is best characterized as a positive situation that arises that you can capitalize on to improve your position within the marketplace and increase your profitability. What external opportunities are currently available or will be coming available that you could use for the benefit of your business? What changes in technologies are now available that could improve your productivity? Are there any forthcoming changes in government regulations that might have a positive impact on your business? List all the external opportunities currently or soon available that you feel you could use to benefit your business.

What external opportunities can your business capitalize on?

_____
_____
_____
_____
_____

Threats

Threats are negative situations that exist or could arise that might damage your position in the marketplace or your profitability. Has a new competitor opened for business in your area? Is your industry in a declining phase? Are there changes coming in government regulations that could have a negative impact on your business? Answering questions such as these will help you to identify the threats that your business currently faces or will soon be facing. Write these down, starting with the biggest external threat.

What external threats is your business facing?

_____
_____
_____
_____
_____

Analyzing the Data and Creating a SWOT Action Plan

The next step is to carefully analyze and prioritize the data collected by identifying your internal strengths and weaknesses and the external opportunities and threats. Do you detect any patterns, such as competitor strengths built on one of your internal weaknesses? Once you have analyzed and prioritized all your data, you will be able to create a SWOT action plan for these strengths, weaknesses, opportunities and threats.

Maximize Strengths. Build on your greatest internal strengths and maximize their positive impact on your business. For instance, if your greatest strength is that you have 20 years of experience in your field, this should become your main competitive advantage and the message that anchors all advertising and marketing activities.

Minimize Weaknesses. Resolve your internal weaknesses or work out ways to minimize the impact that they have on your business. This is one of the greatest benefits of conducting a SWOT analysis. If, for example, you are falling behind your competitors because they are more technologically advanced, hire a technical consultant to advise you on what you need to purchase to even the playing field. Then buy accordingly.

Capitalize on Opportunities. Plan to take action to capitalize on the opportunities that can have an immediate impact.

Eliminate Threats. Create a course of action that will reduce or eliminate external threats. You may even choose to find a way to avoid the threats, if that is possible without damaging your business.

In Chapter 10, "Finding and Keeping Customers," there is a very comprehensive Competition Comparison Worksheet (Figure 10.2) you can copy and use to analyze all your competitors in the marketplace. Answering the questions below (Figure 12.5) will also give you a good start in identifying and analyzing competitors. It is worthwhile to complete both worksheets.

MARKETING OBJECTIVES

The next section of the marketing plan states your Marketing Objectives. If your business is a new startup, you should stay focused on first-year goals. You should give your Marketing Objectives

FIGURE 12.5   Competition Comparison Worksheet

Summarize the research methods and the data sources used in creating the competitor analysis. _____
_____

Based on your research, who are your biggest competitors?

Direct competition:

1. _____

2. _____

3. _____

Indirect competition:

1. _____

2. _____

3. _____

What is the estimated market share of each of your direct competitors? 1. _____% 2. _____% 3. _____%

What is each direct competitor's biggest competitive advantage?

1. _____

2. _____

3. _____

What do you think each direct competitor's greatest strengths and weaknesses are? Why?

Strengths:

1. _____

2. _____

3. _____

Weaknesses:

1. _____

2. _____

3. _____

What opportunities do you see in terms of competing against each direct competitor or filling a niche within the market that they do not? Why?

1. _____

2. _____

3. _____

What is the greatest threat that each direct competitor poses to your business? Why?

1. _____

FIGURE 12.5   Competition Comparison Worksheet, continued

2. _____

3. _____

What is the greatest threat your business poses to each direct competitor? Why?

1. _____

2. _____

3. _____

What is your greatest advantage in terms of competing against each direct competitor? Why?

1. _____

2. _____

3. _____

What does each direct competitor do well enough that you should also be doing?

1. _____

2. _____

3. _____

Now that you know each direct competitor better, what products or services can you provide to their customers to lure them to your business?

1. _____

2. _____

3. _____

What marketing activities can you implement to reach your direct competitor's core target audience?

1. _____

2. _____

3. _____

in easily measured, quantifiable financial terms and set a firm date by which you will achieve each of the objectives. Here's an example.

"Our objective is to increase sales revenues by 10 percent, to $200,000, within 12 months. This will give us a 20-percent share of the current market. To reach our marketing objective, we will be updating our installation equipment at a cost of $11,000, commencing January 15 and completing by February 10. Additionally, to help reach our marketing objective, we will be hiring one additional part-time sales representative in March, who will solely focus on new business generation."

Keep in mind these three key concepts when developing your marketing objectives:

1. If your marketing objectives include expanding into a new geographic territory or expanding a product or service line, do not lose sight

of your current products, services or marketplace. When working hard to reach new goals and objectives, it is very easy to get an extreme case of tunnel vision.

2. Marketing Objectives that do not have the potential to provide a return on the money invested are not really Marketing Objectives. For example, giving away the most helium-filled balloons at Oktoberfest celebrations this year is not a marketing objective. However, it would be a Marketing Objective if you wanted to sell more helium-filled balloons than any other balloon vendor at Oktoberfest celebrations.

3. Marketing Objectives should always revolve around some kind of improvement in your business—training, products, services, customer service, etc. For instance, if your objective is to increase your sales team's closing rate from 30 percent to 50 percent, a strategy would be to retrain your salespeople in their closing skills so that you can meet your objective. In this example, the objective is increasing closing rates and the strategy to be implemented to reach that objective is sales training.

FIGURE 12.6 Marketing Objectives Worksheet

Summarize the research methods and the data sources used in creating your marketing objectives if your business is new. If your marketing objectives are based on (a) previous year(s) in business, mention whether or not past objectives were reached and explain why or why not.

_____

_____

What is your first-year sales objective? What strategies will you put in place to reach your sales objective?

_____

_____

What is your five-year sales objective? _____

_____

_____

List the actions you will take to protect your business. _____

_____

_____

List any improvements you have planned in terms of your business, equipment, technologies, products, services, training, or customer service that will help you reach your marketing objectives.

_____

_____

_____

_____

MARKETING STRATEGY

The Marketing Strategy section of the marketing plan is where things start to get exciting—and creative. You have identified your company's strengths and weaknesses, your competitors, your market size and potential, your primary target customers and the reasons why they buy. You have set your Marketing Objectives. Now it is time to develop marketing and promotional strategies that will enable you to reach those objectives. In other words, it's time to build your marketing game plan. The Marketing Strategy component consists of two parts. Part one is your *positioning strategy*. Part two covers the *four marketing Ps*: product, price, place (distribution) and promotion.

Your positioning strategy is a very important element of your Marketing Strategy. It answers two vital questions: "Where do your business and your products or services fit into the market?" and "How do your target customers view your business and your products or services in relation to your competitors?" You might position your business as the low-price leader in the marketplace or you might choose a "quality first" philosophy. The positioning of your business and the products or services you sell have much to do with competitors and where they are positioned in the market. It also has to do with the perceptions consumers already have of the type of products or services you sell. You can try to alter consumer perceptions and buying habits, but that can be costly. A more logical approach to defining your positioning strategy or philosophy is to analyze the current marketplace (which you have already done), identify what competitors are doing and how consumers are responding, and then make improvements to products or services or how you sell them. In other words, look for a niche market that is being ignored by competitors or make subtle improvements to your products or services in

terms of user benefits to define your positioning strategy. Developing the right positioning strategy for your business is critical; it warrants additional research and a more in-depth understanding. An excellent book to read on positioning, by the men who developed the concept, is *Positioning: The Battle for Your Mind* by Al Ries and Jack Trout (McGraw-Hill), which is available at most booksellers nationwide, as well as on websites like *Amazon. com.*

The second component of your marketing strategy is the four marketing Ps—product, price, place (distribution) and promotion. It is the combination of the four Ps that creates your marketing mix, which is in effect the entire marketing process. The following are a few points that should be discussed in the marketing plan in terms of product, price, place (distribution) and promotion.

Product

The first P is your product (or service), which you want to describe in great detail. There are numerous aspects of your product or service to consider in relation to your marketing strategy, including:

- What is the main benefit that consumers receive from purchasing and using your product or service? Do they save money? Do they make money? Will it make them more fit or healthy? Will they save time? What problem does this product or service solve for your customers? Go into detail about what benefits consumers receive by purchasing and using your product or service.
- Talk about how your product will be packaged to separate it from competitors' packaging.
- Include the warranties and guarantees that you provide—product, workmanship and so on.

Price

Next you want to tackle price issues, which are very important in the marketing mix and your Marketing Strategy. If your prices are too high, you will meet great resistance selling your products or services. If your prices are too low, the same could happen because of perceptions of quality. How you arrive at prices was discussed in Chapter 9, "What Price Will You Charge?" Here, you want to explain your pricing in terms of how and why such a price is fair or a benefit to your customers. Why should your target customers want to pay these prices? What is the benefit relative to the benefit they would get from paying what your competitors charge? Are they getting more for their dollar? Are they spending fewer dollars? Explain the benefits of your pricing for your customers.

Place (Distribution)

Place (distribution) means where your customers can purchase your products and how your products get to your customers. Most home businesses sell their products directly to consumers through their websites, at trade shows or by mail order.

Here you will explain how your customers will find and purchase your products or services. For example, if you design and create one-of-a-kind wedding dresses at home, then logically the dresses should be sold through bridal boutiques and not discount fashion chain stores. If you are selling over the web, you need to explain how your products will be found on your website (which should be very easy to navigate) and how simple it is to order them and then receive them in X number of days. Place is not about where the products or services originate, but how easily your customers can purchase them.

Promotion

In the promotion part of your Marketing Strategy

you describe the various activities you will undertake to promote your products and services. The following is the type of information that you might need to provide here:

- Identify the types of advertising media you will use to promote your products and services, the costs of each, the frequency of each and a description of each advertising medium and its target group(s).
- Describe your personal contact selling strategies, including the number of people in your sales force, how inquiries and presentations are handled, which closing techniques are preferred and how leads and referrals will be generated.
- If you intend to engage in direct marketing promotional activities such as telemarketing, faxing, e-mail blasts, or a direct mail campaign, describe these activities, including costs and expected response rates.
- Discuss public relations and any sponsorships and tell how these will be used to promote your products and services. Include the preferred choice of information release (press release, press conference or expert positioning), charity and activity sponsorships and public speaking opportunities.
- Mention affiliations or memberships in business clubs and associations and how these relationships can be advantageous in the promotion of your products and services.
- Describe your website and whether it will be used solely for promotion or for both sales and promotion. Discuss how you will market the site and what type of information will be available, such as special online promotions, etc.
- List and describe any events such as trade shows, expos and seminars that you will use to promote your products and services—the type of event, where it will be held, the

demographics of the people who will attend the event and the number expected.

- Discuss your plans for using advertising specialties or premiums such as pens, hats and mouse pads that are emblazoned with your business name and promotional message.

Additional information about various promotional methods can be found in the next five chapters—"Advertising and Promotions," "Public Relations and Networking," "Sales," "Event Marketing" and "Internet and E-Commerce."

FIGURE 12.7	Positioning Strategy Worksheet

Positioning

Describe your positioning strategy in detail and why you believe it will work. _____
_____

Describe your main competitor's positioning strategy in detail. _____
_____

Describe how consumers respond to your competitor's positioning strategy. _____
_____

Product

Describe your product in detail. _____
_____

What is the unique user benefit associated with your product? _____
_____

What are the special features of your product? _____
_____

What are the competitive advantages associated with your product? _____
_____

Describe how your product will be packaged. _____
_____

Describe the product warranties and guarantees that you will provide customers, including product warranties, workmanship warranties, third-party warranties and customer service guarantees. _____
_____

Price

Describe your pricing strategy in detail. _____
_____

FIGURE 12.7	Positioning Strategy Worksheet, continued

How much will you charge for your product? How did you arrive at your selling price? _____

How sensitive are your target customers to price and why? _____

How much do competitors charge for their products? _____

List the payment options that you will provide to your customers, including any initial and ongoing fees that your business must pay for offering these payment options. _____

Place (Distribution)

Describe how you sell your products. _____

Describe how consumers receive your products. _____

Describe the management of the distribution system you intend to use. _____

Describe your logistics system, including order fulfillment, warehousing and transportation needs. _____

Promotion

Describe the company marketing materials that you will use in promoting your business, including brochures, business cards and corporate videos. _____

Describe the advertising media you will use to promote your products or services, including print, broadcast, the internet and both outdoor and indoor signage. _____

Describe the tactics you will employ in the direct sales of your goods and services, including personal selling, mail, telephone and electronic. _____

Describe how you will use public relations in promoting your goods and services. _____

FIGURE 12.7   Positioning Strategy Worksheet, continued

Describe how you will use your website for promoting your products and services, for sales or for both. Include any other materials you will use, such as an online newsletter and/or links to other websites.

_____

_____

Describe the types of events you will use to promote your products and services, including trade shows, seminars, expos and sponsorships. _____

_____

Describe the advertising premiums and specialties that you will use to promote your products and services, such as hats, bags, bumper stickers and pens emblazoned with your business name, and promotional message.

_____

_____

MARKETING BUDGET

List the marketing activities described in your marketing plan and discuss how much it will cost to implement, manage and maintain each of these activities. The obvious question is "How much should your Marketing Budget be?" There is only one answer: "How much will it cost to reach your Marketing Objectives?" Every home business owner will have different Marketing Objectives, different Marketing Strategies for achieving those objectives and different timetables for achieving them.

If you are already in business, you have an advantage in setting your Marketing Budget, because you can use sales figures as the basis for calculating your budget. For instance, as a simple approach, if your sales last year were $40,000 and your sales objective for this year is $50,000, 25 percent higher, then you can simply increase your Marketing Budget by 25 percent over last year. If your business is new, then you will have to use a ground-up approach. Break down each marketing activity as defined in your Marketing Strategy by individual cost and add those costs to estimate your Marketing Budget. You also may want to con-

sider using a breakeven analysis. Once you know how much the marketing activity will cost, you can then calculate how many product units or billable service hours will have to be sold to cover the cost of the planned activity and the breakeven point. Breakeven analysis has a way of bringing orbiting marketing ideas down to earth. Once you see how much you have to sell to break even, a marketing activity may no longer seem like such a great idea.

ACTION PLAN

The Action Plan section of your Marketing Plan is really nothing more than a big to-do list broken into marketing categories, with timetables for implementing each promotional activity throughout the calendar year and means for measuring the results. The marketing calendar should be included in your Marketing Plan in this Action Plan section. You may also want to purchase a large wall calendar on which you can write in erasable marker the promotional activities on the relevant dates. This type of calendar is especially handy because it enables you to look at the entire year,

FIGURE 12.8   Marketing Budget Worksheet

List your main marketing activities and the cost of each, including the source of data used to calculate marketing and promotional costs.

1. _____

2. _____

3. _____

4. _____

5. _____

Describe where the money will come from to cover the costs associated with implementing, managing, and maintaining the marketing activities as described in your marketing strategies.

_____

_____

_____

_____

not just each week or month. Remember: It takes time to go from creating a marketing or promotional idea to implementing it and then seeing it in print or in the media. Therefore, you need to plan your marketing well in advance.

Measuring Results

Your Action Plan must include a measurement section that details how and when you will measure the progress and the success or failure of each promotional activity implemented. By measuring results incrementally, you can make sure that the promotional activity is working and that you are on track to achieve your marketing and sales objectives. If you discover that an activity is not working, you can make adjustments to improve the performance or eliminate the activity altogether.

How long should you wait to measure results? That depends. Some promotional activities may take longer than others to produce results, and you do not want to pull the plug too quickly. Your budget will also be a major factor. If marketing money is tight, you certainly cannot afford to waste it on unproductive marketing and promotional activities. You will have to determine what best suits your needs in terms of measuring results during and after the run of a marketing or promotional activity, but at minimum you should measure results at least quarterly, though monthly is preferred.

The key aspect in measuring your activities is to know how many customers you are ultimately getting from each means of advertising, marketing and/or promotion. To do so, you need to find ways of discerning how you got each customer. This can be as simple as asking customers where they heard about your business or including a different code number in each marketing vehicle—website, mail order catalog, brochure and so on.

SUPPORTING DOCUMENTS

The final section of your Marketing Plan is reserved

FIGURE 12.9 Action Plan Worksheet

Describe how each marketing strategy will be implemented. _____

_____

Outline the timetable for implementing each marketing strategy. _____

_____

Who will implement and manage each marketing strategy identified in your marketing plan? _____

_____

Describe the measurement systems you will put in place to track the effectiveness of each marketing strategy.

_____

_____

Outline the timetable for measuring the progress and performance of each marketing strategy.

_____

_____

Describe who will implement and manage the measurement system. _____

_____

for Supporting Documents, such as resumes of the principals (if you are not already including them in your Business Plan), research surveys, market studies, spreadsheets, supplier and vendor agreements, client testimonials and press clippings. Basically, you should include any documents that can help support the research, forecasts, statements, and information contained in your Marketing Plan. Supporting Documents can be especially helpful if you are going to use your Marketing Plan as a tool to help secure investment capital. After reading the Executive Overview of your Marketing Plan, some bankers, accountants and venture capitalists will go straight to the Supporting Documents section to make sure that you have done your homework, that you are committed to the project, and that there is verifiable documentation indicating a great potential to succeed. In short, as with your Business Plan, they want to know that their money is going into

the right venture and will be managed by capable individuals.

Depending on the purpose of your Marketing Plan, you may or may not need to include copies of Supporting Documents. If you do, use this Supporting Document Checklist (Figure 12.10) as a basis for determining which documents to include to support your plan. You can include additional documents, such as the promotional materials, mockups or advertisements.

RESOURCES
Associations

American Marketing Association
311 S. Wacker Drive, Suite 5800
Chicago, IL 60606
(800) AMA-1150 (262-1150), (312) 542-9000
marketingpower.com

FIGURE 12.10 Supporting Document Checklist

Personal Documents

❑ Owner's resume
❑ Sales agent and contractor resume(s)

❑ Partners' resumes
❑ Key personnel resume(s)

Financial Documents

❑ Personal assets statement
❑ Audited financial statement
❑ Breakeven analysis

❑ Sales forecasts
❑ Marketing budgets
❑ Commission estimates

Research Documents

❑ Survey results
❑ PEST analysis

❑ Target customer profile
❑ SWOT analysis

Miscellaneous Documents

❑ Supplier agreement
❑ Press clippings
❑ Client testimonials
❑ Marketing copy, ads, mockups, promotional materials, etc.

❑ Vendor agreements
❑ Competitor price lists, etc.
❑ Better Business Bureau report

Business Marketing Association
1601 N. Bond Street, Suite 101
Naperville, IL 60563
(800) 664-4BMA (4262), (630) 544-5054
marketing.org

Canadian Marketing Association
1 Concorde Gate, Suite 607
Don Mills, ON M3C 3N6
(416) 391-2362
the-cma.org

Marketing Education Association
P.O. Box 27473
Tempe, AZ 85285-7473
(602) 750-6735
nationalmea.org

Marketing Research Association
110 National Drive, 2nd Fl.
Glastonbury, CT 06033-1212
(860) 682-1000
mra-net.org

Suggested Reading

Bangs, David H., Jr. *The Market Planning Guide: Creating a Plan to Successfully Market Your Business, Product, or Service.* 6th edition. Chicago: Dearborn Trade Publishing, 2002.

Hiebing, Roman G., Jr., and Scott W. Cooper. *The Successful Marketing Plan: A Disciplined and Comprehensive Approach.* 3rd edition. New York: McGraw-Hill, 2003.

Kennedy, Dan S. *The Ultimate Marketing Plan.* 3rd edition. Avon, MA: Adams Media Corp., 2006.

Kotler, Philip. *Marketing Management.* 11th edition. Upper Saddle River, NJ: Prentice Hall, 2002.

Stephenson, James, and Courtney Thurman. *Entrepreneur Magazine's Ultimate Small Business Marketing Guide: 1500 Great Marketing Tricks That Will Drive Your Business Through the Roof!* 2nd edition. Irvine, CA: Entrepreneur Press, 2007.

Websites

Entrepreneur Online: Small business information products and services portal featuring marketing planning advice and custom Marketing Calculator software. *entrepreneur.com*

More Business: Marketing plan information, advice and free templates. *morebusiness.com*

MPlans (Palo Alto Software): Marketing plan information, advice, templates and custom software. *mplans.com*

Palo Alto Software: Marketing Plan Pro software enables users to create their own marketing plans and strategies. *paloalto.com*

Society for Marketing Professional Services: Nonprofit association representing professional marketing organizations and consultants. Website visitors can find information about the services provided by marketing professionals. *smps.org*

U.S. Census Bureau: Market demographics information and statistics. *census.gov*

U.S. Small Business Administration: Marketing plan information, advice and samples. *sba.gov/smallbusinessplanner/index.html*

Advertising and Promotions

ADVERTISING IS A MEANS OF REACHING your target customers through various media—newspapers, magazines, Yellow Pages, radio, TV, promotional fliers, and the internet, to name the most commonly used. For most home business owners, advertising is necessary. The challenge is to make sure that you invest your advertising money wisely, that you will reach your target customers and that enough of them will generate sufficient revenue to justify your advertising.

There are three key points in terms of home business advertising—creating advertising buzz, selling the advertising buzz and getting the most mileage possible from it.

Creating the buzz means that it is your opportunity to be creative and motivate people to purchase. Advertising is one way to distinguish your business from your competitors. You might sell the same or similar products and services, but often the business that can create the most buzz through advertising and other promotional efforts captures the largest share of the market.

To make advertising work for you, it is important that you be prepared—before you advertise—to follow up on your advertising by selling your product or service. Too many new entrepreneurs have placed ads and then were unprepared when e-mails or phone calls started coming in. Be prepared for your advertising to succeed.

As for selling your advertising buzz, the amount of selling in your advertising and promotion will depend on the type of product or service, the manner in which it is advertised, and the customers' understanding of your product or service and need for it. In other words, ads will also be more or less descriptive, depending on what you are selling.

For example, if you are selling diapers to new parents, they won't need much convincing to buy your product; they know what they need and will order accordingly.

However, if you are selling a new software program for helping children with their homework, you may need to explain the details of the program and sell parents on how easy it is to use and how much it can help their children.

You also need to maximize your marketing and cross-marketing efforts. For instance, your Yellow Pages advertisement must feature your website URL, your radio spots should mention special events such as trade shows and seminars in which you're participating, and your glossy magazine ad should be reprinted and used as a promotional brochure. If you have artwork or copy created professionally, make sure that it is suitable for a variety of promotional uses throughout your entire marketing campaign. Doing so greatly increases the value of each advertising and promotional activity, while dramatically reducing advertising and promotional costs over the long term. It also maintains consistency throughout your advertising campaign. Often you can lift a short portion of the ad that is in print and use it for web copy or radio spots. Try to use your advertising materials in various forms whenever possible. However, don't run ads that are inappropriate for the chosen media just to save a few dollars.

ESTABLISHING YOUR ADVERTISING BUDGET

How much do you spend on advertising? The answer will depend on the type of business you operate, your growth ambitions and the amount you can afford to spend. Some professionals, such as dentists, attorneys, or specialized business consultants, will rely solely on word-of-mouth referrals and do little or no advertising. However, if you are selling products or services to a wide audience, you will need to advertise.

Some home business operations, such as a yard maintenance service or pet sitting service, can be easily marketed through low-cost and no-cost promotions such as flier drops, knocking on doors, posting notices on bulletin boards, e-mailings and/or word-of-mouth. Home businesses specializing in custom or niche products and services may need to spend a considerable amount of money on advertising to reach and grab the attention of their target customers.

Some advertising specialists suggest using 5 percent of your gross sales for advertising. But in practical terms, this strategy is far too broad. Much will depend on your type of business, marketing objectives and future growth plans. Competition also plays a larger role in determining your advertising budget than you might think. Developing an advertising budget requires balancing your business and marketing objectives, deciding which advertising media are needed to reach your target customers, and determining the amount of money you can afford to invest in advertising. If you have only $1,000 as an advertising budget to get rolling, you would probably be wise to try advertising methods such as low-cost fliers instead of putting your entire ad budget into one newspaper display ad and hoping or praying for the best. Until your business is established and you can begin to test advertising media and promotional activities, you will have to rely on three basic formulas to develop your budget—calculating a percentage of estimated sales, keeping pace with competitors or identifying your objective and creating a budget that ensures you reach it.

YOUR ADVERTISING OBJECTIVES

Before you can create advertising copy or determine where you will advertise, you need to consider what type of message you are trying to present. For example, are you going to sell a simple product that everyone knows and splash your name all over the place for brand identification? Are you introducing a new product or service, so you'll need an advertising campaign that presents the benefits and reasons to buy this product or service? Are you selling a product that is already well known, but a version that is faster, larger or otherwise better? If you're selling a pencil sharpener, you need not explain what it does, but only that yours is solar-powered or sharpens nine pencils at once.

Consider what your target customers already know about your product or service. Determine whether you need to familiarize them with what you're selling or simply make them aware that a new company is now selling something they already know—with a feature or, better, a benefit.

You may have other objectives, such as letting your target customers know that a familiar franchise name is opening a new location or that an old business has been revitalized. What do people need to know from your ad that will get their attention and draw them to you?

CREATING GREAT ADVERTISING COPY

The ability to create clever and convincing advertising copy extends beyond print, broadcast and electronic advertising, and into all areas of your home business operation. Great copy that is informative and sells your products or services is also needed in your business communications, printed fliers, proposals and presentations, catalogs, newsletters and web content. Your copy must grab the attention of your target customers, create interest in what you have to say, build desire for what you have to sell, and compel people to take action and buy or at least contact you for further information.

Creating great copy takes practice. If you are concerned, buy a book on writing copy for advertising and business communications and hone your skills.

Later in this section you will find information and ideas about how to create copy that gets results. Whenever you create any advertising or marketing materials, carefully examine what you are saying and how you are saying it.

You don't want to inadvertently offend anyone. Avoid stereotypes or anything that is not considered politically correct. For example, don't make reference to going to church, as opposed to a more inclusive reference to religious services, unless you are selling materials for strictly a Christian target market.

Also avoid any references to religious and political views and opinions. To write good copy, you have to consider the target customers and what they will take from the message that you present. If you feel your advertising or promotional copy might offend people, don't use it. Find a way of conveying your message that has minimal chance of offending anyone.

Powerful Headline Styles

In writing good advertising copy, the headline is king, because you have only a brief moment to grab the readers' attention and pull them into your message. This is also true of other printed marketing materials, such as newsletters, sales presentations, sales letters and promotional fliers. There are a few powerful headline styles that, when used correctly, can explode responses to ads and promotional materials.

How-To Headlines

One of the best headlines to use in advertising is a How-To headline. People want to know what they can get out of a product or service. Therefore, provide them with a benefit. For instance, a financial planner might create a headline that reads, "New Seminar Reveals How to Retire a Millionaire!"

Promise Headlines

Stating a promise in your headline, such as "Nobody beats our low prices, guaranteed" is another powerful way of grabbing the readers' attention and pulling them into your materials. Of course, the promise that you make will be directly related to what you sell and to your advertising and marketing objectives. The best headline promises are those that offer a specific solution to a problem or otherwise meets the needs of your target customers. Keep in mind, however, that you must make good on your promises. Otherwise, don't go this route.

Question Headlines

Headlines that ask readers a question are also a popular method of capturing attention and drawing them into your message. "Would you like to lose 10 pounds before summer?" This question headline would grab the attention of anyone wishing to shed a few pounds and compel them to read further to find out more.

News Headlines

Creating headlines to look and read like news stories also works well in speaking directly to readers. For instance, a house painting service might create a headline for a newspaper ad that reads, "Local Painting Contractor Helps to Lower the Unemployment Rate," followed by an advertisement informing readers that, because the contractor ensures quality painting at reasonable costs, he has hired more painters to keep up with referral business from satisfied customers. What makes news headlines so effective is that they stand out from the mass of advertisements. Many people are immune to advertisements, skipping right past to the news. By disguising an advertisement as news, you may stand a better chance of getting attention. However, since consumers have become savvier, you may also alienate potential customers who feel tricked.

Numbers in Headlines

People love numbers in headlines. Why do you think so many magazines have headlines such as "10 Tips for a Flatter Stomach" or "The 50 Wealthiest Young Entrepreneurs Under 30"? Thanks to a world of statistics and lists, numbers can be very effective in drawing attention to your advertisement. You might also work a statistic into your headline. The popular "9 out of 10 dentists agree ..." was used to promote toothpaste based on the fact that 90 percent of dentists surveyed agreed that a certain toothpaste or at least the ingredients, were beneficial for teeth. Numbers and percentages grab attention—provided they are accurate.

Humorous Headlines

People love to laugh. If you can say something funny that offends nobody but grabs attention, you can do the same with a headline for your ad. Of course, to be effective, you'll want it to relate to your product. This is not easy. Also, you should make sure people get the joke by test marketing it on some friends and family members.

Photographs and Illustrations

Second to a powerful, attention-grabbing headline in your advertisements and printed business communications is a visually descriptive photograph or illustration. In terms of effectiveness, the old adage that a picture is worth a thousand words is true. Photographs have the unique ability to present the best qualities of a product or service without a word. Include photographs showing your products or services in your advertisements and marketing materials. Photographs and illustrations need not be expensive. If you are good with a camera or have a friend with that skill, there is no reason not to create your own photographs for your copy. You can also go online to find free or inexpensive stock photographs and illustrations. However, these are usually not as distinctive as your own photos—which are so easy to take with digital cameras.

Developing a Single, Clear Message

A common denominator in all great advertising and marketing copy is that it presents a clear and singular message in a simple, straightforward manner. Keep your copy short, to the point, and focused on your headline and main selling point(s). If your main message is quality, this theme should be continued throughout. This message is called your *unique selling proposition*, your statement about why people should buy what you are selling instead of what competitors are selling.

The image or brand you create must be consistent, through design, look, tone, consumer benefit and, once again, message. The reason that brands must be consistent is that they take a long time to build, maintain and evolve. This cumulative consistency is what builds consumer awareness of your brand. This is what makes consumers think of your particular business, service, or product when they have a specific need relevant to what you do or sell.

Including prices in advertisements is not always wise, unless you have major pricing information or discounts to reveal. Pricing issues can become very complex, thus destroying the first rule of great copy—Keep It Simple, Stupid. In general, 10-, 20- or even 30-percent discounts no longer wow consumers when 50-percent-off sales are common. This is especially true for home business owners who cannot afford to get into pricing wars or contests with larger competitors. Instead, keep focused on reaching your primary target groups with your message on what makes your business unique in the marketplace and how people benefit by doing business with you.

Appealing to Your Target Customers

Clever advertising copy appeals to people on an emotional level. It uses emotional triggers, basic feelings, such as the need for friendship, the need for security and the need to achieve. The goal is to combine one or more emotional triggers with copy that is relevant and supports what you sell. For instance, a financial planner might use a photograph of two youthful, healthy, happy baby boomers standing beside their dream beach home to depict the benefits of professional financial planning services. Figure out what emotional trigger best suits your products or services and then build a unique selling proposition around that need.

Also keep in mind the reasons that your target customers buy. These *consumer drivers* include the convenience of shopping, buying image, low price, level of service and quality. Are your customers looking for "a great discount"? Are they seeking something "for discerning tastes"? Your copy must single out and talk directly to your target customers in the same way as they would think and act. That is what great copy does: It reaches the masses but makes everyone in your target group feel as though you are talking directly to him or her as an individual. Also, use the words and phrases that best resonate with your target customers. For example, you might sell a product or service to skateboarders in their teens and retirees in their 60s, but you would write the advertising copy using different wording and phrasing.

Asking for the Sale

The final and perhaps most important aspect of creating great copy is to always ask for the sale. You can have the best attention-grabbing headline, super visually descriptive photographs, a wow sales pitch and an unbeatable offer—and all of it will be for nothing unless you ask your target customers to buy, give compelling reasons to do so and provide what they need to take action.

To motivate people to take the desired course of action, you can build a sense of urgency into your copy and special offers by using an ordering deadline, specifying that the supply is limited or offering a special promotional discount. You can also boost the appeal of your offer with tactics such as extended warranty offers, free delivery or some other freebie, a price discount, or value-added deals such as two-for-ones and no-cost upgrades.

Remember: Regardless of the medium, great copy asks for the sale. Never assume that your reader will know what to do next. Tell them what you want them to do next and give them the means and motivation they need to take action.

ADVERTISING BASICS

Before deciding which media are best for your advertising dollars, you need to keep some advertising basics in mind.

- Advertising is more effective when you run your ads on a consistent basis. A one-time splash typically does not work.
- Using a few media is advantageous, since not everyone reads the newspaper or listens to the radio regularly.
- Be consistent in your tone and style so that readers or listeners become familiar with your business name and what you have to offer.
- Look for package deals. Typically the more you advertise, the cheaper each single ad becomes.
- Stay within your budget.
- Do what fits your product or service. Don't just do whatever some pushy advertising rep suggests.
- Monitor the responses to your ads. When you find that an advertisement and a publication are pulling the desired response and sales, repeat it there over and over.

Newspaper Advertising

Newspaper advertising can be a simple means of getting your message to readers in a given area. Typically it can be effective to run a small ongoing

ad or even a classified ad in local papers or specialty newspapers that your target customers read. For example, if you are running a ticket selling/brokering business from your home, you could advertise sporting events tickets near the sports pages of a local paper. If you are running an auto detailing business, you might opt for a paper that routinely carries ads for used cars. It all depends on your products or services and your advertising budget. Sometimes the best option is to hit the classified section of a newspaper on a frequent basis. A national paper like *USA Today* is generally too pricey for most home business owners. However, local publications can be cost-effective.

To locate newspapers, magazines and specialty publications for advertising, you can visit News Link, at *newslink.org*. This online directory lists publications from the United States, Canada and the rest of the world, indexed geographically and by type of newspaper. If you do business locally or regionally, you can also take the very simple approach of picking up a few newspapers at your newsstand.

Display Advertising

As with all advertising, you need to place ads in newspapers that will be read by your target customers. In the case of display ads, you also need to be careful to place them in the right section of a newspaper and to check out the paper in advance to make sure the section you need is not full of ads. Again, if you sell products, you can make your display ads much more effective if you use powerful, attention-grabbing headlines and give people a reason to take action and contact you.

Newspapers will send you all the information you need about circulation, ad sizes and rates. Use that information to determine if the newspaper targets the people you want to reach. If not, move on until you find a match. There is no sense in advertising in a newspaper if the majority of readers have no need or desire for what you have to sell.

Of course, once you find a newspaper you feel meets your advertising needs, you do not want to pay full price for the ad space. Start by negotiating, since rates are rarely ever set in stone. Try for 30 percent off and settle for 10 percent off. Here are a few other ways to reduce the cost of display advertising.

- *Frequency discounts.* Once you have tested a few publications and find one that is getting the desired results, tell the sales rep that you'll sign up for a year's worth of advertising if you can have a frequency discount. Depending on the publication and the length of advertising term to which you are prepared to commit, frequency discounts can cut your display adverting costs by as much as 75 percent.
- *Free flag advertisement.* Insist on receiving a free flag advertisement every time that you purchase and run a display ad, because that can greatly increase the odds that people will see and read your display ad. A flag advertisement is just a small advertisement (two or three lines), generally in the Classifieds section of the newspaper. The purpose of the flag ad is to grab the readers' attention and direct them to your larger display advertisement for further details and information. For instance, your free flag ad might state, "Get free carpet cleaning from Jim's Carpet Cleaning. See our big ad in today's Real Estate section."

Classified Advertising

Classified advertising is especially accessible to home business owners, because it is easy to create and cheap to run. Again, it will depend on the product or service you are selling, but classified ads can often be much more cost-effective.

For the classified section, you need short, powerful copy that sells, creates an urgency (e.g., by stating a deadline or limited availability), appeals to a basic human emotion (e.g., need, love, family or friendship) and/or, most important, lists the main benefit that a person receives from buying your products.

Again, pick publications that are read by your target customers and choose a classification that they are most likely to check. Because classified ads are cheap and quick to post, continually look for ways to improve your results by testing new ads in various publications read by your target customers. Test your headline, your main sales message and your special offers on a regular basis.

Here are some newspaper advertising tips:

- Proofread everything carefully before you send it to the publication.
- Make sure graphics or photos are very simple, since newspaper photos and graphics are typically not high quality.
- Ask to check the final copy before it goes to print.
- Ask for a tear sheet (the ad or the page on which the ad appears), if not every day, at least the first several times the ad appears, to make sure it is correct and in the right section. If there is an error and it is not your fault, the publisher should make good.
- Be prepared with ads for newspapers at least one to three weeks in advance—ask how far in advance they want the ad copy.

MAGAZINE ADVERTISING

Magazines ads have a definite edge over many other types of advertising: They tend to be around for a while—on a desk, in the waiting room, in the lunchroom or on the coffee table. Because magazines have a longer user shelf life than newspapers, newsletters and fliers, the advertisements are usually seen by the same reader more than once, which means you can reach the same readers through repetition with the same ad, making it very cost effective. However, unlike classified advertisements and direct coupons, you cannot expect immediate results from magazine advertisements. Therefore, you must be patient and not too quick to pull the plug on an ad if the telephone doesn't start ringing the day after the magazine hits newsstands.

Prior to running a magazine ad, you should call to request an editorial calendar for the upcoming issues. This will enable you to better target your advertising related to these issues. For instance, if you operate an ocean kayak tour business and an outdoor recreational magazine is featuring kayak touring in a forthcoming issue, you can contact the magazine and offer to submit an article about ocean kayak touring and your business. You could also offer to be interviewed about ocean kayak tours or for your expertise on the subject and tell the magazine that you will purchase a full-page advertisement in the same issue as an incentive for including you in an interview.

Reaching Your Target Customers

Magazines are unquestionably one of the best advertising media for reaching a specific group because they usually cater to a specific segment of the population, based primarily on interests. The first place to find out more about a magazine's particular target audience is through the publisher's media kit or fact sheet. In the kit you will find information about the people who read the magazine, the number of subscribers and the number of newsstand copies sold, the subscribers' average income, hobbies, education and other demographics. Magazine publishers go to great lengths to compile information about their readers because this is the crucial data that sells advertising space. Therefore, before jumping into signing up for a year's worth of

full-page magazine ads, carefully research the publication's readership to determine if these people meet your target requirements. To locate magazines and other publications that cater to a specific audience, you can check out PubList online, at *publist.com.* PubList is a directory of more than 150,000 print and electronic publications, including magazines, journals, e-journals and newsletters. You can also scan magazine racks at local stores and look for publications that your target customers would read.

Designing the Right Magazine Advertisement

If you have professionally designed artwork that you use in other areas of your business, this can easily be incorporated into your magazine advertisement. But if you do not, it is best to have a professional design your ad, due to the relatively high cost of the advertising; when you invest so much in placing your ads, it makes sense to spend a little more to improve the chances that they will generate the returns you want.

The first place to start looking for a design pro is through the magazine sales representative. Most magazine publishers have in-house design and copy editors who have a great deal of experience in crafting some very elaborate and clever ads for clients. Small publishers that do not offer this service certainly will be able to refer you to a trusted local source. You can also find graphic artists and designers through word-of-mouth and networking with other business owners. Regardless of who designs your advertisement, insist on owning the copyright—and get this in writing. You do not want to pay a royalty every time you use the artwork for other advertising or promotional reasons. Pay a flat fee for the artwork as a one-time payment.

Unlike newspapers or even radio, magazine advertising requires planning well in advance of the publication date. Know the schedule for advertising and the deadlines, which are often three or four months ahead. Therefore, if you wish to run a holiday ad in November, work backward from the deadline to figure out when you need to have it prepared. If the due date for November ad copy to be camera-ready and in the hands of the advertising department is September 1, then you need to start planning your ad in July, so by August you can have it ready to go.

While very popular magazines fill up fast, some magazines scramble for advertisers at the last minute. Therefore, you may have your ad ready to go to your first choice of publication and then call a few other publications at the last second (their due dates) and work a deal, since the editors will likely give you a good percentage off just to get your ad into their magazines, because they need more advertisers. I stress that you must have everything necessary for your ad ready to go in a package that can be couriered or e-mailed to the publisher as soon as you hang up the telephone.

Whenever you run a key or important full-page and full-color ad in a magazine or other specialty publication, make sure to order a lot of reprints of the ad from the publisher. A reprint is like a full-color brochure, but available at a fraction of the cost of designing and printing a full-color brochure. The ad reprints can be used for in wide variety of marketing activities. Include a reprint in all of your mailings, invoices, sales letters, newsletters, letters to the editor, and any other type of mail or business correspondence you send out. You can also use reprints of full-page ads in sales presentations or as promotional handouts at seminars, trade shows and networking meetings.

Advertisement Size, Position and Frequency

There is much debate about which size advertisement is the best: full-page, half-page, third-page, quarter-page and so forth. All have their pros and cons. Full-page advertisements can be costly, but they provide great exposure. Quarter-page ads are much cheaper, but they are often placed near the back of the magazine, with one or more other advertisements on the same page.

If full-page ads are not in your budget, you can try two tactics to increase the exposure of your smaller advertisement. The first tactic is to negotiate for a second ad of the same size to run in the same magazine and issue. Often a second ad discount can be substantial, in the range of 40 percent or greater. The benefit of this tactic is that it doubles the odds that your ad will be seen and read by readers, but the two ads still cost much less than a full-page ad. The second tactic is to negotiate a specific position within the magazine, preferably beside a regular column or feature. Readers will be exposed to your ad for a longer time while they read the feature or column.

Frequency is the number of times that your target readers are exposed to your advertisement; that is, how many times you advertise in the same magazine. Most advertising experts agree that an ad should run a minimum of 3 times, but preferably 6 to 12 times consecutively, for the ad to have real impact for your business.

YELLOW PAGES ADVERTISING

For many years, the Yellow Pages was *the* place you went when seeking a service professional in your neighborhood. Retailers also benefited, but not as much as those providing some type of service. Today, however, the internet has taken a big bite out of the Yellow Pages' hold on homebased information. In fact, many people use the Yellow Pages to build a makeshift booster chair for little children and rarely look anything up unless it doesn't appear on an internet search. Considering that prices can still run upwards of $1,000 per month, depending on the market, Yellow Pages advertising is not the "must" that it once was for promoting a business.

Before taking the plunge, and a small ad is the only plunge you need to take, check with other local business owners and ask what percentage of customers they are pulling from their Yellow Pages ads. You also need to consider your market and the service that you provide. Without question, some service providers need to advertise in the Yellow Pages in a big way, especially service providers who fix emergency problems such as a leaky roof, a broken pipe or a serious pest problem. In such emergency situations, a fair share of homeowners will still reach for the book rather than searching the web. The key to Yellow Pages advertising is that you must design an ad that will last for the entire year, unlike newspaper or magazine ads, which you can change for each season.

Tips for Creating a Great Yellow Pages Advertisement

The Yellow Pages ad that you create and run must present the image you want your business to project. Therefore, your ad must represent the best qualities and most superior advantages that your business has to offer customers. Design your ad from your customers' perspective: Why do they do business with you? What do they like most about your business, products or services? Your answers should be incorporated into your Yellow Pages advertisement so that it will appeal to the majority of your target customers. The following are more tips for creating high-impact and effective Yellow Pages ads.

- Motivate people to contact you by using phrases like "Call now for a free estimate." Give them lots of ways to contact you, with a boldly displayed main telephone number, a toll-free calling option, your web URL, your e-mail address and perhaps your cell phone number—although if you pay for incoming calls, be careful. The purpose of Yellow Pages advertising is to motivate people to call you, not to build brand awareness through long-term repeated exposure to your ad. People do not read the Yellow Pages casually; they read them to find specific products and services that they need. But even though Yellow Pages advertising will make your telephone ring, it is still up to you to make the sale.

- A Yellow Pages display ad is one of the rare advertising occasions when you want to provide as much information as possible. List what you sell, including specific brands; all of the services you provide, including specialized services or authorized services; all the payment options, including credit cards and financing options; your credentials and special training; and any other appropriate information, such as liability insurance coverage, bonding, special certificates or permits and professional association memberships. The more compelling reasons you can give people to call you instead of a competitor, the better.

- Focus on your company's greatest strengths, emphasizing the benefits of your products and services. What need do your products or services fulfill for customers? Spell out your biggest benefits. What is your competitive advantage? Is it quality assurance? Is it convenient 24-hour service? Are you the most qualified to handle the job in the area? Whatever your competitive advantage, you must include it in your ad, making it stand out like a beacon bringing people to your ad through the fog of competitors' ads.

- Be careful about making "lowest price" promises or mentioning specific prices, since the ad will be out there for a year and a lower-priced competitor may open up shop down the road or your costs may rise so that every sale at the advertised prices costs you money. Nonetheless, if you say your prices are lower or you will beat any price, you will have to keep your word so you can retain those customers.

- Make your ad consistent with your business image and the rest of your advertising and marketing activities. Use your logo, consistent fonts and colors and the same sales message. If you are known for a specialty, make your specialty a main feature. Research has also shown that ads with photographs or illustrations greatly outperform ads without. A picture really works well: it can be worth a thousand words—and fit better within the confines of an ad.

RADIO ADVERTISING

One of the key advantages of radio advertising is that radio has the ability to speak to your target customers on a more intimate basis, usually one on one, in their cars, at the office or at home. For that reason, radio has long been a favorite advertising medium for small business owners and marketers.

Still, the key to successful radio advertising is repetition. In radio advertising terms, repetition is frequency, the number of times the station broadcasts an ad. If you choose radio advertising, you must commit to the program for a minimum of three months to realize any benefits. Radio ads cannot create a need for a product or service, thus the importance of repetition. Through repeated exposure to your message and company name, your business will be on people's minds when they need your products or services.

Another big consideration is placement. Ideally, you will want to have the same time slot day in, day out. Most marketers find the morning drive time,

6 a.m. to 10 a.m., or afternoon drive time, 4 p.m. to 7 p.m., slots are the best. These slots cost more, of course.

You should be consistent in your message and stay focused on a central theme.

If you are considering creating your own radio advertisement, make sure that you check with the stations first, because some will include the cost of producing a simple radio spot if you sign up for a minimum 13-week contract. Also, negotiate to get one of their more popular disk jockeys, program hosts, or on-air personalities to record the ad copy. If you opt for something with music or sound effects, which can be effective ways of grabbing attention, you will want to use the radio station's studio to record the spots. They usually make the studio available.

Making Radio Work for You

Two important things should be kept in mind in radio advertising. You are always buying the audience, never the station, regardless of what sales reps might want you to believe. You must find a radio station that matches the image you want to project for your business. Radio stations can provide you with demographic information on their audiences. Match your business up to your target customers. If your target customers are mature, try talk radio and easy listening formats. If your target customers are teens, then urban, pop or rock stations will be a wise choice. If you are selling sporting goods or related items, try a sports talk station. There are radio stations to meet the needs of most entrepreneurs, and even specific shows, hosts or DJs who are particularly appropriate.

Wise entrepreneurs have discovered that using radio advertisements to support other advertising and marketing activities greatly increases the effectiveness of each. An example of cross promotion in a radio ad would be "Drop by our booth at the auto show. Visit our website today. See our full-page advertisement in this Friday's newspaper."

When writing advertising copy, think about conveying a simple message in 15 to 30 seconds. This is where you need your number-one selling point. If you sell flowers, you need not describe what a rose looks like, but state that you can have any number of them in the hands of the intended recipient within one hour or you offer a choice of 12 colors or whatever your main selling point may be. Often, radio ads have a clever banter or a brief sketch that makes the point in a few lines. For example:

Woman #1: Where were you? We've got a meeting in five minutes.

Woman #2: (Angrily) I thought I'd never get here! I had the biggest fight with my husband this morning and I'm so … (Voice changes) Oh my goodness, roses … They're gorgeous!

Announcer: Roses Plus, the fastest way to say, "I'm sorry."

This would be followed by "Roses Plus. Just call …" and the phone number.

The same business could then run ads with other dialogs as examples of other scenarios in which it's important to use Roses Plus to get flowers delivered fast.

Remember: The more you try to pack into your ad, the more likely your listeners will tune out or switch stations. You need to grab people within the first three seconds.

If you are trying to simply make a splash in the region or you have a recognizable name (such as a franchise) you can probably use a 15-second spot to highlight your presence in the market and one phrase that people will remember—something that makes you stand out. If, however, you are trying to advertise a new product or service, you will want to use 30 seconds of copy, which is more expensive, but allows you more time to present

something new.

Radio jingles work extremely well in making your business memorable to listeners. In fact, great jingles can transcend time. Many of us still remember advertising jingles we heard 10, 20 and even 30 years ago. Radio jingles are not necessarily expensive to write, produce and record, especially if you enlist the services of local talent seeking to build a resume.

Finally, radio audiences are extremely loyal to their favorite stations, on-air personalities and programs. Therefore, once you have identified your target customers and the station and programs they prefer, stick like glue to that station, that time slot and that program. You want these listeners to feel the same loyalty to your brand, and this will begin to happen through repeated exposure to your marketing message. In time, you will change your ads or the time slot, since listeners will tire of hearing the same ads after awhile.

FINDING YOUR PLACE ON TV

On average, North Americans now spend more than 30 hours per week in front of the TV, which is only slightly less than the average amount of time people spend working each week. As a result, TV has a very broad reach, crossing all demographics and greatly influencing consumer buying habits and trends.

Before you rush out and get a second mortgage on the house to finance the production of a lavish TV commercial, you should be aware that TV is certainly not a suitable marketing vehicle for most home business owners. It is far too costly for the average home business owner to produce a TV commercial and air it regularly in a way that reaches a mass audience. This is certainly not to say that home business owners should avoid TV advertising, especially those who want to reach smaller audiences in specific regional markets.

The introduction of specialty cable channels over the past decade has increased competition on the airways, which in turn has forced stations to be inventive and create low-cost, yet effective advertising opportunities that will appeal to small business owners and marketers with limited advertising budgets. These new advertising opportunities include crawls (text rolls across the bottom of the screen) and sponsorship of full programs or segments, which generally means the sponsoring business's logo and name will be seen on screen in static billboard fashion or that an on-air personality will read a sponsor's message, ideally both. Another opportunity is airing 15- or 30-second active spots on programs that are produced locally by the station or by cable distributors. The cost to air commercials on locally produced TV is generally a fraction of what the networks charge. It may even be possible to advertise through product placement, which is paying to get your product included as part of a local program, as a prop.

Home business owners can get their names and products on TV through cooperative TV advertising. Ask suppliers if they have any TV commercials that can be broadcast in your local area and to which you can pay to have your business name and sales message added. The majority of these TV commercials will be part of the manufacturer's or supplier's cooperative advertising programs; generally the local business must pay for a portion of the costs of airing the commercial in the local markets. While the lower costs of pre-produced cooperative commercials are attractive, these commercials usually are not best suited for branding your business, one of the key objectives of any good TV advertising campaign.

Of course, if you feel that TV commercials are the best way to showcase your product's or service's unique benefits and will be the most effective and cost-efficient way to reach your target customers, make sure the commercials you create are powerful.

Grab the Attention of Your Target Customers

TV is like any other form of advertising: You have but a precious moment to grab the viewers' attention and pull them into your story. There are various ways to grab attention. Again, much depends on your marketing objectives and the image you want to project. You can use humor, play on an emotional attachment or need or combine music and visual imagery to present your product and the primary features. Presenting a problem and solving it through use of your product is a great way to advertise. Also, tapping into the visual trends that appeal to your audience, whether it is superheros for kids or athletics for the fitness crowd, is a great means of using a common denominator to draw them into buying what you have to offer.

You must identify what your target viewers need and then deliver solutions or benefits directly related to their specific needs. Scream out that you have the right solution, perhaps the only solution available to meet their specific needs. Give them the tools to contact you and a compelling reason to do so immediately and not next week, next month or a year from now. The true power of an active visual medium like TV is that it allows you to fully demonstrate the benefits associated with your products, an advantage that other forms of advertising do not have.

Branding Is Vital for Long-Term, Positive Impact

Mercedes automobiles are synonymous with quality and prestige, while Ford automobiles are known for providing families with reliable and safe transportation at a reasonable cost. Both companies manufacture automobiles, but are dramatically different in consumer perceptions and the image they project.

Branding is the foundation of all marketing and should be consistently delivered in all promotional and advertising activities, including TV commercials. If you are known for low prices, your commercial should deliver that message. If you are known for fast service, that should be the focus of your TV advertisement. Branding also means that the look of your business and products remains constant in all advertising—the same corporate colors, the same logo, the same slogan, the same sales-and-benefits message. You want to project this consistent brand image in your TV ad and make sure that your brand always remains on the screen via signage, logo overlay, uniforms, banners, music and props. This does not mean you cannot change the look of your TV commercial; you can. But your commercials must remain consistent with your overall business image.

Appeal to Emotional Triggers

Key to the success of many well-known TV commercials is their ability to appeal to the emotional triggers of their target audience. Emotional triggers are numerous, including feelings such as the need for physical and financial security, the need to achieve and lead, the need to learn, and the need for friendship and love. Financial planners show youthful and active retired people frolicking on the beach with their children and grandchildren, without a worry, financial or otherwise. These commercials appeal to emotional triggers of their intended target customers: the need for family, the need for physical health and the need for financial security in our golden years. Analyze your product or service to determine which emotional triggers will appeal to your target customers and develop your commercial around these emotional triggers.

DIRECT MAIL

Direct mail is most commonly associated with mail order sales. However, direct mail is really a catchall phrase covering numerous advertising and promotional materials, such as sales letters, postcards, catalogs, newsletters, simple fliers and brochures and product sample packs. The purpose of mailing these items to targeted groups is generally to sell a product or service, but direct-mail campaigns can also be used for other business and marketing activities, such as research surveys, satisfaction polls, special company announcements or holiday greetings. Still, the vast majority of small business owners use direct mail for advertising and promoting products, services and special offers.

One of the main benefits of a direct mail campaign is that, unlike other advertising methods, such as radio or TV, results are often swift, within weeks, if not days. Direct mailing is also more cost-effective.

Not every home business owner will benefit from developing, implementing, and maintaining a direct-mail advertising and promotion program. It can be very costly on a per-contact basis, and not all products and services are suitable for marketing via direct mail. But for marketers of products or services that fill a specific niche in the marketplace, direct mail can be extremely effective. Often products that sell best when direct-mail marketed share a few of the following characteristics:

- They are unique, interesting and not readily available in the marketplace.
- They are easy and inexpensive to pack and ship.
- They have an extended self life.
- They have mass appeal or fill a highly specific niche.
- They have large markup and profit potential.
- They unlock the secrets to a mystery or provide the user with a formula.

■ They are consumable, requiring consumers to regularly reorder.

Developing Your Direct-Mail Package

Developing your direct-mail package will largely depend on the products and services you intend to sell and your marketing objectives. Some products or services can easily be sold with one mailing, while others require numerous mailings and follow-ups with prospects to build a relationship and complete the sales cycle.

To get started, create a plan listing your objective(s), such as to sell, to generate leads or to introduce new products or services. Next, estimate a budget to develop and implement the campaign, taking into account all expenses such as printing, postage, advertising and delivery. Once you have a cost estimate, you can conduct a cost-benefit analysis to ensure that direct mail is the right marketing method to meet your objectives.

If you determine that you want to proceed, the next step is to storyboard your mailing package. Storyboarding enables you to carefully analyze each element of your mailer and make adjustments prior to having your material printed. In the excitement and rush to market, it may be easy to hurry through determining exactly what you want printed. Many small business owners quickly realize the value of storyboarding, proofreading, and creating a complete sample mail package after they have picked up completed print runs—too late. Spelling errors, poor grammar, missed components and last-minute changes are common, leaving you on the hook financially, because printers do not assume responsibility for errors from proofs on which you have signed off before printing.

Stick to printing-industry standard sizes and weights for your paper, envelopes, catalogs, response cards, and all other components of your direct-mailing package. Straying from industry standard sizes or having lots specially die cut and printed can be very costly, easily doubling or tripling your costs.

One of the keys to a successful direct-mail campaign lies in your ability to know which offer and mail package gets the best responses and maximizes your return on investment. There is only one way to know this for sure—test everything. You want to test your mailing list(s), test your product, test your price point and test your special offers. Direct-mail marketing is an ever-evolving process that requires constant testing and management to succeed and generate revenues and profits.

A good source of additional information about direct mail marketing is the Direct Marketing Association, *the-dma.org*, which provides members with helpful information and advice about direct mail and direct marketing. The National Register Publishing Company publishes an annual directory called *Direct Marketing Market Place*, which is packed with information, resources and product and service listings for direct marketers. It can be found online at *dirmktgplace.com*.

Selecting the Right Mailing List

The success of any direct-mail marketing campaign depends on your ability to compile or rent the best mailing list available, the one that will enable you to reach your target customers and achieve your marketing objectives. There are many types of direct-mail marketing lists available.

In-House Mailing Lists

In-house lists are mailing lists that you compile from the names of your current and past customers and prospects. In-house lists are without question the best mailing lists, because the majority of people on the list have purchased from you in the past, are currently purchasing, or are at least familiar with your products or services. The downside to an in-house mailing list is that you must manage and maintain it to keep it current and effective. Managing your list will usually require computer hardware and client management software so that you can customize your list into categories, such as geography, demographics and buying habits, for specific mailing and marketing purposes. A big positive aspect of such lists, however, is that you can have people sign up to be included on them and provide their e-mail addresses. When people want to be included on a mailing list, the response rate usually improves.

Opt-In Mailing Lists

Electronic mailing opt-in lists are compiled from e-mail addresses of people who have given a business, an organization or an individual permission to send them information via e-mail and to share their address with "friends"—a nice way of saying that the lists will be rented, sold and traded to other e-mail marketers.

There are services that will help you to build your own opt-in list, rent you opt-in lists, supply you with electronic message blasting or do all of this. There are also lists being sold that are not opt-in permission-based lists, but lists compiled without permission. These are lists that produce spam—avoid them. Know the company or the individuals from which you are buying or renting lists. Get references from people who have used a list from a specific list provider before you obtain one. You also want to make sure that a list, whether electronic or printed, is updated. You do not want to use a list that wastes a lot of your money because 50 percent of your mailings are returned or bounce back because the addresses or e-mail addresses are old.

Subscription Mailing Lists

Subscription lists are composed of individuals and businesses that subscribe to print or electronic publications—magazines, newsletters, trade journals, industry reports, newspapers, electronic magazines and e-letters. Subscriber lists are generally a good choice for small business marketers, because the names and addresses are usually valid and the people or businesses on the list have expressed an interest in specific topics related to the publication for which the list was compiled.

Event Mailing Lists

These are lists of people who have attended a specific event, such as seminars, trade shows, sports events, concerts, workshops, timeshare pitch sessions and so on. Lists of attendees are available in various configurations based on geography, special interests and even demographics, depending on the event for which the names were gathered. Attendee lists are generally accepted as a good alternative to response lists or an in-house list. Make sure this list does not violate any regulations of the organization that compiled it. A list of attendees may not be for use outside the organization. Make sure it is obtained legally and that the list can be used for mailings.

Assembled Mailing Lists

These lists are compiled from published information sources, such as telephone directories or industry association directories. Assembled lists are generally mailing lists of businesspeople and companies and are usually categorized by industry or profession, such as lawyers, engineers or chiropractors. Assembled lists provide a great opportunity for business-to-business marketing to reach specific target industries, but they are not very valuable for marketing consumer goods. When you rent assembled mailing lists, keep in mind that the only prequalification of the names is that the businesses or individuals on the list belong to a specific industry or profession.

Response Mailing Lists

Response lists are compiled from names of people who have purchased through a direct-mail or other marketing offer in the past. Response lists are usually broken into groups representing various special interests, such as people who play golf or people who own a boat. For direct marketing purposes, a good response list is second only to a good in-house list in terms of the potential to pull a high response rate to the offer. The downside of response lists is that they can be very expensive to rent, up to twice as much as other types of lists, because the quality is generally very high and the names are specific, categorized and targeted.

What You Need to Know About Mailing Lists

Now that you know which types of mailing lists are available, the next step is to understand what you need to know specifically about mailing lists so that you can use them as a powerful marketing tool.

The first issue is that mailing lists are generally rented from the list owner or manager; seldom do list owners want to sell their mailing lists. There are publicly accessible e-mail or opt-in lists, but these are generally not well maintained and include dead addresses and lots of spam addresses. So, unless your budget for mailing lists is extensive (or zero), I would strongly advise you to stay clear of free print or electronic mailing lists. They are generally a waste of precious marketing time.

There are only three reliable sources for mailing lists.

The first option is to use in-house lists, which you have compiled from directories, current customers, prospects, warranty cards, and/or entry forms submitted for a contest or in a drawing.

The second option is to rent mailing lists directly from list owners, lists that marketers and business owners have spent considerable time, money and energy to build and that they often rent to earn extra revenues.

The third option is to rent lists from reputable mailing list brokers, which may own the lists, manage the lists for the owners or represent numerous mailing lists of every type. Finding a source for mailing lists is as easy as doing a web search for "mailing list." You can also visit infoUSA.com at *infousa.com*. This company is billed as the world's largest supplier of mailing lists, which are indexed by consumer, business, industry, hobby, geographic location and demographics.

If you are considering renting a list from any source, you will first want analyze the data card, which provides information about the mailing list, to determine if the list is right for your specific target customers and marketing objectives. On the data card you will find the following information:

- *Cost.* The data card shows the cost per 1,000 names, which can range from about $10 per thousand up to $250 per thousand for highly specialized and targeted lists.
- *Size and minimum order.* The data card shows the total number of names on the list and the minimum number of names that can be pulled from the list and rented, such as 5,000 from 100,000.
- *Profile.* The data card shows details such as the source of the list, history of the list, average value of orders and hotline information, such as the kinds of products or services that people on the list recently purchased.
- *Restrictions.* The data card shows restrictions on use of the list. List owners reserve the right to review and approve or decline your mailing, based on their own criteria, but few uses get declined unless they involve competitive, legal or moral issues.
- *Selections.* The data card shows whether the list can be segmented and, if so, to what degree. Only a certain portion of the list may appeal to you as appropriate for your objectives. This is common, especially when marketers want to target specific businesses, industries or job titles within a specific

industry. Selections information will generally be shown as a percentage indicating the portion of the list that can be selected, such as 25 percent, along with the additional fee for segmenting the list.

Dramatically Increasing Your Response Rate

The higher the response rate, the greater your chances of selling. Also, a person who responds to your mail offers gives you the opportunity to build a profitable ongoing sales relationship. Here are a few time-tested ways to dramatically increase your direct mail response rates.

- *Fill a niche.* The product or service you sell should be something for a dedicated market of consumers who look for expertise in that area, which (of course) your business provides. You can buy almost anything on the internet, so you need to be the expert source.
- *Buying motivation.* You want people to buy immediately, not next week, month or year. In direct-mail marketing, time is critical. You have to create a sense of urgency by limiting the number of products for sale, setting a firm deadline for orders, offering a limited-time financial discount or giving an incentive, such as an upgraded model for free or a free, special bonus gift to the first 50 people who respond to the offer.
- *Simplicity.* Make it as easy as possible for people to respond to your offer and to buy what you are selling. You can allow people to respond by a 24-hour toll-free hotline or through your website. You can also make it easy for people to purchase your products or services by offering a range of payment options, including credit cards, money orders, electronic personal checks, COD, installment plans and bill-me-later options.
- *Reduce buying risk.* People often do not buy

via direct mail because of the potential risks associated with making the purchase. How do they know it's what they want? How do they know your company is legit? You have to go out of your way to eliminate the fear of buying and the risks associated with buying. You can do this by aligning your business with credible organizations such as the Better Business Bureau and by offering bill-me-later payment options or no-risk product trial periods. In an age of identity theft, you should also put your privacy-protection policies on printed materials and on your website, along with information about your business, including address, phone number(s) and e-mail address.

TELEMARKETING

Telemarketing dramatically changed in the United States on October 1, 2003, with the introduction of the National Do Not Call Registry, which is managed by the Federal Trade Commission. (In Canada, the National Do Not Call List is expected to be operational by September 30, 2008.) The National Do Not Call Registry was put into place to protect consumers against fraudulent telemarketing organizations and telemarketing scams. Millions of people have registered. At present only consumers, not businesses, can register, which means that business owners and telemarketers can still randomly telephone businesses and consumers not on the list to market goods and services. The following are a few highlights of the National Do Not Call Registry:

- People volunteer to be registered. Nobody is registered automatically.
- Businesses or telemarketers that violate the Do Not Call rules face fines of up to $11,000 for each violation.
- Business owners can continue to call cus-

tomers who have made purchases within the last 18 months, even if they are on the Do Not Call Registry.

- Business-to-business telemarketing is exempt from the Do Not Call rules, as well as telephone surveys and charity fundraising.
- Business owners and telemarketers can download the entire Do Not Call Registry or any segment of the list, which is indexed by area code.

More information about the National Do Not Call Registry can be found at *donotcall.gov*. Home business owners and telemarketers who would like to download part or all of the Do Not Call Registry can do so by visiting *telemarketing.donotcall.gov*.

Reinforcing Other Marketing Activities

Most people hate telemarketers interrupting them at home or on their cell phones while they are out and about. The proliferation of telemarketers in recent years has prompted the Do Not Call Registry to grow rapidly.

However, there are businesses that hold to the theory that if you call 100 people and 97 of them hang up but 3 purchase something, it's worth the effort. For a strict, all-sales-at-all-costs business, this can work. For businesses that want to build a lasting, positive reputation, random widespread telemarketing is no longer the way to go.

If, however, you define and reach a very carefully targeted group of customers, you may have a chance. For example, if you call outdoor enthusiasts with a great sale on camping gear, you may do well—but you must be reaching the right people with the right product and in a conversational, polite manner.

Steering prospects to some other aspect of your marketing can also work, using a two-step approach. First, about three days before a marketing activity begins, call targeted prospects and cus-

tomers to inform them about it—a special offer, an invitation to your booth at a trade show, the introduction of a new product or service or whatever. The call is to alert prospects and customers to the forthcoming activity and build excitement. Then, three days after the marketing activity has taken place, call those people to follow up. The focus here should be to turn prospects into paying customers, set further appointments and answer questions.

High-Impact Telemarketing Techniques

Telemarketing is nerve-racking work, even for the thick-skinned telemarketing professional. You want results, not rejection, but you will get mostly rejection, so be prepared to grin and bear it. As with direct mail, a 4-percent response rate is terrific.

Here are some high-impact telemarketing tips and techniques:

- *Define your objective.* Before you make calls, clearly define your objective(s). Do you want to set appointments? Are you looking to follow up with prospects or customers? Is your purpose to inform people about a special event or promotion? Know why you're calling and what action you want your prospect or customer to take as a result of the call.
- *Prepare.* Get comfortable before you start making calls, especially if your calling list is long. Have a glass of water handy to avoid dry throat. Sit in your most comfortable chair. Have your script, notes, presentations, and fact sheets ready so you can answer specific questions.
- *Get the right people and the right person.* Make sure you are calling your target customers, the people most likely to need what you have to sell. Random calling can be an exercise in futility. Also make sure you are

talking with the right person, the one who can make the buying decision and pay for the purchase. If the person who answers the phone is not this person, ask for him or her.

- *Get to the point.* Start by clearly stating your business, your name and the purpose of your call. Engage in conversation to get your prospect's immediate involvement. Few people will tolerate rambling without quickly becoming irritated and hanging up. Respect your prospects' and customers' time and never waste it. If the person is not interested, move on to someone else, someone who may need and want to buy what you have to sell.

- *Be polite.* Use please, thank-you, may I?, and you're very welcome.

- *Communicate.* Speak in plain English and avoid using technical terms.

- *Treat people with respect.* Never talk down to the person. Go out of your way to make him or her feel special and important—in other words, the center of the universe at that precise moment.

- *Make it sound natural and conversational.* Even though you may be reading from a script, you want to be able to talk *with* the person and not simply *at* him or her. For this reason, hiring an actor who's between roles is a good idea.

- *Get the name right.* Practice pronouncing people's names before you call. If you pronounce a name wrong, it doesn't bode well for a sale.

- *Go live.* Do not use recorded messages. They can save you time, but they are rarely productive for sales. You are basically telling people that you want money from them but do not have the time or decency to actually talk with them. Recorded messages are, in a word, rude.

CREATING A NEWSLETTER

Newsletters can serve many purposes for the home business owner. They can build a positive image, reinforce brand awareness, promote products and services, position the owner as an expert, introduce new product lines or services, announce important company news and/or all of the above. A newsletter can also be a powerful tool to enhance, complement, and support other advertising and marketing activities. Newsletters are a great way to keep the business name and products or services in front of prospects and keep regular customers in touch with what's new in your business. They are also cost-effective.

Designing, Publishing and Distributing Your Newsletter

Print or electronic format—which is best? There are pros and cons for each format. Printed newsletters cost more, but typically remain longer in the homes or offices of their recipients. E-mail newsletters are inexpensive to create and send, but recipients can skim and delete them very quickly. You will have to consider your target customers, marketing objectives and budget to determine which format would be best for your specific needs. Many businesses offer the choice between print and electronic versions of their newsletters.

Who will create your newsletter? With practice and the appropriate software, you can easily use a template to design and produce print or electronic newsletters yourself. Alternately, you can hire a freelance newsletter writer to provide the copy or a desktop publishing service to handle the entire job. A relatively small production and distribution run of a few hundred print newsletters can easily be done in-house; with suitable computer hardware and software, the number is nearly unlimited for electronic newsletters. Larger print runs or more complicated e-newsletters with audio/visual features should be left to professionals to design. If you tackle the job yourself, most word processing programs such as Microsoft Office and Corel WordPerfect have newsletter templates that can be used for basic design. There is also advanced software available, such as Newsletter Toolkit (*howtowriteanewsletter.com*), which enables you to produce and publish a professional newsletter on your computer.

Content and Layout

The main purposes of your newsletter should be to market and then to communicate.

Newsletters are rarely effective if they are strictly advertising. People tire of ads and move on. You must maintain a balance so that your newsletter does not become aggressive advertisements from beginning to end.

Just as we watch commercial TV or read magazines that are filled with advertising, we are willing to accept advertising as long as we get some content with it. For a newsletter, you need to take the same approach by providing something of interest to your readers. You have to give them information that they would find beneficial and pepper this information with promotional messages and advertisements for your products and services.

Interview customers and include their stories in your newsletter (with permission), especially customers who have benefited from doing business with you. Include their photographs and, if they are in business, thank them by giving them a plug for their products and services, with contact information. Also report news about your industry, joint ventures, impending legislation, statistics and special events. Include stories on local, national and international industry news. Readers like this type of highly specialized information, especially when it revolves around their business, hobbies or interests. Feature monthly product and service

spotlights along with a special discount. Often the most significant aspect of a newsletter is content that tells how to do something, such as "10 Great Low-Fat Holiday Recipes" or "The 20 Best Camp Sites in the Northeast." Stories need not be long, especially in e-newsletters. Often two or three paragraphs will suffice. The key is that you are giving people something useful.

You can include question-and-answer interviews with experts in the industry and "tip of the month." Keep in mind that the content does not have to be all business. You should include some fun stuff—business- or industry-related trivia, crosswords, word games and quizzes. Give a small prize to the first person to correctly answer skill-testing questions. You can also add a small section that regularly features community news, special events and volunteer opportunities. If you are using e-mail, include "forward to a friend" tabs next to great pass-along information. People love sharing recipes, good (tasteful) jokes, fun trivia and short informative articles.

You can also include content that is created around business achievements, such as the number of years you have been in business, the number of customers served or the number of days without a customer complaint or an employee injury on the job. Be careful, however, not to overdo it, because readers are more interested in "what's in it for me?" Therefore, always avoid anything that is self-indulgent, such as news on promoting your spouse from VP to executive VP. Think from their perspective when writing for your target customers.

If you're doing an e-mail newsletter, think about interactivity. Recipients should be able to link to your website and contact you easily with feedback or suggestions. One of the biggest advantages of the web is the ability to interact with your customers and prospects.

To lay out a newsletter, you will typically want

to follow a template, which can be found online or in software programs. For a print newsletter, you'll want to use your front page for content, possibly with a photo and sprinkle some advertising around the outside. You'll then need to find a mix of content and promotional material that fills the pages in such a way that neither is lost. For e-mail newsletters, you'll want a good headline located in the electronic equivalent of "above the fold," so that it comes up in the preview window even before the recipients click to open the e-mail. This will grab their attention. Hook them with good content and, as they scroll down, sell your products and/or services with well-placed promotional materials. A small newsletter can be one page with scrolling. However, people do not like scrolling a lot, so if the page is running long, break some of the articles and insert a link in each so your recipients can click to continue reading the rest of the article on another page. Also, do not make it necessary for your recipients to search for the continuation of an article; it should come up front and center.

Finally, make it very easy to cancel a print newsletter or unsubscribe from an e-mail version. If people need to jump hurdles, you can be sure they won't want to renew their subscription later—and they will feel negatively about your business for setting up those hurdles.

Distribution of Your Newsletter

There are a few options, depending on format, promotional activities, budget and contact information.

- *Mail.* Millions of newsletters are distributed by mail. If your mailing list is large, you will want to use a postage meter and possibly a lower class of mail delivery to reduce postage costs. Also, make sure to include copies of your newsletter in your regular outgoing business mail, press releases, account statements, sales letters, catalogs and presentations.

- *E-mail.* E-newsletters have increased by leaps and bounds in recent years and may have even overtaken printed newsletters. This is because a business can produce three or four electronic versions of a newsletter at far less than the cost of printing a single version. Not only is this the least expensive way to distribute your newsletter, but it is easy to set up and to plug in new material. In fact, it is far and away the best way to stay current, since you can put a story into the newsletter now and your customers and prospects can be reading it almost immediately. You do need to make sure to keep your opt-in subscriber database up-to-date.

- *Handout.* You can hand out your newsletter during sales visits, meetings, seminars, trade shows and networking functions. This method will work only if you are out and about often, in contact with a lot of customers and prospects. Many homebased business owners spend 90 percent of their time at their home offices, in front of their computers or at their desks on the phone. If this is you, then handing it out may not be the best means of distribution.

- *Fax.* Though inexpensive, this is the least preferred method of distributing printed newsletters. If another method is possible, use it. The low cost of distribution by fax is more than offset by the often poor print quality for the recipients. Remember: Image and presentation are important in marketing. Also, fewer and fewer people are using fax machines today, thanks to scanners and e-mail.

Your Target Customers

As a sales and marketing tool, newsletters serve no purpose unless you can get them to people who are likely to buy your products or services or who can influence the buying habits and decisions of other people who are in your target market. In part, your budget and your distribution method determine who receives your newsletter. The following are a few people who should be on your newsletter mailing list.

- Current and past customers and clients
- Current and past prospects
- Suppliers, vendors and subcontractors
- Editors, journalists, producers and reporters
- Business allies
- Employees and their families
- Influential leaders in your community, business associations and industry

Depending on your marketing objectives, you may also want to distribute your newsletter to locations where it could be read by many people, thereby increasing your reach. You could distribute your newsletter to restaurants, waiting rooms, public libraries, schools and community centers—basically, anywhere in the community people read materials while they wait for appointments, eat lunch or take a quiet coffee break. Call it your "idle hands" target group. For this reason, having a printed version of even an e-mail newsletter can be beneficial.

INTERNET ADVERTISING

While having a website is a must for almost all businesses today, you can also advertise on other websites, especially those that feature similar products and attract the people you are targeting. For example, the homebased business owner selling camping gear might want to advertise on a site that provides information and articles about camping or on a general outdoors recreation site.

The cost of banner ads varies by website and the number of visitors the site receives. Ask for demographics and look at "unique visitors" and "return visitors." Then determine whether or not you are reaching enough people for your dollar, which is always part of the advertising equation. There are tons of possible sites, but not many that draw substantial numbers of visitors. Seek those out. Then keep an ad running for at least a couple months to see if you are getting results.

Also, make sure you are not buying pop-up ads, since many browsers allow users to block pop-ups. Look at the site carefully and decide where you want to place your ad. Top banner ads are the most widely seen. You can also buy vertical ads along the right side of the screen or ads that are positioned amid the content. Major search engines sell advertising, such as Google and Yahoo!. Again, make sure you know exactly where the ad will be placed before you pay. (More on internet advertising in Chapter 17, "Internet and E-Commerce.")

CREATING A CATALOG

Like newsletters, product catalogs can be created in print or electronic format. Which format is best for you greatly depends on factors such as the price of the products and services you are selling, your budget and your target customers.

The benefits of an online catalog are obvious. It's cheaper and faster and the orders can start coming in almost immediately.

However, online catalogs often lack the cachet of a good printed catalog that allows potential customers to curl up on the couch and browse. Potential customers must either download the online catalog or visit the website when they want to consult it. Printed catalogs come right to their mailboxes. Yes, the printed catalog is one long business tradition that has stood the test of time, even in the age of the internet.

Printed catalogs are typically specialized to meet the needs of specific groups of people. Victoria's Secret, Lands' End, L.L. Bean, and other popular catalogs all cater to their target customers. The 200-pound massive catalog that sells everything is now a historical artifact.

You can enhance your catalog with good-quality color photos of your products taken with your digital camera. You will also want to include information and highlights of your products, prices and a very easy means of ordering. Many homebased businesses are mail order retailers and a good-quality catalog is essential to their success.

If you choose to put your catalog online, you will need to follow the same basic approach: good photos, clear and easy-to-read descriptions, prices and an easy means of ordering. There is custom software that enables you to create electronic catalogs in-house. One such program is Catalogue Creator at *cataloguecreator.com.*

Regardless of the catalog format you choose, there are four big questions. (1) Who will receive it, current customers and prospects or only new prospects? (2) How you will reach these people? (3) Will you use your in-house mailing list or rent mailing lists? (4) Will you have the catalog delivered by the postal service or electronically through an e-distribution service?

One great aspect of catalogs is that they allow you to fill a very specific niche in the marketplace. You can organize your catalog to feature specific products, by function or by price.

Here are a few tips for improving your catalog:

- Include two order forms with your catalog, a loose insert and a tear-away or cut-out.
- Make it easy for people to order and pay for their purchases. Use toll-free order hot lines, include a complete mailing address, and allow payment by credit cards, e-checks, money orders, COD and installment plans.
- Feature your bestselling and most profitable products near the front of the catalog, because customers and prospects almost always read or at least glance at the first few pages.
- Send out your catalog accompanied by a sales letter with a special offer, even if the offer you are making means selling below cost. One critical aspect of mail order is to get new people to buy. Once people buy and discover how easy the process is, they are likely to continue to buy. So view the initial loss as a business cost that you can recoup through subsequent sales to your new customer.
- Consider using a smaller print catalog to sell your most popular items and to lead people to the larger online catalog. That way you save the cost of printing and sending out pages for lesser-selling products that you can feature online at almost no extra cost.

PRINTED FLIERS: THE HOME BUSINESS OWNER'S BEST FRIEND

The majority of home business owners will find printed fliers represent one of the best advertising vehicles and values available, particularly for start-ups and entrepreneurs working with restricted advertising budgets. Fliers are a fast and frugal, yet highly effective way, to promote a wide range of products and services.

This is especially true if you take the time needed to learn basic design skills so that you can create high-impact promotional fliers in-house. Beginner desktop publishing courses encompassing design and layout for fliers, brochures, reports and presentations are available in just about every community through colleges, continuing education programs or private tutors and generally at very reasonable costs.

There are also desktop publishing programs that include flier templates, which you can customize to suit your specific needs or you can create fliers from scratch using the design tools provided in the software. Adobe, *adobe.com*, and Corel, *corel.com*, are widely known for user-friendly desktop publishing programs. Some of the benefits of creating fliers and other promotional materials yourself are that you can:

- Save time and money
- Experiment and test
- Project a professional image

Save Time and Money

Artwork and layout design are very costly. Most commercial printers charge $60 to $80 per hour for graphic design services for marketing materials like fliers, product brochures, newsletters, and other printed items commonly used for promotions. In addition to saving money, you can also save precious marketing time. You have the ability to create in-house printed promotional materials within a day, perhaps even within a few hours, instead of waiting days or weeks working around the printer's schedule and making numerous trips to proofread and sign off on artwork and copy.

Experiment and Test

Having the equipment and skills to produce your own promotional materials enables you to experiment, at little cost, with various print marketing tools, messages, and special promotions until you find the right mix. On day one, design, print and test two-for-one coupons. On day two, design, print and experiment with a newsletter. On day three, design, print and experiment with a customer service survey. The list goes on. Create, test, and implement marketing messages and activities that will work specifically for your business and your target customers.

Project a Professional Image

Imagine being able to print the name of your cus-tomers on gift certificates and other special promotional materials with the click of a mouse. You can if you have the skills and equipment to do so. You will be able to personalize every correspondence with your best customers: thank-you notes, greeting cards and letters that you have individually created with one customer in mind. That is powerful marketing and customer appreciation.

Flier Distribution and Community Bulletin Boards

Once you have created and printed your fliers, you can have them copied in bulk for as little as 3 cents each at your local copy center or you can invest in a color laser printer for about $400 and keep the printing in-house, too. The great benefit of printed promotional fliers is that they can be used everywhere and for everything.

You can hand out fliers at seminars, trade shows, networking meetings, to the attendees. You can circulate through busy parking lots tucking fliers under windshield wipers. You can hand out fliers outside community gathering places such as movie theaters, sports complexes and convention centers. You can visit local retailers and institutions and ask if you can leave fliers for their patrons. This works well, especially if you purchase "please take one" plastic brochure boxes and leave one in each location. Stock them with your fliers and return weekly to refill them. You can leave your advertising fliers in public transit, like buses and subway cars, for riders to read and take home, as well as in bus stations, train stations, airports and bus shelters.

If you are on a tight advertising budget, you should regard community notice boards as a super valuable source for advertising your business, products and services for free. Stock a supply of promotional fliers and thumbtacks in your car so you can make a weekly run to post the fliers on every community notice board in your area.

Community notice or bulletin boards are typically found in the following locations:

- Supermarkets and public markets
- Convenience stores
- Public libraries
- Community colleges, universities and high schools
- Self-service laundries and dry cleaners
- Automotive service stations
- Community and recreational centers
- Fitness centers and sports complexes
- Religious organizations
- Meeting facilities for clubs or associations

Of course, you can also hire cash-starved students to distribute your fliers and contract with the postal service to have your fliers included in home delivery. Additionally, check with your local newspaper; most offer flier insert programs with home delivery at reasonable rates.

Coupons

Promotional coupons offer home business owners another cost-efficient way to promote their products and services. Once again, with basic skills, a personal computer, desktop publishing software and a printer, you can design, print and distribute your own promotional coupons. Alternately, you can participate in a community marketing campaign in which retailers and service providers join together to create a coupon book that is distributed throughout the community. Coupons can feature a discount in the form of money off (e.g., "Present this coupon and save $25 when you get your carpets cleaned") or in the form of a percentage (e.g., "Get your carpets cleaned before the end of this month and save 25%"). Other uses for coupons include two-for-one specials, free product or service trial periods, and free upgrades with a purchase of the standard product or service. The Association of Coupon Professionals provides information about coupons and about coupon design and distribution services on its website, *couponpros.org*.

Door Hangers

A door hanger is another kind of printed promotional flier, one designed so that it fits over any standard doorknob or handle. The advantage of door hangers is obvious. People can enter their homes without seeing and touching a flier left on the doorstep, but not a door hanger, so hangers generally are read much more often. Door hangers can be multipurpose. Print information about your products or services on the front and a coupon or special offer on the back. Door hangers are cheap, they get noticed, and they don't get lost in a mailbox full of junk mail.

Posters

If you have an artistic flair or know someone who does, posters are a marvelous way to show off what you have to market. Colorful posters are an art form. If you can design something that grabs the attention of passersby, you can benefit from having well-positioned posters. Just make sure, before you hang a poster, that the property owner has no reservations. You can make barter deals with store owners to hang your poster for a free product or service.

Other Means of Advertising

There are still other ways to advertise your business and your products and services:

- Programs at local theater presentations
- Benches, buses and taxies
- Placemats in local eateries
- Elevators, where LCD signs are becoming more popular and
- Local free shopper publications (very effective for service providers)

SIGNAGE NEEDS FOR YOUR HOME BUSINESS

Without question, signs are one of the lowest-cost, yet highest-impact forms of advertising for home business owners. Signs work to promote your business, products or services 24 hours a day, 365 days a year virtually for free, once you've purchased the signs. Your signs tell people at a glance your business name, what you sell, why they should contact you and how they can contact you. That makes signs the ultimate sales reps for your business.

Your signage must be professional, in keeping with the image that you want to project, informative, and yet free from too much secondary information.

Once signs were hand-painted and expensive, but most signs today are designed on a computer, printed and cut on large sheets of vinyl, easily installed, long lasting and very inexpensive. You want to always make a positive first impression, so keep all your signage in top condition. Faded signs, peeling paint, torn banners, or signs that require maintenance in general send out negative messages about your business. Use graphics and pictures of what you do in your signs to lend visual description. Keep your signs consistent with your business image. Use a unified color scheme, the same font and style and a consistent logo and marketing message. More helpful information about business signage can be found online at SignWeb, *signweb.com.*

Signs at Your Home

Installing signs at home is tricky, because there are laws, people and issues that must be taken into account.

There are local bylaws that determine whether signage is allowed at your home and, if so, possibly set restrictions on the size of the sign, placement, style and more. There is no one set of regulations for home business signage; each municipality has its own regulations. Generally, a call to the planning department at city or town hall is all that is required to find out the local laws and regulations on home business signage.

Neighbors are also a consideration. Even if signage is allowed, you want to consult your immediate neighbors to find out how they feel about signs and get their input. You certainly do not want to alienate neighbors over business signs. If you do, expect a backlash in terms of complaints about customer parking, noise, or any other reason that they can find to complain, justified or not. In many residential areas, signage is frowned on, so don't be surprised if you do not succeed with homebased signs.

The final sign issue involves your budget, style and maintenance. Unless you are going to have clients come to your home, you will probably be better off not having signs at all. If you will be having prospects and customers coming to your home, keep your signs in open view, make them tasteful to match not only your business image but also your home and streetscape, perhaps carved wood or brass on stone, and keep lighting to a minimum unless you can incorporate your sign into your exterior house lights or motion lighting.

Vehicle Signs

Some home business owners struggle with the decision about whether to sign their vehicles, especially the vehicles that double as family transportation. My advice is to get magnetic signs that can be quickly installed or removed and stored in the trunk when using your car for family activities. You can also use window signs that can be removed when you are "off duty." However, if you are going to sign your vehicle with semi-permanent stick-on vinyl or with magnetic signs, make sure to have the signs professionally designed. The look of your vehicle signs should be consistent with your business image in style, color, tone, logo and unified marketing message. With computers, even very elaborate signs can be designed and printed inexpensively, making that a worthwhile marketing expenditure. If you sign the vehicle, I would also advise parking in highly visible and high-traffic locations whenever possible, even if this means feeding parking meters. Always think about maximizing the marketing value of these rolling billboards.

Props can also be used in combination with signs to better describe your business and make a more memorable impression. An example is the plumber replacing the door handles on the service van with faucets. Regardless of the signage or props that you use, all signs should include your business name, a brief promotional message that best describes what you do and contact information, including telephone numbers and website URL.

Jobsite Signs

Owners of home businesses that install products or provide services at their customers' homes and offices should consider investing in professional, attention-grabbing jobsite signage, especially if jobs last more than a few days. Jobsite signs come in all sizes and are priced to fit all budgets. Some are metal with metal stands, while others are Coroplastl™, or simple plastic sleeves, similar to political yard signs, but emblazoned with your business name, logo and promotional message. The plastic sleeve signs fits over preformed wire stands, which push easily into the ground, making for fast installation and later removal. Purchased in bulk, the plastic sleeve signs are very inexpensive, less than $5 each and can be reused many times. The metal and Coroplast™ signs tend to be more expensive and much more bulky to move around and install.

Many home businesses—such as landscape services, house painters, interior and exterior designers,

renovation firms and window cleaners—can benefit by actively using jobsite signs. Jobsite signs are without question a very simple and economical way to market your business during work in progress. Business Signs Online, *businesssigns.com*, sells metal and Coroplast™ made-to-order site signs in various sizes. PoliticalLawnSigns.com, *politicallawnsigns.com*, manufactures lightweight plastic site signs.

PLACES WHERE YOU CAN ADVERTISE

The following Advertising Checklist (Figure 13.1) should help you identify places where you can advertise your business, products or services, and provide a few additional advertising ideas that might work for you.

TRACKING YOUR ADVERTISING TO GAUGE EFFECTIVENESS

If you are going to advertise, you will need to gauge the effectiveness of your efforts. This is important, because this information enables you to allocate your advertising dollars more effectively. This way you can continue to benefit from the media that have had the greatest impact in terms of reaching your target audience and generating the most revenue.

Of course, some types of advertising and marketing activities are easier to track than others. For instance, tracking the effectiveness of a coupon drop is much easier than tracking the effectiveness of a TV commercial. You can use multiple telephone extensions, name several people whom customers should request specifically, or give away different special offers or gifts in different ads. But perhaps the easiest way to track your advertising and marketing efforts is to simply ask the people who contact you how they heard about your business. You can create a simple How Did You Hear About Us? form, like the one shown in Figure 13.2,

FIGURE 13.1	Advertising Checklist

Print Advertising

- ❏ Display advertisements in national, regional or local newspapers
- ❏ Classified advertisements in national, regional or local newspapers
- ❏ School newspapers: high school, college, university, trade schools and alumni
- ❏ National or regional magazines
- ❏ Trade and industry newspapers, journals and reports
- ❏ Special-interest and club publications
- ❏ Newsletters: in-house, corporate, organization, union and community
- ❏ Business, consumer and industry directories
- ❏ Yellow Pages
- ❏ Direct-mail promotions
- ❏ Catalogs
- ❏ Coupon books, clip-outs and inserts
- ❏ Seasonal greeting cards and calendars
- ❏ Posters
- ❏ Other

Electronic and Broadcast Advertising

- ❏ Active and static banner advertisements
- ❏ Search engines and search directories
- ❏ Internet directories
- ❏ Reciprocal web links
- ❏ Newsgroups and chat forums
- ❏ Electronic publications: e-zines, e-newsletters and e-reports
- ❏ Radio commercials
- ❏ Radio program and segment sponsorships
- ❏ Event broadcasting
- ❏ Internet radio

- ❏ Network, local or cable TV commercials
- ❏ Infomercials
- ❏ Community and nonprofit TV
- ❏ Telemarketing
- ❏ Telephone on-hold messages
- ❏ LCD Signage
- ❏ Other

Community and Specialty Advertising

- ❏ Cooperative advertising programs: supplier, manufacturers, associations and industry
- ❏ Exterior and interior billboards
- ❏ Transit advertising: bus, light rail, train, subway, taxicab and ferry
- ❏ Community bulletin boards
- ❏ Fliers and door hangers
- ❏ Restaurant placemats, napkin dispensers and menus
- ❏ Community event, sports and charity sponsorships
- ❏ Community "take-one" brochure boxes
- ❏ Tourist and information bureaus
- ❏ Window, point-of-purchase and counter displays
- ❏ Aerial banners, blimps and inflatable advertising
- ❏ Signage: car signs, jobsite signs, portable electronic signs and special event signs
- ❏ Trade and consumer shows, conventions, seminars and expos
- ❏ Amateur sports: team sponsorships and playing field signage
- ❏ Promotional specialties: hats, T-shirts, bags, buttons, pens, magnets, etc.
- ❏ Bumper and specialty stickers
- ❏ Cash register receipts, shopping bags and shopping carts
- ❏ Park benches and garbage receptacles

FIGURE 13.1   Advertising Checklist, continued

- ❑ Human billboards and mascots
- ❑ Movie theater screen shots and event/theater programs
- ❑ Newcomer programs such as Welcome Wagon

- ❑ Free shopper publications (e.g., Pennysavers)
- ❑ Parade floats
- ❑ Score sheets: golf and bowling
- ❑ Product placement in theater, film or TV

listing only advertising and marketing activities that your business does, and complete it every time someone calls. Over time, you will be able to identify patterns, which enable you to focus your efforts on advertising and marketing activities that are working, while ditching the ones that show poor results.

COOPERATIVE ADVERTISING PROGRAMS

Many corporations, manufacturers, and distributors have advertising assistance programs, generally called *advertising* or *marketing cooperative programs*. These programs enable the larger corporations to help their vendors advertise. This is, of course, a beneficial arrangement for both parties.

FIGURE 13.2   How Did You Hear About Us? Form

Advertising or Promotional Source	Additional Information
❑ Newspaper or magazine advertisement	_____
❑ Yellow Pages of telephone directory	_____
❑ Specialty publications	_____
❑ TV or radio advertising	_____
❑ Internet or our website	_____
❑ Publicity or public speaking engagement	_____
❑ Flier, insert or door hanger	_____
❑ Contest or special promotional event	_____
❑ TV or direct mail	_____
❑ Trade show, conference, expo or seminar	_____
❑ Referred by a customer, friend or family	_____
❑ Saw a job in progress or service vehicle	_____
❑ Saw promotional or event signage	_____

Franchises often have cooperative advertising programs. Many franchisors will pay for an ad along with the franchisee, making it more affordable for the franchisee and bringing in the familiar franchise name and products, improving the results of the ad.

Such deals can be arranged with manufacturers if you are selling their products. Even service providers can work a deal. For example, you may be running a home gardening service and team up with the makers of home gardening tools. You help design and plant the garden and their tools can help the owners maintain it. Together you can have a co-op ad featuring their products and your services.

You will want to appeal to your suppliers and business alliances to assist with the following types of advertising through cooperative programs:

- Newspaper display and classifieds advertising
- Magazine advertising
- Spokesperson programs
- Radio commercials and program sponsorships
- TV commercials and program sponsorships
- Transit advertising campaigns
- Outdoor and indoor specialty advertising
- Yellow Pages and business directories
- Internet and e-advertising activities

But don't stop there. Also tap suppliers for additional business and marketing materials, including:

- Special event signs and displays
- Printed marketing and sales materials, including business cards, brochures and catalogs
- Advertising specialties like calendars, pens, hats and notepads
- Contest assistance, including printing and prizes
- Product samples and giveaways
- Educational help, including training and books
- Marketing and business help, advice and guidance

The National Register Publishing, *nationalregisterpub.com*, publishes an annual *Co-op Advertising Programs Sourcebook* that lists hundreds of co-op advertising programs.

CREATING A MEDIA QUESTIONNAIRE

If you know what your customers and target groups like to read, which programs they like on TV or on the radio, which search engines they use, and which websites they visit most often, you can purchase advertising where you know it is most likely to reach them. This greatly increases your odds of getting a better return on your investment.

But how do you find this sort of information? There are a few ways, but perhaps the easiest and least costly is to create a simple media questionnaire and ask your current customers, prospects, and people who fit your target customer profile to kindly complete it. Asking current customers to complete the questionnaire is straightforward. You can give it to them in person, fax it to them, mail it to them, use your opt-in list to e-mail to them or post the questionnaire on your website. Getting the questionnaire into the hands of those with whom you have no contact requires a little more innovation. Set up a survey booth in a mall or other high-traffic area and give away a small gift to people who take the time to complete the questionnaire. Or you can hand-deliver the questionnaire with a stamped return envelope to homes in your community. A discount coupon redeemable toward the purchase of your products or services would be an incentive to get people to respond. Whatever method you use to distribute your questionnaire, if you know what your customers are reading, watching or listening to, you can create effective, targeted advertising campaigns most likely to get the results you want.

Here is a detailed Sample Media Questionnaire you can use as a guideline to create one suitable for your business and advertising objectives. Keep what you want and delete the rest until you are satisfied that you have created the best questionnaire for your specific needs.

FIGURE 13.3 Sample Media Questionnaire

(Print your business name and contact information here.)

We ask that you take a moment to complete the following questionnaire.
Your responses will be used to help us better serve our customers. Thank you.

Optional Information

❑ Mr. ❑ Mrs. ❑ Ms. Name _____

Street Address _____

City _____ State _____ ZIP/Postal Code _____

Home Telephone _____ Work _____ Fax _____ E-Mail _____

May we contact you periodically with information and special offers? ❑ Yes ❑ No

Newspapers

Please list newspapers you typically read, along with your favorite section. Indicate if you have a subscription.

Newspaper Name	Subscription	Favorite Section
1. _____	❑ Yes ❑ No	_____
2. _____	❑ Yes ❑ No	_____
3. _____	❑ Yes ❑ No	_____
4. _____	❑ Yes ❑ No	_____

Magazines

Please list magazines you typically read. Indicate if you have a subscription.

Magazine Name	Subscription
1. _____	❑ Yes ❑ No
2. _____	❑ Yes ❑ No
3. _____	❑ Yes ❑ No
4. _____	❑ Yes ❑ No

FIGURE 13.3   Sample Media Questionnaire, continued

Special-Interest Publications

Please list special-interest publications you frequently read, such as trade journals, newsletters or reports. Indicate if you have a subscription.

Publication Name   Subscription

1. _____   ❑ Yes ❑ No

2. _____   ❑ Yes ❑ No

3. _____   ❑ Yes ❑ No

4. _____   ❑ Yes ❑ No

Radio

Please list radio stations you typically listen to and your favorite programs.

Radio Station Name   Favorite Program

1. _____   _____

2. _____   _____

3. _____   _____

4. _____   _____

Where do you typically listen to the radio? (Check all that apply.)

　　　　❑ Home   ❑ Car   ❑ Office

What time of the day do you typically listen to the radio? (Check all that apply.)

　　　　❑ 6:00 a.m.–9:00 a.m.   ❑ 9:00 a.m.–12:00 noon   ❑ 12:00 noon–3:00 p.m.

　　　　❑ 3:00 p.m.–6:00 p.m.   ❑ 6:00 p.m.–9:00 p.m.   ❑ after 9:00 p.m.

TV

Please list TV stations that you typically watch and specific programs you try not to miss.

Television Station Name   Favorite Program

1. _____   _____

2. _____   _____

3. _____   _____

4. _____   _____

What time of day do you typically watch television? (Check all that apply.)

　　　　❑ 6:00 a.m.–9:00 a.m.   ❑ 9:00 a.m.–12:00 noon   ❑ 12:00 noon–3:00 p.m.

　　　　❑ 3:00 p.m.–6:00 p.m.   ❑ 6:00 p.m.–9:00 p.m.   ❑ after 9:00 p.m.

FIGURE 13.3 Sample Media Questionnaire, continued

Which local news programs do you watch and at which times?

Program	Station	Time
1. _____	_____	❑ a.m. ❑ Noon ❑ p.m. ❑ Late Night
2. _____	_____	❑ a.m. ❑ Noon ❑ p.m. ❑ Late Night
3. _____	_____	❑ a.m. ❑ Noon ❑ p.m. ❑ Late Night
4. _____	_____	❑ a.m. ❑ Noon ❑ p.m. ❑ Late Night

Please list specialty news programs you watch.

1. _____

2. _____

3. _____

4. _____

Internet

Which search engine do you most commonly use to find information, products and services?

❑ Google ❑ Yahoo! ❑ MSN ❑ AltaVista ❑ AOL ❑ Other _____

Do you receive or subscribe to online or electronic publications? If so, please list.

E-Publication Name	Website URL
1. _____	_____
2. _____	_____
3. _____	_____
4. _____	_____

What is the most common type of website you visit?

❑ General News ❑ Financial News ❑ Sports

❑ Shopping ❑ Entertainment ❑ Travel ❑ Other

Which websites do you visit the most? Please list the names and URLs.

Website Name	Website URL
1. _____	_____
2. _____	_____
3. _____	_____
4. _____	_____

FIGURE 13.3   Sample Media Questionnaire, continued

General Questions

What types of advertising medium have the most influence on your buying decisions or habits?

❑ Newspaper   ❑ Magazine   ❑ Radio   ❑ Internet

❑ TV   ❑ Direct Mail   ❑ Live Demonstration

❑ Other _____

Have you ever purchased a product through a mail or e-mail offer? ❑ Yes ❑ No

Do you belong to any shopping clubs, such as a music club or a book club? (Please specify.)

_____

_____

_____

_____

Do you receive any product catalogs? If so, which ones?

_____

_____

_____

_____

Do you clip and redeem coupons and special offers from newspapers and magazines?

❑ Always   ❑ Sometimes   ❑ Rarely   ❑ Never

What do you do with the advertisements that you receive in the mail?

❑ Read and save   ❑ Read and trash   ❑ Straight to recycling without reading

❑ Other _____

Thank you for your cooperation. We appreciate your help.

RESOURCES
Associations

Advertising Photographers of America
P.O. Box 250
White Plains, NY 10605
(800) 272-6264
apanational.com

American Association of Advertising Agencies
405 Lexington Avenue, 18th Fl.

New York, NY 10174-1801
(212) 682-2500
aaaa.org

Association of Canadian Advertisers
95 St. Clair Avenue West, Suite 1103
Toronto, ON M4V 1N6
(416) 964-3805, (800) 565-0109
aca-online.com

Direct Marketing Association
1120 Avenue of the Americas
New York, NY 10036-6700
(212) 768-7277
the-dma.org

International Advertising Association
World Service Center
275 Madison Avenue, Suite 2102
New York, NY 10016
(212) 557-1133
iaaglobal.org

Outdoor Advertising Association of America
1850 M Street NW, Suite 1040
Washington, DC 20036
(202) 833-5566
oaaa.org

Suggested Reading

Briggs, Rex, and Greg Stuart. *What Sticks: Why Most Advertising Fails and How to Guarantee Yours Succeeds*. Chicago: Kaplan Publishing, 2006

Callen, Barry. P*erfect Phrases for Sales and Marketing Copy*. New York: McGraw-Hill, 2007.

Kaplan Thaler, Linda, and Robin Koval, with Delia Marshall. *Bang! Getting Your Message Heard in a Noisy World*. New York: Currency/Doubleday, 2003.

Krause, Jim. *Layout Index*. Cincinnati, OH: North Light Books, 2001.

Lance, Steve, and Jeff Woll. *The Little Blue Book of Advertising: 52 Small Ideas That Can Make a Big Difference.* New York: Portfolio Hardcover (Penguin Group), 2007.

Sissors, Jack Z., and Roger B. Baron. *Advertising Media Planning*. 6th edition. New York: McGraw-Hill, 2002.

Stephenson, James, and Courtney Thurman. *Entrepreneur Magazine's Ultimate Small Business Marketing Guide: 1500 Great Marketing Tricks That Will Drive Your Business Through the Roof!* 2nd edition. Irvine, CA: Entrepreneur Press, 2007.

Whitacre, Claude. *The Unfair Advantage Small Business Advertising Manual.* Wooster, OH: Unfair Advantage Retail, 2007.

Websites

50States.com: Directory of more than 3,300 newspapers in the United States. *50states.com/news*

Ad2Go!: Directory of free advertising opportunities. *adtogo.com*

Adobe Software Corporation: Numerous desktop publishing products for a wide variety of uses—great for creating newsletters, brochures, fliers, reports, presentations, table cards and much more on your desktop computer. *adobe.com*

Advertising Age Magazine Online: Articles from *Advertising Age. adage.com*

AdWeek: Adweek Directories Online: Searchable databases with information on ad agencies, brand marketers and multicultural media. *adweek.com*

Brandweek Magazine Online: Source of news and information in the U.S. marketing industry. *brandweek.com*

Catalogue Software: Online distributor of custom software for designing print and electronic product catalogs. *cataloguecreator.com*

Cheap TV Spots: Full-service TV commercial production company providing scripts, directing, filming, editing, music and narration services and packages. *cheap-tv-spots.com*

Copywriting Course: Downloadable copywriting course for $89. *copywritingcourse.com*

Corel Corporation: Desktop publishing products for a wide variety of uses. *corel.com*

Daily Earth: "The Global Newspaper Directory." *dailyearth.com*

Inc.com: Full small business resource with marketing and advertising sections. *inc.com*

Index Stock Imagery: Online stock photography service offering thousands of royalty-free stock photography images that can be used in your advertising, all available for instant download. *indexstock.com*

National Classified Advertising Group: One-stop resource for advertising in state, regional and national newspapers. *nationalclassifiedadvertising.com*

National Register Publishing: Annual directory listing hundreds of co-op advertising opportunities and programs. *nationalregisterpub.com*

News Link: Online directory of newspapers throughout the world, indexed geographically and by type of newspaper, as well as magazines and radio and TV stations. *nationalregisterpub.com*

Onlinenewspapers.com: Directory of links to newspapers around the world. *onlinenewspapers.com*

Print USA Inc.: One-stop shopping for the best prices for printing projects. *printusa.com*

PubList: Online directory of more than 150,000 print and electronic publications, including magazines, journals, e-journals and newsletters. *publist.com*

Radio Advertising Bureau: "The sales and marketing arm of the radio industry," offering articles on its website covering advertising, radio and competitive media. *rab.com*

Radio-Locator: Online directory linked to more than 10,000 radio stations in the United States and Canada and the rest of the world, indexed by format and geographic location. *radio-locator.com*

SignWeb: Free online information and links covering everything to do with commercial signage and the sign industry. *signweb.com*

SRDS Media Solutions: Publisher of print and online advertising rate card sourcebooks covering media advertising rates for more than 100,000 media properties—magazines, newspapers, TV, direct marketing, radio and online. *signweb.com*

Target Marketing Magazine Online: Source of how-to information for direct marketers. *targetmarketingmag.com*

TV Web Directory: Massive online directory of local, network and cable TV stations in the United States and Canada. *tvwebdirectory.com*

CHAPTER 14

Public Relations and Networking

SMALL BUSINESS OWNERS IN GENERAL tend to shy away from publicity. Few take the time to create and send out press releases. Even fewer actually develop and implement a public relations strategy for their business. Why, when the potential to reach thousands or perhaps even millions of people at little or no cost is a real possibility? Do any of the following excuses sound familiar?

- I don't have any contacts in the media.
- I don't have time to write and send out a press release.
- I don't have any publicity ideas.
- I don't know anything about public relations.
- Only big corporations can benefit from publicity.
- No one wants to hear about my business.
- I don't even know how I'd get started.

Most home business owners fail to realize that every business owner could easily create some sort of news or publicity buzz out of his or her products or services. All that is required is taking the time to understand how public relations works and using a little imagination to develop ways of sharing specialized knowledge and expertise.

Nobody says you need to spend hours developing a full-fledged PR plan. But doing some basic PR can be a very effective way to promote and market your business.

Less than 50 percent of news is generated by news sources. That means half the news we read in publications or on the web, hear on the radio or see on TV was submitted or initiated by people who are not reporters, journalists, producers, editors or media personnel. Who are the people creating the other 50 percent of the news we get? Professional publicists, small business owners and managers, politicians, salespeople, marketing consultants, community leaders, and basically anyone else who has learned that reporting news is one of the best ways to get their message out to a news-hungry public via the media. Each day journalists, editors, reporters, and producers have the daunting task of filling the news pipeline. It's a job that never ends—and with the plethora of news channels and websites dedicated to providing us with the latest information, there is a greater need than ever for more stories.

The need for news has created a problem for media workers. There are not enough people working in the media or enough hours in the day to research, write, film, or record all the stories and get them to the public. This problem creates an excellent opportunity for you to benefit by learning the process of determining which stories will make interesting content for the public to read.

In the preceding chapter, we talked about writing a newsletter. The thought process is very similar. Here, you want to find stories of particular interest, but not just of interest to your customers or other newsletter subscribers, but more generally. No, not everything you do is a news story and it is not cost-effective to send press releases on every little thing that happens. However, it is worth your time and effort to be alert to whatever others might find unique, informative, entertaining or even humorous about your business. Possible newsworthy content can include:

- Opening for business, new management or joint ventures
- Launching new or improved products and services
- Community information, such as events, sponsorships and charity drives
- Winning business awards or receiving special recognition for your business
- Health and safety news and information
- Contests, promotions and special events
- Specialized information, such as poll results or new regulations
- Business milestones, such as five years in business or one thousandth customer served

- Customer success stories as a result of doing business with you
- Celebrities, even local ones, who have benefited from your products or services
- A unique discovery or unorthodox manner of doing something work-related

Another overlooked benefit of developing and implementing a public relations campaign is that a successful campaign enables small businesses to level the playing field and compete against larger and often better-financed competitors. PR costs little outside of time. Yes, it is true that ads in the Yellow Pages can be in front of your target customers longer than a feature newspaper article about your business, product or service. But the newspaper article can be just the tip of the publicity iceberg if you learn to master and apply the art of seeking and securing free or low-cost publicity for your business.

PUBIC RELATIONS BASICS

Home business owners need to plan and implement an ongoing public relations campaign as an active component of their overall marketing plan. We read newspapers, watch television, surf the internet and listen to the radio, and we do so because we want to be entertained, to be informed and to learn. A great movie review in your local newspaper is more likely to pique your interest and pull you into a movie theater than an ad for that movie in the newspaper. That is publicity at work. It grabs your attention, spells out the basic details, creates interest and desire and compels you to take action.

At the core, public relations is much more than clever ways to secure free media attention and exposure for your business. Public relations is really an umbrella that covers many positive image-building techniques aimed at three key audiences: your target market, the media and your community.

Relations with the Target Market

Your first public relations audience is your target market, people who are the most likely to buy your products or services. In terms of relations with your target consumers, you must focus on the message you want to send, the image you want to build, and the level of awareness you want them to have about your business, product or service. Remember: reaching your target market is not limited to channeling a message through the media. Relations with your target market are all-encompassing and include how you present yourself and your business in public and the words and images you choose to present your business in marketing materials.

Relations with the Media

The media is your second key public relations audience and the one with which the vast majority of us are most aware, simply because it is the most publicized use of public relations. It is through print and broadcast media exposure that you gain access to your target market from within the media's broader audience or highly specific or niche audiences. Relations with the media can be ongoing or a one-shot deal, depending on your PR objectives and strategy.

Relations with the Community

The third key audience is the community(s) in which your business operates. Community-related public relations activities include joining business and other associations, volunteering with various community activities and events, and often throwing your small business weight behind local charitable causes. Of course, any time you are out in the community, you are a goodwill ambassador for your business. These community public relations and goodwill activities are generally part of being a good corporate citizen, a common characteristic that every successful small business owner shares.

DEVELOPING YOUR PUBLIC RELATIONS STRATEGY

Developing a PR strategy is a relatively straightforward process, if you follow a logical sequence. The starting point is to determine your PR objectives, your PR message now and in the future, your target market and what you want people to do as a result of your PR message. These are the basic components of a public relations strategy.

Defining Your PR Objectives

Your objectives can cover wanting to increase sales, introduce a new product or service, generate sales leads, repair damage from negative press, or simply build awareness of your business and what you do. Keep in mind that your public relations objectives will never remain static; they will change throughout the year to reflect current and forthcoming business and marketing objectives, strategies and campaigns. So before you actively seek any type of publicity, write down what you want to achieve as a result of the publicity that you are seeking. These are some common objectives:

- Increasing overall awareness of your business, product or service
- Promoting a special business, community or charity event or a sponsorship
- Driving people to your website or toll-free hotline
- Becoming known as an expert within your specific industry or field
- Introducing a new or greatly revamped product or service
- Generating new sales leads
- Changing public perceptions and consumer buying habits
- Announcing information that benefits the local community
- Seeking the public's help to solve an internal problem, such as naming a new product

- Revamping, changing or reinventing your current image

Creating Your PR Message

Every time that you seek publicity or share information with one or more of your key audiences, you will need to devise a central PR message. Your PR message will change depending on your objective, but each time you seek publicity or share information with a key audience, there must be a main message that you want to convey. You cannot have mixed or multiple messages.

If your objective is to secure media exposure for a new product launch, for example, your PR message must revolve around that theme exclusively—nothing else. It should include facts, statistics, benefits, how-to information and other details related to the new product. If your objective is to release information about a community event sponsorship, your PR message should focus on the event, your participation in the event and how your business supports the local community.

Identifying Your PR Target Market

Prior to launching a public relations program or any segment of the program, you have to identify the target market for your message. That target may change, but to effectively reach a target market, you must first identify it. This is a simple process. Break it down into three categories— demographics, location and benefits—and ask yourself questions relevant to the categories. What are the age, sex, education level and income level of the people you want to reach? Where is your target market located geographically? Who will benefit the most from coming in contact with your news by way of media exposure? If you know the answers to these questions, you can properly identify the media that reach the market you want your message to reach.

Identifying the Media

Knowing which market you want to reach helps you identify which media will work best for you. For instance, if your target is business managers, you will want to focus your efforts on securing exposure in media that reach business managers, perhaps industry publications or specific broadcast programs. If your target is high school students, you want to focus your efforts on school publications and other forms of media that regularly cater to this demographic.

Who Will Develop Your PR Program?

Home business owners have three options for developing a PR program. You can do it yourself, hire a freelance public relations specialist as needed or contract with a full-service public relations agency.

Do-It-Yourself Option

The vast majority of home business owners will create and maintain their own public relations program and key campaigns within the program because of the costs associated with hiring a freelance PR specialist or contracting with a full-service PR agency. Doing it yourself requires that you educate yourself in the finer aspects of public relations. But over time and with practice, you will get the results that will help your business grow.

Freelance Option

The second option is to hire a freelance public relations consultant or a marketing/advertising consultant with a strong public relations background. Often freelancers break away from larger firms to build their own agencies; they generally charge 60 to 80 percent less than full-service public relations agencies. To find freelance PR consultants, contact your local chamber of commerce for referrals, do a web search or ask other business owners for recommendations.

Agency Option

The third option is to hire an agency that specializes in creating, maintaining, and growing public relations programs based on each client's individual needs and budget. The downside of hiring a PR firm is that most will not take on small jobs or one-time jobs. They prefer to sign longer-term contracts with monthly payment guarantees and extra billing for services provided over and above the basic agreement. If you are going to hire a professional PR firm, be prepared to shell out at least $2,000 per month—just to get going. It's rare that a home business owner or other small business owner will find this option cost-effective.

A Call to Action

When you develop your PR strategy, one of the decisions you must make is what you want people to do as a result of your PR message. That decision consists of answering two questions. (1) What action do you want them to take? (2) What tools will you give them to take that action? This is commonly called a *call to action*.

In the information you release or share with the media, there must be a compelling reason for people to contact you and there must be ways for them to do it. For instance, if your message is that you want people to come out and support a community cleanup that your business is sponsoring, you must include in your release compelling reasons why people should attend the event and details such as time, place, things they should bring, people they can contact before and during the event and registration information.

Setting a Budget

Though publicity is often considered free adver-

tising, there is still a cost associated with creating, maintaining and growing a PR program. You have to set a PR budget and know where the money will come from to support the program. Like many forms of advertising, it is difficult to track the success of publicity. So once you have committed to the program, follow through and do not let early disappointments dissuade you from further PR endeavors. The budget you set will be in direct relationship to what you can afford. After all, you are operating a small business, probably with limited financial resources, so budget will be a concern.

Creating a Timetable

Sending out a press release in June to inform the media about an ice castle sculpture contest you are hosting in January to raise money for charity will garner little if any attention from the media. It is simply too far in advance to motivate them to take action. You must determine your time line in advance for each segment of your PR program. You must also consider your own schedule. If you are a one-person business, planning a media event or release during your busiest time of the year may be difficult or impossible. Additionally, you will need to know the time line of the media you are trying to interest. Do you want a magazine to publish a holiday-related story about your seasonal carnival?

Send it three or four months in advance. Do you want to get the same information onto a website? You can send it a few days in advance. The point is timing, determining when reaching editors and/or producers will be most effective. Sometimes you simply need to ask. Editors or producers who are deluged by press releases are unlikely to will keep your press materials sitting around for months until the timing is right. On the other hand, you don't want to miss their deadlines.

CREATING A PRESS RELEASE

The press release is the most important PR tool for securing media attention and exposure. Fortunately, with a little practice, it is one that anyone can use.

Practice is the key word. Before you sit down and struggle to put your thoughts into words on paper, research press releases first to get a feel for the style, tone, format, voice and structure commonly used. Simply read other press releases, especially ones that have been picked up and covered by the media. There are numerous websites where you can read press releases, current and archived. One of the best is PRWeb, at *prweb.com*. On PRWeb, you can browse and read through thousands of press releases for free and they are also conveniently indexed by industry. Remember: You don't want to reinvent the wheel; you want to write an effective release that gets picked up. Use what's available as a template for your own information.

Formatting

Press release formatting is very basic. The following overview will give you a guideline that you can use when preparing your press releases.

- *Paper.* Print your press release on company letterhead if you have it; if not, standard 20-pound 8.5-by-11-inch white office paper is totally acceptable. Forget about using fancy, colored or extra heavy paper stock. It's best just to stick with your letterhead or standard office paper. The same applies to envelopes; use a standard white office envelope with no window.
- *Font.* Standard fonts such as Times New Roman or Arial are fine. A good size is 12 points. Avoid fancy fonts, italics or bolding too many words and sentences. Always use black ink on white paper. The only color should be in your business name or logo if you are printing the release on company letterhead.
- *Spacing.* Double spacing makes the release easy to read at a glance. Use 1- to 1.5-inch margins all around.
- *Length.* Generally press releases are one or two pages long. As a rule of thumb, expect to fit roughly 250 words on each page so it won't be hard to read.
- *Templates.* Most of the popular word processing software programs such as Microsoft Office and Corel WordPerfect have press release templates you can customize to suit your particular needs. You can also easily create your own press release template using Notepad, Word, or a similar word processing program and saving it as a document.
- *Proofread.* Always proofread your press release for grammar and spelling errors before sending it out; do not solely rely on your word processor spell-check program. Use exclamation marks sparingly and other punctuation only as required. When you are done proofreading your release, give it to an employee, friend or family member to proofread again.

Contact Information

You should put your contact information at both the top and the bottom of your press release. If you print the release on company letterhead, you will have your full contact information there. If you do not use letterhead, you can print your business name and address at the top of the page, followed by a contact name and the direct telephone number and e-mail address of the contact person. The contact information should then be repeated at the end of the release.

Release Information

Near the top, on the right side, indicate a release date for the news. On the left side, print "FOR IMMEDIATE RELEASE" or, if you have a specific date on which you would like the news or information to be released, write that date in all uppercase letters and underscore, such as "TO BE RELEASED SEPTEMBER 1, 2008." This is not typically done, so have a good reason for setting a specific date for release. When you specify a date, you greatly reduce the odds of securing media exposure. You are telling media personnel to work around your timetable and not to do what is convenient for them.

Headline

The headline is one of the more important aspects of the press release, if not the most important. It grabs attention and makes your press release stand out in the multitude of releases received by media personnel.

Your headline should be bold, in larger type and printed directly across the top of the press release. The headline could be in the form of a question, a statement that reveals part of the news, a quote or a statistic. Use whatever you feel is relevant to your main message and will grab the attention of readers and draw them into the body of the release. Do not be cryptic or attempt to be too clever or subtle in your message. If the reader doesn't get it, then it's trashed. Be clever, but in a manner that does not detract from a straightforward message.

Under the headline, a few lines down, you can use a subhead that reveals more information about your main marketing message or answers the question posed in your headline. The subhead should be used to provide more information and interest the readers more.

Dateline and Lead Paragraph

Start your first paragraph with a dateline. Follow it with your lead into the story. The first paragraph needs to hold the reader by making your message sound compelling without a lot of hype. No, your product is not the greatest thing ever. However, it may be the first to accomplish a task in record time or be the easiest to use or be newsworthy for some other reason. This is where you highlight what it is that you want everyone to know about. What will readers stop and read? What will make TV viewers pay special attention? What will cause people visiting the websites to bookmark your information? This paragraph should be three or four sentences that provide the benefits of your information or show why your information is unique or significant.

Text Information

Follow the lead paragraph with the body of the press release. This should be a few paragraphs long and tell the rest of your story. It basically answers the who, what, why, when, where and how questions. Think of this as the area in which you make your compelling case or argument for the newsworthiness of your release so the media will make your information or story available to the public.

Boilerplate Information

The boilerplate information is a single paragraph that briefly gives some facts about your business, current ownership, company history, significant accomplishments and specialties or features of your business. Include whatever else you feel is relevant to your business.

After the boilerplate paragraph, put three pound signs (# # #) or three Xs (x x x) or simply END to mark the conclusion of the press release.

As mentioned earlier, you should repeat your contact information at the end of your last paragraph and/or at the bottom of the last page in your press release. Typically, the best press releases are one page long, two is fine, but three is usually more than any editor or producer wants to read.

What Makes a Good Press Release?

First, a good press release is about something worth knowing. The fact that you just purchased a new computer system is not important to anyone outside of your home office. The fact that you planted and created the dazzling lawn sculptures in front of the mayor's house that won a prestigious award is newsworthy.

Start out by determining what will generate some attention. The less unique the story is, the more creative you will need to be in writing it. (Again, no hype, just facts.) Editors, producers, reporters, and journalists receive tons of press releases. You have to make yours stand out from the crowd if you want to grab their attention and get the exposure. What you decide is news does not have to necessarily be groundbreaking stuff. Sometimes a new twist on an old story can work well. Also, try to be objective about the information you include in the press release, looking at it from the perspective of the media's target audiences. How will this information benefit them? And think in terms of mass appeal—the more people who would be interested in the information in your press release, the better your odds of securing media exposure.

Include support information or documents with your press release if you feel that it is relevant. These documents can include a fact sheet in bullet format that lists the highlights of your news, a photograph or two or illustrations that will help to paint a complete picture. Again, don't overdo it. Three or four should suffice—and only if you think photos or illustrations will matter.

Media Contacts

The major key to securing media exposure is to make sure that you target the right media and the right media personnel. As mentioned earlier, anyone, with some practice, can learn to write a decent press release. *But* if it does not get into the right hands, it's useless.

Therefore, you need to do your research and find out which media outlets would best serve your purposes. Keep in mind your goals and your target market. Just as you did with advertising, you need to pinpoint the best media outlets and the best editors and producers for your news.

For example, if you provide wedding consulting, you will look for the editors of bridal magazines and the sections of newspapers that cover weddings or special occasions. Perhaps you can interest the editor of a fashion magazine in a new style of wedding gown or a food magazine in the wedding cake of the future.

Whatever your news is, look for where it would best fit and then find out who is the editor or producer for that section. Do not just send blindly to a publication, website or media outlet. Also, don't send it to the editor-in-chief or the executive producer. Narrow your search to the best possible contact. You may call to introduce yourself and inquire whether e-mailed press releases are OK. Most editors and publishers will say yes, but a few old-fashioned types will ask for snail mail.

Try to get a full name and title and then address the release directly to that person. Departments are diverse, including real estate, lifestyles, business and book reviews.

Sourcing out-of-area or national media contacts requires more research. You can purchase media directories like Oxbridge Communication's *Standard Periodical Directory* or subscribe to its online media database at *mediafinder.com*, but these are costly options. A free alternative media directory is NewsLink,

newslink.org. Searching online for area media is also easy. You will find TV and radio stations, as well as newspapers, in every region of the country with a basic search. You can use a contact management software program such as Maximizer, *maximizer.com*; however, it is usually just as simple to set up your own listing with Excel, Word or even paper. Additionally, you can use a simple Media Contact Form (Figure 14.1) to keep track of key media contact people.

Press Release Distribution

Some editors, journalists, and producers still like to receive press releases the old fashioned way, by snail mail or fax. But they are in the minority as more and more prefer e-mail. The internet has transformed the way publicists, marketers, and small business owners can release information to the media. Most print and electronic media directories include e-mail contact information for key media people and companies. Of course, when in doubt, simply call and ask how they prefer to receive a press release or media advisory.

FIGURE 14.1   Media Contact Form

Contact 1 _____

Company _____   Person ❑ Mr. ❑ Mrs. ❑ Ms. _____

Telephone _____   Fax _____   E-mail _____

Comments _____

Contact 2 _____

Company _____   Person ❑ Mr. ❑ Mrs. ❑ Ms. _____

Telephone _____   Fax _____   E-mail _____

Comments _____

Contact 3 _____

Company _____   Person ❑ Mr. ❑ Mrs. ❑ Ms. _____

Telephone _____   Fax _____   E-mail _____

Comments _____

Contact 4 _____

Company _____   Person ❑ Mr. ❑ Mrs. ❑ Ms. _____

Telephone _____   Fax _____   E-mail _____

Comments _____

Contact 5 _____

Company _____   Person ❑ Mr. ❑ Mrs. ❑ Ms. _____

Telephone _____   Fax _____   E-mail _____

Comments _____

FIGURE 14.2   Sample Press Release

[Complete contact information here, including business name, full address and website URL]

<u>FOR IMMEDIATE RELEASE</u>

CONTACT: John Doe

(555) 555-5555

john@doe.com

ENTREPRENEUR MAGAZINE'S ULTIMATE HOMEBASED BUSINESS HANDBOOK IN SECOND PRINTING

The one-stop source of valuable need-to-know business information has been updated with a wealth of new information, including 25% more suggestions for homebased businesses, additional resources, and the latest on high-tech help for homebased entrepreneurs. Just like the original version, released in 2004, the comprehensive guide is specifically written to meet the needs of thousands of entrepreneurial people in North America who are looking forward to starting home businesses.

Unlocking the Mystery of Home Business Success!

For many people, the concept of starting a home business is overwhelming, frustrating and bewildering. Where do they begin? How do they set up a home office? Where should they invest their precious startup dollars? How do they avoid costly mistakes and dead ends? And most important, when will they see needed results? All of that has changed, thanks to *Entrepreneur* Magazine's *Ultimate Homebased Business Handbook*, the most authoritative home business book available today. This book is packed with thousands of useful home office and business ideas that are guaranteed to take new entrepreneurs from start-up to success, painlessly, quickly and for life.

The author of *Entrepreneur Magazine's Ultimate Start-Up Directory* and *Entrepreneur Magazine's Ultimate Small Business Guide*, James Stephenson, invests his 15 years of small business and sales experience into this book. Stephenson promises, "You will discover everything you need to know to get your home business started and, more important, how to generate profits in no time."

Entrepreneur magazine, now in its third decade of providing small business owners with vital business and information know-how, is committed to helping all business owners and managers succeed through timely and expert information in book, magazine and software formats.

#

If you would like more information about this book, a review copy or an interview with the author, call John Doe at (555) 555-5555 or e-mail john@doe.com.

CREATING A MEDIA KIT

A media kit is generally in the form of a decorative folder with an interior pocket that holds various loose information sheets (8.5-by-11-inch). The information sheets are intended to give the reader insights into your business, what you sell or what you do, who is involved and other data that are considered newsworthy or relevant to your business, industry, products or services. The media folder can be basic, but the outside should be imprinted with your business name, logo and contact information, including telephone number, website URL, e-mail address and complete mailing address. These heavy paper presentation folders can be purchased at most office supply stores and in bulk cost about 50 cents each. Some include an indentation where you can insert a business card, a good alternative to printed folders for those on a tight budget.

A variety of information can be included in your media kit. There are no set rules and you can add or delete items as required to meet your own specific needs and objectives. For personalized folder, you can try Presskits at *presskits.com*. They also carry CD/Disk Kits for sending a CD of your business in action, portfolios and more. Whether you use Presskits or another such company, personally designed folders can attract attention and show a touch of class. If, however, you are on a tight budget, you can always add stickers with your information to a plain color folder. Remember to choose colors that fit your business style.

Summary Sheet

A summary sheet is much like a table of contents. It allows the recipient to know at a glance what is in the media kit and what may be of particular interest to him or her. The summary sheet should include the name, address, other contact information of the intended recipient of the media kit, and your contact information or the contact information of the person handling your public relations program. It is always a good idea to print your summary sheet on company letterhead.

Press Releases

Include at least one, if not two or three of the most current press releases in the press kit. The theme or angle of each should be different so you can appeal more broadly in terms of your two target audiences—the media and their markets.

Review Sheet

A review sheet is generally one page that lists the compelling reasons why a reporter, editor or any member of the media should give you coverage. One paragraph can be devoted to describing the product or service. A second paragraph can be devoted to the benefits that using the product or service will deliver. A third paragraph can be used to describe how the product or service can solve a problem and any competitive advantages associated with it. The review sheet is the place for fascinating facts and figures about your product or service.

Company Fact Sheet

A company fact sheet can be included with the media kit. It briefly describes the history of your company and your vision for the future. You can also use this sheet to mention awards your company has won and to point readers to your company website.

If you are going to put a fact sheet in your media kit, make sure it includes your company mission statement. Your mission statement will instantly give the recipient a clear understanding of what your company does, why you do it, and what people get out of doing business with your firm. You can use a highlighter pen to draw attention to key information on the company fact sheet and other information sheets in the kit, but don't go overboard. You can also include biographical information about yourself, key employees and important business allies. Remember to keep everything brief.

Testimonials

Include in your media kit glowing testimonials that you have received from clients. Make sure to give complete information about the people who wrote them. This information should include their company and title, how they can be contacted, what solutions your products or services provided them and how they benefited as a result. Be aware that there is a fair chance that the recipient (media personnel) will contact the people whose testimonials you include to check on your claims.

Press and Support Materials

This is why they are called *press kits,* because you include articles and photos that have been published about your business. At first, you won't have much to put here, so you can use some of your own photos, perhaps a web screenshot or some general articles, opinion polls and charts about the industry. However, once you have succeeded in landing a few stories about your business, these are what you should include.

If stories are on newspaper pages with other articles, you may cut out the story, put it on a plain piece of paper and run copies of your article without the various other stories. Typically, you'll put the articles in order of publication, from the most recent to the oldest.

If you have TV or radio exposure on talk shows or in the news, you might want to include a CD of your media appearances. If you have been featured on other websites, run a hard copy of the page or pages and include it.

Your press materials are very important. They show producers and editors that you are already newsworthy. Once one editor or producer has featured you, others are more likely to follow.

PUBLIC RELATIONS TIPS, TECHNIQUES AND GREAT IDEAS

Home business owners can never have enough public relations tools, tips, strategies or ideas in their toolbox. After all, for the most part, publicity is free, valuable and yours for the taking, especially when you know how to get it.

Start a Great Public Relations Ideas Folder

One of the main reasons that most home business owners do not actively seek free publicity and media exposure for their businesses is a lack of great publicity ideas. What makes information news and not merely a promotional plug for your business that sounds like an advertisement? One of the easiest ways to figure this out is to profit from the great publicity and news-making ideas of others. Start collecting public relations ideas. Every time you see, hear or read a great publicity idea, write it down in detail or clip it out and put it into your PR ideas folder or box. Take a few moments each week to go through your collection for ideas you think would work to secure media exposure for your business. Encourage staff and friends to collect great ideas for your folder or box.

Media Advisory

A media advisory differs a little from other forms of contacting the media discussed in this chapter. Media advisories or alerts are prepared and sent to the media outlining an event that will be taking place. In other words, a media advisory is very much like an invitation that spells out the details of the event you believe should be covered by the media in print, on air or as a good photo opportunity. The details in the media advisory should include:

- *What.* The type of event—a special promotion, a charity event, a publicity stunt, etc.
- *Where.* The location of the event and directions, including parking facilities and a map if the location is difficult to find.
- *When.* The day, month, year and time of the event. If the event consists of various activities, include a schedule or itinerary.
- *Who.* Indicate the people expected to attend—customers, politicians, celebrities, company executives, contest winners or children getting their picture taken with Santa. Basically, for whom is the event being staged? Ultimately, that is what will spark the interest of the media.

- *Why.* Why is the event taking place—to raise money for charity, draw a contest winner or present an award? More important, why do you think the media should attend? The event could be good for a human-interest story, a photo opportunity or something that benefits their audience and the community.
- *How.* Ways for the media to get further information about the event—telephone, appointment, website, press conference before the event, e-mail or a combination.

Media advisories can be mailed or e-mailed to the media you want to target. They can be printed on company letterhead or standard office paper. Send out your media advisory at least a week prior to the event. There is no reason why you cannot follow up with members of the media to check on whether they will be attending.

Speeches

Another great way to share your expertise with others is through giving speeches and hosting workshops. There are business associations, agencies, and clubs in every community throughout the United States and Canada. Most of them have one thing in common: They all have expert speakers come in to give presentations on business and business-related topics. Many also hold conferences and seminars that include speakers.

These business clubs provide opportunities for you. Contact them and offer to share your expertise. If you're a marketing consultant, offer to give a presentation on marketing or conduct an informational workshop. If you operate a copyediting service, offer to talk about the importance of great copy and the positive effects it can have on business sales letters and brochures. You are offering your expertise for free, but you are getting opportunities to generate business from people in attendance or from referrals.

Of course, you need to be a fairly good speaker to get up in front of a room of people and hold their attention. You need to prepare your presentation and have several key points to discuss. Don't try to wing it. Pace yourself, so that you cover all your main points within a reasonable timeframe. Typically, you will have a half hour or 40 minutes. If you have more time, you can invite questions. Be prepared with answers for the most obvious ones and try not to sound stumped on the more offbeat questions. If someone leads you off topic, try to find a way to bring all tangential questions back to the topic at hand.

Speaking in public takes practice. You need to be confident, likable and even entertaining up there, so that you don't put your audience into a trance. Appropriate humor sprinkled into your speech, in the form of an anecdote or humorous comment, can help you keep your audience engaged. You can get some practice speaking in public by asking questions at other conferences and seminars and at meetings.

Connect with your audience by looking at the people and not at your notes or a PowerPoint screen. Don't look at your watch; if you appear bored, they will also be bored.

There are many books and some websites with information on public speaking, such as *speaking-tips.com*, where you'll find many articles on the subject.

The key is to sound authoritative yet likable and engaging … and never let them see you sweat. You may want to take a class on public speaking to hone your skills.

If you are really good and word spreads, you can make money as a professional speaker. This is taking it to a much higher level, where you can generate some pretty good additional income. If you feel you are ready to speak professionally, make a CD of a speaking engagement and seek out speakers' bureaus. They are highly critical and don't take on many clients to represent, so make sure you are very good.

Talk Radio

Talk radio represents a potential publicity windfall for savvy home business owners who take the time to develop a strategy for being featured on talk radio programs locally and nationally. Start by researching the radio show and its audience; nothing will scare off a producer faster than if you present ideas for topics that are not even close to being relevant to the station or the program's format, style and target audience. Next, develop a story idea, something that would interest the producer and the audience. If you can tie it into current world, national or local events, all the better.

Once you have developed your idea, put it on paper in the form of a pitch letter, which is basically a professional business letter that tells about your story and why you should be invited to discuss the topic on air. Along with your pitch letter, include a background sheet that clearly spells out your qualifications and expertise on the topic. Back this up with facts or statistics and perhaps even a customer testimonial or describe special work you have done for a recognized person or business. Of course, if you have written books or articles, taught classes or courses or done anything else in the topic area, let the producer know about it in your bio sheet. List anything that would constitute credentials.

Send your pitch letter or set up an appointment to meet with the producer in person. If you are an experienced public speaker and carry yourself well, I strongly suggest pitching in person. Producers like to know that they will be booking an exciting, knowledgeable and engaging guest. Additionally, you might try to develop an overall angle or concept that could secure subsequent appearances. However, you should do this after your first appearance or two, so that you've already shown what you can offer.

You can visit *radio-locator.com*, an online directory with links to more than 10,000 radio stations, indexed by format and geographic location in the United States and Canada (and the world), to find talk radio stations and then specific programs.

TV

Just like radio, TV talk shows use experts as guests. The difference, however, is that television is more difficult to do successfully. Sure, the pros make it look easy. However, it may be advisable to take some media training classes at a local college or from a media trainer in your area before venturing onto TV. If you think you can manage it on your own, a few here are a few things to remember.

- Sit up straight. Slouching is a sign of insecurity and does not instill confidence.
- Wear solid colors that will not "bleed" or glare.
- Avoid shiny jewelry that can glare.
- Keep your hands still, at your side, on your lap or on the desk if there is one. Hand gestures or fidgeting can be distracting.
- Most stations will have someone do your makeup. Let them do it, even if it is just a little touch-up. Also, let them know if you are allergic to anything. Sneezing attacks on camera are not good for business.
- Project when you speak. Do not rush through your sentences. Speaking in an engaging manner at a normal pace will suffice. Practice.
- Look at the host and be responsive. Avoid talking at the same time by not interrupting.
- Smile as appropriate throughout your interview.

- Bring samples of what you do, what you make or what you sell.
- If you are asked to give a demonstration of what you make, bring a finished product or other evidence of the results, since you may not have enough time to demonstrate, for example, how you cook and cater a meal for 40 from your home kitchen. Also, explain clearly. Remember KISS: Keep It Simple, Stupid.

Press Conference

A press conference is simply inviting reporters, journalists, editors and broadcasters to gather so that you can release special news, make an important announcement, answer questions, and hand out related print materials to media personnel as a group, rather than contacting each individually. Few home business owners will ever have the type of groundbreaking news required to draw major media players to a press conference. But almost all home business owners can create or generate news that is interesting enough to draw secondary media sources. These secondary media sources can include school newspapers, business associations, community TV and radio stations, special interest groups that publish magazines or journals (in print or electronically) and local politicians. Sometimes media coverage can go beyond being featured in traditional big media and include word-of-mouth coverage or print coverage in smaller publications.

If you plan on doing a press conference, the following ideas can help ensure that your press conference is successful:

- Do not host the press conference at your home office. Find a suitable location, like a small banquet room, the Chamber of Commerce or a supplier's office or warehouse. You will need chairs, a PA system and

basic refreshments like water, coffee and a snack tray.
- Plan your conference for a convenient time when media people are more likely to be able to attend. 10:00 p.m. will draw few, if any, but 10 a.m. will definitely attract the interest of more than a few.
- Always think "photo opportunity" from the media's perspective when arranging the location for the conference. Make sure that products, logo, business name and anything else that can identify your business or products will be included in photographs or film footage.
- Don't give long speeches. If appropriate, include demonstrations. Showing a video may be more practical than doing it live. Try to have on hand a credible expert who can answer questions and back up any claims that you may make about a product, a service or featured information.
- Create a media kit that you can hand out at the conference. Consider handing out sample products, photographs and promotional materials. Basically, do anything you believe will help to present your message and product or service most appropriately.

What Do You Have to Offer?

Every homebased business owner has expertise or valuable information that he or she can offer to the media in exchange for free publicity. For example, consider these careers:

- *Travel agent.* Contact the local TV station and go on air once a week or even daily. Talk about travel information, tips, destinations and the best travel deals of the day.
- *Financial planner.* Write a weekly column for the local newspaper, providing information and advice on investing, planning for retire-

ment and college education funds. Include information about your business—at least the name and contact information.

- *Fix-it services.* Be a guest expert on local talk radio to answer home repair questions from listeners who call.

The key to securing media exposure is to develop a news or story angle that will appeal to a large segment of the media's target audience. The media love this stuff because it's cheap to produce and feature, it appeals to their target audiences, and they need good news, information and activities to fill the airwaves and publications.

Expert Postcards

Creating expert postcards is a clever way for media-savvy business owners and professionals to become known as experts in their fields or industries among members of the local and even national media. Expert postcards are large versions of business cards and state all of your qualifications, training, special permits, and anything else that can substantiate your credentials as an expert for media personnel. Expert postcards should be professionally printed in high-gloss color like regular postcards. You may even want to put your photograph or a photograph relevant to your business, industry, product, or service on the front and your information on the back. Expert postcards can be sent to members of the media along with a brief introduction letter asking them to file your expert postcard for future reference and stating that, whenever they need someone in your field of expertise, you welcome any and all questions, interviews and inquiries. Update your expert postcard annually and send the new version to all of your media contacts.

Photo Opportunities

Often when thinking about how to secure public-

ity, it is very easy to be so focused on creating a news story or angle as to overlook the obvious—creating a photo opportunity instead. Print and television media love a good photo opportunity, and it is often much easier to create a great photo opportunity than a good news story.

There are two ways to contact the media about your photo opportunity. You can send a press release or a media advisory. Call or meet in person to pitch the photo opportunity and explain why you think it's worthy. You also can take the photograph yourself and send it to newspapers and magazines, along with a paragraph or two of explaining the situation. The photo opportunity and accompanying story must be something that will appeal to a large segment of the media's target audience, of course. Great photo opportunities can be created around:

- Contests and prize awards
- Community and charity events
- Business grand opening ceremonies
- Company achievements
- Winning industry, business or community awards
- Team sponsorships, especially sports teams that win a big game or a major tournament
- Holiday events such as Christmas decorations, Santa visits or Easter egg hunts

E-Public Relations Page

Design a public relations page for your website. Your PR page should be listed in your navigation bar and linked from the home page. It should include current and past press releases and a downloadable full media kit in PDF format. Also include the latest news about your business, key personnel, and detailed information about your products and services. Provide information about the unique benefits and competitive advantages associated with these products and services.

Update your PR web page regularly. When you send out press releases and media kits, mention that you have a PR page on your website.

Web Columns and Blogs

Web sites are always in need of content and, in some cases, columnists. What better way to promote yourself as an expert and get publicity for your business than by writing for the web?

Find topics of interest to you that you feel would also interest your target customers. Contact the editors of sites that you feel could benefit from your content. Pitch them ideas and send some sample stories to see if they are interested. Keep the stories brief, to the point and informative. Remember: The editors want to appeal to their readers.

You are not advertising your business, but writing about a related topic. For example a homebased auto detailer might write about how to keep a car looking good in the winter, providing a few expert tips. At the end of the article it will say "By Joe Smith, owner of Detailing Works" and give some contact information, including the URL for the Detailing Works website. You can also exchange web links with the site for which you are writing.

In addition, you might consider starting a blog. Essentially, blogs are like online journals in which someone writes about topics of interest. You can promote your blog on your website and even link to other sites. The key to a successful blog is not to be too self-indulgent—write about things of interest to your readers, update often, and be informative, entertaining, enlightening and engaging in your writing. Rambling or complaining wears thin very quickly.

There are websites that tap into bloggers. For example, on the Industry Centers of *AllBusiness. com* you'll find regular blogs on industries (e.g., construction, restaurant, retail trade, medical practices, manufacturing) and other business topics.

Reading these can give you an idea of how you write a blog.

Letters to the Editor

Writing letters to the editor is another simple method for home business owners to secure exposure. Keep in mind that your letter cannot be an outright advertisement for your business, so perhaps you can tie your letter into a local hot topic or position yourself as an expert on a particular subject. A home alarm installer might write a letter to the editor on the topic of break-ins and how not to become a victim. The letter should be signed and give the business name and telephone number. Published letters can provide you with free advertising. Sometimes a letter will be the focus of letters from other readers. In fact, your letter will stand a better chance of getting published if it is related to a recent article or letter featured in the publication.

Editorial Calendars

Media people use editorial calendars for planning, usually a year in advance. For instance, a newspaper might plan a 10-page feature section to run in October on pre-winter car maintenance information and feature sections for April on camping and other outdoor recreational activities. Media calendars give you the opportunity to fashion your news and publicity efforts around upcoming media events and features. For instance, if you operate a homebased career consulting service, you could create a news angle around finding the right career to match your personality type and submit it to media outlets that are creating a features section on career planning and searches.

Invent an Event

One of the best ways for small business owners to secure positive publicity is by creating a special annual event. The event could be tied into charity, such as a 10K run every August to support the American Cancer Society or a just-for-fun event, such as a restaurant hosting an annual hotdog-eating contest. The key idea behind inventing an event is, of course, to name it after your business or your products or services, such as "Joe's Restaurant Annual Hotdog-Eating Contest." Some home business owners take advantage of working from home to stage a backyard cookout for their regular customers. Others look to draw new business by holding a street fair (with the required permits from the municipality or county and the OK of the local neighborhood association). The festivities can include activities for the kids, food, music and demonstrations of your products or services.

Public Opinion Polls

Public relations specialists have long relied on public opinion polls and surveys to secure media exposure for their clients. You can do likewise for your business.

If there is one thing that media love to deliver to their readers, listeners and viewers, it's the results of public opinion polls and surveys. The media and the public have a love affair with statistics and numbers, mainstream or way out there. It doesn't matter, just as long as there are numbers. This is a fantastic opportunity for home business owners to develop and conduct their own public opinion polls and surveys and then release the results to the media. For example, a homebased income tax accountant could poll 500 taxpayers to find out their biggest pet peeve about taxes, tabulate the responses, and release the results to the media in January, as the income tax return season is beginning.

Breaking Records

Attempting to break a world record is an interest-

ing and fun way to promote your business and perhaps get valuable media exposure in the process. Go through the *Guinness Book of Records* to determine if there is a record that is suitable to break. If there is not a record that you feel comfortable trying to break, start inquiring locally to find out if any residents in the community are attempting to set a world record in the near future. If so, offer to be the "official sponsor" for that person or group of people. World record attempts attract lots of media attention and exposure, so this can be a good strategy, no matter how odd it may seem at first. Even if the attempt fails, the media exposure, lingering goodwill, and word-of-mouth advertising can be very beneficial for your business. Before sponsoring any record-breaking attempt, make sure that your liability insurance will cover you in case of unfortunate circumstances or that the party attempting the record is covered and signs a waiver releasing you from any liability.

GETTING STARTED WITH NETWORKING

Networking is one of the best and easiest ways to form long-term and profitable business relationships with like-minded businesspeople and new prospects who can be turned into customers. Networking gives you the power to build one-to-one relationships that few other methods of marketing or advertising can match.

Most successful small business owners understand the power of networking and make an effort to include networking activities into their schedules. In fact, they create a networking plan so they know who can have the biggest and most positive impact on their business and build business relationships with those individuals. There is no question that networking works and will take you a long way toward your marketing and business objectives.

Start by Setting Objectives

As with any business or marketing activity, you will get the most out of networking if you know why you are doing it and what you want to achieve. Your networking objectives will vary depending on your needs, but common networking objectives and goals include:

- Generating new sales leads
- Selling products and services
- Making new business contacts and form new business alliances
- Introducing new products or services
- Finding new suppliers, vendors or employees
- Conducting business and marketing research
- Branding your business and building a positive image within the community
- Becoming known as an expert in your industry or field
- Seeking new business and joint venture opportunities
- Keeping informed about current issues facing your business, industry and community

Business Card Networking

Business cards are an inexpensive and a very powerful networking tool when used correctly. If you are selling products, you should get into the habit of handing out 10 business cards a day, since you never know where new customers will come from. Tack a few business cards onto every community bulletin board in your community. Arrange with other businesses to leave a plastic cardholder with a supply of your business cards in their reception areas. Of course, don't forget to leave a business card behind every time you go to restaurants, gas stations, dry cleaners, grocery markets or movie theaters. And most important, every time you hand out a business card, let the person know that you are always seeking and appreciating new business.

If, however, you are providing a specialized service, you may not want to hand out business cards to everyone in sight, because you can't take the time to answer an endless stream of callers who cannot use your service.

Become a Great Conversationalist

The ability to converse effectively with others is important in networking. Poor conversationalists tend to interrupt or argue when they disagree, talk when they should be listening, and offer lots of opinions without being asked. On the other hand, great conversationalists listen well, take great interest in what other people have to say, and frequently address others by name. Most important, enter into conversations knowing what they would like to say and learn, but without preconceptions or judgments about the other person. Great conversationalists know that you control the conversation by asking questions and carefully listening to what people are really saying. Talking is not controlling. The best conversationalist is not the person who talks the most. Listening helps you remain in control because you are able to guide others toward revealing the information that you would like to know. You should take mental notes and then, after the conversation ends, write them down in your networking notepad.

Community Networking

People like to do business with people they know and like. They also like to refer other people to businesses run by people they know and like. In terms of building a positive business image and gaining loyal customers, no marketing effort can match getting involved with the community that supports your business and success. Get out and shake hands, smile and pitch in and help out for a good cause. Be genuine in your efforts: Get involved because you want to help out your community, not because you want to promote your business. Don't worry about the upside, because over time your business will benefit. Best of all, the people in the community who benefit from your involvement will promote your business for you.

Expand Your Networking Reach

Build friendships and alliances with people outside your ethnic, social, economic and cultural background. Develop a wide net of valuable relationships to broaden your networking circle and increase your opportunities for referrals and word-of-mouth marketing. At some point, staying within your current networking circle will produce diminishing returns. You will be able to make better use of networking time by enlarging your circle to include new people and places. You might join a new club or association—business, social, sports, hobbies or just about anything. Getting involved with a local charity is also a good option. Basically, find ways to make new contacts in new places so that you can broaden your marketing reach through new networking activities.

Network Online

Take advantage of the internet by going online and networking for new customers and business contacts. Join online discussion groups, post messages in chat rooms, and join online communities with people who share similar interests or fit your target profile for your products or services.

Networking via the internet can be a great way to find new prospects and customers and to build valuable business relationships. But be aware it will take time to establish a network and many of the people you meet will also be networking. So expect to hand out referrals and advice to others when they ask you to do so. The following are a few popular online business networking associations and their websites.

- The Virtual Handshake, *onlinebusinessnetworking.com*
- NetParty, *netparty.com*
- Networking for Professionals, *networkingforprofessionals.com*

Of course, you can always find discussion boards and chat groups on your own.

One thing to keep in mind: Online, people are not always who they seem to be. Therefore, be very careful before giving out any personal contact information.

Create a Contact List and Follow-Up System

Fully capitalize on business cards and personal information you collect while networking by developing a contact list so you can stay in touch with your new prospects by sending them your newsletter, a special offer through the mail or your monthly e-zine if you publish one. You can build your contact list using Word or Excel or using customer and prospect management software, such as Maximizer, *maximizer.com*.

One of the most valuable mailing and contact lists you can use for marketing purposes is the one you have created, a compilation of the names of people with whom you have personally been in contact. This *house list* must be considered as one of your most valuable business assets. The first time you mail to a new prospect, be sure to remind him or her where you met. Say it was a pleasure to meet them and you enjoyed the conversation you shared. Remember that effective networking is not meeting someone today and then calling 10 years later to see how things are going. Effective networking is a three-part strategy: make contact, follow up with the person almost immediately, and stay in contact with your new business alliance or customer for the long term. Update your lists periodically, since people move around a lot.

RESOURCES
Associations

Canadian Public Relations Society
4195 Dundas Street West, Suite 346
Toronto M8X 1X4
(416) 239-7034
cprs.ca

Network Professional Association
1401 Hermes Lane
San Diego, CA 92154
(888) NPA-NPA0 (672-6720)
npanet.org

Public Relations Society of America
33 Maiden Lane, 11th Floor
New York, NY 10038-5150
(212) 460-1400
prsa.org

SOHO America (Small Office Home Office)
P.O. Box 941
Hurst, TX 76053-0941
(800) 495-SOHO (7646)
soho.org

Small Office Home Office Business Group (SOHO)
P.O. Box 49266
Suite 1, 1680 Lloyd Avenue
North Vancouver, BC V7P 2N6
(604) 929-8250, (800) 290-SOHO (7646)
soho.ca

Suggested Reading

Aronson, Merry, Don Spetner, and Carol Ames. *The Public Relations Writer's Handbook: The Digital Age.* 2nd edition. San Francisco, CA: Jossey-Bass, 2007.

Baber, Anne, and Lynne Waymon. *Make Your Contacts Count: Networking Know-How for Business and Career Success.* 2nd edition. New York, NY: AMACOM, 2007.

MacInnis, J. Lyman. *The Elements of Great Public Speaking: How to Be Calm, Confident, and Compelling.* Berkeley, CA: Ten Speed Press, 2006.

Mackay, Harvey. *Dig Your Well Before You're Thirsty: The Only Networking Book You'll Ever Need.* New York: Currency/Doubleday, 1999.

Mintzer, Richard. *Public Speaking for Wimps: Staying Cool When Stage Fright Strikes.* New York: Sterling Publishing, 2005.

Pinskey, Raleigh. *101 Ways to Promote Yourself.* New York, NY: Avon Books (HarperCollins), 1999.

Scott, David Meerman. *The New Rules of Marketing and PR: How to Use News Releases, Blogs, Podcasting, Viral Marketing and Online Media to Reach Your Buyers Directly.* Hoboken, NJ: John Wiley & Sons, 2007.

Stephenson, James, with Courtney Thurman. *Entrepreneur Magazine's Ultimate Small Business Marketing Guide: 1,500 Great Marketing Tricks That Will Drive Your Business Through the Roof!* 2nd edition. Irvine, CA: Entrepreneur Press, 2007.

Yudkin, Marcia. *6 Steps to Free Publicity.* Revised edition. Franklin Lakes, NJ: Career Press, 2003.

Websites

24-7 Press Release: Press release distribution service with the small to midsized business in mind. *24-7pressrelease.com*

BNI: Billed as the world's largest referral organization, with more than 2,600 chapters worldwide and thousands of members. *bni.com*

Canadian Welcome Wagon Association: Community newcomer programs. *welcomewagon.ca*

Comstock Images: Source of stock photo images. *comstock.com*

Council of Public Relations Firms: Free online directory service listing public relations firms and consultants. *prfirms.org*

InternetNewsBureau.com: Subscription-based online press release distribution service. *internetnewsbureau.com*

NewsLink: Free online media directory service providing contact information for print and broadcast media companies, indexed geographically. *newslink.org*

OnlinePressReleases.com: Custom software for building a media database and creating and distributing press releases via e-mail. *onlinepressreleases.com*

MediaFinder: Publishers of print and electronic CD-ROM media directories covering magazines, newsletters, journals and newspapers and a subscription-based online media directory service. *mediafinder.com*

PRWeb: Free online press release distribution service. *prweb.com*

Welcome Wagon Association (United States): Community newcomer programs. *welcomewagon.com*

Presskits: Company featuring original press kit folders designed to meet the needs of the individual business. *presskits.com*

CHAPTER 15

Sales

I N THIS CHAPTER YOU WILL DISCOVER MANY advanced selling techniques that top business and sales professionals use to find more prospects, sell more goods and services and win more customers for life. Many of these will not apply to homebased business owners who will be selling through a website and not making major in-person sales presentations and/or who will be selling low-cost items. However, there are important general concepts throughout that apply to all business owners, such as prospecting, closing, negotiating and getting referrals.

Here are the selling skills featured in this chapter:

- Preparation
- Sales communications
- Prospecting
- Qualifying
- Presentations
- Trial closing
- Overcoming objections
- Identifying buying signals
- Closing
- Negotiations
- Referrals
- Follow-up

Don't feel overwhelmed or intimidated by these selling skills. After all, the vast majority of those who start home businesses are not professional salespeople nor do they have to be to succeed. But you must understand that it is sales that drive the growth of your business and help you generate your income.

Of course, there are different ways of looking at sales and approaches to selling. A high-end consultant, making thousands of dollars from a few key clients, will not have a "sell to anyone and everyone you meet on the street" attitude like a late-night "real estate at no money down" hawker. Likewise, some salespeople will do very well selling with integrity and concern for the environment, while others will do anything and everything to make a sale, whether it is ethical or not. The point is that you and only you can define the approach you wish to take as a salesperson and this will be influenced in part by the products or services you sell and in part by your integrity.

It is not the end of the world if you are not a master of the essential selling skills. What is important is that you are aware of the basic selling skills and that you recognize the importance of discovering your own sales strengths and weaknesses. Through education and practice, you can improve your selling skills.

PREPARE TO SELL

Preparation is the starting point for all selling, much like a family vacation. In sales, there is knowledge you need to acquire to get from prospecting to closing to building lifetime business relationships with customers. You need to know what you are selling, to whom you are selling it, who else is selling it or something similar, and what will help you in the selling and closing process. Preparation can be divided into four main categories: products or services, customers, competitors and sales tools.

1. *Products or services.* You have to know what you are selling inside out and upside down. Knowledge about your products or services can be acquired from research, specialized training, suppliers, information in print or on the internet, feedback from customers and hands-on experience. The better you know your products or services, the more you will be able to identify potential customers and sell them what they need. Product and service knowledge must also extend to your business and how products and services are delivered and guaranteed.
2. *Customers.* You must know who needs what you are selling, where those people are located, how much they buy and how often they buy.

You must also know things about those people, such as the clubs they belong to, the newspapers they read and the cars they drive. Customer knowledge also includes how prospects and customers view or rate your goods and services and the level of service your business provides in delivery and follow-up. Perhaps more important, sales preparation means you know the answers to the questions your prospects and customers have before they ask them. More information about customer profiling and customer service can be found in the research, planning and customer service sections of this book.

3. *Competitors.* Sales preparation means that you know your competitors thoroughly—how long they have been in business, their managers and key employees, what people like and dislike about their businesses, their prices, their guarantees and the level of their customer service as compared with yours and how they promote their business, gain customers and build long-term relationships with their customers. Basically, you need to know how your business stacks up against direct and indirect competitors, today, tomorrow and in the future. More information about identifying and conquering competitors can be found in the competition section of this book.
4. *Sales tools.* The final aspect of sales preparation is to be ready to use great sales tools to grab your prospects' attention, create interest and desire and motivate them to buy. Sales tools include product or service literature, product samples, customer testimonials, training and knowledge about your products, services, customers and competitors. Presentation systems are all important to the sales process. Your sales tools must be in good condition, plentiful and unique to your particular business.

SALES COMMUNICATIONS

Sales communications are any and all contact you have with prospects and clients, regardless of the method—telephone, letter, personal visit, e-mail or fax. The importance of communication as an essential selling skill cannot be overstated. It is the communication between you and prospects that ultimately determines your success. If you cannot effectively communicate with prospects and customers, regardless of contact method, you will not close sales. It is that simple. Below you will find helpful advice to enable you to communicate more effectively in your selling endeavors.

Mastering the Art of Listening

Effective listening is one of the most important skills to learn, master and apply. Being able to understand what prospects and customers are telling you, so that you can meet their expectations and needs, is the cornerstone for all selling. It is how you learn the most and become able to close more sales because of what you have learned. You can ask the greatest qualifying questions in the world, but unless you carefully listen to what prospects and customers are telling you, your qualifying questions will be of no value. To be an effective listener, you must be prepared to shut up. Stop talking and start listening. Many salespeople have a hard time doing this. They mistakenly believe that selling means bombarding the listener with information. This isn't really selling, but badgering, which is not usually very effective. To listen effectively, you need to get rid of any distractions; try to minimize interruptions. Give people your full and undivided attention and politely ask that they do the same. When you set up sales meetings and presentations, ask if you can be located where you will not be interrupted. Here are a few more helpful hints:

- Never finish others' thoughts or sentences during a conversation. Be patient and allow them to articulate fully.

- Avoid being argumentative, even if you disagree. If you must show exaggerated emotions, make them positive ones—excitement, appreciation or happiness. As the wise old saying goes, "It is impossible to win an argument with a prospect or customer, even when you know you are right and they are wrong."

- Be empathetic. Pay attention to what other people are telling you. Look at the situation from their point of view and never assume that any concern they have is small. People don't mention concerns or objections unless they consider them important.

- Ask questions to completely flush out all their needs, motivations and objections. The more clearly you can get your prospects or customers to let you know what they want, the better positioned you will be to help.

- Make mental notes, starting with their name and continuing with what they are telling you. Since we process information more successfully through repetition, you can even repeat key words and phrases to yourself, which should help you remember them.

Creating Effective Sales Letters

How do you get prospects to buy, customers to buy more frequently and close a whole lot more sales? One way is to create powerful sales letters aimed at grabbing attention, demanding action and bolstering sales.

- Develop a central sales theme that is focused on your prospects' needs, desires, benefits, hopes and dreams. Focus on emotional appeal when targeting consumers and on logistical appeal when targeting business owners and managers. Before you send the letter, know the answer to the question that every prospect asks before making a purchase: What is in it for me? The answer should be the central theme of the letter.

- Address the recipient by name. Single out the prospect as an individual; make him or her important, special. Make the prospect your second-highest priority. The first is the main benefit he or she will receive by taking the desired action. Of course, the two should go hand in hand, as in "Helen, I guarantee that you will save $2,349 annually by using recycled ink!"

- Grab attention right away with a bold headline at the top of your letter that solves a problem, creates a fantastic opportunity, states a special limited offer, expresses controversial or provocative ideas or highlights an important and informative statistic about the prospect's business, industry or target market. Increase the impact of your headline by including the prospect's name whenever possible and using subheads throughout the letter to introduce other interesting information you know will benefit the prospect. Subheads work incredibly well at keeping the skimmers interested and involved in your letter.

- Keep the content of the sales letter relevant to the topic or purpose, particularly when you discuss the action you want your prospect to take. Be brief, to the point and perfectly clear. If content is not 100-percent relevant to your objective, your prospect and your main message, get rid of it. It is a waste of valuable selling space.

- Always write to sell, even if the message or theme is not selling. The subtext should be leading the reader on a path to the close. Every contact you make with your prospect—be it a letter, a telephone call or a personal appointment—should take you and your prospect one step closer to making the sale. Handing out information is useless unless it helps you reach your ultimate marketing objective, which is always to sell.

- Based on the letter you have drafted, ask, "Would I buy?" If your answer is yes, list the reasons. What is the appeal? What is the advantage? What is the motivation? What is the urgency to buy? If your answer is no, list the reasons why not. Figure out what's missing.

- Use action-oriented power words and powerful sales phrases, such as "free samples," "call now," "make an appointment," and "guaranteed." Action words and phrases get the prospect instantly involved in the message of the letter and make him or her want to learn more.

- If your letter is more than one page long, do not end a sentence on the bottom of the page or in the last paragraph. Instead, force the prospect to continue reading by starting an incentive or special offer at the bottom of the first page and completing it on the next. Use an additional benefit that your product or service provides as a way to keep the prospect involved in the letter. Basically, be it an incentive, guarantee or second big benefit, use something that is powerful and important enough to the prospect that he or she stays involved.

- Make sales letters visually appealing with bright color, graphics, and bold paragraph headings on impressive, professionally printed letterhead emblazoned with your business logo and unified marketing message. Also make sure that your color selection, font and logo are all consistent with the rest of your printed materials. People visually link consistent styles with a business when they are continually exposed to a unified corporate image. Your prospects and customers will begin to instantly identify your business just by the envelope, letterhead, logo and/or color scheme you use in your marketing and promotional activities.

- Make the letter easy to read and understand. Skip the technical jargon; never make prospects feel stupid by using language or terms they could not possibly understand. Nothing will turn them off faster. Check spelling, grammar and structure. If time allows, let the letter sit for a few days; then return to complete the editing. You will almost always find something else you want to include and something you want to delete.

- Always tell the prospects what you want them to do next: "Call me," "Stop by our trade show booth," "Order now," or "Log onto our website for more information." Always make sure you give them whatever they need to take the desired action—full contact information, an incentive coupon, a customer testimonial if you want them to contact happy customers, a self-addressed stamped envelope if you want them to respond by mail, your web URL or your toll-free order hotline. The easier you make it for people to do what you want them to do, the more people will do it.

- Include a postscript that reinforces the benefits and values of your main offer or the key elements and message of the letter. For example, "P.S. We have the best widgets in the industry. If you call now, I'll prove it by sending you 10 free samples by overnight courier and give you $100 credit toward your first order. But only if you call before the end of the week!"

Productive Cold Calling

Telephone cold calling can be a tough grind, but there are a few cold-calling techniques that are productive and secure more sales appointments and meetings. Of course, this is applicable only for businesses that set up sales appointments. For most home business owners who are selling items online or offering a service, cold calling has gone the way of eight-track tapes.

Start by knowing your objective. To set up a fact-finding or presentation appointment? To send promotional literature or samples? To introduce your company, products or services? To find out who are the decision makers within the organization? Plan what you are going to say and write it down in brief script format. Anticipate objections to your pitch, and be ready to answer and overcome those objections during the conversation.

When you call, start by identifying yourself, your company and your reason for calling. As soon as possible, state the main benefit of your product or service and how this relates to your prospect. Be very clear about this. Your prospect must benefit directly; if not, you will soon lose his or her interest. But give only enough information to get your prospect interested and involved in the conversation. There is power in mystery, so use mystery to reach your objective. Ask for an appointment in a way that it is assumed the prospect will agree, such as "Which is best for you, Thursday at 10:00 or Friday at 11:00?" With this type of assumptive question, the choice becomes when to meet; not meeting is no longer an option.

Leaving Messages That Get Returned

Leaving a voice-mail message is easy; getting people to return the call is an entirely different story. One of the best ways of leaving a voice-mail message that will get returned is to anticipate leaving a message. Knowing exactly what to say, why you are calling and why the person should call you back is one of the keys to getting your calls returned. If you are caught off guard and leave behind a broken string of mumbo jumbo, the person will not return your call. Here are a few more helpful tips:

- Speak clearly and slowly so that the person will understand exactly what you are saying without having to guess. Spell out any words that are difficult to pronounce.
- Use your voice effectively and with energy and enthusiasm, as if you have some earth-shaking information that he or she needs to know. Excitement and mystery combined will almost always get your call returned.
- Leave your main contact telephone number at least twice, near the beginning of your message and repeated at the end.
- State a best call-back time or a block of time; e.g., "I will be in the office Tuesday afternoon between noon and four in the afternoon and would appreciate if you would call me back then."
- State the main reason why you are calling. Your reason should be something that will benefit the person, so that he or she will be motivated to call you back right away. The benefit should be your biggest selling point, something the person could not possibly resist. Make it believable. There are too many "You may have just won the sweep-stakes" letters and phone calls for anyone with half a brain to take them seriously any-more. Get to the point and make it realistic, not something that sounds like the multi-tude of phony "get rich quick" schemes. People know you're not going to make them rich or provide some miracle cure. However, you can provide something they need: For example, "Feel healthier and more energetic with a full body massage from a professionally trained and skilled masseuse" is better than "We will change your life for-ever!"

Other good examples:

- "Make your carpets look brand new again with a state-of-the-art professional cleaning."
- "Offer your guests sumptuous dining at an affordable cost. Let Margo's Masterful Caterers cater your next party or event."
- "Want that showroom-fresh look on your cars? Bring in one car for a full detailing and we'll detail your second car for half the price."

HIGH-IMPACT PROSPECTING

Typically, three things define good prospects:

1. They need your product or service.
2. They have the ability to pay for it.
3. They have the authority to purchase it.

Identifying and initially qualifying a prospect is outlined in the next section of this chapter. This section is aimed at prospecting techniques and skills that can help overcome the common home business owner's complaint: "Business is always feast or famine. I have no business or I have more business than I can handle." Feast or famine can be eliminated entirely or at least regulated, through constant and consistent prospecting to keep your sales pipeline flowing regularly. Prospecting for new customers serves two main needs, depending on your situation.

If your business is just starting up, prospecting for customers most likely will dominate your ini-tial marketing efforts. You lack a customer base and, because your marketing budget is probably tight, you're likely to be making telephone calls, sending e-mails, and making personal visits to drum up new business.

If your business is established, there are many reasons for continuing to prospect for new busi-ness. Regardless of how busy your sales schedule is presently or how rosy your sales future looks, you always want to systematically prospect to ensure that your business pipeline remains full. It's important to keep looking to add new customers.

Whatever your business stage, prospecting remains the foundation for all selling. You must keep your level of potential customers steady at all times. With time, you get a sense of who your best customers are, the people who buy products or services from you frequently, always pay on time and in full, refer others to your business and rarely complain. Leading businesspeople take the time to identify their best customers and then set out to find other people like them. They identify common characteristics of their best customers and use this information to develop marketing and action plans aimed at finding similar people. They find out information such as the publications they read, radio and TV programs they like and other key facts on education, income, family and career. You can use this information to identify patterns, things your best customers have in common. Perhaps a high percentage of them subscribe to the same newspaper; then it would be wise to advertise your business in that newspaper. Or maybe a high percentage of them belong to particular community associations; logically, you would want to join these associations and network with their members. There is much wisdom to the old adage "Birds of a feather flock together." Identify the feathers your best customers have in common and you won't be far from discovering where the entire flock is located. More information about target customer demographics and profiling can be found in the research section of this book.

Prospect and Customer Management Database

There are numerous database management software programs available. However, your database is only as good as the information you enter and manage, so here are a few ideas for maintaining a good prospect and customer relationship management database.

- Create two rating systems: one for customers and one for prospects. Both should use a system such as A, B and C—A for your best customers and hottest prospects and C for your least frequent customers and coldest prospects. This saves time and money when it comes to sending out direct mail marketing materials, telemarketing to present new offers or following up.

- Update your database regularly, focusing on inputting information on new customers and prospects. Update files and delete outdated information as needed.

- Include only information that is helpful in terms of your objectives, information that helps you recognize your customers and prospects as individuals, such as birthdates, hobbies and family members. This data is especially important when developing presentations and proposals that will appeal to each individual based on needs and wants.

- Develop and maintain a system for entering and recalling information—by company name, by personal name, alphabetically or in order of importance. Although the type of information that you choose to capture and record about your customers will change depending on your marketing objectives, you should capture the bare minimum, which includes individual or company name, full address and contact information, buying history, job title or occupation, demographic information (including age, sex and level of education) and special requests.

Eight Prospecting Laws

The following eight laws have been developed to help you get the most benefit from the time you invest in prospecting.

1. *Set prospecting goals.* The first law of prospecting is to set goals. How many new contacts do you want to make each day, each week and each month? Setting numerical goals is the only logical way to ensure that you are constantly making new contacts.

2. *Get facts.* The second law of prospecting is to treat initial contact with new prospects strictly as a fact-finding mission. Most business owners spend far too much time trying to sell during the first contact, instead of carefully listening and asking well-crafted questions to identify what the prospect needs.

3. *Avoid preconceptions.* The third law of prospecting is to never prejudge a person's ability to buy and pay for a purchase until careful questions and answers have established what they need, when they need it, if they can make the buying decision and if they can pay for it. Until you've asked these questions and have received answers, consider every prospect equally, regardless of appearance, clothing, behavior, speech, race, religion, ethnicity, etc.

4. *Keep it simple.* The fourth law is that your product or service and how you market it must be clear and easy to understand and grasp in moments. Consequently, you must focus on clarity when developing your sales message to appeal to your target market. Make it plain English, easy to understand, and free of boring technical jargon that only works to confuse the vast majority of people.

5. *Make it beneficial.* The fifth law of prospecting is that what you sell has to benefit the person to whom you are trying to sell it. Living in balmy Vancouver, I have little use for a snowmobile, no matter how many features and how much horsepower. But a rain jacket would be very beneficial here on the "wet coast" of Canada. Appeal to your prospects by giving them what they need—help them fix a problem, make them rich, save them money or make them feel better. Selling is about matching what you have to sell with the people who need it.

6. *Provide value.* The sixth law of prospecting says that what you sell has to represent value to your prospect. Regardless of the price, prospects must be able to see (and therefore justify) a direct correlation between what you're offering, what it costs and what it will do for them. Products and services are worth only what people will pay for them. The more value (benefits) a person can derive from buying a product or service, the more likely he or she is to pay a premium and not object to the price.

7. *Never sell only what you like.* The seventh law of prospecting is that no one cares what products or services you like. You're not the one who will be using them and paying for them. If you sell based only on your likes, then you are not listening to what the prospect wants. Sell what your prospects need and like, even if you don't agree with their choices. If they're happy with their choices and are prepared to pay for them, get the contract signed, thank them for their support, ask for referrals, and tell them that you look forward to doing more business with them in the near future.

8. *Manage your prospecting time.* The eighth law of prospecting is to manage your time well to ensure maximum productivity. The better you manage your time, the more time you will be able to devote to prospecting for new business. Therefore, employ time management tactics such as these:

   - Set aside a block of time each day strictly for prospecting, creating new ways to promote your products or services, and finding unique ways to position what you sell in the marketplace.

- Prepare your daily to-do list the evening before. Make an effort to check every item off before you call it quits the following day.
- Develop a scheduling system and stick to it. Prospect the same time each day, when you are most likely to reach your target audience in some manner. Group your sales presentations and meetings to save time and stay in the same focused mindset.
- Carry around a folder of hot prospects so you can benefit from any unexpected down time by calling them or working on solutions to fix their product or service problems.
- Take notes. Inspirational ideas are lost if they are not written down in an easily retrievable format.
- Keep your prospecting goals and objectives written down and in front of you as a daily motivator.

Simple Lead-Generation Ideas and Techniques

One way to secure fresh sales leads is to develop a customer list and lead swap program with business owners and sales professionals in your area who represent noncompeting, but compatible, products and services. For example, if you sell home renovation products and installation services, swap your customer and prospect list with an appliance store owner. The businesses are not in competition, but share common characteristics that could benefit each. In this example, it's likely that customers and prospects for both businesses own a home and the lifecycle of many building products, such as bathroom fixtures, is approximately 20 years, the same as major appliances. Therefore, it's a safe assumption that someone having a washroom renovated would also need new appliances. Customer list and lead exchange programs are a very efficient way to prospect for

new business, because they greatly reduce the time you spend finding and qualifying new prospects.

Here are six more great lead-generation ideas.

1. *Stage contests.* Contests are a way to generate sales leads from the information you capture on the entry forms. Strike a deal with a local retailer to host the contest and install the ballot box at that location. Alternately, send out entry forms in the mail or insert the form as an advertisement in the newspaper and ask people to complete the forms and return them by mail. Use trade shows and other marketing events to host contests and collect sales leads from the forms. Make sure that you conform to local laws or regulations about running contests.

2. *Apply for a job.* Calling all consultants, freelancers and independent contractors! It is time to tap into the thousands of employment advertisements that appear in print newspapers and employment websites daily. Get started by creating a specialized resume and an introduction letter that explains the benefits of your service, including a few client success stories. Send your consulting service package to companies that are seeking to fill specialized positions in your area of consulting expertise. Attend job and career expos to make introductions and network with business owners and managers who could also benefit from hiring your service as opposed to hiring an employee. Just because a corporation, organization, or small business is advertising for an employee doesn't mean that they are not actually in need of the services of a highly skilled consultant. Maybe all it will take is for you to explain in depth how hiring your consulting service or bringing you in as a freelancer or contractor will be more beneficial and productive than hiring an employee. Remind them that they do not need to pay you the same benefits as a full-

time employee and that when you've completed the job you can move on.

3. *Give your service away for free.* If you strategically provide a service for free in the presence of potential paying customers, you can generate new customers. For example, if you operate a carpet cleaning service and offer to do the carpet in the lobby of the building, you can generate attention from tenants as they pass by and by putting door hangers on apartment doors or fliers under doors. Likewise, if you detail a car of the owner of a business in front of the building, then everyone coming and going will see the job you do and you can hand out coupons for 25 percent off to all passersby.

4. *Try life-cycle prospecting.* Life-cycle prospecting opportunities are abundant, but only if you take the time required to identify them. Every product has a definable life span, both in use and time. Here's an example. About 90 percent of all homes built in the last 60 years have been constructed in subdivision developments. A residential housing subdivision that is 15 years old represents a wealth of life-cycle prospecting opportunities because almost all building products and fixtures have a definable lifespan of 15 to 20 years. Consider the vast numbers of products used in the construction of these homes that are reaching the end of their useful life span. There are roofing, kitchen and bathroom fixtures, appliances, windows, fencing and the list goes on.

The greatest benefit of life-cycle prospecting is that most contacts you make in this way are already qualified to a certain degree. Because every product and even most services have a definable life cycle, the key to successful life cycle prospecting is knowing exactly the life span of your product or service and then planning strategies to capitalize. Life-cycle prospecting simply means seeking prospects with products or services that are nearing the end of their useful life span before these people contact you and your competitors for bids.

5. *Do demonstration prospecting.* For centuries, street performers have been using demonstrations as a successful way to prospect for new business. A juggling street performer sets up in a busy park and begins to juggle bowling balls (demonstration). Soon people start to take notice and crowd around to watch (prospects). Some people leave, while others stay to watch (qualifying). The performer continues to demonstrate juggling skills to an amazed audience (presentation). The juggler completes the presentation and takes a bow as people drop lose change into a box (closing). By doing no more than demonstrating a service (entertainment), the juggler has attracted prospects, qualified some, presented to a crowd and closed a few sales. It's a complete sales cycle, all in a matter of minutes. The point is that most products and services can be demonstrated in public—in more than the usual demonstration forums of trade shows and seminars. For instance, if you operated a martial arts training facility and took the class to a local park for a training session, it would not be long until a crowd gathered and began asking questions about your school. Many products have generated attention in this manner, such as Razor Scooters: the company offered kids a chance to to ride around and demonstrate the product. Local performers in a theater group may do song-and-dance numbers at a local mall to sell tickets. At restaurants and other locations, models may walk around in the latest fashions. The employees of a massage business may set up tables in the lobby of a busy office building or at a mall and give some free massages to demonstrate their skills.

These are all examples of showing or demonstrating products or services.

7. *Prospect through expertise.* Prospecting does not always mean searching for new customers. It can also mean developing prospecting strategies that have people seeking you out for your expertise. Society in general accepts the notion that published authors or speakers on specific topics and issues are mostly experts within their field. Therefore, it makes sense to capitalize on your expertise and persuade people to come to you. Get started with a newspaper column or a magazine article or actively seek out places where you can speak on topics related to your specialty. Becoming known as an expert not only distinguishes you from the competition; it also means that people will most likely seek your advice when they are trying to solve a problem or need advice or help in a decision, all of which can be turned into selling opportunities.

QUALIFYING PROSPECTS

Qualifying prospects in the sales cycle is the process of asking carefully crafted questions and using the responses to determine if prospects need, want and can afford what you are selling. The importance of qualifying cannot be overstated. The better qualified a prospect, the greater the chance of closing the sale.

Business owners often feel uncomfortable asking qualifying questions because they wrongly think they are being pushy, nosy or aggressive. Asking questions enables you to better help other people determine what they need. Doctors ask questions about symptoms so that they can make an informed diagnosis. A fitness trainer will ask about specific goals to develop an exercise program that will help the individual achieve those goals. It is the only way you will be able to determine if you can help a prospect and if he or she truly wants and can afford what you are selling.

Another aspect of qualifying often overlooked is that you can make one generalized assumption—seldom do people stray too far from what they already have, are comfortable with or understand. For instance, most people currently driving a family vehicle such as a minivan or station wagon will purchase a similar vehicle when it comes time to buy a new vehicle. People, in general, are creatures of habit, so consumers are transparent in terms of the products and services they purchase and use. Knowing this can help you in the qualifying process, because much of your work is already done if you take the time to ask people what they are currently using.

Are You Asking Open-Ended Questions?

Key to the success of effective prospecting is asking open-ended qualifying questions. A common example of a closed-ended question is a sales clerk asking a shopper, "Is there anything I can help you find?" This is a closed-ended question that will elicit a yes or a no. Even an open-ended question such as "What brought you into our store today?" is a vast improvement, because the shopper must then reveal information the clerk can use to determine if he or she can help the shopper.

By asking open-ended questions, you involve your prospect in the conversation and sales process. Try experimenting with various open-ended questions related to what you do or sell and keep a log detailing the success or failure rates of each question. This will enable you to build a repertory of open-ended questions you know will be effective more times than not. Here are a few examples of open-ended sales questions: "How did you hear about our company?" "Who else will be involved in this decision?" "What budget has been established for this purchase?"

Who Makes the Buying Decisions?

It's important to deal with the person making the buying decision. However, since many executives have others do the scouting and the shopping before they put their stamp of approval on a sale, you cannot dismiss those who come to you scouting for a good deal. While it is advantageous to deal with the decision maker, you could be dealing with the right-hand man or woman for Donald Trump or someone else who probably will not be calling you directly. Find out who is making the decision; if you cannot speak directly with that person, make sure you get the best possible information into his or her hands.

The best way to find out who makes the decisions is to simply ask your prospect questions such as "Who will be making the purchasing decision?" or "Will you be making the decision on your own or will there be other people involved in the purchasing decision?"

Do They Need It?

It is important to determine whether or not a prospect needs what you are selling. If he or she needs it, your job is that much easier. However, most products and services sold are not actual needs in the sense of food, shelter or clothing. Most people don't actually need sporting equipment, high-tech gadgets, party planners, designer jeans or most of what is sold. Therefore, it is up to you to make the prospect buy based on his or her desire or an emotional appeal. Few people need a sports car, a vacation home or a cruise to the Bahamas, yet many people sure want these luxuries. You cannot base sales solely on needs, but work on what people want.

There was a popular electronics chain of stores in New York City in the 1970s in which the salespeople would ask you what you needed shortly after you passed through the front doors. If you didn't have a quick response, they would not bother with you. The trick was to sell customers on the pleasure of owning new high-tech state-of-the-art systems. The salespeople, in looking for those customers in need, lost out on all of those customers who sat on the fence, since nobody really needs a new sound system. By the early 1980s, that electronics chain had filed for bankruptcy.

Here's the point. Most people don't know what they need or want. It is your job to ascertain what they could use and benefit from and show them the benefits of something new.

Can They Afford It?

Many small business owners feel extremely uncomfortable asking people questions about their personal or business financial situation. Of course, if you are selling low- to mid-priced items, this should not be a factor. You need not know someone's financial status to sell him or her a few books, a $99 software program or a dog-walking service. If, however, you are selling higher-end products or services, you will want to get an idea of what the prospect can afford. Therefore, you must get comfortable asking prospects about their ability to pay for what you are selling or their ability to secure credit. Ask your prospects if they have the money put aside to pay for the purchase, if they will be using credit cards or would like to arrange for financing, or if you can take the liberty of arranging financing for them. Second, you have to be realistic about your prospects' purchasing power and always be prepared with a less expensive option should finances become an obstacle to closing the sale. If you spend all your time focused on one product or service and suddenly money becomes an issue, you have little latitude. However, if you keep in mind that money could become an obstacle and have a plan in place, you are ready to save the sale and still do business with your prospect.

When Do They Want It?

When is your prospect in the market to buy what you are selling and how committed is he or she to this buying schedule—very committed, somewhat committed, or just tentative based on other factors that could influence the final buying decision? You can learn more in terms of timing by asking easy open-ended questions such as "How soon do you need the _____?" or "When will you be ready to have the product installed?" or "What is your time frame for completing this project?" or "When would you like to take delivery?" These are non-threatening questions.

The beauty of asking timeline questions early is that the answers give you a good indication how open the prospect might be to an early close in the sales cycle. If your prospect answers positively to your qualifying timeline question, then echo with a trial close question. So, for example, if the prospect asks, "Can I get this before the end of the week?" you would reply, "If I can arrange delivery before the end of the week are you prepared to make the purchase?"

What Other Obstacles Stand in the Way?

Effective qualifying means you are carefully listening and watching for other obstacles that can stand between you and making the sale. Other obstacles are usually the quiet deal killers, things that you overlooked during the initial qualifying process because you did not think to look for them or the prospect was not forthcoming with information about potential obstacles. These other obstacles could include things such as your prospect's health, his or her level of training or education to use your product or service or personal priorities. While a person might be genuinely interested in purchasing a new car, is the leaky roof at home that needs to be replaced the true priority, rather than the new car?

Whatever the obstacle, the trick is to listen carefully to what your prospect is telling you so that you will be able to identify potential obstacles. Sometimes they will be subtle; other times they will be obvious. Of course, if you think there might be a hidden obstacle, it is always best just to come out and ask.

WINNING PRESENTATIONS

Generally the objective of the sales presentation is to close the sale, but not always. Other objectives can include booking a second meeting, introducing a new or improved product or service, or conducting research to get valuable feedback.

The reason I mention this is that all presentations must be built on a clear objective. You must know what you want to accomplish and what your prospect is expecting to happen at the presentation. Nine times out of 10, of course, your objective is to sell. It is during the presentation stage of the sales cycle that you deliver to your prospect the full impact of your product or service and the benefits associated with owning it. Call it "delivery of the total package," including samples, colorful brochures, testimonials and demonstrations.

Home business owners have one disadvantage to overcome that businesspeople with an office or storefront do not—lack of personal contact presentation space. As a general rule, clients, prospects and sales representatives feel extremely uncomfortable traipsing through your home for a meeting unless they know you very well. Therefore, you'll want to meet at the client's office or boardroom. You might also meet in the offices of a local business association, such as the Chamber of Commerce, where members can often rent meeting rooms or office facilities. Depending on the product or service you are selling, you can meet in a convenient but quiet restaurant or, if there is potential for significant funding, in a rented space. The truly innovative entrepreneur can even take clients to unusual places for meetings—to the park, on a boat ride or even a drive through the country.

Key Presentation Points

While a lot goes into developing great sales presentations, at the core there are four key presentation fundamentals: (1) keeping your prospects' attention, (2) focusing on your prospects' needs and wants, (3) making your presentations memorable, and (4) leading your prospects to the action you want them to take.

Attention

Seldom will a piece of paper, such as a brochure, estimate or proposal, close the sale. Closing is left up to you and the interaction you establish and maintain with your prospects. For that reason, it's important that you keep your prospect's attention at all times during presentations. A good way to do this is not to distribute sales materials or a typed presentation at the beginning of the meeting. Hold printed sales materials back until the end of the presentation; distribute them to prospects after you have presented your information and conducted demonstrations. The focus of the sales presentation should be on persuading the prospect to buy through questions, answers and demonstrations. None of this can be achieved if your prospect is busy flipping through and concentrating on printed sales material. Your words and actions are lost. And worse, prospects form opinions and make decisions based on what is in print; unfortunately, all these printed words cannot show the best and biggest benefits of your product or service.

Focus

During the presentation, stay focused on your prospect's needs and on the results you want. Your entire presentation should be based on needs—how what you sell fills their needs, solves their

problems or, for business clients, creates new opportunities they need to compete or it increases productivity they need to be profitable. Common needs include the need to make more money, save more money, increase productivity, expand market share and improve their health. Also focus on results. Never assume your prospects saw, heard, read, or understood what you wanted them to during the presentation. Instead, restate the benefits of your product or service in terms of fulfilling their needs.

Action

Your presentation must end with some sort of action, preferably the action you want your prospect to take, such as buying. Therefore, always end your presentation by asking your prospect to take action. The action might be to buy, buy more, buy more frequently, set up a follow-up meeting or whatever you determine. The desired action should be directly related to the initial objective of the presentation. Remember: People are not mind readers. Unless you specifically tell them what you want them to do next, do not expect that they will automatically take action.

Customer Testimonials

Few consumers want to sail into uncharted waters alone. We all want to know that someone has gone before us and that everything worked out just fine. That's the benefit of customer testimonials; they prove that others have purchased your product or service and that everything has worked out just fine.

Share customer success stories with your prospects to show them that they are not alone. Use customer testimonials to remove buying anxiety, doubt and fear. Without question, client testimonials are one of the best sales and marketing tools for home business owners. And there are ways to maximize the positive impact that a testimonial can have on prospects.

- Customer testimonials should include the full name of the author, printed and signed. This carries much more clout than just a first name or an initial and a last name. Whenever possible, include a photograph of the person(s) giving the testimonial, because this will appeal to emotions. People love to hear and read about good things that happen to people who don't look so different from them, their family members and their friends.
- If you have a client who is well known in your community, ask that person to write a shining testimonial about your business. Celebrity testimonials can be used as a wonderful icebreaker, as most people feel especially at ease if the others who have gone before include a person they know and trust. The community celebrity could be the police or fire captain, school principal, city councilor, bank manager, minister or head of a local charity.
- Business client testimonials should include the name, the business name, and mailing address and the contact telephone number printed on their company letterhead, if possible. This makes the testimonial much more tangible and credible than a testimonial with a few words followed by an illegible signature.
- Ask the person providing the testimonial to list or give short quotes about the things he or she likes about your product or service and the benefits of doing business with you. Make sure you get permission to copy the testimonial and use it in other forms of marketing and advertising.

Supporting Documents

Much like client testimonials, you can use supporting documents and certificates to build confi-dence, credibility and trust with your prospects. These documents might include:

- Business and vendor licenses and permits
- Liability and special insurance coverage
- Training certificates and/or professional accreditation certificates
- Workers' compensation coverage
- Industry, association and Better Business Bureau memberships
- Business and customer service awards
- Publicity or media spotlights
- Product patents or intellectual property trademarks and copyrights
- Customer security and privacy policies

Supporting documents should be included in the presentation phase of the sales cycle and copies of appropriate documents should be given to your prospects and customers. Not only will you be building confidence and credibility with your prospects, you also be showing your commitment to your business. It is an icebreaker and a great way to separate your presentation from those of competitors.

TRIAL CLOSING THE SALE

What is trial closing and when should you use it? Trial closing means asking prospects for the sale early in the sales cycle or presentation.

There are two reasons for asking a trial close question early in the sales process. One, your prospect might be just as eager as you to move forward and close the deal, but you will never know unless you ask. Two, few people will take it upon themselves to offer you the sale unless they are asked to do so. Whether you are meeting prospects face to face, talking over the telephone or communicating through sales letters, you should always attempt at least one trial close early in the sales process. The following are a few trial-closing techniques you might find useful.

Trial Close by Assuming the Sale

The first rule of trial closing is to simply assume that every prospect with whom you come into contact will buy what you are selling. Act on this assumption by making statements like "I will have this shipped to you by the end of the week" or "I just need your signature on this agreement so we can start processing your order." If the response or action is favorable, then complete the paperwork, restate the benefits and value of your goods or service, thank the prospect for his or her business and move on to your next appointment. If your prospect raises objections, you will know exactly what obstacles stand in the way of closing the sale and can start overcoming them with the appropriate response and information.

Trial Close by Being Quiet

Always ask for the sale early, but then be quiet. Even if you feel you have more to say, resist the urge to speak. The goal of the quiet trial close is to place your prospect in the position of having to make a decision or at least respond to the trial-close question with an answer, objection or question. If you choose to talk after you ask for the sale, you negate the trial-closing question; your prospect is no longer bound to answer or respond to the question. The vast majority of people do not like to be placed on the hot seat, especially if all around them is uncomfortable silence. This can lead to a "Yes, let's proceed" just to escape the pressure. This technique should be used any time you ask a closing question.

Trial Close by Offering an Alternate Choice

As the name suggests, this technique is nothing more than giving your prospect more than one option in terms of the product or service you sell. By doing so and by asking a question like "So which desk would you prefer, the maple finish or the oak finish?" you pull the prospect into making a buying decision and selecting one of the options. Not buying is no longer an available option with the alternate-choice trial-closing question. Alternate-choice questions can also be used effectively to increase the quantity of an item you want your customer to buy. For instance, "Would you like one bookcase to go with your new maple desk or two matching maple bookcases so you can balance the look of your office?" Once again, this question pulls your customer into a buying decision. The question is no longer "Will you buy?" but rather "How many are you going to buy?"

Trial Close with Incentives

Offering incentives is also an excellent way to approach a trial-close situation: "Mr. Jones, I just wanted to let you know that for a limited time we are offering a 15 percent discount to any new customer who signs up for our monthly pool maintenance service. Would you like to take advantage of this valuable time-sensitive offer?" A percentage discount, free delivery, a two-for-one offer or a trip to Spain—incentives work well at speeding up the sales cycle, at creating buying excitement and urgency and, more important, for attempting a trial close early in the sales process.

OVERCOMING OBJECTIONS

When your prospects start raising objections or providing reasons why they shouldn't buy from you, don't give up. Instead, welcome and even encourage these objections. Prospects raise objections simply as a way of telling you they are interested in what you are selling. If they were not, they would tell you they are not interested, a flat refusal. When prospects raise objections, they are asking you to do two things. First, they have points (objections) that they do not fully understand about your product or service or the buying process. They need you to explain these points in greater detail before they can commit to buying. Second, they are giving you a signal for you to do your job and persuade them that buying is the right decision. If you are not prepared to answer and overcome objections, you will lose sales. Consequently, prior to sales meetings and presentations, you must anticipate objections and develop a four-step strategy to overcome these objections.

Step one. Never sidestep an objection. If you do, you will sidestep closing the sale. You must listen to, confirm, and answer every single objection that prospects raise. Often due to lack of confidence or experience, many home business owners sidestep objections by ignoring them or by quickly changing the topic or rushing to the next point in the presentation. Generally, this happens because they have not planned for objections and therefore cannot overcome them or they are not giving weight to the objection. Both are deadly, because prospects seldom forget about the objections they raise; they are there as a constant reminder of why they should not buy.

Step two. Listen to the objection. Never assume you know exactly what objections your prospect will raise. You must anticipate objections, but a prospect may raise an objection you have not anticipated. You must give your prospects the opportunity to voice their objections and you must be prepared to listen with an open mind. You must consider the validity of the objection to determine if it is a major or minor obstacle in the way of the sale and decide how to respond.

Step three. Confirm every objection so you fully understand what the prospect is saying and how it relates to what you are selling. Ask the prospect to restate the objection and relevant details or why he or she feels the objection is valid. Doing this gives you the opportunity to understand the objection from the prospect's perspective. It also gives you

extra time to consider how to respond and overcome the objection. And sometimes in restating the objection, the prospect will realize that he or she has misunderstood something and will answer the objection before you even have to respond, clarify or explain.

Step four. The last step in the objection process is to answer and, hopefully, overcome the objection by revealing additional information about your offering that will satisfy your prospect. Once you have answered his or her objections, make sure that the prospect is happy with your response by asking if he or she understands and agrees with your explanation.

Overcoming Price Objections

It should come as no surprise that most people will automatically respond to your offer or closing question with "The price is too high." More often than not, most people have not even considered if the price is too high. They just say that because it comes naturally for many of us. Perhaps the best way to deal with this response is simply to ask, "The price is too high in comparison with what?" This throws most people off balance, especially if they have not actually considered why the price is too high. Another strategy for overcoming price objections is to agree with your prospect that indeed your price is higher than what competitors charge and then explain why. Perhaps it is higher quality, a longer warranty, specialized training, or some other competitive advantage that justifies charging more. By justifying your price through valid reasons and explanations, you can actually increase your prospects' desire to buy. They better understand the value of your offering in relation to the price. Explain to your prospects they are not buying price or even a product or service; they are buying a solution, something that will benefit them immensely and help solve a problem, make them money, save them money or improve their health. When you can clearly demonstrate the benefits or results far outweigh the price, it will become less of an obstacle.

Overcoming No-Money Objections

When prospects tell you that they cannot afford to buy, ask them why. You cannot overcome the no-money objection unless you know all the details and the reasons for their decisions so that you can develop workable solutions that might otherwise go unnoticed. Clearly demonstrate the benefits of buying are so important to their particular situation that a no-money objection would not be wise. In other words, the cost of not buying far outweighs the cost of buying. In a business-to-business selling environment, the first way to overcome a no-money objection is to make sure that you are calling on business prospects and making proposals when they are planning their budgets for the forthcoming year, not when they are spending their budgets for the current year.

Overcoming Let-Me-Think-About-It Objections

When a prospect says he or she wants to think about whether or not to buy, suggest that you go over things again while the details are fresh in his or her mind. This works because going over the details of the product or service and the offer gives you another opportunity to open the lines of communication and persuade the prospect to buy.

Another way to overcome the let-me-think-about-it objection, especially if you feel you are at the end of the line with your prospect, is to offer an incentive for closing on the spot. Justify the incentive to your prospect as a way to save time for both parties by not having to meet later. However, be firm. Say in no uncertain terms your incentive—whether it is a discount, a better model at the same

price, an extended warranty or something else—is only valid right then and there and the prospect must make a decision to buy immediately to take advantage of it.

You can also try to overcome let-me-think-about-it by trying the Benjamin Franklin closing technique. List the advantages of a decision to buy in one column and the disadvantages in a second column. When prospects can see in black and white that the pros of buying far outweigh the cons, that is often all the persuasion they need to make a buying decision. If, however, you are going to use this closing technique to overcome the let-me-think-about-it objection, just make sure that the advantages really do outweigh the disadvantages. If not, you will lose any chance of closing the sale.

CLOSING THE SALE

Only 1 percent of your time spent selling is devoted to closing, yet success depends 100 percent on closing the sale. This fact perfectly illustrates the importance of closing; it is an essential selling skill. No matter how much closing may intimidate you, it is nothing more than the natural progression in the sales cycle. You prospect, you qualify, you present and you close. Therefore, if you have followed the logical steps in the sales cycle, asking for the sale should be nothing more than a formality.

Below are a few time-tested and proven closing techniques.

Summary Closing

The summary close is perhaps the most common and easiest closing technique to master. Carefully note the benefits and features that your prospect found the most valuable and useful during your initial contact and sales presentation. Then use these hot buttons to close the sale by summarizing them to your prospect at the end of the presentation. In doing so, you place positive emphasis on all the things your prospect finds beneficial about your product or service while conveniently leaving out any disadvantages. Constantly remind your prospect about these hot-button benefits throughout the presentation and get him or her to reconfirm that these are the most important and beneficial aspects.

Fear Closing

Fear is an extremely powerful closing tool—the fear of missed opportunity, fear of poor health, or fear of what other people think about us. Fear can represent many different things to many different people, yet this emotion is an influential component of the decision-making process for us all at one point or another. The fear close is obviously more productive for some than for others. It is difficult to make someone fear not buying a new lawnmower. But when a seasoned stockbroker uses this closing technique, watch the success rate soar.

Chip-Away Closing

You can gently lead prospects to make a buying decision by getting them to agree to small or minor points about your product or service during the sales presentation. What makes the chip-away close powerful is that you are subconsciously reducing buying risk. You are not placing your prospect in the situation of having to say yes to the entire deal all at the end or at any time during the presentation, but only leading him or her to agree to pieces along the way. These small pieces of the deal could include the color of the item or various product features. Try to get your prospect to agree to at least four or five minor points during the sales presentation. Then, prior to asking for the sale, restate the benefits of these minor points. Often you will find the prospect becomes accustomed to saying yes and along the way a trust relationship begins to form as you eliminate risk and doubt and show the

prospect that saying yes does not have to be difficult or cause dire consequences.

Convenience Closing

People will often buy based on no more than the overall convenience of the buying process. How many times have you chosen to buy at one shop instead of another because there was free parking, convenient shopping hours, or free delivery and setup? If you are like most people, the answer is probably often because you based your buying decisions on convenience. Consequently, as a home business owner, it is wise to make it as easy as possible for all prospects to say yes by making it convenient. For instance, if permits or licenses are required to buy what you are selling, secure them or help your prospects secure them. Meet with prospects at times and in locations that are convenient for them.

Suggestion Closing

Not all people are comfortable with making decisions. Often in a sales presentation this discomfort can cause your prospects to seem uninterested, when they may just be unsure and uncomfortable with the process and with making buying decisions. If your prospect seems uncomfortable, ask "Do you mind if I make a suggestion?" More times than not, you will see a look of relief. We have all made bad decisions and wished that at the time someone had helped us see the way to the right decision by making a suggestion.

Maximum-Benefits Close

With this closing technique, you go to great lengths to ensure that your prospect will get the maximum benefit by owning and using your product or service. Think of the maximum benefit as the ace that you pull from your sleeve precisely at the right time to wow the prospect and close the deal. For instance, a recreational vehicle dealer might include a driver training program with every new or used motor home sold and use this maximum benefit to close more sales. The driving training course would be a maximum benefit to buyers because it could save their lives in hazardous driving conditions. The driver safety course also ensures the buyers get the maximum benefit from their RV because knowing how to operate and maintain the RV properly means they will provide many years of safe travel enjoyment for the entire family. Creating your own maximum benefit can also be a great way to distinguish your business, products and services from your competitors'.

Last-One-In Close

This is a very simple closing strategy. The last-one-in close means getting a commitment from your prospects that they will not make a buying decision until they have spoken with you last. Believe it or not, this strategy can work. First, they don't know why you want to speak with them last. To offer a special offer or what? Mystery and suspense are great for keeping prospects involved and invested in the sales process. Second, if you have done all your homework and have established a trust relationship with your prospects, then to a certain degree they will feel obligated to talk with you one last time. Being the last one in enables you to play the devil's advocate in terms of competitors' bids and also gives you one last opportunity to persuade your prospects to buy from you.

NEGOTIATE LIKE A PRO

The ability to negotiate effectively is unquestionably a skill that every home business owner should strive to master. In business, negotiation skills are used daily. You negotiate with prospects and clients to sell your goods and service for a higher price. You negotiate with suppliers to receive a lower cost per unit or better payment terms. Or you negotiate with your bank to secure lines of operating capital or lower credit card merchant rates.

Keep in mind that in every negotiation there must be two winners, you and the person with whom you are negotiating. Never go into negotiations expecting to get everything you want while the other side gets nothing. If you do, expect to close fewer sales, be constantly searching for new suppliers, and face a revolving door with business alliances. In every successful negotiation, both sides must win for the relationship to be mutually beneficial. Generally this requires some compromise; without it, one side will feel cheated, which is no good for any long-term customer or business relationship. Win-win negotiations means that both sides benefit, that long-term relationships are established, and that multiple issues on each side are resolved at the table through fair and honest negotiations. Never try to negotiate with someone who is unwilling to find a win-win solution. If you do, the negotiating effort will be for nothing; in the future, that person will expect to get everything on his or her terms.

Be Prepared to Negotiate

The more information you have, the stronger your position becomes for getting what you want and at the terms and conditions you want. Information is the cornerstone of preparation. Find out as much as you can about your prospect's wants and needs and how these wants and needs are prioritized—by budget, by benefits, by ability to solve a problem or by schedule. Make sure you understand what your prospect is trying to achieve through negotiations; e.g., a better price, faster delivery, more features for free or a longer warranty. Be prepared with all the relevant documents and data; nothing will kill a negotiation faster than having to come back with one missing element at a later date. The act of negoti-ation serves no purpose unless you can take advantage of the exact moment you have success-fully negotiated to close. Otherwise, never be drawn into negotiating. Being prepared also means you are prepared mentally to negotiate—your mood is good, your confidence is high, and your rapport with your prospect is excellent.

Set Your Objectives

Know exactly what you want before you negotiate and set your objectives. You might want to get the sale at any price because of the potential for repeat or referral business or you might want to get your current customer to order more products or order more frequently. The key is to write down, before meeting with the other party, what you want the outcome to be. If you do so, you know exactly what you want to achieve and have a plan in place to help you pursue your objectives.

Position Your Value

Price is relative. If you really need a product or service, then the price becomes secondary. If you do not, then the price will always be too high.

Before you reach the negotiation stage with any prospect, you must position the value of your product or service. This is a critical step in the negotiation process. If you properly position your product or service in terms of value, it gives you increased leverage and power to get what you want out of the negotiation without having to concede on a major point or give away money. But you do not want to place value on the wrong things, such as the price or specific features. You want to value the benefit your prospects will receive as a result of buying—what your product or service will do for them, how they will benefit from using and own-ing it or what problem it will fix. If you do not clearly position the value of your product or serv-

ice in terms of the benefit to the potential cus-tomer, you lose the ability to justify your price rel-ative to the value of your product or service for the prospect.

For example, I am selling a car with a five-star safety rating and my prospect has a family. Before negotiating the sale, I want to position the value of this five-star safety rating as being first priority with my prospect (protect the family). In doing so, I would place myself in a strong negotiating posi-tion because you cannot put a price on safety, thus justifying a higher price.

Develop a "Yes" Strategy

Early in negotiations, get your prospect to say yes to a few small issues. Perhaps there is a time issue regarding delivery of the product; use this to your advantage early in the negotiations and ask "If I can ensure early delivery, do you still want that?" Your prospect will say yes because he or she has already indicated he wants early delivery. Therefore you have asked a question guaranteed to get a yes. Continue to ask questions about small issues you know will elicit a positive response, such as product colors, features and warranty informa-tion. In the end, try to narrow the negotiations to a single point. Doing this will make it much easier for you to make one small compromise, if any at all, and for your prospect to accept that compro-mise and feel that he or she has won. Additionally, use questions that begin with what: "What would you suggest?" "What are the alternatives?" "What would you think about if …?" By asking what questions, you force your prospect to reveal what he or she wants and, therefore, you weaken his or her position in the process.

Do Not Accept First Offers

Never accept your prospect's first offer. If you do, I can almost guarantee that you will be leaving money on the table or paying too much for a product or service. Few people will walk away from negotiations when you decline a first offer and say you need more money or you need to pay less money in order to go ahead. If you automatically accept first offers, most people will begin to doubt the entire negotiation process.

Keep Your Emotions in Check

Always strive to control your emotions during negotiations. Never react in an argumentative way with a prospect or client over a price objection or any other aspect of the negotiation or sales process. Whatever the emotion, it can take over and greatly reduce your ability to think clearly. Stick with your plan and don't let emotions weaken your negotiating abilities.

Use Incentives as a Powerful Negotiating Tool

Incentives are a great way to help motivate prospects to buy or entice current customers to buy more frequently. But to be an effective negotiating tool, the incentive you offer must provide real value and be relative to your main offering. If you were not including this incentive in the deal, would the incentive be valuable enough that it could actually be sold as a separate product or service? Ideally, the incentive you offer to motivate your prospect to buy should be something you sell. A good example is including an extended warranty in the deal for free. You can actually indicate the value of the incentive in terms of dollars and the benefit to your prospect in terms of the extra security and peace of mind that extended warranties provide. Other examples of valuable incentives that could be sold individually include more product or service for the same price, free upgrades or a free $50 gift certificate to be applied toward future purchases on other

products and services you sell. Strong incentives that add real value to your main offering should also increase buying motivation and urgency, benefit the buyer and improve your offer. Avoid discounts, whether straight cash or percentages, because they reduce the perceived value of your product or service. Giving cash discounts can become a habitual negotiating and closing technique and quickly devour your profits. Just make sure your incentives do not cost you more than you are making on the sale.

Confirm and Reconfirm the Details

I cannot overstate the importance of confirming all the details once negotiations are complete and both parties have reached an agreement. These details must be recorded and it is best if both parties also sign off on each major point in the deal or at least initial it. Handshakes and verbal agreements are fine on small jobs or orders if you have an established working relationship with a client. If not, you must get all the details on paper and then, when you're done, reconfirm these details step by step with your customer. It's equally important to reconfirm for your clients that they have made a wise purchasing decision and that you appreciate their business. Confirming the details works to strengthen the business relationship and close negotiations and the meeting in a very professional manner. All of these actions can increase repeat and referral business.

Learn When to Walk Away

If necessary, be prepared to walk away from negotiations if you are positive that you have nothing to gain by continuing.

GETTING MORE REFERRALS

Which type of sales lead would you prefer—cold, warm or hot? Cold leads require knocking on doors or calling on the phone. Warm leads are prospects who contact you directly as a result of your advertising, a special promotional activity or publicity your business has received. Hot leads are people who seek you out because one of your customers or a business alliance has recommended your business. Obviously, you want the hot leads.

A surefire way to increase sales and profits, while reducing sales cycle time and costs of finding new prospects and developing profitable business relationships, is to secure more referrals. In fact, for home business owners, referral business is often the primary means of generating leads. Therefore, the importance of ensuring that you get referrals cannot be overstated.

The first step toward securing more sales referrals is simply to set a target amount of referrals you want to secure and create a recording system so you track how many referrals your business is getting from whom. Most home business owners do neither, so they have no way to measure how they're getting referrals and how these referrals are affecting their closing rate, revenues and profits. By setting sales referral targets, you make securing referrals an ongoing, conscious effort, as it should be at all times. Once you have set targets, you can implement strategies to hit those targets and secure more referrals. You will also, of course, receive more referrals by providing excellent service, quality products, value and benefits and by keeping your word to all customers.

Never let an opportunity pass to ask people for referrals—prospects, customers, suppliers, alliances and friends and family members. Basically, whenever you are in contact with people, you have to get comfortable with asking them for the names and contact information of people who would benefit from what you have to sell. Figure 15.1 is a Sample Referral Form. Use it as a template to develop your own referral form to hand out.

Thank the Ones Who Got Away

Another way to secure more referrals is to thank prospects who did not purchase anything by sending them a "sorry" letter. This is simply a letter sent to prospects who did not buy. Of course, this is for higher-end products and services, since you would not be sending letters to every online customer who inquires about your sunglasses but does not buy a pair. You should send a "sorry" letter within two days of learning of the negative decision. Thank the prospect for the opportunity to fulfill his or her product or service needs. Restate the value and benefits of your product or service and your offer. Close by stating that if he or she should have a change of mind or future needs, you would like the opportunity to earn his or her business. You might be surprised to learn how useful this practice is.

Offer Referral Rewards

Offering incentives for referrals is truly a win-win situation. Your incentives could be a gift certificate, product or service discounts or even cash payments. Much depends on the circumstances and the value of the goods or services you sell. I used to send all customers a simple referral form along with a self-addressed return envelope, asking them to kindly complete the form and return it. With the referral form I enclosed a discount coupon related to what I sold that the customer could give to a friend, along with a letter stating that if any referrals led to new work I would send him or her a gift certificate for dinner at a nice restaurant. The incentive was basic, but month after month the referral forms would pour in and I would make new contacts and close new sales as a direct result of those forms.

FIGURE 15.1	Sample Referral Form

(Your Business Name Here)

Please identify any person who would might be interested in our products and services.

❏ Mr. ❏ Mrs. ❏ Ms.

Name: _____ Occupation: _____

Address: _____

City: _____ State/Province: _____ ZIP/Postal Code: _____

Telephone: (home) _____ (work) _____ Fax: _____

E-mail: _____ Website: _____

How do you know this person?   ❏ Personal Friend   ❏ Family Member   ❏ Co-Worker

❏ Current/Past Customer   ❏ Business Associate

May we let this person know you referred them to us?   ❏ Yes   ❏ No

Additional Comments: _____

Referred by: ❏ Mr. ❏ Mrs. ❏ Ms.

Name: _____ Occupation: _____

Address: _____

City: _____ State/Province: _____ ZIP/Postal Code: _____

Telephone: (home) _____ (work) _____ Fax: _____

E-mail: _____ Website: _____

May we contact you with special offers and information?   ❏ Yes   ❏ No

If so, which contact method do you prefer?   ❏ E-Mail   ❏ Fax   ❏ Ground Mail   ❏ Telephone

Thank you! We appreciate your help.

PROFITING FROM FOLLOW-UP

There are two types of follow-up: following up with prospects who have not yet bought, to turn them into customers, and following up with current customers, to strengthen the relationship so they will buy more and buy more frequently. Briefly, follow-up enables you to turn prospects into customers, increase the value of each sale and increase buying frequency.

With so much to gain, it should be obvious that you can never procrastinate. Follow-up is as important as any other part of the sales cycle or continuing customer relationship.

Prospects

Following up with prospects after a sales meeting or presentation can be done by e-mail, fax, telephone or letter. The benefits of immediate follow-up are many. First, it is an opportunity to compile all the information that was discussed at the meeting and to reconfirm the information, right down to the smallest detail. Second, it shows your prospects you are interested in their needs, you want to solve their problems, and you conduct business in a very professional manner. Third, immediate follow-up provides you with a great opportunity to reconfirm all the details with your prospect so there will be no missed communications when you get back together for the sales presentation.

Customers

The real work begins after the sale. It is easy to sell a prospect, but it takes effort to retain a customer for life. According to the SBA, more than 60 percent of consumers stop doing business with a company because they feel they are being ignored and forgotten after the original sale. Couple that startling statistic with the fact that it costs 10 times as much to find and sell to a new customer than to serve and keep current customers, and I am sure you see why the real work begins after the sale. Never be deluded into thinking that once you have made a sale, it's over. It isn't. After you make a sale, you should follow up regularly, provide great customer service and maintain a close working relationship with your customer for life. It is what you do once you make a sale that will determine its true value.

Survey Lost Sales

Even lost sales should be followed up with a survey form. Ask prospects who did not buy from you to complete the survey and send it back. Ask questions on the survey form to help you better understand why your prospects did not buy. The questions you ask will be relevant to your business, industry and your products or services. Consider the type of information you would benefit from knowing and ask the questions that would elicit it. Obviously you would have preferred to close the sale. But if you survey prospects to find out why

they did not buy, you can get insights so you can make changes in the way you sell your products and services.

The 30-Minute Follow-Up Close

Another closely guarded follow-up secret that professionals use is the 30-minute follow-up closing technique. More often than not, people will have made a decision about whether to buy within 30 minutes after the sales meeting or presentation, especially with consumer goods. Therefore, it is wise to follow up with all prospects within 30 minutes after a sales presentation. Call your prospect and let him or her know it is your policy to place a courtesy call to ensure 100 percent customer service and complete understanding of the products or services presented. Not only will this follow-up call open the lines of communication with the prospect once more, it will also provide an incredible opportunity for you to take advantage of the situation and close on the sale.

RESOURCES
Associations

American Marketing Association
311 S Wacker Drive, Suite 5800
Chicago, IL 60606
(800) AMA-1150 (262-1150), (312) 542-9000
marketingpower.com

Canadian Marketing Association
1 Concorde Gate, Suite 607
Don Mills, ON M3C 3N6
(416) 391-2362
the-cma.org

Direct Marketing Association
1120 Avenue of the Americas
New York, NY 10036-6700
(212) 768-7277
the-dma.org

Sales and Marketing Executives International
P.O. Box 1390
Sumas, WA 98295-1390
(312) 893-0751
smei.org

Suggested Reading

Blackman, Jeff. *Stop Whining! Start Selling!: Profit-Producing Strategies for Explosive Sales Results.* New York: John Wiley & Sons, 2004.

Carnegie, Dale. *How to Win Friends and Influence People.* Reissue. New York: Pocket Books (Simon & Schuster), 1998.

DeSena, James. *The 10 Immutable Laws of Power Selling: The Key to Winning Sales, Wowing Customers, and Driving Your Profits Through the Roof.* New York: McGraw-Hill, 2004.

Dyche, Jill. *The CRM Handbook: A Business Guide to Customer Relationship Management.* Boston: Addison-Wesley, 2002.

Fisher, Roger, and William Ury. *Getting to Yes: Negotiating Agreement Without Giving In.* 2nd edition. New York: Penguin, 1991.

Fox, Jeffrey J. *How to Become a Rainmaker: The People Who Get and Keep Customers. (The Rules for Getting and Keeping Customers and Clients.)* New York: Hyperion Books, 2000.

Gregory, Kip. *Winning Clients in a Wired World: Seven Strategies for Growing Your Business Using Technology and the Web.* New York: John Wiley & Sons, 2004.

Groth, Robert. *Data Mining: Building Competitive Advantage.* 2nd edition. New York: Prentice Hall, 2000.

Hopkins, Tom. *How to Master the Art of Selling.* Revised and updated edition. New York: Warner Business Books, 2005.

Parinello, Anthony. *Secrets of Vito (Very Important Top Officer): Think and Sell Like a CEO.* Irvine, CA: Entrepreneur Press, 2006.

Porter-Roth, Bud. *Writing Killer Sales Proposals: Win the Bid and Close the Deal.* Irvine, CA: Entrepreneur Press, 2004.

Stephenson, James, with Courtney Thurman. *Entrepreneur Magazine's Ultimate Small Business Marketing Guide: 1500 Marketing Tips and Tricks That Will Drive Your Business through The Roof!* Irvine, CA: Entrepreneur Press, 2003.

Websites

BNI: Billed as the world's largest referral organization, with more than 2,600 chapters worldwide and thousands of members. *bni.com*

Brian Tracy International: Sales and motivational expert, coaching, information, products, programs and services. *briantracy.com*

Guerilla Marketing Online: Weekly online magazine for small businesses, entrepreneurs, sales people and marketers. *gmarketing.com*

Sales & Marketing Management Magazine: Information, products and services for improving sales and marketing. *salesandmarketing.com*

Securetenders.com: Online service connecting buyers and sellers worldwide. *securetenders.com*

Selling Power Magazine Online: Information, products and services aimed at improving sales abilities. *sellingpower.com*

CHAPTER 16

Event Marketing

I N ADDITION TO TRADITIONAL SALES AND marketing activities, home business owners can benefit from event marketing to help drive revenues and profits. In this chapter we cover:

- Trade and consumer shows
- Seminars
- Public speaking
- Contests
- Sponsorships

TRADE AND CONSUMER SHOWS

For the home business owner, few marketing activities are as effective as trade and consumer shows for showcasing your products, services and expertise to a large and captive audience at one time and in one place, relatively cost-effectively. Over the course of one day to a few weeks, depending on the show, you can make personal contact with hundreds, if not thousands, of qualified prospects, affording numerous opportuni-

ties to sell your products or services.

Trade and consumer shows are one of the best ways to generate well-qualified sales leads. In fact, depending on how you generate and qualify leads at the show, it is possible to collect thousands of leads at a single event, which can easily be turned into profit-generating sales through post-show follow-up and presentations. The trade and consumer show environment is also a great forum for introducing new or improved products and services to a wide and qualified audience. This is especially true at the more specialized industry shows, exhibits, conferences and expos, which can substantially drive down your marketing and personal presentation costs.

You can take advantage of the many contacts you make exhibiting at trade and consumer shows to build or expand your database. You can also network within your field and meet people in tangential businesses who can be of benefit to you, including suppliers, vendors and consultants.

Home business owners on tight research budgets should also consider trade and consumer shows as great ways to collect information about competitors, the industry, customers, new trends and your business, products and services. Trade shows are almost always covered by media outlets, giving you the opportunity to meet members of the media in person and possibly get valuable free media exposure for your business, which can be turned into new sales.

Well-conceived exhibits, displays, in-show seminars and demonstrations also enable you to showcase your expertise in the industry. Of course, showcasing your expertise in this fashion builds a brand image so you can position your business, products, and services within your industry and in your customers' and prospects' minds. Many entrepreneurs use trade shows to support their field reps, agents and vendors. They use trade shows to generate leads, hold training and education workshops, or to introduce and demonstrate new or improved products and services you plan to make available to your business team in the near future.

In sum, trade and consumer shows provide home business owners with so many opportunities to expand their business that it is nearly impossible to list all the potential benefits.

How to Locate the Right Show

Once you have made the decision to exhibit at trade and consumer shows, expos and other types of special marketing events, the next step is to locate shows that will meet your marketing and exhibiting objectives. When you consider there are more than 10,000 trade and consumer shows annually in North America, this task could be overwhelming were it not for the internet. Fortunately, the internet makes finding trade shows and expos relatively easy, saving time over

reading through print trade show directories and making telephone calls to industry associations. Now you can search for trade shows in your industry and click through hundreds of tradeshow listings online in no time, gain valuable insights into each show and, most important, learn more about the people who attend to make sure they match your primary target market. There are online tradeshow directories such as Tradeshows.com, *tradeshows.com* and Trade Show News Network, *tsnn.com*. These directories can help you find the times, locations, costs, and additional information for trade shows in your industry.

You need to plan well in advance if you are going to be part of a trade show, since most fill up quickly.

To help you keep track of basic trade shows and other events, use the Trade Show Contact Form (Figure 16.1).

Follow the KISS Formula in Designing Your Exhibit

When designing your trade show booth and displays, follow the time-tested and proven marketing concept—Keep It Simple, Stupid (KISS). You want your booth and displays to be simple and straightforward, grab the attention of passing prospects, stimulate their interest in your products or services, instantly create a desire for what you sell, and make prospects take action and inquire about more information or buying. The purpose of your exhibition booth and display is to attract attention and project the appropriate image for your company, products and services. At a glance people should be able to know what your company does or sells.

You should not, however, display every single product or service you sell; you do not want your booth to appear cluttered and disorganized. Keep

FIGURE 16.1   Trade Show Contact Form

Event 1

Event Name _____ Date _____

Location _____

Contact Person ❑ Mr. ❑ Mrs. ❑ Ms. _____

Telephone _____ Fax _____

E-Mail _____ Website _____

Duration of Event _____ Booth Size _____ Booth Cost _____

Number of Exhibitors _____ Expected Gate Attendance _____

Event 2

Event Name _____ Date _____

Location _____

Contact Person ❑ Mr. ❑ Mrs. ❑ Ms. _____

Telephone _____ Fax _____

E-Mail _____ Website _____

Duration of Event _____ Booth Size _____ Booth Cost _____

Number of Exhibitors _____ Expected Gate Attendance _____

Event 3

Event Name _____ Date _____

Location _____

Contact Person ❑ Mr. ❑ Mrs. ❑ Ms. _____

Telephone _____ Fax _____

E-Mail _____ Website _____

Duration of Event _____ Booth Size _____ Booth Cost _____

Number of Exhibitors _____ Expected Gate Attendance _____

your booth lean. Move displays and tables back and to the sides so you have lots of space to greet prospects and engage in sales conversation. Far too many exhibitors try to arrange their booths and product displays like a retail store or office and restrict the flow of passersby, creating a funnel effect that makes people uncomfortable. As a result, passersby may skip those booths altogether.

There is no one set of standard rules for designing trade show booths and displays. Exhibitors have their own sales and marketing objectives, specific budgets and reasons for exhibiting their goods and services. But here are a few ideas you can use to grab attention and maximize the interest of your target audience:

- Use attention-grabbing devices such as a computer monitor, LCD screen, or TV running a corporate advertisement or product or service video. Perhaps you can have a service display taking place or something eye-catching, from giant inflatables to a greeter handing out your brochures and urging people to check out the booth. Your choice will depend on the type of business you run, the image you want to present and your budget.

- Create a freestanding durable product display, preferably a working model of what you sell, that can be used for interactive demonstrations. Interactive computer terminals on swivel bases also work well for presentations and demonstrations.

- Keep a whiteboard and markers handy in case you have to construct diagrams to respond to unique questions from visitors.

- Display products, scale models, and photographs and graphics at eye level, i.e., about five feet from the floor to the key focal point or feature of the product or display.

- If you are not a one-person operation, have some of your team members present. However, make sure not to pounce on passersby as they stop at your booth. Let people take in the display and then introduce yourself.

- Spread your display out—use the entire booth. Position your products and yourself so that you are not blocking your products if you are talking with prospective clients. You might set up a few chairs toward the back of the booth so that someone from your team can sit comfortably and talk with prospective clients or network with people in the industry.

Booths with exciting product or service demonstrations draw considerably more interest and larger crowds than static booths without demonstrations. Therefore, consider ways you can demonstrate your products or services in the booth to grab attention and build interest.

Invite the Media to the Event

Trade shows and expos are favorite places for members of the media to get news and information about products and services for their target audiences. Take advantage of this fact. Sing your praises in a dynamic media invitation outlining the special features and benefits of your products or services. Provide details on the trade show. Send the invitation to media outlets two to three weeks prior to the show. Let reporters know in advance the why, what, when, where, who and how of the event and your products and services. Remember, the media needs news for their viewers, readers and listeners. Good reasons to invite the media to your booth include the following:

- New or improved product or service launches
- Specialized demonstrations or in-show information seminars
- Celebrity or expert guest appearances in your booth
- Company milestones, such as number of years in business
- Publicity stunts at the show, such as attempts at breaking records, events, contests or product trade-in exchanges

Additional information about working with the media and securing free publicity can be found in Chapter 14, "Public Relations and Networking." Use the Media Invitation Form (Figure 16.2) to list the media outlets you will invite to your next trade show, seminar or expo and to remember to follow up with them before the event.

FIGURE 16.2 Media Invitation Form

Media Company	Contact Person	Date Invitation Sent	Date Followed Up
1.			
2.			
3.			
4.			
5.			

Presenting and Selling in the Booth

The trade show pace can be fast and furious, with time always too short. Therefore, it is important to prepare an effective and well-rehearsed sales plan. It should revolve around five key elements—engage, qualify, generate leads, present and close. Four of these sales elements are discussed here; lead generation is discussed in depth in a following section. Remember: Rarely will your booth, exhibit, or display do the selling in the trade show environment. That job is up to you and your staff through the personal contacts you make with prospective customers in the booth and through follow-up after the event. In a matter of moments, you must be able to engage prospects, qualify by asking questions and listening to the answers, generate a lead, present and close.

Engage

There are three main types of exhibitors. There are exhibitors who stand back in their booth and do and say nothing as prospects look over their products and displays. There are those who approach prospects with irrelevant questions or opening statements. Then there are exhibitors who are proactive and greet approaching prospects with well-prepared opening questions designed to provoke meaningful conversation and qualify each prospect's level of interest. I cannot stress the importance of decisive in-booth engagement. You must be direct and engage in conversation focusing on what you sell and how it meets their need.

Qualify

You know what you sell, who your target customers are and what your target customers need. That knowledge should guide you in developing a series of qualifying questions you can ask prospects to determine if they are hot prospects or cold fish. In addition to qualifying questions specific to the products or services you sell, remember to cover the basic, important qualifying information. That information includes prospects' need for your goods or services, their ability to make the buying decision, their ability to pay for the purchase and other companies competing with you.

Don't dismiss potential sales prospects too soon. The person who is not a great candidate for your product or service today may be ideal in six weeks or six months, so do not ignore people to whom you cannot sell immediately.

Present

Presenting in the booth is much different from presenting outside the trade show environment, where you typically might spend 30 minutes to a few hours with your prospect in a sales presentation. In the trade show booth, you are often limited to five minutes or less to give your sales presentation. Any longer and you risk losing qualified prospects who will wander away because you are not taking care of them. Prior to the show, you must scale down your standard sales presentation to only a few moments, while still delivering the same high-impact message.

Close

Closing in the booth is straightforward: simply ask for the sale. Most people who attend trade and consumer shows do so with the intention of making a purchase at the show or within a few weeks after the show. If you spend time qualifying and presenting in the booth and then let prospects get away before asking for the sale, all you have accomplished is educating your prospects. Maybe they will use that knowledge to buy from a competitor or maybe they will return to you if your competitor is interested only in selling and makes no effort to connect with them as you have done. You must give prospects a very strong reason for buying at the show. This is best achieved by creating buying urgency.

Lead Generation in the Booth

Next to selling in the booth, the second most common trade show objective is collecting leads that can be turned into sales after the show. Actually, in many industries and at many shows, this is a primary function of exhibiting, since not all shows draw a buying crowd and many potential buyers are not willing to commit until they have visited all the displays. Therefore, you can build up numerous leads and sell after the show.

As with any marketing activity, there are a few key points to consider—lead forms, generating leads and lead follow-up—prior to collecting leads.

Lead Forms

Lead generation in the booth starts with a system to capture prospect information—a lead form, either paper or electronic, with a computer in the booth. Regardless of the format, the form should do the same things.

- Get complete name and contact information, including telephone number and e-mail address. Some people may or may not want to provide home addresses, out of heightened security concerns; that is why electronic communications are so vital. You might want to also ask prospects to indicate their business or occupation.
- Use a checklist of qualifying questions relative to what you sell.
- Ask for the best manner of contacting the prospects, the best times to contact (day of the week and morning, afternoon or night) and best contact telephone numbers for those times.
- Rank each lead so that when the event is over you'll be able instantly to identify the hottest prospects and contact them immediately. Ranking leads is as easy as assigning a number, such as 1 for the hottest, 2 for good, and 3 for cool or poor quality. If you do not want people to catch you ranking leads, develop an alternate ranking system, such as placing hot leads in a red file folder, good leads in a green file folder, and cool or poor-quality leads in a blue folder.
- Request additional information so you understand each prospect's unique situation and needs during follow-up.

Figure 16.3 is an example of a simple lead form you can use to collect names, qualify and rank prospects. The sample is for a window replacement company. You can use this sample form as a guide in creating your own lead form relevant to your business and the products or services you sell.

FIGURE 16.3   Lead Form for a Window Installation Service

Prospect Information

❑ Mr. ❑ Mrs. ❑ Ms. Name: _____

Business Name (Business Customer): _____

Street Address: _____

City: _____ State/Province: _____ ZIP/Postal Code: _____

Telephone: (home) _____ (work) _____ Fax: _____

E-mail: _____ Website: _____

What is the best day and time to contact you?

Day _____ Time _____

Contact Number _____

Questions

Do your current windows need to be replaced? ❑ Yes ❑ No

Do you own the home where the windows are to be replaced? ❑ Yes ❑ No

What is wrong with your current windows? ❑ Steaming/condensation ❑ Poor condition ❑ Not energy-efficient

How old are your current windows? ❑ Less than 10 years ❑ 10–20 years ❑ 20+ years

What type of windows do you currently have? ❑ Wood ❑ Aluminum ❑ Vinyl ❑ Other

When do you want to have the windows replaced? ❑ 1–3 months ❑ 3–6 months ❑ 6–12 months ❑ 12+ months

Have you established a budget for replacing your windows? ❑ Yes ❑ No

Do you want one of our qualified window replacement experts to give you a no-obligation free quote to replace your windows? ❑ Yes ❑ No

Have you received or will you be getting other quotes to replace your windows? ❑ Yes ❑ No

Have you heard of our company before today? ❑ Yes ❑ No

How did you hear about our company?

    ❑ Print advertising ❑ Yellow Pages ❑ Radio/television advertisement ❑ Referral

    ❑ Job in progress/site sign ❑ Other: _____

May we include you on our mailing list and send you valuable information periodically? ❑ Yes ❑ No

By: ❑ Mail ❑ Fax ❑ E-Mail

Rank: ❑ Hot ❑ Warm ❑ Cold

Additional Comments: _____

_____

Generating Leads

Depending on your marketing objectives, you can talk with every prospect personally and generate leads based on the conversations or you can assemble a lead-generation station where prospects complete lead forms, either on paper or electronically. Both methods have pros and cons. While personally talking with each prospect and completing the lead form yourself generally results in better qualified leads, the process can be very time-consuming and you will generate fewer leads during the event. On the other side, asking people to complete the lead form by way of a contest entry ballot or similar promotion without talking with you generally means you will have to spend much more time after the show personally qualifying each lead or spending a bundle on direct marketing to reach and qualify every lead.

Contests and special promotions, such as the old favorite "Trade Show Special Discount," are great ways to lure people into your booth. These gimmicks are productive only when they are self-explanatory. If you have to take time out to explain contest details or how your special promotion works, either don't bother with the promotion or create one that is less involved. The time, energy, and money you spend on exhibiting are not to promote a contest; the contest is to help you meet your marketing objective. Get contact information on the entry form to generate a lead. Many contests at trade shows ask for a business card as the entry form for the contest; this is smart because it saves people the time it would take to fill out an entry form and it reduces the congestion around your booth. As prizes, you want to award something that will draw your target customers, rather than something generic.

Lead Follow-Up

Generating leads at trade shows is often easy, because you can generate hundreds of them at one event. But what do you do with them once you've got them? Obviously, you follow up and attempt to turn as many of the leads into sales as quickly as possible to maximize the value of the leads and to get the highest rate of return on the money you invested in exhibiting at the show.

Develop a lead follow-up package before the show so when it ends you're ready to start following up on the hottest leads immediately. The follow-up package should include sales letters, telemarketing scripts, presentation templates, and just about any other item or service required to maximize the value of the leads by contacting and re-qualifying prospects right away. Remember that competitors at the show are probably chasing the same leads as you. You'll want to carefully gauge the progress you make with each prospect: too fast or too slow and competitors could scoop them away from you. The key to beating your competitors is to position your follow-up with your prospect so you can maximize your chances of closing the sale.

SEMINARS

Much like trade shows, seminars are a great forum for home business owners to market their goods and services, showcase their specific expertise and present the main benefits of their products or services to a select and captive audience. Best of all, seminars need not be formal or conducted in fancy, high-rent rooms. On the contrary, seminars and workshops can be informal and hosted in just about any location imaginable—a banquet room, a living room, a supplier's warehouse or a local restaurant. The specific place will depend on the audience, the objective of the event and the topic or subject matter. Regardless of the location, seminars provide home business owners with many marketing and business-building opportunities.

Unlike a trade show, where the purpose is to

show off your goods and services, a seminar is typically designed to present information and educate people. Nobody wants to attend a seminar that turns into one long sales pitch. People will feel that they have been duped and start walking out. You must include content and provide something for those attending to take away, while working your sales benefits into the presentation or into the supporting materials that you hand out.

A seminar should have a theme, an educational or informational purpose and provide content that meets the needs of those attending. Your selling point is that you can teach them something about your products and/or services. For example, teach them how to take better care of their cars and then let them know what a full detailing job can do for them, as a detailer with years of experience. Plan out, very carefully, what your seminar will be about and what people can learn from it.

When you consider that you should develop every marketing activity with sales in mind, then seminars should be near the top of the list. Use your seminar as a means of selling, but remember, unlike a trade show, buying is not the primary reason people attend and most people cannot be fooled that easily. One well-known public speaking guru ran a seminar in New York City in the late 1990s on how to be a better public speaker. Halfway through the "seminar," it became apparent this was not about learning anything, but simply an ongoing advertisement for her book, her speakers' bureau, and the books and products of her associates. Three quarters of the way through, most of the audience had exited.

Prospect and build a powerful database. Through seminar events, it is possible to generate a wealth of well-qualified leads by using the attendee list or by staging a contest and using information captured on the entry ballot for direct marketing purposes. Collect as much information as possible, including full names, job titles, complete addresses, and information specific to your goods or services and their needs. Remember, of course, that people are not likely to provide long descriptions or explanations or give personally identifying information to someone they do not know, so ask for e-mail addresses and follow up with a thank-you for attending and a link to your website. Prospect building is not a matter of hitting people over the heads or cornering them in a room, but starting off communications with respect for the prospect. Remember: In an age of identity theft and security concerns, the more personal information you try to get, the less likely you are to win a prospect.

Seek publicity and showcase your expertise. Use seminars to position yourself as an expert in your industry or specific field. Becoming an expert is relatively easy. It is maintaining your status as an expert that can prove difficult, which is what makes seminars such a great forum for maintaining your expert status. You can reach a large audience very effectively, giving more substantial amounts of information or advice than you can through other formats, such as print advertisements. Seminars also present a fantastic opportunity to involve the media and get publicity. Send a press release to the media with the seminar details about three weeks prior to the event and follow up the first mailing with a telephone call or a second mailing as a reminder a week prior to the event.

Support, recruit and educate. Seminars can be perfect for recruiting employees, sales agents, suppliers, vendors and, most important, customers. It is a highly effective and cost-efficient way to recruit people for every role. You can also use the seminar format to train or educate a group of people cost-effectively and to inform customers or your business team members about the details of your products or services. One on one, this type of training or education would be far too costly for most home business owners, but in a seminar the cost of training or educating each person is dramatically reduced.

Location, Location, Location

Before you can plan and promote your seminar, you need a place to hold it. For homebased business owners, this typically means finding a facility, unless you are daring and don't mind inviting 50 people into your home. Typically, neighborhood associations, schools and universities, churches and temples, or libraries make rooms available for free or for a minimal fee. You need to make sure that the facility is easily accessible, accommodates people with limited mobility, has parking nearby, and is not too hard to find with relatively simple directions. Remember to print basic directions on fliers and posters and post them on your website.

Once you secure the location, make sure someone from the facility will be there to let you in and make sure you have whatever you need. Your needs are fairly simple—chairs, a podium, a microphone with speakers (you can always rent a sound system elsewhere) and access to bathroom facilities. Keep in mind technical needs that must be accommodated. You must then make sure you are in and out of the facility in the time specified and you leave the facility in the same condition as you found it.

Plan everything in advance. If you are allowed to serve food and/or beverages, it is advantageous to provide coffee, tea and water, and cookies or cakes after you speak. This is not only a nice gesture for your audience, but also a way to enable networking and to meet people up close and personal. If they liked your seminar, people will be more than happy to meet with you—this is your opportunity to sell your products and/or services.

Promoting Your Seminar on a Shoestring Budget

Fortunately for small business owners with tight marketing budgets, seminars can be promoted effectively and successfully for little cost—if you are prepared to roll up your sleeves and do the hard work yourself rather than hiring out the job. The ideas presented below are best suited for promoting a free seminar, one that creates revenues and profits through sales at the time of the seminar or through follow-up of sales leads collected during the seminar.

Handouts

Design a basic, yet colorful, promotional flier on your computer. List the details of your seminar or workshop event, print a few dozen copies, and post the fliers on free notice and bulletin boards throughout your community. These free boards are usually located in community centers, churches, temples, schools, libraries, grocery stores, self-service laundries and post offices. You can also enlist students to hand out the fliers door to door or tuck them under windshield wipers on parked cars.

Posters

Posters attract attention. You might have an art student or a freelance artist design the poster. Look for places that allow you to post. If a business owner will let you put up a poster, go for it!

Telemarketing

Devote a few hours each day before the seminar to calling past and current clients and hot prospects to inform them about your seminar and invite them to attend. Maximize the impact of this shoestring budget marketing method by asking them to bring a friend or two to the seminar. You can even offer special incentives to people who bring others to the event.

Word of Mouth

Let everyone with whom you come in contact

know about the event and ask them to spread the word by telling others. This is an especially effective technique for informal seminars, for which people are not asked to register in advance, just to show up on the day of the seminar with a friend, co-worker or family member. Word-of-mouth marketing is the home business owner's best and by far most effective marketing weapon.

Media

Create a news release about your seminar event and send it to local media outlets. Also invite key members of the media to the seminar, as the coverage they might provide afterward can be just as valuable as the exposure before the event.

Outbound Communications

Include details about the seminar in all your outbound business communications and correspondences, including telephone voice messages, company newsletters, invoices and sales receipts, faxes and e-mails.

Your Website

Not only can you promote your seminar on your website, you can also request feedback from those who attended, which is a way of starting up communication with attendees and turning them into possible clients. In addition, you can post a downloadable version of the seminar for those who missed it. Have visitors sign up with their e-mail address to download the seminar and then contact them to thank them for doing so and to offer an incentive for signing up for your online newsletter.

Securing Speakers and Sponsors

Before organizing and hosting a seminar, you will need to decide who will speak at the event and if you will try to find people or businesses to sponsor or co-produce the event.

Speakers

Every seminar requires a presenter—one person or a number of people to speak at the event who have the expertise or qualifications to do so. Depending on the seminar, you may need to pay speakers. Paid professional speakers are available to speak at any occasion, anywhere in the country. Their fees vary from about $250 per day to as much as six figures per day plus expenses. Obviously, the majority of small business owners cannot afford to pay professional speakers and will have to rely on speakers who, like you, are looking to impart knowledge and generate clients or leads. While you do not want direct competition, you want speakers on tangential subjects who can draw more attendees who will also fit into your target audience.

Sponsors

Planning and hosting seminars can be costly and time-consuming. Because of this, many small business owners forgo using seminars to market their goods or services. However, before you eliminate seminars from your potential marketing toolbox, consider securing an event sponsor to share in the time, energy, and financial investment required to plan and host the event. Sponsors can be active or inactive. As the word suggests, active sponsors take an active role in planning and presenting at the seminar. An example of an active sponsorship match would be a real estate broker who hosts a seminar for first-time homebuyers, which is co-sponsored by a home inspector and a mortgage broker. All have similar target audiences and each can benefit from being in contact with people at the seminar. Inactive sponsors can benefit from the exposure associated with the event, but do not necessarily want to play an active role in the event beyond financial sponsorship. These sponsors typically include financial institutions, manufacturers, and insurance brokers that want to be associated with the event and recognized through signage, advertisements and articles in the printed seminar guide. Securing inactive sponsors requires time, planning and a formal presentation. You must be able to demonstrate successfully that sponsorship will be worthwhile. The only real way to do this is by showing prospective sponsors how you will draw attendance, since all that truly matters is how many people see their signage, especially people who fit their target profile. Let the prospective sponsors know how you will be marketing the seminar, the background of the speakers and the location, which must be one that will draw people.

Three Key Considerations for Success

In addition to deciding on the topic of your seminar and ways to promote the event, while creating your seminar action plan to achieve your key objectives and secure a return on investment, there are three critical considerations to keep in mind.

Competition. The success of your seminar event can be adversely affected by competition for your audience's time and attention—not literally by way of competing seminars on the same day, same topic, with the same target audience, but more by distractions that can lure your target audience away. These distractions can be, for example, a legal holiday, the Super Bowl, political elections or a local community parade or fair. Therefore, before planning a seminar, check the date and time against the calendar and community schedules to make sure you will not face much competition.

Timing. Most seminar and professional meeting consultants agree that the best time to plan and host a seminar is in the spring, between late March and very early June or in the fall, from early September to mid-November. Of course, the timing of your event will depend greatly on your seminar topic, your industry and your marketing objective. Other timing considerations include holidays and target audience availability. If you want to reach businesspeople, a midweek daytime seminar works best. If you want to reach other consumers, plan your event for when your target customers are not at work; generally Tuesday through Thursday evenings are considered the best time.

Accessibility. This issue encompasses everything from uncontrollable situations, such as poor weather conditions and unexpected traffic congestion, to controllable issues, such as parking and transit availability. Ideally, you want the seminar location to be central for most of the people expected to attend. If people will be attending from out of town, the location should also be central to hotels and to the airport.

PUBLIC SPEAKING

If you can't get up and speak in public, how will you speak at your seminar? Public speaking is a highly effective way for small business owners to showcase their expertise, brand their business and market their goods or services. Yet public speaking is one of the most underutilized marketing activities, mainly because the vast majority of people are scared to death at the prospect of speaking in front of an audience. Fortunately, there are techniques you can use to reduce or eliminate fear of public speaking that can improve your skills. We will discuss this issue in the next section.

Many home business owners will find themselves in the position of being asked to speak publicly—at the local Chamber of Commerce, industry or trade meetings, business schools or community clubs and organizations. It is a common practice for these groups and organizations to bring in experts to speak to their members, guests and students. Before committing time and resources to free public speaking, there are a few requests that you should make for the benefit of your business:

- You should request a copy of the guest list, including some type of contact information. If there is no advance signup, as is often the case, ask your host to distribute a signup sheet and give you a copy.
- If appropriate, ask if you can sell or demonstrate your products or services during or after the event.
- Ask for permission to take printed promotional literature about your business to hand out or place on all seats before the event.
- Ask for a display advertisement promoting your business, product, or service in the function schedule and other printed literature handed out to guests at the event or mailed to guests before or after the event.
- Ask to be included in any pre-event press releases and post-event mailings to guests.

Overcoming the Fear of Public Speaking

The fear of speaking in public is real. In fact, that fear is shared by more American adults than any other fear or phobia. Fortunately, there are proven methods to help you overcome the fear of public speaking. This is especially important for small business owners who want to capitalize on public speaking as a highly effective method of marketing their products or services.

Here are some simple ways to overcome the fear of public speaking. Arrive early at the speaking location so you can familiarize yourself with the room. Walk around the stage or dais to get comfortable in your surroundings. Test all audio and visual equipment before guests arrive. Introduce yourself to the organizers of the event and their staff. Know the key people involved so if any problems arise you'll know whom to turn to for help. If possible, get to know the audience before you speak by greeting people as they arrive. You'll find it much easier and more relaxing to speak if you can look at the audience and see a few familiar and friendly faces smiling back.

You should also understand that everyone in the audience will be sympathetic to your task. Public speaking can be difficult and nerve-racking even for the most experienced professional speakers. Therefore, remember that the people attending the event are behind you; they support you and want you to be informative and entertaining and, most of all, to succeed.

Of course, the fear is often more deep-rooted than these basic helpful hints can alleviate. Therefore, you may want to talk with a psychologist to help you determine what is holding you back and how you can summon the confidence and courage to speak.

The Advanced Public Speaking Institute offers visitors to its website, *public-speaking.org*, additional information and advice for overcoming the fear of public speaking and advice on public speaking in general.

Tips for Professional Public Speaking

As mentioned above, public speaking is hard work and requires much practice. Where do you begin?

One good starting point is with the length of your speech, which will depend on the situation and the information you want or need to share. As a rule of thumb, however, after 30 continuous minutes of listening, the majority of the audience will start to lose interest unless there are pre-planned breaks or intermissions. You will want to talk at the educational level of the audience or slightly below, never above. Skip technical jargon that might be lost on the audience; and use plain, easy-to-understand English.

Here are a few more public speaking tips that can help you in public speaking.

- Prepare and know your material in advance. Being prepared and confident in what you have to say is half the battle. Even the most experienced professional speakers cannot successfully "wing it," so don't think that you can.

- Rehearse. No, not just standing in front of a mirror, but while driving in your car or waiting in a long line (rehearse to yourself). Also, rehearse with some distractions, since you will likely not have absolute quiet.

- Make eye contact with members of the audience as you look around. Talk to individuals and to the audience as a whole. Look out at them and get them to acknowledge you.

- Tools such as charts, props, and printed handouts can help when appropriate. However, don't overdo it or you'll lose your audience to the printed matter. Also, if referring to a screen, look at your audience, not at the screen, so you do not turn your back to them.

- Know the central message and theme of your speech inside out and upside down, but don't try to memorize your speech word for word. If you do, you will come off as manufactured, rigid and boring. Instead, know all of your key points and get to them in a comfortable manner.

- Avoid rocking back and forth as you stand at the podium. Try to use normal hand gestures and voice fluctuations in your tone and pacing. Be slightly animated and move as you would naturally. A podium is always good because it gives you a place on which to rest your hands and a means of staying centered. Just don't lean on it.

- Avoid talking too fast, rambling on beyond the point made, and speaking in a high pitch or monotone. Practice with a tape recorder and play it back. Don't worry about how you sound on tape; nobody sounds perfect. Just listen for inflection and speed. Take momentary pauses, to allow information to set in. If

you listen to news and sports commentators, such as Bob Costas, you will notice that generally they speak in short segments, rather than a stream.

- Avoid talking so quietly that people cannot hear or so loudly the audience feels as though you are scolding. Using slang, profanity, poor grammar, and politically incorrect humor is inappropriate for any audience, regardless of the topic or situation.

- Basic breathing and relaxation exercises and techniques can be beneficial before speaking engagements.

- Use rhetorical questions and/or an entertaining anecdote to draw your listeners from the beginning. People love a good story. Make sure it fits the theme of your speech. A joke or two can also lighten the mood. Make it current and appropriate to the occasion and do not use religious, political or offensive material.

- Ask for questions at the end. Provide short responses that answer the question without going off on tangents. Don't let one person dominate the Q&A session, if there is one. If you cannot answer a question, let the questioner know you will find the answer and get back to him or her.

- Have a glass of water or juice on hand while you speak.

CREATING AND STAGING PROFITABLE CONTESTS

Contests have long been a favorite promotional tool for small business owners as a way to generate sales leads, increase exposure and build awareness about their business, products or services. But, long before you decide what type of contest to hold, you first should identify the objective for holding the contest.

Ask yourself, "What do I want to achieve as a result of staging the contest?" Keep in mind that increasing sales is not an objective, but a potential result of an objective. What do you want? To capture and qualify leads from the completed entry ballots? To generate publicity and media coverage as a result of the contest? To build or update your database for direct marketing purposes from the information you collect? To use the contest to introduce a new product or service or to celebrate a company milestone, such as an anniversary? To support a local charity or organization? To build goodwill within the community or cross-promote your business with other businesses or organizations by becoming an official sponsor of a contest? There are lots of reasons to create and host a contest. Once you have determined your objective, you will be in a better position to decide which type of contest is best suited to achieve it. There are, of course, many other points to consider before creating and holding a contest, as discussed below.

What Type of Contest?

The type of contest you stage must be relevant to your business and marketing objectives. And you must be able to execute it successfully within your event budget and support structure. There is no point in staging a labor-intensive contest when you are a one-person operation.

One simple contest for small business owners is an entry ballot contest: contestants complete a ballot and deposit it into an on-site box or mail or e-mail it in. Entry ballot contests are a wise choice for small business owners, because you can use the information you collect on the entry form to build a prospect database, which can be used for direct marketing. The best way to get a lot of people to sign up is to make the process very simple, asking for minimal information—name and contact information. Then you can build from there by establishing communication.

Other contests include scratch cards that reveal prizes, counting games and customer interactive contests such as celebrity look-alike costumes or essay contests. You can purchase insurance if you decide that you want to stage high-stakes contests, such as million-dollar hole-in-one or basketball free-throw competitions. If a participant wins, the insurance company covers the prize value. National Indemnity, *nationalindemnity.com*, offers insurance packages to cover up to $1 million in prize money for contests involving shooting a hole-in-one, kicking a field goal, or shooting a basketball from half court, as well as insurance programs to cover other types of unique contests and promotional risks. The website offers visitors a free and instant online quote service.

What Is the Prize?

What will you award as the grand prize? Will there also be secondary or participation prizes? If you partner with other businesses, you can combine to create a grand prize package. In any case, the prize(s) should be relevant to your business and complement the products or services you sell. For instance, if you operate a landscaping service, a "backyard landscaping makeover" would be a suitable grand prize. Above all, the prize should enhance and complement your core product line and be valuable enough that it compels people who are not otherwise customers to want to enter for a chance to win. The reason the prize should be complementary to your core business, products, or services is that the people who enter but do not win will be, to a certain degree, qualified prospects. You can follow up with these leads after the drawing and persuade them to buy your goods or services. Therefore, it is a safe assumption that the people who enter the "backyard landscaping makeover" contest will have backyards that need landscaping.

Consider All the Legal Issues

Once you have determined the type of contest you will be holding and the prize that you will be awarding, the next step is to seek legal advice to make sure you will not be placing yourself, your business, your family, contestants, or contest promotional partners in a position of liability as a direct result of the contest or prize. In most cases, the lawyer who advises you on business matters should be qualified to advise you on the contest and potential liabilities associated with hosting it. In addition to seeking legal advice on larger contests, be sure to call your insurance broker and inquire about liability insurance to cover the event and matters relating to the contest. Once again, you do not want to be left with a liability if something goes wrong. Be proactive and make sure you are protected. It should also be noted that not every state is created equal when it comes to the rules and regulations surrounding promotional contests. Check with state government agencies before conducting any contests to make sure you comply with state rules.

Establish a Contest Budget

The contest budget is a major consideration for most small business owners. You will have to cover not only the cost for the contest prize(s), but also the costs of promotion, the drawing, publicity, time, and labor to cover the event, interruption of your business organizing the event, legal work, liability insurance, and collecting and recording the information you receive through the entry forms. The budget will depend on your marketing objectives, the prize and promotion of the contest. There is no one standard financial formula to be used when establishing a contest budget. Your contest budget will directly reflect what you can afford to spend and what you plan to get in return. Of course, one method for reducing costs

is to ask suppliers to furnish the prize free or at a reduced cost.

As a cautionary note, understand that if you cannot afford to create, implement and manage a contest properly, you will be better off not staging one at all. Reaching your objective is the goal of the event. If financial restrictions hamper that effort, the result will not be what you need.

Promoting the Contest

Promoting a contest should be an extension of promoting your business. Include the contest in your ads, in your fliers, on your website, and anywhere else you would normally promote your business.

Regardless of the contest budget, be sure to seek free publicity and media exposure for the contest by contacting local media through a press release, e-mails, a media advisory, telephone calls or a personal visit. Let local media know that your contest will be a great photo opportunity for a human-interest story and will benefit their audience.

Awarding the Prize

Awarding the prize is the final important consideration. You want the maximum promotional bang possible. Contact local media and get them interested in covering the official award ceremony. Don't forget your camera. Take pictures of the winner and the event and use these pictures on your website and in your printed promotional materials throughout the year. Ask the prizewinner to submit a testimonial about how happy he or she was to win, why he or she entered the contest and a few nice comments about your business. Basically, seek ways to make awarding the prize a grand event. The more people, media and interest you can create, the more exposure your contest and your business will receive. Always make a big deal out of every contest you hold, regardless of the size of the prize. The more fanfare, the better.

SPONSORSHIP OPPORTUNITIES

Sponsoring community associations, organizations, and events by donating money, products, or services is yet another method for small business owners to promote and market their goods and services. It should be noted that marketing via sponsorships requires a long-term commitment to realize a return on investments of time, money and energy. There are three main categories of sponsorships—charity, sports and community events. Often it is common for the three types of sponsorships to become entwined. For instance, you might sponsor a community pancake breakfast, the proceeds of which are donated to a charity or a number of charities and the event is hosted by a local youth sports association. In this example, all three main types of sponsorships are connected through the single event.

Charity Sponsorships

Great wisdom can be found in the old saying "Charity begins at home"—especially for small business owners. Support the community that supports your business by picking a worthwhile local charity or charitable event and help out any way you can—financially or with other resources at your disposal. You can gain much goodwill by contributing to a charity within your community and over the long run it will benefit your business through the contacts you make and the relationships you build. One of the best ways to support a charity is to create a charitable event hosted annually under your banner, but includes others from the business community, such as a 10-mile run for cancer or an annual drive to collect nonperishable foods for the local food bank.

The charity sponsorship options are nearly unlimited. Advertise the fact that you support or sponsor one or more local charities and watch customer loyalty and repeat business grow expo-

nentially because of your acts of kindness. Even home business owners on tight financial budgets can get involved by donating products or services to a charity or charitable event or by providing assistance in organizing the event, finding transportation or even providing a location to host the event.

Community Sports Sponsorships

Most amateur sports teams and leagues have business sponsorship packages available to small business owners based on the team budget and sponsorship needs. Your sponsorship may only partially cover a team's requirements to compete, such as uniforms or, if your sponsorship is more extensive, the team's entire needs. If you can afford to get involved with sports sponsorship, do it. It helps to build a good corporate image and shows that you support the community that supports your business.

Don't forget it is not enough just to have your business name emblazoned across the backs of the team jerseys; you also have to get out to the games and cheer your team on. I think that is the most gratifying aspect of sponsoring a local sports team. Consider the following advice to ensure the biggest bang for your sports sponsorship bucks:

- Try to have the team you sponsor named after your business, which can usually be arranged with full sponsorships. Check with league officials. The team uniforms should boldly display your business name as the sponsor of the team.
- Have a banner made promoting your team and business and fly it at all games, home and away. Also consider setting up product or service displays and demonstrations at games, especially during tournaments. Attend games and network by handing out business cards, product samples (if allowed

by the team rules and regulations) or coupons and your monthly newsletter.

- If you sell products, arrange to have a prize drawn at every home game. Make sure the announcer names your business at least twice during the drawing and subsequent awarding of the prize.
- Have team pictures taken and display the pictures in your office, newsletter and printed promotional materials. Let your customers and prospects know that your business is a proud sponsor of community sports.
- Pay to have game rosters and schedules printed for distribution that include your business name, logo, and marketing message across the header of all pages. Printed promotional opportunities can extend to ticket stubs and player cards. Also be sure to give away tickets for special tournaments to your best customers as an appreciation gift or to your hottest prospects.
- Create team and individual player awards, with trophies and certificates. Ensure that your business name and sponsorship are engraved or printed on them. Likewise, consider sponsoring an end-of-season celebration for players, parents, fans and coaches and inviting the local media for coverage and photo opportunities.
- Inquire about advertising opportunities around the playing field or the arena, in the stands or on the scoreboard. These opportunities can include signs, banners and displays, branding your business, products or services with those in attendance.
- Look for ways to turn sponsorship into media or publicity events. Send out press releases about the team, write a weekly community sports column for the local newspaper or get the scores out to radio disc jockeys

to read on air, along with your business name, of course.

Community Event Sponsorships

Sponsoring community events is much like sponsoring charities; ultimately you want the event to help people and organizations in your community through raising money, awareness, products or service depending on the event and its goals. And you want your business name to be associated with the event.

Once again, if you have the financial resources and the time necessary, try to create an annual event and take ownership of it. For example, even something as simple and inexpensive as a community cleanup day in which you supply school-age kids with garbage bags to stash trash from school yards and playing fields can have an extremely positive benefit on your business. Other forms of community sponsorships and events include raising money for community buildings, such as renovations of the library or expansion of the community center, planting trees in local parks, or raising money to send a local choir to competitions. Community sponsorships can be small things, such as donating a park bench with an engraved plaque naming your business as the donating sponsor. Whichever sponsorship avenue you choose, make sure you support the community that supports you and your business.

RESOURCES
Associations

American Seminar Leaders Association
2405 E. Washington Boulevard
Pasadena, CA 91104
(800) 801-1886
asla.com

American Training and Seminar Association
P.O. Box 1003
Cleveland, TN 37364-1003
(866) 572-0142
americantsa.com

Canadian Association of Exposition Management
2219-160 Tycos Drive, Box 218
Toronto, ON M6B 1W8
(416) 787-9377, (866) 441-9377
caem.ca

Exhibit Designers and Producers Association
1100 Johnson Ferry Road, Suite 300
Atlanta, GA 30342
(404) 303-7310
edpa.com

National Speakers Association
1500 S. Priest Drive
Tempe, AZ 85281
(480) 968-2552
nsaspeaker.org

Trade Show Exhibitors Association
McCormick Place
2301 S. Lake Shore Drive, Suite 1005
Chicago, IL 60616
(312) 842-TSEA (8732)
tsea.org

Suggested Reading

Abrams, Rhonda, and Betsy Bozdech. *Trade Show in a Day: Get It Done Right, Get It Done Fast!* Palo Alto, CA: The Planning Shop, 2006.

Carnegie, Dale. *The Quick and Easy Way to Effective Speaking.* (Revision by Dorothy Carnegie of Public Speaking and Influencing Men in Business.) New York: Pocket Books (Simon & Schuster), 1990.

Esposito, Janet E. *In the Spotlight: Overcome Your Fear of Public Speaking and Performing.* Southbury, CT: In the Spotlight/Strong Books, 2000.

Gleeck, Fred. *Marketing and Promoting Your Own Seminars and Workshops.* Henderson, NV: Fast Forward Press, 2001.

Jolles, Robert. *How to Run Seminars and Workshops: Presentation Skills for Consultants, Trainers, and Teachers.* 2nd edition. New York: John Wiley & Sons, 2001.

Miller, Steve. *Stop Wasting Your Time at Trade Shows and Start Making Money.* Federal Way, WA: HiKelly Productions, 2006.

Miller, Steve, and Robert Sjoquist. *How to Design a "Wow!" Trade Show Booth Without Spending a Fortune.* Federal Way, WA: HiKelly Productions, 2002.

Mintzer, Richard. *Public Speaking for Wimps.* New York, NY: Sterling Publishing, 2005.

Stephenson, James, with Courtney Thurman. *Entrepreneur Magazine's Ultimate Small Business Marketing Guide: 1500 Great Marketing Tricks That Will Drive Your Business Through the Roof!* 2nd edition. Irvine, CA: Entrepreneur Press, 2007.

Websites

Advanced Public Speaking Institute: Public speaking portal providing products, services, information, resources and links related to public speaking. *public-speaking.org*

Contests and Sweepstakes Directory: Lists to which visitors can add their contests and/or get ideas about types of contests that can be held. *sweepstakes-contests.com*

National Seminars Training: Seminar industry information, resources and links, as well as products and services to assist in planning and hosting seminars and workshops. *nationalseminarstraining.com*

Toastmasters International: Nonprofit organization offering opportunities to develop public speaking skills through 11,300 clubs in 90 countries. *toastmasters.org*

TradeShow Week Online: Print and electronic magazine serving the trade show, consumer show and convention industry with information, product and service listings, resources and helpful links. *tradeshowweek.com*

Tradeshows.com: Online directory listing trade shows, conventions and expos worldwide, indexed by country and providing information and resources for improving trade show performance. *tradeshows.com*

Internet and E-Commerce

I T IS ALMOST IMPOSSIBLE TO COMPETE IN THE business world today without a presence on the web. Most businesses at all levels have a website or at least a web page on someone's site. The internet is where people go to find whatever they need.

The homebased business owner can use a website in three ways. (1) It can be your primary location for selling your products and/or services. (2) It can be an adjunct means of selling your products and/or services in conjunction with catalogs or other means of making sales. (3) Finally, it can serve strictly as a means of promoting your business and presenting information. Numerous businesses benefit from using websites in all three ways.

The internet is unique in that a website can provide home business owners and marketers from all walks of life, geographic regions, and financial budgets a level playing field with larger and often better-financed competitors. The internet enables home business owners to reach a wider and broader audience, sell to more people, share more information with more people, inform and service their current customers better, and test new products, services, and markets inexpensively, quickly and effectively—all with the click of a mouse. It is also the most immediate means of communicating with your customers or clients, as it is an interactive tool and you should use it as such.

The internet has forever changed the way the world does business and shares information and it will only continue to expand and prosper with new online technology.

To truly benefit from operating a website, you must first determine what you want your site to do for your business. As noted above, there are several possibilities. Let's look at those more closely.

Your website can:

- *Serve as your primary source of selling.* If you are starting a web business, setting up a first-rate site must be your primary objective. Your focus will need to include how the site is set up, how it is designed, how it will function and how you will maintain it. Running an e-business means that this is your one gateway to the world and that you must build your site like you would build a bricks-and-mortar business, from the ground up, taking into account all possible details. Of course, a website has two big advantages—cost and accessibility. It's far less expensive to build and maintain a global website than a local retail store. Your business can be open 24/7 and can send information to customers in minutes, not hours, days or weeks. Plus you can update or alter your marketing message and strategy quickly, conveniently and very inexpensively if necessary.

- *Support your business.* To support your business and sell, you want to have a website that will tie into your other forms of marketing and vice versa. When you have established contact with customers or prospects, you can direct them to your website to learn more about your business and potentially buy. Just as bricks-and-mortar stores also have websites, you can use your site to sell products even when you are sound asleep. It can significantly boost your sales opportunities while supporting other means of sales.

- *Promote your business and share information.* Many small service-based businesses use their websites to promote what they do. If, for example, you are a local caterer, you are not going to be selling your services globally. Therefore, it is not worthwhile to set up your site to sell. However, like millions of restaurants, you can post your menu and show photos of your catering specialties. In essence, your website is promoting your business. In this case, you'll want your phone number front and center and put your e-mail address in a prominent location, as well.

Other uses for websites, in conjunction with the above, include:

- *Branding.* The internet can help you brand your company and products and help build awareness of your company and products— for a fraction of the cost it would take to attain the same exposure in the bricks-and-mortar world.

- *Support.* Through your website you can support contractors, sales agent and your customers by hosting virtual workshops and training seminars and with specialized product and service information and customer service support features.

- *Research.* You can use the internet and, more specifically, your website to conduct research on important issues affecting your business via online polls, surveys, questionnaires and research forums. Discover how your customers view your products or services in comparison to competitors' products or services, what other types of products or services your customers would be willing to purchase from you, and what customers think about the level of customer service you provide.

- *Expand.* The internet presents incredible opportunities to expand your business by selling your products or services to people outside your geographical trading area, by finding new employees or distributors to market your products and services or by finding new joint venture opportunities that can help expand your business.

BUILDING YOUR PLACE ON THE WEB

Before you can launch a website, you will need to consider the following:

- What is your budget for building your website?
- Who will build your website?
- Who will maintain your website and how much will it cost?
- Who will host your website and how much will it cost?
- What type of content and interactive web tools do you need?
- Where will you get these tools and how much will they cost?

Who Will Build, Host and Maintain Your Site?

Your first option is to design, build and maintain your website yourself. There are a plethora of website-building software programs and websites available to enable novice webmasters to build and maintain their own sites. You will need to be familiar with computers and the internet if you choose this option, regardless of the "no experience required" advertisements. The cost to maintain your site will vary by the content you feature, how often you update the site and the objectives of the site. In terms of hosting, costs will also vary depending on the services you select—e-commerce shopping carts, payments systems, order tracking, website statistics and database storage options. There are services that will host your website for free, but in exchange they will put their banner advertisements and other types of advertising on your site and attach ads to e-mails initiated from your site.

The second option is to hire a professional to design and build your website. This can run you anywhere from $1,000 to $20,000, depending on the size and complexity of the site.

Which is best for you? If you are putting up a simple site just to let people know you exist and to show some of your products or services, you can probably go it alone and create the website yourself. Search the web and you'll find plenty of opportunities and tools to create and build a site. For example, visit Decisive Web Sites, *decisivewebsites.com,* to get an idea of how you can build a site and have it hosted for around $120 a year.

For anything more than a basic promotional site, you should use a professional to build and maintain your website. For online selling, a site must be more complex and you do not want to risk losing sales. The investment in a site designer will pay for itself, especially if you are selling via the internet only.

Choosing the Right Domain Name

Choosing your domain name or URL (uniform resource locator, still known as universal resource locator) is more difficult than you might think. In the first place, short, high-impact dotcom designations are becoming increasingly difficult to acquire. Second, the domain name you select must suit the image you want your business to project. Ideally, you will want your business name and domain name to match. For instance, if you operate Jim's Pool Cleaning, you would try to acquire the right to use the URL *jimspoolcleaning. com* or perhaps *jimspoolcleaning.net.* The top-level domain *com*, however, is by far the primary designation used by commercial enterprises, especially in North America, with *net* being an alternative, yet not a first choice for most businesses. Any other top-level domain (such as *org* or *biz*) is far less likely to be considered a "legitimate" business by many potential customers.

Before conducting a domain name search, you will want to consider several alternatives, such as *jimspools.com* or *jpcleaning.com.* Because of the rapid expansion of the Internet, it's important to choose a name and a domain name at the same time, especially if you are selling primarily online.

The domain name that you select should also be short, preferably 15 letters or fewer, easy to remember, easy to spell and something that best describes the type of business that you operate, the products you sell or the services you provide. With *jimspoolcleaning.com*, there is no mistaking that Jim provides pool cleaning services.

Additionally, make sure that you register your domain in your business name, instead of using any one of the numerous extension services offered on the web. You want the security of knowing that your domain name is yours and under your control. Good names are hard to acquire. Ones that have not already been selected or that become available go fast. Don't worry if your site is not ready. Once you pay a domain registration fee, you can park the domain until your site is built and ready to be put onto the web. Domain name registration fees vary greatly, from a low of $7 per year to as much as $100+ per year, depending on the designation (top-level domain) and the registration service you choose. The majority of domain registration services will conduct a search and provide customers with various additional Internet and e-commerce services and packages, ranging from website design to hosting and maintenance services. The following are a few of the most popular domain registration services:

- NetworkSolutions, *networksolutions.com*
- Register.com, *register.com*
- Domain Direct, *domaindirect.com*
- Domain-It!, *domain-names.com*
- Dotster, *dotster.com*
- Aplus.Net, *domains.aplus.net*
- ActiveDomain.com, *active-domain.com*
- MyDomain.com, *mydomain.com*
- Triple.com, *triple.com*

You may also consider registering close misspellings of your name if they are not taken. If you register a misspelling, any user who enters that misspelling in a web browser will be directed to your site, not to a site registered later by another person or company. Consider that *gogle.com*, *gooogle.com* and *googel.com* will all get you to the Google home page, *google.com*.

While you always want to do a domain check, in the event that someone owns a name and is not yet using it, you can get an idea what is available simply by typing in the URLs you want to register.

You can use the Domain Name Tracker (Figure 17.1) to record your preferred domain name choices. Don't let anyone sell you on anything in the top-level domain other than *com* or *net*, even if they tell you that another designation will soon be the hottest one. They were saying that several years ago and no other designations became popular for businesses in the United States. If you are operating solely in Canada, you might use *ca*, but it may limit you, since it is more often used for associations and government activities.

Elements of a Website

All successful websites share qualities that make them tops in their industry and with their customers and visitors. Many elements go into building a great site that will appeal to your target audience, create a sense of online community, be easy to navigate and use and be consistent in providing beneficial content, products and services to fill the needs of your target audience.

Keep Your Content Fresh

If a site looks stale, it will lose visitors. Therefore, you need to update your website and keep it fresh. If you are a web-based business, you will need to update the site daily, just as you would maintain a bricks-and-mortar store. If you are not selling exclusively via the web, you can update a little less often, but you should never let a week go by without updating your website in some manner.

FIGURE 17.1 Domain Name Tracker

Possible Domain Names	Check If Available	
www. _____	❏ .com	❏ .net
www. _____	❏ .com	❏ .net
www. _____	❏ .com	❏ .net
www. _____	❏ .com	❏ .net
www. _____	❏ .com	❏ .net
www. _____	❏ .com	❏ .net
www. _____	❏ .com	❏ .net
www. _____	❏ .com	❏ .net
www. _____	❏ .com	❏ .net
www. _____	❏ .com	❏ .net

For businesses that focus on information as the cornerstone of their online marketing strategy, it is critical to remember that content is king. Use bold, attention-grabbing headlines and subheads that spell out clearly how your visitors benefit from the information or products or services you are promoting. Try to keep articles and explanations brief, powerful and to the point. Use bullet lists, photographs and illustrations to make the site stand out. Edit your content for spelling and grammar errors. Avoid using all capital letters and too many exclamation points. Above all, provide information that visitors and customers cannot get anywhere else. If people can get the same information elsewhere, they are much less likely to return to your site, which means fewer selling opportunities.

If you absolutely do not have the time to constantly update your website content, you can get content for a fee or sometimes for free. The following companies provide content:

- YellowBrix, *yellowbrix.com*
- HotPlugins, *hotplugins.com*
- FreeSticky.com, *freesticky.com*

Since this can be a means of finding a vast supply of mediocre content, you are probably better off finding people in your area who are happy to write for credit to build a portfolio or for a low fee. You can also stockpile material from such original sources and run content when you have an opportunity. Many sales-oriented sites have limited content, some of which is in the form of testimonials or letters from their customers. This, too, is a way of including content on your site. Look through your mail for letters from customers and ask for permission to use their letters on your site.

Appeal to Your Target Audience

Everything you feature in your website—including content, products, services, interactive web tools, links and resources—must appeal to your primary target market. Keep this in mind, especially when building your site. There are so many cool and easy plug-in tools and features available that it is easy to get sidetracked and lose sight of your target market and your online marketing objectives. Perhaps the best way to design a site packed with information and tools that appeal to your target market is to use competitors' sites as examples.

Looking at other sites, even those of companies not competing against yours, is a great way to determine what you do and do not like. Make a list of design elements and features that you would like on your site. Then draw your site on storyboards. No, you need not draw very well or fill in the content; just put boxes where photos will go, columns where content will be and so on. Remember to feature your company name and your products and services in prominent places, such as front and center on the home page and around content on other pages.

Consistency

Consistency is critical in two areas. Your website should be consistent throughout—the look of its pages, the content and tools, the sales message and entire site functions. Your site should also be consistent with your offline business image—the central sales message, the use of identifying marks such as a logo and a central color scheme, and the business philosophy, such as "lowest priced" or "highest quality." Building an online and offline image and branding your business is a long process that requires hands-on management. Therefore, it makes sense to develop and stick with a consistent image so people will recognize your business instantly and favorably.

Keep Your Site User-Friendly

As a rule of thumb, people will stay longer and return more often to sites that are user-friendly and fast, so make sure to build your site to meet these important criteria. Start by using a white or very light-color background with dark letters, preferably black, in a font that is easy to read. Create a site map and include it in the navigation bar on each page,

because with keyword searches visitors may not enter your site on your home page. Also put a link to your home page in an obvious location on every page. Even small issues such as a frequently asked questions (FAQ) page and automatic formatting for printing text only, with a printer-friendly button, make a big difference in terms of visitor usability. You also want to keep your site fast, so avoid large, slow-loading graphics, long and detailed introduction pages, scrolling messages and other features that will slow down your site.

White space can be your friend. Use some white space to separate the photos and the written material on your pages. Do not pack a page so it is cluttered. Some web pages are so full that visitors feel overwhelmed and confused and they leave.

A Sense of Community

Many websites have created and maintained a sense of community for their customers and visitors. People enjoy visiting and using these websites because they feel they are part of an online community of like-minded site visitors. Building community is not as easy as it may sound; it requires research, finding the right mix of content and tools through trial and error and hands-on management to perfect. Creating community is a combination of elements, such as beneficial content, products or services that fill specific needs and interactive tools, such as discussion boards, chat rooms and online workshops, to unite visitors, convert them to customers and keep them returning, not only as repeat customers but also as active members of your online community.

Registering with Search Engines and Directories

The number-one way people find the information, products, and services on the Internet is by keyword and phrase searches on search engines and search directories. In fact, some studies suggest that as many as 90 percent of internet users search for information, products and services this way. Because you never know which search engine or directory people will use, your website and web pages need to be listed or registered with all the major players. However, before you start registering with every search engine, you should know the basics of *web optimization*, which essentially means how to make your website pop up earlier than others on a search.

Search engines such as Google are indexed by *bots* or *spiders*, which extract specific information from websites and web pages and use that information for indexing. Most major search engines and directories use both mechanical and human power to build and index information.

Many entrepreneurs new to internet marketing find registering their websites and pages with search engines and directories frustrating because there is no one set of rules, regulations or guidelines for registering. Most search engines and directories have their own particular submission policies. Because 90 percent of web surfers use search engines and directories, you would be well advised to learn how to submit to each engine and directory for registration purposes or use one of the companies that automatically submit or register your website with all major search engines and directories.

Listed below are a few of the more popular search engine submission and optimization services:

- Add Me, *addme.com*
- SubmitToday.com, *submittoday.com*
- AddPro.com, *addpro.com*
- Submit Express, *submitexpress.com*
- Submitawebsite.com, *submitawebsite.com*

If you plan on using your site to sell products and services, take the time to select the right submission and maintenance service.

Remember: Your goal is to secure a top search ranking or result on all the major search engines and directories, preferably on the first page, ideally in the top-10 search results. You can do this on your own by optimizing your website, as discussed, and contacting the following web search engines/directories for their specific requirements:

- Google, *google.com*
- Yahoo!, *yahoo.com*
- Excite, *excite.com*
- Ask, *ask.com*
- Lycos, *lycos.com*
- dmoz Open Directory Project, *dmoz.org*
- Microsoft Network, *msn.com*
- Dogpile, *dogpile.com*
- AllSearchEngines.com (international search engine directory), *allsearchengines.com*
- Big Search (international search engine directory), *big-search.com*

Use the Search Engine and Directory Tracking Form (Figure 17.2) to list search engines and directories with which you want to register your website and the cost of registration.

Optimizing Your Site

Because 90 percent of internet users search via keywords and phrases, you need to optimize your website for keyword searches. (A keyword is word used by a search engine to find relevant web pages.) Most online marketing specialists suggest that you aim for a keyword density of about 5 percent, meaning that 5 out of every 100 words of your content will be keywords. You will also want to include keywords in your page titles, headers, meta tags and hyperlinks. (A *meta tag* is a special coding element that provides information about a web page but without affecting how the page displays. Many search engines use information in meta tags when building indices.) Each page is unique in terms of the information featured and

FIGURE 17.2   Search Engine and Directory Tracking Form

Search Engine/Directory	Fees	Comments	Registered
_____	$ _____	_____	❑
_____	$ _____	_____	❑
_____	$ _____	_____	❑
_____	$ _____	_____	❑
_____	$ _____	_____	❑
_____	$ _____	_____	❑
_____	$ _____	_____	❑
_____	$ _____	_____	❑

its marketing objective; be sure to select different keywords for each subsequent page in your site. Be very descriptive when selecting your keywords and phrases. Keep in mind that few people type in single search words, so it's wise to combine keywords into short descriptive phrases. A good starting point is to list what you sell and try doing searches using variations of the descriptive words you use to describe your products or services. For example, a closet-cleaning and -organizing company based in Cleveland might list words and phrases such as the following:

Closet cleaning
Closet organizing
Closets
Organizing
Straightening
Cleveland closet cleaning
Home organizing

Compile all the possible words and phrases that you think someone would use to search for your business. Then use your keywords in content; do not insert them randomly or the search engines will catch on. Search engines often penalize a site if they detect *keyword stuffing*; some search engines will even drop web pages from their search results if they seem guilty of keyword stuffing. Don't try to fool them; it doesn't work.

There are also keyword generators and keyword creation services that will optimize your keyword selection on your website for a fee. Here are some of the more popular services:

- Wordtracker, *wordtracker.com*
- The Handbook of Keyword Selection, *keywordhandbook.com*
- 1st Position Keyword Generator, *1stposition.net/keyword-generator.html*

You can also try searching online for businesses like yours. When your search generates results that rank businesses selling similar products or services among the first sites, you know you are choosing the right keywords. Narrow the field until you have found suitable matches. Then repeat this exercise for each page in your site. Always include the maximum number of keywords the search engines allow. Directories base ranking more on the quality of the content and not just on keywords, so concentrate on quality content.

Also make sure to include keywords in your meta tags.

Creating a Linking Strategy

Much like developing a keyword strategy, it is also very beneficial to develop a linking strategy for your website. Many popular search engines use links found within your site as part of the formula to establish search result rankings; the greater the number of links relevant to the keywords or phrases found within your site, the higher it gets ranked in search results. Incoming links are also helpful when optimizing, so try reciprocal linking with other businesses. Make sure, however, you do not mind if your visitors click away from your site to visit their pages. Obviously, you do not want to link to competitors' sites. Also, avoid linking with sites that are not reputable.

In addition, provide customers and visitors links to additional sources of information, products and services. This is a great way to help build your online community. Once again, the more needs and wants you can fulfill at your site, the greater the odds that visitors will return.

Ideally, you want your site and link featured on sites visited by people who match your target profile. To do this, create a list of websites to which you would like your site linked, like the Website Linking Worksheet (Figure 17.3). Then, contact each site's webmaster and ask to be linked. You can use this handy form for listing the sites to which you want your site to be linked and check off "Completed" each time you succeed in linking.

Test Your Website Before You Launch

When you build or revise your website, always make sure to totally debug the site and ensure that everything is working properly before you publish your site, so your visitors and customers aren't guinea pigs. You can enlist friends, workers, and family members to test every aspect of your website. Ask them to proofread content, order products, test links, submit keyword searches to search engines, and directories to check the resulting rankings and aggressively test all the other functions and features of your site. Since there are more and more people accessing the internet on notebooks and even cell phones, you will want to make sure that graphics, colors and font sizes work for a

FIGURE 17.3 / Website Linking Worksheet

URL	Comments	Completed
www.		☐
www.		☐
www.		☐
www.		☐
www.		☐
www.		☐
www.		☐
www.		☐
www.		☐
www.		☐

variety of monitors and screens. You'd be surprised at how different web pages can appear on a smaller screen. Don't panic; just have your site designer make the appropriate adjustments or, if you know how, do it yourself.

MARKETING YOUR WEB BUSINESS

Building a website puts your business out there. Then you need to work at drawing people to your site. You have to create an online marketing strategy that outlines the promotional methods and activities you will use to achieve your online marketing objectives. You will also need to develop a budget that shows how much each marketing strategy will cost, where the money will come from and what you estimate for your return on investment. Ideally, you will tie your internet marketing plan in with your overall business plan and marketing plan as discussed in Chapters 6 and 12, respectively.

Once you have identified your objectives, mapped out a strategy and developed a budget, your options for marketing and promoting your website, products or services are almost unlimited, especially if you combine online and offline promotional activities. Online marketing activities featured in this section include online grand openings, banner advertising, electronic publications, pay-for-performance keywords, opt-in lists, securing repeat visits and permission-based marketing.

However, it is offline promotional activity that will draw people to your site. Therefore, you will need to include your URL on all printed materials and make sure it is always part of any marketing that you do.

Your E-Grand Opening

Once you've tested your website to make sure it is working properly, the next logical step is to host an online e-grand opening. You will want to have a "soft" launch first, which means simply putting the website up before announcing the grand launch. That way people won't try your URL and find nothing.

You will then want to create special incentives and offers to lure visitors to your site and get them to purchase or ask for additional information, much like you would if you were opening a retail shop or showroom in the bricks-and-mortar world. First, you will need to draw people to your site in the real world. This might be with a launch party at a restaurant or another location. You can use conventional promotional methods, such as balloons for the kids with your URL on them. Plan your launch party carefully and try to draw the media, friends, family, other business contacts and, if possible, the general public to the location for "something exciting."

Additionally, you will want to promote your grand opening on the web. The following ideas should help:

- *Post an announcement* of your party on other websites that attract people who match your target profile. Have them put it into their newsletters, in exchange for a mention of their site on your new site and in your upcoming newsletters or other barter deals.
- *Contact the media.* Send out electronic and print news releases, media advisories and letters to the editor to announce the opening of your new site. Follow the guidelines for standard news releases and make your release read like news, not like an advertisement for your site. Make sure your e-mail announcement does not appear as spam or it will get deleted by spam filters.
- *Newsgroups.* Post messages in Usenet newsgroups and on discussion boards. Talk up the new site in chat rooms related to your business, products, services and industry. You might even want to post messages about your new site to competitors' discussion

forums, message boards and chat rooms.

■ *Advertise.* Purchase advertising space on websites and in e-publications where people who fit your target profile will find your ads. Include a link to your site. Also consider purchasing advertising space in print publications that are read by people in your target market.

■ *Consider banner ads.* This type of advertising, mentioned earlier in the book, is still popular, but people are more cautious about believing the promises of banner ads.

Banner Advertising Basics

Before you put money into banner ads, you should first understand the basics and most common terms.

■ *CPM, cost per thousand (impressions)*, is used to calculate the fee charged for the number of times the banner is displayed on a website or within a network of sites multiplied by the number of visitors exposed to the banner. If the CPM of a banner on a particular site is $30 and the number of impressions is 5,000, the cost to the advertiser is $150 (5M x $30). Costs per thousand impressions range from a few dollars to a few hundred dollars.

■ *CTR, click-through rate*, is the number of times visitors to a site click on a banner ad or text message to follow the link to the advertiser's website, expressed as a percentage of the number of visitors to the site displaying the link. For instance, if 100 people click on a banner advertisement that has been displayed 10,000 times, then the click-through rate for the banner would be 1 percent. Click-through rates vary greatly, from almost zero on untargeted or poorly targeted sites to as high as 10 percent on perfectly targeted websites. The cost per lead

(click) can be calculated by dividing the number of clicks by the number of impressions you purchased and then multiplying the result by the CPM. For instance, if you received 100 clicks and you purchased 10,000 impressions at a CPM of $25, your CTR would be 1 percent (0.01), which you would multiply by $25 to get a cost per lead (click-through) of $0.25.

■ *CPC, cost per click*, is an alternative to CPM for calculating the fee for a banner ad or text message ad. You might agree on a CPC rate for your ad and pay for each time a visitor clicks on your link to visit your site.

■ *ROS, run of site*, and *RON, run of network*, are terms describing how an ad will be displayed. If it's ROS, the ad can appear on any page of a targeted website. If it's RON, the ad can appear on any website within a network of sites. Few banner advertising services and programs guarantee placement on any one page or site unless the contract specifies guaranteed placement.

■ A *static banner* is one that remains on one web page within a site until the term of the advertising contract ends or the agreed-upon number of impressions has been reached.

■ A *rotating banner* is one that moves throughout the website or the network of sites where you are advertising. The banner can be set to rotate on a specific time loop or each time there is a new visitor to the page.

■ An *animated banner* is one that moves, which can mean anything from a changing promotional message or graphic to flashing colors, lights and icons. Animated banners can be *static* or *rotating*, depending on the advertising contract.

With a better understanding of the more common banner advertising terms, you can begin to map out your strategy. Start by keeping your target market in mind when renting banner advertising space. While cheap run-of-site or run-of-network deals might be alluring in terms of your budget, your results can suffer dramatically if you are not presenting your advertising message to your primary target market. Also, bigger is not always better. While brand-name sites and search engine sites attract untold numbers of visitors, those numbers do not necessarily make those the right sites for your message.

Once again, it's all about reaching your target market and achieving your online marketing objectives. Studies have shown that banners created to resemble web forms and polls pull a higher click-though rate. You can dramatically increase your click-through rate by using words and phrases such as "Click Here" or "Start Here" in your banner. Also, think carefully about the page where you want click-through visitors to land.

There are online services that create banner advertisements for a fee; some services also offer banner advertising posting and placement packages. If you search for banner ad packages, you will find plenty of them. Compare deals before making any buying decision.

Banner Advertising Exchange Programs

Over the past few years, banner exchange programs have become extremely popular among web entrepreneurs with tight advertising budgets, mainly because the programs are cheap, yet highly effective. Most banner exchange programs are similar. In exchange for allowing other website owners to put banner ads on your website, you are allowed to place banner ads on their sites.

Each banner exchange program has its own specific criteria, ranging from a points-and-credits placement system to exchange ratios ranging from 1:2 to 1:5 and other criteria that define the program. Few programs swap one for one, because to earn revenue the services sell the excess advertising space to advertising marketers, brokers, corporations and small business owners.

Before you commit to a banner exchange program, check with the operator to make sure there are restrictions limiting the banners displayed on sites to tasteful ads from reputable businesses. Likewise, make sure there are also size restrictions so your site is not burdened with gigantic banners that are slow to download. You can visit the following websites to find out more about the banner exchange programs they provide:

- Ad Server Solutions, Banner Exchange Program, *bannerexchangeprogram.com*
- e-bannerx.com, *e-bannerx.com*
- Free-Banners, *free-banners.com*
- Trade Banner Ads, *tradebannerads.com*
- IBannerExchange, *ibannerexchange.com*
- 123Banners, *123banners.com*
- Bpath, *bpath.com*

E-Zine Advertising

Home business owners in particular have found advertising in electronic magazines to be highly effective for reaching their target markets for a very modest cost. I say "highly effective," because even though there are an estimated 100,000 e-publications distributed monthly worldwide, these e-publications cover specific areas of interest, such as small business, travel or entertainment. Within these areas of interest, there are subcategories that allow for even more focused marketing.

Before committing to advertising in any e-zines or other e-publications, you will want to know the basics, the statistics for circulation and demographics. This information will be featured on the publisher's data or media card. You also want to know its policies for competing advertisers. A larger subscriber base is not necessarily better, because e-zines with large subscriber bases often contain more advertisements.

One of the best ways to determine if a particular e-zine is right for you is to subscribe to it and track the featured ads. If an ad runs continuously, that generally means it is getting the desired response for the advertiser. You might even want to contact a few advertisers and inquire about their success rate with that particular e-zine.

Not unlike advertising in a print magazine, you always want to make sure to track the results of your ads, especially if you are advertising in more than one e-zine at a time. Knowing which ads in which e-zines are pulling the best response rates will help you to spend your advertising dollars where you will get the best results. Because there are so many e-zines published, the best starting point for narrowing the field for advertising is to visit a few e-zine directories to track down those e-zines most suited for your target market:

- New-List, *new-list.com*
- The Ezine Directory, *ezine-dir.com*
- The Book of Zines, *zinebook.com*

Of course you can also do a web search for e-zines and newsletters in your industry to find others.

Pay-Per-Click Advertising Programs

Another form of advertising on the internet is through pay-per-click programs. Google's AdWord program, *https://adwords.google.com/select/advantages.html*, is the biggest and arguably most effective.

How do pay-per-click programs work? When someone uses a search engine, the words or phrases used in the search can cause ads to appear with the search results, generally along the right or above the results and labeled "sponsored links." You have no doubt noticed these links. To use a pay-per-click program, advertisers specify the words that should trigger their ads—words each advertiser believes his or her target customers will

use when searching for the advertiser's products or services—and the maximum they are willing to pay per click. The order in which these sponsored links appear depends on the amounts bid by the advertisers and the quality score of all ads triggered by a given search.

For instance, if you sell movie DVDs, you would want to bid on prime keywords such as "DVDs," "movies," and "celebrities." Pay-per-click programs have different requirements and rules in terms of how you select your words and how they make sure your site is relevant or optimized for the keywords you select or bid on. However, the programs are similar in the way you bid for the keywords you want. For instance, you can bid $1 for a specific keyword; if that is the highest bid, you win and your ad appears first among the sponsored links triggered by that keyword in a search. On the other hand, if you bid $0.20 and other marketers bid more for the same keywords, your ad will appear lower. Google charges an advertiser only when the person doing the search clicks on that advertiser's ad, that is, the ad generates a click-through.

Targeted pay-per-click advertising can greatly increase your search result rankings and dramatically increase your click-through rate. Still you will want to research these programs, carefully reading the information provided to make sure that participation in a program will meet your online marketing objectives and fit your advertising budget. Such programs can become very costly and are not advisable for home business owners.

Surefire Ways to Keep Customers and Visitors Coming Back

Online marketing comprises three separate but equally important elements: attracting visitors to your site, turning visitors into paying customers and ensuring that customers return to your site frequently. Studies have shown beyond a doubt that the more often people visit a site, the more likely they are to do business with the company. Therefore, to increase your selling opportunities, you have to provide reasons for customers and visitors to return to your site frequently. Online marketing gurus refer to this as developing your website's *stickiness*, which is done through the use of content, features and web tools, all of which benefit customers and visitors.

Ask Visitors to Bookmark Your Site

One way to lure back customers and visitors is to simply to ask them to bookmark your site and specific pages within your site. Do this by displaying a "Bookmark Us" button on all your web pages. This is one of the easiest ways to increase the number of repeat visits. How many times have you visited a website and later wanted to return, but couldn't remember the URL or even how you found your way to the site? Plenty, I am sure. Bookmarking a site is a way of keeping it handy for returning often. Smart website owners make it easy for visitors to bookmark.

Provide Useful Tools

Another effective way to keep visitors and customers coming back to your site is to provide useful interactive tools. Is there a calculator or customizable template you can provide that would benefit visitors, make their jobs or lives easier or solve specific challenges? What tools can you provide that would be appropriate for people whom you want to target for what your business sells? For example, if you do tax returns from your home, that handy online calculator is a plus.

Of course you can also provide downloads to products or service popular with your target audience. Make sure the downloads work before you offer them, of course.

Bravenet, *bravenet.com*, is home to lots of free interactive tools, sticky content and community

building plug-ins.

Indicate What's New

Adding a "What's New" page or a "Daily Update" is a great way to draw visitors regularly so they can get updated on the latest news and information related to your industry. Ideally, this should be at the top right side of your home page, so visitors can find it quickly or click to read it. Obviously, you'll need to update it daily.

You can have a daily trivia column or any type of updated content that would appeal to your audience and bring them back to your site every day.

Give Expert Advice

Providing visitors with an online ask-an-expert service is a powerful community-building tool that can be extremely effective for encouraging repeat visits. Securing experts to answer questions and provide advice about topics related to your business and target market should not prove difficult, providing, of course, there is a benefit, such as a link to their website or free advertising for their products or services. For instance, if you sell antique car parts online, enlist an expert in the classic car restoration field to answer questions through an "e-mail letter of the week" feature. Post the answers and invite people to send their questions.

Hold Contests

Another way to increase repeat visits is to hold regular contests—daily, weekly or monthly, depending on your marketing objectives and budget. Prizes need not be expensive, just something valuable to your target customers, perhaps extended warranties, special downloads, free consultations or gift certificates for products.

There are also pooled contest services: many online marketers sponsor a contest together so they can offer bigger prizes and more frequent drawings. Pooled contests are very inexpensive in comparison with the value of the prizes awarded. One such service is ePrize, *eprize.net*.

If contests are going to be part of your online marketing strategy, be sure to get listed in contest directories such as ContestHound.com, *contesthound.com*. Most contest services and directories also offer free legal advice about online contests and sweepstakes, which is great if you are going to use these services or get listed in the directories. Online contest have their own set of rules, since they transcend state and national boundaries, so consult with an attorney who knows about online contests.

Remember: Your website is global. If you run a local business based in Des Moines, there is no point in having a winner in Hong Kong. You will need to limit eligibility.

Provide News, Weather and Sports

You can also make your site stickier and get more repeat visits by providing up-to-date news headlines, sports scores and other information, international and local weather forecasts and stock market information. There are literally hundreds of online suppliers for this type of content; many will customize content packages to suit your specific business and marketing needs. The problem is that you are competing with a plethora of sites in the business of providing news, weather and sports, so people won't likely go to your furniture site to get the day's top headlines. Therefore, you would be better served with the latest industry news.

Entertain

Providing visitors with some fun stuff to read and doing it on your site can be a big draw in luring visitors back often. Entertainment information and activities can include trivia, interactive games, columns, lists and quizzes to test skills or knowledge. Regardless of the type of entertainment you provide, fun stuff can be a great way to build a loyal

visitor base for your site. FreeSticky, at *freesticky.com*, is an online provider of free and fee-based content, plug-ins and live feeds, which include games and entertainment features. Keep your entertainment content relevant to your site and entertaining to people in your target market. If, for example, your business is all about gardening, you might have quizzes that test knowledge of plants and planting.

Host Interactive Forums

Installing interactive forums on your site is one of the best ways to keep customers and visitors returning to participate in your online community. These interactive forums can include discussion boards, message boards, chat rooms, workshops and private offices, free classified advertising, letters-of-the-day submitted by visitors and other items submitted by visitors.

Marketing Through Usenet Newsgroups

Usenet newsgroups are discussion groups on the internet that focus on specific subjects or topics, such as business, sports, computers or entertainment. At present it is estimated there are more than 100,000 newsgroups on the web, each composed of members who share an interest in the newsgroup topic. The most common newsgroup categories include:

alt	Any conceivable topic
humanities	Fine art, literature and philosophy
biz	Business products, services and opportunities
news	Information about Usenet newsgroups and administration
rec	Games, hobbies and sports
talk	Current news issues, general conversation and debates
comp	Computer hardware and software

In terms of marketing and promoting your

business, Usenet newsgroups can be very powerful, because they are usually free and many consist of thousands of members. That gives a broad reach for your promotional message.

Be aware, however, that many newsgroups are monitored. Before your message gets posted, it will be reviewed to make sure it fits the theme of the group. If it does not, it will be rejected. Unmonitored newsgroups generally post any message in the forum unchecked for content. There are newsgroups that allow and encourage commercial or marketing postings while others do not. You can find out by tracking groups that meet your target profile or are relevant to your products and service. Research is required to make sure you devote time to the right newsgroup. It is very time-consuming to post and track discussions in the group, so read other posts carefully so you can better understand what the people in the group are seeking in terms of information, products and services. To promote your business, you can also sign off each message using a signature that includes a link to your website.

The following are a few popular newsgroup directories and services:

- DMOZ Open Directory Project, *dmoz. org*
- Google Groups, *groups.google.com*
- Usenet, *www2.webmagic.com/usenet.org*
- Message Board Blaster, *messageboardblaster.com*
- AllTheNewsGroups.com, *allthenewsgroups.com*

Permission-Based Marketing

Permission-based marketing is a term used to describe asking and securing permission from your website customers and visitors to send them information via e-mail. Providing they give you permission, the information you send can be about anything, ranging from simple e-special offers to elaborate e-newsletters and e-catalogs, depending on your marketing objectives. It is usually in your best interest to ask people to sign up specifically for a newsletter or a catalog so they anticipate it and don't delete it.

Remember: If you do not gain the permission of the recipients, you are spamming them, which is not only illegal, but will hurt your online credibility. Even if you gain the permission of recipients, don't abuse the privilege. It's very easy for them to hit the delete button, so rather than bombarding people because they agreed to let you send them e-mails, start with a plan that will interest potential customers and build accordingly.

If people ask to be included in your electronic mailings, they most likely have an interest in your products or services. That immediately lets you get past the "hit them over the head" selling approach and begin with some intriguing offers via e-mail. You can then introduce a sample newsletter and ask the recipients if they would like to sign up for more. Yes, you have their permission initially, but you don't want to make them regret giving it to you. The point is to establish a level of trust and a means of communication. Then they will be long-time customers.

There are many ways to get permission from visitors to your website to send them electronic information and special offers. One way is to create a weekly e-publication and ask your visitors to subscribe for free. You can offer special incentives to people who sign up for your e-mails. Much will depend on your marketing objectives and the type of information you are planning to send. One of your main online goals should always be to get as many visitors as possible to agree to receive information via e-mail. The value of building an in-house permission-based mailing list cannot be overstated in terms of marketing and customer relationships.

You will need to compile, store and manage your subscriber base. Fortunately there are numerous contact and customer management software programs to enable you to build your permission-based opt-in list. Alternately, you might want to have your contact list managed by an online contact list management service from a remote server location. The cost for this type of service generally starts at about $10 per month and increases based on size and usage. The benefits of a list management service is that it supplies the subscription form link from your web pages and automatically signs up visitors who want to join.

Renting Opt-In Lists for E-Mail Blasting

Electronic opt-in lists are name lists of people that have requested to receive by e-mail specific information or offers on one or more subjects or topics of interest. The list could be specific to people with an interest in cars, sports, entertainment or about any conceivable topic. The words *opt-in* means people have requested or given their permission to receive information by way of e-mail; since they choose to receive it, it is not spam. Remember: Although the laws are not routinely enforced, spamming is illegal.

Renting well-targeted opt-in lists is a challenge faced by most online marketers. You might want to ask other home business owners and online marketers about their sources for opt-in lists and their success rate with these lists. The next challenge is trying to distinguish between a great opt-in list and a mediocre one. List quality is the difference between success and failure in reaching your target market and between meeting your marketing objectives and coming up short.

Before you consider renting an opt-in list, rather than building your own, consider the amount of junk e-mails you receive daily. The big question regarding opt-in lists is this: If an individual gave permission six months ago for XYZ Company to send him or her e-mails, does that mean he or she wants or even expects e-mails from you? What typically happens is that the person who signed up for the opt-in list has long forgotten about it or anticipated receiving e-mails from only one source. Very few people, if any, knowingly sign up for lists that can result in tons of unexpected e-mails showing up in their in-box—even if those e-mails are not technically spam. Unless someone opts in to be specifically on *your* list, you may as well be sending spam. Therefore, while you are not actually spamming, your e-mail has the same effect and will often be perceived as spam by people on these rented opt-in lists. The result? Your reputation will suffer and people are likely to delete any e-mail from your business.

Try Word-of-Mouse Marketing

Through the decades, small business owners have relied heavily on word-of-mouth advertising and referrals to promote and grow their businesses. You can greatly increase your odds of online e-commerce success by making it as easy as you can for your visitors and customers to promote your business and spread the word about your website by adding a simple, yet highly effective "Forward to a Friend" button to the end of feature articles and special-interest content on your site. When visitors click on the "Forward to a Friend" button, a simple form appears that instructs the visitor to enter the name and e-mail address of anyone to whom they want to send the information. A click of the mouse sends the information to the identified recipient.

At the same time, to really increase the effectiveness of this simple marketing trick, you can ask if they would like to subscribe to your e-newsletter or special offers. In fact, you can add "Forward to a Friend" button to as much content as you like—contests, columns, newsletters, games, special offers, coupons, workshops and tips-of-the-day.

There are certain types of content that people enjoy sharing, such as jokes, recipes and, of course, e-cards. If you can create some specialized e-cards for holidays that are perfect for your target market, you can get people to forward them to others and thus help you market. Just make sure your company name is on them.

An added benefit of this powerful marketing technique is that there is software that enables you to customize the e-mail that customers and visitors send to friends. In addition to the information sent, you can include a promotional message or special offer in the e-mail as a headline over the information. Use this space to promote a sale, introduce a new product, ask people to sign up for your newsletter or e-zine or just say, "Hello, and thank you for the interest in our website." However you use this powerful tool, you can greatly increase your odds of success when there are people who promote your e-business through word-of-mouse marketing. For a variety of other word-of-mouth marketing ideas, both online and offline, you can visit the Word of Mouth Marketing Association, *womma.org.*

Figure 17.4 is a checklist of ideas that will help you drive traffic to your website and ultimately improve sales and profits.

SELLING ONLINE

Marketing online and selling online are two entirely different things. Marketing means getting people to your website, using any of the promotional methods discussed in this chapter. Selling is getting people to buy once they get to your site.

There are steps that you must take, beyond offering a great product or service, to maximize the odds of turning your web visitors into paying customers and ideally forging long-term selling relationships. You have to create credibility. You have to reduce or eliminate buying doubt and fear.

You have to provide strong guarantees. You have to provide an efficient and easy-to-use shopping cart if you are actually selling online. If you are not selling via the internet, turning visitors into customers means persuading them to pick up the phone and call to order or make an appointment. All the while, you have to provide great customer service.

Creating Online Credibility

Before you can consider shopping carts, online payment systems or communicating in any manner with potential customers, the first order of business is creating online credibility. How do you gain the trust of consumers in the faceless world of cyberspace?

One common means of creating some credibility is to include the "About Us" page, which should provide a history of your business: when you started, information about yourself and any partners or employees, perhaps even some photographs. The faces behind a website make a business more real in the minds of visitors and reassure them. Remember: online you are trying to appeal to a global market.

It is very important that you include real-world contact information. People generally do not like doing business with websites lacking an address and a phone number.

Let your visitors know who you and any key people within your organization are, what you and they do and how you can be contacted directly by e-mail, snail mail, fax and telephone. If you are not confident enough to let people know who wants their business, how they can contact you, and what steps you take to ensure their security and privacy, you may as well shut down your cyber venture and hit the road. Remember: people do business with people—and they want to know who is the person behind your business.

FIGURE 17.4 Driving Traffic to Your Website Checklist

❏ Register your site with major search engines and search directories and smaller search engines that serve a niche market relative to your business, products or services.

❏ Link your site and pages to other appropriate sites. Use linking services to increase the number of sites to which your site is linked.

❏ Purchase targeted keyword advertising at the major search engines and use keyword-generating services and software to optimize your keyword selections to improve your search rankings and results on all of the major search engines.

❏ Publish a monthly e-zine or e-newsletter peppered throughout with promotions and links to your site.

❏ Ask your site visitors to subscribe to your electronic publications and offer an incentive to motivate them to do so, with additional incentives if they help recruit subscribers.

❏ Write articles, as an expert, for online and offline publications and include your byline and your URL.

❏ Create an e-mail signature for all outgoing e-mail that includes a link to your site.

❏ Start an affiliate program, enlisting other web marketers to promote and sell your products or services on their sites and in their e-publications.

❏ Use direct marketing techniques such as snail mail, public speaking engagements and personal visits to promote your site.

❏ Ask all visitors to bookmark your site for their convenience.

❏ Purchase online and offline display and classified advertising in print newspapers and magazines, as well as in electronic publications, promoting your site, products and services.

❏ Include your URL in all online and offline business communications, such as letters, faxes, voice-mail messages, business cards, sales presentations, receipts and brochures.

❏ Join professional, business and industry associations and have your URL listed in their print and online member directories and newsletters.

❏ Create press releases around a news event or information posted on your site.

❏ Add a "Forward to a Friend" button to content and information featured in your site.

❏ Create e-coupon discount offers and e-gift certificates. Get listed in online coupon sites and gift certificate portals and sites.

❏ Use paid banner advertisements and banner exchange programs to increase click-through traffic to your site.

❏ Build an in-house opt-in list and e-mail valuable offers to everyone on your list routinely. Also ask recipients to share the information and offers with others by forwarding the e-mails to friends and family members.

❏ Create and host online contests and list your events in online directories of contests, with links back to your site.

❏ Participate in online discussion groups and chat rooms.

❏ Start a blog on your site.

❏ Give away free stuff and get listed in websites and portals featuring free stuff and giveaways.

❏ Make sure your site is listed in web directories.

Privacy

Create a privacy policy that clearly spells out the steps you take to ensure privacy and protect security for all visitors and customers alike. Every page on your website should link to your privacy and security policy page. If you do not share customer information with others, clearly state that fact. If you employ the latest encryption technologies to ensure secure online financial transactions, let customers know. Have an attorney review your privacy policy to make sure you have covered all bases. And do not breech your own policy. If your best friend is starting a website and asks for your list of customers and tells you not to worry because they will never know where he or she obtained the list, *do not* give it to him or her, even if it causes a dispute. Maintaining your customers' privacy is essential. If you are cited in an identity fraud scheme, you will have far more legal problems than customers.

Alliances

Establish alliances with larger, better-known companies, organizations, and associations by offering them free advertising on your website and by joining their affiliate vendor programs. When your visitors see your business is aligned with these well-known and trusted companies and organizations, that link will lend you instant credibility. Join professional business associations relevant to your business and industry, as well as consumer-protection organizations such as the Better Business Bureau. Not only will this contribute to building trust with visitors, but many of these organizations and associations also have well-known logos and graphics that can be displayed on your site, lending further credibility.

Testimonials

Create a client testimonial page on your site and try to feature at least three or four testimonials from your happiest and best customers. To get the maximum benefit from the testimonial, for each customer give the full name, business and title (if any), provide contact information such as an e-mail link and display his or her photograph. Update the testimonial page twice per year with your newest and greatest customer testimonials. Client testimonials are without question one of the best ways online marketers can establish credibility for their business, products and services. Remember: the testimonials must, by law, be legitimate, so don't be tempted to get creative.

Expertise

Go the extra mile to make your website a one-stop source for expert information relevant to your business, products, services and industry. Write articles and columns in your area(s) of expertise for other online news and general information websites and link your articles on those sites to your site. A ton of credibility comes with being known as an expert in your field or industry.

Charities

Include a page on your website that lists and describes in detail all charities your business supports, including fundraising activities and ongoing charity causes so that visitors can also become involved. To really increase credibility, show a dollar amount. If your business has raised $10,000 through fundraising and donation activities for charitable causes, let your visitors know.

Awards

Enter your business and website in competitions that bestow awards on businesses that provide the best customer service, have the most user-friendly websites or offer the best products or services. Proudly display all awards won by your business, products, services or website. Winning awards boosts your credibility and earns the trust of customers.

Show Me the Money

Unlike the real world, where customers can personally hand you a check, cash or a credit card to pay for their purchases, on the internet you have to provide customers with online payment options that are safe and secure. To cover all consumer payment preferences, your online payment options should include electronic money transfers, credit cards, electronic checks and offline payment.

Credit Cards

Credit cards are by far the most popular way to pay for online purchases. They provide their credit card information during the checkout phase of the purchase. For online retailers, providing customers with a credit card payment option is essential. Without it, there is a good chance your online retailing venture will not succeed, simply because consumers will choose to buy from competitors that accept credit cards. Online credit card merchant account services include:

- Charge.com, *charge.com*
- USA Merchant Account, *usa-merchantac-count.com*
- Merchant Accounts Express, *merchantex-press.com*
- Monster Merchant Account, *monstermer-chantaccount.com*
- Network Solutions Merchant Accounts, *merchantaccounts.networksolutions.com*

Money Transfers

Money transfers, like the one pioneered and perfected by PayPal, have become very popular for consumers—and for online retailers because of the low cost to participate, easy bookkeeping, and relatively quick processing time that gives them access to their money very quickly. Here's how online money transfers work: People deposit money into an electronic bank account; they can then use funds in that account like cash to pay for purchases they make online, providing, of course, that the retailer accepts this payment option. Some of the companies that provide this service are:

- PayPal, *paypal.com*
- VeriSign, *verisign.com*
- WorldPay, *worldpay.com*
- PaySystems, *paysystems.com*

E-Checks

A third option is to provide customers with e-check payment options, which work much like cash or a debit card in the real world. If the customer has adequate funds in a checking account to pay for a purchase from your site, after the purchase and payment amount have been verified, the funds are deposited directly into your bank account electronically.

- PayByCheck, *paybycheck.com*
- Zytransact, *.e-checkprocessing.com*
- Alpha Check Express, *alphacheckexpress.com*

Offline Options

Finally, even if you incorporate the latest and greatest encryption technology on your website to ensure safe and secure online shopping options for all customers, you will still find that some people are reluctant to give out credit card or other financial information online. For that reason, don't take a chance on limiting potential sales and profits; make it easy for all your visitors to give you money by providing them with offline product ordering and payment options.

Offline payment options should include a 24-hour toll-free telephone order hotline and/or mail-in payments. Post the details on your website. In both cases you can enlist fulfillment services to answer the telephones, to check post boxes for orders and checks, and to store and ship products to your customers for a fee, which is charged on a per-customer order. These companies can often do this for less than it would cost a business to set up and provide these services. Fulfillment services work on a volume basis, serving many business clients at one time. In our super-competitive online marketplace, often all that separates the winners from the losers is which business empowers consumers to make choices that fill their individual needs. This is possible only by providing people with numerous payment options so they can decide which suits them best.

Finally, you can provide an address where people can send you a paper check. Wait until it clears before sending the merchandise. Give notice of this policy on your website.

Choosing a Shopping Cart

One of the greatest challenges facing online e-tailers today is shopping cart abandonment. The shopping cart is too complicated or simply too unreliable, so shoppers give up on the process and abandon their cart before checking out and paying. So it stands to reason that the shopping cart program you select is important to your online sales, perhaps one of the more important e-decisions you will have to make. Do a search for "shopping cart software" and you will be overwhelmed by the results: thousands of choices—but which shopping cart program is best for your specific e-business?

The shopping cart decision will be based largely on your business needs and your budget. There are free shopping cart programs and services, but most are unreliable and ultimately will cost you sales. (Remember, poor reliability is the number-one reason online consumers abandon their shopping carts and do not complete the sale.) Thus they are not a good value. There are shopping carts you can rent and that operate from a remote server location. Some of these are very good quality, have a good reputation, a terrific performance record, and can be subscribed to for less than $100 per month.

Another option is to purchase your own shopping cart program and server and operate the program in-house. You will need to purchase the software, an investment that in time will prove worthwhile.

Today, many host services and internet providers offer shopping carts. They are typically reliable, since this is a major part of their business. Check all possibilities and ask your website designer what he or she would recommend.

Whichever you choose, make sure your shopping cart is safe, secure, fast, easy to use, reliable and cost-effective for your needs. If a cart does not meet all these criteria, keep looking. The following are a few popular shopping cart programs and services:

- eCartsoft, *ecartsoft.com*
- NetworkSolutions E-Commerce websites, *ecommerce.networksolutions.com*
- ShopFactory, *shopfactory.com*
- CoolCart, *coolcart.com*

How to Turn Visitors into Paying Customers

Let's face it, if you are selling products and services online and you have 10 million hits a year on your site, you must develop ways to turn a portion of these visitors into paying customers or you will not remain in business for long. There are many reasons why people will choose not to buy, such as doubt or lingering questions about the products or services offered. Remember: They cannot touch and feel fabrics or try on sizes. Therefore, you need to make buying—and returning—a product as painless as possible.

Removing Fear and Doubt

One of the best ways to motivate your online visitors to buy is to remove the fear or doubt associated with making a purchase. In the bricks-and-mortar world, consumers can pick up and examine the goods; they cannot do the same in cyberspace. Even if the product you are selling is relatively well known and accepted, it will always be, to a degree, intangible. Potential customers may doubt or fear that it might not work as advertised, might not fit or might be too expensive. Doubt and fear are the two biggest obstacles all online sellers face—period. You can, however, remove or substantially reduce consumer doubt and fear by:

- Having a simple and straightforward return policy. Determine in advance how this will work, whether they get credit or cash back, and make it easy to return or exchange products.
- Offering free, no-obligation product or service trial periods (depending on the product).
- For higher-priced items, dividing the total cost into installments over a fixed period; $20 per month for 12 months appears much less risky than a one-time payment of $240.
- Having accessible, polite, and knowledgeable customer service reps available by e-mail and by telephone. This can be your strongest manner of closing sales: reassuring customers that you are there to meet their needs.

- Making shipping options easy to understand and doing the calculations for the customers. Shipping and handling is one place that loses many potential customers. Have your customer service hotline number there in case anyone is confused.
- Having an easy-to-find link to your privacy policy, which should assure customers you will not sell their personal information or let it be used by anyone for any reason other than the purchase of a product or service from your business.

Fear and doubt are major stumbling blocks to online sales. By reducing or eliminating them, you will be able to dramatically increase your online sales revenues.

Value-Adding

Adding value to your online offers is another way to entice people to buy. For instance, instead of offering a one-year product warranty, increase the value of the product and your offer by upping the warranty to two years. If you sell widgets for $10 each, increase the value by offering three widgets for $20. The most powerful way to make your value-added incentives irresistible to your site visitors is to give away something for free that enhances the value of the product or service being sold and that you would normally charge for as a stand-alone item. For example, if you sell computers online, offer a free extended warranty that protects the customer's purchase for two years instead of one; if you sell gift items or clothing, add something small and as simple as free gift wrapping, which is a biggie over the year-end holiday season. You are offering an incentive that is relevant to your main offer and that greatly increases the value of your offer. Think through your offers before making them. Offering a "free installation" online, for example, could come back to haunt you if your business is located in Sacramento and the buyer is in Vermont.

Presenting Your Products and/or Services

Packing more items onto a web page does not sell more products; it simply clutters the page and confuses the potential buyer. Do not crowd your pages. Use strong, clear photographs that visitors can click on to enlarge. You may even offer various views of certain products. You then need to include the features, prices and all other pertinent data.

If this is too much to put on one page, have customers click to a landing page, where they find more information about a product or service. Most people, in stores or online, do not pick up a product and immediately buy it unless they know exactly what they wanted before entering the store or the website. Therefore, your landing page is the place to build your sale. If you rush people to a shopping cart without providing the details, they will get nervous and leave. Amazon.com provides a great example of landing pages. When you search for books on a topic or by an author or a title, you will get a lengthy list. You can click on the title of the book to go to a landing page with all sorts of information, from an overview to a sample table of contents to reviews and sometimes even some sample pages. This is designed to sell you on the book. Amazon.com also presents similar books on the topic, in case you want to check out other titles. Take a cue from this mega website and provide information and even appropriate similar products.

You want to make it easy for shoppers to find what they are looking for by cross-categorizing your goods and/or services. For example, if you are selling clothing, you might list items by category, by size and by designer or manufacturer. This way the customer can choose the manner in which he or she would prefer to shop.

One of the advantages an online business has is that it can accommodate various styles of shopping. Therefore, the price-conscious shopper can shop for price and the person interested in the latest features can look up specific features and find items grouped in that manner.

Make the shopping experience as customer-friendly as possible.

Affiliate Programs

Affiliate programs are alliances with other online businesses to sell their products or services via your website and receive a commission ranging from 5 to 25 percent, depending on the program and profitability of what is being sold. You can also pay other online businesses a commission on your products and services they sell through their websites. Amazon.com was one of the first major players to embrace the affiliate system. The program has proven to be so successful that the number of affiliate sellers has grown to more than 900,000.

There are basically two ways to profit from affiliate programs: (1) you sell your affiliates' products and services and (2) your affiliates sell your products and services. But "selling" is not really the best description of the activity. You do not actually warehouse and ship goods or even collect payment. The main role of affiliates is to promote each other's products or services on their websites via advertisements, banners, or text messages that take visitors away to the affiliates' websites to make their purchases. Each affiliate is assigned a code so that any affiliate that makes a sale to a visitor coming from an affiliate's website knows where the purchase originated and can attribute the commission to that affiliate. In most cases there are no or low fees to join affiliate seller programs, but the potential to earn extra revenues from your website is quite substantial. More information on affiliate programs as well as affiliate program directories can be found at the following websites:

- AssociatePrograms.com, *associateprograms.com*
- AffiliateMatch.com, *affiliatematch.com*
- AffiliatesDirectory.com, *affiliatesdirectory.com*
- AssociateSearch.com, *associatesearch.com*
- ClicksLink Affiliate Program Directory, *clickslink.com*

Great Online Customer Service Tips

First, resolve all customer challenges as quickly as possible. Complaints can move much more swiftly on the internet than in the real world. An unhappy cyber customer can tell other people about a negative experience with your business in a matter of moments with a click of the mouse. If possible, interact with your customers and visitors through your online discussion boards and chat rooms on your site. This will go a long way to making customers and visitors feel as though they are part of your online community. Here are a few other online customer service tips that will go a long way in building long-term and profitable selling relationships with all your customers:

- Give customers and visitors lots of choices, a wide selection of products and services, multiple payment options and specialized web tools and information on your site.
- Give customers and visitors options beyond e-mail for contacting you, including telephone, fax and traditional mail. Add an online FAQ page to provide answers to the most frequently asked questions. But do not assume this covers all questions and answers. This is a mistake made by many websites: an FAQ often does not solve a customer's problem. The

additional contact information helps when it's not possible to immediately reach a human being on the phone.

- If you have a phone number so they can call you (and you should), make it easy to reach a real person. Yes, you may have voice mail to differentiate between calls that involve technical problems with the website and calls relating to your products or services, but do not lead customers along a string of push-button options. There's nothing more infuriating than having a problem (online or off) and being forced to play the push-button phone game for 10 minutes—only to end up leaving a voice-mail message. This loses customers. If you have a site for selling, then have someone ready to answer the phone even if it means only politely taking a message so someone can call the customer back.
- Get into the habit of returning calls and responding to all of your e-mails (from customers, vendors and suppliers) within 24 hours.
- Get into the habit of e-mailing customer satisfaction questionnaires a few days after the order has been delivered. Ask questions relevant to your business, website, industry and products or services. Use the responses to identify weak areas of your business so you can improve.
- Stay in regular contact with customers by creating an e-publication and sending it out weekly or monthly, along with the occasional greeting card to let them know you are thinking about them.
- Tell your customers and visitors how much you appreciate their business and their continued support. Show your appreciation by delivering great service and access to products, services, and information that are beneficial and meet their needs.

ELECTRONIC COMMUNICATIONS

Online communications are the premiere way of reaching people worldwide. No other medium can reach so many people in so many places, so quickly or at such a low cost.

So how can home business owners use the internet to communicate with customers, prospects, alliances, suppliers and vendors cheaply and effectively? Along with your website, you can develop an electronic newsletter to keep your business team and customers up-to-date on your latest business news. You can send out daily e-mails featuring company information and special offers. In short, the internet provides every home business owner with an incredibly cheap, yet highly effective means of communicating with customers, employees, alliances and everyone else associated with your business. Volumes could be written on the numerous electronic communications options and the benefits associated with each. Here we will consider only three options—e-mail signatures, electronic publications and automatic e-mail responders.

E-Mail Signature

An e-mail signature is a text message, a link, and/or an image automatically attached at the bottom of your outgoing e-mails. Most e-mail programs give you the option of setting up an e-mail signature. Look under "Tools" or "Toolbar" for "new signature" or "set up new mail signature options," click, and follow the instructions. If you have problems setting up an e-mail signature file, consult the tutorial section of your e-mail program for guidance.

In your e-mail signature, include your business name, title and contact information, such as telephone and fax numbers and mailing address. You can also include a text link in your signature that links directly to your website or an alternate site where you would like to send your reader. But perhaps one of the biggest benefits of an e-mail signature is that you can develop a new marketing message every day and attach it to all outgoing e-mails automatically. Announce a sale or a special offer, introduce a new product, promote a forthcoming event, include company or industry news, or provide any type of information or announcements that you think your customers and prospects need and want.

Creating an E-Publication

Home business owners that operate e-commerce sites or sell products and services online and offline should consider creating and maintaining some sort of e-publication, such as an electronic newsletter, an e-zine, or a simple weekly e-alert that can be sent on a regular basis. Not only can your e-publication be a useful tool to market your website and your products or services, it also can help you stay in touch with all your customers and prospects effortlessly, building stronger customer relationships and substantially increasing selling opportunities.

Of course, like any publication, it needs content. Fortunately, there are numerous options for content to include. The first option is to write the content yourself, which means you can create content of interest and benefit to your customers and target market. The downside is that writing the content can become time-consuming. The second option is to subscribe to a content service and pay for content. This option will be out of reach for web marketers on restricted budgets and very often the content is stale by the time you receive it or it's already posted on 25 other websites. A good option is to get content directly from writers. You can hire content writers for a low fee to provide some quality material or even get some writing students or people starting out who want only a byline. If you advertise for writers, be prepared to be inundated by e-mails from anyone who thinks they can write a sentence. It can take forever to sift through these to find a couple of good writers. Therefore, ask around, look for people who can write, check out the bylines in local newspapers and find a few writers on your own if possible.

E-publications can be very powerful marketing and customer service tools, but they require subscribers in order to flourish. In addition to asking current customers and prospects to subscribe, you can try a few of the following ideas to motivate visitors to your website to subscribe to your e-publication:

- Make special offers and discounts to people who subscribe to your e-publication.
- Hold an exclusive new-subscriber contest, open only to people who subscribe to your e-publication.
- Give away free gifts, such as T-shirt emblazoned with your logo or a free upgrade on a product order to people who subscribe to your e-publication.

Automatic E-Mail Responders

Autoresponders are a must for all entrepreneurs serious about building a powerful and efficient online presence and an electronic communications network. You can respond automatically to hundreds of e-mail inquiries painlessly by installing an autoresponder program or by using a remote e-mail autorespond system integrated with your website, e-mail and/or electronic publication or a combination.

Perhaps one of the greatest benefits of autoresponders for marketing and customer service is that the program will automatically send follow-up e-mail offers to customers after they have purchased or inquired about products and service. You can personalize your messages with mail-merge features so you can single out and write directly to a person by using his or her first name in all electronic correspondence. Many autorespond systems also contain tracking mechanisms so you will know which recipients are opening your messages and clicking through on included web links.

Even web entrepreneurs with limited experience will find most autorespond programs very simple to use. In no time you will be changing or updating your communications or marketing message within moments and as often as you like. Autoresponders help you stay in touch with thousands of customers, prospects and visitors in moments rather than days. Just beware of free autorespond systems and programs because some feature advertisements from other companies that show up on the e-mails automatically responded to through your e-mail. You can ask your hosting service about autoresponders or visit GetResponse, *getresponse.com*, for information, products and links of interest about e-mail autoresponder marketing and communications. E-mail and e-business automation software and services can be found online at *marketingtips.com/mailloop*.

A Source of Web Income

You can make money not only through selling products and services on your website, but also through selling advertising space. Just as your banner ads appear on other websites, other companies can post their ads atop your site or along the right-hand column or on your newsletter to help you offset the cost.

There are two keys to selling ad space:

Do not post ads for competing businesses (obviously), disreputable websites or those that may not appeal to your target customers. Review the website carefully before posting its ads and check in on the site periodically to ensure its content has not changed.

While you want to make money by displaying ads from other companies, you do not want ads to dominate your website or newsletter. If the ad distracts from your site, then it may not be right for you.

Rather than selling ad space yourself, you may work with a web advertising broker who can find qualified clients and charge accordingly.

RESOURCES
Associations

eMarketingAssociation
224 Post Road, #129
Westerly, RI 02891
(401) 315-2194
emarketingassociation.com

Federal Communications Commission (FCC)
445 12th Street SW
Washington, DC 20554
(888) 225-5322
fcc.gov

International Internet Marketing Association
P.O. Box 4018
Vancouver Main
349 W. Georgia Street
Vancouver V6B 3Z4
(866) 281-IIMA (4462)
iimaonline.org

International Webmasters Association
119 E. Union Street, Suite F
Pasadena, CA 91103
(626) 449-3709
iwanet.org

Web Design and Developers Association
8515 Brower Street
Houston, TX 77017-2429
(435) 518-9784
wdda.org

Word of Mouth Marketing Association
65 E. Wacker Place, Suite 500
Chicago, IL 60601
(312) 853-4400
womma.org

Suggested Reading

Brelsford, Harry, Michael S. Toot, Karishma Kiri, and Robin Van Steenburgh. *Connecting to Customers: Strategies and Solutions for Growing Your Business Online.* Redmond, WA: Microsoft Press, 2002.

Brown, Bruce C. *How to Use the Internet to Advertise, Promote and Market Your Business or Website with Little or No Money.* Ocala, FL: Atlantic Publishing Co., 2006.

Davidson, Jeffrey P. *101 Internet Marketing Tips for Your Business: Increase Your Profits and Stay Within Your Budget.* Irvine, CA: Entrepreneur Press, 2002.

Davis, Harold. *Google Advertising Tools: Cashing in with AdSense, AdWords, and the Google APIs.* Sebastopol, CA: O'Reilly Media, 2006.

Eisenberg, Bryan, Jeffrey Eisenberg, with Lisa T. Davis. *Call to Action: Secret Formulas to Improve Online Results.* Nashville, TN: Thomas Nelson, 2006.

Grappone, Jennifer, and Gradiva Couzin. *Search Engine Optimization: An Hour a Day.* San Francisco: Sybex; Indianapolis, IN: Wiley Publishing, 2008.

Gregory, Kip. *Winning Clients in a Wired World: Seven Strategies for Growing Your Business Using Technology and the Web.* New York: John Wiley & Sons, 2004.

Scott, David Meerman. *The New Rules of Marketing and PR: How to Use News Releases, Blogs, Podcasting, Viral Marketing and Online Media to Reach Buyers Directly*. Hoboken, NJ: John Wiley & Sons, 2007.

Sweeney, Susan. *101 Ways to Promote Your Web Site: Filled with Proven Internet Marketing Tips, Tools, Techniques and Resources to Increase Your Web Site Traffic*. 6th edition. Gulf Breeze, FL: Maximum Press, 2006.

Websites

American E-Commerce Association: Nonprofit association representing American electronic merchants and marketers. *aeaus.com*

Animation Online (Meher Software): Online banner-generation program with free and paid services available. *animationonline.com*

AssociatePrograms.com: Directory service listing associate and affiliate reseller programs. *associateprograms.com*

Bravenet: Gigantic source of interactive website tools and content. *bravenet.com*

ClickZ: Daily electronic newsletter providing information on e-commerce and internet marketing. *clickz.com*

eCommerce Times: E-commerce and internet marketing portal providing daily news, features, advice, links and special reports. *ecommercetimes.com*

Ezine Directory: E-zine directory service index by topic. *ezine-dir.com*

Free Sticky: Providers of free and paid content and online tools. *freesticky.com*

Institute of Certified E-Commerce Consultants: E-commerce training programs, products and services and directory listing certified independent e-commerce consultants. *eccertified.com*

InternetNews.com: Leading online resource center for internet trends and internet statistics. *internetnews.com*

LinkLeads.com: website linking, link management and advertising service. *linkleads.com*

Message Board Blaster: Software that automatically submits your message to more than 1,300 online message boards and Usenet newsgroups. *messageboardblaster.com*

newsClicker.com: Providers of automatically updated free and low-cost news, weather, sports and business content. *newsclicker.com*

Systran Software: website and e-communications language translation software. *systransoft.com*

Webopedia: Online dictionary and search engine for computer and internet technology. *webopedia.com*

CHAPTER 18

Home Business Startup Ideas and Home Franchise Opportunities

THIS CHAPTER OF THE *ULTIMATE Homebased Business Handbook* features 125 great home business startup ideas. The information included about these opportunities is brief, intended only as a snapshot of the venture, to get you thinking about these and other home business enterprises—and ultimately one that is right for you.

Of course, all new home business ventures require a business license or permit. A major component of starting a home business is to research all the legal aspects of the business venture, including licenses and permits, liability insurance, zoning and building-use codes, fire and health regulations, employee regulations and certificates of training. A successful entrepreneur carefully researches and plans every aspect of a new business venture, including the financial investment needed to start a business and the working capital required to achieve a positive cash flow. While keeping all of that in mind, why not browse these 125 ideas and begin thinking about the possibilities for your own homebased business?

125 GREAT HOME BUSINESS STARTUP IDEAS

1. Mystery Shopping Service

Go undercover and learn the secrets of businesses for the sake of your clients. Mystery shoppers assess all sorts of valuable information for clients, such as management trends, operational procedures and customer service policies. In the past decade, more companies, organizations, and retailers have introduced mystery shopper programs into their business, and for good reason. Such programs uncover problems within large operations and enable the business owners to solve those problems. Generally, on completing one or more visits, the mystery shoppers prepare a document detailing their findings, relaying their experiences and making recommendations to clients. Expanding the business is as easy as hiring additional mystery shoppers to work on a subcontract-as-needed basis. Of course, these people need to be trained. The industry is competitive, so the more relevant experiences and training you can bring to the table, the better. These experiences could include managerial training, customer service postings, human resources experience and work as an operations specialist. There are even mystery shopper training courses available.

The Mystery Shopping Providers Association, *mysteryshop.org:* Members receive industry information, advice and support.

Home requirements include basic software programs for scheduling your appointments and a word processing program for writing up your findings. You'll also need transportation for visiting locations. This type of business typically offers a flexible schedule.

2. Inflatable Advertising Rentals

Twenty-foot high inflatable gorillas, holiday reindeer and cartoon characters get noticed by traffic, especially when these large inflatables are sitting on a retailer's rooftop with a "sale in progress" sign emblazoned across them. Renting inflatable advertising objects is a fantastic home business venture. You can operate the business full or part time. A potential client list can include retailers, sports teams, community organizations, or just about anyone else who wants to draw attention to a sale or special occasion. Currently, new inflatables are retailing at around $5,000. To reduce startup

investment, you can purchase secondhand inflatables in good condition for half the cost of new. Rental rates range from $100 to $500 per day, including delivery and setup. You can start with half a dozen and build as you receive income from renting those out. Make sure to get a deposit to cover your cost in advance and hold it until the inflatable is safely back in storage.

Windship International, *windship.com:* Manufacturers of hot- and cold-air advertising inflatables.

Home requirements include appropriate insurance in the event that an inflatable falls and hurts someone. You also need a place to store inflatables and a means of transporting them safely and inflating them. Keeping track of orders and pickups is your other main concern, which can be done manually or on a computer.

3. Public Relations Specialist

An outstanding PR person is essential for representing individuals, businesses, politicians and products or services. The main duty of a public relations specialist is to promote the client in a positive and informative manner. Promotion techniques and services include creating press releases, press kits, organizing media conferences and special events, performing damage control services, and networking around the clock on the client's behalf. Getting started in the business can be difficult, as the public relations industry is fiercely competitive. The problem is that public relations firms and consultants are often selected by clients based on *whom* they know and not *what* they know. Therefore, the key question is: Do you know a lot of editors and producers in any given region or town? If so, you can help local businesses looking to grow in that market. As they grow, you can also expand your contact base. Learning how to write press releases is easy; having those important contacts is much tougher. However, if you have dealt with newspaper and magazine editors, TV producers and reporters and other people in the media, you may want to use all of your resources for this endeavor. Do you have a nephew at a radio station? An old friend who works in TV news? A former girlfriend or boyfriend who's a newspaper reporter? These are all contacts to use.

As an entry point, consider starting small and representing one or two clients on a local basis until you have mastered the art.

Public Relations Society of America, *prsa.org:* Members receive industry information, advice and support.

PRWeb, *prweb.com:* Free online press release distribution, industry information, resources and links.

Home requirements are minimal. You need a quiet environment to be at your computer writing press releases and sending e-mails, as well as on the phone, constantly building and maintaining your communications base.

4. Manufacturer's Representative

Using print and online manufacturers' directories can identify products not being offered for sale in your community, better-quality products for businesses and consumers at lower costs. Using this information you can establish a home business as a manufacturer's representative. Once you have identified the right products and conducted a market analysis into their viability in your area, you use the directory to contact the manufacturers of these products. Working as a manufacturer's representative means you promote and market the products on a city, state or even a national basis. You sell the manufacturer's products to the target audience, be it businesses or consumers. Always try to negotiate exclusive service contracts with the manufacturers so you rep-

resent them within geographic boundaries specified in the agreement. Remuneration can be by way of a commission charged on total sales or you can mark up your wholesale costs on the goods to set a price. A background in sales and marketing is a plus for this field. Also, you'll want to have a good working knowledge of and an interest in the type of products you may be selling or reselling.

National Association of Manufacturers, *nam.org:* Association representing American manufacturers.

Home requirements are basically having the computer and phone lines ready at all times. If you are storing the products, you will need a storage facility, large basement or empty garage. Unless the items you are selling are small, this is where you can begin having problems with your neighbors. So, before you try storing pianos, look for a nearby storage facility. Also, take precautions for any items that could be affected by storage in a warm, cold or damp climate.

5. Energy Management Consultant

Corporations and homeowners spend billions of dollars annually on energy to light, heat and air-condition their homes and buildings. Imagine how much healthier the environment would be and how much money each of us could save every year if we all could reduce our energy consumption by a mere 10 percent. Working as an energy management consultant from a home office, you can teach home and business owners practical and useful energy management tips for reducing energy consumption and eliminating energy waste. Getting this enterprise off the ground will require a great deal of research, planning and perhaps training, depending on your background and experience in this area. However, with energy costs continuing to soar, taking care of the environment and saving money have become significant concerns for everyone. The future for energy management consulting looks very bright, but you will need to take the time and effort to become an expert in the field. Many universities are now offering courses and training programs on how to get "greener" in business and at home.

United States Department of Energy, *energy.gov:* Government website featuring energy management and conservation programs, information, resources and links. You should also look at the Energy Management Institute, *energyinstitution.org.*

Home requirements include the basic computer needs and some space to build and maintain a library of the latest periodicals and books on energy conservation.

6. Personal Chef Service

Take your pots and pans, cooking skills and love of food, and hit the road as a personal chef for hire. Prepare gourmet meals for people hosting house parties, special-occasion events such as birthdays and anniversaries and corporate luncheons—basically anywhere there is a kitchen on-site. Personal chefs are becoming a very popular alternative for people who do not have the budget for full-scale catering or who are hosting small events that do not require complete catering services. The advantages for startup are apparent: low overhead and initial investment, full-time or part-time operating hours and easy management from home. Promote the service by joining business associations and community social clubs to network and spread the news about your service. Once established, the business can easily be supported by word-of-mouth advertising and repeat business, providing the food is great and the service is second to none. You need to have an array of specialties that you have expertise in preparing—and can make for 10,

20 or even 50 people, which is much different from cooking for 4. Your biggest cost will probably be a larger freezer and perhaps a new line of the latest in cooking accessories.

Also, people are eating healthier now and there are many special diets to consider. Therefore, you should hone your skills in several genres of food and with various ingredients, especially considering the number of people with food allergies.

Typically rates are quoted on each job and vary according to factors such as the supply of food, the type of menu requested, and the market in which you are cooking. You can charge more in markets like Beverly Hills or Greenwich, Connecticut. In fact, if your prices are too low, customers in high-end areas will look elsewhere. Earnings are in the range of $35 to $100 per hour plus the cost of the foods.

United Stated Personal Chef Association, *uspca.com:* Members receive industry information, advice and support.

Home requirements, along with computer basics for scheduling, e-mailing and storing numerous online recipes, will include a place for cookbooks and all of the utensils and appliances for your business. You will also want to have a database of waiters and kitchen helpers in case a small job turns into a larger catering job. Although a personal chef is not a catering service, you always want to be able to help out a client.

7. E-Zine Publisher

Electronic e-zine publishing and distribution has exploded over the past decade, with no fewer than 100,000 e-zine publications being distributed to millions of readers monthly. Best of all, there is lots of room for startups. Develop your e-zine based on what you know and like; it could be a monthly covering model trains or a weekly offering career advice and information. E-zines are generally free to subscribers and supported by advertisers interested in targeting your subscribers. For instance, if you publish and distribute a monthly camping e-zine featuring great camping tips and information, logical advertisers would include camping equipment retailers, travel agents and tour operators. The key to success is to serve a well-defined niche market, provide interesting and informative content that readers cannot get anywhere else, and build a large and solid subscription base that will appeal to advertisers.

The second way to build this type of business, once you have your own e-zine out, is to do e-zines for other business owners or clients from associations or clubs who want such an online publication or a newsletter and need someone to put it together, edit it and manage it. Using a few basic templates, you can build monthly or bimonthly e-zines or newsletters sponsored by your clients and distributed on their mailing lists. Writing, editing and publishing experience are a big plus here. Learning to do layout is a must.

EmailUniverse.com, *emailuniverse.com:* "Ezine Strategies for Email Newsletter Publishers."

E-ZineZ.com, ezine-dir.com: Online e-zine directory listing hundreds of electronic publications index by topic.

For information on templates, you can go to *e-zinez.com/handbook/template.html.*

Home requirements include the latest in desktop publishing programs.

8. Graffiti Removal Service

Graffiti is everywhere—walls, sidewalks and fences—which makes a graffiti-removal service a very timely and in-demand startup. This business does not require much work experience and the market is unlimited, largely untapped and constantly being renewed. The equipment required is a portable water pressure washer and portable sandblaster, both which can be conveniently mounted on a trailer for easy transport to job sites. One marketing option is to visit businesses that are often the victims of graffiti vandalism and offer them a low-cost graffiti-removal solution. Provide clients with a monthly graffiti-removal option in which, for a fixed monthly fee, you will check once a week to see if there is graffiti to be removed. Additionally, graffiti-removal services can be marketed to schools, libraries, and just about any other location with graffiti problems.

Home requirements include a place to keep your cleaning supplies and towels.

9. Wedding Planner

The Association of Bridal Consultants estimates that consumers spend a whopping $33 billion on their weddings every year. The cost of a typical wedding today can easily exceed $20,000 or even $50,000, depending on the size of the function. There are myriad details to consider, which lead couples to either elope or hire professional help. Wedding planners earn a median income of just over $50,000 annually, using their expertise for anywhere from $500 to $5,000 per event. The key word here is "expertise." First, you need to know everything possible about wedding planning. This includes everything from the music to the menus to the décor to the latest in bridal party fashions and gifts. Second, you need to develop a long list of key contacts in the wedding industry and related fields in the region in which you plan to operate your business. This is a must, since you will need to call florists, wedding bands and caterers constantly. Third, you need excellent organizational and communications skills plus the ability to work very well under pressure, since it will be up to you to rectify all last-minute problems—and there will always be a few.

The wedding consulting industry is competitive, with more than 8,000 professional wedding planners in the United States, so you need to be good at what you do.

The National Association of Wedding Professionals, *nawp.com:* Members receive industry information, advice and support.

Home requirements, besides a fast computer, include multiple phone lines, perhaps even a couple of cell phone lines, since you will constantly be receiving and making calls. You also need some sturdy shelves to collect every bridal magazine and directory available and, if possible, space to keep samples of the offerings of vendors. You can elect to meet clients at their homes or decorate your office in the wedding-friendliest motif to let clients know that you are all about weddings. And finally, have a very good database of contacts.

10. Garage and Estate Sales Promoter

Weekend profits await entrepreneurs with good marketing and organizational skills who become garage and estate sale promoters. Garage, lawn, and estate sales are hugely popular events in every community across North America. As a promoter, you can provide clients who do not have the time or gumption to hold their own sale with the service of organizing and conducting the sale for them. Duties include promoting, organizing, selling items and cleaning up after everyone has gone home. In exchange for providing this valuable service, you can obtain a small flat fee and retain a percentage of the total revenues generated, 25 percent for larger sales, even more for the largest. Once you have secured a client, be sure to canvass the immediate neighborhood and solicit additional items. Why hold a small sale if you can increase revenues and profits by enlisting neighbors to provide items, too? Promote the sales with professional site signage and in community newspapers that do not charge for small classified ads or garage sale postings. Of course, you'd better know the area or find out the laws and ordinances of running and promoting a sale in each neighborhood you cover.

Best Yard Sales, *bestyardsales.com:* A national yard sale directory, with information and resources pertaining to garage sales.

Home requirements include storage space for accumulating items until the weekend occasions and dedicated transportation for these items.

11. Local Tour Guide

If you are living in an area frequented by tourists, you can start a business as a personal tour guide. It can be managed from home, it can be started for peanuts, and it has the potential to generate an income that can easily top $50,000 per year. The first key to success is to promote your service aggressively by building contacts with businesses and individuals who can refer your tour guide services to their clients, such as coach and taxi drivers, event planners, hotel concierges and travel agents. Currently, personal tour guides are charging $150 to $200 for half-day tours and up to $350 for full-day tours plus the cost of transportation and tickets to events and attractions. The second key to success is to provide clients with incredible service and an unforgettably fun experience. This means doing research and knowing all about the areas in which you are providing tours. It also means getting to know the key attractions and how to get inside those unique landmarks, trendy shops, and fashionable eateries that discerning clients want to visit. This takes building up communications and discounting a little off that half- or full-day rate, if necessary, to help build up your reputation.

World Federation of Tourist Guide Associations, *wftga.org:* A not-for-profit organization for tourist guide associations and individual tourist guides where no association exists, providing its members with industry information and support as well as a listing in the association's directory, which features tourist guide associations worldwide, indexed geographically.

Home requirements include little more than the basic computer, phone needs, and a desktop publishing program for fliers and maps.

12. Mobile Art Gallery

Take a traditional art gallery and place wheels on it and you have this home business opportunity in a nutshell. You will want to work with artists who work in all sorts of media: paint, photography, prints and sculpture. Once you have selected the artists, begin to establish locations where you can display the artwork for sale. These locations should include doctor's office waiting rooms, office lobbies and reception areas, restaurants, hospitals and other high-traffic places. Each piece of art can be displayed along with a small place card that reads, "This art is for sale. For further information call … (your business name and toll-free 1-800 number)." I would suggest giving the artist 50 percent of the selling price and the host location 10 percent, taking the balance (40 percent) for yourself. On a volume basis, there is enormous potential to profit. However, the key to the success of the business will be your ability to work with artists who produce great art and your ability to find high-traffic locations in which the art can be displayed.

World Artist Directory, *worldartistdirectory.com:* Directory service listing thousands of artists in all media, indexed geographically.

Home business requirements include a vehicle in which to transport art and some protective materials for keeping each item safe. Also, check your insurance coverage or determine what coverage you may need in the event a work of art gets damaged or destroyed.

13. Disaster Preparation Service

Earthquakes, floods, hurricanes, tornadoes, blizzards and wildfires wreak havoc and destruction of enormous magnitude. We cannot control these forces of nature, but with careful planning we can be prepared when disaster strikes. Being prepared for a natural disaster can literally mean the difference of life or death. While you cannot establish an emergency services business to react to such emergencies, since law enforcement will be in charge of such a situation and you are not going to make money from a disaster (nor should you try to), being prepared is another story. You can provide the necessary tangible items, such as emergency lighting, blankets, nonperishable food and water and even storm windows. Services can include one-on-one consulting with clients to identify potential threats in disaster situations and drafting emergency action plans to respond to a wide variety of natural disaster situations.

The requirements for starting this specialized sales and consulting service are numerous, including disaster response training and a full understanding of the needs of disaster victims. You can even specialize. Some businesses provide off-site computer data backup for other businesses. This can prove to be extremely valuable to businesses hit by hurricanes, fires and other disasters.

Given the frequency and widely publicized severity of many natural disasters, successfully marketing this type of business should not prove difficult.

Federal Emergency Management Agency, *fema.gov:* FEMA has disaster preparation, and relief information, programs, education, training, resources and links.

Home requirements range from computer banks for storing client data to a place to store supplies or access to a nearby 24-hour storage facility.

14. Gift Basket Sales

Gift baskets are extremely easy to assemble. Simply select items such as specialty foods, flowers, or personal health products and arrange them in attractive wicker baskets or similar containers, wrap in foil or colored plastic, and the gift basket is complete. The real secret to success in operating a homebased gift basket service is not so much in the gift basket, but in the sales and marketing of the baskets. I suggest concentrating your marketing efforts on gaining repeat corporate clients, professionals, small business owners and sales professionals, such as real estate agents. Basically, market to individuals or companies that would have reason to regularly send out gift baskets to current and new clients. Promote the business using your website, on web directories, through direct mail brochures, and by networking with your target audience at business and social functions. Be sure to provide local clients with free local delivery of the gift baskets and to arrange low-cost delivery outside the local area. Focus on holiday themes and baskets for special occasions. This is a nice business for involving family members as helping hands, since putting together gift baskets is relatively simple. Marketing is the bigger challenge.

Gift Basket Review Online, *festivities-pub.com:* Print and electronic magazine serving the gift basket industry with information, resources and links.

Home requirements, along with computer basics, include space for keeping your baskets and stocking the contents, room for making baskets, and a vehicle for transport.

15. Party Tent Rentals

Party tents are in demand in warmer weather for outdoor events in backyards and/or local parks. Potential clients include wedding planners, catering companies, event and corporate planners, charity organizations, retailers hosting under-the-tent sales and clearance events, sports teams, and local homeowners who want to throw that special party in their backyard.

Large party tents cost $3,000 to $7,000 or more retail, while secondhand party tents can generally be found in good condition for about half that cost. As a rule of thumb, party tents require about one hour for two people to set up and about the same time to take down. Currently, party tent rental rates range from $200 to $600 per day, depending on tent size. Additional revenues can be earned by renting tables, chairs, lighting and PA systems.

Celina Tent, *celinatent.com:* Manufacturer and distributor of a wide range of party tents.

Home requirements, besides your computer for scheduling, include a place for storing the tents and poles and a van or truck for transport. You'll also want to review your insurance policies and make sure you have coverage should a tent collapse on the heads of your clients.

16. Embroidery Services

Recent technology changes in the embroidery industry have made it very easy for even a novice to start an embroidery service. Embroidery machines are now available in single or multihued units, enabling the operator to embroider six items at a time or more. Modern embroidery equipment is computer-assisted. Designs can be created using specialty software and automatically transferred to the embroidery machine to complete the stitching of the design onto the garment. The business can easily be operated from a homebased location. However, there should be a small showroom established, even if it is in the home, to display items that can be embroidered as well as samples of embroidery options and designs. Marketing is as easy as creating a product catalog and marketing brochure and distributing the promotional package to potential customers, such as sports associations, schools, corporations, government agencies, organizations and charities. You'll also want to have samples on your website. Consider hiring a subcontract commission salesperson to solicit for new business, preferably one with appropriate contacts.

Impressions Magazine, *impressionsmag.com*: "One-stop source for authoritative business and technical information crucial to starting up and building a profitable decorated apparel business."

Home requirements include an embroidering machine, space for your embroidering machine and all other equipment, and possibly a small showroom area.

17. Cartridge Recycling

Ink and toner cartridges used in most photocopiers, fax machines, and printers can be recycled by simply replenishing the ink or toner supply. This fact creates a wonderful home business opportunity for energetic entrepreneurs to start toner cartridge recycling businesses. Requirements are basic: simple tools, reliable transportation and the ability to refill cartridges with new ink, which is easily learned. Your competitive advantage over retail operations selling new ink and toner cartridges is that you can offer clients fast service and bring the recycled cartridges right to their office or home. In addition, clients can save as much as 50 percent by purchasing recharged ink and toner cartridges rather than new cartridges. Promote your business via brochures, your website and posters about recycling.

Recharger Magazine Online, *rechargermag.com*: Print and electronic magazine serving the cartridge recycling industry with information, resources and links.

Home business requirements include a work area that can get dirty from ink and a place to keep cartridges and any other supplies.

18. Mobile Boat Broker

In most areas of North America, certification is not required to start a professional boat brokerage business. That is good news if this is the type of business venture that gets you thinking, "What if?" Thousands of pre-owned motorboats, sailboats and personal watercrafts are bought and sold annually in North America. Securing just a tiny portion of this very lucrative market may be easier than you think, especially when you consider that you can operate from home and travel to marinas to show clients boats for sale. The business could be a general boat brokerage business or you could specialize in one particular type of boats such as wooden sailboats or commercial fishing boats and equipment. Generally, boat brokerage or boat sales consultants charge the owner of the boat a 10-percent fee on sale and transfer of the boat. However, the commission rate can be as high as 25 percent for boats with a value of less than $5,000 and as low as 3 percent when selling boats in the million-dollar price range.

Obviously you will need to learn as much as possible about boats, what constitutes "good" condition, and the costs of buying and selling boats.

Home business requirements include a simple office for making calls and sending e-mails to locate boat buyers and sellers, plus transportation to see the boats you are brokering. You'll also want your lawyer to help with paperwork so that you steer clear of any liability or responsibility for the safe transport of the boats.

19. Handyperson Service

This business opportunity requires little explanation. The main requirement for starting such a service is, of course, you are handy with tools and have a good understanding and working knowledge of many trades, that is, be a jack-of-all-trades. Currently, handyperson billing rates are in the range of $25 to $85 per hour, plus materials. The service can be promoted and marketed to both residential and commercial clients through advertising and marketing means such as the web, the Yellow Pages, newspaper ads, fliers and door hangers, site and vehicle signage, door-knocking, home and garden shows and word-of-mouth referrals. If you are not very handy, but have a knack for marketing and promoting a service, you can always be responsible for the phones and the e-mails and contract with 5 to 10 people to handle the tools. This means you will only take a commission from each job, but through volume you will probably come out ahead. Of course, you'll need to find good people, some of who may be part-timers who are retirees and/or students. You'll want to have them bonded.

Home business requirements include the tools of the trade (literally) for yourself and possibly for your staff, plus liability insurance for yourself and anyone you send out to do a job.

20. Trophy and Award Sales

Millions of trophies and custom-engraved awards are given every year to winning sports teams, game MVPs and people being recognized for outstanding achievements in sports, work and community participation. Consumer demand for trophies and awards is a proven winner, making this an excellent choice as a home business venture. The business can be started for less than $5,000. Purchasing trophies and awards wholesale should not prove difficult, as there are hundreds of trophy and award manufacturers worldwide. Of course, ingenious entrepreneurs could also design and manufacture their own custom trophies and awards to separate their products from those offered by competitors. The equipment needed for engraving name plaques for the trophies is inexpensive and available at most building supply centers.

Awards and Engravers Magazine Online, *nbm.com/ae:* Print and electronic magazine serving the trophy and award industry with information, resources and links.

Home business requirements include tools for engraving, a place to store awards and a quiet place for engraving.

21. Homebased Manufacturing Business

Your options are endless in terms of what can be easily manufactured from a simple homebased workshop—picnic tables, birdhouses, picture frames, wind chimes, custom furniture, toys, specialty soaps and candles are just a few ideas to get you thinking. Of course, some creative design and handyperson skills will be needed as well as basic tools and equipment. Depending on what you manufacture, you can sell the end products at craft shows, through retailers on consignment or wholesale, directly to commercial users or directly to consumers at trade shows, by mail order and online. You must ensure that your workshop meets zoning codes and you have taken all fire and safety precautions, for your safety and that of your neighbors. Also, be aware of environmental concerns, including waste removal.

The key is to focus on a product you know a lot about and can create in a relatively short time for a reasonable cost without destroying your home.

American Home Business Association, *homebusiness.com:* Members receive home business information, access to specific products and services, advice and support.

Home business requirements include the tools of your specific trade, storage space, insurance in the event of a mishap or injury, and transport to move your goods to various locations.

22. Dog-Walking Service

A dog-walking service is perfectly suited for the person who has the time, patience and love for dogs. Best of all, a dog-walking service can be launched for a few hundred dollars. There are various styles of multi-lead dog-walking collars and leashes so several dogs can be walked at the same time without becoming tangled in the leash. This equipment is important because it will reduce frustration and enable you to walk more than one dog at a time and so increase revenues and profits. To secure clients for the service, simply design a promotional flier that explains your dog-walking service and qualifications and distribute the flier to businesses are frequented by dog owners, such as grooming locations, kennels, pet food stores, community animal shelters and town halls. Once word is out about your dog-walking service, it should not take long to establish a base of 20 or 30 regular clients. A second word of caution: clean up after them or you will be paying fines. To expand the business, you can also hire other canine lovers to help out and pay you a percentage of their fees. Additional income can come from selling doggie toys and accessories to owners who feel guilty for not having the time, energy or physical ability to walk their dogs themselves.

Home business requirements include leashes, doggie treats and plenty of bags for cleanup.

23. Home Office Planner and Organizer

Functional room design is more important for a home office than you might think. "Where is my …?" "I can't work with all this noise." Many first-time attempts to work or operate a business from home meet with frustration and a feeling of "What do I need and where do I start?" These very common problems are the basis of starting a home office planning service, with the focus on helping employees or business owners establish or transition to a homebased office. In such a business, you will work one-on-one with clients to develop successful work and organization plans and programs tailored to specific needs. The home office planning service can include assisting employees and business owners with homebased office solutions, such as office layout design, ergonomics, security systems and devices, storage solutions, recycling programs, work routine schedules, computer and technology integration, communications systems, and suitable equipment and supplies requirements. Remember to market this service to corporations, because many are allowing key employees to work from home, as telecommuters. For additional profit, you can bill yourself as an organizer, meaning you can come back every three or six months to help reorganize for the many folks who have a hard time maintaining order. If you are skilled in technology, you can also earn money by helping to upgrade computer systems. To be effective in this capacity, you obviously need a very strong sense of organization, excellent computer proficiency, and a knowledge of the high-tech tools of the modern office.

Organize Tips Online, *organizetips.com:* website offering visitors hundreds of home office planning and organization tips and ideas.

Life Organizers.com, *lifeorganizers.com:* This website has hundreds of articles and tips to provide ideas on how to rid clutter from every part of your life, including your home office.

National Association of Professional Organizers, *napo.net:* The premier national association dedicated to the field of organizing.

Home business requirements include a workspace to draw and blueprint office designs and layouts for clients, as well as the usual computer basics. You'll also want to keep plenty of basic tools and supplies on hand for setting up high-tech equipment for your clients.

24. Mobile Car Wash

A mobile car wash service is perfectly suited for the entrepreneur who is seeking a simple, profitable and low-investment opportunity. The business requires only basic equipment and supplies and can be operated from a van, pickup truck or enclosed trailer. The market potential is enormous, with more than 130,000,000 motor vehicles registered in the United States. However, the real target market for this service is to establish monthly car and truck washing and cleaning accounts with companies, organizations and government agencies that have fleets of automobiles, such as a limousine or taxi service. Before embarking on this venture, you need to make sure you will not be violating any local environmental laws regarding water runoff or the disposing of chemicals into sewer drains.

To enhance your appeal and raise your income, you can offer detailing, which is a more specific (detailed) cleaning. You'll need to learn the tricks of detailing from an expert.

Car Wash Equipment Directory, *car-wash-equipment.net*: Online directory of manufacturers and suppliers of car wash equipment.

Detail City, *detailcity.com*, and Detail King, *detailking.com:* Two places to buy detailing equipment.

Home business requirements include a water reclamation system, which can cost upwards of $2,500, plus a wide range of cleaning supplies and a van or flat-back truck in which to keep them.

25. Home Inspection Service

If you have construction experience and are prepared to invest some money and time in a training course to qualify you as a certified home and property inspector, you can earn a very good living from owning and operating an inspection service. Millions of homes and properties are bought and sold each year in North America. As a condition of

sale, most of these homes must be inspected by a professional home inspector for major structural or mechanical problems. Currently, home and property inspection rates range from $150 for a small and basic residential home to well over $1,000 for larger commercial buildings and complexes. A home and property inspection service can be managed from a home office with minimal monthly overhead costs, making this business startup a wise choice.

National Association of Home Inspectors, *nahi.org:* Nonprofit association in the United States to promote and develop certified and licensed home inspectors.

Canadian Association of Home and Property Inspectors, *cahpi.ca:* Association to promote and develop the home inspection profession in Canada.

Home business requirements are little more than your basic computer and communications needs.

26. Disc Jockey Service

Not only are mobile disc jockey services in high demand, the business can be launched on a modest investment, often less than $10,000, and the monthly operating overheads are minimal. There are still a few basic requirements for starting and operating a mobile disc jockey service successfully. These include an excellent and varied music selection, DJ equipment, reliable transportation, an outgoing personality and a talent for public speaking. You'll also need to be current on the latest in fashion so that you are dressed accordingly. Clients can include event and wedding planners, tour operators, restaurant and nightclub owners, and individual consumers wanting disc jockey services for a celebration or special event. Today's disc jockey services typically provide plenty of amenities, if requested, such as party favors and games for bar mitzvahs and bat mitzvahs, Sweet Sixteen parties and Quincea-ñeras, not to mention special lighting, video screens and dancers. From basic DJ services at a corporate function, simply providing some music, to a full-fledged high school or college graduation party with all the trimmings, DJ services rake in anywhere from $400 to $4,000 and more per party.

Disc Jockey Online, *discjockeyonline.com:* Website serving the professional mobile disc jockey industry with information, resources and links.

Home business requirements include a fair amount of storage space for equipment and party favors, plus an office for meeting clients and showing them some of your work on CD (which can also be done via your website). You'll need good organizational programs on your computer and a rotary card file or database with names of dancers and/or other performers, if requested by your clients, as well as vendors for giveaways.

27. Online Researcher

Do you spend hours every day surfing the web? If so, why not start an internet research service? Since it is too easy to conduct research on the web, you will not likely be able to sell material, but instead you will be hired by small business owners, writers/editors, students, professionals and anyone else who needs information but does not have the time to look for it.

Billing rates for the services vary, depending on how much research time is required to compile the data; however, many internet research services have base billing rates of $25 to $35 per hour.

Association of Internet Researchers, *aoir.org:* Academic association providing industry information, resources and links for professional researchers.

Home business requirements include the fastest computer and internet connection you can

find and an offsite backup source for data. This way you'll never lose a job if you have a power outage.

28. Promotional Product Sales

The business world spends billions of dollars annually on embossed and printed promotional items such as T-shirts, pens, calendars, tote bags, umbrellas, caps, and visors as promotional giveaways for customers and potential clients. Securing just a small portion of this very lucrative market can make you rich. The key to success in the promotional products marketing industry for the small or homebased operator is not to manufacture and print the items yourself, but simply to market them, using the services of manufacturers and printers to fill the orders. This is a business opportunity that requires excellent sales and marketing abilities.

Aim to achieve yearly sales of $300,000 with a 50 percent markup on all products sold and the result will be a homebased business that generates a pretax and expense earnings of $100,000.

Promotional Products Directory, *promotionalproductsdirectory.com:* Directory service listing promotional product manufacturers, printers and distributors.

Home business requirements include some storage space for the goods, plenty of shipping materials and all the basic computer and communication tools.

29. Marketing Consultant

Without marketing, a business cannot survive. Top-notch marketing consultants are in high demand across North America. Many specialize in one particular marketing discipline, while the more experienced consultants handle the full range of marketing activities for their clients. You can secure business by promoting the service at networking meetings, initiating a direct-mail advertising campaign, through a well-promoted website, or working the telephone and setting appointments with business owners and professionals to present and explain the benefits of your services. Of course, this is not something you simply decide to do overnight, unless you have several years of experience in the marketing field and are willing to take courses to keep current.

Marketing consultants with proven results in internet marketing are earning as much as $100+ an hour.

Direct Marketing Association, *the-dma.org:* Association serving the direct marketing industry, including mail order, telemarketing and direct sellers.

Home business requirements include little more than a fast computer, communication tools, and some shelves or files for the latest in marketing books and magazines.

30. Retail Display Specialist

Retailers often must rely on elaborate window displays to grab the attention of passersby and draw them into the store, where exciting in-store displays promote their goods. Start a business that specializes in creating effective window and in-store merchandise displays for retailers. Marketing the service can be as easy as approaching local retailers and offering a free trial period so the owners realize the benefits and increased sales from a well-designed product display. Photos of the free displays you create can be used to market your services to other shop owners. Build an inventory of interesting props, signage, and lighting so you can provide clients with an all-inclusive display service. To be effective in this endeavor, you'll need to have some design and creative experience. You can also take classes in design and marketing to get up to speed.

National Retail Federation, *nrf.com:* Association serving retailers and shop owners nationwide.

Home business requirements include some room to map out your display designs on paper. Along with computer graphics programs, you'll want to have tools and supplies for creating displays, plus basic display fixtures and props, although most of your clients will supply you with these basics.

31. Cosmetics Retailing

For the innovative entrepreneur, there are numerous ways to sell cosmetics and make a profit, including home cosmetics parties, online, mail order, temporary kiosks set up in malls and fashion shows, and in-home personal sales visits. Ever since the first Avon Lady began ringing doorbells, there has been a growing market for cosmetics. The first step is to source a quality and reputable supply. You can create your own cosmetics brand and have it manufactured under a private labeling agreement. However, this is very difficult and an awful lot of work. The other (far more common) option is to strike a deal with a cosmetics manufacturer and distributor to market its line in an exclusive territory of your choosing. In either case, you need to know about cosmetic manufacturers and distributors. Expand the business by hiring cosmetic sales representatives and paying them a commission on the sales they generate. This home business is easy to set up and has the potential to earn huge profits.

Independent Cosmetic Manufacturers and Distributors Inc., *icmad.org:* Directory service listing cosmetic manufacturers and distributors, as well as providing industry information, resources and links of interest.

Home business requirements include little more than a computer, solid listings of potential customers and some storage space for the cosmetics.

32. Window-Cleaning Service

Window-washing is perhaps the granddaddy of all home-managed service businesses. The advantages are apparent:

- Proven consumer demand, with millions of potential clients
- Low startup investment and low fixed operating overheads
- No special skills or business experience required
- Flexible operating hours
- No need to stock or warehouse costly inventory
- Year-round operation by offering interior and exterior window cleaning
- Potential to generate a very good income
- Unlimited growth potential and possibly the opportunity to franchise
- Repeat customers, since windows get dirty again and again and again

Promoting a window-washing service is just as easy as starting one: print and distribute fliers detailing your service, run low-cost classified ads under home services, network with potential customers at business association functions and social events, and piggyback your service with other businesses, such as house painters, window installers, property managers, real estate agents and renovation contractors.

Window Cleaning Network, *window-cleaning-net.com:* Window-washing information, resources and links, as well as a directory of window-washing equipment suppliers.

Home business requirements are minimal. Along with the cleaning supplies, plenty of towels and a couple of ladders and step stools, you'll probably want a basic computer file for maintaining your customer lists.

33. Valet Parking Service

Starting a valet parking service is very easy. Basically, if you have a driver's license and can secure third-party and automobile liability insurance, you are in business. A valet parking service can be marketed directly to businesses. However, a more logical approach is to offer the service to entertainment industry professionals, such as event and wedding planners, trade show organizers and charity groups and organizations for their special functions. The business can be started with a minimal capital outlay. The profit potential is also excellent, as current rates for valet parking services are range from $50 to $70 per hour for a two- to three-person crew and the cash tips can really add up.

ValetPark.net, *valetpark.net:* Website serving the valet parking industry with information, resources and links.

Home business requirements are minimal: a good list of possible valets who are trustworthy and a basic computer setup for planning your marketing materials.

34. Human Billboard Advertising

Silly and embarrassing, but potentially profitable, human billboards are people who hold signs or banners emblazoned with promotional messages in high-traffic areas of the community—usually outside, in front of or close to the business they are promoting. They advertise everything from new housing developments to car dealerships to restaurant openings and are really catching on as a highly effective, cost-efficient method of promoting services and products. The objective of a human billboard is to grab the attention of passing motorists and pedestrians and get them to visit the business being promoted. Your human billboard staff can include homemakers, students, actors, musicians, and basically anyone who is available to work part time, as needed. Marketing the service can be as easy as setting up appointments with local business owners to explain and promote the benefits of your service. Joining local business networking clubs is also a good way to get the word out. Rates for human billboards vary, based on factors such as the number of people (billboards), the length of the promotion and other items like signage and special costumes.

American Association of Advertising Agencies, *aaaa.org:* Members receive industry information, business advice and support.

Home business requirements are nothing more than the basic communications tools, a computer for e-mails, phones for calling clients and—of course—sandwich boards.

35. Product Demonstration Service

We have all seen people in grocery stores offering free samples of food or cleaning products to shoppers. These people are generally not employed by the supermarket, but by a product demonstration company. The idea is to get consumers to try these products and then start buying them. Typically, product demonstration services are awarded to operators by contract, with the contract specifying a certain number of demonstration hours and outlets. Currently, product demonstration rates range from $7 per hour to $15 per hour, with employee demonstrators making 75 percent. The business must therefore, secure a lot of product demonstration contracts to realize sufficient revenues and profits.

ThomasNet, *thomasregister.com:* Online and print directories of manufacturers.

Home business requirements basically include communication tools for working with companies.

36. Cloth Diaper Service

Ah, the not-so-sweet smell of success. Disposable diapers are not environmentally friendly and can often irritate a baby's skin. The solution? Environmentally friendly cloth diapers made of natural fibers. A baby can go through as many as 4,000 diapers before being fully toilet trained, which creates an outstanding home business opportunity. Depending on your business startup budget, there are two methods of pursuing this venture. You can offer a complete service, including diaper supply, delivery, pickup and cleaning. Or you can simply supply delivery and pickup services of the diapers and have a commercial laundry clean them at a reduced or bulk rate. If startup capital is plentiful, the first option is probably more profitable than the second over the long term. Word-of-mouth marketing will be your main promotional weapon, so get out and start promoting by talking with as many new parents as possible. Fliers in ob-gyn offices (with permission) and in maternity shops are also good promotional options.

Diaper Pin Online, *diaperpin.com:* Extensive online directory serving the cloth diaper industry with information, products, services, resources and links.

Home business requirements are minimal. If you are supplying and cleaning the diapers yourself, then obviously you will need to stock up on diapers and cleaning supplies and, if possible, have a washer and a dryer dedicated to your business.

37. Instruction Classes

Capitalize on your knowledge, experience and special skills by starting a homebased instruction business. Depending on your skills, you could offer clients instruction classes on cooking, gardening, home improvement, dog training, self-defense, survival, music lessons, languages, sewing or anything you have mastered yourself. Of course, knowing about something doesn't mean you can teach it. You will need to create a lesson plan, decide on how many students you can accommodate (a rented space can typically accommodate more students, although then you will be paying a fee for the facility), and decide the level of the instruction—beginning, intermediate or advanced. You will also have to practice your public speaking.

You can teach in your home, if it's suitable or you can arrange to teach at your clients' locations or in a rented facility. If you teach in your home, make sure you have sufficient insurance coverage in the event one of your dance students falls and breaks something, whether an ankle or a table. Market the classes with print advertisements, promotional fliers and word-of-mouth networking. Specialized instruction training is one of the best home businesses to start because in most cases the product (your skill) helps others solve a problem, improve themselves or both. Charge for what the service is really worth; in most cases it will be higher than you think.

National Tutoring Association, *ntatutor.org:* Members receive industry information, advice and support.

Home business requirements include space enough for teaching a class. If teaching at home, you will also need to make sure you have parking available that does not interfere with your neighbors. If you are teaching outside of your home, then home requirements are minimal, but include a desktop publishing program to run off fliers.

38. Business Plan Consulting

Did you know that a recent survey of 250 new business owners revealed that fewer than 25 percent had created a business plan for their new venture? When asked why they had not, the number-one reason was that they simply did know how. According to the SBA, approximately 750,000 new businesses are started each year in the United States. This creates an outstanding opportunity for the ingenious entrepreneur to capitalize by starting a business that researches and creates business plans for owners of new and established businesses.

The key to success is being an expert on business plans and having some experience with them. Therefore, start by studying everything possible on the topic. Once you are confident that you are an expert on business plans, do some low-cost consulting to new entrepreneurs who are in the process of writing business plans. Once you have worked on several plans, you can start up your business.

Market your service by attending business networking meetings. Also attempt to obtain a list of all new and renewal business registration licenses through your local business service center.

Business Plan Writer Online, *business-plan-writer-online.com:* Website dedicated to the business plan writer, including information, resources and links.

Home business requirements include computer basics and a place to house all of the books and magazines on business plans that you find.

39. Recycling Consultant

Taking the time to educate yourself on recycling industrial and household materials can really pay off, especially if you apply that knowledge and become a recycling consultant. Millions of homeowners and companies now recycle waste materials. However, millions more could. But what can be recycled and where do you start? This is the point where you put your recycling knowledge to work by teaching homeowners, business owners and employees how to recycle, what to recycle and where it can be recycled. Charge corporations and homeowners a fee to design a recycling plan for their particular needs. In addition to creating the recycling program, you can also provide brief instruction on their new recycling program and on recycling in general. The timing has never been better, because the need for everyone to practice recycling has never been more apparent. Potential income ranges from $50 to $150 per hour plus markup on products sold.

Solid Waste Association of North America, *swana.org:* Recycling and environmental issues, information, education, training, resources and links.

Home business requirements include electronic files and hard copies of research papers, books and magazines on recycling.

40. Bartender for Hire

Starting a bartending service is a fantastic way to get into business for yourself, without breaking the bank. You can market your services as an independent bartender to catering companies, event and wedding planners, and hotels and pubs for relief duties. The business requires only a few hundred dollars of seed capital to initiate and can return $150 to $200 per day plus gratuities. Ideally, the entrepreneur who starts a bartender-for-hire service will have experience mixing drinks and outstanding social skills. An option is to book bartenders for events. This means building up a very large contact list of caterers, wedding and party planners and anyone else who may be throwing a party, including corporate event planners. Next you begin assembling a list of a dozen or so experienced bartenders who are looking for part-time gigs. Make sure they are up on all the latest drinks and have the personality and ear for listening required of bartenders.

A bartender-for-hire service with some regular clients has the potential to generate annual revenues that can easily top $50,000.

Bartender Online, *bartender.com:* Official site of *Bartender Magazine,* with plenty of information on bartending.

Home business requirements include some bartending outfits and tools of the trade plus a computer and a good scheduling program.

41. Property Manager

Here is the perfect new business venture for someone who wants to start a homebased business on a limited budget. Becoming a property manager is relatively straightforward. Find residential and commercial landlords who are seeking the services of a property management firm, negotiate a service contract and start managing. The duties of a property manager include working with handypersons to conduct repairs, receiving and answering inquiries from tenants and owners, leasing or renting vacant units, and negotiating lease terms and details. A property management service is ideal for a person with a real estate background. However, anyone can start this venture on a full- or part-time basis and gain valuable on-the-job experience, which can be leveraged to grow the business.

National Property Management Association, *npma.org:* Members receive industry information, advice and support.

Home business requirements are minimal, including basic computer software to maintain lists of tenants, handypersons and various tasks that need to be completed.

42. Flier Distribution Service

Small business owners, salespeople and marketers of all sorts have used promotional fliers for decades as a fast and frugal, yet highly effective, method of advertising their products and services. A home-based flier distribution service is easy to start and operate, yet it has the potential to generate a great full-time or part-time income and requires no more than a telephone and a good pair of walking shoes to get started. Rates range from a few cents for each flier handed out to $1 for each flier posted on community notice and bulletin boards, commonly found in supermarkets, self-service laundries and schools. As a method of increasing revenues, consider hiring students or retirees to deliver fliers during busy times. Of course, if you also design and run off fliers, you can make significantly more money.

Corel Corporation, *corel.com,* and Adobe Inc., *adobe.com:* Leading software development companies with desktop publishing products available for a wide range of applications.

Home business requirements include the computer basics for keeping up with client needs, plus graphics programs if you choose to include layout and design of fliers.

43. Bed-and-Breakfast

If you don't mind sharing your home with overnight guests, you stand to profit substantially by turning your home into a bed-and-breakfast operation. B&B rates are typically from $40 to $140 per night per person, depending on the location, amenities and historical aspect of the setting, typically including a light breakfast. Promote your B&B through local tourist associations, via online lodging directories and by establishing alliances with independent travel agents and brokers. Of course, the biggest obstacle to overcome may be zoning regulations. Some municipalities encourage B&Bs, while others prefer to keep guest accommodations within commercial zones. You'll need to check with your local planning and zoning department.

American Bed and Breakfast Association, *abba.com,* BBCanada.com, *bbcanada.com,* and Canadian Bed and Breakfast Guide, *canadian-bandbguide.ca:* Organizations dedicated to promoting B&Bs. Most states and provinces have organizations that provide members with information, advice and support.

Home business requirements include at least one furnished, clean guest room, a relatively quiet household, amenities for guests and sufficient insurance coverage.

44. Boat Cleaning Service

If you don't want to get into the highly competitive residential or commercial cleaning industry but would like to start a cleaning service, why not consider a boat cleaning service? The competition is minimal and, providing you choose the right area, the number of potential customers is nearly unlimited. Starting a boat cleaning service could not be easier, as there are no special skills or equipment required to operate the business and marketing the service requires no more than some printed fliers and a little bit of legwork to distribute them around marinas and boating clubs. Considering that a boat cleaning service can be started on an initial investment of less than $1,000, the income potential at $20 to $30 per hour is excellent. Additionally, if you have the equipment and necessary skills, you could also expand the business and offer clients additional services, including in-the-water bottom cleaning, sailboat rigging, haul-out bottom painting and woodwork or brightwork refinishing.

Mer-maids Products, Inc., *mermaid.com:* Manufacturers and distributors of boat-cleaning products and supplies.

Home business requirements include all the tools and cleaning products necessary, plus some room around the house, in the basement or in the garage to store them.

45. Bicycle Repair Service

Consider all of the advantages of starting a home-based bicycle repair service:

- Low initial startup investment and minimal monthly operating overheads;
- Potential to earn $30 per hour and more;
- Part-time or full-time opportunity with flexible working hours;
- Repair skills needed are minimal and can be learned quickly on the job or through specialized training courses.

One key aspect of marketing is making sure that you establish alliances with bicycling clubs and organizations in the community because the members of these clubs can become customers if you promote your services a little. You can also work for established bike retailers and repair shops on a subcontract basis to handle their overflow work in the busy season.

United Bicycle Institute, *bikeschool.com:* Training school in Ashland, Oregon, offering certification courses in bicycle mechanics.

Home business requirements include the tools of the bike repair trade and possibly a garage workshop, if you are bringing bikes home for repair. For extra income, you might consider selling bicycling accessories from water bottles to helmets.

46. Medical Billing Service

The medical billing industry is extremely competitive. However, for the determined entrepreneur, there is still a good opportunity to earn $40,000 or more per year operating a medical claims billing service from a home office. All medical claims billing is processed electronically and sent directly to Medicare clearinghouses, so computer equipment and the ability to use medical billing software programs are required. Additionally, you will need to familiarize yourself with the diagnostic and procedure coding system used on medical claim forms by doctors and health care professionals to indicate the type of service being billed. Currently, medical billing services charge clients $2 to $3 per claim processed; the profit potential for the service is good, providing you can process enough claims. There is a fairly steep leaning curve for operating this service and careful research and planning techniques are necessary to ensure initial and continued success. Additionally, you must guarantee confidentiality and not allow personal patient information to fall into the wrong hands.

American Medical Billing Association, *ambanet.net/AMBA.htm:* Information on the industry and regulations, support and networking opportunities for members.

Home business requirements include medical billing software programs, secure data backup and good filing systems for electronic and hard copies.

47. Proposal Writer

Government agencies on the federal, state, and local levels put thousands of RFPs (requests for proposals) out for bid annually. Proposals can range from construction of new buildings to supplying computer equipment for government offices and just about anything in between. These proposals can be very lucrative for companies and individuals that bid successfully for contracts. Many small to medium-sized contractors do not complete the proposal and bid forms because the process is extremely involved and usually requires technical drawings, action plans and contingency plans. Business owners and managers rarely have the time or abilities to complete them. A proposal writer compiles and completes the proposal documents for the contractor. Experienced proposal writers charge fees based on the amount of time it takes to complete the proposal, typically from $40 to $75 per hour; some will even charge a commission based on the value of the contract should their client's bid be accepted. Furthermore, most proposal writers specialize in one area, such as nonperishable goods, construction, services or maintenance. A proposal writer must have access to a wide range of research resources and, in almost all cases, strong technical writing experience.

Association of Proposal Management Professionals, *apmp.org:* Members receive industry information, advice and support.

Home business requirements include a quiet place in which to work (since this can be complicated), the latest software programs for proposal writing and plenty of room for offline research reports and materials.

48. Independent Sales Consultant

Some of the highest-earning professionals in any industry are independent sales consultants working freelance for clients. Freelance sales consultants represent companies that sell products and services ranging from manufactured goods to home improvement services. Securing clients to represent is easy, simply because freelance sales consultants generally supply all the tools of the trade—transportation, communications requirements and computer hardware. Many independent sales consultants also generate and qualify their own sales leads. To put it differently, clients have little to lose by having freelance sales consultants representing their business. Remuneration for products and services sold is always by way of commission, which will range between 10 and 25 percent of the total sales value, depending on what is being sold.

Entrepreneur Online, *entrepreneur.com:* Online resource center for small business owners and sales professionals.

Home business requirements include computer

and communications tools for building your client base.

49. Budget Decorating Service

This is a service for the millions of people who don't want to hire a high-priced interior decorator. If you can master the many methods of decorating and designing on a shoe-string budget, you can become a valuable resource for homeowners.

Start honing your skills by reading up on design and decorating theories and then look for ways to follow the trends and apply the tips on a limited budget. Spend time at garage and estate sales and in flea markets and scan local newspaper classified ads for wacky decoration items, recycled building materials, and unique home furnishings that you can purchase and then sell to clients for a profit while you redecorate rooms or entire homes. Start by decorating a few homes for free to get some before-and-after photos of your work and build your portfolio. Market your service through home and garden shows and by creating colorful before-and-after brochures and a website that illustrates your decorating talents.

Rental Decorating Digest, *rentaldecorating.com/Budget%20Decorating.htm:* Plenty of budget decorating ideas.

International Interior Design Association, *iida.org:* Members receive industry information, advice and support.

Home business requirements include all the basic tools of the trade—rulers, scissors, markers, staple guns, etc. You'll also need a workspace for sketching out room designs and an area for storing items you buy here and there.

50. Survey Service

Businesses often rely on public opinion surveys to discover more about their products, services and customers. Politicians rely on opinion polls to gauge what voters feel are the most important issues. Just about every level of government agency relies on public opinion polls to find out what services taxpayers want and need. Public opinion polls and surveys can be conducted on the telephone, by mail, by e-mail or in face-to-face interviews, making this service a great opportunity for a home business. Capitalize on your communication, organizational and marketing skills to make this business successful. To start, create, and conduct a few polls on topics that would be interesting to the public. Send the results to local media in the form of a press release or media alert, to use the media coverage as a marketing tool to attract clients.

Marketing Research Association, *mra-net.org:* Members receive industry information, advice and support.

Home business requirements are fairly simple. You'll need good communications tools and a means of keeping current on trends and hot topics of public concern.

51. Interior and Exterior House Painting

Heights, ladders, and slow, tedious labor-intensive work are enough reasons to scare off even the most hardcore do-it-yourself homeowners and make a house-painting service a wise startup for entrepreneurs with the required skills. House painting is a very simple business to start and requires only a small investment. As with most labor-intensive business ventures, you can pretty much be guaranteed work, regardless of economic conditions. Providing free value-added services, such as cleaning the rain gutters or windows while on the job site, is a great way to distinguish your company from competitors. Often free value-added services will increase the number and the quality of refer-

rals your business receives. Before launching the business, learn some house-painting techniques from books, articles, and websites and then practice a little by touching up your home office.

Painting and Decorating Contractors of America, *pdca.org:* Members receive industry information, advice and support.

Home business requirements include ladders, rollers, brushes of various sizes, and a good relationship with local paint suppliers for good prices. Also make sure you have the necessary insurance coverage.

52. Silk-Screening Service

Silk-screen printing equipment can be set up in your garage, basement, or any spare room and used for printing logos and images on a wide variety of products, such as T-shirts, mouse pads, bumper stickers, hats, sweatshirts, heat transfers, shower curtains, binder covers, furniture, and sports and corporate uniforms. Best of all, the profit potential is great. For example, basic T-shirts can be purchased in bulk for less than $5 each and the ink used to print the image costs only a few cents per printed item. If you secure orders for 500 printed T-shirts a week and charge only $10 each for the shirt and printing, you can generate gross profits in excess of $100,000 per year! It's more than a compelling reason to start a homebased silk-screening business, wouldn't you agree?

U.S. Screen Print & Inkjet Technology (formerly U.S. Screen Printing Institute), *screenprinters.net:* Company offering books, videos, DVDs, hands-on workshops and software solutions for screen printers and industry information, resources and links.

Home business requirements include the silk-screening equipment, a place for storing the items on which you will be printing, and materials for shipping and packaging.

53. Employee Training

The demand from employers for specialized employee training is enormous, so a homebased employee training service could be a terrific new business venture. The key to success in this business is specialization: your service should focus on one particular training style or method that you have mastered or can quickly master. Popular employee training course topics include computer and software training, customer service, working without distraction, multitasking, handling money, sales, theft reduction and coping with stress. The training course can be conducted at the client's site. The service can be marketed through networking meetings and a direct mail program explaining the service and course curriculum. Make sure you have gained significant expertise in the areas in which you are conducting training. You'll want to keep classes to a size you can manage. You can also conduct online training courses as well from the comfort of your home.

Training Registry, *trainingregistry.com:* Online directory of professional business, management and employee training consultants, as well as training courses and training products, all indexed geographically and by topic.

Home business requirements include the necessary equipment for each type of course plus desktop publishing software to create and print course-related materials.

54. Catering Service

If you can cook for large groups of people and if you have access to wheels for transport and helping hands for serving, you can start a small-scale catering business. Unlike the personal chef, who cooks at clients' homes and offices, a caterer supplies a selection of favorites off his or her menu for parties, meetings and other occasions.

You can offer a variety of possibilities, from romantic catering for 2 to parties for 30, or whatever number you can manage to cook for in your kitchen. Obviously a love of cooking and the skills to make various dishes are prerequisites for a catering business. You can start marketing by creating a brochure featuring photos of the tempting treats and delightful dishes you make. Small businesses, offices, associations and community groups are all in your primary market. You'll also want to put your menu up on your website. Include prices for various selections, based on size, cost of ingredients and time to prepare. If you can find some interesting themes, you can stand out from other local catering operations. For example, if you are near a college or pro sports stadium, you might offer a football season tailgate catering package delivered to the stadium parking lot.

Association of Catering and Event Professionals, *acep.com:* Association dedicated to the planning and catering industry, offering information and contacts.

Home business requirements include plenty of kitchen space for cooking and preparing, which may mean installing some new home appliances—and making sure not to overload any circuits. You'll also need plenty of trays and other means of transporting and presenting foods and a van or SUV for transport.

55. Deck Building

One of the fastest-growing segments of the home improvement industry is designing and building custom sundecks that can retail for as much as $20,000 and include features such as built-in planters, hot tubs, glass or cast iron handrails, atmosphere lighting, and custom-manufactured wood patio furniture to match the deck's design. The most profitable way to operate the business is to sell the sundecks directly to the consumer. However, this method is also the most expensive to start and market. Additional ways to get started include subcontracting for established building and renovation companies, building alliances with landscape designers and architects, and marketing your sundecks directly to consumers via home and garden shows. In most areas, the installation of a sundeck requires a building permit, which must be issued prior to installation. There are also building codes for the construction specifications of sundecks. Starting this business requires significant construction experience and skills, as well as creative design abilities. Equipment, such as table saws, miter saws, drills and a host of hand tools, will be required, but much of this can be rented at first to keep startup costs to a minimum.

Deck Industry Association, *deckindustry.org:* Members receive industry information, advice and support.

Home business requirements include insurance to cover any damages to customers' homes or to yourself. You'll also need to clear an area to clean and house your construction tools.

56. Collectible Clothing Sales

The value and popularity of collectible clothing has been increasing steadily for the past decade and the demand for collectible clothing from the 1940s to the 1980s shows no signs of diminishing. Working full or part time from home, you cannot go wrong buying collectible and vintage clothing and reselling it for a profit. Collectible clothing can be purchased at garage sales, auctions and estate sales, and through classified ads in newspapers and online. The clothing can then be sold to collectors through vintage clothing shows and fashion events, at home collector clothes parties and on clothing collectors' websites. Of course you can also establish and promote your own website to sell your items.

Collecting Network, *collectingnetwork. com:* Site providing antiques and collectibles information, resources, valuation guides and links.

Home business requirements include a safe, moth-free location in which to store the clothing, and basic internet service to help you find and sell your wares, as well as communicate with other collectors.

57. Temporary Employment Agency

There are thousands of businesses that employ temporary help ("temps") to assist in completing projects, fill in for full-timers who are out or handle a work overflow. Ideally, your homebased temporary help agency should specialize in supplying qualified workers to a few industries. Construction, home-care, domestic, office, and warehouse workers are all frequently needed by businesses. Recruiting people qualified and prepared to work on a temporary basis should not prove difficult. Target students, early retirees, homemakers, or anyone looking for full- or part-time employment. Often people between jobs will take temp work, hoping that it will lead to a full-time position. Even other homebased business owners seeking additional income may become clients. Marketing the service can be as easy as creating information packages describing your service and the temps available, and mailing them to businesses and companies that occasionally need temps. You'll want a website that attracts both employers and people seeking temporary employment. Temp companies usually charge the employers a percentage based on the salary of the job. This varies by market and industry.

Of course, to be successful, you'll need to carefully screen both temps and employers to make sure both are reputable so that you can create good matches. This will require running background checks on employees and researching employers. Your reputation will be on the line every time you send a temporary worker off to a client, so being able to discern the more skilled and reliable temps from the slackers will be a key to your success. Likewise, you'll need to know employers who are reputable.

American Staffing Association, *staffingtoday.net:* Members receive industry information, advice and support.

Home business requirements include strong, reliable computer and communications tools for organizing, promoting, marketing and managing the business. You'll also need to be knowledgeable and keep up-to-date on employment law.

58. Website Design and Maintenance

More than 1,000 websites a day are added to the internet and you can cash in by starting a web design service. The key here is learning as much as possible about the differences between high-quality and substandard websites. What makes one site more effective than another and why? You'll need to be able to answer that question and know the technical tricks of the trade to succeed in this highly competitive field. Of course, if you create several sites that "wow" people, you can make good money, since there are not only people looking for site designers to build sites, but also people wanting to update and/or improve their sites.

Market yourself via your own website and through direct mail, e-mail and word-of-mouth to small business owners, since most of them have websites and many would love better ones. Clubs and associations are also a good source of business. Additionally, you'll want to obtain the names of new business owners who may be seeking web designers. See what business licenses were recently obtained in your area and contact these new entrepreneurs to set up an appointment to meet with the business owner to show him or her some samples on your notebook computer and explain what

you can do from a technical perspective. The key to success, however, is listening to what the client wants and making his or her dream website a reality. Many web designers have the "we know what we're doing, so just let us do it for you" approach, which results in clients dissatisfied with what the designers create.

Additional revenues can be generated by hosting sites, web optimization and maintaining sites. You might also get into providing content and creating online marketing programs, but this can take more time than it is worth.

Web Design and Developers Association, *wdda.org:* Industry information, advice and support.

Home business requirements include the latest in web design software and a notebook computer.

59. Vending Routes

The snack vending business is a multibillion-dollar industry in North America and continues to grow. Getting started in the vending industry is easy: purchase a few vending machines, stock them and locate them—and you're in business, right? Wrong. The vending industry has one of the highest failure rates, due to heavy competition and shady operators selling newcomers inferior equipment and vending routes that don't exist. As a result, it is very difficult for most new operators to secure high-traffic and potentially profitable locations for their machines. Therefore, the key to success in vending is the same as in opening a retail store: location, location, location. Research and source the right locations and you'll find that vending machines will not only make money, but be profitable for years. Seek out uncharted, safe, secure routes that are high-traffic areas and sell those routes to new vending machine businesses. Of course, this isn't easy, so you will have to first learn the business, so you'll know what makes a good location for a vending machine, and then do plenty of legwork to find routes that will be safe and profitable. Getting some business experience in this industry is also fairly important, to instill trust.

National Automatic Merchandising Association, *vending.org:* Members receive industry information, advice and support.

Home business requirements include good communications tools and trustworthy transportation, since you will be out and about often, scouting for routes.

60. Homebased Rental Business

From animals to zeppelins, people will rent almost anything if they need it. With that in mind, you can start a rental business. Like most businesses, the rental industry is based on supply and demand, so you will need to determine what types of items you will rent out, based on the needs of either the public at large or a specific industry. You could rent tables and chairs for catered events, meetings and other gatherings. You could rent camping and outdoor equipment to outdoor enthusiasts. You could rent costumes for school plays, local theater productions and, of course, Halloween, or rent props to movie studies and commercial production companies. Perhaps you could even start a seasonal rental business, with sporting equipment by summer, for example, and holiday decorations in the winter. All of this will depend on the market in which you are doing business and the availability of rental items in that market.

Research your geographic area and find out what is not easily rentable. Then, if there is a demand for such items, you can fill it. Of course, the larger the equipment, the less likely you will be able to store it in your home.

Market your rental items by advertising in local newspapers, printing and distributing two-for-one rental coupons, networking at business and social functions, and being in Yellow Pages directories and, of course, on your website.

You'll want to take deposits on all rental items and you'll need to make sure all equipment that you rent remains in good shape. You'll also want to look into insurance, to protect yourself if your rented equipment malfunctions and causes an injury or damage to a home or business.

American Rental Association, *ararental.org:* National association of rental operators, renting a wide range of equipment and products.

Home business requirements include storage for whatever you are renting, a well-maintained database for tracking who has what and when it will be returned, and good communications tools to stay in touch with rental clients.

61. Awning-Cleaning Service

In the past decade, more and more business owners have switched to commercial awning signs, as opposed to traditional box signs, to advertise their businesses. All of these awnings have one thing in common: they all have to be cleaned regularly to project a good corporate image for the businesses. This creates a great opportunity for the enterprising entrepreneur to start an awning-cleaning service. The best way to gain clients is simply to put on some comfortable walking shoes and start knocking on doors. Visit all the shops and offices in your area that have awning signs and present your service. Explain about the benefits of good first impressions. This may seem to be an old-fashioned and time-consuming way to promote the business, but if you set an objective of talking with 10 potential customers a day and can close two of these presentations, you will then have 40 new clients within a month and be well on your way to establishing a solid and profitable business. Carry around a small portfolio of your work, including before-and-after photos of awnings you have cleaned. If necessary, clean a few for free before launching your business, just for the sake of taking photos. Hint: look for the dirtiest awnings in town for your "before" shots and then work your tail off cleaning them.

National Register of Professional Awning Cleaners, *awningpro.com:* Members receive industry information, advice, support and a listing in the association's online guide.

Home business requirements include storage space for your cleaning equipment and supplies, plus ladders and other tools of the trade.

62. *Landscaping Service*

A basic one- or two-person landscaping service can be set in motion for less than $10,000 and many of the skills needed to run it successfully can be learned on the job. However, operating a landscaping service still requires some landscaping experience to give clients peace of mind. Most landscaping business owners worked for some time for another landscaping company before launching their own companies. This allowed them to gain experience and knowledge of the business and see firsthand how things are done—and to decide how they might want to do things as owners. Potential customers for a landscaping service include commercial property owners, residential property owners, contractors and property developers. While an established landscaping service can compete for work in all categories, a new service should focus on one particular type of customer until the business has established a reputation. Most landscaping contracts are completed based on an estimate prior to starting the work, so practice your estimating (hourly) skills, as it is easy to underbid and overbid, both of which can be very costly in terms of profits. In the beginning, you'll want to start with some small

jobs and even do some free landscaping work for local associations, clubs, churches or temples. Such volunteer opportunities can allow you to take photos of your work for your printed literature and your website. Marketing is largely word-of-mouth, so make sure to take your time and do excellent work.

PLANET, the Professional Landcare Network, *landcarenetwork.org:* Members of this association, formed when the Associated Landscape Contractors of America and the Professional Lawn Care Association of America merged in 2005, receive industry information, advice and support.

Home business requirements include plenty of insurance coverage, lots of gardening tools, a good database for customer names and appointments, and storage space for all of your landscaping equipment.

63. *Mobile Screen Repair*

Starting a mobile screen-repair-and-replacement business could put you on the road to riches. Getting started will require basic tools and materials, such as a miter saw, screen rollers, screen replacement parts and a selection of fiberglass and aluminum screen rolls in various widths. The business can be operated from an enclosed trailer or van, to provide protection from inclement weather. To market a mobile screen-repair service, you should establish alliances with companies and individuals needing screen repairs and replacements on a regular basis. These include residential and commercial property management firms, condominium strata corporations, apartment complexes, government institutions and renovation contractors. The profit potential is excellent, since competition is limited and the demand for screen repairs and replacements is proven.

ScreenMobile, *screenmobile.com:* Major screen dealer and franchiser.

Home business requirements include a selection of screens and storage space for your equipment. You may also want to set up a workshop to repair screens in your basement or garage.

64. Used Fitness Equipment Sales

The time has never been better than now to start a home business that buys and resells used fitness equipment. Millions of people across North America are striving to become more fit and are buying fitness equipment such as treadmills, steppers, elliptical trainers and exercise bikes. Fitness equipment can be purchased at garage sales, gym closeouts, auctions and estate sales and via newspaper classified ads. Reselling the fitness equipment for a profit is also very easy, because it can be advertised for free in many community newspapers, on community bulletin boards, on your website and through fliers. This is a business that will eventually be promoted by word-of-mouth. The key is first learning about the latest fitness equipment (how it works and how it is assembled) and then finding and evaluating equipment to make sure it is in good shape. You will likely need to hire some local helpers to carry some of the heavier equipment.

Fit4Sale.com, *fitnessequipmenttrader.com:* Online fitness equipment auction and classified ads service bringing together buyers and sellers of fitness equipment and related equipment.

Home business requirements include insurance to cover you from liability in case a treadmill that you sold sends someone flying at warp speed, a large storage area (likely in a self-storage rental facility), a van or truck for moving exercise equipment and tools for disassembly and reassembly.

65. Pool and Hot Tub Cleaning Service

There are millions of swimming pools and hot tubs in North America, all with one thing in common—they must be cleaned and maintained regularly to work properly and be safe for use. A pool and hot tub maintenance service can be marketed in all traditional advertising media and by all promotional methods. However, for a fast start to getting customers, consider distributing fliers or coupons throughout your community to offer free pool and hot tub water safety tests for owners. The safety test would simply consist of checking the water for toxins and recommending corrective measures to fix the problem. The true purpose of the free water safety test is, of course, to gain clients for the service on a monthly basis. Before launching your business, learn everything you can about pools, pool maintenance and health department regulations.

Pool and Spa Online, *poolandspa.com:* Swimming pool and spa supplies, chemicals, industry information, resources and links.

Home business requirements include all the tools of the trade, any special licensing necessary in your area to work with cleaning chemicals and to dispose of them properly, insurance coverage and storage for your tools.

66. For-Sale-By-Owner Consultant

Many people attempt to sell their own homes, properties and cottages every year. Some succeed, but many do not. This fact creates a great opportunity to start a for-sale-by-owner consulting business to help people sell their homes quickly and for top dollar. You would tell clients how to prepare their home for listing, help them establish a value, teach them how to market their property, instruct them in the finer points of hosting an open house, and provide them with template forms that can be used to write an offer-and-sale agreement. This venture is ideal for entrepreneurs with significant real estate experience. Securing clients is as easy as calling people who currently have their homes for-sale-by-owner and by advertising locally in the newspaper in the Real Estate section. Charge clients a flat fee for the service and charge separately for extras like printing fliers, creating For-Sale and Open-House signs, and listing on your homes-for-sale-by-owner website and in any for-sale-by-owner publications that you print and distribute. Of course, if you end up charging more than a real estate broker would get from a sales commission, why would a seller choose to work with you? Therefore, you need to watch your fees and show potential clients the benefit of selling the home on their own with some basic guidance from you.

Owners.com, *owners.com:* "The Largest 'For Sale by Owner' Marketplace for Buyers and Sellers," a source of insight into the market.

Home business requirements, beyond your computer and communication tools, are minimal.

67. Mail Order Sales

Like manufacturing, listed earlier, this is a broad category that can encompass any number of products. After many years, mail order sales remain one of the best opportunities for a homebased business. More and more people are shopping from the comfort of their homes, via catalogs, toll-free numbers and websites, so you can sell almost anything by mail order. However, you want products that allow high profit margins, that pack and ship well, that have mass appeal within a niche target market, and preferably that can be the first of many such products that your customers purchase. Good possibilities include vitamins, herbs and home remedies, fishing lures and other products, kitchen items, collectibles and popular hobby favorites, wine and home or car repair tools.

You can reach your target audience for your products by launching a direct mail campaign,

advertising in publications read by your target audience and promoting your goods on websites visited by the consumers you're targeting. Mail order entrepreneurs cross-market between their websites and their printed catalogs. Smaller, niche-oriented catalogs have replaced massive mail order catalogs and many now provide just a sampling of the merchandise, with much more available on a website.

National Mail Order Association, *nmoa.org:* Membership organization with a lot of information, contacts, books, links and more.

infoUSA.com, *infousa.com:* Billed as the world's largest supplier of mailing lists, all of which are indexed by consumer, business, industry, hobby, geographic and demographic classifications.

Home business requirements may include extra phone lines for orders, high-speed internet access, and sturdy shelves to keep a wide variety of other catalogs to study the industry and your competition. You'll also need storage space and a fulfillment house as you grow your business.

68. Home Crafts Business

Another broad category is home crafts, making and selling. You can use your creative skills to create a multitude of nifty craft items that can be sold for big profits to those of us who are less crafty. From a simple home workspace, you can create items like specialty soaps, scented candles, jewelry, pottery, woodcarvings and turnings, Christmas decorations, woven baskets or stained glass items. You can then sell these craft items and decorations online, through mail order, at craft shows and by renting kiosk space in malls during the holidays. Invest the initial profits you earn into more equipment and inventory so that you can grow from part time into full time.

Crafts Reports Magazine Online, *craftsreport. com:* Print and electronic magazine serving the crafts industry by providing information, products, services, resources and links.

Home business requirements include a workshop in which to create and house your tools and a safe area in which to keep the fruits of your labor.

69. Packing Service

Let's face it: the worst aspect of moving is packing and unpacking—slow, tedious and back-breaking work. That's great news if you do not mind rolling up your sleeves and doing a little hard work. Moving companies will be one source of work, because they can subcontract with you to provide packing services or refer you to their clients. However, since many moving companies want to do everything themselves (which often results in some breakage), you should also contact home buyers and sellers who may soon need your services. Your billing rate could range from $15 to $40 per hour, depending on what you are packing. For example, for fine china, works of art and/or antiques, you might charge more. You might also look into targeting a certain niche, such as seniors who may require more help packing and often have valuables that they are very concerned will be broken during the move. Prior to starting such a business, you should get to know all the best packing techniques; it's not as obvious as it may appear and you want to be "the expert."

Uline Shipping Supplies, *uline.com:* Provider of packing materials.

Home business requirements include additional insurance and plenty of materials, from packing peanuts to boxes of various sizes, box cutters, tape, labels, etc.

70. Web Sales

Talk about a broad category! In essence, online product sales are a type of mail order sales, since that is how customers receive their goods. Nonetheless, it has taken on a life of its own as a means of running a business. It is also a major reason for the growth of homebased businesses.

The real question is not what can be sold online for a profit, but what *cannot* be sold. The answer: not much. New, used, overstocked, slightly damaged or one of a kind—just about anything can be sold over the internet, as confirmed by eBay, which has already helped hundreds of people become millionaires and thousands more make six-figure incomes selling everything from boats to little knickknacks on the wildly popular shopping and auction site. But just as in the bricks-and-mortar shopping world, to truly succeed, you must be selling things that fill a niche, are highly desirable or collectible or are priced low enough to spur impulse buying. You also have to decide whether to create your own e-tailing site or sell through eBay.

Do a *lot* of research and discover what market you may be able to tap into. There are numerous websites for almost any product out there. To make a splash, you'll need to offer something different, which could mean personalizing the items you sell or having another strong selling point, such as added bonuses for shopping on your site. In some cases, providing more detail about products and better customer service than the mega sites may win you steady customers. Running a website from your home is the easy part. Finding products that can make your business profitable and marketing the site are the hard parts. One reason so many people use eBay to sell is that eBay is a household word, so a major portion of the marketing is already done for you.

eBay, *ebay.com:* Online auction and retail cyber storefronts, offering an opportunity to sell almost any product.

Amazon, *amazon.com:* Online retailer of books, music, clothes and lots more, offering an opportunity to sell products in any of the categories covered.

Home business requirements include a fast and reliable internet connection, a well-designed site, various means of communications (including a toll-free number for customer support), and a place for storing and shipping your products (such as your garage or a fulfillment house).

71. Hand-Painted Products

Capitalize on your artistic abilities by starting a home business that involves hand-painting objects for resale in the retail and corporate gifts industry. You can specialize in watercolors, acrylics, oils or all paint media and depict landscapes, people, abstracts or any subject that tickles your fancy. You can paint calendars, greeting cards, report covers, flowerpots, wood and metal crafts and glassware. You can place painted household, craft and garden items on consignment with local retailers or sell them to retailers on a bulk and wholesale basis or to consumers directly at craft shows, through mail order and via online malls. Hand-painted items that are intended for the corporate gift market can be promoted through business networking meetings and through a direct marketing campaign aimed squarely at companies and professionals that routinely send out gifts to clients. The main requirement to ensure success is, of course, artistic ability.

CreateForLess, *createforless.com:* Wholesale craft supplies, industry information, resources and links.

Home business requirements include a workspace conducive to quiet, creative, artistic expression and storage space for products and art supplies.

72. Yard Maintenance Service

You need not be a landscaper to offer clients a host of yard and property cleanup services by starting a general yard maintenance business. Cut grass, remove rubbish, trim trees and hedges, aerate lawns and till gardens. Concentrate your marketing efforts at securing customers who might need regular service and offer financial incentives to persuade them to sign up for it. Most of the equipment needed to operate a yard maintenance service is relatively inexpensive to purchase. To keep startup costs to a minimum, you can purchase this equipment secondhand or rent it as needed. Averaged out, you should have no problem charging $20 to $30 per hour. Yard maintenance can be hard work, so there should be no shortage of homeowners prepared to part with a few dollars per month to have their yards maintained professionally, providing that you offer great service at fair rates.

HomeContracting, *home-contracting.com:* National online referral service, indexed geographically, so consumers can find qualified yard maintenance contractors.

Home business requirements include a place to house all the tools of the trade, plus gloves, goggles and other safety equipment. You'll also want to upgrade your liability insurance.

73. Wood Floor Sanding and Repairs

Many do-it-yourself homeowners are happy to stain and finish hardwood floors. However, when it comes to sanding off old finishes, repairing and fixing deep scratches in floors, that's another story entirely. Let's face it: sanding hardwood floors can be a back-breaking task and require a certain amount of experience and skill to do the job right. These are good reasons for starting a sanding and repair service. Of course, you need skills, but with practice on your own hardwood floors and those of willing friends and relatives, you can acquire this skill in a relatively short time. To keep startup costs to a minimum, you can rent floor-sanding equipment as needed until the business is established and generating revenues. Floor sanding is billed per square foot; call around to find out rates in your area.

Floorsanding.com, *floorsanding.com:* Floorsanding equipment and supplies for sale, as well as industry information, resources and links.

Home business requirements include room for the sanding equipment and necessary protective gear, plus insurance in case you have a mishap on the job.

74. Power Washing Service

A power washing service can be extremely profitable. The only fixed costs are a telephone, liability insurance, transportation and the occasional equipment repair. The income will depend on the amount of work, but there are hundreds of items that can be cleaned using power washing equipment, including:

- Concrete, pavement and paving stone driveways, walkways and parking lots
- Recreational vehicles, mobile homes, cars, trucks and boats
- Store signs, awnings and outdoor furniture
- Decks, patios, siding and metal roofs
- Construction and farm equipment

The key to success will be your ability to secure repeat clients. Remember: it costs 100 times as much to find 100 clients than to find 1 client and selling him or her 100 times. By far the best approach is to focus marketing on companies and individuals that could become regular customers.

ePowerWash.com, *epowerwash.com:* Website dedicated to serving professionals in the power washing industry with information, products, services, support, resources and links of interest.

Home business requirements include a high-

quality power washer (they cost between $500 and $750), a place to keep it and all the necessary accessories, along with a good database (online or offline) of contacts and regular clients.

75. Computer Repair Service

The toughest part of this business is staying one step ahead of the ever-changing computer technology. If, however, you are a whiz with computers, a true "computer geek," and are constantly on top of all that is new in the industry, you can make a good living fixing computers in the comfort of your own home … or in the homes or small businesses of others. Knowledge is more significant than startup cash. The key is to do a good job, do it quickly and listen to the needs of the client. If clients feel confident that you can help them quickly and cost-effectively in their homes or businesses, they will be happy to call you, rather than schlepping their computers to Best Buy's Geek Squad locations. Too many computer experts price their house calls too high and lose the business. If you can undercut the big players with lower-cost visits, you can build a reputation and eventually start raising your rates. Don't focus only on the big jobs; there's a tremendous need for people to handle the little catastrophes that slow down small businesses and homebased businesses.

National Association of Computer Repair Business Owners, *nacrbo.com:* Trade association of computer repair business owners, "dedicated to the advancement of the computer repair business through the building of trust and professionalism of its members."

Home business requirements include state-of-the-art computers, all the tools for repairing computers, and a cool, dry, clean location for housing them. You'll also need an abundance of cables and a reliable vehicle for making house calls.

76. Small Business Advertising Agency

Put your advertising skills and experience to good use by starting an advertising agency focused on helping home business and small business owners create campaigns that get results. Creating cost-effective advertising campaigns is one of the toughest challenges for most small business owners, because advertising is an all-encompassing task that requires experience and creative skills that most small business owners either do not have or have little time to apply. Capitalizing on your advertising experience, you can create campaigns for clients that will reach their target market directly and within their budget. Advertising is costly; small business owners cannot waste money on advertising that does not hit their target. By charging business owners for what they need, rather than an extravagant, high-cost campaign, you can help them reach prospective clients cost-effectively.

American Association of Advertising Agencies, *aaaa.org:* Members receive advertising industry information, advice and support.

Home business requirements are minimal, since your creativity and knowledge of the business are your most significant assets. Nonetheless, the latest in computer graphics programs, a portfolio (online and off) and a comfortable office space in which to create are important in this homebased business.

77. Photography Service

If you have the necessary skills and equipment, there are a multitude of photography-related home businesses that can you could start and operate successfully—commercial, aerial, portraits, weddings and special events (photography and videography), pets, extreme sports (videography), headshots and portfolios for actors and models, video editing and security identification photos. Market your photography service by networking at business and social functions, advertising in your local newspaper and telephone directory, featuring some of your work on your website, and establishing alliances with business-people in areas such as planning weddings and other events who can help spread the word.

International Freelance Photographers Organization (American Image Press), *aipress.com:* Members receive industry information, advice and support.

Advertising Photographers of America, *apanational.com:* Members receive industry information, advice and support.

Wedding and Event Videographers Association International, *weva.com:* Members receive industry information, advice and support.

Home business requirements include state-of-the-art photography equipment, including a variety of cameras and lenses and digital software to edit your work. You'll also need special lighting, and perhaps a location for darkroom if you are a photo traditionalist (unless you have a trusty photo lab), which can be a converted walk-in closet or a specially built room within your home. If possible, you would like to set up a small studio space for portraits and headshots. If not, you can work strictly on location.

78. Home Security

Much like a photography business, home security offers innovative entrepreneurs a nearly unlimited number of related startups, such as sales and installations of window security bars and roll shutters, home alarm sales and installations, locksmith, crime prevention training, security engraving service or the latest in state-of-the-art closed-circuit surveillance cameras and full home-integration security systems. Of course, the prerequisites for most will be training, experience and, generally, certification in the field. Home security is one of the fastest-growing segments of the home services and home products industry. The latest trends, however, require a great deal of technical know-how, especially for high-end systems. Therefore, unless you have an extensive background in the security field, you will need to train yourself or take training classes in all the latest crime deterrents.

Market your home security business through traditional forms of advertising, as well as by offering free security seminars in your field of expertise to secure sales leads. Also consider writing a home security column for your local newspaper, because the weekly exposure is great publicity for your business and positions you as an expert in the industry. Your website should be updated regularly as new products emerge.

Check local laws about becoming certified to do this type of work.

International Association of Professional Security Consultants, *iapsc.org*: Members receive industry information, advice and support.

Home business requirements include a location for storing the security systems you sell and all of the tools to install them. Since many of the latest security systems require codes and proprietary information with which to repair and reactivate them, you will need a secure location for storing data online and offline.

79. Fashion Design and Manufacturing

Independent fashion designers, manufacturers and merchandisers have been springing up all over the country in the past few years. Much of this growth can be attributed to the internet. Now these junior fashion houses have a way to get their designs in front of a global audience, leveling the playing field with their larger competitors. From a homebased design and manufacturing workspace

(e.g., spare bedroom), you can design, manufacture and market custom handbags, hats, jackets, bathing suits, belts, costume jewelry, shoes, shirts, elegant formal wear, business wear or casual social wear. Remember: At the root of the fashion industry is buzz. Therefore, spend considerable time figuring out how you will get your fashion creations and/or accessories to someone that can create the buzz. This "someone" could be an entertainment or sports celebrity or anyone who writes about fashion. As much as the fashion industry is about creating great fashions, it is equally about creating great publicity. Along with trying to get your fashions in the hands of celebrities (even local ones) and the media, you can set up local fashion shows at all your favorite restaurants.

Fashion Group International, Inc., *fgi.org*: A global, nonprofit, professional organization with a mission to be the pre-eminent authority on the business of fashion and design and to help its members become more effective in their careers.

InfoMat Inc., *infomat.com*: "Fashion Industry Search Engine" that provides "guides for navigating the business of fashion," news, information on trends and publications.

Home business requirements include that special room in which to create your masterpieces, complete with all the latest in fashion-making tools and equipment. You will also want to have a second area in which to keep everything safe and clean for upcoming fashion shows.

80. Antique Furniture Sales

Dig through garage sales, attend estate sales and scan your local newspaper classifieds to find truly outstanding antique and collectibles bargains. Resell these items for a profit by placing selected ads in antique-related magazines and newspapers, featuring them on your website, listing them on other websites and consigning your best items to well-attended auctions of antiques and col-lectibles. Selling antique furniture and collectibles is a fantastic home business venture. Work your own hours. Keep your present job if you choose. The investment to start is minimal and so is the operating overhead. It's the perfect home business for people who know antique bargains when they find them. You will need a van or a truck for trans-porting your inventory. Used trucks in good con-dition can be bought for a few thousand dollars. Also, if you have the credentials, skills and equip-ment, you can earn extra revenue by doing appraisals of antiques and collectibles and even restoring antiques, although that requires addi-tional skills and some training.

Antiques and Collectibles National Association, *antiqueandcollectible.com:* Members receive indus-try information, advice and support.

Home business requirements include a pickup truck or van, storage space for your collection, pol-ishes and cleaners and the basic computer and communications tools to constantly be seeking and finding new opportunities to buy and sell antiques.

81. Cleaning Service

Cleaning services still rank as the most common new home business startups, and with good rea-son. They're cheap to get going, easy to operate, able to generate excellent revenues and profits, easy to expand, in high demand in a growth industry, and light on special skills to master. You can oper-ate a residential cleaning service focused on homes and apartments, a commercial cleaning service focused on stores and offices, or a more specialized cleaning service, providing any number of options from carpet cleaning to ceiling cleaning to blind cleaning and construction site cleanup. Your options are wide open. On average, most cleaners charge $30 or more per hour, depending on spe-

cialized services like floor stripping and waxing or restaurant hood cleaning. This also depends on the market in which you are working. Many cleaning service owners start out handling some of the jobs themselves, but typically move to running the business, hiring reliable individuals to handle the moving and heavy lifting. This means being or becoming an excellent judge of people, recogniz-ing who would be a dependable, trustworthy employee and who would not. After all, you'll want to have employees bonded before they enter homes or offices.

Promoting the business requires fliers for com-mercial clients. Residential cleaners can rely on print ads, fliers and coupons to get the word out, although much of your business will come via word-of-mouth, so make sure that you and/or your staff do good work.

Cleaning and Maintenance Management Magazine Online, *cmmonline.com:* Print and elec-tronic magazine featuring cleaning industry infor-mation, resources and links.

Home business requirements include a variety of cleaning tools and first-rate equipment for yourself and/or as many people as you choose to send out on jobs.

82. Homebased Travel Agent

Once upon a time it was easy to find storefront travel agencies in every town or city. Today, aside from the large players, such as Liberty Travel, there are very few left. The glut of online budget travel operations is part of the reason. The other reason is that state-of-the-art computers once reserved for industries like travel are now in homes. Therefore, homebased travel businesses, once reserved for "specialty" trips, are now the norm in the industry. Once you get your travel agent license, you can launch a business from your home office. Typically, you will want to affiliate yourself with a host agency, which is a large travel agency that serves as a wholesaler to some degree, buying in bulk from tour distributors and enabling you to get excellent deals on packages to wherever your clients want to go. Host agencies are also on the inside track for airline reservations, since the airlines pulled commissions for travel agents out of the mix a few years ago, another cause of the demise of many storefront travel agencies.

It's always a good idea to specialize. With that in mind, you can book anything from eco-friendly tours of the rain forest in Brazil to senior excursions to cruises exclusively on Carnival, Norwegian and other leading ocean lines. Why does someone choose a travel agent when it's possible to book on Orbitz or one of the other online travel discount sites? Good question. With the proliferation of web travel sites, more and more discerning travelers have discovered the limitations of these sites: changing itineraries when necessary often became a nightmare, making connections was not always easy, and photos of rooms on the internet often did not represent the actual accommodations. Thus, many people have opted to contact the ever-growing number of homebased (licensed) travel agents to make sure that their one vacation in the middle of a busy schedule would be rewarding and enjoyable, rather than disappointing.

Market your adventure vacation packages through your own website, company newsletters, online chat rooms and forums and e-mail to regular clients can work wonderfully. Remuneration is typically earned by charging clients a fee for making arrangements and organizing the vacation. Once a travel business is established, the owner can earn a substantial living by arranging vacations for people who are seeking personal attention rather than gambling on a website to make their vacation plans. Yes, there is still a very large market, especially if you work with corporate travel, as well as family vacations.

National Association of Commissioned Travel Agents, *nacta.com:* Association for independent travel agents, providing members with industry information, advice and support.

Home business requirements include first-rate computer and communications tools and all the literature you can get from host agencies and on your own about the trips and packages you sell.

83. Freelance Writer

Some writers' websites peg the number of freelance writers in the United States at more than 100,000 at any given time. While the competition certainly is steep, the rewards can be excellent financially and you can enjoy a very fulfilling career, if you can make it in the field. When asked, most successful freelancers will tell you that if you want to succeed, you should specialize. While some generalists do very well, it can be beneficial having one or a couple of broad areas in which you have expertise, such as business writing, travel, health, entertainment or technical writing.

You will start out by writing and pitching stories for any and every small publication, e-zine or website from which you can get exposure. Do not start out shooting for the moon, but rather build a portfolio of published work. You'll want to market yourself by sending out queries, proposals and, if they are looking for regular contributors, sample columns to publications and websites that fit your writing prowess. Do a lot of digging for new outlets. They are out there, but the paying ones are often harder to find. Books like *Writer's Digest* and e-mail newsletters like *Writer's Weekly* (*writersweekly.com*) can be very helpful.

Rates can be based on a per-word scale or per-feature article. Expect to write a few freebies to get your name out there while building your publication credits. The best-paying markets tend to be major monthly magazines, midsized to large book publishers and the top websites. (Small websites and newspapers generally do not pay well.) There is also a large market in corporate and technical writing. If you are well versed in computers, keep in mind that there is always someone out there looking for a writer for an instruction manual or for computer game directions.

American Society of Journalists and Authors, *asja.org:* Long-standing organization offering plenty of articles, resources and contacts for newcomers, plus an annual convention in New York City open to all.

Home business requirements include a comfortable setting in which to write and excellent computer and communications tools for writing, maintaining a contacts list and staying in touch with editors and publishers.

84. Event Planner

Attention to detail, a knack for organization, good communication skills, and a creative flair are all personal traits shared by event planners. If this describes you, perhaps you should consider starting an event planning service. Event planners are responsible for organizing and hosting special events for their clients, with duties that can include creating and sending out invitations, selecting the event location, acquiring decorations and props, arranging entertainers and speakers, selecting caterers and creating menus, and just about everything else necessary for staging a special event without a hitch. You can specialize in social events such as wedding anniversaries, birthdays, graduations and award ceremonies or you can focus on corporate events, including luncheons, parties, grand openings, investor meetings and trade shows. Networking, networking and more networking will be your main marketing tool for attracting and securing new business.

Event Planner Online, *event-planner.com:*

Directory service listing event planners, with information about the industry and starting and marketing an event-planning service.

Home business requirements are minimal, but they include strong communications tools and a good database of contacts, since you will spend a great deal of time going back and forth with clients and service providers.

85. Masseur/Masseuse

The tension and stress of the fast pace world have many people looking for a relaxing massage, at work or in their home. This is a growing and potentially very lucrative business, one for which you can train and receive certification as a masseuse or masseur or hire several individuals with such training and book them with clients. Of course, if you train to become a massage therapist, you can acquire more clients and possibly collect from insurance companies if clients are referred to you by physicians. Other options for a licensed masseur or masseuse are to provide special types of massages, such as hot stone and Swedish massages.

Massages will typically range from $25 to $75 per hour and startup costs are fairly minimal. Once trained, you may want to practice your techniques on some friends and relatives. After that, you can promote your business through fliers, on your website, at wellness seminars, through health food stores, and in gyms and fitness centers if they do not already have a masseur or masseuse on staff.

American Massage Therapy Association, *amtamassage.org:* Membership association dedicated to providing the latest information on massage therapy.

Home business requirements include limber hands and at least one massage table, the appropriate lotions, scents and other accessories of the craft. If you do massages in your home, you'll need a very quiet room.

86. Pet-Sitting Business

If you love pets, you do not want to see them boarded in kennels while their owners travel. It is, therefore, a great idea to start a pet-sitting business. It can consist of scheduling someone to check in on animals large and small while their owners are away, to feed them, walk them or provide any other specific pet needs. Other than being trustworthy, reliable and responsible and having a good rapport with animals world (not being scared really helps!), there is not much more to know about handling this business, other than doing what is requested by the pet owner. You can provide the service yourself or you can hire students, retirees or others seeking some part-time cash.

You can advertise by handing out fliers to people out walking their dogs and by placing notices on bulletin boards in pet stores, supermarkets or other shops.

The key to success is to have several clients per day in a nearby area, so you can make your rounds and return home to field calls from new or returning customers. Obviously the most popular travel months, summer and school vacation time, will be your busiest times of year.

You can make additional income by selling pet-related products, such as fancy dog collars, fun pet toys and even doggie shampoo.

National Association of Professional Pet Sitters, *petsitters.org:* All the information for pet sitting in one place, plus a certification program that can up your rates and number of clients.

Home business requirements include having some brushes, leashes, and other pet accessories on hand in case they are needed. (Typically everything is provided by the owner.) You'll also want to have excellent scheduling software and reliable transportation available at all times.

87. College Consultant/Advisor

It has never been more competitive than it is today to get into college. Students are feeling the pressure as soon as they start high school, with so much riding on grades, SAT and ACT scores and eventually their college applications. Therefore, if you immerse yourself in the world of colleges and college entry, you can make $100,000 a year in this rapidly growing field. The key is to become an expert; this does not happen without a lot of initial research and legwork. And while it helps to have a background in education, it is also very helpful to be able to relate well to high school students—and their parents (which is the toughest part).

A good college consultant will start meeting with students in the 10th grade (sometimes earlier) and guide them toward schools that might be right for them based on their interests, passions, academic achievements, future goals and personalities. You'll need to know a lot about universities all over the country and even tour some of them. Next you will need to determine what the parents and students want in a school and try to match the school with the family's plans. When the time comes to apply for colleges, you will help with applications, which are now very involved and detailed and usually require essays.

Along with the money, there are great rewards when you see your students getting accepted by the college of their choice and then graduating.

Independent Educational Consultants Association, *educationalconsulting.org:* Members counsel students and their families in the selection of educational programs, based on each student's needs and talents.

Home business requirements include fast internet access for going online often for the latest news on college programs and offerings, as well as excellent communications tools for staying in contact with deans of admissions, students and parents. You will likely want to have a nicely decorated, comfortable office space, since your clients will be primarily visiting you.

88. Literary Agent

It's easy to run this type of business from a home office, since almost all of your time is spent on the phone, reading manuscripts, or scheduling and going to appointments and meetings to discuss projects. Typically, literary agents specialize in the types of books or scripts (film or television) they represent, based on their connections in the industry. And that is one of the keys to success—*connections*. To make it as a literary agent, you need to have very close ties within the industry; those usually come from working for a publishing house, production facility or TV network. It takes time to build up a database of good contacts who will be willing to read the work of your clients. The second requirement is to know the genre or genres you represent inside out. If you represent mystery novels, for example, you need to know without a doubt the difference between a great, compelling story that will fly off the shelves and one about which publishers simply won't care "who done it."

If you have the contacts and experience, you can do very well, while setting your own hours. You can seek new clients at writers' association gatherings and through newsletters and websites for writers.

Association of Authors' Representatives, *aar-online.org:* Not-for-profit organization of independent literary and dramatic agents.

Home business requirements include excellent computer and communications tools and an ever-expanding list of contacts.

89. Rehearsal Coordinator

Whether it's for a play, a dance recital or a band,

there is always a demand for rehearsal space. This opens up an opportunity to solve the problem for those who are seeking a place to work on their performances.

If you have a garage that you can convert, by soundproofing, reflooring and adding proper lighting, you may be able to handle smaller needs. However, your real money will be in finding all the local studios and other facilities that could make excellent rehearsal spaces. Once you know about those places, you will serve as the central clearinghouse, putting those in need of a space into locations that fit their needs. Meeting the needs of the group and making sure the facilities are well maintained are your two tickets to success.

Making a percentage off each rehearsal booking can become lucrative, as there is typically not much competition in this field and you can become *the* person to contact for all rehearsal needs. Market yourself through fliers and brochures to theater and dance groups, classes, schools, production companies and even the circus if it is coming to town.

Soundproofing101, *soundproofing101.com:* Introductory information, plus courses and links regarding soundproofing.

Home business needs are minimal. You'll need very good computer and communications tools to maintain schedules and stay in touch with rehearsal studio and facility owners and managers. If you opt to use space within your home or an addition for a rehearsal studio, check with local zoning laws and keep soundproofing and safety concerns as your two major priorities.

90. Interior Decorating

If you have a flair for color schemes, design and décor, this might be the ideal homebased business for you. Training, experience, and certification are typically required if you are serious about this field, but once you have proven your skills and have a stellar portfolio (online and off) to back up your abilities, you can make very good money.

Most interior decorators specialize in either residential or commercial circles, although some cross the lines. The key is to know what the client wants and build relationships with suppliers to get materials at a good cost.

Once you're certified, you'll want to start out by doing some gratis work to build a portfolio. You can then market yourself through fliers leading people to your website. Word-of-mouth is the key to success, so consider each job well done to be part of your marketing strategy: take before-and-after photos.

American Society of Interior Designers, *asid.org:* Site featuring education, information, knowledge sharing, advocacy, community building and outreach for more than 35,000 members in the field.

International Interior Design Association, *iida.org:* Members receive industry information, advice and support.

Home business requirements include workspace for mapping out ideas and laying out designs, interior design software and excellent tools for communicating and storing your database of suppliers and industry affiliations.

91. Specialty Cakes

If you love baking and have a flair for the artistic, you can start a business right in your own kitchen, creating and designing specialty cakes for special occasions. This can be a part-time or full-time endeavor, depending how far and wide you market your culinary masterpieces. From catering facilities to associations to large corporations to individuals holding backyard parties, there are plenty of opportunities. The more creative your cakes are, the more attention they will generate

from brochures and website photos. If you can make cakes that are both tasty and healthy, all the better!

American Bakers Association, *americanbakers. org:* Organization representing "all segments of the grain-based foods industry before the U.S. Congress, state legislatures and domestic and international regulatory authorities."

Home business requirements include at least one oven exclusively for baking, plus a large kitchen workspace and storage for the tools of the trade.

92. Speakers' Bureau

There seems to be a never-ending need for public speakers, whether for awards functions, conventions, seminars or graduations. Running a speakers' bureau can be very lucrative if you put the right speakers in front of the right audiences. To do so, you'll need to listen to speakers present and choose only the best to represent. You will also need to market yourself to all businesses, associations, and clubs with upcoming conventions, as well as schools and social groups. Include bios of your speakers on your website and have marketing material to hand out and send out to all potential clients.

Since most speakers' bureaus have a penchant for booking only high-end, very high-priced speakers, you might find a great deal of business booking mid-priced speakers. You make money by charging the client a fee for booking the speaker and/or a percentage of what the speaker earns per appearance. You'll do excellent word-of-mouth business if your speakers are dynamic and entertaining.

Advanced Public Speaking Institute, *public-speaking.org:* A wealth of information about public speaking.

Home business requirements include all means of playing speaker presentations (CD, DVD, tape, etc.) and excellent communications tools. You might also have microphones and other tools of the speaking trade on hand for those who need or wish to make a demo tape with your assistance.

93. Illustrator

Can you draw? If you are good at it, you can have a career as a professional illustrator and run your business from your own home. Illustrators are used in the fashion industry, in book and magazine publishing, as well as in the medical field, although medical illustrating is a more complicated specialty.

A good illustrator will need to establish a portfolio of his or her best work and use that to get the business off the ground. Fees and rates range dramatically, depending on the type of illustrations. A children's book illustrator, for example, might have a 50/50 split with the author of the book on the advance and subsequent royalties from the publishing house. Some illustrators are paid per drawing. It all depends on the project.

Picture Book Artists Association, *picturebookartists.org:* An independent association of professional children's book illustrators from around the world.

Association of Medical Illustrators, *ami.org:* International organization promoting the study and advancement of medical illustration.

Home business requirements focus primarily on a quiet space in which to work and the necessary tools for drawing and coloring.

94. Home Day-Care Center

If you saw the movie *Daddy Day Care*, don't panic: it does not have to be like that. A day-care center can be run in a home for a small number of children (of similar ages) with the right guidance and a background in child care. The toughest part is not

promoting a day-care facility or transforming part of your home into a child-friendly environment. The challenging aspect is to make sure you meet all of the requirements. In most areas of North America, day-care centers and staff require certification. It is very important that you meet or exceed these legal requirements. You will also need to carry liability insurance and have on-site safety equipment such as first-aid kits, fire safety equipment and emergency action plans. You will also need to determine how many children you can accommodate. Typically the ratio of adults to children needs to be high (such as one adult to three infants and toddlers or one to five for preschoolers) to gain the trust of parents and possibly to satisfy licensing requirements. This means you must hire reliable people, preferably with a background in child care or early childhood education. College or graduate students majoring in education or simply good with kids may be a good fit. Screen all applicants carefully. If your approach is professional and very well planned, you will have no difficulty in charging a premium over competing day-care services in your community.

Homebased day-care facilities can cost as little as $5,000 to establish, while full-scale day-care centers operating from an independent business location can cost as much as $100,000 to start. Of course, zoning laws may prevent you from starting a homebased day-care business, so before doing anything, check them out first.

National Childcare Association, *nccanet.org:* Organization providing information and education to the private, licensed child-care industry.

National Association of Child Care Resource & Referral Agencies, *naccrra.org:* Organization that works with more than 800 state and local child care resource and referral agencies to promote the quality of child care services.

National Child Care Information Center, *nccic.org:* A service of the U.S. Department of

Health and Human Services, Child Care Bureau, Office of Family Assistance, "a national clearinghouse and technical assistance center that links parents, providers, policy-makers, researchers and the public to early care and education information."

National Network for Child Care, *nncc.org:* An outreach program that shares "knowledge about children and child care from ... landgrant universities with parents, professionals, practitioners and the general public."

Child Care Law Center, *childcarelaw.org*: National nonprofit legal services organization that serves as a legal resource for the local, state and national child-care communities.

Home business requirements include a large child-safe space, plenty of child-friendly activities, all safety measures taken inside and outside, all the necessary insurance, a knack for taking care of children, and a lot of patience.

95. Fabric Restoration

If you can learn how to restore fabric, you can start your own business without the need for very much startup funding. From leather repair to fabric dying to reupholstering, there is a need for experts who maintain the look and feel of fine furniture.

You can start by offering your services in handouts and on your website and as you build your business, continue learning and expanding your restoration expertise.

Ads on bulletin boards, in furniture dealerships, and in local free shopper publications will help you spread the word, but good-quality work that leads to word-of-mouth marketing will generate much more business. Additional income can come from restoring carpets, cleaning blinds and steam-cleaning upholstered furniture.

Fabrics.net, *fabrics.net*: Fabric information and all about fabric care.

Home business requirements include a workshop with all the necessary tools and a reliable vehicle for transporting furniture.

96. Career Coaching

There are many people looking to change careers and many other recent graduates trying to determine where that archaeology or philosophy degree can place them in the real world. If you have your finger on the pulse of the career market and a knack for working with people to determine what they would most like to accomplish, you might consider training to become a career consultant. Your goal is not to find jobs, but to help individuals find the best career opportunities. Oddly enough, this is a career in which you work to put yourself out of work, by finding the client a good career path on which he or she moves on without further assistance from you.

Career shows, employment agencies and colleges and universities can all benefit from your services, meaning you'll want to target these as possible marketing locations. You'll also want to advertise in traditional media and put your coaching philosophy on your website.

Career Management Alliance, *careermanagementalliance.com:* Formerly Career Masters Institute and the International Association of Career Coaches.

Home business requirements include a well-appointed office, since most clients will come to you, and a wealth of resources on a wide range of occupations.

97. Tax Returns

Talk about your seasonal business. From January until April 15 (in the United States) or April 30 (in Canada), you can be rather busy doing tax returns and making good money for your efforts.

Depending on the complexity of the return and the time involved, you can make from $100 to several hundred per return and you need not be a certified public accountant to do so. As long as you are trained in the tax laws (H&R Block offers training courses, *hrblock.com* or *hrblock.ca*), you can do tax returns from the comfort of your home office. Considering that a number of clients will need extensions to finish their returns, you can have some work at other times of the year as well.

Once you have taken a course and feel that you are knowledgeable and ready to prepare tax returns, you should have your ads set to go by the start of the year. Use all traditional print advertising methods and set up a website. Staying on top of the ever-changing tax laws and making people feel comfortable working with you are the two primary requirements of this business.

If you study bookkeeping and add that to your repertoire, handling the books for small businesses, you can end up with a lucrative full-time business.

National Association of Tax Professionals, *natptax.com:* Nonprofit professional association formed to serve professionals who work in all areas of tax practice, including individual practitioners.

American Accounting Association, *aaahq.org:* Organization promoting excellence in accounting education, research and practice, with a vision of being a "Thought Leader in Accounting."

Home business resources include the latest in accounting software and a quiet office space for deciphering the latest in tax laws from Congress or Parliament.

98. Laundry Service

Yes, there are self-service laundries out there for an ongoing parade of individuals armed with quarters. You, however, can provide local laundry service to small businesses that require employees to wear uniforms, which could include service station attendants, fast-food restaurant employees or even hotel staffers. Add to that school sports uniforms and costumes for theatrical productions and you have a laundry business, provided your home can handle the extra plumbing load.

Advertise locally and provide pickup and drop-off at specific times so you do not have people coming and going from your home at all hours. You can charge by the load and by your time commitment, meaning that you charge more if you have to travel across town to pick up and drop off uniforms. While the learning curve is minimal, you have to know how to do laundry without shrinking anything or turning home white uniforms into visiting road colors.

American Laundry News, *americanlaundrynews.com:* Online and print newspaper with plenty of information on the industry.

Home business requirements include top-of-the-line washer(s) and dryer(s), with plumbing that can support them, plus a space for folding uniforms and ironing. You'll also need to have reliable transportation that can accommodate several bags of laundry.

99. Online Dating Service

While many of them may not admit it, there are still plenty of singles who will sign up with an online dating service in hopes of meeting someone special. To run such a service, you'll need a high-speed, reliable computer plus a well-designed website and plenty of marketing and promotion. The key is to provide a service where people with similar interests and personalities can discover one another and communicate online until they feel comfortable meeting in person. For your efforts, you will receive payment from each person who signs up with your service, which should be for adults 18 or 21 and over only.

Prior to setting up such a service, you'll need to make sure you have a contract in place that absolves you from all responsibility when clients decide to meet in person. Of course, if your service gains a bad reputation, you'll need to rethink your application and screening process. Remember to include same-sex dating and encourage senior dating with a section for individuals over 60. If you set up and maintain it correctly and promote it everywhere, this can be a lucrative business, with very little overhead.

StyleCareer.com, *stylecareer.com/professional_matchmaker.shtml:* A "How To" guide to get started in the dating service (matchmaking) business.

Online Dating Magazine, *onlinedatingmagazine.com:* An internet publication dedicated to in-depth coverage of the online dating services industry

Home business requirements include top-of-the-line computer and communications tools.

age based on the number of students that sign up. Make sure to set a minimum for sign-ups (or the class will be canceled) and a maximum based on the number of students the room and the course can accommodate. Typically such courses have 7 to 15 students.

Once you line up the instructors and the locations, you'll need to put together a catalog that can be posted online and distributed offline. Market using all the conventional means, including fliers, posters, local radio ads, web advertising and so on. If you can find instructors to teach courses on the latest and hottest trends, your adult learning center can become very popular.

The American Association for Adult and Continuing Education, *aaace.org:* Association providing the latest research and information in the adult education industry.

Home business requirements include excellent computer and communications tools.

100. Adult Learning Center

There are always people who want to learn more, beyond their years of formal schooling. Adult learning centers provide courses and seminars on a wide range of subjects, including cooking, personal finance, pilates, yoga, fiction or nonfiction writing, ballroom dancing and more. Thanks to computers, e-mail and other communications tools, running such a learning center can be done from the comfort of your own home. No, you do not host courses in your home, but instead find course locations and instructors (subject-matter experts) interested in teaching. Many adult learning centers use school classrooms and community centers in the evening for such classes, usually for a fee. Typically courses run from one to six sessions and students pay accordingly, usually by credit card. You work out arrangements with your teachers that they will receive a flat fee and/or a percent-

101. Fundraising Consultant

Working with charities and charitable individuals can be both profitable and very rewarding. Your job will be to help such groups and organizations raise the necessary funds to reach their goals. The first step required for establishing a fundraising service is to build alliances with local or national charities. When a charity hires you as a fundraising consultant, you will then establish a fundraising program, similar to a business plan, outlining how the funds will be raised. It should also state the fee you will charge for your service. Typically, fundraising consultants charge a fee for basic services and a commission for services based on a percentage of the total amount of money raised, such as 10 percent on amounts in excess of $50,000, for example. Be careful not to take too big a bite or the organization will use volunteers instead of hiring you, even if they do not have your expertise.

The best way to build a reputation is to start small, running this as a side business by raising funds for a few smaller local charities. As is the case with many businesses, you are only as good as your track record and you will need to establish one to get started.

Association of Fund-Raising Distributors and Suppliers, *afrds.com:* International organization "devoted exclusively to the product fundraising industry" and "dedicated to promoting professionalism and integrity in product fundraising."

Home business resources include excellent computer and communications tools and a well-appointed office for meeting with clients.

102. Gift Items

Calendars, picture frames, candleholders, and numerous other small gift items can bring you a very good part-time or even full-time income if you are good at marketing and selling. The advantages are that you can buy in bulk, keeping the price down, and that you have a lower overhead than the nearby storefront gift shop. You'll use your home office to contact vendors and suppliers and set up sales appointments. While you can sell to friends, family, neighbors and anyone else, especially with a website featuring your gift selection, you can make more money by selling to companies that are looking for gift items for clients, suppliers and employees. You can also set up house parties, where, much like the Tupperware® sales force, you play some games, eat some food and sell plenty of gift items. You'll also want to arrange, well in advance, for booths at gift shows and gift fairs. Bulk up on inventory and market heavily in the spring during bridal shower time and prior to the holidays, when people need those small gift items for teachers, friends and others and for stocking stuffers.

Global Sources Gifts & Premiums, *gifts.global-sources.com:* Suppliers of gifts and premiums.

Gift Shop Magazine, *giftshopmag.com:* Online and print publication for gift retailers, offering information, products, ideas and inspiration.

Home business requirements include excellent computer and communication tools, plus storage space for your inventory and reliable transportation for getting your goods to and from gift parties or shows.

103. Resume Writing Service

With the exception of a professional athlete, it's hard to find a profession in which job seekers do not need resumes to get jobs. Writing a great resume, one that presents the individual in the best light and provides the pertinent information in a concise manner that jumps off the page, is an art. If you can write winning resumes, you can start a resume service from the comfort of your home office. With some good marketing at job fairs, ads in newspapers and other traditional sources, along with a good website and word-of-mouth marketing, you can make a good income while spending very little money other than on advertising and marketing.

Depending on the complexity of the resume and your market, you can make anywhere from $60 to $150 per resume. If you can turn around 10 per week at $100 each, you can make over $50,000. To expand on this, learn the art of writing a good cover letter and practice, practice, practice. For $35 to $50 more, you can include this service, as well.

National Résumé Writers' Association, *nrwaweb.com:* Nonprofit organization "dedicated to promoting the highest standards of excellence in resume writing through certification, education and mentoring programs."

Home business requirements include a reliable computer with the latest software for resume writing and a nicely appointed office for client visits.

104. Editor/Proofreader

Writers and publishers want their work to look good in print, which means the need for editors and proofreaders remains very important, especially with the glut of misspellings and poor grammar showing up on websites. You can start a lucrative career by editing and proofreading texts of all kinds—manuscripts, articles, screenplays, corporate reports, business plans, resumes, school essays, web content and anything else being written for others to read.

Rates will vary according to the complexity of the materials, with medical and highly technical materials commanding more money than mainstream magazine articles. Obviously, you will need a good command of the English language to excel in this business. Being proficient in other languages can help you garner more work. You'll want to market your services to all types of publishers, authors, and anyone else responsible for putting printed material in the hands of readers or viewers.

American Society of Business Publication Editors, *asbpe.org:* Association that provides information to its members, runs competitions and holds an annual conference.

Editorial Freelancers Association, *the-efa.org:* National nonprofit professional organization of "self-employed workers in the publishing and communications industries" (including editors, proofreaders and writers), offering on its website a wide variety of resources.

Home business requirements are little more than a good editing program, reliable data backup (including offline) and a good database of clients who will need editing and/or proofreading services regularly, such as publishing houses.

105. Gourmet Chocolates

There's a huge market of chocolate lovers who are always seeking out delectable delights. If you can create, design and package a wide array of chocolates, you can start a mouthwatering business that can turn chocolate into dough. Making delicious candy is only half the work. You'll want to present it in unique shapes and forms and package it in ways that make ideal gift boxes for clients. There is a very large corporate market, as well as schools, associations and the general public.

Chocolate flavors may include such favorites as *dulce de leche*, champagne, cappuccino, creamy caramel, dark, espresso, hazelnut, raspberry, coconut, coffee and lavender. Such variety will spice up your selection and possible sales. Assorted gourmet chocolates in beautiful boxes can be sold for upward of $75 for a selection of 36 pieces. You can also sell chocolate bars, hot chocolate, and other variations on your way to the sweet smell of success.

Chocolate Manufacturers Association, *chocolateusa.org:* Membership organization dedicated to improving the methods and means of making chocolate products.

Home business requirements include a dedicated oven for your craft, reliable suppliers and shippers for ingredients, and storage space for those ingredients and packaging materials, a space for designing your goodies and reliable transport for shipping.

106. Contractor

If you have the skills as a carpenter or a contractor, you can run a very profitable business from your home. Every year, numerous homeowners remodel or add to their homes, while others get their homes into better condition to sell them. A contractor's license and the appropriate tools and skills to handle a variety of jobs let you provide valuable services to homeowners and small business owners.

You can advertise at home shows and through all the traditional means, including a website with a menu of your services. You'll want to network and build relationships with specialists in areas where you can use assistance and for larger jobs. Before starting out, you should check the going rate for contractors in your market and charge accordingly.

Associated Builders and Contractors, *abc.org:* Membership association offering education, training, safety information and contacts in the industry.

Home business requirements include a place for housing and cleaning all the necessary tools, a good database for supplier names and numbers, and, of course, all the necessary insurance.

107. Personal Shopper

Let's face it: There are those who love to shop and those who hate it. Then there are those who always need some personal attention—and for whom you can work if you have a good eye for fashions, style, trends and bargains and you love to shop.

As a personal shopper, you will typically help high-end shoppers with discerning tastes find what they want. The modern personal shopper uses the internet and visits the stores on a regular basis, earning $50 to $100 an hour, which makes shopping that much more fun!

The value of a personal shopper isn't just as a time saver, but also as a knowledgeable assistant. Therefore, you need to know where to find items quickly, where to get the best deals, and all the tricks of the shopping trade. Having a background in retail is a definite plus, since it will help you keep up with the wealth of products and brands available. Also, you must be a good listener and understand that you are trying to meet the shopping needs and tastes of someone else. Once you've got the knack, you can hire and train others to be personal shoppers, too.

FabJob.com, *fabjob.com/PersonalShopper.asp:*

Web page devoted to what you need to know to become a personal shopper.

Homebased business requirements include excellent computer and communications tools plus all the latest store and mail order catalogs.

108. Ticket Broker

There is a big market for those who can score hard-to-get tickets for discerning clients willing to pay top dollar for sporting events, area concerts and theatrical productions. Of course to make this business work, you need to be cunning and have the inside track to legally obtaining tickets to these events.

If it's legal to broker tickets in your area, you need to start by establishing contacts with stadiums, theaters, and other event venues to purchase blocks of tickets or be on the list to receive tickets to sell on consignment. In addition, you will need to build up a large network of movers and shakers in your town as well as season ticket holders for sports teams, theaters, ballet companies and so on—anyone who might have tickets to sell.

If there is a great demand for tickets, you can sell them at a significant markup, with in-demand tickets bringing in hundreds and sometimes thousands of dollars. On the other hand, you may find yourself stuck with tickets for events that are not sold out and lack the appeal of the latest Broadway hit show. This business is, therefore, very risky to start, so start small, with a limited inventory, until you get the hang of the business and the wheeling and dealing.

Some areas do not allow ticket brokering or have specific laws regarding where and how you can run such a business. Make sure you know the laws.

National Association of Ticket Brokers, *natb.org:* Organization focused on concerns of the brokering industry, including maintaining a positive image of brokers.

Home business requirements are minimal, with good computer and communications tools at the top of the list, plus a database of numerous contacts and, if necessary, an appropriate license.

109. Film and Television Extras Agency

The vast majority of those "background" folks in film and television scenes are known as "extras"—and they receive payment for being in the scenes. If you are near a major market where there is significant film and/or television production, you can start an agency that finds the people to put into the scenes for production companies. The key is being able to get enough people to the right place at the right time, often on short notice.

You'll need to advertise heavily to build up a wide range of individuals who "want to be in pictures" and collect their headshots and resumes (although you don't need much of a resume to be an extra). On the other side of the equation, you need to have contacts in production companies, studios and advertising agencies (which also use extras).

InsideHollywood.info, *insidehollywood.info/index.php?pg=movie-extra-tv-extra:* Web page on how to be an extra.

Home business requirements are primarily excellent computer and communications tools for maintaining a large database of names and numbers and getting in touch with your clients and your extras.

110. Neighborhood Directory

Online or in print, running a neighborhood directory can be profitable, especially if you cover several neighborhoods, each with its own directory. Listing stores, restaurants, community and after-school centers, and other homebased businesses can prove beneficial for the neighborhood residents and profitable for you. There are several ways you can make money. You can charge businesses to be listed, charge for advertisements, charge for the directory or all of the above. It's important that you remain up to date, staying current on all businesses in the areas you represent. A background in publishing, primarily in layout, is helpful.

Home business requirements include a good publishing program, such as QuarkXPress, and an excellent database to build up and maintain your contact listings.

111. Expert Witness Service

Expert witnesses are experts in their fields who are retained by lawyers to give professional testimony in court or other legal proceedings. These expert witnesses may include medical doctors, psychologists, transportation experts, communications professionals, or just about any other professional who can be deemed an expert in their respective fields. Your job is to find these experts and have them ready for lawyers should they be needed in court cases. In some manner, you are like an agent for these individuals, except it is important that you use high-security measures and protect your clients and witnesses. You can set presentation appointments with lawyers to introduce them to your service and discuss their needs for experts to testify.

You can collect a fee from attorneys for using your service or charge clients a commission based on the amount of money received for providing expert testimony.

Starting this type of business requires very careful planning. Partnering with a lawyer may be a consideration. However, the effort and expense to properly research and establish this business could be well rewarded financially, as expert witnesses can receive as much as five figures in some situations.

HGExperts.com, *hgexperts.com/hg/expert-witness-articles.asp:* Website providing articles pertaining to expert witnesses.

Home business requirements are minimal, primarily requiring good communications, a computer and data storage tools.

112. Yoga Instructor

The popularity of yoga has soared in recent years. If you are experienced in any school of yoga, you can make excellent money running classes as a trained instructor. Typically, you will want to find a location outside your home in which to run the classes, since the best times for many nine-to-fivers will be at night and on weekends, when your home may be noisy if you have a family. You can teach some daytime classes from your home. If you are using a facility such as a school or community center, you will need to secure the time and make sure the space is generally quiet at the time selected.

Once you are trained and even certified in yoga instruction, running the business means marketing your course in all traditional media and through word of mouth.

Yoga Alliance, *yogaalliance.org:* Association representing the yoga community and providing information on training and certification, insurance and so on.

Home business requirements include yoga mats, appropriate musical selections, necessary insurance (especially if you are teaching from your home), good communications for reaching out to possible students, current students and corporate clients, and a database for storing contact information.

113. Freelance Translator/Interpreter

As businesses large and small continue to expand into the global marketplace, there is a growing need for multilingual individuals to provide translation. If you are bilingual or trilingual, you can start a business as a translator and/or interpreter. This can include translating documents, creating

multilingual instructions and/or serving as an in-person translator for meetings, functions, conferences, conventions, hospitals, colleges and universities and major corporations. You can also work for the government. In fact, individuals who are classified as specialists for the U.S. government earn more than $65,000 annually, on average.

Of course, your pay rate will depend in large part on the languages in which you are fluent. For example, according to the American Translators Association, translators fluent in Chinese and Japanese typically earn the highest hourly rate.

As a freelancer, you will need to be very good at scheduling your time as you move from job to job. It will also be important to constantly promote and market your skills through advertising, networking and your website.

For additional income, you can locate and book other translators, provided you have developed a list of clients. You can add translators for other languages, if you discover a demand for those languages.

The American Translators Association, *atanet.org:* Organization providing various services and a wealth of data to translators.

Home business requirements are minimal, since this business is based on your skills. However, you will need to have first-rate communications tools at your disposal, including bilingual software programs.

114. Tailor, Dressmaker or Seamstress

For more than 500 years, the tailoring profession has had a great history and tradition. If you have strong sewing skills and are good at marketing your abilities, you can make a part-time or even full-time income as a tailor, dressmaker or seamstress.

You'll want to market yourself to places in which uniforms are worn, including hospitals, various types of businesses and schools with sports teams, marching bands and cheerleaders. You'll also want to promote your business to wedding parties, theatrical troupes, and groups or associations that have presentation dinners or other special occasions. Custom tailoring and dressmaking can also be particularly lucrative if you market yourself to high-end stores and their customers.

Custom Tailors & Designers Association of America, *ctda.com:* Organization providing education, resources and unity with the custom tailoring profession.

Home business requirements include the latest in sewing machines, the necessary materials and supplies, and a well-lit and comfortable room in which to use your skills. You'll also need reliable transportation for dropping off 200 band uniforms or whatever threads you have been working on.

115. Financial Planner

No, it is not easy to figure out where to put money today to make it grow for retirement and other needs. For this reason, the financial planning industry has grown by leaps and bounds over the past decade.

This is a field that requires significant training and one of several certifications. It also requires that you work for one of the larger financial companies to get your feet wet and gain practical experience before anyone will call on you for your financial know-how.

However, once you have honed your skills and can post your certificate on the wall, you can make a very good income by charging flat fees and/or a percentage of the client's funds.

It is to your advantage to have a defined strategy and yet plenty of flexibility, since the key to success as a financial planner is to listen to the needs of your clients and help them achieve their goals. This is particularly important because, after

your initial marketing and networking, most clients will come via word-of-mouth. If you can show you can make money for your clients, rather than simply mirroring an index through good and bad times, you can be a busy financial planner. After all, it's easy to advise clients in a bull market, since almost anything works. However, in a bear market or during market downturns, can you still make money for your clients or at least not lose any? A good financial planner with various strategies can be a star if he or she can guide clients through the tough times so they come out without losing their shirts.

There are many rules and regulations (the SEC in the United States, provincial securities commissions or administrators in Canada) that you must be aware of, not only for investing, but also for marketing.

Financial Planning Association, *fpanet.org:* Membership organization with services, support and resources for financial planners in the United States.

Advocis, The Financial Advisors Association of Canada, *advocis.ca:* Organization (formed by the merger of the Canadian Association of Insurance and Financial Advisors and the Canadian Association of Financial Planners) that "prepares, promotes and protects financial advisors in the public interest" and offers a full range of education programs.

Home business requirements include top-notch computer and communication tools. You'll also need to stay on top of the financial industry at all times.

116. Set Designer

The proliferation of independent producers and filmmakers and the growth of local cable television and regional theater make this a business with great potential if you know how to work within a budget and arrange the scenery and properties (props) to best suit the needs of the producers, writers, directors and others involved in the production.

To effectively design sets, you should have decorating skills and an artistic flair, plus a proficiency in carpentry and woodworking to build sets.

To start out, you'll want to do some mock sets and take photos for a basic portfolio. You can then build your portfolio by volunteering to do the sets for nonprofit groups and schools staging plays. Once you have some solid experience under your tool belt, you'll move to more designing and probably less building (depending on the budget) as you start marketing yourself to all sorts of producers and directors. You can also make money by designing trade show booths, which are often like mini-sets.

Typically, with commercial productions, you can earn $40,000 to $50,000 with little operating expense other than marketing yourself, and much of that will come from networking and word-of-mouth within the industry.

Justin's Theatre Links, *theatrelinks.com/set.htm:* Theater link site with set design section.

Association of Theatrical Artists and Craftspeople, *atacbiz.com:* "Professional trade association for artists and craftspeople working in theatre, film, television advertising, display and education."

United States Institute for Theatre Technology Inc., *usitt.org:* Association of design, production and technology professionals in the performing arts and entertainment industry.

Entertainment Services and Technology Association, *esta.org:* "Nonprofit trade association representing the entertainment technology industry dedicated to a core mission of Building the Business of Show Business."

Home business requirements include plenty of tools, a dedicated workshop (which can be in your garage until your business outgrows it), and a solid database of industry contacts.

117. Tropical Fish Sales

There's a large market for tropical fish sales. You can tap into it if you know how to breed and care for these exotic fish. You'll need to purchase large breeding tanks or build ponds, if you have room on your property. Other equipment will include water and air circulatory machines and perhaps filters. You start with a few species of breeding tropical fish and you're in business. Some tropical fish breeds sell for as much as $100 each, so this can become a very profitable business. You can market to pet stores that buy wholesale and sell to fish collectors and/or you can seek out collectors yourself.

To run this business effectively, you must read up on how to care for the fish. It's very easy to lose more fish than you breed if you do not know what tropical fish require.

Tropical Fish Find, *tropicalfishfind.com:* Extensive site, including suppliers, forums, clubs and links for more information.

Home business requirements include the breeding tanks and/or ponds plus the equipment to maintain the tank or aquarium. You'll also need to stock up on fish food and other tools of the trade.

118. Dog Sweaters and Accessories

Do you want to make a fashion statement in the canine world? By designing, manufacturing and/or buying dog sweaters and other pet clothing items wholesale, you can launch a canine clothing business from the comfort of your own home. Add the latest in leashes, personalized collars, toys and other accessories and you can enjoy a profitable business with the many dog owners in your region.

You can market your goods via your website

and by taking fliers and/or brochures and handing them out to anyone walking a dog. You can seek out potential customers at dog shows and even sell homemade or wholesale items to pet stores. Word-of-mouth will also market your business once dogs and their owners see the quality of your products. You can earn more money by making customized sweaters with dog names on them.

If you are also a cat fancier, you can make toys for cats and even scratching posts.

PetWholesaler.com, *petwholesaler.com:* Online wholesaler of pet products, a source for accessories.

Home business requirements include the knack for creating products and all the tools needed to make them. You'll also need to set aside a workspace and a storage area.

119. Identity Theft Consultant

Identity theft is the fastest-rising crime in the world. In the past four years, more than 12 million Americans have been victims of identity theft. These sobering facts mean that an identity theft consultant can be a blessing to the millions of potential victims.

If you have a background in security, this is a potentially lucrative business. By researching, studying, and reviewing all of the means by which identity theft occurs, you can become an expert in the field. Your objective is to learn how to outsmart the identity thieves and pass the knowledge on to businesses and individuals through consulting work and speaking engagements.

While you cannot act in a law enforcement capacity, you can provide preventative measures to businesses through seminars or personal consultation. You can charge as much as $125 for an hour of specialized consultation and $100 and up for conducting two-hour seminars.

The key is to gather the facts on this area of sig-

nificant concern and spread the word through your marketing efforts (brochures, fliers, your website) that you have concrete solutions to identity theft problems. Prepare a good presentation that holds the attention of your audience and people will listen.

Association of Independent Consultants, *aiconsult.ca:* A community of consultants who share information and ideas while also providing workshops, plus articles and a discussion board on the website.

Business requirements are minimal, including a good computer, an internet connection and communication tools.

120. Party Decorations and Favors

One entrepreneur, who also worked on Wall Street, ran a lucrative part-time business designing party decorations from the comfort of his home. If you have a flair for decorating and plenty of clever ideas for creating centerpieces, balloon arches and unique invitations or place cards, you can be working with event and party planners. If you can meet the needs of theme parties, you'll be a big hit, since it often takes some careful scouting to find the right goodies for certain gatherings.

Get your name and number into the hands of caterers and party planners, with some photos highlighting what you can create. You can also drum up business by advertising in free shopper publications and other local newspapers and magazines.

The way to truly succeed is to wow people with décor that is one step above the competition. Practice honing your skills and take photos to show your work. You may even do a party or two gratis before launching your business.

Accent the Party.com, *accenttheparty.com:* Low-priced party favors and gifts plus ideas for making your own.

Home business requirements include a space

for creating, designing and making your decorations. You'll also need a place for storing the necessary supplies and party favors.

121. Auction and Auctioneer Service

More than 70,000 auctions take place in the United States every year—and that's not including those on eBay. There are many groups that stage auctions, especially in the nonprofit sector. Your job is to organize the auction and supply the goods and the auctioneer. Like many auction houses, you may specialize in one area, such as art or sports memorabilia. Typically the auction house retains a percentage of the profits of each sale, with the rest going to the organization staging the event.

This will vary depending on the value of the items being auctioned and the market. If you have the skills of a professional auctioneer or can learn them, you can make money running the auctions yourself. Becoming certified as an auctioneer is not difficult; the course takes less than two weeks and costs only a few thousand dollars. If you don't have the skills, you can book the auctioneers and take a commission for serving as the intermediary.

While this may sound simple enough, be forewarned that hosting and promoting auction sales can be costly. You have to pay wages for employees and the costs of transportation, advertising and promoting the sales and administration. Securing clients can also be difficult, simply because this is a very competitive industry and sellers want as much for their products as possible, especially commercial clients. Therefore, you need to do plenty of research and find a niche in the vast auction market. You may elect to start small on a part-time basis, to establish yourself as a player in this exciting and potentially very lucrative industry.

National Auctioneers Association, *auctioneers. org:* Information and links as well as certification programs.

Home business requirements include plenty of space to house items for auctions and a good vehicle (truck or van) for transporting the items.

122. Personal Trainer

If you are fitness-minded and know how to shape up, you can become a certified personal fitness trainer. You can have clients at your home or visit theirs, while determining the best workout program for each individual's needs.

Typically, you will work with clients to help them lose weight, build muscles, improve endurance and/or increase flexibility. Unless specifically trained, you are generally not in a position to work with physical injuries or disabilities.

There are a number of places to find out about accreditation, including the American College of Sports Medicine, the American Council on Exercise, the National Council on Strength and Fitness and the National Federation of Professional Trainers.

The three keys to success are developing specific programs for each individual, taking all safety precautions against injuries, and knowing the limitations of each client. It also helps to have a positive, outgoing personality to make clients feel good about training.

Depending on where you are located, the going rates vary from roughly $30 to $150 per hour, with long-term programs (three or six months) being worked out at specific rates. Check the rates in your market.

National Federation of Professional Trainers, *nfpt.com:* Information about certification and courses toward certification.

American College of Sports Medicine, *acsm.org:* Organization that "promotes and integrates scientific research, education and practical applications of sports medicine and exercise science to maintain and enhance physical performance, fitness, health and quality of life."

American Council on Exercise, *acefitness.org:* Nonprofit organization "committed to enriching quality of life through safe and effective exercise and physical activity."

National Council on Strength and Fitness, *ncsf.org:* Organization that provides "support services, educational programs, public outreach and professional credentialing for the personal training profession."

Home business requirements include a specially equipped space for working out. This should be comfortable, with temperature and humidity regulated and with safety precautions in place. You'll need to review additional insurance needs with your broker. A storage area for equipment is also important.

123. Medical Transcription Service

From a homebased office, you can start a medical transcription business and make a nice income. You will be transcribing the dictated recordings of doctors, dentists, chiropractors, physical therapists, and even veterinarians to create electronic patient records. Material can include examination and operation reports, diagnostic studies, ongoing patient progress notes and even material for seminars, journal articles, books and other printed materials.

To excel in this type of business, you will need a strong knowledge of medical terminology, anatomy and physiology. Certificate and associate degree programs are easily found to help you acquire the necessary skills.

Seventy percent of the work typically comes from hospitals or private physicians' offices. Medical and diagnostic laboratories, outpatient care centers and offices of physical, occupational and speech therapists can also provide you with clients. One of the fastest-growing fields in the United States, with more than 100,000 medical transcribers, makes this a very promising business.

Association for Healthcare Documentation Integrity, *ahdionline.org:* Association providing advocacy, networking, resources and professional development in the field of medical data entry.

Home business requirements include the latest in technology for playing recorded information plus excellent computer and communications equipment and a reliable system of secure data backup.

124. Babysitting/Nanny Service

As the number of two-income families increases, so does the need for those hard-working couples to get away from their children for an evening now and then. You can help them secure a reliable care for their kids by running a babysitting service. Additionally, you can provide nannies for the hours when the parents are working. By screening and representing sitters and nannies, you can help them secure more jobs and at a higher rate. You can also provide peace of mind for parents who are unsure how to find good sitters. Of course, you'll want to screen the clients to make sure your sitters are entering a safe environment.

For your service, you could charge a flat fee or receive a percentage of the pay. The key to success is to work in volume, providing plenty of reliable sitters and experienced nannies for regular customers.

Association of Professional Nannies, *nannyassociation.com:* Organization that provides nanny support and information and holds an annual national conference.

Home business requirements include insurance coverage, strong communication skills and a solid database for sitters, nannies and clients.

125. Data Backup and Recovery Service

Protecting data is of extreme importance to businesses of all sizes. If you have a background in computers and understand the various data backup methods or are willing to learn, you can have a lucrative business securing and, when necessary, recovering important data.

Your automated data services can provide compressed duplicated backups in a secure off-site system with the highest level of security and end-to-end encryption. Additionally, you can provide data archiving plus disaster relief and immediate recovery via the internet or by disk/CD.

To make this business work, you need to be able to offer a variety of data storage and recovery options, depending on the needs of the clients. You will need to ensure the utmost in security. It's also important that you offer availability and customer service as close to 24/7 as possible, meaning you will want to hire some help so you can sleep.

Network and Systems Professionals Association, *naspa.com:* Organization that provides its members with services and benefits, such as peer networking, member discounts, job placement, technical information and *Technical Support* magazine.

Home business requirements focus primarily on top-of-the-line data centers for backup and secure data recovery. You may want to have a backup facility off location to further secure data. You will need to ensure climate control, fire safety and general security for your data banks and to use a backup power supply so that you are never in the dark.

ENTREPRENEUR MAGAZINE'S ULTIMATE START-UP DIRECTORY

Additional home business startup ideas can be found in *Entrepreneur Magazine's Ultimate Start-Up Directory* by James Stephenson (2nd edition, with Rich Mintzer, Entrepreneur Press). The *Ultimate Start-Up Directory* features 1,500 great business startup ideas, representing more than 30

industries, such as retail, manufacturing, advertising, sports, recreation, travel and transportation, includings hundreds of home business opportunities. The *Ultimate Start-Up Directory* is available online from Entrepreneur Press, *entrepreneurpress.com,* Amazon, *amazon.com,* Barnes and Noble, *barnesandnoble,* and at bookstores nationwide.

GETTING STARTED WITH 101 HOME FRANCHISE OPPORTUNITIES

The following 101 home franchise opportunities represent various industries, budgets and skill levels. This list was compiled by *Entrepreneur* Magazine and *entrepreneur.com.* Therefore, while we do not endorse or promote any one franchise, these have been found to be reputable companies that are considered the best franchise options.

A major component of starting a home business is to research all the legal elements and aspects of the venture, including licenses and permits, liability insurance, zoning and building-use codes, fire and health regulations, employee regulations, certificates of training, and, for a franchise, the franchisor. A successful entrepreneur carefully researches and plans every aspect of a new business venture, whether an independent business or a franchise, including the financial investment needed to start the home business and the working capital required to achieve positive cash flow.

It's also important to remember that franchises vary considerably. There are many beyond this list of 101, some of which are intended not for selling products or services as much as for selling franchises and leaving the franchisees high and dry. Therefore, before choosing a franchise, it is important to look at listings from reputable sources and find out what other franchisees have to say.

Along with this list, *Franchise Business Review, franchisebusinessreview.com,* is an excellent place for gathering information on franchise companies. "There are a lot of franchise companies out there where the franchisor makes a lot of money and does very well and the franchisees just sort of struggle and get by," explains Eric Stite, founder and president of *Franchise Business Review*. "It is up to you to do your research and not get involved with these companies, but instead to look for the better opportunities for you as a franchisee." With that in mind, *Franchise Business Review* also rates top franchises *(franchisebusinessreview.com/reports)*.

ENTREPRENEUR'S TOP 101 HOMEBASED BUSINESS FRANCHISE OPPORTUNITIES

1. Jani-King
Commercial cleaning
16885 Dallas Parkway
Addison, TX 75001
(800) 552-5264
Startup cost: $11.3K–34.1K+

2. Jan-Pro Franchising International, Inc.
Commercial cleaning
11605 Haynes Bridge Road, #425
Alpharetta, GA 30004
(678) 336-1780
Startup cost: $3.3K–49.9K

3. Matco Tools
Distributor of professional hand tools and
    equipment
4403 Allen Road
Stow, OH 44224
(800) 368-6651
Startup cost: $79K–182K

4. Servpro Industries Inc.
Insurance/disaster restoration and cleaning
801 Industrial Boulevard
Gallatin, TN 37066
(800) 826-9586, (615) 451-0600
Startup cost: $97.3K–154.7K

5. Chem-Dry Carpet Drapery and Upholstery Cleaning
Carpet-cleaning service
1530 N. 1000 West
Logan, UT 84321
(877) 307-8233
Startup cost: $25.3K–213.6K

6. Budget Blinds Inc.
Window covering retailer and installer
1927 N. Glassell Street
Orange, CA 92865
(800) 420-5374
Startup cost: $79.7K–153.1K

7. Bonus Building Care
Commercial cleaning
P.O. Box 300
Indianola, OK 74442
(800) 931-1102
Startup cost: $7.8K–13.4K

8. ServiceMaster Clean
Commercial and residential cleaning and disaster
    restoration
860 Ridge Lake Boulevard
Memphis, TN 38120-9417
(800) 633-5703, (800) 255-9687, (901) 597-7500
Startup cost: $21.1K–111.1K

9. Jazzercise Inc.
Dance/exercise classes
2460 Impala Drive
Carlsbad, CA 92008
(760) 476-1750
Startup cost: $2.99K–33.1K

10. CleanNet USA Inc.
Commercial cleaning
9861 Broken Land Parkway, #208
Columbia, MD 21046
(800) 735-8838, (410) 720-6444
Startup cost: $3.9K–35.6K

11. Heaven's Best Carpet & Upholstery Cleaning
Carpet and upholstery cleaning
247 N. First East
P.O. Box 607
Rexburg, ID 83440
(800) 359-2095
Startup cost: $44.9K–65.9K

12. WSI Internet
Internet services
5580 Explorer Drive, #600
Mississauga, ON L4W 4Y1
(888) 678-7588, (905) 678-7588
Startup cost: $58.4K–163.2K

13. Home Helpers
Nonmedical care services
10700 Montgomery Road, #300
Cincinnati, OH 45242
(800) 216-4196
Startup cost: $41.7K–73.3K

14. Snap-on Tools
Professional tools and equipment
2801 80th Street
P.O. Box 1410
Kenosha, WI 53141-1410
(877) 476-2766
Startup cost: $19.8K–276.4K

15. Novus Auto Glass
Windshield repair and replacement
12800 Highway 13 S., #500
Savage, MN 55378
(800) 944-6811
Startup cost: $14.9K–190K

16. Coverall Cleaning Concepts
Commercial cleaning
5201 Congress Avenue, #275
Boca Raton, FL 33487
(800) 537-3371, (561) 922-2500
Startup cost: $6.3K–35.9K

17. Coffee News
Weekly newspaper distributed at restaurants
P.O. Box 8444
Bangor, ME 04402-8444
(207) 941-0860
Startup cost: $8.5K

18. Candy Bouquet
Floral-like designer gifts and gourmet confections
423 E. Third Street
Little Rock, AR 72201
(877) 226-3901
Startup cost: $9.9K–52.4K

19. Comfort Keepers
Nonmedical inhome care
6640 Poe Avenue, #200
Dayton, OH 45414
(888) 329-1368, (888) 801-1121
Startup cost: $56.4K–88.8K

20. Cruise Planners Franchising LLC/American Express
Cruise/tour travel agency
3300 University Drive, #602
Coral Springs, FL 33065
(888) 582-2150, (954) 227-2545
Startup cost: $1.9K–19.6K

21. Vanguard Cleaning Systems
Commercial cleaning service
655 Mariners Island Boulevard, #303
San Mateo, CA 94404
(800) 564-6422, (650) 594-1500
Startup cost: $6.6K–32.9K

22. CertaPro Painters Ltd.
Residential and commercial painting
P.O. Box 836
Oaks, PA 19456
(800) 462-3782
Startup cost: $129K–144K

23. Lawn Doctor

Lawn, tree and shrub care; pest control
142 Highway 34
Holmdel, NJ 07733-0401
(800) 452-9637
Startup cost: $97.9K–118.3K

24. Homes & Land Magazine

Real estate advertising magazine
1830 E. Park Avenue
Tallahassee, FL 32301
(800) 458-9520
Startup cost: $50K–125K

25. ActionCoach

Business coaching, consulting and training
5781 S. Fort Apache
Las Vegas, NV 89148
(702) 795-3188
Startup cost: $82.3K

26. Interiors by Decorating Den

Mobile interior decorating service
8659 Commerce Drive
Easton, MD 21601
(410) 822-9001
Startup cost: $49.9K

27. Club Z In-Home Tutoring Services

Inhome tutoring services
15310 Amberly Drive, #185
Tampa, FL 33647
(800) 434-2582
Startup cost: $32K–65.5K

28. 1 800 905 GEEK

On-site computer services (formerly known as
    Geeks on Call)
814 Kempsville Road, #106
Norfolk, VA 23502
(757) 466-3448
Startup cost: $59.2K–90.5K

29. Bark Busters Home Dog Training

Inhome dog training
250 W. Lehow Avenue, #B
Englewood, CO 80110
(877) 300-2275
Startup cost: $71.1K–96.4K

30. Pillar To Post

Home inspections
14502 N. Dale Mabry Highway, #200
Tampa, FL 33618
(877) 963-3129
Startup cost: $35.7K–73.7K

31. Aussie Pet Mobile

Mobile pet grooming
34189 Pacific Coast Highway, #203
Dana Point, CA 92629
(949) 234-0680
Startup cost: $63.4K–124.6K

32. American Leak Detection

Water, gas and sewer leak detection
888 Research Drive, #100
Palm Springs, CA 92262
(800) 755-6697, (760) 320-9991
Startup cost: $73.3K–157.1K

33. Rooter-Man

Plumbing, drain and sewer cleaning
268 Rangeway Road
North Billerica, MA 01862
(800) 700-8062
Startup cost: $46.8K–137.6K

34. Mr. Handyman International LLC

Home maintenance and repairs
3948 Ranchero Drive
Ann Arbor, MI 48108
(800) 289-4600
Startup cost: $91.2K–132.3K

35. United Shipping Solutions

Transportation services
6985 Union Park Center, #565

Midvale, UT 84047
(866) 744-7486, (801) 352-0012
Startup cost: $53.7K–103.5K

36. CruiseOne Inc.
Cruise travel agency
1415 N.W. 62nd Street, #205
Fort Lauderdale, FL 33309
(800) 892-3928
Startup cost: $9.8K–25.4K

37. Proforma
Printing and promotional products
8800 E. Pleasant Valley Road
Cleveland, OH 44131
(800) 825-1525, (216) 520-8400
Startup cost: $2.5K–32K

38. Weed Man
Lawn care
11 Grand Marshall Drive
Scarborough, ON M1B 5N6
(888) 321-9333
Startup cost: $60.1K–80.3K

39. AmeriSpec Home Inspection Services
Home inspection service
3839 Forest Hill Irene Road
Memphis, TN 38125
(888) 327-0269, (901) 597-8500
Startup cost: $26.6K–64.8K

40. Pop-A-Lock Franchise System
Mobile locksmith and roadside assistance services
1018 Harding Street, #101
Lafayette, LA 70503
(337) 233-6211
Startup cost: $120K+

41. Window Gang
Window and pressure cleaning services
1509 Ann Street
Beaufort, NC 28516
(877) 946-4264
Startup cost: $85K–250K

42. Padgett Business Services
Financial, payroll, consulting and tax services
160 Hawthorne Park
Athens, GA 30606
(800) 723-4388, (706) 548-1040
Startup cost: $67.9K

43. Mr. Rooter
Plumbing, drain and sewer cleaning
1020 N. University Parks Drive
Waco, TX 76707
(800) 298-6855
Startup cost: $51.7K–142K

44. National Property Inspections Inc.
Home and commercial property inspection
service
9375 Burt, #201
Omaha, NE 68114
(800) 333-9807
Startup cost: $30.5K–35K

45. The HomeTeam Inspection Service
Home inspection
575 Chamber Drive
Milford, OH 45150
(800) 598-5297
Startup cost: $21.2K–56.1K

46. American Poolplayers Association
Administrator of recreational billiard leagues
1000 Lake St. Louis Boulevard, #325
Lake St. Louis, MO 63367
(636) 625-8611
Startup cost: $11.9K–14.7K

47. MARS International Inc.
Auto appearance reconditioning services
1360 Post and Paddock
Grand Prairie, TX 75050
(972) 647-6277
Startup cost: $500–49K

48. V2K Window Decor & More

Blinds, shades and shutters
13949 W. Colfax Avenue, #250
Lakewood, CO 80401
(800) 200-0835
Startup cost: $40.1K–82.3K

49. WIN Home Inspection

Home inspection services (formerly known as
    World Inspection Network)
6500 6th Avenue N.W.
Seattle, WA 98117
(800) 967-8127
Startup cost: $27.8K–46.3K

50. Money Mailer Franchise Corp.

Direct mail advertising
12131 Western Avenue
Garden Grove, CA 92841
(888) 446-4648
Startup cost: $59.7K–86.5K

51. Computer Troubleshooters

Computer services and support
755 Commerce Drive, #412
Decatur, GA 30030
(877) 704-1702, (404) 477-1300
Startup cost: $24.8K–35.5K

52. System4

Commercial cleaning
10060 Brecksville Road
Brecksville, OH 44141
(440) 746-0440
Startup cost: $5.5K–37.8K

53. Stanley Steemer Carpet Cleaner

Carpet and upholstery cleaning
5500 Stanley Steemer Parkway
Dublin, OH 43016
(800) 848-7496, (614) 764-2007
Startup cost: $91.5K–216.7K

54. N-Hance

Wood floor and cabinet renewal systems
1530 N. 1000 West
Logan, UT 84321
(435) 890-1010
Startup cost: $31.5K–94.7K

55. The Growth Coach

Small business coaching and mentoring
10700 Montgomery Road, #300
Cincinnati, OH 45242
(888) 292-7992
Startup cost: $38.2K–58.4K

56. The Alternative Board

Discussion groups for business administrators
    and entrepreneurs
11031 Sheridan Boulevard
Westminster, CO 80020
(800) 727-0126, (303) 839-1200
Startup cost: $47.4K–111.4K

57. Rescuecom

Computer repair services
2560 Burnet Avenue
Syracuse, NY 13206
(800) 737-2837
Startup cost: $36.5K–53.1K

58. Anago Cleaning Systems

Commercial cleaning services
3111 N. University Drive, #625
Coral Springs, FL 33065
(800) 213-5857
Startup cost: $8K–350K

59. Stretch-n-Grow International Inc.

Fitness program for preschool children
P.O. Box 7599
Seminole, FL 33775
(727) 596-7614
Startup cost: $23.6K

60. PuroSystems Inc.
Property restoration and reconstruction services
   (formerly known as Purofirst International,
   Inc.)
6001 Hiatus Road, #13
Tamarac, FL 33321
(800) 247-9047
Startup cost: $81.5K–122.4K

61. BuildingStars Inc.
Commercial cleaning
11489 Page Service Drive
St. Louis, MO 63146
(314) 991-3356
Startup cost: $2.2K

62. Mr. Appliance Corp.
Household appliance service and repair
1020 N. University Parks Drive
Waco, TX 76707
(800) 290-1422
Startup cost: $37.7K–76.95K

63. Dr. Vinyl & Associates Ltd.
Leather and vinyl repair; bumper repair and dent
   removal service
201 N.W. Victoria Drive
Lee's Summit, MO 64086
(800) 531-6600, (816) 525-6060
Startup cost: $55.8K–84.95K

64. FiltaFry
Fryer management/mobile filtration services
7075 Kingspointe Parkway, #1
Orlando, FL 32819
(407) 996-5550
Startup cost: $73.1K–80.8K

65. The Screenmobile
Mobile window and door screens
72050-A Corporate Way
Thousand Palms, CA 92276
(800) 775-7795
Startup cost: $61K

66. Colors on Parade
Mobile automotive appearance services
642 Century Circle
Conway, SC 29526
Phone: (800)726-5677
Startup cost: $45.1K–180.2K

67. Aire Serv Heating & Air Conditioning Inc.
Heating, ventilation and air conditioning services
1020 N. University Parks Drive
Waco, TX 76707
(800) 583-2662
Startup cost: $39.8K–147K

68. HouseMaster Home Inspections
Home inspection
421 W. Union Avenue
Bound Brook, NJ 08805
(800) 526-3930
Startup cost: $35.5K–59.5K

69. TSS Photography
Youth and youth sports photography (formerly
   known as Sports Section)
2150 Boggs Road, #200
Duluth, GA 30096
(866) 877-4746
Startup cost: $34.3K–77.2K

70. Sandler Sales Institute
Sales and sales management training
10411 Stevenson Road
Stevenson, MD 21153
(800) 669-3537, (410) 653-1993
Startup cost: $72.2K–88.8K

71. Complete Music
Mobile DJ entertainment service
7877 L Street
Omaha, NE 68127
(800) 843-3866, (402) 339-0001
Startup cost: $20.4K–33.7K

72. Visiting Angels

Nonmedical home care agencies
28 W. Eagle Road, #201
Havertown, PA 19083
(800) 365-4189, (610) 924-0630
Startup cost: $32.99K–58.95K

73. Furniture Medic

On-site furniture repair and restoration
3839 Forest Hill Irene Road
Memphis, TN 38125-2502
(800) 255-9687, (901) 597-8600
Startup cost: $37K–81.9K

74. The Mad Science Group

Provider of science activities for children
8360 Bougainville Street, #201
Montreal, QC H4P 2G1
(800) 586-5231
Startup cost: $38.4K–80.2K

75. High Touch-High Tech

Educational consulting service
P.O. Box 8495
Asheville, NC 28814
(800) 444-4968, (828) 277-5611
Startup cost: $42K–46K

76. CHIP–The Child I.D. Program

Children's ID and school safety program
705 Lakefield Road, Building G
Westlake Village, CA 91361
(805) 557-0577
Startup cost: $10.99K–14.99K

77. Friendly Computers

Computer service and sales
3440 W. Cheyenne, #100
North Las Vegas, NV 89032
(800) 656-3115
Startup cost: $59.3K–219K

78. SuperGlass Windshield Repair

Windshield repair services
6101 Chancellor Drive, #200
Orlando, FL 32809
(407) 240-1920
Startup cost: $9.9K–31K

79. Scotts Lawn Service

Lawn, tree and shrub care; pest control
14111 Scottslawn Road
Marysville, OH 43041
(800) 264-8973
Startup cost: $81.4K–279K

80. OpenWorks

Commercial cleaning
4742 N. 24th Street, #300
Phoenix, AZ 85016
(800) 777-6736
Startup cost: $15.2K–150K+

81. Christmas Decor Inc.

Holiday and event decorating services
P.O. Box 5946
Lubbock, TX 79408-5946
(800) 687-9551
Startup cost: $16.95K–59.4K

82. Mr. Electric

Electrical services
1020 N. University Parks Drive
Waco, TX 76707
(800) 290-1422
Startup cost: $69.2K–162K

83. Miracle Method Surface Restoration

Bathroom restoration services
4239 N. Nevada, #115
Colorado Springs, CO 80907
(800) 444-8827, (719)594-9196
Startup cost: $50K

84. Spring Green Lawn Care

Lawn and tree care
11909 Spaulding School Drive
Plainfield, IL 60544
(800) 777-8608, (815) 436-8777
Startup cost: $87.7K–94.8K

85. Kitchen Tune-Up

Kitchen remodeling business specializing in cabinet reconditioning and refacing
813 Circle Drive
Aberdeen, SD 57401
(800) 333-6385, (605) 225-4049
Startup cost: $83K–90K

86. Kitchen Solvers LLC

Kitchen and bathroom remodeling services specializing in custom cabinet refacing and recoloring
401 Jay Street
La Crosse, WI 54601
(800) 845-6779, (608) 791-551
Startup cost: $113K–177K

87. OctoClean Franchising Systems

Janitorial services
5225 Canyon Crest Drive, #71-339
Riverside, CA 92507
(951) 683-5859
Startup cost: $9.5K–182.2K

88. Critter Control Inc.

Wildlife control service
9435 E. Cherry Bend Road
Traverse City, MI 49684
(800) 699-1953
Startup cost: $10.3K–69K

89. Precision Door Service

Garage door repairs and installation
2395 S. Washington Avenue, #5
Titusville, FL 32780
(888) 833-3494, (321) 225-3500
Startup cost: $53.2K–320.9K

90. StrollerFit Inc.

Interactive fitness programs, classes and products
   for parents and babies
4700 Ridge Avenue
Cincinnati, OH 45209
(866) 222-9348
Startup cost: $4.9K–13.2K

91. Computer Explorers

Computer-based learning for child-care centers,
   preschools and public and private schools
12715 Telge Road
Cypress, TX 77429
(888) 638-8722, (281) 256-4100
Startup cost: $62.9K–73.3K

92. Aire-Master of America Inc.

Restroom deodorizing and cleaning services
1821 N. Highway CC
P.O. Box 2310
Nixa, MO 65714
(800) 525-0957, (417) 725-2691
Startup cost: $43.1K–111.4K

93. Jantize America

Commercial cleaning
14452 Bruce B. Downs Boulevard, #104
Tampa, FL 33613
(888) 540-0001
Startup cost: $9.6K–43.1K

94. Adventures in Advertising Franchise Inc.

Promotional product consulting and design
800 Winneconne Avenue
Neenah, WI 54956
(800) 460-7836
Startup cost: $15K–55K

95. Duraclean International

Residential and commercial cleaning service
220 Campus Drive
Arlington Heights, IL 60004
(800) 251-7070, (847) 704-7100
Startup cost: $51K–91.5K

96. Pressed4Time Inc.

Mobile dry cleaning pick-up and delivery service
8 Clock Tower Place, #110
Maynard, MA 01754
(800) 423-8711, (978) 823-8300
Startup cost: $31.3K–38K

97. Drama Kids International Inc.

Drama classes for children
3225-B Corporate Court
Ellicott City, MD 21042
(410) 480-2015
Startup cost: $17.3K–51.9K

98. Service Team of Professionals Inc.

Carpet cleaning and disaster restoration
10036 N.W. Ambassador Drive
Kansas City, MO 64153-1362
(800) 452-8326, (816) 880-4746
Startup cost: $25.4K–99.4K

99. Truly Nolen

Pest and termite control and lawn care
3636 E. Speedway
Tucson, AZ 85716
(800) 458-3664, (520) 977-5817
Startup cost: $61K–226.5K

100. Interface Financial Corp.

Provides short-term working capital for businesses through invoice discounting
2182 Dupont Drive, #221
Irvine, CA 92612-1320
(800) 387-0860
Startup cost: $88.3K–139.3K

101. Handyman Matters Franchise Inc.

Handyman services
12567 W. Cedar Drive, #250
Lakewood, CO 80228
(866) 448-3451
Startup cost: $44.1K–103.9K

Home Business Resources

UNITED STATES GOVERNMENT AGENCIES AND BUSINESS ASSOCIATIONS

United States Small Business Administration (SBA)
409 Third Street SW
Washington, DC 20416
(800) 827-5722
sba.gov
The SBA provides new entrepreneurs and established business owners with financial, technical and management resources to start, operate and grow a business. Find the local SBA office in your region at *sba.gov/localresources/ index.html.*

SBA Services and Products for Entrepreneurs

Small Business Start-Up Kit
sba.gov/starting/indexstartup.html

Business Training Network
sba.gov/services/training/index.html

Business Plan: Road Map to Success
sba.gov/indexbusplans.html

Business Financing and Loan Program
sba.gov/financing

United States Patent and Trademark Office

Commissioners of Patents and Trademarks
P.O. Box 9
Washington, DC 20231
(800) 786-9199
uspto.gov

United States Copyright Office
Library of Congress
101 Independence Avenue SE
Washington, DC 20559-6000
(202) 707-3000
copyright.gov

Internal Revenue Service (IRS)

United States Department of the Treasury
1111 Constitution Avenue, NW
Washington, DC 20224
(202) 622-5164
irs.gov

United States Department of Labor

200 Constitution Avenue NW, Room S-1032
Washington, DC 20210
(866) 4-USA-DOL (487-2365)
dol.gov

SCORE

409 Third Street, SW, 6th Floor
Washington, DC 20024
(800) 634-0245
score.org

SCORE (formerly known as Service Corps of Retired Executives) is a nonprofit association in partnership with the SBA. SCORE provides aspiring entrepreneurs and business owners with free business counseling and mentoring programs. The association consists of more than 11,000 volunteer business counselors in 389 regional chapters throughout the United States—seasoned professionals, mostly retired, from a wide range of business experiences and backgrounds, from bank executives to CEOs of major international corporations. SCORE offers monthly workshops and informational publications. Member coaches can help you directly with a one-on-one coaching session to answer specific business questions and problems. SCORE members are also well versed in all sales and marketing methods and the organization offers many publications and training programs for increasing revenues and profits. By tapping into the SCORE network, you will be tapping into a wealth of free business knowledge and experience.

United States Chamber of Commerce

1615 H Street NW
Washington, DC 20062-2000
(202) 659-6000
uschamber.com

The U.S. Chamber of Commerce represents small businesses, corporations and trade associations from coast to coast. Visit its website to locate a regional branch office.

National Business Incubation Association

20 E. Circle Drive, Suite 37198
Athens, OH 45701-3571
(704) 593-4331
nbia.org

In the United States, there are more than 900 business incubation programs and NBIA provides links to them. Additionally, NBIA assists entrepreneurs with information, education and networking resources in both the early stages of business start-ups and the advanced stages of business growth.

National Association of Women Business Owners

8405 Greensboro Drive, Suite 800
McLean, VA 22102
(800)-55-NAWBO (556-2926)
nawbo.org

NAWBO provides women business owners support, resources, and business information to help them grow and prosper in business.

American Home Business Association

965 East 4800, Suite 3C
Salt Lake City, UT 84117
(866) 396-7773
homebusinessworks.com

National Association for the Self-Employed

P.O. Box 612067
DFW Airport
Dallas, TX 75261-2067
(800) 232-6273
nase.org

SOHO America, Inc. (Small Office Home Office)

P.O. Box 941
Hurst, TX 76053-0941
(800) 495-SOHO (7646)
soho.org

International Franchise Association

1501 K Street NW, Suite 350
Washington, DC 20005
(202) 628-8000

franchise.org

International Franchise Association members include franchisors, franchisees, and service and product suppliers for the franchising industry.

Canadian Government Agencies and Business Associations

Canada Business/Entreprises Canada

CB/EC offers a wide range of products and services to help Canadian entrepreneurs start, grow and manage their businesses. The federal government of Canada has partnered with provincial governments and private industry to develop CB/EC centers in all provinces and territories. CB/EC products, services, and publications can be accessed on the CB/EC website at *canadabusiness.ca* or at any CB/EC provincial center. Services offered to entrepreneurs include:

Interactive Business Planner, an online interactive software application with which you develop and prepare a comprehensive business plan.

Online Small Business Workshops, developed to help entrepreneurs start, finance, and market new business ventures or improve operating businesses.

Info-Guides, brief overviews of industries, free of charge.

Business Information System, a business resource databank containing more than 1,200 documents pertaining to business programs, services and specific regulations, all free of charge and available at *canadabusiness.ca* or at any CB/EC provincial center.

CANADA BUSINESS/ENTREPRISES CANADA PROVINCIAL OFFICE LOCATIONS

Alberta Business Link

100-10237 104th Street NW
Edmonton, AB T5J 1B1
(800) 272-9675, (780) 422-7722
250-639 5 Avenue SW

Calgary, AB T2P 0M9
(800) 272-9675, (403) 221-7800
canadabusiness.ca/alberta

British Columbia Business Service Center

601 West Cordova Street SW
Vancouver, BC V6B 1G1
(800) 667-2272 (in BC), (604) 775-5525
smallbusinessbc.ca

Manitoba Business Service Center

250-240 Graham Avenue
P.O. Box 2609
Winnipeg, MB R3C 4B3
(800) 665-2019, (204) 984-2272
canadabusiness.ca/manitoba

New Brunswick Business Service Center

570 Queen Street
Fredericton, NB E3B 6Z6
(506) 444-6140, (888) 576-4444
canadabusiness.ca/nb

Newfoundland and Labrador Business Service Center

90 O'Leary Avenue
P.O. Box 8687, Station A
St. John's, NF A3I 3T1
(709) 772-6022, (888 576-4444)
canadabusiness.ca/nf

Northwest Territories Business Service Center

P.O. Box 1320
5201 - 50th Avenue, 7th Fl.
Yellowknife, NT X1A 3S9
(867) 873-7958, (888) 576-4444
canadabusiness.ca/nwt

Nova Scotia Business Service Center

1575 Brunswick Street
Halifax, NS B3J 2G1
(902) 426-8604, (800) 668-1010
canadabusiness.ca/ns

Nunavut Business Service Centre

Inuksugait Plaza
P.O. Box 1000, Station 1198
Parnaivik Building
Iqaluit, NU X0A 0H0
(877) 499-5199, (867) 975-7860
Siniktarvik Building, Bag 002
Rankin Inlet, NU X0C 0G0
(877) 499-5199, (867) 645-5067
Hamlet of Cambridge Bay, Box 16
Cambridge Bay, NU X0B 0C0
(877) 499-5199, (867)-983-2337
canadabusiness.ca/nunavut

Ontario Business Service Center

151 Yonge Street, 3rd Fl.
Toronto, ON, M5C 2W7
(800) 567-2345, (416) 775-3456
canadabusiness.ca/ontario

Prince Edward Island Business Service Center

Jean Canfield Building
191 University Avenue, 1st Fl.
Charlottetown, PE C1A 4L2
(902) 368-0771, (888) 576-4444
canadabusiness.ca/pe

Quebec Business Service Center/Info Entrepreneurs

380 St-Antoine Ouest, bureau 6000
Montréal, QC H2Y 3X7
(888) 576-4444, (514) 496-4636
infoentrepreneurs.org

Saskatchewan Business Service Center

#2 - 345 Third Avenue South
Saskatoon, SK S7K 1M6
(306) 956-2323, (888) 576-4444
canadabusiness.ca/sask

Yukon Business Service Center

101-307 Jarvis Street
Whitehorse, YT Y1A 2H3
(888) 576-4444, (867) 633-6257

canadabusiness.ca/yukon

Canadian Intellectual Property Office

Place du Portage I
50 rue Victoria, C-114
Gatineau, QC K1A 0C9
(866) 997-1936
cipo.gc.ca

Canada Revenue Agency

333 Laurier Avenue West
Ottawa, ON K1A 0L9
(800) 959-2221, (888) 576-4444
cra-arc.gc.ca

Information and resources pertaining to small business taxes, corporate tax, tax rebates and programs, payroll deductions, and goods and services tax/harmonized sales tax (GST/HST).

Business Development Bank of Canada

BDC Building
5 Place Ville Marie, Suite 400
Montréal, QC H3B 5E7
(877) BDC-BANX (232-2269)
bdc.ca

BDBC provides financial services and programs to Canadians seeking to start or grow a business. Loan applications can be ordered by calling the BDBC or by visiting the website.

Canadian Chamber of Commerce

360 Albert Street, Suite 420
Ottawa, ON K1R 7X7
(613) 238-4000
chamber.ca

The Canadian Chamber of Commerce represents small businesses, corporations and trade associations from coast to coast. Log on to its website to locate a regional branch office.

Small Office Home Office Business Group (SOHO)

SOHO Business Group
Suite 1, 1680 Lloyd Avenue
North Vancouver, BC V7P 2N6

(604) 929-8250, (800) 290-SOHO (7646)
soho.ca

SOHO is a nonprofit small business organization founded in 1995 that provides members with networking, education and incentive programs and opportunities.

Canadian Franchise Association

5399 Eglinton Avenue West, Suite 116
Toronto, ON M9C 5K6
(416) 695-2896, (800) 665-4232
cfa.ca

Women Entrepreneurs of Canada

720 Spadina Avenue, Suite 202
Toronto, ON M5S 2T9
(416) 921-5150, (866) 207-4439
wec.ca

BUSINESS MAGAZINES

Advertising Age
Crain Communications, Ad Age Group
Subscriber Services
1155 Gratiot Avenue
Detroit, MI, 48207-2912
(313) 446-1665
adage.com

Barter News
P.O. Box 3024
Mission Viejo, CA 92690
(949) 831-0607
barternews.com

Black Enterprise
130 Fifth Avenue, 10th Fl.
New York, NY 10011-4399
(212) 242-8000
blackenterprise.com

Business 2.0 (online)
money.cnn.com/magazines/business2

Business Travel News
770 Broadway
New York, NY 10003
(646) 654-4500
btnonline.com

Business Week
800-635-1200
businessweek.com

Canadian Business
1 Mount Pleasant Road, 11th Fl.
Toronto, ON M4Y 2Y5
(416) 764-1200
canadianbusiness.com

eBusiness Advisor
5675 Ruffin Road
San Diego, CA 92123
(858) 278-5600
ebusiness-advisor.com

Enterprise Magazine (formerly Small Business Canada Magazine)
P.O. Box 31010
Barrie, ON L4N 0B3
(705) 722-9692
enterprisemag.com

Entrepreneur
2445 McCabe Way, Suite 400
Irvine, CA 92614
(949) 261-2325, (800) 274-6229
entrepreneur.com

Family Business
1845 Walnut Street, Suite 900
Philadelphia, PA 19103
P.O. Box 41966
Philadelphia, PA 19101-1966
(800) 637-4464, (215) 567-3200
familybusinessmagazine.com

Forbes
90 Fifth Avenue
New York, NY 10011

(212) 366-8900

forbes.com

Franchise Times
2808 Anthony Lane S.
Minneapolis, MN 55418
(612) 767-3200, (800) 528-3296
franchisetimes.com

Hispanic Business
425 Pine Avenue
Santa Barbara, CA 93117-3709
(805) 964-4554
hispanicbusiness.com

Home Business
20711 Holt Avenue, PMB 807
Lakeville, MN 55044
(800) 734-7042
homebusinessmag.com

Home Business Report
2625 Alliance Street, Suite A
Abbottsford, BC V2S 3J9
(604) 854-5530, (604) 857-1788, (800) 672-0103
*impactcommunicationsltd.com/HBR/
main.htm*

Inc.
7 World Trade Center
New York, NY 10007-2195
(212) 389-5377
inc.com

Marketers Forum
383 East Main Street
Centerport, NY 11721-1538
(631) 754-5000
forum123.com

My Business Magazine
National Federation of Independent Business
3322 West End Avenue, Suite 700
Nashville, TN 37203
(615) 690-3419
mybusinessmagazine.com

PC Magazine
Ziff Davis Media Inc.
28 East 28th Street
New York, NY 10016-7930
(212) 503-3500
pcmag.com

Small Business Opportunities
Harris Publications
1115 Broadway
New York, NY 10010
(202) 807-7100
sbomag.com

World Trade Magazine
4711 Rodman Street, NW
Washington, DC 20016
(202) 237-8011
worldtrademag.com

BUSINESS NEWSPAPERS

United States

The Wall Street Journal
wsj.com

Washington Business Journal
washington.bizjournals.com/washington

San Francisco Business Journal
sanfrancisco.bizjournals.com/sanfrancisco

Canada

Financial Post
financialpost.com

Business in Vancouver
biv.com

Ottawa Business Journal
ottawabusinessjournal.com

WEBSITES OF INTEREST

AllBusiness.com

allbusiness.com

Articles and advice on all areas of forming and running a small business.

Association of Coupon Professionals

couponpros.org

Industry trade organization for marketing professionals interested in the consumer promotion business.

BizBuySell

bizbuysell.com

Billed as the Internet's largest business-for-sale site, with over 20,000 listings.

Business Know-How

businessknowhow.com

Small business information, advice and links.

Business Network International

bni.com

Billed as the world's largest referral organization, with more than 2,600 chapters worldwide.

eBay

eBay.com

The most prominent global auction website and home to numerous small business owners.

Entrepreneur Online

entrepreneur.com

Small business information, products and services portal.

Franchise Direct

franchisedirect.com

Comprehensive listings of franchise opportunities and general information on franchising.

Franchise Expo

franchiseexpo.com

Franchise opportunities in the United States and worldwide.

Franchise Online

franchise.com

Franchise and franchisee information and services and directory service of franchise opportunities.

Franchise Works

franchiseworks.com

Online directory of franchise opportunities, business opportunities, franchises, home business franchise opportunities and franchise information.

Guerrilla Marketing Online

gmarketing.com

Small business marketing tips, information, seminars, books and links.

Independent Computer Consultants Association

icca.org

Members are information technology consultants who provide consulting, implementation, support, training, strategic planning and business analysis services.

International Business Brokers Association

ibba.org

Links to more than 1,800 business brokers in North America, Asia and Europe.

International Customer Service Association

icsa.com

Offering members information, products, services and education to improve customer service skills and relationship building.

International Licensing Industry Merchants' Association

licensing.org

Representing 1,000 member companies and individuals engaged in the marketing of licensed properties, as agents and/or as property owners: manufacturers, consultants, publications, lawyers, accountants and retailers in the licensing business.

MarketResearch.com

marketresearch.com

Billed as the most comprehensive collection of published market research available on demand.

Marketing Source

marketingsource.com/associations

Online directory listing more than 37,000 business associations indexed by industry.

National Mail Order Association

nmoa.org

Entrepreneurial organization providing education, information, ideas and business connections to small and midsize direct marketers around the world.

National Venture Capital Association

nvca.org

Association membership consisting of venture capital firms and organizations that manage pools of risk equity capital designated to be invested in young, emerging companies.

NewsLink

newslink.org

An online newspaper directory serving the United States, Canada, Mexico and South America, indexed geographically and by type of newspaper.

Nolo

nolo.com

Online legal self-help information, products, services, resources and links for consumers and business owners.

PowerHomeBiz.com

powerhomebiz.com

Home business information portal.

SmallBusinessLoans.com

smallbusinessloans.com

Online loan applications for financing new business startups and financing established businesses to help growth.

SmartBiz

smartbiz.com

Small business information.

Trade Show Exhibitors Association

tsea.org

Online news and information about marketing products and services at trade shows and special events.

vFinance

vfinance.com

Directory of venture capital firms and angel investors.

HOME OFFICE ONLINE BUYERS' GUIDE

Business Books

Amazon
amazon.com
Retailer of new and used books.

Barnes and Noble
barnesandnoble.com
Retailer of new and used books.

Chapters/Indigo
chapters.indigo.ca
Canadian bookseller.

Entrepreneur Press
entrepreneurpress.com
Small business and management books, startup guides and business software.

Powell's Books
powells.com
Retailer of new and used books.

SmallBizBooks.com (Entrepreneur Magazine)
smallbizbooks.com
Industry and business specific startup guides, manuals and software.

Office Supplies

Business Supply, *business-supply.com*

Discounted Office Supply, *discountedofficesupply.com*

Office Depot, *officedepot.com*

OfficeMax, *officemax.com*

Staples, *staples.com*

Desktop/Notebook Computers

Apple Computers, *apple.com*

Dell Computers, *dell.com*

Gateway Computers, *gateway.com*

Hewlett-Packard Compaq, *hp.com*

IBM Computers, *ibm.com*

Panasonic, *panasonic.com*

Sony, *sonystyle.com*

Toshiba, *toshiba.com*

Inkjet and Laser Printers

Brother, *brother.com*

Canon, *usa.canon.com*

Epson, *epson.com*

Hewlett-Packard, *hp.com*

Lexmark, *lexmark.com*

Business Software, Shareware and Downloads

Find Accounting Software *findaccountingsoftware.com*

CNET Shareware, *shareware.com*

BizRate, *bizrate.com*

Computers, Printers and Peripherals

Best Buy, *bestbuy.com*

Circuit City, *circuitcity.com*

CompUSA, *compusa.com*

SuperWarehouse, *superwarehouse.com*

Promotional Products

Branders, *branders.com*

CaféPress.com, *cafepress.com*

Global Sources, *globalsources.com*

Killer Promotions, *killerpromotions.com*

PromoMart, *promomart.com*

Custom Printing

Print USA, *printusa.com*

PrintingForLess.com, *printingforless.com*

Quebecor, *quebecorworldinc.com*

ThePrintGuide.com, *theprintguide.com*

Home Office Furniture

Home Office Direct, *homeofficedirect.com*

Ikea, *ikea.com*

Office by Design, *officebydesign.com*

OfficeFurniture.com, *officefurniture.com*

Index